T0336699

Interdisciplinary Research and Applications in

Bioinformatics, Computational Biology, and Environmental Sciences

Limin Angela Liu
Shanghai Jiao Tong University, China

Dong-Qing Wei
Shanghai Jiao Tong University, China

Yixue Li
Shanghai Center for Bioinformation Technology, China

MEDICAL INFORMATION SCIENCE REFERENCE

Hershey · New York

Director of Editorial Content:	Kristin Klinger
Director of Book Publications:	Julia Mosemann
Acquisitions Editor:	Lindsay Johnston
Development Editor:	Christina Bufton
Typesetter:	Casey Conapitski
Production Editor:	Jamie Snavely
Cover Design:	Lisa Tosheff

Published in the United States of America by
Medical Information Science Reference (an imprint of IGI Global)
701 E. Chocolate Avenue
Hershey PA 17033
Tel: 717-533-8845
Fax: 717-533-8661
E-mail: cust@igi-global.com
Web site: http://www.igi-global.com

Library of Congress Cataloging-in-Publication Data

Interdisciplinary research and applications in bioinformatics, computational biology
and environmental sciences / Limin Angela Liu, Dongqing
Wei and Yixue Li, editors.
    p. cm.
  Includes bibliographical references and index.
  Summary: "This book presents cutting-edge research in the field of
computational and systems biology, presenting studies ranging from the
atomic/molecular level to the genomic level and covering a wide spectrum of
important biological problems and applications"--Provided by publisher.
  ISBN 978-1-60960-064-8 (hardcover) -- ISBN 978-1-60960-066-2 (ebook) 1.
Computational biology. 2. Bioinformatics. I. Liu, Limin Angela, 1974- II.
Wei, Dongqing. III. Li, Yixue, 1955-
  QH324.2.C66 2010
  570.285--dc22
                    2010021428

British Cataloguing in Publication Data
A Cataloguing in Publication record for this book is available from the British Library.

List of Reviewers

Munib Ahmed, *University of Texas, Arlington, USA*
Tatsuya Akutsu, *Kyoto University, Japan*
Angel Ariel Caputi, *Instituto de Investigaciones Biológicas Clemente Estable, Uruguay*
Paola Causin, *Universita' degli Studi di Milano, Italy*
Nagasuma Chandra, *Indian Institute of Science, India*
Kun-Mao Chao, *National Taiwan University, Taiwan*
Yuhui Cheng, *University of California, San Diego, USA*
Zhengjun Cheng, *China West Normal University, China*
Flávio Codeço Coelho, *Gulbenkian Institute of Science, Portugal*
Pietro Cortona, *Laboratoire Structure, Propriété et Modélisation des Solides, France*
Yongsheng Ding, *Donghua University, China*
Dmitry Dmitriev, *Illinois Natural History Survey, USA*
Todor Dudev, *Academia Sinica, Taiwan*
Andreas Fuerholz, *Nestlé Research Center, Switzerland*
Omar Gaci, *Le Havre University, France*
Jean-François Ganghoffer, *LEMTA – ENSEM, France*
Dietlind Gerloff, *University of California, Santa Cruz, USA*
Leonardo L. Gollo, *Instituto de Física Interdisciplinar y Sistemas Complejos, Spain*
Wenzhi He, *Tongji University, China*
David Holcman, *Ecole Normale Superieure, France*
James A. Holzwarth, *Nestlé Research Center, Switzerland*
Zeti Azura Mohamed Hussein, *Universiti Kebangsaan Malaysia, Malaysia*
Timo Jacob, *Abteilung Elektrochemie, Universität Ulm, Germany*
Yiannis N. Kaznessis, *University of Minnesota, USA*
Samee Ullah Khan, *North Dakota State University, USA*
Jens Lagergren, *The Royal Institute of Technology, Stockholm Bioinformatics Center, Sweden*
Gianluca Lattanzi, *International School for Advanced Studies, Italy*
Wei Lei, *Sun Yat-Sen University, China*
Yingchun (Spring) Liu, *Harvard Medical School, USA*
Wei-Hong Lu, *Harbin Institute of Technology, China*
Thomas Manke, *Max Planck Institute for Molecular Genetics, Germany*
Jason McDermott, *Computational Biology and Bioinformatics Group, Pacific Northwest National Laboratory, USA*

Table of Contents

Section 2
Biological Networks and Systems Biology

Section 3
Computational Predictions of Drug Properties

Section 4
Medical Signal Processing and Analysis

Section 5
Computational Biology

Section 6
Structure and Modeling

Section 7
Problems and Solutions in Environmental Sciences

Detailed Table of Contents

Section 1
Method Development and Application in Bioinformatics

Chapter 1

    Xin Chen, Zhejiang University, China
    Hangyang Xu, Zhejiang University, China

Prediction of various functional properties of proteins has long been a central theme of bioinformatics in the post-genomic era. Statistical learning, in addition to analysis based on sequence similarity, was proven successful to detect complex sequence-function associations in many applications. JFeature is an integrated Java tool to facilitate extraction of global sequence features and preparation of example sets, in statistical learning studies of sequence-function relationships. With a user-friendly graphical interface, it computes the composition, distribution, transition and auto-correlation features from sequence. It also helps to assemble a negative example set based on the most-dissimilar principle. The Java package and supplementary documentations are available at http://www.cls.zju.edu.cn/rlibs/software/jfeature.html.

Chapter 2

    Jian Yu, Tongji University, China
    Jun Wu, Shanghai Center for Bioinformation Technology, China
    Miaoxin Li, Shanghai Center for Bioinformation Technology, China
    Yajun Yi, Vanderbilt University, USA
    Yu Shyr, Vanderbilt University, USA & Yixue Li Shanghai Center for Bioinformation
        Technology, China
    Lu Xie, Shanghai Center for Bioinformation Technology, China

Integrative analysis of microarray data has been proven as a more reliable approach to deciphering molecular mechanisms underlying biological studies. Traditional integration such as meta-analysis is usually gene-centered. Recently, gene set enrichment analysis (GSEA) has been widely applied to bring gene-level interpretation to pathway-level. GSEA is an algorithm focusing on whether an a priori defined set of genes shows statistically significant differences between two biological states. However, GSEA does not support integrating multiple microarray datasets generated from different studies. To overcome this, the improved version of GSEA, ASSESS, is more applicable, after necessary modifications. By making proper combined use of meta-analysis, GSEA, and modified ASSESS, this chapter reports two workflow pipelines to extract consistent expression pattern change at pathway-level, from multiple microarray datasets generated by the same or different microarray production platforms, respectively. Such strategies amplify the advantage and overcome the disadvantage than if using each method individually, and may achieve a more comprehensive interpretation towards a biological theme based on an increased sample size. With further network analysis, it may also allow an overview of cross-talking pathways based on statistical integration of multiple gene expression studies. A web server where one of the pipelines is implemented is available at: http://lifecenter.sgst.cn/mgsea//home.htm.

Chapter 3

Zu-Guo Yu, Xiangtan University, China & Queensland University of Technology, Australia
Guo-Sheng Han, Xiangtan University, China
Bo Li, Xiangtan University, China
Vo Anh, Queensland University of Technology, Australia
Yi-Quan Li, Xiangtan University, China

The mitochondrial genomes have provided much information on the evolution of this organelle and have been used for phylogenetic reconstruction by various methods with or without sequence alignment. In this paper, we explore the mitochondrial genomes by means of the chaos game representation (CGR), a tool derived from the chaotic dynamical systems theory. If the DNA sequence is a random collection of bases, the CGR will be a uniformly filled square; on the other hand, any pattern visible in the CGR contains information on the DNA sequence. First we use the Markov chain models to simulate the CGR of mitochondrial genomes. Then we model the noise background in the genome sequences by a Markov chain. A simple correlation-related distance approach without sequence alignment based on the CGR of mitochondrial genomes is proposed to analyze the phylogeny of 64 selected vertebrates.

Chapter 4

Ruofei Wang, Xiangtan University, China
Xieping Gao, Xiangtan University, China

Classification of protein folds plays a very important role in the protein structure discovery process, especially when traditional sequence alignment methods fail to yield convincing structural homologies. In this chapter, we have developed a two-layer learning architecture, named TLLA, for multi-class protein folds classification. In the first layer, OET-KNN (Optimized Evidence-Theoretic K Nearest Neighbors) is used as the component classifier to find the most probable K-folds of the query protein. In the second layer, we use support vector machine (SVM) to build the multi-class classifier just on the

K-folds, generated in the first layer, rather than on all the 27 folds. For multi-feature combination, ensemble strategy based on voting is selected to give the final classification result. The standard percentage accuracy of our method at ~63% is achieved on the independent testing dataset, where most of the proteins have <25% sequence identity with those in the training dataset. The experimental evaluation based on a widely used benchmark dataset has shown that our approach outperforms the competing methods, implying our approach might become a useful vehicle in the literature.

Chapter 5

Ren-Xiang Yan, China Agricultural University, China
Jing Liu, China Agricultural University, China
Yi-Min Tao, China Agricultural University, China

Profile-profile alignment may be the most sensitive and useful computational resource for identifying remote homologies and recognizing protein folds. However, profile-profile alignment is usually much more complex and slower than sequence-sequence or profile-sequence alignment. The profile or PSSM (position-specific scoring matrix) can be used to represent the mutational variability at each sequence position of a protein by using a vector of amino acid substitution frequencies and it is a much richer encoding of a protein sequence. Consensus sequence, which can be considered as a simplified profile, was used to improve sequence alignment accuracy in the early time. Recently, several studies were carried out to improve PSI-BLAST's fold recognition performance by using consensus sequence information. There are several ways to compute a consensus sequence. Based on these considerations, we propose a method that combines the information of different types of consensus sequences with the assistance of support vector machine learning in this chapter. Benchmark results suggest that our method can further improve PSI-BLAST's fold recognition performance.

Chapter 6

Dan Wei, Xiamen University, China & Fujian Key Laboratory of the Brain-like Intelligent
*   Systems (Xiamen University), China*
Qingshan Jiang, Xiamen University, China
Sheng Li, Xiamen University, China

Similarity analysis of DNA sequences is a fundamental research area in Bioinformatics. The characteristic distribution of L-tuple, which is the tuple of length L, reflects the valuable information contained in a biological sequence and thus may be used in DNA sequence similarity analysis. However, similarity analysis based on characteristic distribution of L-tuple is not effective for the comparison of highly conservative sequences. In this paper, a new similarity measurement approach based on Triplets of Nucleic Acid Bases (TNAB) is introduced for DNA sequence similarity analysis. The new approach characterizes both the content feature and position feature of a DNA sequence using the frequency and position of occurrence of TNAB in the sequence. The experimental results show that the approach based on TNAB is effective for analysing DNA sequence similarity.

Huan Yang, Jilin University, China

Yan Wang, Jilin University, China

Trupti Joshi, University of Missouri, USA

Dong Xu, University of Missouri, USA

Shoupeng Yu, Changchun Institute of Technology, China

Yanchun Liang, Jilin University, China

MicroRNAs (miRNAs) are endogenous single-stranded non-coding RNAs of ~22 nucleotides in length and they act as post-transcriptional regulators in bacteria, animals and plants. Almost all current methods for computational prediction of miRNAs use hairpin structure and minimum of free energy as characteristics to identify putative pre-miRNAs from a pool of candidates. We discovered a new effective feature named "basic-n-units" (BNU) to distinguish pre-miRNAs from pseudo ones. This feature describes pairing continuity of RNA secondary structure. Simulation results show that a classification method, called Triplet-SVM-classifier, achieved an accuracy of 97.24% when this BNU feature was used. This is a 3% increase caused solely by adding this new feature. We anticipate that this BNU feature may increase the accuracy for most classification methods.

Fuge Zhu, Jiangsu University, China

Xiaoli Tan, Jiangsu University, China

Juan Li, Jiangsu University, China

Mingyu Wei, Jiangsu University, China

Lili Yu, Jiangsu University, China

Long chain acyl-coenzyme A synthetases (LACSs) activate free fatty acid to acyl-CoA thioesters, and play important roles in the biosynthesis and degradation of lipids. In this study, four cDNAs (Complementary DNA) encode long chain fatty acyl-CoA synthetase activity has been found in Brassica napus. Sequence analysis indicated that the four LACSs possessed typical molecular characteristics of LACS. Compared with low oil content varieties seed, the four genes are strongly expressed in high oil content varieties seeds at 35 days after pollination (DAP). The expression pattern suggested that the four LACSs might be involved in the biosynthesis of lipids and oil accumulation in rapeseed.

Section 2
Biological Networks and Systems Biology

Xuning Chen, Shanghai University, China

Weiping Zhu, Shanghai University, China

Axonal outgrowth is usually guided by a variety of guidance factors, such as netrins, ephrins, slits and semaphorins, and is one of the critical steps for the proper formation of neural networks. However, how the signal molecules function and why some of these play more important roles than others in guiding the axonal directional outgrowth has not been fully understood. In this study, we try to solve the problem by using the complex network analysis method. The signal molecules and interactions are treated as the nodes and edges to construct the axon guidance network model for Homo sapiens. The data of the model are taken from the KEGG database, and an analysis workbench named Integrative Visual Analysis Tool for Biological Networks and Pathways (VisANT) is employed to analyze the topological properties, including the degree distribution and the top co-expressed genes of the axon guidance network. This study has just opened a window into understanding the mechanism of axon guidance.

Chapter 10

Tingzhe Sun, Nanjing University, China
Meihong Cai, Nanjing University, China
Jun Cui, Nanjing University, China
Pingping Shen, Nanjing University, China

The tumor suppressor protein p53 predominantly serves as a sequence specific transcription factor that may be activated upon exposure to diverse stimuli. One potent death inducer, p53-upregulated mediator of apoptosis (PUMA), is transcriptionally induced by p53. Once released into the cytoplasm, PUMA can lead to the activation of Bcl-2 apoptotic network. The cytoplasmic proapoptotic roles of p53 have recently been discovered, and these findings have placed p53 into the chemical interaction network with Bcl-2 family members. PUMA can also relieve p53 from the sequestration of antiapoptotic members. Released p53 further enters the nucleus and induces PUMA expression. We proposed that this positive feedback loop could lead to bistability. Further sensitivity analysis suggested that the system which covers the interactions between p53 and BCL-2 family members is considerably sensitive to p53 production rate. Meanwhile, downstream network components are much more affected by certain parameters than upstream effectors. Therefore, this newly discovered positive feedback loop might play critical roles in apoptotic network.

Chapter 11

Lin Ji, Capital Normal University, China
Haiyan Wang, Capital Normal University, China

Signals in transduction cascades are widely exposed to stochastic influences. In this work, we investigate the effects of agonist release noises on calcium signaling. Besides the usually considered "amplitude noise", the case of "frequency noise" is also discussed. Simulation results show that the transduction cascades may amplify these noises when its intensity is bigger than certain critical value. The amplified noise show constructive effect to maintain the calcium signaling in critical signal-free cases. Moreover, the signal is more sensitive to the "frequency noise" than to the "amplitude noise". This suggests frequency fluctuations in signaling cascades may have greater influence than the amplitude ones, which is an important finding for signal transduction in complex pathways. Since biological systems are inherently stochastic, this work demonstrates how the calcium system takes advantage of the environmental fluctuations to maintain signaling, and therefore provide effective, sensitive signal communication.

Section 3
Computational Predictions of Drug Properties

Chapter 12

Ruifa Jin, Chifeng University, China
Hongzheng Bao, Chifeng University, China
Yin Bai, Chifeng University, China
Xiuhua Li, Chifeng University, China

Hydroxyanthraquinone derivatives are a large group of natural polyphenolic compounds found widely in plants. The cytotoxic activities of hydroxyanthraquinone derivatives have been demonstrated using cancer cell lines. The pharmacological effect can be explained by their antioxidant activity and their inhibition of certain enzymes. There are two main kinds of mechanism, H-atom transfer and one-electron transfer, by which antioxidants can play their role. The structural and electronic properties of hydroxyanthraquinone derivatives, alizarin, purpurin, pseudopurpurin, and their radicals were investigated using density functional theory. It turned out that these three molecules appear to be good candidates for high antioxidant activity species, particularly for pseudopurpurin. Taking this system as an example, we present an efficient method for the investigation of antioxidant activity for such kind of hydroxyanthraquinone derivatives from theoretical point of view. With the current work, we hope to highlight the antioxidant activity of hydroxyanthraquinone derivatives and stimulate the interest for further studies and exploitation in pharmaceutical industry.

Chapter 13

Aixia Yan, Beijing University of Chemical Technology, China
Zhi Wang, Beijing University of Chemical Technology, China
Jiaxuan Li, Beijing University of Chemical Technology, China
Meng Meng, Beijing University of Chemical Technology, China

In the development of drugs intended for oral use, good drug absorption and appropriate drug delivery are very important. Now the predictions for drug absorption and oral bioavailability follow similar approach: calculate molecular descriptors for molecules and build the prediction models. This approach works well for the prediction of compounds which cross a cell membrane from a region of high concentration to one of low concentration, but it does not work very well for the prediction of oral bioavailability, which represents the percentage of an oral dose which is able to produce a pharmacological activity. The models for bioavailability had limited predictability because there are a variety of pharmacokinetic factors influencing human oral bioavailability. Recent study has shown that good quantitative relationship could be obtained for subsets of drugs, such as those that have similar structure or the same pharmacological activity, or those that exhibit similar absorption and metabolism mechanisms. In this work, using MLR (Multiple Linear Regression) and SVM (Support Vector Machine), quantitative bioavailability prediction models were built for four kinds of drugs, which are Angiotensin Converting Enzyme Inhibitors or Angiotensin II Receptor Antagonists, Calcium Channel Blockers, Sodium and Potassium Channels Blockers and Quinolone Antimicrobial Agents. Explorations into subsets of compounds were performed and reliable prediction models were built for these four kinds of drugs. This work represents an exploration in predicting human oral bioavailability and could be used in other dataset of compounds with the same pharmacological activity.

Chapter 14

Zhi Wang, Beijing University of Chemical Technology, China
Aixia Yan, Beijing University of Chemical Technology, China
Jiaxuan Li, Beijing University of Chemical Technology, China

The ability of penetration of the blood-brain barrier is an important property for the development of Central Nervous System drugs, which is commonly expressed by logBB (logBB = log(Cbrain/Cblood). In this work, a support vector machine was used to build quantitative models of blood brain barrier permeability. Molecular descriptors for 182 compounds were calculated by ADRIANA.Code and 12 descriptors were selected using the automatic variable selection function in Weka. Based on two common physicochemical descriptors (xlogP and Topological Polar Surface Area (TPSA)) and 10 2D property autocorrelation descriptors on atom pair properties, an SVM regression model was built. The built model was validated by an external test set. The reliable predictions of the test set demonstrate that this model performs well and can be used for estimation of logBB values for drug and drug-like molecules.

Section 4
Medical Signal Processing and Analysis

Chapter 15

Zhiqiang Zhang, Sichuan University, China
Bo Gao, Sichuan University, China
Guojie Liao, Sichuan University, China
Ling Mu, West China Hospital, China
Wei Wei, West China Hospital, China

In this chapter, the transesophageal oxygen saturation (SpO2) monitoring system was proposed based on the early experiments, to provide a new program of SpO2 acquisition and analysis and avoid the limitation of traditional methods. The PPG (photoplethysmographic) signal of descending aorta and left ventricular was monitored in the experiment. The analysis of the peak-to-peak values, the standard deviation and the position of peaks in signal waveforms showed that in vivo signal was more stable and sensitive; and the physiological information was reflected in the left ventricular PPG waveform. Therefore, it can be concluded that the transesophageal SpO2 monitoring technology has better guidance in clinical applications.

Chapter 16

Fanpeng Zhou, East China University of Science and Technology, China
Jianjun Yan, East China University of Science and Technology, China
Yiqin Wang, Shanghai University of Traditional Chinese Medicine, China
Fufeng Li, Shanghai University of Traditional Chinese Medicine, China
Chunming Xia, East China University of Science and Technology, China
Rui Guo, Shanghai University of Traditional Chinese Medicine, China
Haixia Yan, Shanghai University of Traditional Chinese Medicine, China

Digital auscultation of Traditional Chinese Medicine (TCM) is a relatively new technology which has been developed for several years. This system makes diagnoses by analyzing sound signals of patients using signal processing and pattern recognition. The paper discusses TCM auscultation in both traditional and current digital auscultation methods. First, this article discusses demerits of traditional TCM auscultation methods. It is through these demerits that a conclusion is drawn that digital auscultation of TCM is indispensable. Then this article makes an introduction to voice analysis methods from linear and nonlinear analysis aspects to pattern recognition methods in common use. Finally this article establishes a new TCM digital auscultation system based on wavelet analysis and Back-propagation neural network (BPNN).

Chapter 17

Rui Guo, Shanghai University of Traditional Chinese Medicine, China
Yiqin Wang, Shanghai University of Traditional Chinese Medicine, China
Haixia Yan, Shanghai University of Traditional Chinese Medicine, China
Fufeng Li, Shanghai University of Traditional Chinese Medicine, China
Jianjun Yan, East China University of Science and Technology, China
Zhaoxia Xu, Shanghai University of Traditional Chinese Medicine, China

From the perspective of hemodynamics principles, the pressure pulse wave marked in the radial artery is the comprehensive result of pulse wave propagation and reflection in the arterial conduit. The most common pulse charts (also called pulse wave) obtained by Traditional Chinese Medicine (TCM) pulse-taking technique, if quantified and standardized, may become a universal and valuable diagnostic tool. The methods of feature extraction of TCM pulse charts currently involve time-domain analysis, frequency-domain analysis and time-frequency joint analysis. The feature parameters extracted by these methods have no definite clinical significance. Therefore, these feature parameters cannot essentially differentiate different types of TCM pulse. In this chapter, the harmonic analysis method was applied to analyze the common TCM pulse charts (plain pulse, wiry pulse, slippery pulse). Velocity and reflectivity coefficients of pulse were calculated. We found that wave velocities and reflection coefficients of different TCM pulse have different distributions. Furthermore, we studied the clinical significance of velocities and reflection coefficients. The result suggests that wave velocity and reflection coefficient are the feature parameters of TCM pulse with physiological and pathological significance, which can be used to interpret formation of Chinese medicine pulse. Our study reveals the mechanism of TCM pulse formation and promotes non-invasive TCM pulse diagnostic method.

Section 5
Computational Biology

Chapter 18

Houye Liu, Wenzhou University, China
Weiming Wang, Wenzhou University, China

Amplitude equation may be used to study pattern formation. In this chapter, we establish a new mechanical algorithm AE_Hopf for calculating the amplitude equation near Hopf bifurcation based on the method of normal form approach in Maple. The normal form approach needs a large number of variables and intricate calculations. As a result, deriving the amplitude equation from diffusion-reaction is a difficult task. Making use of our mechanical algorithm, we derived the amplitude equations from several biology and physics models. The results indicate that the algorithm is easy to apply and effective. This algorithm may be useful for learning the dynamics of pattern formation of reaction-diffusion systems in future studies.

Chapter 19

Feng Rao, East China Normal University, P.R. China

Predator–prey models in ecology serve a variety of purposes, which range from illustrating a scientific concept to representing a complex natural phenomenon. Due to the complexity and variability of the environment, the dynamic behavior obtained from existing predator–prey models often deviates from reality. Many factors remain to be considered, such as external forcing, harvesting and so on. In this chapter, we study a spatial version of the Ivlev-type predator-prey model that includes reaction-diffusion, external periodic forcing, and constant harvesting rate on prey. Using this model, we study how external periodic forcing affects the stability of predator-prey coexistence equilibrium. The results of spatial pattern analysis of the Ivlev-type predator-prey model with zero-flux boundary conditions, based on the Euler method and via numerical simulations in MATLAB, show that the model generates rich dynamics. Our results reveal that modeling by reaction-diffusion equations with external periodic forcing and nonzero constant prey harvesting could be used to make general predictions regarding predator-prey equilibrium,which may be used to guide management practice, and to provide a basis for the development of statistical tools and testable hypotheses.

Chapter 20

*Junran Zhang, Southwest Science and Technology University and The Forth Military
    Medical University, China*
Yongguo Han, Southwest Science and Technology University, China
Guangcan Xiao, Southwest Science and Technology University, China
Sanjue Hu, The Forth Military Medical University, China

In neural science, different action potential (AP) firing patterns are typically considered to be dominated by different dynamical mechanisms. Different AP firing patterns in unmyelinated fibres can contribute to pain and sensory information transmission. Experiments in rabbit unmyelinated nerve (axon) show some interesting phenomena, mainly concerned with the AP firing patterns that changed regularly. Investigating the dynamical mechanism of unmyelinated fibre during various kinds of AP firing patterns is useful to understand the neural information processing in axon and pain information transmission. Here, we reproduced these phenomena by constructing a mathematical model, where the discharge of the Hodgkin-Huxley (H-H) neuron under square wave stimulation was studied by simulation. It is shown that square wave can induce bursting firing, especially with long time-course duration. This is different from the popular theory that explained repetitive and bursting firing due to stimulus intensity and instantaneous fluctuation. Through dynamical analysis, we found that the mechanism of the action potential pattern changed according to Hopf bifurcation, a dynamical behavior that emergence and stability of limit cycles of bifurcating from a stable equilibrium. The finding may support the neural information coding hypothesis in unmyelinated axon.

Chapter 21

Lixin Luo, South China University of Technology, China
Fang Zhu, South China Universityof Technology, China
Si Deng, South China University of Technology, China

Many enzymes have been widely used in industrial production, for they have higher catalytic efficiency and catalytic specificity than the traditional catalysts. Therefore, the performance of enzymes has attracted wide attention. However, due to various factors, enzymes often cannot show their greatest catalytic efficiency and the strongest catalytic ability in industrial production. In order to improve the enzyme activity and specificity, people become increasingly interested in the transformation and modification of existing enzymes. For the structure modification of proteinase, this chapter introduces a computational method for modelling error-prone PCR. Error-prone PCR is a DNA replication process that intentionally introduces copying errors by imposing mutagenic reaction condition. We then conclude about the mathematical principle of error-prone PCR which may be applied to the quantitative analysis of directed evolution in future studies.

Section 6
Structure and Modeling

Chapter 22

Guo-Xiang Pan, Huzhou Teachers College, China
Feng Cao, Huzhou Teachers College, China
Pei-Song Tang, Huzhou Teachers College, China
Hai-Feng Chen, Huzhou Teachers College, China
Zhe-Ming Ni, Zhejiang University of Technology, China
Jin-Tian Yang, Huzhou Teachers College, China
Li-Geng Wang, Zhejiang University of Technology, China
Min-Hong Xu, Huzhou Teachers College, China

Interlayer structure, hydrogen-bond, hydration and swelling properties of glycine intercalated layered double hydroxides (LDHs-Gly) were investigated with molecular dynamics (MD) methods. The results show that the interlayer spacing dc increases as hydration level increases. The computed hydration energies reach the most negative values at low water contents and change rapidly over the range $1 \leq NW \leq 6$, and slowly and gradually approach the potential energy for bulk SPC water at $NW > 6$. But there are no local minima in the energy over the entire hydration range. This result suggests that LDHs-Gly tend to absorb water continuously in water-rich environments and enhance swelling to delaminate the hydroxide layers. The interlayers of LDHs-Gly exhibit complex hydrogen-bond network. With water content increasing, the glycine molecules progressively change their orientation from parallel to the layers to nearly perpendicular. Water molecules firstly form hydrogen-bond with M-OH layers at low water contents. While the hydroxide layers gradually get to saturation state at $Nw > 3$. And then water molecules continuously fill the interlayer to expand interlayer spacing.

Chapter 23

Ming Du, Harbin Institute of Technology, China
Lu Zhang, Harbin Institute of Technology, China

Hydrogenase plays an important role in the process of biohydrogen production. Hydrogenases have very unique active sites and are classified into three groups according to the metal composition of the active sites: the [Ni-Fe] hydrogenase, [Fe-Fe] hydrogenase, and [Fe-only] hydrogenase. In this paper, the crystal structures and active sites of three kinds of hydrogenases are examined and compared. These enzymes have an unusual structural feature in common. Their similar active site indicates that the catalytic mechanism of hydrogen activation is probably similar. The understanding of the catalytic mechanisms for the three kinds of hydrogenases may help achieve the industrialization process of hydrogen energy production. Moreover, the future research direction about the hydrogenases from auto-aggregative bacteria and the chemical mimic of hydrogenases structure is discussed.

Section 7
Problems and Solutions in Environmental Sciences

Chapter 24
    Shengkui Cao, Qinghai Normal University & Chinese Academy of Sciences, China
    Qi Feng, Chinese Academy of Sciences, China
    Jianhua Si, Chinese Academy of Sciences, China
    Yonghong Su, Chinese Academy of Sciences, China
    Zongqiang Chang, Chinese Academy of Sciences, China
    Haiyang Xi, Chinese Academy of Sciences, China

Foliar δ13C values are often used to denote the long-term water use efficiency (WUE) of plants whereas long-term nitrogen use efficiency (NUE) are usually estimated by the ratio of C to N in the leaves. Seasonal variations of δ13C values, foliar nitrogen concentration and C/N ratios of Populus euphratica and Tamarix ramosissima grown under five different microhabitats of Ejina desert riparian oasis of northwestern arid regions in China were studied. The results indicated that T. ramosissima had higher δ13C value compared with that of P. euphratica. The N concentration and C/N ratios of two species were not significantly different. The seasonal pattern of three indexes in two species was different. The δ13C values and N concentration decreased during the plant's growth period. However, the change of C/N ratios was increased. Among microhabitats, there were higher δ13C values and N concentration as well as lower C/N ratios in the Dune and Gobi habitats. Foliar δ13C values significantly and positively correlated with N concentration in P. euphratica and T. ramosissima, whereas a significantly negative correlation between δ13C values and C/N ratios was found for P. euphratica. This relation in T. ramosissima was weak, but there was a significant quadratic curve relationship between δ13C values and C/N ratios, which revealed that there was a trade-off between WUE and NUE for P. euphratica and in natural condition, P. euphratica could not improve WUE and NUE simultaneously. T. ramosissima could simultaneously enhance WUE and NUE. The above characters of WUE and NUE in two plants reflected the different adaptations of desert species to environmental condition.

Chapter 25
    Yongzheng Tian, Chinese Academy of Sciences, China & Alxa League of Inner Mongolia
        Autonomous Region, China
    Jianhua Si, Chinese Academy of Sciences, China
    Qi Feng, Chinese Academy of Sciences, China
    Shengkui Cao, Qinghai Normal University, China & Chinese Academy of Sciences, China

Plant root water uptake is a key way to transfer soil water to the atmosphere. It is an important part of the research on water transforming patterns in the SPAC (Soil-Plant-Air Continuum). So understanding the water absorption patterns of plant root system is a base to recognize the SPAC. Recently there are many studies on the water absorption patterns of plant root system. However, the researched plants are mostly crops and the main researched areas are regions with adequate precipitation. There are only a few studies on the water absorption of natural plants in extreme arid desert regions. This paper studied the root water absorption patterns of Populus euphratica and established the corresponding mathematical model based on the data of root density and soil water dynamics in root zone in desert riparian forest in extreme arid region. The finite difference method was used to discretize the soil water movement equation with evaporation boundary conditions. Numerical simulation analysis of soil water movement in root zone of Populus euphratica showed that the simulated values were consistent with the measurement values with 92-98% precision. This work provides a theoretical basis for the study of water movement in the SPAC.

Yaqun He, China University of Mining and Technology, China
Hua Wei, China University of Mining and Technology, China
Weiran Zuo, China University of Mining and Technology, China
Xiaobing Wu, China University of Mining and Technology, China
Xin Ge, China University of Mining and Technology, China
Shan Wu, China University of Mining and Technology, China
Baofeng Wen, China University of Mining and Technology, China

Based on the analysis of five factors affecting energy risks, including supply and demand, economy, environment, transport, and disaster, this chapter establishes the prior-warning index system of the energy risk by covering 3 sub-systems and 37 indexes. The three sub-systems are the coal sub-system, the petroleum and natural gas sub-system, and the integrated factors sub-system. Fuzzy synthesis evaluation was applied to confirm the internal estimated index weight of the sub-systems. Moreover, the risk prior-warning model of the energy sub-systems was established by the method. The weights of the three sub-systems were determined through the concept of entropy weight, and the prior-warning indexes of energy risk were applied to evaluate the total energy security of the three sub-systems. Finally, the prior-warning model of energy risk in China was established. The entire situation of energy safety of China was summarized via empirical analysis.

Jingfeng He, China University of Mining and Technology, China
Yaqun He, China University of Mining and Technology, China
Nianxin Zhou, China University of Mining and Technology, China
Chenlong Duan, China University of Mining and Technology, China
Shuai Wang, China University of Mining and Technology, China
Hongjian Zhang, China University of Mining and Technology, China

Waste printed circuit boards (PCBs) contain a number of valuable constituents. It is of great significance to separate precious metals and non-metallic constituents from waste PCBs with appropriate methods for resource recycling and environment protection. A novel flowsheet for the recycling of waste PCBs using physical beneficiation methods was constructed. Waste PCBs were disassembled into substrates and slots firstly. The substrates were crushed to the size below 1mm through wet impact crushing and separated with a tapered column separation bed. The results indicated that products with integrated separation efficiency of 93.9% and metal recovery ratio of 93.7% were obtained by the primary separation with the water discharge of 5.5 m3/h, feed-rate of 250g/min and inclination angle of 35°. Waste PCBs slots components were crushed to the size of 0.5-5mm through impact crushing and separated with an active pulsing air classifier. The separation results showed that products with integration separation efficiency of 92.4% and metal recovery ratio of 96.2% were obtained with the airflow velocity of 2.90m/s and pulsing frequency of 2.33Hz. Precious metals could be obtained by further separation and purification of the metal components and the non-metal components could be used as refuse derived fuel. The flowsheet has great potential to be applied in the field of waste PCBs treatment and recycling.

Preface

Bioinformatics and computational biology are quickly advancing fields over the past decade, thanks to the Human Genome Project and the development of many high-throughput technologies. Biological and medical sciences have blended their traditional boundaries with many other disciplines, such as computer science, mathematics and statistics, physical sciences, engineering, etc., in becoming a more quantitative and precise science. Establishing a mathematical model in describing a life phenomenon and using statistical tools in inferring probable outcome of living systems or guiding future experiments are becoming common practice around the world. Nonetheless, despite such exciting progress of these fields, how our genome is organized, how our genes perform their pertinent functions, how diseases develop, etc., are all complex and hard questions that remain to be solved.

Therefore, we believe it is of great significance and importance to summarize and present some of the most recent research carried out in these fields to encourage and guide future research. The book *Interdisciplinary Research and Applications in Bioinformatics, Computational Biology, and Environmental Sciences* is created with this exact purpose.

This book is a collection of conference submissions to the 1st Annual Annual International Conference on Computational and Systems Biology, Shanghai, China, October 2009. Among over 40 submissions, 27 manuscripts were accepted to appear in this book. These 27 chapters are contributed by world-leading researchers from a broad range of disciplines, such as biological and medical sciences, chemistry, mathematics, environmental sciences, etc. The topics discussed in the book are in bioinformatics, computational biology, environmental sciences, and their related interdisciplinary fields.

The chapters, including 26 research articles and a short review, are written to highlight the most recent advances and breakthroughs in these subject fields. In order to improve the readability of the book, each chapter includes an "Additional Reading" section and a "Key Terms and Definitions" section.

TARGETS AND OVERALL OBJECTIVES OF THE BOOK

This book aims to provide a platform of communication for researchers in the fields of bioinformatics and computational biology and to foster the continuing development of these interdisciplinary fields. We hope that this book may serve the research community in bioinformatics and computational biology by presenting some of the most exciting and frontier research work in these fields. The prospective audience of the book would be scientists, researchers, and students actively working in these fields and related disciplines. We hope by reading this book, the readers may get a sense of where these fields are and what limitations there may be in existing work. Interested readers may then be empowered to formulate new ideas for future research and push the fields forward by embarking on such innovative work.

ORGANIZATION OF THE BOOK

The 27 chapters of the book are divided into 7 sections:

- Method Development and Application in Bioinformatics
- Biological Networks and Systems Biology
- Computational Predictions of Drug Properties
- Medical Signal Processing and Analysis
- Computational Biology
- Structure and Modeling
- Problems and Solutions in Environmental Sciences

A broad range of topics in bioinformatics and computational biology are covered by the book, including protein functional classification by a novel software tool (Chapter 1), a novel method for microarray data integration (Chapter 2), a novel representation of genomes by chaos game theory (Chapter 3), protein fold classification and recognition (Chapters 4 and 5), DNA sequence similarity analysis (Chapter 6), a novel feature for microRNA representation and classification (Chapter 7), a combined experimental and bioinformatics study of lipid enzymes (Chapter 8), biological networks and pathways in systems biology and their computational modeling (Chapters 9, 10, and 11), drug properties and delivery (Chapters 12, 13, and 14), medical signal analysis (Chapter 15), standardization and modernization of traditional Chinese medicine diagnostic methods (Chapters 16 and 17), computational models for ecological system (Chapters 18 and 19), neural science (Chapter 20) and the evolution of proteins (Chapter 21), molecular modeling of bio-materials (Chapter 22), and a short review on the structures of bacteria hydrogenases (Chapter 23). The book also contains four chapters in the field of environmental sciences, covering several important topics ranging from plant adaptation to water shortage, plant water uptake model, China's energy risk analysis (Chapter 26), and novel methods for the recycling of electronic waste (Chapter 27).

A brief description of each of the chapters follows:

Section 1: Method Development and Application in Bioinformatics

Chapter 1: *JFeature: A Java Package for Extracting Global Sequence Features from Proteins for Functional Classification,* by Xin Chen and Hangyang Xu

Prediction of various functional properties of proteins has long been a central theme of bioinformatics in the post-genomic era. Statistical learning, in addition to analysis based on sequence similarity, was proven successful to detect complex sequence-function associations in many applications. JFeature is an integrated Java tool to facilitate extraction of global sequence features and preparation of example sets, in statistical learning studies of sequence-function relationships. With a user-friendly graphical interface, it computes the composition, distribution, transition and auto-correlation features from sequence. It also helps to assemble a negative example set based on the most-dissimilar principle. The Java package and supplementary documentations are available at http://www.cls.zju.edu.cn/rlibs/software/jfeature.html.

Chapter 2: *Cross-Platform Microarray Data Integration Combining Meta-Analysis and Gene Set Enrichment Analysis,* by Jian Yu, Jun Wu, Miaoxin Li, Yajun Yi, Yu Shyr, Yixue Li, and Lu Xie

Integrative analysis of microarray data has been proven as a more reliable approach to deciphering molecular mechanisms underlying biological studies. Traditional integration such as meta-analysis is usually gene-centered. Recently, gene set enrichment analysis (GSEA) has been widely applied to bring gene-level interpretation to pathway-level. GSEA is an algorithm focusing on whether an a priori defined set of genes shows statistically significant differences between two biological states. However, GSEA does not support integrating multiple microarray datasets generated from different studies. To overcome this, the improved version of GSEA, ASSESS, is more applicable, after necessary modifications. By making proper combined use of meta-analysis, GSEA, and modified ASSESS, this chapter reports two workflow pipelines to extract consistent expression pattern change at pathway-level, from multiple microarray datasets generated by the same or different microarray production platforms, respectively. Such strategies amplify the advantage and overcome the disadvantage than if using each method individually, and may achieve a more comprehensive interpretation towards a biological theme based on an increased sample size. With further network analysis, it may also allow an overview of cross-talking pathways based on statistical integration of multiple gene expression studies. A web server where one of the pipelines is implemented is available at: http://lifecenter.sgst.cn/mgsea//home.htm.

Chapter 3: *Chaos Game Representation of Mitochondrial Genomes: Markov Chain Model Simulation and Vertebrate Phylogeny,* by Guo-Sheng Han, Zu-Guo Yu, Bo Li, Vo Anh, and Yi-Quan Li

The mitochondrial genomes have provided much information on the evolution of this organelle and have been used for phylogenetic reconstruction by various methods with or without sequence alignment. In this paper, we explore the mitochondrial genomes by means of the chaos game representation (CGR), a tool derived from the chaotic dynamical systems theory. If the DNA sequence is a random collection of bases, the CGR will be a uniformly filled square; on the other hand, any pattern visible in the CGR contains information on the DNA sequence. First we use the Markov chain models to simulate the CGR of mitochondrial genomes. Then we model the noise background in the genome sequences by a Markov chain. A simple correlation-related distance approach without sequence alignment based on the CGR of mitochondrial genomes is proposed to analyze the phylogeny of 64 selected vertebrates.

Chapter 4: *A Two-layer Learning Architecture for Multi-Class Protein Folds Classification*, by Ruofei Wang and Xieping Gao

Classification of protein folds plays a very important role in the protein structure discovery process, especially when traditional sequence alignment methods fail to yield convincing structural homologies. In this chapter, we have developed a two-layer learning architecture, named TLLA, for multi-class protein folds classification. In the first layer, OET-KNN (Optimized Evidence-Theoretic K Nearest Neighbors) is used as the component classifier to find the most probable K-folds of the query protein. In the second layer, we use support vector machine (SVM) to build the multi-class classifier just on the K-folds, generated in the first layer, rather than on all the 27 folds. For multi-feature combination, ensemble strategy based on voting is selected to give the final classification result. The standard percentage accuracy of our method at ~63% is achieved on the independent testing dataset, where most of the proteins have <25% sequence identity with those in the training dataset. The experimental evaluation based on a widely used benchmark dataset has shown that our approach outperforms the competing methods, implying our approach might become a useful vehicle in the literature.

Chapter 5: *Improving PSI-BLAST's Fold Recognition Performance through Combining Consensus Sequences and Support Vector Machine*, by Ren-Xiang Yan, Jing Liu, and Yi-Min Tao

Profile-profile alignment may be the most sensitive and useful computational resource for identifying remote homologies and recognizing protein folds. However, profile-profile alignment is usually much more complex and slower than sequence-sequence or profile-sequence alignment. The profile or PSSM (position-specific scoring matrix) can be used to represent the mutational variability at each sequence position of a protein by using a vector of amino acid substitution frequencies and it is a much richer encoding of a protein sequence. Consensus sequence, which can be considered as a simplified profile, was used to improve sequence alignment accuracy in the early time. Recently, several studies were carried out to improve PSI-BLAST's fold recognition performance by using consensus sequence information. There are several ways to compute a consensus sequence. Based on these considerations, we propose a method that combines the information of different types of consensus sequences with the assistance of support vector machine learning in this chapter. Benchmark results suggest that our method can further improve PSI-BLAST's fold recognition performance.

Chapter 6: *A New Approach for DNA Sequence Similarity Analysis Based on Triplets of Nucleic Acid Bases,* by Dan Wei, Qingshan Jiang, and Sheng Li

Similarity analysis of DNA sequences is a fundamental research area in Bioinformatics. The characteristic distribution of L-tuple, which is the tuple of length L, reflects the valuable information contained in a biological sequence and thus may be used in DNA sequence similarity analysis. However, similarity analysis based on characteristic distribution of L-tuple is not effective for the comparison of highly conservative sequences. In this paper, a new similarity measurement approach based on Triplets of Nucleic Acid Bases (TNAB) is introduced for DNA sequence similarity analysis. The new approach characterizes both the content feature and position feature of a DNA sequence using the frequency and position of occurrence of TNAB in the sequence. The experimental results show that the approach based on TNAB is effective for analysing DNA sequence similarity.

Chapter 7: *MicroRNA Precursor Prediction Using SVM with RNA Pairing Continuity Feature,* by Huan Yang, Yan Wang, Trupti Joshi, Dong Xu, Shoupeng Yu, and Yanchun Liang

MicroRNAs (miRNAs) are endogenous single-stranded non-coding RNAs of ~22 nucleotides in length and they act as post-transcriptional regulators in bacteria, animals and plants. Almost all current methods for computational prediction of miRNAs use hairpin structure and minimum of free energy as characteristics to identify putative pre-miRNAs from a pool of candidates. We discovered a new effective feature named "basic-n-units" (BNU) to distinguish pre-miRNAs from pseudo ones. This feature describes pairing continuity of RNA secondary structure. Simulation results show that a classification method, called Triplet-SVM-classifier, achieved an accuracy of 97.24% when this BNU feature was used. This is a 3% increase caused solely by adding this new feature. We anticipate that this BNU feature may increase the accuracy for most classification methods.

Chapter 8: *Four Long-Chain Acyl-Coenzyme A Synthetase Genes That Might be Involved in the Biosynthesis of Lipids in Brassica Napus,* by Fuge Zhu, Xiaoli Tan, Juan Li, Mingyu Wei, and Lili Yu

Long chain acyl-coenzyme A synthetases (LACSs) activate free fatty acid to acyl-CoA thioesters, and play important roles in the biosynthesis and degradation of lipids. In this study, four cDNAs (Complementary DNA) encode long chain fatty acyl-CoA synthetase activity has been found in Brassica napus. Sequence analysis indicated that the four LACSs possessed typical molecular characteristics of LACS. Compared with low oil content varieties seed, the four genes are strongly expressed in high oil content varieties seeds at 35 days after pollination (DAP). The expression pattern suggested that the four LACSs might be involved in the biosynthesis of lipids and oil accumulation in rapeseed.

Section 2: Biological Networks and Systems Biology

Chapter 9: *Topological Analysis of Axon Guidance Network for Homo Sapiens,* by Xuning Chen and Weiping Zhu

Axonal outgrowth is usually guided by a variety of guidance factors, such as netrins, ephrins, slits and semaphorins, and is one of the critical steps for the proper formation of neural networks. However, how the signal molecules function and why some of these play more important roles than others in guiding the axonal directional outgrowth has not been fully understood. In this study, we try to solve the problem by using the complex network analysis method. The signal molecules and interactions are treated as the nodes and edges to construct the axon guidance network model for Homo sapiens. The data of the model are taken from the KEGG database, and an analysis workbench named Integrative Visual Analysis Tool for Biological Networks and Pathways (VisANT) is employed to analyze the topological properties, including the degree distribution and the top co-expressed genes of the axon guidance network. This study has just opened a window into understanding the mechanism of axon guidance.

Chapter 10: *Evaluation of Coupled Nuclear and Cytoplasmic p53 Dynamics*, by Tingzhe Sun, Meihong Cai, Jun Cui, and Pingping Shen

The tumor suppressor protein p53 predominantly serves as a sequence specific transcription factor that may be activated upon exposure to diverse stimuli. One potent death inducer, p53-upregulated mediator of apoptosis (PUMA), is transcriptionally induced by p53. Once released into the cytoplasm, PUMA can lead to the activation of Bcl-2 apoptotic network. The cytoplasmic proapoptotic roles of p53 have recently been discovered, and these findings have placed p53 into the chemical interaction network with Bcl-2 family members. PUMA can also relieve p53 from the sequestration of antiapoptotic members. Released p53 further enters the nucleus and induces PUMA expression. We proposed that this positive feedback loop could lead to bistability. Further sensitivity analysis suggested that the system which covers the interactions between p53 and BCL-2 family members is considerably sensitive to p53 production rate. Meanwhile, downstream network components are much more affected by certain parameters than upstream effectors. Therefore, this newly discovered positive feedback loop might play critical roles in apoptotic network.

Chapter 11: *Agonist Fluctuation Maintained Calcium Signaling in a Mesoscopic System*, by Lin Ji and Haiyan Wang

Signals in transduction cascades are widely exposed to stochastic influences. In this work, we investigate the effects of agonist release noises on calcium signaling. Besides the usually considered "amplitude noise", the case of "frequency noise" is also discussed. Simulation results show that the transduction cascades may amplify these noises when its intensity is bigger than certain critical value. The amplified noise show constructive effect to maintain the calcium signaling in critical signal-free cases. Moreover, the signal is more sensitive to the "frequency noise" than to the "amplitude noise". This suggests frequency fluctuations in signaling cascades may have greater influence than the amplitude ones, which is an important finding for signal transduction in complex pathways. Since biological systems are inherently stochastic, this work demonstrates how the calcium system takes advantage of the environmental fluctuations to maintain signaling, and therefore provide effective, sensitive signal communication.

Section 3: Computational Predictions of Drug Properties

Chapter 12: *Theoretical Study on the Antioxidant Activity of Alizarin, Purpurin, and Pseudopurpurin*, by Ruifa Jin, Hongzheng Bao, Yin Bai, and Xiuhua Li

Hydroxyanthraquinone derivatives are a large group of natural polyphenolic compounds found widely in plants. The cytotoxic activities of hydroxyanthraquinone derivatives have been demonstrated using cancer cell lines. The pharmacological effect can be explained by their antioxidant activity and their inhibition of certain enzymes. There are two main kinds of mechanism, H-atom transfer and one-electron transfer, by which antioxidants can play their role. The structural and electronic properties of hydroxyanthraquinone derivatives, alizarin, purpurin, pseudopurpurin, and their radicals were investigated using density functional theory. It turned out that these three molecules appear to be good candidates for high antioxidant activity species, particularly for pseudopurpurin. Taking this system as an example, we present an efficient method for the investigation of antioxidant activity for such kind of hydroxyanthraquinone derivatives from theoretical point of view. With the current work, we hope to highlight the antioxidant activity of hydroxyanthraquinone derivatives and stimulate the interest for further studies and exploitation in pharmaceutical industry.

Chapter 13: *Human Oral Bioavailability Prediction of Four Kinds of Drugs*, by Aixia Yan, Zhi Wang, Jiaxuan Li, and Meng Meng

In the development of drugs intended for oral use, good drug absorption and appropriate drug delivery are very important. Now the predictions for drug absorption and oral bioavailability follow similar approach: calculate molecular descriptors for molecules and build the prediction models. This approach works well for the prediction of compounds which cross a cell membrane from a region of high concentration to one of low concentration, but it does not work very well for the prediction of oral bioavailability, which represents the percentage of an oral dose which is able to produce a pharmacological activity. The models for bioavailability had limited predictability because there are a variety of pharmacokinetic factors influencing human oral bioavailability. Recent study has shown that good quantitative relationship could be obtained for subsets of drugs, such as those that have similar structure or the same pharmacological activity, or those that exhibit similar absorption and metabolism mechanisms. In this work, using MLR (Multiple Linear Regression) and SVM (Support Vector Machine), quantitative bioavailability prediction models were built for four kinds of drugs, which are Angiotensin Converting Enzyme Inhibitors or Angiotensin, Receptor Antagonists, Calcium Channel Blockers, Sodium and Potassium Channels Blockers and Quinolone Antimicrobial Agents. Explorations into subsets of compounds were performed and reliable prediction models were built for these four kinds of drugs. This work represents an exploration in predicting human oral bioavailability and could be used in other dataset of compounds with the same pharmacological activity.

Chapter 14: *In Silico Prediction of Blood Brain Barrier Permeability: A Support Vector Machine Model*, by Zhi Wang, Aixia Yan, and Jiaxuan Li

The ability of penetration of the blood-brain barrier is an important property for the development of Central Nervous System drugs, which is commonly expressed by logBB (logBB = log(Cbrain/Cblood). In this work, a support vector machine was used to build quantitative models of blood brain barrier permeability. Molecular descriptors for 182 compounds were calculated by ADRIANA.Code and 12 descriptors were selected using the automatic variable selection function in Weka. Based on two common physicochemical descriptors (xlogP and Topological Polar Surface Area (TPSA)) and 10 2D property autocorrelation descriptors on atom pair properties, an SVM regression model was built. The built model was validated by an external test set. The reliable predictions of the test set demonstrate that this model performs well and can be used for estimation of logBB values for drug and drug-like molecules.

Section 4: Medical Signal Processing and Analysis

Chapter 15: *The Study of Transesophageal Oxygen Saturation Monitoring*, by Zhiqiang Zhang, Bo Gao, Guojie Liao, Ling Mu, and Wei Wei

In this chapter, the transesophageal oxygen saturation (SpO2) monitoring system was proposed based on the early experiments, to provide a new program of SpO2 acquisition and analysis and avoid the limitation of traditional methods. The PPG (photoplethysmographic) signal of descending aorta and left ventricular was monitored in the experiment. The analysis of the peak-to-peak values, the standard deviation and the position of peaks in signal waveforms showed that in vivo signal was more stable and sensitive; and the physiological information was reflected in the left ventricular PPG waveform. Therefore, it can be concluded that the transesophageal SpO2 monitoring technology has better guidance in clinical applications.

Chapter 16: *Digital Auscultation System of Traditional Chinese Medicine and Its Signals Acquisition-Analysis Methods,* by Fanpeng Zhou, Jianjun Yan, Yiqin Wang, Fufeng Li, Chunming Xia, Rui Guo, and Haixia Yan

Digital auscultation of Traditional Chinese Medicine (TCM) is a relatively new technology which has been developed for several years. This system makes diagnoses by analyzing sound signals of patients using signal processing and pattern recognition. The paper discusses TCM auscultation in both traditional and current digital auscultation methods. First, this article discusses demerits of traditional TCM auscultation methods. It is through these demerits that a conclusion is drawn that digital auscultation of TCM is indispensable. Then this article makes an introduction to voice analysis methods from linear and nonlinear analysis aspects to pattern recognition methods in common use. Finally this article establishes a new TCM digital auscultation system based on wavelet analysis and Back-propagation neural network (BPNN).

Chapter 17: *Pulse Wave Analysis of Traditional Chinese Medicine Based on Hemodynamics Principles*, by Rui Guo, Yiqin Wang, Haixia Yan, Fufeng Li, Jianjun Yan, and Zhaoxia Xu

From the perspective of hemodynamics principles, the pressure pulse wave marked in the radial artery is the comprehensive result of pulse wave propagation and reflection in the arterial conduit. The most common pulse charts (also called pulse wave) obtained by Traditional Chinese Medicine (TCM) pulse-taking technique, if quantified and standardized, may become a universal and valuable diagnostic tool. The methods of feature extraction of TCM pulse charts currently involve time-domain analysis, frequency-domain analysis and time-frequency joint analysis. The feature parameters extracted by these methods have no definite clinical significance. Therefore, these feature parameters cannot essentially differentiate different types of TCM pulse. In this chapter, the harmonic analysis method was applied to analyze the common TCM pulse charts (plain pulse, wiry pulse, slippery pulse). Velocity and reflectivity coefficients of pulse were calculated. We found that wave velocities and reflection coefficients of different TCM pulse have different distributions. Furthermore, we studied the clinical significance of velocities and reflection coefficients. The result suggests that wave velocity and reflection coefficient are the feature parameters of TCM pulse with physiological and pathological significance, which can be used to interpret formation of Chinese medicine pulse. Our study reveals the mechanism of TCM pulse formation and promotes non-invasive TCM pulse diagnostic method.

Section 5: Computational Biology

Chapter 18: *A New Mechanical Algorithm for Calculating the Amplitude Equation of the Reaction-Diffusion Systems*, by Houye Liu and Weiming Wang

Amplitude equation may be used to study pattern formation. In this chapter, we establish a new mechanical algorithm AE_Hopf for calculating the amplitude equation near Hopf bifurcation based on the method of normal form approach in Maple. The normal form approach needs a large number of variables and intricate calculations. As a result, deriving the amplitude equation from diffusion-reaction is a difficult task. Making use of our mechanical algorithm, we derived the amplitude equations from several biology and physics models. The results indicate that the algorithm is easy to apply and effective. This algorithm may be useful for learning the dynamics of pattern formation of reaction-diffusion systems in future studies.

Chapter 19: *Pattern Formation Controlled by External Forcing in a Spatial Harvesting Predator-Prey Model*, by Feng Rao

Predator–prey models in ecology serve a variety of purposes, which range from illustrating a scientific concept to representing a complex natural phenomenon. Due to the complexity and variability of the environment, the dynamic behavior obtained from existing predator–prey models often deviates from reality. Many factors remain to be considered, such as external forcing, harvesting and so on. In this chapter, we study a spatial version of the Ivlev-type predator-prey model that includes reaction-diffusion, external periodic forcing, and constant harvesting rate on prey. Using this model, we study how external periodic forcing affects the stability of predator-prey coexistence equilibrium. The results of spatial pattern analysis of the Ivlev-type predator-prey model with zero-flux boundary conditions, based on the Euler method and via numerical simulations in MATLAB, show that the model generates rich dynamics. Our results reveal that modeling by reaction-diffusion equations with external periodic forcing and nonzero constant prey harvesting could be used to make general predictions regarding predator-prey equilibrium,which may be used to guide management practice, and to provide a basis for the development of statistical tools and testable hypotheses.

Chapter 20: *Repetitive Firing and Bursting due to Different Bifurcation Mechanism in Unmyelinated Fibre,* by Junran Zhang, Yongguo Han, Guangcan Xiao, and Sanjue Hu

In neural science, different action potential (AP) firing patterns are typically considered to be dominated by different dynamical mechanisms. Different AP firing patterns in unmyelinated fibres can contribute to pain and sensory information transmission. Experiments in rabbit unmyelinated nerve (axon) show some interesting phenomena, mainly concerned with the AP firing patterns that changed regularly. Investigating the dynamical mechanism of unmyelinated fibre during various kinds of AP firing patterns is useful to understand the neural information processing in axon and pain information transmission. Here, we reproduced these phenomena by constructing a mathematical model, where the discharge of the Hodgkin-Huxley (H-H) neuron under square wave stimulation was studied by simulation. It is shown that square wave can induce bursting firing, especially with long time-course duration. This is different from the popular theory that explained repetitive and bursting firing due to stimulus intensity and instantaneous fluctuation. Through dynamical analysis, we found that the mechanism of the action potential pattern changed according to Hopf bifurcation, a dynamical behavior that emergence and stability of limit cycles of bifurcating from a stable equilibrium. The finding may support the neural information coding hypothesis in unmyelinated axon.

Chapter 21: *The Mathematical Modeling and Computational Simulation for Error-Prone PCR*, by Lixin Luo, Fang Zhu, and Si Deng

Many enzymes have been widely used in industrial production, for they have higher catalytic efficiency and catalytic specificity than the traditional catalysts. Therefore, the performance of enzymes has attracted wide attention. However, due to various factors, enzymes often cannot show their greatest catalytic efficiency and the strongest catalytic ability in industrial production. In order to improve the enzyme activity and specificity, people become increasingly interested in the transformation and modification of existing enzymes. For the structure modification of proteinase, this chapter introduces a computational method for modelling error-prone PCR. Error-prone PCR is a DNA replication process that intentionally introduces copying errors by imposing mutagenic reaction condition. We then conclude about the mathematical principle of error-prone PCR which may be applied to the quantitative analysis of directed evolution in future studies.

Section 6: Structure and Modeling

Chapter 22: *Molecular Dynamics Simulation of Interlayer Structure and Hydration Properties of Glycine Intercalated Layered Double Hydroxides*, by Guo-Xiang Pan, Feng Cao, Pei-Song Tang, Hai-Feng Chen, Zhe-Ming Ni, Jin-Tian Yang, Li-Geng Wang, and Min-Hong Xu

Interlayer structure, hydrogen-bond, hydration and swelling properties of glycine intercalated layered double hydroxides (LDHs-Gly) were investigated with molecular dynamics (MD) methods. The results show that the interlayer spacing dc increases as hydration level increases. The computed hydration energies reach the most negative values at low water contents and change rapidly over the range $1 \leq NW \leq 6$, and slowly and gradually approach the potential energy for bulk SPC water at $NW > 6$. But there are no local minima in the energy over the entire hydration range. This result suggests that LDHs-Gly tend to absorb water continuously in water-rich environments and enhance swelling to delaminate the hydroxide layers. The interlayers of LDHs-Gly exhibit complex hydrogen-bond network. With water content increasing, the glycine molecules progressively change their orientation from parallel to the layers to nearly perpendicular. Water molecules firstly form hydrogen-bond with M-OH layers at low water contents. While the hydroxide layers gradually get to saturation state at $Nw > 3$. And then water molecules continuously fill the interlayer to expand interlayer spacing.

Chapter 23: *Structure of Hydrogenase in Biohydrogen Production Anaerobic Bacteria*, by Ming Du and Lu Zhang

Hydrogenase plays an important role in the process of biohydrogen production. Hydrogenases have very unique active sites and are classified into three groups according to the metal composition of the active sites: the [Ni-Fe] hydrogenase, [Fe-Fe] hydrogenase, and [Fe-only] hydrogenase. In this paper, the crystal structures and active sites of three kinds of hydrogenases are examined and compared. These enzymes have an unusual structural feature in common. Their similar active site indicates that the catalytic mechanism of hydrogen activation is probably similar. The understanding of the catalytic mechanisms for the three kinds of hydrogenases may help achieve the industrialization process of hydrogen energy production. Moreover, the future research direction about the hydrogenases from auto-aggregative bacteria and the chemical mimic of hydrogenases structure is discussed.

Section 7: Problems and Solutions in Environmental Sciences

Chapter 24: *Seasonal Trade-Off between Water- and Nitrogen-Use Efficiency of Constructive Plants in Desert Riparian Forest in Hyperarid Region of China*, by Shengkui Cao, Qi Feng, Jianhua Si, Yonghong Su, Zongqiang Chang, and Haiyang Xi

Foliar δ13C values are often used to denote the long-term water use efficiency (WUE) of plants whereas long-term nitrogen use efficiency (NUE) are usually estimated by the ratio of C to N in the leaves. Seasonal variations of δ13C values, foliar nitrogen concentration and C/N ratios of Populus euphratica and Tamarix ramosissima grown under five different microhabitats of Ejina desert riparian oasis of northwestern arid regions in China were studied. The results indicated that T. ramosissima had higher δ13C value compared with that of P. euphratica. The N concentration and C/N ratios of two species were not significantly different. The seasonal pattern of three indexes in two species was different. The δ13C values and N concentration decreased during the plant's growth period. However, the change of C/N ratios was increased. Among microhabitats, there were higher δ13C values and N concentration as well as lower C/N ratios in the Dune and Gobi habitats. Foliar δ13C values significantly and positively correlated with N concentration in P. euphratica and T. ramosissima, whereas a significantly negative correlation between δ13C values and C/N ratios was found for P. euphratica. This relation in T. ramosissima was weak, but there was a significant quadratic curve relationship between δ13C values and C/N ratios, which revealed that there was a trade-off between WUE and NUE for P. euphratica and in natural condition, P. euphratica could not improve WUE and NUE simultaneously. T. ramosissima could simultaneously enhance WUE and NUE. The above characters of WUE and NUE in two plants reflected the different adaptations of desert species to environmental condition.

Chapter 25: *Root Water Uptake Model of Populus Euphratica in Desert Riparian Forest in Extreme Arid Region,* by Yongzheng Tian, Jianhua Si, Qi Feng, and Shengkui Cao

Plant root water uptake is a key way to transfer soil water to the atmosphere. It is an important part of the research on water transforming patterns in the SPAC (Soil-Plant-Air Continuum). So understanding the water absorption patterns of plant root system is a base to recognize the SPAC. Recently there are many studies on the water absorption patterns of plant root system. However, the researched plants are mostly crops and the main researched areas are regions with adequate precipitation. There are only a few studies on the water absorption of natural plants in extreme arid desert regions. This paper studied the root water absorption patterns of Populus euphratica and established the corresponding mathematical model based on the data of root density and soil water dynamics in root zone in desert riparian forest in extreme arid region. The finite difference method was used to discretize the soil water movement equation with evaporation boundary conditions. Numerical simulation analysis of soil water movement in root zone of Populus euphratica showed that the simulated values were consistent with the measurement values with 92-98% precision. This work provides a theoretical basis for the study of water movement in the SPAC.

Chapter 26: *The Fuzzy Integrated Energy Prior-warning Model Based on Entropy Weight*, by Yaqun He, Hua Wei, Weiran Zuo, Xiaobing Wu, Xin Ge, Shan Wu, and Baofeng Wen

Based on the analysis of five factors affecting energy risks, including supply and demand, economy, environment, transport, and disaster, this chapter establishes the prior-warning index system of the energy risk by covering 3 sub-systems and 37 indexes. The three sub-systems are the coal sub-system, the petroleum and natural gas sub-system, and the integrated factors sub-system. Fuzzy synthesis evaluation was applied to confirm the internal estimated index weight of the sub-systems. Moreover, the risk prior-warning model of the energy sub-systems was established by the method. The weights of the three sub-systems were determined through the concept of entropy weight, and the prior-warning indexes of energy risk were applied to evaluate the total energy security of the three sub-systems. Finally, the prior-warning model of energy risk in China was established. The entire situation of energy safety of China was summarized via empirical analysis.

Chapter 27: *A Novel Flowsheet for the Recycling of Valuable Constituents from Waste Printed Circuit Boards,* by Jingfeng He, Yaqun He, Nianxin Zhou, Chenlong Duan, Shuai Wang, and Hongjian Zhang

Waste printed circuit boards (PCBs) contain a number of valuable constituents. It is of great significance to separate precious metals and non-metallic constituents from waste PCBs with appropriate methods for resource recycling and environment protection. A novel flowsheet for the recycling of waste PCBs using physical beneficiation methods was constructed. Waste PCBs were disassembled into substrates and slots firstly. The substrates were crushed to the size below 1mm through wet impact crushing and separated with a tapered column separation bed. The results indicated that products with integrated separation efficiency of 93.9% and metal recovery ratio of 93.7% were obtained by the primary separation with the water discharge of 5.5 m3/h, feed-rate of 250g/min and inclination angle of 35°. Waste PCBs slots components were crushed to the size of 0.5-5mm through impact crushing and separated with an active pulsing air classifier. The separation results showed that products with integration separation efficiency of 92.4% and metal recovery ratio of 96.2% were obtained with the airflow velocity of 2.90m/s and pulsing frequency of 2.33Hz. Precious metals could be obtained by further separation and purification of the metal components and the non-metal components could be used as refuse derived fuel. The flowsheet has great potential to be applied in the field of waste PCBs treatment and recycling.

Editors:
Limin Angela Liu, Shanghai Jiao Tong University, China
Dong-Qing Wei, Shanghai Jiao Tong University, China
Yixue Li, Shanghai Center for Bioinformation Technology, China

Editorial Assistant:
Huimin Lei, Shanghai Jiao Tong University, China

May, 2010

Section 1
Method Development and Application in Bioinformatics

Chapter 1

JFeature:
A Java Package for Extracting Global Sequence Features from Proteins for Functional Classification

Xin Chen
Zhejiang University, China

Hangyang Xu
Zhejiang University, China

ABSTRACT

Prediction of various functional properties of proteins has long been a central theme of bioinformatics in the post-genomic era. Statistical learning, in addition to analysis based on sequence similarity, was proven successful to detect complex sequence-function associations in many applications. JFeature is an integrated Java tool to facilitate extraction of global sequence features and preparation of example sets, in statistical learning studies of sequence-function relationships. With a user-friendly graphical interface, it computes the composition, distribution, transition and auto-correlation features from sequence. It also helps to assemble a negative example set based on the most-dissimilar principle. The Java package and supplementary documentations are available at http://www.cls.zju.edu.cn/rlibs/software/jfeature.html.

INTRODUCTION

In the last decade, genome projects have been generating a huge amount of sequences at an exponential rate. By the year 2009, more than 500 species have been sequenced, whereas the characterization of newly discovered genes is lagging far behind. Computational approaches are usually sought to predict function or functional class of many new genes yet to be studied experimentally.

Sequence similarity based approaches, in the forms of global alignment, local alignment or hidden Markov model, are extensively used to assign putative functions for new genes. Recent studies show that statistical learning approaches could be an effective alternative and/or supplement, especially in the case of predicting function of distantly-related proteins or homologous proteins with different functions (Cai et al., 2003). Their successful applications have also been reported in predicting protein functional classes (Karchin et al., 2002), protein-protein interactions (Bock &

DOI: 10.4018/978-1-60960-064-8.ch001

Gough, 2001), sub-cellular localizations (Zhang, 2006) and many other functional aspects of proteins from sequences.

Statistical learning approaches construct statistical models, such as neural network models or support vector machine (SVM) models, trained from known examples of the target sequence-function relationship. The models are then used to predict the functions of unknown sequences. The learning algorithms, in most cases, only deal with encoded representations of the examples sequences (known as the feature vectors), instead of the raw sequences themselves. Moreover, they usually require both positive and negative examples (sequences with and without a certain function) for training.

The feature vectors representing example sequences are usually required to have a fixed length for most learning algorithms. Therefore, researchers often compute global sequence features to build a feature vector with the same number of components. In this case, each component (a global feature) describes sequence characteristics on a whole protein level. A global feature is typically a real-valued function of some physicochemical property and / or sequential order of the residues in the sequence. Four types of functions have been demonstrated to be useful in extracting informative features for functional classifications. They are the composition, distribution, transition and auto-correlation functions. The four different function types, in combination with the over 500 different amino acid properties (Kawashima & Kanehisa, 2000), result in thousands of possible global features. A set of the most discriminative features is often chosen empirically to form the feature vector. Moreover, many rounds of optimizations are usually necessary.

In many applications, we want to predict proteins with certain functions, for instance, the prediction of potential allergen proteins. This requires both allergen (positive) and non-allergen (negative) protein examples to train. While positive examples are usually reported in literatures

and can be collected, there is hardly any primary data source where negative examples can be found. Without much knowledge on the potential distributions of negative examples in a particular objective, many researchers resort to the intuitively solution of constructing a negative example dataset that is most unlike the positive one. Such an approach has produced satisfactory results in many applications, including the prediction of drug-target likeness (Xu et al., 2007), protein-protein interactions (Ben-Hur and Noble, 2005; Gomez, et al., 2003; Zhang, et al., 2004), and proteins functional classes (Lin, et al., 2006). In addition, similar to positive examples, negative examples are better to be sampled from all potential negative examples uniformly without any bias. Empirical evidence suggests that positive examples are usually clustered in association with their protein family classifications. Assuming the same for negative examples, protein family based sampling of negative examples would help to get an unbiased sampling of negative examples. This is the idea implemented for negative example preparations in several recent studies (Cai, et al., 2003; Lin, et al., 2006; Xue, et al., 2004). In the above example, satisfactory results classifying allergen and non-allergen proteins were achieved by assembling negative examples from randomly picked PFam families that do not show sequence similarities to any of the allergic effect-causing proteins (Cui, 2007).

Till 2009, many software tools and packages are available to facilitate statistical learning analysis. However, there is still no convenient software package assisting the extraction of sequence features and preparation of negative examples. Therefore, the *JFeature* toolbox was developed as a bridging tool for efficient statistical learning studies on sequence-function relationship.

THE *JFEATURE* TOOLBOX

JFeature is implemented in Java. Its current version (1.0) contains two main functional modules: extracting features from protein sequences and assembling negative examples from a classification system. It supports a multitude of data formats providing seamless integration with major statistical learning tools and packages for downstream research work.

The composition, transition and distribution features are calculated based on protein sequences encoded by residue properties. Taking hydrophobicity as an example, all residues can be categorized as hydrophobic (L), neutral (N), or hydrophilic (H). Therefore, an arbitrary sequence can be coded by the three category letters as shown in Figure 1. Composition (C) refers to the percentage of amino acids in a particular category (in this case, $C_H=11/30=36.67\%$, $C_L=11/30=36.67\%$ and $C_N=8/30=26.67\%$). Transition (T) characterizes the frequency in percentage that amino acids of a particular category are followed by amino acids of a different category (for example, there are overall 22 transition events. $T_{H/L}=10/22=45.45\%$, $T_{H/N}=5/22=22.73\%$ and $T_{L/N}=7/22=31.82\%$). Distribution (D) measures the position where the n_{th} percentile of the amino acids of a particular category is located. Usually the 1_{st}, 25_{th}, 50_{th}, 75_{th} and 100_{th} percentiles are used (in this case, $D_{H1}=1/30=3.33\%$, $D_{H25}=6/30=20\%$, $D_{H50}=18/30=60\%$, $D_{H75}=24/30=80\%$ and $D_{H100}=29/30=96.67\%$). Details of the algorithms can be found in the User's Guide (http://www.cls.zju.edu.cn/rlibs/software/JFeature_User_Guide.pdf).

Auto-correlation features describe the sequential relationship of residues. They are calculated based on continuous property values. As different physicochemical property scales differ much in value range. Usually the property values need to be normalized before auto-correlation (such as in Equation 1). Then auto-correlations features are calculated with equations like Equation 2.

$$H(i) = (H^0(i) - \bar{H}) / \sigma$$

where $\bar{H} = \dfrac{1}{20}\sum_{i=1}^{20} H^0(i)$,

$$\sigma = \sqrt{\frac{1}{20}\sum_{i=1}^{20}(H^0(i) - \bar{H})^2} \quad (1)$$

$$I(d) = \frac{\dfrac{1}{N-d}\sum_{i=1}^{N-d}(H(R_i) - \bar{H})(H(R_{i+d}) - \bar{H})}{\dfrac{1}{N}\sum_{i=1}^{N}(H(R_i) - \bar{H})^2} \quad (2)$$

JFeature allows a flexible choice of properties in the AAindex database for the computation of auto-correlation features. It also supports user-specified property values. In these equations, $H^0(i)$ ($i=1...20$) is the original AAindex property value for each of the 20 residues. $H(i)$ represents the normalized property value of the i_{th} residue in the protein sequence (Kawashima & Kanehisa, 2000). A protein sequence can therefore be represented as a property value sequence [$H(1)$, $H(2)$, $H(3)...H(L)$], where L is the total length of the protein sequence. $I(d)$ reflects sequential correlation between all pairs of d_{th} neighboring

Figure 1. An arbitrary example for feature extraction

```
Category Sequence: H L H N L H L L H N L N H L N N L H H L H N L H H N N L   H   L
   Sequence Index: 1         5          10          15          20          25          30
      Index for H: 1   2       3         4           5         6 7   8       9 10          11
      Index for L:   1     2   3 4     5       6       7         8       9         10 11
      Index for N:         1           2       3     4 5           6           7 8
    H/L Transition: 1       2 3   4           5         6 7 8       9           10 11
    H/N Transition:       1           2       3                   4         5
    L/N Transition:     1           2 3     4   5           6           7
```

residues. Besides the above method, *JFeature* provides many other algorithms for normalization and auto-correlation calculation, such as the Moreau-Broto method, the Moran method, and the Geary method. More information on the available algorithms can be found in the User's Guide.

Another major function of *JFeature* is to facilitate assembling a negative example set based on a designated protein classification system. By default, *JFeature* uses the NCBI blast tool (Altschul, et al., 1990) to determine whether a positive sequence shall be associated with a pFam family. The NCBI blast tool requires all sequences in the pFam database formatted in its native blastdb format. This is a once for ever work. After the pFam database is formatted, all subsequent negative example generation jobs can use the same formatted database files. Note that because of a limitation inherited from the NCBI blast tool, file paths to the database files and blast executables (formatdb and blastall) cannot include spaces, e.g. "D:\\Program Files\Blast\bin\blastall.exe" is not allowed. JFeature also allows the use of custom protein classification system other than pFam. Users may prepare a custom classification specification file in the FASTA format. In the description line of each Fasta sequence, there should be a sequence ID and a family ID, separated by a space. For example, in a sequence with a description line ">Q9XZV0_9CILI/2-235 PF00244.9;14-3-3", the sequence ID is "Q9XZV0_9CILI/2-235" and its family ID is "PF00244.9;14-3-3". Then, *JFeature* calls the external standalone NCBI blast tool to search sequences similar to any of the positive example sequences. Sequences less than 50 amino acids long would be ignored for computational reasons. Based on tunable criteria of E-value, identity, and match length, protein classes containing any hits are marked as positive classes. Negative examples are then randomly sampled from the remaining classes uniformly.

The interoperability between *JFeature* and major statistical learning tools is implemented by its abundant data exporting features. Its can write data files for Weka, MLC and LibSVM. It can also export data in the Excel CSV format and a number of other flat-file formats.

APPLICATION

The usefulness of *JFeature* was demonstrated with an interesting application to predict drug targets, regardless of their associated drugs or diseases. It has been observed that small chemicals have shared certain structural properties to be a successful drug, which is known as the property of "drug likeness". An appealing proposition is therefore that drug targets, as the binding partner of drugs, shall also display disease-independent similarities corresponding to the "drug-likeness" properties of small chemicals. As protein structures and functions are determined by sequences, it was expected that the "drug-target likeness" might be observed with sequence features.

Positive examples of known drug targets were collected from DrugBank (Wishart et al., 2006). Negative examples were assembled by *JFeature*. Composition, distribution, and transition features were extracted from example sequences based on nine physicochemical properties. Then, the examples represented in feature vectors were handed to the Weka software (Gewehr et al., 2007) for an SVM classification experiment. Detailed treatment of data and the algorithms used were fully expanded in the User's Guide. In a 10-folds cross-validation evaluation, the optimal SVM model recorded 67.1% for sensitivity and 96.1% for specificity. This observation strongly suggested that "drug-target likeness" does exist and that our feature extraction approach was usefulness to detect it. More details can be found in (Xu et al., 2007). Below describes in detail how JFeature streamlined this study.

Collection of Positive Examples

Drug targets are collected from the Drugbank database (Wishart et al., 2006).

1. Go to Drugbank http://redpoll.pharmacy. ualberta.ca/drugbank/
2. Click "Download" in the top right corner of the home page to get to the download page. Find the data set that contains "Approved Drug Target Protein Sequences". Click "Non-redundant" to download the raw positive set.
3. Clean this dataset by removing sequences that were too similar (>70% identity) or too short (less than 50 residues). We have 520 protein sequences left. This data cleaning procedure will help to get better accuracy.

We provided an example positive data set (positive.txt) in the example directory of the *JFeature* package (http://www.cls.zju.edu.cn/ rlibs/software/example_data.tar.gz).

Assembling of the Negative Examples

With positives examples ready, we can now assemble a negative example dataset based on the most-dissimilar principle. The negative example generation interface is illustrated below.

1. In "Menu Bar" (A), select "Tools/Negative Examples Generator".
2. In "File Path Section" (C), specify the paths of

> formatdb program executable (e.g. D:\JFeature\Blast\bin\formatdb.exe),
> blastall program executable (e.g. D:\JFeature\Blast\bin\blastall.exe),
> database file (e.g. D:\JFeature\pfam\ Pfam-A-full-new.fasta),
> and positive example file (e.g. D:\JFeature\example\positive.txt).

3. Specify desired number of negative examples (e.g. 5000) in (E).

Figure 2. The negative example generation interface

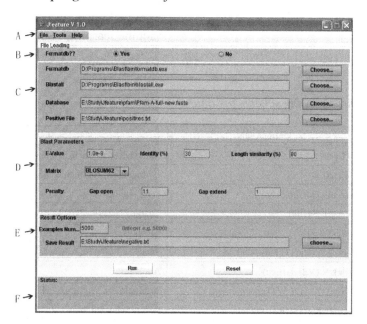

4. Specify the output file for storing the negative example set (e.g. D:\JFeature\example\negative.txt) in (E).

5. Click "Generate".

Specify Custom Property Scale

We used a 9-category coding scheme to extract CTD features (Table 1).

This custom coding scheme was specified in the "Custom property index specification" interface (Figure 3) and this coding scheme was selected for computing the CTD features in the property selection interface (Figure 4).

1. Select "Tools/Feature Vector Generator" in "Menu Bar" (A).

2. Click the "Custom" button (I).

3. In "Description", type in "Test Index", fill in other blanks as in Figure 3. Click "Save".

4. Type "Test" in "Search Text Bar" (G). Click "Search".

5. Find the right property index name in search results. Check "CTD", then click "OK".

6. Click "Submit". In the confirmation interface, click "Next".

Extracting Feature Vectors

The feature vector extraction interface was shown in Figure 5.

1. Click "Load" button in "File Input" (J). Specify the positive data file path (e.g. D:\JFeature\example\positive.txt). In the "Class Label" field, change the drop-down list to "Positive".

2. Click "Load" again, specify the negative data file path (e.g. D:\JFeature\example\negative.txt). In the "Class Label" field, change the drop-down list to "Negative".

3. In "C.T.D. Parameters" (K), change "Number of Groups" to 9.

4. In "Output Format" (N), check .arff (Weka).

5. Click "Run" and specify the output file path in the pop-up window. (e.g. D:\JFeature\example\result).

Statistical Learning Analysis

Now with the example dataset ready, we could proceed to the downstream statistical learning analysis. We use the well-known package Weka to demonstrate the processes. The detailed instructions on how to install and use Weka for machine learning researches can be found in its

Table 1. The 9-category encoding scheme for amino acids

Category	Amino Acids	Description
1	C (Cys)	Strongly conserved in evolution
2	M (Met)	Hydrophobic, sulfur containing
3	N (Asn), Q (Gln)	Polor, amides
4	D (Asp), E (Glu)	Charged, acids
5	S (Ser), T (Thr)	Alcohols
6	P (Pro), A (Ala), G (Gly)	Small
7	I (Ile), V (Val), L (Leu)	Aliphatic
8	F (Phe), Y (Tyr), W (Trp)	Aromatic
9	H (His), K (Lys), R (Arg)	Positive charged, base

Figure 3. The custom property index specification interface

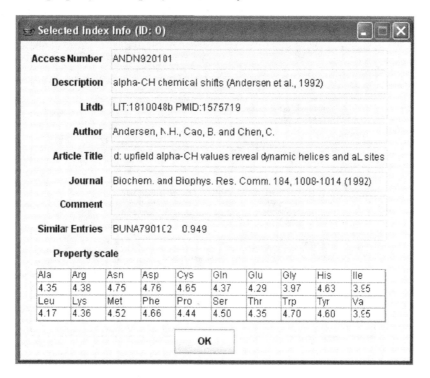

Figure 4. The property selection interface

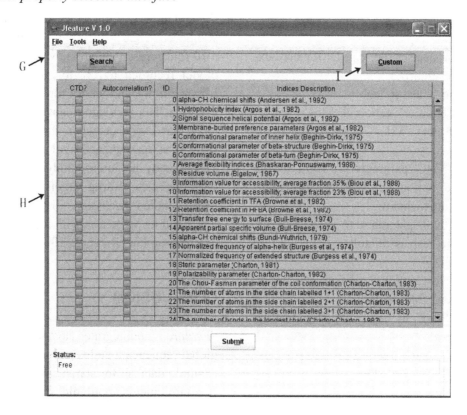

Figure 5. The feature vector extraction interface

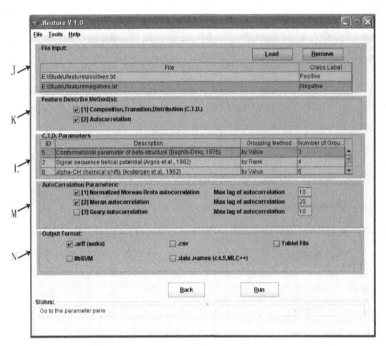

website (http://www.cs.waikato.ac.nz/~ml/weka/index.html).

1. Start weka/Explorer.
2. Open the dataset file, e.g. D:\JFeature\example\result.arff.
3. Click the "Classify" tab.
4. In the "Classifier" section, click the "Choose" button. Select "Weka/Classifiers/functions/SMO".
5. Click "SMO parameters", right to the "Choose" button. This will open the parameter-settings window.
6. Set c=100.0, gamma=0.6, useRBF=True, leave the rest as default. Click "OK" to continue.
7. In the "Test options" section, set "cross-validation" folds to 10.
8. Click "Start" to begin the classification experiment.

Results and Brief Analysis

We obtained a training set of 5520 examples composed of 520 positives and 5000 negatives. In a 10 folds cross-validation evaluation, the SVM model recorded 67.1% for sensitivity, 96.1% for specificity, and 93.4% for overall prediction accuracy. This was significant enough to demonstrate that drug targets share disease-independent features at the sequence level and further studies to accurately and interpretably define this shared characteristics of drug targets was encouraged. More detailed discussions on "drug-target likeness" and its prediction with the SVM approach can be found in (Xu et al., 2007).

CONCLUSION

JFeature is an integrated Java tool for extracting global sequence features and preparing negative example data set for statistical learning studies. It complements available statistical learning tools and makes the study of sequence-function relationship much easier. With a large number of tunable parameters and a friendly interface, it offers great flexibility and extensibility to experiments with different features proven useful in previous studies. Its usefulness is illustrated by an example of predicting drug targets from their sequences, based on the CTD features extracted by the *JFeature* software.

ACKNOWLEDGMENT

This toolbox is developed under the support of the National Natural Science Foundation of China (NSFC) grant 30600039.

REFERENCES

Altschul, S. F., Gish, W., Miller, W., Myers, E. W., & Lipman, D. J. (1990). Basic local alignment search tool. *Journal of Molecular Biology*, *215*(3), 403–410.

Ben-Hur, A., & Noble, W. S. (2005). Kernel methods for predicting protein-protein interactions. *Bioinformatics (Oxford, England)*, *21*(Suppl 1), i38–i46. doi:10.1093/bioinformatics/bti1016

Bock, J. R., & Gough, D. A. (2001). Predicting protein-protein interactions from primary structure. *Bioinformatics (Oxford, England)*, *17*(5), 455–460. doi:10.1093/bioinformatics/17.5.455

Cai, C. Z., Han, L. Y., Ji, Z. L., Chen, X., & Chen, Y. Z. (2003). SVM-Prot: Web-based support vector machine software for functional classification of a protein from its primary sequence. *Nucleic Acids Research*, *31*(13), 3692–3697. doi:10.1093/nar/gkg600

Cui, J., Han, L. Y., Li, H., Ung, C. Y., Tang, Z. Q., & Zheng, C. J. (2007). Computer prediction of allergen proteins from sequence-derived protein structural and physicochemical properties. *Molecular Immunology*, *44*(4), 514–520. doi:10.1016/j.molimm.2006.02.010

Gewehr, J. E., Szugat, M., & Zimmer, R. (2007). BioWeka-extending the Weka framework for bioinformatics. *Bioinformatics (Oxford, England)*, *23*(5), 651–653. doi:10.1093/bioinformatics/btl671

Gomez, S. M., Noble, W. S., & Rzhetsky, A. (2003). Learning to predict protein-protein interactions from protein sequences. *Bioinformatics (Oxford, England)*, *19*(15), 1875–1881. doi:10.1093/bioinformatics/btg352

Karchin, R., Karplus, K., & Haussler, D. (2002). Classifying G-protein coupled receptors with support vector machines. *Bioinformatics (Oxford, England)*, *18*(1), 147–159. doi:10.1093/bioinformatics/18.1.147

Kawashima, S., & Kanehisa, M. (2000). AAindex: amino acid index database. *Nucleic Acids Research*, *28*(1), 374. doi:10.1093/nar/28.1.374

Lin, H. H., Han, L. Y., Zhang, H. L., Zheng, C. J., Xie, B., & Chen, Y. Z. (2006). Prediction of the functional class of lipid binding proteins from sequence-derived properties irrespective of sequence similarity. *Journal of Lipid Research*, *47*(4), 824–831. doi:10.1194/jlr.M500530-JLR200

Wishart, D. S., Knox, C., Guo, A. C., Shrivastava, S., Hassanali, M., & Stothard, P. (2006). DrugBank: a comprehensive resource for in silico drug discovery and exploration. *Nucleic Acids Research*, *34*(1), D668–D672. doi:10.1093/nar/gkj067

Xu, H., Lin, M., Wang, W., Li, Z., Huang, J., Chen, Y., & Chen, X. (2007). Learning the drug target-likeness of a protein. *Proteomics*, *7*(23), 4255–4263. doi:10.1002/pmic.200700062

Xue, Y., Yap, C. W., Sun, L. Z., Cao, Z. W., Wang, J. F., & Chen, Y. Z. (2004). Prediction of P-glycoprotein substrates by a support vector machine approach. *Journal of Chemical Information and Computer Sciences, 44*(4), 1497–1505. doi:10.1021/ci049971e

Zhang, L. V., Wong, S. L., King, O. D., & Roth, F. P. (2004). Predicting co-complexed protein pairs using genomic and proteomic data integration. *BMC Bioinformatics, 5*, 38. doi:10.1186/1471-2105-5-38

Zhang, T. L., & Choua, K. C. (2006). Prediction of protein subcellular location using hydrophobic patterns of amino acid sequence. *Computational Biology and Chemistry, 30*(5), 367–371. doi:10.1016/j.compbiolchem.2006.08.003

Zhang, H. L., Lin, H. H., Tao, L., Ma, X. H., Dai, J. L., Jia, J., & Cao, Z. W. (2008). Prediction of Antibiotic Resistance Proteins from Sequence Derived Properties Irrespective of Sequence Similarity. *International Journal of Antimicrobial Agents, 32*(3), 221–226. doi:10.1016/j.ijantimicag.2008.03.006

Zhu, F., Han, B. C., Kumar, P., Liu, X. H., Ma, X. H., & Wei, X. N. (2010). Update of TTD: Therapeutic Target Database. *Nucleic Acids Research, 38*(1), D787–D791. doi:10.1093/nar/gkp1014

Zhu, F., Han, L. Y., Chen, X., Lin, H. H., Ong, S., & Xie, B. (2008). Homology-Free Prediction of Functional Class of Proteins and Peptides by Support Vector Machines. *Current Protein & Peptide Science, 9*(26), 70–95.

ADDITIONAL READING

Cai, C. Z., Han, L. Y., Ji, Z. L., Chen, X., & Chen, Y. Z. (2003). SVM-Prot: Web-based support vector machine software for functional classification of a protein from its primary sequence. *Nucleic Acids Research, 31*(13), 3692–3697. doi:10.1093/nar/gkg600

Wishart, D. S., Knox, C., Guo, A. C., Shrivastava, S., Hassanali, M., & Stothard, P. (2006). DrugBank: a comprehensive resource for in silico drug discovery and exploration. *Nucleic Acids Research, 34*(1), D668–D672. doi:10.1093/nar/gkj067

Xu, H., Lin, M., Wang, W., Li, Z., Huang, J., Chen, Y., & Chen, X. (2007). Learning the drug target-likeness of a protein. *Proteomics, 7*(23), 4255–4263. doi:10.1002/pmic.200700062

KEY TERMS AND DEFINITIONS

AAIndex: An amino acid index is a set of 20 numerical values representing a particular physicochemical or biological property of the 20 different amino acid residues.

Auto-Correlation: Auto-correlation is defined as the simple linear correlation of a time series with its own past; that is, the correlation of the sequence of values x(t) with the sequence of values x(t+w) occurring w units of time later. The time displacement is called the lag. The auto-correlation function is a function of the variable lag. We here borrow the auto-correlation concept to describe the sequential correlation between protein residues.

Feature Vector: A real number vector whose elements are different sequence features describing the same sequence. A feature vector can be considered an encoded representation of a protein sequence.

Machine Learning (Supervised): Deducing a function from training data (consisting example objects and their desired outputs). This function is able to predict the desired outputs for new objects.

Positive and Negative Examples: In machine learning tasks where the desired outputs are class labels in a two-category classification system, the examples in the two categories are called positive examples and negative examples. Often the positive label is given to the category of interest.

Sequence Feature: A real number describing one specific characteristic of a protein sequence.

12

Chapter 2
Cross–Platform Microarray Data Integration Combining Meta–Analysis and Gene Set Enrichment Analysis

Chapter 2
Cross–Platform Microarray Data Integration Combining Meta–Analysis and Gene Set Enrichment Analysis

Jian Yu
Tongji University, China

Jun Wu
Shanghai Center for Bioinformation Technology, China

Miaoxin Li
Shanghai Center for Bioinformation Technology, China

Yajun Yi
Vanderbilt University, USA

Yu Shyr
Vanderbilt University, USA & Yixue Li Shanghai Center for Bioinformation Technology, China

Lu Xie
Shanghai Center for Bioinformation Technology, China

ABSTRACT

Integrative analysis of microarray data has been proven as a more reliable approach to deciphering molecular mechanisms underlying biological studies. Traditional integration such as meta-analysis is usually gene-centered. Recently, gene set enrichment analysis (GSEA) has been widely applied to bring gene-level interpretation to pathway-level. GSEA is an algorithm focusing on whether an a priori defined set of genes shows statistically significant differences between two biological states. However, GSEA does not support integrating multiple microarray datasets generated from different studies. To overcome this, the improved version of GSEA, ASSESS, is more applicable, after necessary modifications. By making proper combined use of meta-analysis, GSEA, and modified ASSESS, this chapter reports two workflow pipelines to extract consistent expression pattern change at pathway-level, from multiple microarray

DOI: 10.4018/978-1-60960-064-8.ch002

datasets generated by the same or different microarray production platforms, respectively. Such strategies amplify the advantage and overcome the disadvantage than if using each method individually, and may achieve a more comprehensive interpretation towards a biological theme based on an increased sample size. With further network analysis, it may also allow an overview of cross-talking pathways based on statistical integration of multiple gene expression studies. A web server where one of the pipelines is implemented is available at: http://lifecenter.sgst.cn/mgsea//home.htm.

INTRODUCTION AND BACKGROUND

Gene expression profiling has become an important tool for biological research, creating exponentially increasing amount of microarray data. However, several studies have shown that when identifying Differentially Expressed Genes (DEGs) in two groups of tissues (such as cancer vs. normal), the consistency of results among different labs or even batches was rather poor (Choi, 2004). This would cause confusion in follow-up experimental research. The direct comparison of various microarray studies is restricted by different protocols, microarray platforms, and analysis techniques, etc. (Warnat, 2005). Integrative analysis of multiple microarray data has always been both an attraction and a challenge.

There have been some studies using statistical and computational methods to integrate gene expression data (Warnat, 2005; Cheadle, 2007; Bosotti, 2007; Li 2006). The most typical integrative approach at gene level is meta-analysis. In statistics, a meta-analysis combines the results of several studies that address a set of related research hypotheses. In statistics, a meta-analysis combines the results of several studies that address a set of related research hypotheses. Meta-Analysis has been widely used in public health research (Berry, 2000). Rhodes (2002) and Choi (2004) were the first to apply meta-analysis in cross-platform microarray data integration. They identified the concordance of significantly differentially expressed genes among several microarray datasets of prostate cancer and hepatocellular carcinoma (HCC). It was demonstrated that meta-analysis increased the sensitivity of analysis and allowed for small but consistent expression changes to

be detected. More applications of meta-analysis in gene expression studies were reported in the following studies (Hong, 2006; Conlon, 2007; Marot, 2009; Pihur, 2009).

Although meta-analysis succeeded in combining results from different datasets, it has its limitations. First limitation is, only overlapping genes represented in all platforms could be used in the analysis. Therefore it is more suitable for integration of studies using the same miroarray platform. Same platforms indicate that the microarray chips are from the same manufacturer, same probe type (cDNA or oligo nucleotides) and same probe set design. Another limitation of meta-analysis is, it is an integrative analysis at single gene level, which means, results are often demonstrated as long lists of statistically significant genes without meaningful biological interpretations.

Recently, a gene set-level approach named Gene Set Enrichment Analysis (GSEA) has been widely applied in microarray study. It is a powerful technique to determine whether members of a predefined gene set, e.g., genes that belong to the same pathway or share the same cellular function or component are significantly changed in two groups of tissues based on the whole-genome gene expression data (Subramanian, 2005). For biological research, "pathway" gene sets are often chosen. Therefore, in this chapter, gene set-level is often referred to as pathway-level.

These existing studies suggest that for datasets from same microarray platform, meta-analysis plus GSEA may be a good approach for integrative analysis at pathway-level. In fact, that is our proposed Pipeline I in this chapter.

However, the situation may be more complex for integrative analysis across different microarray platforms. Platforms from the same manufacturer but with different probe sets or platforms from different manufacturers are defined as different platforms. For data generated using different platforms, a large amount of gene expression information would be lost if only genes present in all platforms are used, as required by meta-analysis. Therefore meta-analysis can not be directly performed. As for GSEA, one good example was shown by Subramanian (2005) who performed GSEA on two independent studies of gene expression profiling of lung adenocarcinoma patients with good or poor clinical outcome, and he identified overlap among the significantly enriched gene sets in the patients with good prognosis. It is shown in this example that only resulting gene set lists are comparable if GSEA is performed directly on individual dataset; there can be no real integration of original data.

However, GSEA provides a framework for further integrative analysis, for it can extract the gene-level expression data to pathway-level so that it has the potential to bypass gene-by-gene mapping among all datasets. In GSEA, an Enrichment Score (ES) and a corresponding p-value are calculated for each pathway to represent whether this pathway is enriched or not. An improved application of GSEA, ASSESS (Analysis of Sample Set Enrichment Scores) (Edelman, 2006), makes it possible to estimate each sample's contribution to the ES. Although ASSESS originally aims to assay the variation of pathway activity for different samples, this method may facilitate meta-analysis among different platforms. By defining an ES for each sample, the traditional expression profile at gene level becomes an "enrichment score profile" at pathway level. In this kind of profile, an ES which indicates the pathway activity is just like an ordinary expression value which shows the gene abundance in microarray profile for each sample. Naturally, meta-analysis can be introduced to the "enrichment score profiles" to perform integrative analysis as it is done on gene expression profiles. This is our proposed Pipeline II in the

chapter, combining ASSESS and meta-analysis. Integration across different platforms can thus be performed on predefined pathway-level datasets extracted from original gene-level expression profiles.

MAIN FOCUS OF THE CHAPTER

Issues, Controversies, Problems

As microarray data accumulate rapidly, integrative analysis is expected to be an efficient approach to extract information from different studies. Meta-analysis is a useful approach, but it can only integrate common genes among all datasets. Moreover, it is gene-centered. The output is a long list of DEGs, to which further functional classification is needed to imply the biological significance. GSEA, an outstanding gene-set analysis approach, can bring gene-level interpretation to pathway-level. There are two different issues we have to face in microarray data integration, the first from same platforms (same manufacturer, same probe type, same probe sets design), and the second from different platforms (different probe type or probe sets design). Different work pipelines need to be developed to achieve real integration of original data and at biologically meaningful pathway-level. For example, for different microarray platforms, neither meta-analysis nor GSEA can be performed directly to obtain real integration on original data.

Solutions and Recommendations

In order to overcome the flaws of meta-analysis and gene-set level analysis, and to deal with both cross-same platform and cross-different platform situations, in this chapter, two workflow pipelines were constructed: Pipeline I combines meta-analysis and GSEA, and deals with microarray data integration from same platforms. Pipeline II combines ASSESS and meta-analysis, and works on microarray data integration from different platforms. ASSESS is the improved version of GSEA, which can bring original gene-level data from individual microarray experiment to gene set level. With a common gene set list, data across different microarray platforms can be integrated with meta-analysis. We further modified ASSESS to ASSESS', to make it more applicable to our study (will be described in another session below).

In the first case, meta-analysis is applied to calculate a transformed z-score for each gene across the platforms. Z-score is derived from the average effect size. The z-score corresponding to a p-value of 0.05 in a two-sided normal distribution is 1.96. (For the measure of differential expression of a gene, a standardized mean difference is obtained as an effect size index. See Choi, 2003 for details).

A list of ranked Z-scores that are related to the phenotypes of two classes are given as input for GSEA software to obtain the enriched gene sets (pathways) (See Pipeline I, Figure 1).

For the second case, our approach is to transform the dataset of each platform from gene level to gene set level by using the modified ASSESS (designated as ASSESS' below). For each individual sample in one platform, E-Scores (Enrichment Score, indicating the pathway activity of each sample) for gene sets are obtained. Then in all datasets, the output ES of ASSESS' for all samples represented an "enrichment score profile". Meta-analysis is finally performed on these profiles to obtain the enriched gene sets

Figure 1. Schematic representation of two workflows for integrative analysis cross the same platforms and different platforms

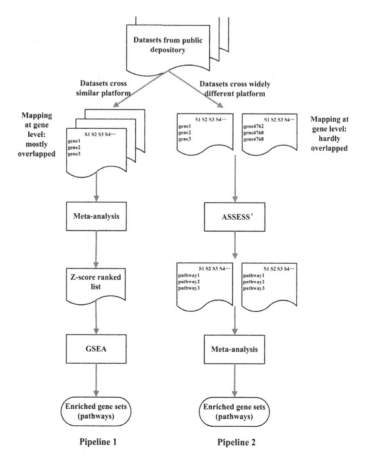

across different platforms (See Pipeline II, Figure 1).

Two publicly available breast cancer datasets and two HCC gene expression datasets are investigated for the two pipelines respectively.

Pipeline I Incorporating Meta-Analysis and GSEA

For meta-analysis we used GeneMeta (Choi, 2003), an R (R is a free software environment for statistical computing and graphics, for more details, please refer to http://www.r-project.org) package that can be freely downloaded from Bioconductor homepage (http://www.bioconductor. org/packages/2.3/bioc/html/GeneMeta.html). The GSEA software (v2.0.1) is obtained from Broad Institute website (http://www.broad.mit.edu/ gsea/). The corresponding predefined sets of genes (Molecular Signature Database, MSigDB v1.1) are also downloaded from the GSEA website. We used the C2 (Curated gene sets) of MSigDB in our study for it corresponds to widely investigated biological pathway by domain experts, which is more reliable. An online web server--Meta Analytic Gene Set enrichment Analysis (MGSEA) has been constructed for Pipeline I based on Apache and is implemented with PHP. It is composed of R scripts of meta-analysis and GSEA. Users can accomplish integrative analysis across two or

three datasets and receive the enriched gene sets as the final result directly from the web site. The web server is freely available at http://lifecenter. sgst.cn/mgsea//home.htm.

Pipeline II Modification for ASSESS

ASSESS is an improved application of GSEA approach. In GSEA, the variations in gene set enrichment over individual samples are not considered. In ASSESS gene set enrichment scores for each sample is calculated based on likelihood ratio to form an "enrichment score profile", in which each row is a gene set and each column is an individual sample. By introducing likelihood ratio, ASSESS quantifies the contribution of each sample to the ES rather than just returns a unique ES for all dataset in GSEA. Then meta-analysis is performed on the transferred datasets to retrieve enriched gene sets. However, in order to ensure the meta-analysis can be conducted in such "enrichment score profile", the process of ES generation must be phenotype independent and every ES must be normalized, just like ordinary microarray expression profile. As ASSESS does not aim to perform integrative analysis, the Matlab scripts retrieved from ASSESS website make use of phenotype label information of each sample when estimating ES of a gene set for itself and do not calculate a normalized enrichment score

Table 1. Information of the microarray datasets used in pipeline integration study

Cancer	Dataset	Study	Platform	Sample	Genes	Pipeline
Breast cancer	GSE1561	Farmer, 2005	Affymetrix Chip	Estrogen Receptor positive (27): negative (22)	22215	Pipeline I
	GSE2944	Yu, 2006	Affymetrix Chip	Estrogen Recpetor positive (57): negative (39)	22215	
HCC	D2	Choi, 2004	Incyte Genomics cDNA dual channel array	HCC (23): adjacent non-tumor tissues (23)	4097	Pipeline II
	GSE3500	Chen, 2002	non-commercial cDNA dual channel array	HCC (104): adjacent non-tumor tissues (75)	18098	

(NES) for gene sets. Our modification is focused on overcoming the two limitations and detailed description can be found in the additional file:

http://cid-5701384154d622dd.skydrive.live. com/self.aspx/.Public/AdditionFile.doc

RESULTS

As the application of Pipeline I is more straightforward, we provide a simple web server--Meta Analytic Gene Set enrichment Analysis (MG-SEA), where datasets can be uploaded directly, and meta-analysis and GSEA can be run contiguously and automatically. For different microarray platforms, Pipeline II is recommended, which is slightly more complicated than pipeline I and may require some programming experience. Modified ASSESS' script source code can be provided to users upon request.

Four cancer microarray datasets are chosen to demonstrate our integrative analysis workflows. The information of the four datasets is listed in Table 1.

GSE1561 and GSE2294 are two breast cancer related datasets downloaded from Gene Expression Omnibus database (GEO). They both are generated on Affymetrix GeneChip HG-U133A. GSE1561 contains 27 Estrogen Receptor (ER) positive and 22 ER negative breast cancer samples; while GSE2294 contains 57 ER positive and 39 ER negative samples. We used them for Pipeline I, i.e. integration cross similar platforms.

Dataset D2 is initially presented in one integrative analysis of multiple HCC expression profiles (Choi, 2004). Microarray studies of 23 HCC tissue and 23 non-tumor liver tissues are performed on spotted microarray containing 10,000 cDNA clones from Incyte Genomics. GSE3500 (downloaded from GEO) is an array experiment consisting of 104 HCC tissue and 75 non-tumor liver tissue samples performed on printed microarray of 23,075 human cDNA clone set. Although two datasets are both from cDNA chips, the number of overlapped genes is only 2133. We chose these

two datasets for integrative analysis across different platforms, i.e. for Pipeline II.

Data preprocessing is performed for these four publicly available datasets as follows: for within-array replicates we calculated the mean expression value for each gene; all genes with missing expression values in greater than 50% of the samples are filtered out; for the remaining genes, we replaced their missing expression values using the KNN (K-nearest neighbor, k=10) (Troyanskaya, 2001) method.

Cross Similar Platforms (Pipeline I)

Although GSE1561 and GSE2294 come from two different studies (Lustig, 2003), the microarray platform they used are the same--Affymetrix GeneChip HGU133A. Pipeline I was used to integrate these two datasets. First the two datasets were imported into GeneMeta to calculate Z-score for each gene. Z-score indicates the extent of gene expression difference in both datasets. Then a ranked Z-score list was given as an input file for the GSEA software. GSEA returned twenty pathways which are significantly enriched at a nominal P-value less than 0.01 and FDR less than 0.25 (Table 2). FDR (False Discovery Rate) was estimated to address the multiple testing problem in statistical test by adapting the core algorithm of SAM (Tusher, 2001). When using GSEA on single non-integrated dataset of GSE1561 and GSE2294 based on the same criteria, no pathway was significantly enriched. Figure 2A demonstrates the top 10 pathways of GSEA implemented on single dataset or after integration with Pipeline I. The top gene set CK1PATHWAY in GSE1561 and top gene set PTENPATHWAY in GSE2294 with insignificant p-value or FDR, are able to be detected significantly enriched after integration. Our results imply that the sensitivity of detecting enriched pathways by GSEA is significantly increased by pipeline I, and the integrative analysis gains the ability to detect small but consistent

Table 2. List of enriched gene sets after integrative analysis with pipeline I, under the statistical criteria of p<0.01 and FDR<0.25

	Gene Sets	NES	NOM p-val	FDR q-val
1	PYK2PATHWAY	2.29	0	0
2	AT1RPATHWAY	2.07	0	0.021
3	ERK5PATHWAY	1.92	0	0.073
4	PTENPATHWAY	1.84	0	0.134
5	CREBPATHWAY	1.83	0	0.117
6	CK1PATHWAY	1.83	0	0.099
7	ST_DIFFERENTIATION_PATHWAY_IN_PC12_CELLS	1.76	0	0.101
8	MEF2DPATHWAY	1.69	0	0.14
9	CCR3PATHWAY	1.69	0	0.128
10	EDG1PATHWAY	1.68	0	0.131
11	RASPATHWAY	1.68	0	0.121
12	OXIDATIVE_PHOSPHORYLATION	1.66	0	0.126
13	GPCRPATHWAY	1.64	0	0.128
14	HDACPATHWAY	1.64	0	0.121
15	ST_P38_MAPK_PATHWAY	1.58	0	0.14
16	MTORPATHWAY	1.57	0	0.143
17	CIRCADIAN_EXERCISE	1.55	0	0.148
18	CXCR4PATHWAY	1.54	0	0.145
19	MRNA_PROCESSING_REACTOME	1.47	0	0.195
20	AKTPATHWAY	1.45	0	0.211

expression changes based on multiple datasets at the pathway level.

Validation of Enriched Pathways on an Independent Breast Cancer Dataset

The gene signature constituting each enriched pathway was further validated on an independent microarray dataset of breast cancer by hierarchical clustering. The testing dataset consisted of 8 ER positive samples and 8 ER negative samples (Weigelt, 2003). Our results show that gene signatures of some enriched pathways from our Pipeline I analysis could sufficiently distinguish ER positive and ER negative breast cancers in the independent testing dataset. Figure 3 is an example: with expression pattern of twenty three gene members

in CREBPATHWAY ER positive and ER negative samples in the new dataset clustered correctly according to their phenotypes but one.

Cross Different Platforms (Pipeline II)

D2 and GSE3500 are datasets from different platforms, the number of overlapping genes of the two datasets are only 2133. For such different platforms, we applied the pipeline II for data integration and compared the result with that by just overlapping their GSEA enrichment gene sets lists. First, each set of gene expression data was transformed from gene level to gene set (pathway) level by using ASSESS' (modified ASSESS) separately. As recommended by GSEA, only gene sets with the size of 15 to 500 genes

Figure 2. A. Pipeline I integration of two breast cancer microarray datasets: GSE1561 and GSE2294, compared to GSEA result on each dataset alone; B. Pipeline II integration of two liver cancer microarray datasets: D2 and GSE3500, compared to GSEA result on each dataset alone.

GSE1561

Enriched pathway	NES	NOM p-val	FDR q-val
CKIPATHWAY	1.560	0.020	1.000
CARM_ERPATHWAY	1.540	0.000	1.000
HSP27PATHWAY	1.540	0.039	0.779
PEPTIDE_GPCRS	1.480	0.000	1.000
GAMMA_HEXACHLOROCYCLOHEXANE_DEGRADATION	1.450	0.149	1.000
CERAMIDEPATHWAY	1.430	0.041	1.000
OVARIAN_INFERTILITY_GENES	1.410	0.020	1.000
CIRCADIAN_EXERCISE	1.400	0.042	0.963
RARRXRPATHWAY	1.400	0.104	0.893
BADPATHWAY	1.390	0.017	0.823

GSE2294

Enriched pathway	NES	NOM p-val	FDR q-val
PTENPATHWAY	1.52	0.017	1
CCR3PATHWAY	1.45	0.111	1
OXIDATIVE_PHOSPHORYLATION	1.4	0.175	1
CHOLESTEROL_BIOSYNTHESIS	1.26	0.234	1
AKTPATHWAY	1.21	0.319	1
CIRCADIAN_EXERCISE	1.18	0.213	1
IGF1RPATHWAY	1.16	0.218	1
METPATHWAY	1.15	0.261	1
SA_PTEN_PATHWAY	1.13	0.388	1
BREAST_CANCER_ESTROGEN_SIGNALING	1.1	0.278	1

Enriched pathway	NES	NOM p-val	FDR q-val
PYK2PATHWAY	2.290	0.000	0.000
AT1RPATHWAY	2.070	0.000	0.021
ERK5PATHWAY	1.920	0.000	0.073
PTENPATHWAY	1.840	0.000	0.134
CREBPATHWAY	1.830	0.000	0.117
CKIPATHWAY	1.830	0.000	0.099
CALCINEURINPATHWAY	1.820	0.026	0.089
IGF1RPATHWAY	1.790	0.022	0.095
ST_DIFFERENTIATION_PATHWAY_IN_PC12_CELLS	1.760	0.000	0.101
NDKDYNAMINPATHWAY	1.750	0.031	0.095

A   **Results of enriched pathways before and after integration with Pipeline I**

D2

Enriched pathway	NES	NOM p-val	FDR q-val
PEPTIDE_GPCRS	1.48	0.055	1
PROTEASOME_DEGRADATION	1.47	0.064	0.759
PYRIMIDINE_METABOLISM	1.46	0.052	0.514
MRNA_PROCESSING_REACTOME	1.46	0.065	0.401
P53_SIGNALING	1.39	0.066	0.502
APOPTOSIS_KEGG	1.31	0.149	0.649
DNA_DAMAGE_SIGNALING	1.31	0.097	0.572
G2PATHWAY	1.3	0.144	0.502
BREAST_CANCER_ESTROGEN_SIGNALING	1.25	0.118	0.592
ST_DIFFERENTIATION_PATHWAY_IN_PC12_CELLS	1.23	0.207	0.583

GSE3500

Enriched pathway	NES	NOM p-val	FDR q-val
CELL_CYCLE	2.02	0.002	0.013
DNA_REPLICATION_REACTOME	1.97	0	0.013
CELL_CYCLE_KEGG	1.87	0.009	0.033
G1_TO_S_CELL_CYCLE_REACTOME	1.86	0.002	0.026
HCC_SURVIVAL_GOOD_VS_POOR_DN	1.83	0.007	0.031
RNA_TRANSCRIPTION_REACTOME	1.8	0.01	0.038
RHOPATHWAY	1.75	0.014	0.054
G1PATHWAY	1.7	0.014	0.073
SIG_REGULATION_OF_THE_ACTIN_CYTOSKELETON_BY_RHO_GTPASES	1.64	0.009	0.112
G2PATHWAY	1.57	0.043	0.186

Enriched pathway	Z score	FDR
CELL_CYCLE_CHECKPOINT	-3.8203	0.0008
CIRCADIAN_EXERCISE	-3.4148	0.0036
TOB1PATHWAY	-3.0642	0.0096
NFKBPATHWAY	-2.5501	0.0427
TALL1PATHWAY	-2.5048	0.048
AKTPATHWAY	-2.4865	0.0487

B   **Results of enriched pathways before and after integration with Pipeline II**

were selected, and 323 pathways were found to be overlapped across D2 and GSE3500. The two datasets, now at the level of pathways, have the same format as the gene expression dataset, containing pathway (gene set) name in rows like gene IDs and enrichment scores for all the samples in columns like gene expression profiles. Thus, we could integrate these 2 datasets by performing meta-analysis. The Z-score corresponding to the p-value 0.05 in two-sided normal distribution

Figure 3. Unsupervised clustering analysis of an independent dataset using the gene signature from CREBPATHWAY (left column to the clustering graph) showed a clear separation of ER negative (black bar at the bottom) and positive tissues (bottom blue). In the graph red color stands for over-expression and green color stands for down-regulation. The colored version of this figure is available at http://cid-5701384154d622dd.skydrive.live.com/self.aspx/.Public/AdditionFile.doc

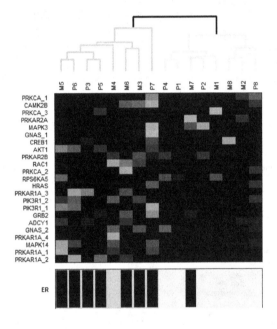

(-1.96) and FDR at 0.05 were chosen as the cutoff values (A looser threshold of FDR is also available, but 0.05 appears to be accepted in a wide range of studies). Combining two criteria (Z<-1.96 and

FDR<0.05), six significantly enriched gene sets in HCC after Pipeline II integration were found and listed in Table 3. As a contrast, using GSEA with the same criteria on single dataset produced no significant gene set in D2, and six different gene sets in GSE3500 with higher FDR values (Figure 2B). This implies that the six pathways identified in pipeline II are more reliable, due to the increased sample size.

Biological Implication of Enriched Pathways in Liver Cancer

By using our strategy to integrate two different liver cancer datasets by Pipeline II, three gene sets that had been reported before in extensive HCC related studies were found: Cell Cycle Checkpoint gene set, NFkB signaling pathway and AKT pathway. The Cell Cycle Checkpoint gene set is the most significant pathway in our study, and the relevance of which gives an idea of the general perturbations intrinsic to tumor cells (Edelman, 2008). NFkB signaling pathway regulates the expression of hundreds of genes that are involved in different cellular processes such as cell proliferation and survival, and its activation has been found in many types of tumor (Cortés, 2008). AKT pathway is one of the most frequently involved pathway in tumorigenesis (Zender, 2008) and it is reported to accelerate c-myc-induced liver neoplastic development in vivo (Factor, 2001). AKT pathway is now considered as

Table 3. The enriched gene sets after integration cross two microarray datasets of HCC under the statistical criteria of Z-score <-1.96 and FDR < 0.05

Gene Sets	Z-score	FDR
CELL_CYCLE_CHECKPOINT	-3.8203	0.0008
CIRCADIAN_EXERCISE	-3.4148	0.0036
TOB1PATHWAY	-3.0642	0.0096
NFKBPATHWAY	-2.5501	0.0427
TALL1PATHWAY	-2.5048	0.0480
AKTPATHWAY	-2.4865	0.0487

a major potential target for anti-cancer therapies (Garcia-Echeverria, 2008).

The other three gene sets have not been reported previously to be directly related to HCC, including: CIRCADIAN-EXERCISE gene set, TOB1 pathway and TALL1 pathway, suggesting unrevealed roles of their potential function in HCC progression. For CIRCADIAN-EXERCISE gene set, researches from different fields have revealed the complexity and ubiquitous nature of circadian regulation in the past several years, uncovering intriguing associations between clock components and cellular pathways implicated in tumorigenesis (Gery, 2010). TALL1, also known as BAFF, has gained increasing interest, in view of their role in cell protection, differentiation and growth. Although there remains no direct evidence between the aberrant expression of BAFF and HCC, studies have shown that BAFF dependent mechanism may play a role in the development of certain types of cancer cells, such as breast cancer (Pelekanou, 2008) and osteosarcoma

(Kohno, 2008). As for TOB1PATHWAY, the situation is a little complicated. According to the microarray data (Figure 4), the TOB1 expression is decreased in liver cancer tissue, but the pathway it regulates is activated (Table 3). TOB1 itself encodes a member of anti-proliferative proteins that have the potential to regulate cell growth. When exogenously expressed, this protein suppresses cell growth in tissue culture. In this sense, TOB1 is a tumor suppressor gene, which is concordant with its gene-level expression. However, TOB1 is also a factor identified recently that represses T cell activation and IL-2 expression (Figure 4). When the gene is down-regulated, the immune cells, especially T cells are activated and IL-2 expression is increased, which may bring immune response against cancer cells. This is concordant with the pathway-level results, that TOB1 pathway is activated in HCC. This may suggest that TOB1 may function as a tumor suppressor through modulation and regulation of multiple signaling pathways and a recent study on breast

Figure 4. TOB interacts with the TGF-beta activated transcription factor SMAD4 and SMAD3, increasing their binding to the IL-2 promoter, and helping to repress IL-2 expression in unstimulated state. Our result shows that the expression of TOB is down-regulated (marked green/within the ellipse) and IL-2 is up-regulated (marked red/right to the ellipse) in tissues of HCC comparing to non-tumor liver tissues.

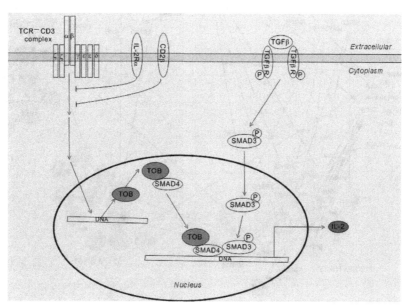

cancer provides sufficient experimental evidence to support this idea (O'Malley, 2009). Therefore, TOB1 pathway is a good example to illustrate that pathway-level analysis may help to reveal novel pathways relevant to specific tumorigenesis.

Then we sought to analyze relationships among all enriched pathways in liver cancer on a network level. STRING, a web-server to retrieve and display the repeatedly occurring neighborhood of genes was used to obtain a combined gene-network of these six pathways (von Mering, 2005). As graphed in Figure 5, the relationship between nodes (genes) refers to the confidence coefficient that is predicted by STRING according to their occurrence in several databases. The genes belonging to each pathway cluster in different sub-network. There are many interrelationships between the sub-networks of each pathway. Particularly densely connected nodes involve *SMAD3*, one of the genes identified in TOB-

1PATHWAY, and also *RELA, MAPK3 and P53*. This may implicate that each of the six pathways not only works on its own, but may also function together through cross-talking to other pathways.

DISCUSSIONS AND CONCLUSION

In our work, by distinguishing the integration approaches into cross-same microarray platforms and cross-different microarray platforms, two workflow pipelines have been constructed by different combinations of meta-analysis, gene set enrichment analysis (GSEA), ASSESS (advanced version of GSEA), and ASSESS' (our modification of ASSESS). The applications of these two pipelines were demonstrated by cancer gene expression datasets.

The results of Pipeline I--cross-same platform analysis demonstrated that: the sensitivity of

Figure 5. The number on each linked line between nodes (genes) refers to the association confidence coefficient that is predicted by STRING according to the occurrence of gene-interaction in curated databases

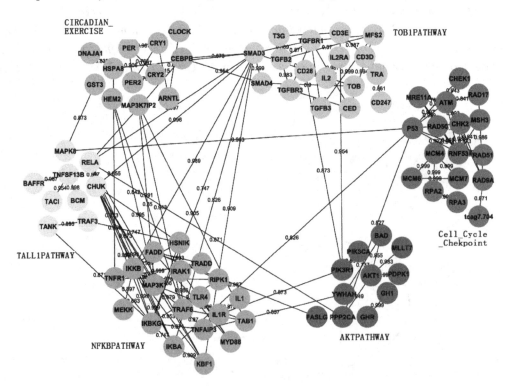

GSEA is low for small dataset. GSEA on single breast cancer microarray dataset could not identify changed pathways between ER positive and ER negative patients. By integrating two original datasets using meta-analysis, twenty significantly changed pathways were discovered; some could be verified on an independent breast cancer dataset of the same molecular pathological categories. Therefore gene set level integration analysis is possible for labs which runs only a small set of samples on microarray, as long as similar studies can be found in public resources or through collaborations. By integration, the sample size investigated can be increased.

More intractable a problem is the comparison of data from different microarray platforms. Because of the different design of probe sets, on one hand, the overlapping genes may be much fewer than total gene numbers. On the other hand, GSEA on individual dataset may generate such different results that no overlapping can be found, thus no integrative analysis is feasible. This was actually shown in our case of two liver cancer microarray study datasets used for Pipeline II analysis. Therefore for Pipeline II--cross-different platform integration, our strategy was to combine ASSESS and meta-analysis. ASSESS summarizes gene expression change to gene set level by giving an ES to each gene set under each sample. We modified ASSESS to ASSESS', to exclude the use of each sample's phenotype information when calculating gene set ES for that sample, and to add normalized enrichment score. These modifications facilitated further meta-analysis to realize integration across different platforms. However, it should be warned that when integrating different microarray platform studies, careful design of biological theme and appropriate parsing of original data may be indispensable to generate meaningful integration result.

Overall, when there exit multiple microarray studies for a similar biological theme it is worthwhile to consider appropriate integrative analysis either before or after one's own research. The choice of original datasets and integrative approaches are important, as stated in this chapter. After integration, the consistently changed pathways in different studies may be identified and some may be explored more in detail experimentally. Moreover, the cross talks among these pathways may be viewed on network level, as demonstrated by our analysis on six pathways extracted from two liver cancer microarray datasets. This will allow more systematic overview of a biological theme based on statistical integration of multiple gene expression studies.

REFERENCES

Berry, D. A., & Stangl, D. K. (2000). *Meta-Analysis in Medicine and Health Policy*. Boca Raton, FL: CRC Press.

Bosotti, R., Locatelli, G., Healy, S., Scacheri, E., Sartori, L., & Mercurio, C. (2007). Cross platform microarray analysis for robust identification of differentially expressed genes. *BMC Bioinformatics*, *8*(Suppl 1), S5. doi:10.1186/1471-2105-8-S1-S5

Cheadle, C., Becker, K. G., Cho-Chung, Y. S., Nesterova, M., Watkins, T., & Wood, W. III (2007). A rapid method for microarray cross platform comparisons using gene expression signatures. *Molecular and Cellular Probes*, *21*(1), 35–46. doi:10.1016/j.mcp.2006.07.004

Choi, J. K., Choi, J. Y., Kim, D. G., Choi, D. W., Lee, K. H., & Yeom, Y. (2004). Integrative analysis of multiple gene expression profiles applied to liver cancer study. *FEBS Letters*, *565*(1-3), 93–100. doi:10.1016/j.febslet.2004.03.081

Choi, J. K., Yu, U., & Kim, S. (2003). Combining multiple microarray studies and modeling interstudy variation. *Bioinformatics (Oxford, England)*, *19*(Suppl 1), i84–i90. doi:10.1093/bioinformatics/btg1010

Conlon, E., Song, J., & Liu, A. (2007). Bayesian meta-analysis models for microarray data: a comparative study. *BMC Bioinformatics*, *8*(80).

Cortés, S. M., Rodríguez, F. V., Sánchez, P. I., & Perona, R. (2008). The role of the NFkappaB signalling pathway in cancers. *Clinical & Translational Oncology*, *10*(3), 143–147. doi:10.1007/s12094-008-0171-3

Dennis, G., Sherman, B. T., Hosack, D. A., Yang, J., Gao, W., Lane, H. C., & Lempicki, R. A. (2003). DAVID: Database for Annotation, Visualization, and Integrated Discovery. *Genome Biology*, *4*(5), 3. doi:10.1186/gb-2003-4-5-p3

Edelman, E., Porrello, A., Guinney, J., Balakumaran, B., Bild, A., Febbo, P. G., & Mukherjee, S. (2006). Analysis of sample set enrichment scores: assaying the enrichment of sets of genes for individual samples in genome-wide expression profiles. *Bioinformatics (Oxford, England)*, *22*(14), 108–116. doi:10.1093/bioinformatics/btl231

Edelman, E. J., Guinney, J., Chi, J. T., Febbo, P. G., & Mukherjee, S. (2008). Modeling cancer progression via pathway dependencies. *PLoS Computational Biology*. .doi:10.1371/journal.pcbi.0040028

Factor, V., Oliver, A. L., Panta, G. R., Thorgeirsson, S. S., Sonenshein, G. E., & Arsura, M. (2001). Roles of Akt/PKB and IKK complex in constitutive induction of NF-kappaB in hepatocellular carcinomas of transforming growth factor alpha/c-myc transgenic mice. *Hepatology (Baltimore, Md.)*, *34*(1), 32–41. doi:10.1053/jhep.2001.25270

Garcia-Echeverria, C., Sellers, & W. R. (2009). Drug discovery approaches targeting the PI3K/Akt pathway in cancer. *Oncogene*, *27*(41), 5511–5526. doi:10.1038/onc.2008.246

Hong, F., Breitling, R., McEntee, C. W., Wittner, B. S., Nemhauser, J. L., & Chory, J. (2006). RankProd: a bioconductor package for detecting differentially expressed genes in meta-analysis. *Bioinformatics (Oxford, England)*, *22*(22), 2825–2827. doi:10.1093/bioinformatics/btl476

Kim, J., Chu, J., Shen, X., Wang, J., & Orkin, S. H. (2008). An extended transcriptional network for pluripotency of embryonic stem cells. *Cell*, *132*(6), 1049–1061. doi:10.1016/j.cell.2008.02.039

Li, S., Li, Y. H., Wei, T., Su, E. W., Duffin, K., & Liao, B. (2006). Too much data, but little interchangeability: a lesson learned from mining public data on tissue specificity of gene expression. *Biology Direct*, *1*, 33. doi:10.1186/1745-6150-1-33

Marot, G., Foulley, J., Mayer, C., & Jaffrézic, F. (2009). Moderated effect size and P-value combinations for microarray meta-analyses. *Bioinformatics (Oxford, England)*, *25*(20), 2692–2699. doi:10.1093/bioinformatics/btp444

O'Malley, S., Su, H., Zhang, T., Ng, C., Ge, H., & Tang, C. K. (2009). TOB suppresses breast cancer tumorigenesis. *International Journal of Cancer*, *125*(8), 1805–1813. doi:10.1002/ijc.24490

Pihur, V., Datta, S., & Datta, S. (2009). RankAggreg, an R package for weighted rank aggregation. *BMC Bioinformatics*, *10*(62).

Rhodes, D. R., Barrette, T. R., Rubin, M. A., Ghosh, D., & Chinnaiyan, A., M. (2002). Meta-Analysis of Microarrays: Interstudy Validation of Gene Expression Profiles Reveals Pathway Dysregulation in Prostate Cancer. *Cancer Research*, *62*(15), 4427–4433.

Subramanian, A., Tamayo, P., Mootha, V. K., Mukherjee, S., Ebert, B. L., & Gillette, M. A. (2005). Gene set enrichment analysis: a knowledge-based approach for interpreting genome-wide expression profiles. *Proceedings of the National Academy of Sciences of the United States of America*, *102*(43), 15545–15550. doi:10.1073/pnas.0506580102

Tusher, V. G., Tibshirani, R., & Chu, G. (2001). Significance analysis of microarrays applied to the ionizing radiation response. *Proceedings of the National Academy of Sciences of the United States of America*, *98*(9), 5116–5121. doi:10.1073/pnas.091062498

Warnat, P., Eils, R., & Brors, B. (2005). Cross-platform analysis of cancer microarray data improves gene expression based classification of phenotypes. *BMC Bioinformatics*, *6*, 265. doi:10.1186/1471-2105-6-265

Weigelt, B., Glas, A. M., Wessels, L. F., Witteveen, A. T., Peterse, J. L., & van't Veer, L. J. (2003). Gene expression profiles of primary breast tumors maintained in distant metastases. *Proceedings of the National Academy of Sciences of the United States of America*, *100*(26), 15901–15905. doi:10.1073/pnas.2634067100

Yoshida, Y., Nakamura, T., Komoda, M., Satoh, H., Suzuki, T., & Tsuzuku, J. K. (2003). Mice lacking a transcriptional corepressor Tob are predisposed to cancer. *Genes & Development*, *17*(10), 1201–1206. doi:10.1101/gad.1088003

Zender, L., & Kubicka, S. (2008). Molecular pathogenesis and targeted therapy of hepatocellular carcinoma. *Onkologie*, *31*(10), 550–555. doi:10.1159/000151586

Zheng, Q., & Wang, X. J. (2008) GOEAST: a web-based software toolkit for Gene Ontology enrichment analysis. *Nucleic Acids Res, 36*(Web Server issue):W358-63. Retrieved from http://omicslab.genetics.ac.cn/ GOEAST/index.php

ADDITIONAL READING

Alles, M. C., Gardiner-Garden, M., Nott, D. J., Wang, Y., Foekens, J. A., & Sutherland, R. L. (2009). Meta-analysis and gene set enrichment relative to er status reveal elevated activity of MYC and E2F in the "basal" breast cancer subgroup. *PLoS ONE*, *4*(3), e4710. doi:10.1371/journal.pone.0004710

Barrett, T., Suzek, T. O., Troup, D. B., Wilhite, S. E., Ngau, W. C. Ledoux, P., Rudnev, D., Lash, A. E., Fujibuchi, W., & Edgar, R. (2005). NCBI GEO: mining millions of expression profiles--database and tools. *Nucleic Acids Res, 1*(33) (Database issue), D562-6.

Chen, X., Cheung, S. T., So, S., Fan, S. T., Barry, C., & Higgins, J. (2002). Gene Expression Patterns in Human Liver Cancers. *Molecular Biology of the Cell*, *13*, 1929–1939. doi:10.1091/mbc.02-02-0023.

Gentleman, R. C., Carey, V. J., Bates, D. M., Bolstad, B., Dettling, M., & Dudoit, S. (2004). Bioconductor: Open software development for computational biology and bioinformatics. *Genome Biology*, *5*(10), R80. doi:10.1186/gb-2004-5-10-r80

Guo, Z., Zhang, T., & Li, X. (2005). Towards precise classification of cancers based on robust gene functional expression profiles. *BMC Bioinformatics*, *6*(58).

Hardiman, G. (2004). Microarray platforms--comparisons and contrasts. *Pharmacogenomics*, *5*(5), 487–502. doi:10.1517/14622416.5.5.487

Irizarry, R. A., Warren, D., & Spencer, F. (2005). Multiple-laboratory comparison of microarray platforms. *Nature Methods*, *2*(5), 345–350. doi:10.1038/nmeth756

Kuhn, A., Luthi-Carter, R., & Delorenzi, M. (2008). Cross-species and cross-platform gene expression studies with the Bioconductor-compliant R package 'annotationTools'. *BMC Bioinformatics*, *17*(9), 26. doi:10.1186/1471-2105-9-26

Larkin, J. E., Frank, B. C., & Gavras, H. (2005). Independence and reproducibility across microarray platforms. *Nature Methods*, *2*(5), 337–344. doi:10.1038/nmeth757

Menssen, A., Edinger, G., Grün, J. R., Haase, U., Baumgrass, R., & Grützkau, A. (2009). SiPaGene: A new repository for instant online retrieval, sharing and meta-analyses of GeneChip expression data. *BMC Genomics*, *10*(98).

Rhodes, D. R., Yu, J., Shanker, K., Deshpande, N., Varambally, R., & Ghosh, D. (2004). Large-scale meta-analysis of cancer microarray data identifies common transcriptional profiles of neoplastic transformation and progression. *Proceedings of the National Academy of Sciences of the United States of America*, *101*(25), 9309–9314. .doi:10.1073/pnas.0401994101

Shi, L., Reid, L. H., & Jones, W. D. (2006). The MicroArray Quality Control (MAQC) project shows inter- and intraplatform reproducibility of gene expression measurements. *Nature Biotechnology*, *24*(9), 1151–1161. doi:10.1038/nbt1239

Smith, D. D., Saetrom, P., Snøve, O. Jr, Lundberg, C., Rivas, G. E., Glackin, C., & Larson, G. P. (2008). Meta-analysis of breast cancer microarray studies in conjunction with conserved cis-elements suggest patterns for coordinate regulation. *BMC Bioinformatics*, *9*(63).

Troyanskaya, O., Cantor, M., Sherlock, G., Brown, P., Hastie, T., & Tibshirani, R. (2001). Missing value estimation methods for DNA microarrays. *Bioinformatics (Oxford, England)*, *17*, 520–525. doi:10.1093/bioinformatics/17.6.520

Xu, M., Kao, M. C., Nunez-Iglesias, J., Nevins, J. R., West, M., & Zhou, X. J. (2008). An integrative approach to characterize disease-specific pathways and their coordination: a case study in cancer. *BMC Genomics*, *9*(Suppl 1), S12. doi:10.1186/1471-2164-9-S1-S12

Xu, M., Li, W., James, G. M., Mehan, M. R., & Zhou, X. J. (2009). Automated multidimensional phenotypic profiling using large public microarray repositories. *Proceedings of the National Academy of Sciences of the United States of America*, *6*(30), 12323–12328. doi:10.1073/pnas.0900883106

Yajun, Y., Chun, L., Clay, M., & Alfred, L. G. Jr. (2007). Strategy for encoding and comparison of gene expression signatures. *Genome Biology*, *8*(7), R133. doi:10.1186/gb-2007-8-7-r133

Yu, Y., Tu, K., Zheng, S., Li, Y., Ding, G., & Ping, J. (2009). GEOGLE: context mining tool for the correlation between gene expression and the phenotypic distinction. *BMC Bioinformatics*, *25*(10), 264–270. doi:10.1186/1471-2105-10-264

Zhu, Y., Zhu, Y., & Xu, W. (2008). EzArray: a web-based highly automated Affymetrix expression array data management and analysis system. *BMC Bioinformatics*, *9*(46).

KEY TERMS AND DEFINITIONS

Microarray: A multiplex technology used in molecular biology and in medicine. It consists of an arrayed series of thousands of microscopic spots of DNA oligonucleotides, called features, each containing picomoles of a specific DNA sequence. This can be a short section of a gene or other DNA element that are used as probes to hybridize a cDNA or cRNA sample (called target) under high-stringency conditions. Probe-target hybridization is usually detected and quantified by detection of fluorophore, silver, or chemiluminescence-labeled targets to determine relative abundance of nucleic acid sequences in the target.

Meta-Analysis: In statistics, a meta-analysis combines the results of several studies that address a set of related research hypotheses. This is normally done by identification of a common measure of effect size, which is modeled using a form of meta-regression. Resulting overall averages when controlling for study characteristics can be considered meta-effect sizes, which are more powerful estimates of the true effect size than those derived in a single study under a given single set of assumptions and conditions.

HCC: Hepatocellular carcinoma, a primary malignancy (cancer) of the liver.

FDR: False Discovery Rate is an estimation of false positive rate in statistical test by computational method. It is a statistical method used in multiple hypotheses testing to correct for multiple comparisons. In a list of rejected hypotheses, FDR controls the expected proportion of incorrectly rejected null hypotheses (type I errors). It is a less conservative procedure for comparison, with greater power than familywise error rate (FWER) control, at a cost of increasing the likelihood of obtaining type I errors.

GSEA: Gene Set Enrichment Analysis, a computational method that determines whether an a priori defined set of genes shows statistically significant, concordant differences between two biological states (e.g. phenotypes).

ASSESS: Analysis of Sample Set Enrichment Scores. Given gene sets defined by prior biological knowledge or genes co-expressed in an experiment with a specific genetic or molecular perturbation, and a data set of expression profiles from samples belonging to two classes, ASSESS provides: a measure of the enrichment of each gene set in each sample and a confidence assessment. This extends the methodology developed in GSEA to annotate individual samples.

MSigDB: Molecular Signatures Database, a collection of gene sets for use with GSEA software.

Chapter 3

Chaos Game Representation of Mitochondrial Genomes:
Markov Chain Model Simulation and Vertebrate Phylogeny

Zu-Guo Yu
Xiangtan University, China

Guo-Sheng Han
Xiangtan University, China & Queensland University of Technology, Australia

Bo Li
Xiangtan University, China

Vo Anh
Queensland University of Technology, Australia

Yi-Quan Li
Xiangtan University, China

ABSTRACT

The mitochondrial genomes have provided much information on the evolution of this organelle and have been used for phylogenetic reconstruction by various methods with or without sequence alignment. In this paper, we explore the mitochondrial genomes by means of the chaos game representation (CGR), a tool derived from the chaotic dynamical systems theory. If the DNA sequence is a random collection of bases, the CGR will be a uniformly filled square; on the other hand, any pattern visible in the CGR contains information on the DNA sequence. First we use the Markov chain models to simulate the CGR of mitochondrial genomes. Then we model the noise background in the genome sequences by a Markov chain. A simple correlation-related distance approach without sequence alignment based on the CGR of mitochondrial genomes is proposed to analyze the phylogeny of 64 selected vertebrates.

DOI: 10.4018/978-1-60960-064-8.ch003

INTRODUCTION

The availability of long genomic sequences opens a new field of research devoted to the analysis of their structure. Singular short-word frequencies in the genome sequences have been reported for various species and shown to be species-specific (Deschavanne et al., 1999). It was shown that the dinucleotide relative abundance values vary less within a genome than among species and that closely related organisms display more similar dinucleotide composition than do distant organisms (Karlin et al., 1997).

As a form of fractal images, the chaos game representation (CGR) of a DNA sequence originally proposed by Jeffrey (1990) offers a handy approach for dealing with such large amount of data. Goldman (1993) used CGRs to explain the observed patterns by calculating the dinucleotide and trinucleotide frequencies and proposed two Markov Chain models to simulate the CGRs of long DNA sequences. Deschavanne et al. (1999) detailed genomic comparisons involving parts of the genome or the whole genome, and some constructions of molecular phylogenies based on the CGR. Later on the CGR technique was used to compare genomes by Almeida et al. (2001) and Joseph & Sasikumar (2006). The idea of CGR of DNA sequences proposed by Jeffrey (1990) was generalized and applied for visualizing and analyzing protein sequences and structures (Fiser et al., 1994; Basu et al.,. 1998; Yu et al., 2004; Yang et al., 2009). Yu et al. (2008) proposed an iterated function system to simulate the CGR of linked protein sequences of prokaryote genomes.

When complete genomes are considered, mitochondrial DNA has been proved to be a powerful tool for phylogenetic reconstruction (Reyes et al., 1998). Mitochondrial genes and genomes have long been a major focus in molecular evolution, and these genomes are excellent candidates for demonstrating the power of evolutionary genom-ics. They have the advantage that they are present in high concentrations in many tissues, reliably amplified by PCR, and can easily be enriched by purification of the mitochondria prior to DNA extraction (e.g., Dowling et al., 1996). Mito-chondrial genomes also have a strong advantage over nuclear genes in that they are unlikely to experience many intraspecific recombination events (Pollack et al., 2000). The mitochondrial gene order breakpoints were used to discuss early eukaryote evolution (Sankoff et al., 2000). Due to the problems caused by the uncertainty in alignment (Wong et al. 2008), existing tools for phylogenetic analysis based on multiple alignment could not be directly applied to the whole-genome comparison and phylogenomic studies. There has been a growing interest in alignment-free methods for phylogenetic analysis using complete genome data (Wu et al. 2009).

In the present study, we study the CGR of mitochondrial genomes. First we use the Markov Chain models proposed by Goldman (1993) to simulate these CGRs. Then a simple correlation approach without sequence alignment based on the CGR of mitochondrial genomes is proposed to analyze the phylogeny of 64 selected vertebrates.

MATERIALS AND METHODS

Genome Data Set

In order to explore the feasibility of our method, we used the 64 complete mitochondrial genome data set used by Stuart et al. (2002). The whole DNA sequences (including protein-coding and non-coding regions) of these complete genomes were obtained from the NCBI genome database (http://www.ncbi.nlm nih.gov/genbank/ge-nomes). Species represented in the analysis are shown in Table 1.

Markov Chain Models to Simulate the CGR of Mitochondrial Genomes

Chaos Game Representation of DNA Sequences

DNA sequences are composed of four different kinds of monomers (nucleotides): adenine (A),

cytosine (C), guanine (G), and thymine (T). Based on a technique from chaotic dynamics, Jeffrey (1990) proposed a chaos game representation of DNA sequences by using the four vertices of a square in the plane to represent A, C, G and T. One point is plotted for each site of the sequence: the first point is placed halfway between the centre of the square and the corner corresponding to the

Table 1. The names and their abbreviations of organisms in the analysis

name	Abbrev.	Name	Abbrev.
Alligator mississippiensis	Amis	*Artibeus jamaicensis*	Ajam
Aythya Americana	Aame	*Balaenoptera musculus*	Bmus
Balaenoptera physalus	Bphy	*Bos taurus*	Btau
Canis familiaris	Cfam	*Carassius auratus*	Caur
Cavia porcellus	Cpor	*Ceratotherium simum*	Csim
Chelonia mydas	Cmyd	*Chrysemys picta*	Cpic
Ciconia boyciana	Cboy	*Ciconia ciconia*	Ccic
Corvus frugilegus	Cfru	*Crossostoma lacustre*	Clac
Cyprinus carpio	Ccar	*Danio rerio*	Drer
Dasypus novemcinctus	Dnov	*Didelphis virginiana*	Dvir
Dinodon semicarinatus	Dsem	*Equus asinus*	Easi
Equus caballus	Ecab	*Erinaceus europaeus*	Eeur
Eumeces egregius	Eegr	*Falco peregrinus*	Fper
Felis catus	Fcat	*Gadus morhua*	Gmor
Gallus gallus	Ggal	*Gorilla gorilla*	Ggor
Halichoerus grypus	Hgry	*Hippopotamus amphibius*	Hamp
Homo sapiens	Hsap	*Latimeria chalumnae*	Lcha
Loxodonta africana	Lafr	*Macropus robustus*	Mrob
Mus musculus	Mmus	*Mustelus manazo*	Mman
Myoxus glis	Mgli	*Oncorhynchus mykiss*	Omyk
Ornithorhynchus anatinus	Oana	*Orycteropus afer*	Oafe
Oryctolagus cuniculus	Ocun	*Ovis aries*	Oari
Paralichthys olivaceus	Poli	*Pelomedusa subrufa*	Psub
Phoca vitulina	Pvit	*Polypterus ornatipinnis*	Porn
Pongo pygmaeus abelii	Ppyg	*Protopterus dolloi*	Pdol
Raja radiata	Rrad	*Rattus norvegicus*	(Rnor
Rhea americana	Rame	*Rhinoceros unicornis*	Runi
Salmo salar	Ssal	*Salvelinus alpinus*	Salp
Salvelinus fontinalis	Sfon	*Scyliorhinus canicula*	Scan
Smithornis sharpei	Ssha	*Squalus acanthias*	Saca
Struthio camelus	Scam	*Sus scrofa*	Sscr
Talpa europaea	Teur	*Vidua chalybeata*	Vcha

first nucleotide of the sequence and successive points are plotted halfway between the previous point and the corner corresponding to the base of each successive sequence site. The method produces a visualization of a DNA sequence which displays both local and global patterns. If the DNA sequence is a random collection of bases, the CGR will be a uniformly filled square; on the other hand, a pattern visible in the CGR represents some information on the DNA sequence (Goldman, 1993). Self-similarity or fractal patterns were found in these plots. Some open questions from the biological point of view based on the CGR were proposed (Jeffrey, 1990).

Once we get the CGR of a DNA sequence, a question in computational biology is how to simulate it using mathematical models. Goldman (1993) proposed to use first-order and second-order Markov chain models to simulate the CGR. The *first-order Markov chain model* is a four-state discrete time Markov chain. In this model, a 4×4 matrix P defines the probabilities with which subsequent bases follow the current base in a DNA sequence. If the base labels A, C, G and T are equated with the numbers 1, 2, 3 and 4, then P_{ij}, the jth element of the ith row of P, defines the probability that base j follows base i. The row sum of P must be equal to 1. Using this matrix, a simulated DNA sequence may be obtained by selecting the first base randomly, according to the frequencies of the bases in the DNA sequence under study. If this is base i, then the probabilities P_{i1}, P_{i2}, P_{i3} and P_{i4} are used to select the next base, and so on, until the simulated sequence is of the same length as the original DNA sequence. Goldman (1993) proposed to estimate the probabilities in the matrix P by direct calculation from the sequence's dinucleotide frequencies. If the dinucleotide xy is observed n_{xy} times in the sequence, then the probability P_{xy} is estimated by $n_{xy} / (n_{xA} + n_{xC} + n_{xG} + n_{xT})$. If the first-order Markov chain model is not sufficient, Goldman (1993) proposed to use the *second-order Markov*

chain model. In this model, each base depends on the previous bases. The probability that base z follows the dinucleotide xy, P_{xyz}, is estimated directly from the DNA trinucleotide frequencies n_{xyz} as $P_{xyz} = n_{xyz} / (n_{xyA} + n_{xyC} + n_{xyG} + n_{xyT})$. So there are in total 64 P_{xyz} values for each DNA sequence. Using these P_{xyz} values, a second-order Markov chain model simulating a DNA sequence may be obtained by selecting the first base randomly according to the frequencies of the bases, and the second base randomly according to the first base and the frequencies of dinucleotides staring with the first base in the DNA sequence under study. If the previous two bases are i and j, then the probabilities P_{ij1}, P_{ij2}, P_{ij3} and P_{ij4} are used to select the third base, and so on until the simulated sequence is of the same length as the original DNA sequence. The CGR for the simulated DNA sequence using first-order or second order Markov chain model is regarded as a simulation of the CGR of the original DNA sequence.

Simple Correlation-related Distance Approach for Vertebrate Phylogeny Based the CGR of Mitochondrial Genomes

Considering the points in a CGR of a genome, we can define a measure μ by $\mu(B) = \#(B) / N_l$, where $\#(B)$ is the number of points lying in the subset B of the CGR and N_l is the length of the genome sequence. We can divide the square $[0,1] \times [0,1]$ into meshes of sizes 64×64, 128×128, 512×512, 1024×1024, 2048×2048 or 4096×4096 (we use the classification of the species published in literatures as criteria to evaluate the trees. In our method, a mesh of 4096x4096 can give us satisfactory tree already. The optimal mesh size problem still needs further investigation). This results in a measure for each mesh. We then obtain a 64×64, 128×128, 512×512, 1024×1024, 2048×2048 or 4096×4096 matrix A, where each matrix element is the measure value of the corresponding mesh. We call *A* the measure matrix of the genome. Then for the first-order or second order Markov chain model simulation of the original CGR, we can also get a 64×64, 128×128, 512×512, 1024×1024, 2048×2048 or 4096×4096 matrix A^s. As pointed out in Qi et al. (2004) and Yu et al. (2005), in the composition vector method for phylogenetic analysis, a key step is to remove the random background before performing a cross-correlation analysis. We regard A^s as the random background of the genome here like in Yu et al. (2004). We fix the same size for *A* and A^s. Denoting $A = (A_{ij})$ and $A^s = (A^s_{ij})$, we then subtract the random background by defining $A^d = (A^d_{ij})$; here

$$A^d_{ij} = A_{ij} - A^s_{ij}. \qquad (1)$$

The matrix A^d will be used for correlation analysis.

For matrices $A^d = \left(A^d_{ij}\right)_{n\times n}$ and $B^d = \left(B^d_{ij}\right)_{n\times n}$ of two different mitochondrial genomes, with n=64,128, 512, 1024, 2048 or 4096, we consider two random variables A^d and B^d with sample values A_{ij} and B_{ij}, respectively. We denote

$$<A^d> = \frac{1}{n^2}\sum_{i=1}^{n}\sum_{j=1}^{n} A^d_{ij}, \ <B^d> = \frac{1}{n^2}\sum_{i=1}^{n}\sum_{j=1}^{n} B^d_{ij}, \qquad (2)$$

$$\delta(A^d) = \sqrt{\frac{1}{n^2}\sum_{i=1}^{n}\sum_{j=1}^{n}(A^d_{ij} - <A^d>)^2},$$

$$\delta(B^d) = \sqrt{\frac{1}{n^2}\sum_{i=1}^{n}\sum_{j=1}^{n}(B^d_{ij} - <B^d>)^2}. \qquad (3)$$

Then the sample covariance of A^d and B^d is

$$Cov(A^d, B^d) = \frac{1}{n^2}\sum_{i=1}^{n}\sum_{j=1}^{n}(A^d_{ij} - <A^d>)(B^d_{ij} - <B^d>)$$

(4) and their sample correlation coefficient is

$$\rho(A^d, B^d) = \frac{Cov(A^d, B^d)}{\delta(A^d)\delta(B^d)}. \qquad (5)$$

Asymptotically, $-1 \leq \rho(A^d, B^d) \leq 1$. If it is equal to zero, A^d and B^d are uncorrelated. We next define the *chord distance* between these two genomes by $D_{chord}(A^d, B^d) = \sqrt{2[1 - \rho(A^d, B^d)]}$. (6)

The chord distance is defined on the set of unit vectors in a vector space as the length of the chord constructed from two unit vectors. We proved that the chord distance is a proper distance metric in strict mathematical sense (i.e. it satisfies the 3 conditions of a distance metric) in Yu et al. (2010). This distance performed well in simulations of tree-building algorithms by Takezaki & Nei (1996). It has also been used to analyze microarray gene expression data (Causton et al., 2003).

Once we get the distance matrix for all genomes under study, we can construct their phylogenetic tree using the neighbour-joining (NJ) method (Saitou & Nei, 1987) in the software *SplitsTree4* V4.10 (Huson & Bryant, 2006) based on the distance matrix.

RESULTS AND DISCUSSIONS

First we derived the CGRs for all 64 selected mitochondrial genomes. For example the CGR for human mitochondrial genome is given in Figure 1(A). Then we used the first-order and second-order Markov chain models to simulate the CGRs of these mitochondrial genomes. As an example, the simulations of the CGR of human mitochondrial genome are given in Figure 1(B) and Figure 1(C) for first-order and second-order Markov chain models, respectively. Corresponding estimated probabilities in the two Markov chain models are given in Tables 2 and 3 respectively.

By comparing the simulated CGRs with the original CGRs, we see that the Markov chain models simulate the CGR of mitochondrial genomes very well (see Figure 1 as an example). The first-order Markov chain model is a special

Figure 1. (A) The CRG of the human mitochondrial genome. (B) The CGR of the simulated human mitochondrial genome using the first-order Markov chain model. (C) The CGR of the simulated human mitochondrial genome using the second-order Markov chain model.

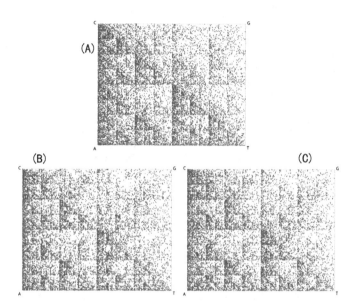

case of the second-order Markov chain model. It is obvious that the second-order Markov chain model is more refined than the first-order Markov chain model and also simulates the CGRs of the mitochondrial genomes better. We can also confirm this fact by comparing the figures in Figure 1. Goldman (1993) also gave some examples to show this fact. We find that the vertebrates with close phylogenetic relationships have similar probability matrices in first-order and second-order Markov chain models for these mitochondrial genomes.

Table 2. Probability matrix of the first-order Markov chain model for the human mitochondrial genome

Second base A C G T			
A	0.311754	0.292392	0.1566590	0.239194
First C	0.295840	0.342643	0.0845532	0.276965
base G	0.282240	0.328591	0.1959610	0.193208
T	0.334802	0.294175	0.1253060	0.245717

Now we study the phylogentic relationships of the 64 vertebrates using the distance method described in Section 2 based on the CGRs of their mitochondrial genomes. We constructed the trees based on the 64×64, 128×128, 512×512, 1024×1024, 2048×2048 and 4096×4096 measure matrices of the CGRs of genomes and using the CGRs simulated by the first-order or second-order Markov chain model as random background, respectively. We found that the phylogenetic tree based on the 4096×4096 measure matrices and using the CGR simulated by the first-order Markov chain model as random background is the best tree. We show this tree in Figure 2.

The phylogenetic tree (Figure 2) shows that the mitochondrial genomes are separated into three major groups except *Dinodon semicarinatus* (Dsem). One group contains mammals; one group contains fish; and the third group contains Archosauria (including birds and reptiles). The tree is largely in agreement in topology with the current known phylogenies of vertebrates.

Table 3. Probability matrix of the second-order Markov chain model for the human mitochondrial genome

Second base A C G T		
A	0.327478 0.30803 0.131117 0.233375	A
C	0.298328 0.346488 0.0802676 0.274916	C
First	0.222222 0.355805 0.218477 0.203496	G
base	0.298446 0.300082 0.130826 0.270646	T
	0.302083 0.295573 0.13151 0.270833 0.260259 0.355256 0.0798201 0.304666	A
	0.28246 0.357631 0.182232 0.177677	C
G	0.363004 0.290682 0.125869 0.220445	G
T		T
	0.323577 0.281301 0.213008 0.182114 0.291899 0.378492 0.0782123 0.251397	Third
	0.288056 0.355972 0.168618 0.187354 0.36342 0.254157 0.135392 0.247031	A base
	0.298977 0.275585 0.189327 0.236111 0.347754 0.297837 0.100666 0.253744	C
	0.369863 0.238748 0.195695 0.195695 0.326693 0.308765 0.113546 0.250996	G
		T
		A
		C
		G
		T

Figure 2. NJ tree of mitochondrial genomes based on the whole DNA sequences using the 4096×4096 measure matrices and the simulated CGRs by the first-order Markov chain model as random background

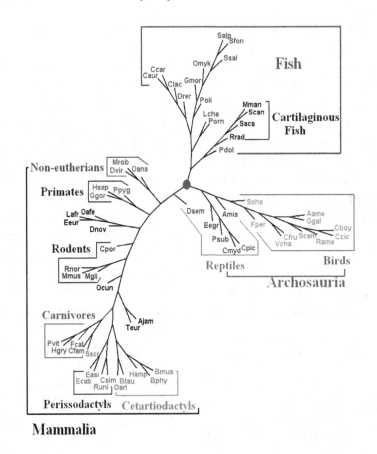

In the non-mammalian group, the fish and birds cluster as distinct groups as expected (Figure 2). In the cluster of fish, the chondrichthyes (cartilaginous fish) cluster as a group; osteichthyes (bony fish) belong to one branch except for *Protopterus dolloi* (Pdol). The relationships among cartilaginous fish are similar to those in Stuart et al. (2002). The overall phylogeny of fish, including the relationship between cartilaginous fish and bony fish, is currently uncertain (Stuart et al., 2002). Within the reptiles, they group together except for *Dinodon semicarinatus* (Dsem), the three turtles (Cmyd, Cpic and Psub) group together as a branch and the *Alligator mississippiensis* (Amis) stays closer to birds than the other reptiles as expected (Stuart et al., 2002 and references therein) in Figure 2. Within the mammals in Figure 2, perissodactyls, carnivores and cetartiodactyls group together as expected except for *Sus scrofa* (Sscr) (Stuart et al., 2002 and references therein). These three groups form the ferungulates, together with the mole (Teur) and the bat (Ajam), as observed in recent independent analyses (Mouchaty et al., 2000; Nikaido et al., 2000; Stuart et al., 2002). For the rest of the mammals, primates, rodents and non-eutherians cluster together and the non-eutherians [Marsupalia (Dvir and Mrob) and Monotremata (Oana)] are located at the root of all the mammals included in the study, which is the same as the results previously reported (Stuart et al., 2002). The rabbit (Ocun) is found to be close to rodents as expected in Figure 2. Because all rodents do not gather as a branch, our methods did not provide an answer on the unsolved issue on the monophyly of rodents (Reyes et al., 2000). In the trees presented by Li et al. (2001) and Stuart et al. (2002), the guinea pig (Cpor) does not group with the other rodents either.

In this phylogenetic analysis, we have seen that using the CGRs simulated by the first-order Markov chain model as the random background can give better results than those CGRs simulated by the second-order Markov chain model. This seems reasonable because the paths of first-order Markov chain model are more random than those of the second-order Markov chain model. If we regard the observation (DNA sequence) = biological information + noise background, we have shown that the second-order Markov chain model can simulate the observation better than the first-order Markov chain model, i.e. the second-order Markov chain model can capture more biological information while the first-order Markov chain model is closer to the noise background. Since phylogenetic analysis is based on biological information, it is reasonable that we should subtract the first-order Markov chain which simulates the background noise.

It seems that alignment-based distance methods (Wong et al. 2008) are not suitable for complete genome data, and also there is no acceptable bootstrap method for alignment-free phylogenetic approaches as asserted by Stuart et al. (2002). The problem of how to use cophenetic correlation (Sokal & Rohlf 1962; Rohlf & Fisher 1968) to replace the bootstrap for alignment-free phylogenetic approaches still needs further investigation. The cophenetic correlation is a measure of how faithfully a dendrogram preserves the pairwise distances between the original unmodeled data points. It has been most widely applied in the field of biostatistics (typically to assess cluster-based models of DNA sequences, or other taxonomic models) (Sokal & Rohlf 1962, Rohlf & Fisher 1968).

CONCLUSION

The Markov chain models can simulate very well the CGR of mitochondrial genomes. The second-order Markov chain model is more refined than the first-order Markov Chain model in simulating the CGR of the mitochondrial genomes.

The original CGR of mitochondrial genomes can be used to analyze the phylogeny of vertebrates. The CGR simulated by the first-order Markov chain model can be used to represent the random background, which is then removed from the original CGRs to enhance phylogenetic information in the mitochondrial genomes. An analysis of the phylogeny of 64 selected vertebrates supports the working of this approach.

ACKNOWLEDGMENT

This research was supported by the Chinese Program for New Century Excellent Talents in University grant NCET-08-06867 and the Fok Ying Tung Education Foundation grant 101004 (Z.-G. Yu), the Australian Research Council (grant no. DP0559807) (V.V. Anh).

REFERENCES

Almeida, J. S., Carrico, J. A., & Maretzek, A., Nobl,e P. A., & Fletcher, M. (2001). Analysis of genomic sequences by Chaos Game Representation. *Bioinformatics (Oxford, England)*, *17*(5), 429–437. doi:10.1093/bioinformatics/17.5.429

Basu, S., Pan, A., Dutta, C., & Das, J. (1998). Chaos game representation of proteins. *Journal of Molecular Graphics & Modelling*, *15*(5), 279–289. doi:10.1016/S1093-3263(97)00106-X

Causton, H. C., Quackenbush, J., & Brazma, A. (2003). *Microarray gene expression data analysis: A beginner's guide*. Blackwell Science Ltd.

Deschavanne, P. J., Giron, A., Vilain, J., Fagot, G., & Fertil, B. (1999). Genomic Signature: Characterization and Classification of Species Assessed by Chaos Game Representation of Sequences. *Molecular Biology and Evolution*, *16*(10), 1391–1399.

Dowling, T. E., Moritz, C., Palmer, J. D., & Rieseber, L. H. (1996). *Nucleic acids III: analysis of fragments and restriction sites*. Sunderland, Mass.: Sinauer.

Fiser, A., Tusnady, G. E., & Simon, I. (1994). Chaos game representation of protein structures. *Journal of Molecular Graphics*, *12*(4), 302–304. doi:10.1016/0263-7855(94)80109-6

Goldman, N. (1993). Nucleotide, dinucleotide and trinucleotide frequencies explain patterns observed in chaos game representations of DNA sequences. *Nucleic Acids Research*, *21*(10), 2487–2491. doi:10.1093/nar/21.10.2487

Huson, D. H., & Bryant, D. (2006). Application of Phylogenetic Networks in Evolutionary Studies, *Mol. Biol. Evo.*, *23*(2), 254-267. *Software*: http://www.splitstree.org.

Jeffrey, H. J. (1990). Chaos game representation of gene structure. *Nucleic Acids Research*, *18*(18), 2163–2170. doi:10.1093/nar/18.8.2163

Joseph, J., & Sasikumar, R. (2006). Chaos game representation for comparision of whole genomes. *BMC Bioinformatics*, *7*(243), 1–10.

Karlin, S., Mrazek, J., & Campbell, A. M. (1997). Compositional biases of bacterial genomes and evolutionary implications. *Journal of Bacteriology*, *179*(12), 3899–3913.

Li, M., Badger, J. H., Chen, X., Kwong, S., Kearney, P., & Zhang, H. (2001). An information-based sequence distance and its application to whole mitochondrial genome phylogeny. *Bioinformatics (Oxford, England)*, *17*(2), 149–154. doi:10.1093/bioinformatics/17.2.149

Mouchaty, S. K., Gullberg, A., Janke, A., & Arnason, U. (2000). The phylogenetic position of the Talpidae within eutheria based on analysis of complete mitochondrial sequences. *Molecular Biology and Evolution*, *17*(1), 60–67.

Nikaido, M., Harad, M. M., Cao, Y., Hasegawa, M., & Okada, N. (2000). Monophyletic origin of the order chiroptera and its phylogenetic position among mammalia, as inferred from the complete sequence of the mitochondrial DNA of a japanese megabat, the ryukyu flying fox *Pteropus dasymallus*. *Journal of Molecular Evolution*, *51*(4), 318–328.

Pollack, D. D., Eisen, J. A., Doggett, N. A., & Cummings, M. P. (2000). A case for evolutionary genomics and the comprehensive examination of sequence biodiversity. *Molecular Biology and Evolution, 17*(12), 1776–1788.

Qi, J., Wang, B., & Hao, B. (2004). Whole proteome prokaryote phylogeny without sequence alignment: a K-string composition approach. *Journal of Molecular Evolution, 58*(1), 1–11. doi:10.1007/s00239-003-2493-7

Reyes, A., Pesole, G., & Saccone, C. (1998). Complete mitochondrial DNA sequence of the fat dormouse, *Glis glis*: further evidence of rodent parahyly. *Molecular Biology and Evolution, 15*(5), 499–505.

Reyes, A. C., Gissi, C., Pesole, G., Catzeflis, F. M., & Saccone, C. (2000). Where do rodents fit? Evidence from the complete mitochondrial genome of *Sciurus vulgaris. Molecular Biology and Evolution, 17*(6), 979–983.

Rohlf, F. J., & Fisher, D. L. (1968). Test for hierarchical structure in random data sets. *Systematic Zoology, 17*, 407–412. doi:10.2307/2412038

Saitou, N., & Nei, M. (1987). The neighbor-joining method: a new method for reconstructing phylogenetic trees. *Molecular Biology and Evolution, 4*(4), 406–425.

Sankoff, D., Bryantd, D., Deneault, M., Lang, B. F., & Burger, G. (2000). Early Eukaryote Evolution Based on Mitochondrial Gene Order Breakpoints. *Journal of Computational Biology, 7*(3-4), 521–535. doi:10.1089/106652700750050925

Sokal, R. R., & Rohlf, F. J. (1962). The comparison of dendrograms by objective methods. *Taxon, 11*, 33–40. doi:10.2307/1217208

Stuart, G. W., Moffet, K., & Leader, J. J. (2002). A comprehensive vertebrate phylogeny using vector representations of protein sequences from whole genomes. *Molecular Biology and Evolution, 19*(4), 554–562.

Takezaki, N., & Nei, M. (1996). Genetic distances and reconstruction of phylogenetic trees from microsatellite DNA. *Genetics, 144*(1), 389–399.

Wong, K. M., Suchard, M. A., & Huelsenbeck, J. P. (2008). Alignment uncertainty and genomic analysis. *Science, 319*(5862), 473–476. doi:10.1126/science.1151532

Wu, G. A., Jun, S. R., Sims, G. E., & Kim, S. H. (2009). Whole-proteome phylogeny of large dsDNA virus families by an alignment-free method. *Proceedings of the National Academy of Sciences of the United States of America, 106*(31), 12826–12831. doi:10.1073/pnas.0905115106

Yang, J. Y., Peng, Z. L., Yu, Z. G., Zhang, R. J., Anh, V., & Wang, D. S. (2009). Prediction of protein structural classes by recurrence quantification analysis based on chaos game representation. *Journal of Theoretical Biology, 257*(4), 618–626. doi:10.1016/j.jtbi.2008.12.027

Yu, Z. G., Anh, V. V., & Lau, K. S. (2004). Chaos game representation, and multifractal and correlation analysis of protein sequences from complete genome based on detailed HP model. *Journal of Theoretical Biology, 226*(3), 341–348. doi:10.1016/j.jtbi.2003.09.009

Yu, Z. G., Shi, L., Xiao, Q. J., & Anh, V. (2008). Simulation for chaos game representation of genomes by recurrent iterated function systems. *J. Biomedical Sci. and Eng., 1*(1), 44–51. doi:10.4236/jbise.2008.11007

Yu, Z. G., Zhan, X. W., Han, G. S., Wang, R. W., Anh, V., & Chu, K. H. (2010). Proper Distance Metrics for Phylogenetic Analysis Using Complete Genomes without Sequence Alignment. *International Journal of Molecular Sciences, 11*(3), 1141–1154. doi:10.3390/ijms11031141

Yu, Z. G., Zhou, L. Q., Anh, V., Chu, K. H., Long, S. C., & Deng, J. Q. (2005). Phylogeny of prokaryotes and chloroplasts revealed by a simple composition approach on all protein sequences from whole genome without sequence alignment. *Journal of Molecular Evolution, 60*(4), 538–545. doi:10.1007/s00239-004-0255-9

ADDITIONAL READING

Goldman, N. (1993). Nucleotide, dinucleotide and trinucleotide frequencies explain patterns observed in chaos game representations of DNA sequences. [About the Markov chain model to simulate the chaos game representation of DNA sequences]. *Nucleic Acids Research, 21*(10), 2487–2491. doi:10.1093/nar/21.10.2487

Huson, D. H., & Bryant, D. (2006). Application of Phylogenetic Networks in Evolutionary Studies, *Mol. Biol. Evol., 23*(2), 254-267. *Software*: http://www.splitstree.org. (the software *SplitsTree4* V4.10 to plot the phylogenetic tree).

Jeffrey, H. J. (1990). Chaos game representation of gene structure. [For the chaos game representation of DNA sequences]. *Nucleic Acids Research, 18*(18), 2163–2170. doi:10.1093/nar/18.8.2163

Stuart, G. W., Moffet, K., & Leader, J. J. (2002). A comprehensive vertebrate phylogeny using vector representations of protein sequences from whole genomes. [About reasons to use mitochondrial genomes to refer the vertebrate phylogeny]. *Molecular Biology and Evolution, 19*(4), 554–562.

Yu, Z. G., Zhou, L. Q., Anh, V., Chu, K. H., Long, S. C., & Deng, J. Q. (2005). Phylogeny of prokaryotes and chloroplasts revealed by a simple composition approach on all protein sequences from whole genome without sequence alignment. *Journal of Molecular Evolution, 60*(4), 538–545. doi:10.1007/s00239-004-0255-9

KEY TERMS AND DEFINITIONS

Mitochondrial Genome: The complete DNA located in organelles called mitochondria, structures within cells that convert the energy from food into a form that cells can use.

Chaos Game Representation: Using the four vertices of a square in the plane to represent A, C, G and T. One point is plotted for each site of the sequence: the first point is placed halfway between the centre of the square and the corner corresponding to the first nucleotide of the sequence and successive points are plotted halfway between the previous point and the corner corresponding to the base of each successive sequence site. The method produces a visualization of a DNA sequence which displays both local and global patterns.

Markov Chain Model Simulation: Simulating the data using Markov chain model. A Markov chain model is a discrete random process with the Markov property. A discrete random process means a system which can be in various states, and which changes randomly in discrete steps. It can be helpful to think of the system as evolving through discrete steps in time, although strictly speaking the "step" may have nothing to do with time. The Markov property states that the probability distribution for the system at the next step (and in fact at all future steps) only depends on the current state of the system, and not additionally on the state of the system at previous steps. Since the system changes randomly, it is generally impossible to predict the exact state of the system in the future. However, the statistical properties of the system at a great many steps in the future can often be described. In many applications it is these statistical properties that are important.

Vertebrate Phylogeny: The phylogenetic relationships among vertebrates. In biology, phylogenetics is the study of evolutionary relatedness among various groups of organisms (for example, species or populations), which is discovered through molecular sequencing data and morphological data matrices.

Chapter 4
A Two-Layer Learning Architecture for Multi-Class Protein Folds Classification

Ruofei Wang
Xiangtan University, China

Xieping Gao
Xiangtan University, China

ABSTRACT

Classification of protein folds plays a very important role in the protein structure discovery process, especially when traditional sequence alignment methods fail to yield convincing structural homologies. In this chapter, we have developed a two-layer learning architecture, named TLLA, for multi-class protein folds classification. In the first layer, OET-KNN (Optimized Evidence-Theoretic K Nearest Neighbors) is used as the component classifier to find the most probable K-folds of the query protein. In the second layer, we use support vector machine (SVM) to build the multi-class classifier just on the K-folds, generated in the first layer, rather than on all the 27 folds. For multi-feature combination, ensemble strategy based on voting is selected to give the final classification result. The standard percentage accuracy of our method at ~63% is achieved on the independent testing dataset, where most of the proteins have <25% sequence identity with those in the training dataset. The experimental evaluation based on a widely used benchmark dataset has shown that our approach outperforms the competing methods, implying our approach might become a useful vehicle in the literature.

INTRODUCTION

The successful completion of many genome sequencing projects produces a massive number of putative protein sequences. However, the number of known three-dimensional (3D) protein structure is growing at a much slower pace. This situation has challenged us to develop computational methods by which the 3D protein structure could be predicted timely from its sequence.

Many computational methods have been developed, which are used for assigning folds to protein sequences. Traditional similarity-based methods, such as sequence-structure homology recognition methods (Shi et al., 2001), align target sequence onto known structural templates and calculate

DOI: 10.4018/978-1-60960-064-8.ch004

their sequence-structure compatibilities using either profile-based scoring functions (Kelley et al., 2000) or environment-specific substitution tables (Shi et al., 2001). The scores obtained for different structural templates are then ranked. And the template, which gives rise to the best score, is assumed to be the fold of the target sequence. Although these methods can accurately recognize protein folds when proteins have close evolutionary relationship (Yu et al., 2006), they are not efficient when proteins are structurally similar, but have no significant sequence similarity. Threading methods have demonstrated promising results in detecting the latter type of relationship. However, these methods also yield poor accuracies perhaps due to the difficulty of formulating reliable and general scoring functions (Jones, 1999).

In recent years, the taxonomic approach without relying on sequence similarity, such as those using machine learning methods (Ding & Dubchak, 2001; Huang et al., 2003; Nanni, 2006; Shen & Chou, 2006; Guo & Gao, 2008), plays a critical role in protein folds recognition. This approach assumes that the number of protein folds is limited according to the SCOP (Structural Classification of Proteins) database (Andreeva et al., 2004), therefore, the protein fold recognition problem can be viewed as a fold classification problem, where a query protein can be classified into one of the known folds. Ding and Dubchak (2001) investigated support vector machine (SVM) and artificial neural network (ANN) methods for protein folds classification. Shen and Nanni studied ensemble classifiers based on nearest neighbor and K-local hyperplane (Shen & Chou, 2006; Nanni, 2006), respectively. Guo and Gao (2008) developed a novel ensemble classifier using GAET-KNN. These taxonomic approaches have achieved much better performance than the traditional similarity-based methods.

Most current taxonomic approaches assign the fold of a query protein to one of the most populated 27 folds in the SCOP (such as globin-like, cupredoxins, beta-trefoil, etc.). Protein folds prediction

in the context of this large number of folds presents a rather challenging classification problem. Huang and Lin (2003) developed a hierarchical learning architecture (HLA). In the first level of HLA, it classifies the protein sequence into four major structural classes. And in the next level, it further classifies the protein sequence into 27 folds. This two step strategy reasonably reduced the number of folds to classify. HLA obtained higher accuracy than those methods which classify the query protein into 27 folds in one step. Hence, reducing the number of probable folds of the query protein is instructive to achieve better accuracy. Toward this goal, in the article, a two-layer learning architecture (TLLA) is presented. In the TLLA, we first use Optimized Evidence-Theoretic K Nearest Neighbors (OET-KNN) to find the most probable K-folds, then build the multi-class classifier just on the K-folds based on SVM. Finally, the query protein is tested on the multi-class classifier and its fold type is predicted. The standard percentage accuracy of our method at ~63% is achieved on a widely used independent testing dataset, which is better than the competing methods. Therefore, we suggest that TLLA can be used for fold-wise classification of unknown proteins discovered in various genomes.

MATERIALS

Datasets for Training and Testing

The working (training and testing) datasets studied here were taken from Ding and Dubchak (2001). The training dataset was selected from the database built for 128-fold prediction problem (Dubchak et al., 1999). This database is based on PDB-select sets where two proteins have no more than 35% of the sequence identity for the aligned subsequences longer than 80 residues. 27 most populated SCOP folds in the database with seven or more proteins were utilized, which represented four major structural classes: all alpha-helices (all-α), all beta-strands (all-β), alpha/beta (α/β), and alpha+beta (α+β). There are 313 proteins in the training dataset. The independent testing dataset was derived from PDB-40D set which was developed by the authors of the SCOP database (Andreeva et al., 2004). Using the same 27 SCOP folds, 385 proteins were selected, and any PDB-40D protein having more than 35% sequence identity with the proteins in the training dataset was excluded. The follow-up study by Shen and Chou (2006) excluded two training proteins (2SCMC and 2GPS) and two testing proteins (2YHX_1 and 2YHX_2) due to lacking sequence information. We follow Shen and Chou's study and adopt the two datasets without these four proteins. So, we have 311 proteins for training dataset and 383 proteins for testing dataset (for details see Table A1 in APPENDIX).

The SCOP database, created by manual inspection and abetted by a battery of automated methods, aims to provide a detailed and comprehensive description of the structural and evolutionary relationships between all proteins whose structure is known. As such, it provides a broad survey of all known protein folds, detailed information about the close relatives of any particular protein, and a framework for future research and classification. Its principal level includes family, superfamily and fold (Andreeva et al., 2004). In our study, we mainly focus on fold level. Proteins are defined as having a common fold if they have the same major secondary structures in the same arrangement and with the same topological connections. Different proteins with the same fold often have peripheral elements of secondary structure and turn regions that differ in size and conformation. In our study, we used SCOP v1.73.

Feature Space Representation

In order to use machine learning methods, feature vectors are extracted from protein sequences. There are two main kinds of feature used in this study: sequence-based feature and structure-based feature. Detailedly, sequence-based feature is the amino acid composition, which contains 20 components, with each representing the occurrence frequency of one of the 20 native amino acids in a given protein. As to structure-based feature, it includes five features: (1) predicted secondary structure, (2) hydrophobicity, (3) normalized van der waals volume, (4) polarity, and (5) polarizability. For structure-based feature, three descriptors: composition (C), transition (T), and distribution (D) are used to describe the global composition of a given amino acid property in a protein, the frequencies with which the property changes along the entire length of the protein, and the distribution pattern of the property along the sequence, respectively (Dubchak et al., 1995). These five features, each contains 21 dimensions. (Dubchak et al., 1999; Ding & Dubchak, 2001). All six features presented above are listed in Table 1.

METHOD

Our Proposed Two-Layer Learning Architecture (TLLA)

The proposed classification method developed in this article consists of two layers. In the first layer, we use OET-KNN (Optimized Evidence-Theoretic K Nearest Neighbors) (Zouhal & Denoeux, 1998) as the component classifier. For a query protein fed into the first layer, using the OET-KNN classifier, we obtain the most probable K-folds which the query protein belongs to. In the second layer, support vector machine (SVM), a supervised binary classification, is adopted as the component classifier. We use One-versus-One method to extend SVM to multi-class classification. In this process, we build the multi-class classifier just on the K-folds, generated in the first layer, rather than on all the 27 folds. Considering there are varieties of features, voting-based ensemble strategy, which combines predictions from different kinds of feature space, is selected to give the final output result.

Table 1. List of six features extracted from protein sequences. The dimension and symbol of each feature are also shown

Feature	Symbol	Dimension
Amino acid composition	C	20
Predicted secondary structure	S	21
Hydrophobicity	H	21
Normalized van der waals volume	V	21
Polarity	P	21
Polarizability	Z	21

Optimized Evidence-Theoretic K Nearest Neighbors (OET-KNN)

For reader's convenience, a brief introduction of the OET-KNN classifier is given below. In our study, we consider a problem of classifying N entities into 27 classes (fold type), which can be formulated as

$$S = \{c_1, c_2, \cdots, c_{27}\} \tag{1}$$

The training set, which contains N n-dimensional patterns $x^{(i)}$, can be denoted by

$$\Gamma = \{(x^{(1)}, c^{(1)}), (x^{(2)}, c^{(2)}), \cdots, (x^{(N)}, c^{(N)})\} \tag{2}$$

The class label $c^{(i)}$ takes value in the set S. The similarity between patterns is measured by Euclidean distance. If the distance is small, two vectors are deemed as belonging to the same class. On the contrary, their classes are completely irrelevant. The training sample with the smallest distance is deemed as the nearest neighbor for a query. According to the ET-KNN rule, every neighbor of the query protein x is considered as an item of evidence supporting certain hypotheses concerning the class membership of the query. So, K nearest neighbors with the smallest distance are used to determine the fold of the query protein. A

basic belief assignment (BBA) is assigned to every neighbor. The resulting BBA is obtained through aggregating the BBA of the K nearest neighbors using the Dempster's rule. Consequently, a BBA can be defined by (Denoeux, 1995).

$$m(\{c_u\} \mid x^{(i)}) = \alpha \exp(-\gamma_u d^2(x, x^i)) \tag{3}$$

$$m(S \mid x^{(i)}) = 1 - \alpha \exp(-\gamma_u d^2(x, x^i)) \tag{4}$$

where $d(x, x^{(i)})$ is the Euclidean distance between x and $x^{(i)}$, c_u is the class of $x^{(i)}$, α is a fixed parameter ($0 < \alpha < 1$), and γ_u is a positive parameter associated to the class c_u.

According to Dempster's rule, a resulting BBA m regarding the class of the query x can be formulated by

$$m = m(\cdot \mid x^{(i_1)}) \oplus (\cdot \mid x^{(i_2)}) \oplus \cdots \oplus (\cdot \mid x^{(i_k)}) \tag{5}$$

Where $\oplus$ denotes the orthogonal sum. $I_k = \{i_1, i_2 \cdots i_k\}$ is the indexical set of the K nearest neighbors of x.

Thus, m can be shown as the following expression

$$m(\{c_u\}) = \frac{1}{w}(1 - \prod_{i \in I_{k,u}} (1 - \alpha \exp(-\gamma_u d^{(i)}))) \times \prod_{r \neq u} \prod_{i \in I} (1 - \alpha \exp(-\gamma_r d^{(i)})) \tag{6}$$

where w is a normalized factor.

Therefore, the predicted class for the query x is c_u, if

$$m(\{c_u\}) = Max\{m(\{c_1\}), m(\{c_2\}), \cdots, m(\{c_{27}\})\} \tag{7}$$

where *Max* means taking the maximum one among those in the brackets.

The tuning of the parameter vector γ has significant influence on the classification accuracy. In 1998, an optimization procedure to determine the optimal or near-optimal parameter values was proposed from the data by minimizing an error function (Zouhal & Denoeux, 1998). It was observed that the OET-KNN rule obtained through such an optimization treatment would lead to a substantial improvement in classification accuracy.

Support Vector Machine (SVM)

SVM is a promising binary classification method and widely used for many pattern recognition problem based on the statistical learning theory. It uses training data as inputs to generate a decision function as an output to classify unknown data. Suppose there are N training data $x_i \in R^n, i = 1, 2, \cdots, N$, where each of data belongs to one of the two classes. As a decision function to classify input data, SVM finds a hyperplane separating two classes with maximum distance from the hyperplane to support vectors. SVM supports both linearly separable data and linearly non-separable data. If data is separable linearly, SVM finds the following hyperplane using Lagrangian multiplier approach

$$f(X) = \sum_{i=1}^{N_s} \alpha_i y_i x_i \cdot X + b \qquad (8)$$

where N_s is the number of support vectors. Depending on the sign of $f(X)$, the input data is classified to either of the two classes. In addition, for many linearly non-separable problems, SVM can be extended to handle them through a kernel function. Please refer to Vapnik (1998) for details.

RESULTS AND DISCUSSION

Evaluation of the Protein Folds Classification

There are many measures to assess the performance of protein folds classification method. True Positive Rates (TPR) and False Positive Rates (FPR) are usually designed for two-class classification problem. In our paper, we use the standard Q percentage accuracy (Baldi, et al., 2000), generalized to handle true positives and false positives, since the protein folds classification is a multi-class problem. Suppose n_i denotes the number of testing proteins in the *ith* fold. Out of n_i proteins c_i are correctly and uniquely recognized. Then the accuracy for class i is $Q_i = c_i / n_i$. Individual Q_i relates to the overall Q in a very simple way. An individual class contributes to overall accuracy in proportion to the number of proteins in its class, and thus has a weight $w_i = n_i / N$. Therefore the overall accuracy Q equals the weighted average over individual classes:

$$Q = \sum_{i=1}^{K} w_i Q_i = C / N \qquad (9)$$

Where N is the total number of proteins in the testing set, C is the total number of proteins which are correctly recognized, and K is the number of classes.

Experiments on the Two-Layer Learning Architecture (TLLA)

When a query protein is presented to TLLA, OET-KNN in the first layer generates a K-dimension vector, which represents the label set of its most probable K-folds. In the second layer, SVM is adopted as the component classifier. In practice, there are usually four kinds of kernels: Linear, Polynomial, Radial basis function (RBF), and

Gaussian. We choose RBF kernel for the SVM as it gives the best result in our experiments.

Once the classification system is built and trained, we test it against a widely used dataset which is independent of the training dataset, where none of proteins in the testing dataset has >35% sequence identity to those in the training dataset.

In the first layer of TLLA, we set the number of the nearest neighbors in OET-KNN as 8. We have tried a series of K, and the tuning of K has little influence on classification accuracy. For single feature input vector (C, S, H, P, V, and Z), where each character represents a feature listed in Table 1, our proposed approach obtains classification accuracy: 54.0%, 52.9%, 45.2%, 40.3%, 41.1%, and 35.3%, respectively. Additionally, different combinations of features were also used as input vectors fed into TLLA. They are C, C+S, C+S+H, C+S+H+P, C+S+H+P+V, C+S+H+P+V+Z, and symbol "+" means combination. Each of them achieved 54.0%, 59.6%, 62.8%, 61.2%, 59.3%, 58.5% classification accuracy correspondingly.

Among the 27 folds, belonging to four major structural classes: all-α, all-β, α/β, α+β, the average accuracy for all-α class is ~75%, for all-β class is ~55%, for α/β class is ~49% and for α+β class is ~38%. The folds that belong to all-α and all-β structural classes are easier to classify, while folds that belong to α/β and α+β classes

are more difficulty to correctly recognize. This is expected as the feature space, especially the predicted secondary structure, should be able to successfully represent proteins that contain mainly α-helices and β-strands. In contrast, the extracted feature space is less efficient in capturing long range interaction that is characteristic of parallel and anti-parallel β-strands. Our experiment on independent testing dataset showed that the amino acid composition is the most effective feature, followed by the predicted secondary structure, and then hydrophobicity. It is consistent with the previous research result.

Comparison with Competing Prediction Methods

The features in the taxonomic methods (Ding & Dubchak, 2001; Nanni, 2006; Shen & Chou, 2006) are the same listed in Table 1. Therefore, the comparison between these methods and TLLA can provide a relative reasonable ranking (see Table 2, Table 3). Take notice that AvA-SVM is the best method in (Ding & Dubchak, 2001), we only list it for comparison in Table 3. Considering these taxonomic methods (Ding & Dubchak, 2001; Nanni, 2006; Shen & Chou, 2006) classify the query protein into the 27 folds directly, we call them single layer approaches. As we can see from

Table 2. Classification accuracy comparison of the proposed TLLA and single layer approaches based on different combination of features

Feature space	Single layer approaches (%)					TLLA (%)
	OvO-ANN#	OvO-SVM#	uOvO-SVM#	AvA-SVM#	OET-KNN*	
C	20.5	43.5	49.4	44.9	42.7	54.0
C+S	36.8	43.2	48.6	52.1	49.7	59.6
C+S+H	40.6	45.2	51.1	56.0	53.8	62.8
C+S+H+P	41.1	43.2	49.4	56.5	51.6	61.2
C+S+H+P+V	41.2	44.8	50.9	55.5	49.8	59.3
C+S+H+P+V+Z	41.8	44.9	49.6	53.9	48.3	58.5

refer to (Ding & Dubchak, 2001)

* refer to (Shen & Chou, 2006). The value of K in the OET-KNN is 8.

Table 3. Classification accuracy comparison of the proposed TLLA and single layer approaches based on individual feature

Feature space	Single layer approaches (%)		TLLA (%)
	AvA-SVM #	OET-KNN *	
C	44.9	46.7	54.0
S	35.6	42.9	52.9
H	36.5	37.0	45.2
P	32.9	29.8	40.3
V	35.0	32.5	41.1
Z	32.9	24.2	35.3

\# refer to (Ding & Dubchak, 2001)

* refer to (Shen & Chou, 2006). The value of K in the OET-KNN is 8.

the comparison between TLLA and single-layer approaches, the performance of our method TLLA is much better on both individual feature and different combination of features. We also make a comparison between our method and the popular two steps approach-HLA (Huang & Chen, 2003). HLA adopted SVM as the constituent classifiers, and the kernels of SVM used MLP (Multilayer Perceptron) and RBFN (Radial Basis Function Network) respectively (see Table 4).

We have compared the performance between our approach TLLA and single layer approaches, two steps approach-HLA (see Table 2, Table 3, and Table 4). For the sake of completeness, we have also shown the classification accuracy of other methods including template based methods in the literature, which include THREAD (Jones et al., 1992), FUGUE (Shi et al., 2001), SPARK (Zhou et al. 2004), 3DPSSM (Kelley et al., 2000) and FOLDpro (Cheng et al., 2006). Next are popular taxonomic methods, including SVM(AvA) (Ding & Dubchak, 2001), RBFN (Huang et al., 2003) and SE (Nanni, 2006) (see Figure1). As evident from Figure 1, the classification accuracy of our approach TLLA is the highest.

In our classification system, only the second layer needs training process for SVM since the first layer directly generates the most probable K-folds of a query protein sequence. As a result of high convergence of SVM, the training time required is about a minute or so, where the training was performed on a personal computer with the Intel Pentium4 CPU. This is almost the same as single layer approaches based on SVM and

Table 4. Classification accuracy comparison of the proposed TLLA and two steps approach-HLA based on different combination of features

Feature space	Two steps approach (HLA) (%)		TLLA (%)
	MLP	RBFN	
C	32.7	44.9	54.0
C+S	48.6	53.8	59.6
C+S+H	47.5	53.3	62.8
C+S+H+P	43.2	54.3	61.2
C+S+H+P+V	43.6	55.3	59.3
C+S+H+P+V+Z	44.7	56.4	58.5

Figure 1. The overall prediction accuracy for protein folds recognition by different methods. THREADER (Jones et al., 1992), FUGUE (Shi et al., 2001), SPARK (Zhou et al. 2004), 3DPSSM (Kelley et al., 2000) and FOLDpro (Cheng et al., 2006) are template based methods, where their overall prediction accuracy are <30%. The following taxonomic methods are much higher, and our method TLLA is the best. SVM(AvA) refer to (Ding & Dubchak, 2001); RBFN refer to (Huang et al., 2003); SE refer to (Nanni, 2006).

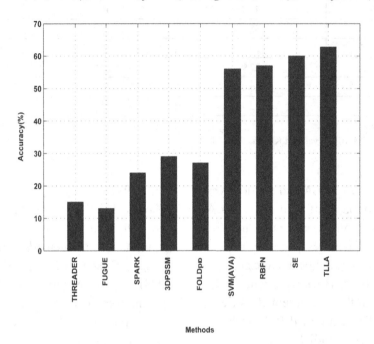

OET-KNN. So our classification system is also very efficient.

CONCLUSION

In this study, we have developed a two-layer learning architecture (TLLA) for multi-class protein folds classification. In the first layer, OET-KNN (Optimized Evidence-Theoretic K Nearest Neighbors) was used to find the probable K-folds which the query protein belongs to. In the second layer, we further predict the final fold of the query protein among the probable K-folds. As a result of the reduction of the number in its probable folds, compared to directly classifying the query protein to one of all the 27 folds, it improves the classification accuracy. The experimental evaluation based on a widely used benchmark dataset has also

shown that our approach outperforms the competing methods. This would provide good insights for fold-wise classification of unknown proteins discovered in various genomes. Our method can be extended to other protein prediction tasks, e.g. prediction of structural class, secondary structure content, membrane protein type or enzyme family with a defined secondary structure etc., to improve their accuracies.

Our method, as a kind of taxonomic methods, based on machine learning techniques, also has its limitation. It can't accurately predict the fold pattern for a query protein sequence, whose structure is brand-new, not deposited in the SCOP.

In our study, we focus on 27 populated SCOP folds, but in biological universe, the number of fold is close to one thousand. So in future work, we will consider a more complicated situation, such as the recognition of hundreds of fold. As we can see, feature extraction is quite important for protein fold prediction. So seeking new features that could better reveal the relationship between protein sequence and its structure would improve the classification accuracy.

ACKNOWLEDGMENT

We would like to thank Chris Ding for sharing the datasets and Guo Xia for her constructive comments.

REFERENCES

Andreeva, A., Howorth, D., Brenner, S. E., Hubbard, T. J., Chothia, C., & Murzin, A. G. (2004). SCOP database in 2004: refinements integrate structure and sequence family data. *Nucleic Acids Research*, *32*(Database issue), D226–D229. doi:10.1093/nar/gkh039

Baldi, P., Brunak, S., Chauvin, Y., Andersen, C. A., & Nielsen, H. (2000). Assessing the accuracy of prediction algorithms for classification: an overview. *Bioinformatics (Oxford, England)*, *16*(5), 412–424. doi:10.1093/bioinformatics/16.5.412

Cheng, J., & Baldi, P. (2006). A machine learning information retrieval approach to protein fold recognition. *Bioinformatics (Oxford, England)*, *22*(12), 1456–1463. doi:10.1093/bioinformatics/btl102

Denoeux, T. (1995). A k-nearest neighbor classification rule based on Dempster-Shafer theory. *IEEE Transactions on Systems, Man, and Cybernetics*, *25*(5), 804–813. doi:10.1109/21.376493

Ding, C. H., & Dubchak, I. (2001). Multi-class protein fold recognition using support vector machines and neural networks. *Bioinformatics (Oxford, England)*, *17*(4), 349–358. doi:10.1093/bioinformatics/17.4.349

Dubchak, I., Muchnik, I., Holbrook, S. R., & Kim, S. H. (1995). Prediction of protein folding class using global description of amino acid sequence. *Proceedings of the National Academy of Sciences of the United States of America*, *92*(19), 8700–8704. doi:10.1073/pnas.92.19.8700

Dubchak, I., Muchnik, I., Mayor, C., Dralyuk, I., & Kim, S. H. (1999). Recognition of a protein fold in the context of the Structural Classification of Proteins (SCOP) classification. *Proteins*, *35*(4), 401–407. doi:10.1002/(SICI)1097-0134(19990601)35:4<401::AID-PROT3>3.0.CO;2-K

Guo, X., & Gao, X. P. (2008). A novel hierarchical ensemble classifier for protein fold recognition. *Protein Engineering, Design & Selection*, *21*(11), 659–664. doi:10.1093/protein/gzn045

Huang, C. D., Lin, C. T., & Pal, N. R. (2003). Hierarchical learning architecture with automatic feature selection for multiclass protein fold classification. *IEEE Transactions on Nanobioscience*, *2*(4), 221–232. doi:10.1109/TNB.2003.820284

Jones, D. T. (1999). Protein secondary structure prediction based on position-specific scoring matrices. *Journal of Molecular Biology*, *292*(2), 195–202. doi:10.1006/jmbi.1999.3091

Jones, D. T., Taylor, W. R., & Thornton, J. M. (1992). A new approach to protein fold recognition. *Nature*, *358*(6381), 86–89. doi:10.1038/358086a0

Kelley, L. A., MacCallum, R. M., & Sternberg, M. J. (2000). Enhanced genome annotation using structural profiles in the program 3D-PSSM. *Journal of Molecular Biology*, *299*(2), 499–520. doi:10.1006/jmbi.2000.3741

Nanni, L. (2006). A novel ensemble of classifiers for protein fold recognition. *Neurocomputing*, *69*(16-18), 2434–2437. doi:10.1016/j.neucom.2006.01.026

Shen, H. B., & Chou, K. C. (2006). Ensemble classifier for protein fold pattern recognition. *Bioinformatics (Oxford, England)*, *22*(14), 1717–1722. doi:10.1093/bioinformatics/btl170

Shi, J., Blundell, T. L., & Mizuguchi, K. (2001). FUGUE: sequence-structure homology recognition using environment-specific substitution tables and structure-dependent gap penalties. *Journal of Molecular Biology*, *310*(1), 243–257. doi:10.1006/jmbi.2001.4762

Vapnik, V. (1998). *Statistical Learning Theory*. New York: Wiley.

Yu, Y. K., Gertz, E. M., Agarwala, R., Schaffer, A. A., & Altschul, S. F. (2006). Retrieval accuracy, statistical significance and compositional similarity in protein sequence database searches. *Nucleic Acids Research*, *34*(20), 5966–5973. doi:10.1093/nar/gkl731

Zhou, H., & Zhou, Y. (2004). Single-body residue-level knowledge-based energy score combined with sequence-profile and secondary structure information for fold recognition. *Proteins*, *55*(4), 1005–1013. doi:10.1002/prot.20007

Zouhal, L., & Denoeus, T. (1998). An evidence-theoretic k-NN rule with parameter optimization. *IEEE Transactions on Systems, Man, and Cybernetics*, *28*(2), 263–273. doi:10.1109/5326.669565

ADDITIONAL READING

Baldi, P., & Brunak, S. (1998). *Bioninformatics: the Machine Leanrning Approach*. Cambridge: MIT Press.

Baxevanis, A., & Oullette, F. (2004). *Bioninformatics: a practical guide to the analysis of genes and proteins*. New York: Wiley.

Brenner, S. E., Chothia, C., & Hubbard, T. J. (1998). Assessing sequence comparison methods with reliable structurally identified distant evolutionary relationships. *Proceedings of the National Academy of Sciences of the United States of America*, *95*(11), 6073–6078. doi:10.1073/pnas.95.11.6073

Burges, C. (1998). A Tutorial on Support Vector Machines for Pattern Recognition. *Knowledge Discovery and Data Mining*, *2*(2), 121–167. doi:10.1023/A:1009715923555

Chou, K. C., & Zhang, C. T. (1995). Prediction of protein structural classes. *Critical Reviews in Biochemistry and Molecular Biology*, *30*(4), 275–349. doi:10.3109/10409239509083488

Durbin, R., & Eddy, S. (2004). *Biological Sequence Analysis*. New York: Cambridge University Press.

Goutte, C. (1997). Note on Free Lunches and Cross-Validation. *Neural Computation*, *9*(6), 1245–1249. doi:10.1162/neco.1997.9.6.1245

Holm, L., & Sander, C. (1999). Protein folds and families: sequence and structure alignments. *Nucleic Acids Research*, *27*(1), 244–247. doi:10.1093/nar/27.1.244

Larranaga, P., Calvo, B., Santana, R., Bielza, C., Galdiano, J., & Inza, I. (2006). Machine learning in bioinformatics. *Briefings in Bioinformatics*, *7*(1), 86–112. doi:10.1093/bib/bbk007

Onuchic, J. N., Luthey-Schulten, Z., & Wolynes, P. G. (1997). Theory of protein folding: the energy landscape perspective. *Annual Review of Physical Chemistry*, *48*(3), 545–600. doi:10.1146/annurev.physchem.48.1.545

Vapnik, V. (1995). *The Nature of Statistical Learning Theory*. New York: Springer.

KEY TERMS AND DEFINITIONS

SCOP: Structural Classification of Proteins, created by manual inspection and abetted by a battery of automated methods, aims to provide a detailed and comprehensive description of the structural and evolutionary relationships between all proteins whose structure is known.

TLLA: Two-Layer Learning Architecture. Once it is trained well on the training dataset, it can predict its fold pattern of a query protein sequence in two steps.

OET-KNN: Optimized Evidence-theoretic K Nearest Neighbors, for a test sample (input), it can give its class label (output) through aggregating the basic belief assignment (BBA) of K nearest neighbors of the training dataset.

Protein Fold: A common three dimensional pattern with the same major secondary structure elements in the same arrangement.

Protein Structure Classes: Mainly include four classes: all alpha-helix (all-α), all beta-strands (all-β), alpha/beta (α/β) and alpha+beta ($\alpha+\beta$) in the SCOP. The all-α and all-β classes represent structures that consist of mainly α-helices and β-strands, respectively. The α/β and $\alpha+\beta$ classes contain both α-helices and β-strands where the α/β class includes mainly parallel β-strands and $\alpha+\beta$ class includes anti-parallel β-strands.

Artificial Neural Network: This refers to a graphical structure with artificial neurons as nodes. The node value of each node is determined by the input signals of the connected nodes passing through a nonlinear transfer function.

MLP: Multilayer Perceptron, a classic and widely used NN model. Such a network can solve nonlinear regression, and construct global approximation to the nonlinear input–output mapping.

RBFN: Radial Basis Function Network, a three layer network. The hidden layer nodes use a basis function, the Gaussian function, as the activation function. When data are fed into the network, the sum square error (SSE) will be calculated with the cost function, and the backpropagation (BP) learning rule is used to minimize the SSE until the restrict number of nodes or the preset value of SSE arrived.

APPENDIX

Table 5. The non-redundant 27 SCOP folds used in the article

Fold	Index	N_{train}	N_{test}
all-α			
Globin-like	1	13	6
Cytochrome c	3	7	9
DNA-binding 3-helical bundle	4	12	20
4-helical up-and-down bundle	7	7	8
4-helical cytokines	9	9	9
EF-hand	11	6	9
all-β			
Immunoglobulin-like	20	30	44
Cupredoxins	23	9	12
Viral coat and capsid proteins	26	16	13
ConA-like lectins/glucanases	30	7	6
SH3-like barrel	31	8	8
OB-fold	32	13	19
Trfoil	33	8	4
Trypsin-like serine proteases	35	9	4
Lipocalins	39	9	7
α/β			
(TIM)-barrel	46	29	48
FAD(also NAD)-binding motif	47	11	12
Flavodoxin-like	48	11	13
NAD(P)-binding Rossmann fold	51	13	27
P-loop cntaining nucleotide	54	10	12
Thioredoxin-like	57	9	8
Ribonuclease H-like motif	59	10	12
Hydrolases	62	11	7
Periplasmic binding protein-like	69	11	4
α+β			
β-grasp	72	7	8
Ferredoxin-like	87	13	27
Small inhibitors, toxins, lectins	110	13	27

: number of *each fold in the training dataset.*
: number of *each fold in the testing dataset.*

Chapter 5

Improving PSI–BLAST's Fold Recognition Performance through Combining Consensus Sequences and Support Vector Machine

Ren-Xiang Yan
China Agricultural University, China

Jing Liu
China Agricultural University, China

Yi-Min Tao
China Agricultural University, China

ABSTRACT

Profile-profile alignment may be the most sensitive and useful computational resource for identifying remote homologies and recognizing protein folds. However, profile-profile alignment is usually much more complex and slower than sequence-sequence or profile-sequence alignment. The profile or PSSM (position-specific scoring matrix) can be used to represent the mutational variability at each sequence position of a protein by using a vector of amino acid substitution frequencies and it is a much richer encoding of a protein sequence. Consensus sequence, which can be considered as a simplified profile, was used to improve sequence alignment accuracy in the early time. Recently, several studies were carried out to improve PSI-BLAST's fold recognition performance by using consensus sequence information. There are several ways to compute a consensus sequence. Based on these considerations, we propose a method that combines the information of different types of consensus sequences with the assistance of support vector machine learning in this chapter. Benchmark results suggest that our method can further improve PSI-BLAST's fold recognition performance.

DOI: 10.4018/978-1-60960-064-8.ch005

INTRODUCTION

Alignment between two protein sequence profiles is a fundamental technique in bioinformatics. Profile is a richer encoding of a protein versus raw sequence and can be used to improve remote homology detection and fold recognition performance (Kelley et al., 2000; Ginalski et al., 2003; Anand et al., 2005; Jaroszewski et al., 2005; Zhang et al., 2005). Sequence-sequence alignment can detect homology with significant sequence identity (i.e., identity >40%) (Needleman & Wunsch, 1970; Smith & Waterman, 1981; Altschul et al., 1997). Profile-sequence or sequence-profile alignment is usually more effective and sensitive than sequence-sequence alignment, and it can recognize distant homology with lower sequence identity (i.e., identity > 20%) (Altschul et al., 1997). Profile-profile alignment approaches may be the most effective approach among the alignment methods and even can create accurate alignments in the twilight zone (i.e., identity <10%) (Yona & Levitt, 2002). Generally speaking, alignment methods should accurately identify and align the homologous proteins, and the results can be used to predict a query protein's three-dimensional structure or to infer its biological function. Here, we can distinguish three classes of alignment approaches: sequence-sequence alignment, profile-sequence alignment and profile-profile alignment. Sequence-sequence alignment methods, such as BLAST (Altschul et al., 1997), Smith-Waterman (Smith & Waterman, 1981) or Needleman-Wunsch (Needleman & Wunsch, 1970) dynamic programming are relatively faster while less sensitive when compared with profile-profile alignment methods. Profile-profile alignment approaches or HMM-HMM comparison algorithms (Remmert et al., 2009) are more sensitive but relatively slower. PSI-BLAST (Altschul et al., 1997), a typical profile-sequence alignment method, is more sensitive than sequence-sequence alignment and much faster than profile-profile alignment. Currently, PSI-BLAST has become one of the most popular tools in bioinformatics and it is widely used in life science research. The improvement of PSI-BLAST's performance is still required. A profile can be used to represent the mutational variability at each sequence position of a protein by using a vector of amino acid substitution frequencies, which usually provides more information than a single sequence. The vector of a profile can be simplified to a consensus sequence by picking the most frequent or the most informative amino acid at each position of a protein. Several ways can be employed to generate a consensus sequence (Przybylski & Rost, 2008). And profile-consensus alignment (i.e., align a profile to a consensus sequence) can significantly improve PSI-BLAST's performance (Przybylski & Rost, 2008). Profile-consensus alignment can be considered as a method that mimicks profile–profile alignments (Przybylski & Rost, 2008). Based on this observation, we also compared consensus sequence based methods with COMPASS (Sadreyev & Grishin, 2003) in this paper. COMPASS is a local profile–profile alignment method, which can analytically estimate e-values for the detected protein similarities. And we also tried to improve PSI-BLAST's remote homology and fold recognition performance by combining search results that are generated by alignments between a profile and different types of consensus sequences with the assistance of support vector machine learning.

COMPUTATIONAL MODELS AND METHODS

Dataset

The protein sequences were extracted from the SCOP ASTRAL Compendium (Andreeva et al., 2004) database (1.73 version) filtered by 10% sequence identity and *an* e-value threshold of 0.01. Moreover, we also excluded sequences that only contained a single superfamily member and sequences that are too short (< 60 amino acid).

And every family of proteins was reserved only a representative one. Membrane proteins, small proteins, multi-domain proteins were removed. Finally, 1754 protein sequences remained. The dataset was named as SCOP1754, which covers 409 different superfamilies and 294 different folds.

Methods to Generate Consensus Sequences from a Profile

The sequences in the NR database (Wheeler et al., 2008) were removed redundancy using CD-HIT (Li & Godzik, 2006) method with 0.9 identity cut-off. Three different ways were used to compute consensus residue at a given position *i* of a sequence: maximal frequency, the residue with the highest frequency ratio of PSSM frequency and corresponding background residue frequency, and maximal relative entropy term. Maximal frequency-based method is to adopt consensus residue *j* have the highest occurrence frequency *fij* in the profile column. When consider maximal relative entropy-based method, we chosen the residue *j* with the highest relative entropy term *fijln (f ij/bj)* with respect to the background frequency *bj*. Employing maximal ratio of frequencies is using the residue with the highest frequency ratio *fij/bj*. Detailed on how to calculate the consensus sequences can be found in (Przybylski & Rost, 2008). The background residue frequencies were calculated based on the NR90 database. We named these consensus sequences derived from the above three strategies as consensus sequence Type I, Type II and Type III. And we constructed three databases by using these three type's consensus sequences instead of the raw sequences. Searching a query sequence against a database of consensus sequences rather than raw sequences is a simple add-on that boosts performance surprisingly well (Przybylski & Rost, 2008).

Combine the Information of Different Types of Consensus Sequences with SVM

In this work, we searched every sequence against NR database iteratively three times by using PSI-BLAST program to generate a profile. Three types of consensus sequences can be calculated from a profile. Then, we created three databases using three types' of consensus sequences. To search a query sequence's PSI-BLAST profile against these databases instead of raw sequences using leave one out protocol. We derived descriptors from the search results. The SVM discrimination method can be used to predict the similarity between proteins using these descriptors. We labeled positive instances where the protein pairs that in the same superfamily level and negative instances that protein pairs in the different superfamily. Here, we have 1754*(1754-1)/2 protein pairs. The similarity score of the pair *(A, B)* is considered identical to *(B, A)*. We evaluated our method using the five-fold cross-validation technique. The ratio of positive instances to negative instances is imbalanced in the training set. The optimized ratio of positives and negative was set to 1:1.5.

The PSI-BLAST's search result of every type of consensus sequence is *e-value (i.e. (A,B))*, which corresponding to the similarity between A and B. The e-value similarity score was finally evaluated according to the following equation:

$$e\_value\_sim(A,B) = -log(E(A,B)) \qquad (1)$$

We adopted a maximum cut-off as 100 for the *E(A,B)* value. And score value in the search result was used as a parameter. The descriptor derived from one type of consensus sequence search result includes four parameters: *PSI-BLAST_ bit_score(A,B)*, *PSI-BLAST_bit_score(B,A)*, *e_value_sim(A,B)*, *e_value_sim(B,A)*. These four parameters were combined by using support vector machine learning. The SVM package applied in our study is Libsvm (Chang & Lin, 2001). And

Figure 1. The flow chart of our method. A sequence was PSI-BLASTed for three iterations with a cut-off e-value of 0.001 on the NR90 database to generate a profile.

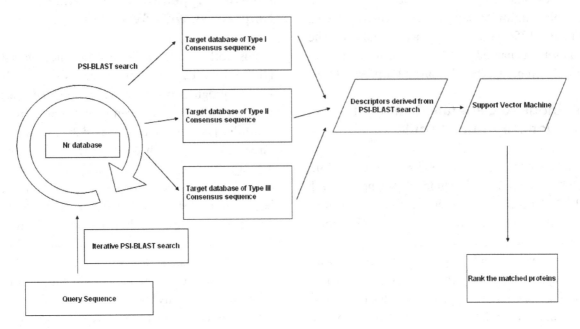

the employed kernel function was linear kernel with default parameters. The SVM models were trained to predict the similarity among proteins. This kind of usage of SVM can refer to (Zhang et al., 2005). The flow chart of our method is shown in Figure 1.

We extracted the multiple alignments that were generated by the last iteratively search of PSI-BLAST's for all SCOP1754 sequences. The multiple alignments can be transformed to numerical profile and search by COMPASS.

RESULT

We evaluated the performance of different methods using ROC (receiver operating characteristic) analysis (Gribskov & Robinson, 1996) across all sequences. The ROC curves that focus on identification of sequences in superfamily level were shown in Figure 2. The top hit for a query sequence was assigned a true positive instance or a false positive instance according to the top hit

protein and the query protein are from the same superfamily or not based on the SCOP (Andreeva et al., 2004) classification scheme. And we ranked the instances by the similarity scores predicted by SVM. True positive instances versus false positive instances were conducted to examine the number of true positives identified by varying similarity

Figure 2. Detection performance of remote homology in superfamily level when employing different methods. Descriptor of PSI-BLAST-based search include four parameters.

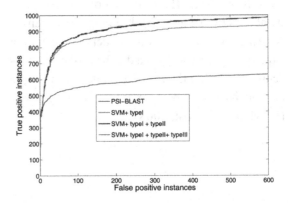

Figure 3. Detection performance of remote homology in fold level when employing different methods. Descriptor of PSI-BLAST-based search include four parameters.

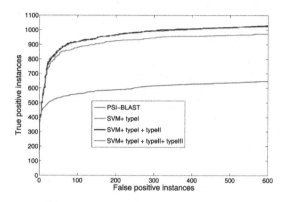

scores. Figure 3 is ROC analysis that focuses in fold level identification performance. The Figures suggest that profile-consensus alignment methods can significantly improve PSI-BLAST's performance. And descriptors derived from profile-consensus alignment results can improve profile-consensus alignment-based remote homology detection. As can be seen in Table 1, the rate of PSI-BLAST's remote homology identification increased about

5% sensitivity in fold and superfamily level when compared with the profile-consensus alignment method. We repeated the 5-fold cross-validation process for 5 times, and all results listed in Table 1 were assigned used by average scores and standard deviation. The ROC curves in Figure 2 and Figure 3 were drawn using average scores.

DISCUSSION AND CONCLUSION

With the increasing number of protein sequences and structures, it is high time for the establishment of a fast and sensitive homology detection method. The work of Przybylski & Rost (2008) has proved that profile-consensus alignment can significantly improve PSI-BLAST's remote homology and fold recognition performance. In this study, we found an interesting result: combining information that was derived from different consensus-based profile-consensus alignments could further improve PSI-BLAST's performance. Taking a protein pair A and B using one type consensus sequence as an example, the corresponding four parameters are *PSI-BLAST_bit_score(A,B)*, *PSI-*

Table 1. Sensitivity of remote homology detection in superfamily and fold levels using different methods

	Superfamily Sensitivity (%)	Fold Sensitivity (%)
PSI-BLAST	37.229	38.312
C1[A]	49.885	51.254
C2[B]	48.404	50.456
C3[C]	49.885	51.710
SVM[D]+C1	54.389±0.001[E]	56.271±0.002[e]
SVM+C1+C2	56.602±0.002[e]	58.814±0.001[e]
SVM+C1+C2+C3	56.556±0.001[e]	58.689±0.002[e]
COMPASS	59.977	62.713

A. C1 stands that search a PSI-BLAST profile against type I consensus sequence database.

B. C2 stands that search a PSI-BLAST profile against type II consensus sequence database.

C. C3 stands that search a PSI-BLAST profile against type III consensus sequence database.

D. The descriptor derived from every type of consensus sequence search result contains four parameters. Take a protein pair *(A,B) for example*, parameters derived from one type of consensus sequence search result include *PSI-BLAST_bit_score(A,B), PSI-BLAST_bit_score(B,A), e_value_sim(A,B)*, and *e_value_sim(B,A)*. The corresponding measurements were represented as the average value ± standard deviation.

BLAST_bit_score(B,A), *e_value_sim(A, B)* and *e_value_sim(B,A)*. We also compared our method with COMPASS, which is a typical profile-profile alignment approach. The COMPASS is by far the most sensitive approach among the methods examined in this study, which indicates that the full substitution frequencies of the PSSM provide more information regarding remotely homologous proteins than consensus sequences.

The consensus sequence can be considered as a simplified representation of a profile, which can significantly improve PSI-BLAST's remote homology detection and fold recognition performance. The results may tell us that consensus sequence is an important feature of a profile and different types of consensus sequences can be combined to obtain better results of protein alignment.

ACKNOWLEDGMENT

We thank the anonymous referees and Dr. Limin Liu at Shanghai Jiao Tong University for their constructive comments are very helpful in improving the quality of this work. We extend our gratitude to Dr. Ziding Zhang at China Agricultural University for the numerous discussions on this topic.

REFERENCES

Altschul, S. F., Gish, W., Miller, W., Myers, E. W., & Lipman, D. J. (1990). Basic local alignment search tool. *Journal of Molecular Biology*, *215*(3), 403–410.

Altschul, S. F., Madden, T. L., Schaffer, A. A., Zhang, J., Zhang, Z., Miller, W., & Lipman, D. J. (1997). Gapped BLAST and PSI-BLAST: a new generation of protein database search programs. *Nucleic Acids Research*, *25*(17), 3389–3402. doi:10.1093/nar/25.17.3389

Anand, B., Gowri, V. S., & Srinivasan, N. (2005). Use of multiple profiles corresponding to a sequence alignment enables effective detection of remote homologues. *Bioinformatics (Oxford, England)*, *21*(12), 2821–2826. doi:10.1093/bioinformatics/bti432

Andreeva, A., Howorth, D., Brenner, S. E., Hubbard, T. J., Chothia, C., & Murzin, A. G. (2004). SCOP database in 2004: refinements integrate structure and sequence family data. *Nucleic Acids Research*, *32*(Database issue), D226–D229. doi:10.1093/nar/gkh039

Chang, C. C., & Lin, C. J. (2001). *LIBSVM: a library for support vector machines*. Computer Program.

Ginalski, K., Pas, J., Wyrwicz, L. S., von Grotthuss, M., Bujnicki, J. M., & Rychlewski, L. (2003). ORFeus: Detection of distant homology using sequence profiles and predicted secondary structure. *Nucleic Acids Research*, *31*(13), 3804–3807. doi:10.1093/nar/gkg504

Gribskov, M. a. R., N. L. (1996). Use of receiver operating characteristic(ROC) analysis to evaluate sequence matching. *Computers & Chemistry*, *20*(1), 25–33. doi:10.1016/S0097-8485(96)80004-0

Han, S., Lee, B. C., Yu, S. T., Jeong, C. S., Lee, S., & Kim, D. (2005). Fold recognition by combining profile-profile alignment and support vector machine. *Bioinformatics (Oxford, England)*, *21*(11), 2667–2673. doi:10.1093/bioinformatics/bti384

Jaroszewski, L., Rychlewski, L., Li, Z., Li, W., & Godzik, A. (2005). FFAS03: a server for profile-profile sequence alignments. Nucleic Acids Res, 33(Web Server issue), W284-288.

Kelley, L. A., MacCallum, R. M., & Sternberg, M. J. (2000). Enhanced genome annotation using structural profiles in the program 3D-PSSM. *Journal of Molecular Biology*, *299*(2), 499–520. doi:10.1006/jmbi.2000.3741

Li, W., & Godzik, A. (2006). Cd-hit: a fast program for clustering and comparing large sets of protein or nucleotide sequences. *Bioinformatics (Oxford, England)*, *22*(13), 1658–1659. doi:10.1093/bioinformatics/btl158

Needleman, S. B., & Wunsch, C. D. (1970). A general method applicable to the search for similarities in the amino acid sequence of two proteins. *Journal of Molecular Biology*, *48*(3), 443–453. doi:10.1016/0022-2836(70)90057-4

Przybylski, D., & Rost, B. (2008). Powerful fusion: PSI-BLAST and consensus sequences. *Bioinformatics (Oxford, England)*, *24*(18), 1987–1993. doi:10.1093/bioinformatics/btn384

Sadreyev, R., & Grishin, N. (2003). COMPASS: a tool for comparison of multiple protein alignments with assessment of statistical significance. *Journal of Molecular Biology*, *326*(1), 317–336. doi:10.1016/S0022-2836(02)01371-2

Sadreyev, R. I., Tang, M., Kim, B. H., & Grishin, N. V. (2007). COMPASS server for remote homology inference. Nucleic Acids Res, 35(Web Server issue), W653-658.

Schaffer, A. A., Wolf, Y. I., Ponting, C. P., Koonin, E. V., Aravind, L., & Altschul, S. F. (1999). IMPALA: matching a protein sequence against a collection of PSI-BLAST-constructed position-specific score matrices. *Bioinformatics (Oxford, England)*, *15*(12), 1000–1011. doi:10.1093/bioinformatics/15.12.1000

Smith, T. F., & Waterman, M. S. (1981). Identification of common molecular subsequences. *Journal of Molecular Biology*, *147*(1), 195–197. doi:10.1016/0022-2836(81)90087-5

Soding, J., Biegert, A., & Lupas, A. N. (2005). The HHpred interactive server for protein homology detection and structure prediction. Nucleic Acids Res, 33(Web Server issue), W244-248.

Wheeler, D. L., Barrett, T., Benson, D. A., Bryant, S. H., Canese, K., & Chetvernin, V. (2008). Database resources of the National Center for Biotechnology Information. *Nucleic Acids Research*, *36*(Database issue), D13–D21. doi:10.1093/nar/gkm1000

Yona, G., & Levitt, M. (2002). Within the twilight zone: a sensitive profile-profile comparison tool based on information theory. *Journal of Molecular Biology*, *315*(5), 1257–1275. doi:10.1006/jmbi.2001.5293

Zhang, Z., Kochhar, S., & Grigorov, M. G. (2005). Descriptor-based protein remote homology identification. *Protein Science*, *14*(2), 431–444. doi:10.1110/ps.041035505

ADDITIONAL READING

Abagyan, R., Frishman, D., & Argos, P. (1994). Recognition of distantly related proteins through energy calculations. *Proteins*, *19*(2), 132–140. PubMed doi:10.1002/prot.340190206doi:10.1002/prot.340190206

Anand, B., Gowri, V. S., & Srinivasan, N. (2005). Use of multiple profiles corresponding to a sequence alignment enables effective detection of remote homologues. *Bioinformatics (Oxford, England)*, *21*(12), 2821–2826. PubMed doi:10.1093/bioinformatics/bti432doi:10.1093/bioinformatics/bti432

Bernsel, A., Viklund, H., & Elofsson, A. (2008). Remote homology detection of integral membrane proteins using conserved sequence features. *Proteins*, *71*(3), 1387–1399. PubMed doi:10.1002/prot.21825doi:10.1002/prot.21825

Brenner, S. E., Koehl, P., & Levitt, M. (2000). The ASTRAL compendium for protein structure and sequence analysis. *Nucleic Acids Research*, *28*(1), 254–256. PubMed doi:10.1093/nar/28.1.254doi:10.1093/nar/28.1.254

Busuttil, S., Abela, J., & Pace, G. J. (2004). Support vector machines with profile-based kernels for remote protein homology detection. *Genome Inform*, *15*(2), 191–200. PubMed

Damoulas, T., & Girolami, M. A. (2008). Probabilistic multi-class multi-kernel learning: on protein fold recognition and remote homology detection. *Bioinformatics (Oxford, England)*, *24*(10), 1264–1270. PubMed doi:10.1093/bioinformatics/btn112doi:10.1093/bioinformatics/btn112

Falquet, L., Pagni, M., Bucher, P., Hulo, N., Sigrist, C. J., Hofmann, K., & Bairoch, A. (2002). The PROSITE database, its status in 2002. *Nucleic Acids Research*, *30*(1), 235–238. PubMed doi:10.1093/nar/30.1.235doi:10.1093/nar/30.1.235

Fontana, P., Bindewald, E., Toppo, S., Velasco, R., Valle, G., & Tosatto, S. C. (2005). The SSEA server for protein secondary structure alignment. *Bioinformatics (Oxford, England)*, *21*(3), 393–395. PubMed doi:10.1093/bioinformatics/bti013doi:10.1093/bioinformatics/bti013

Ginalski, K., Pas, J., Wyrwicz, L. S., von Grotthuss, M., Bujnicki, J. M., & Rychlewski, L. (2003). ORFeus: Detection of distant homology using sequence profiles and predicted secondary structure. *Nucleic Acids Research*, *31*(13), 3804–3807. PubMed doi:10.1093/nar/gkg504doi:10.1093/nar/gkg504

Hadley, C., & Jones, D. T. (1999). A systematic comparison of protein structure classifications: SCOP, CATH and FSSP. *Structure (London, England)*, *7*(9), 1099–1112. PubMed doi:10.1016/S0969-2126(99)80177-4doi:10.1016/S0969-2126(99)80177-4

Han, S., Lee, B. C., Yu, S. T., Jeong, C. S., Lee, S., & Kim, D. (2005). Fold recognition by combining profile-profile alignment and support vector machine. *Bioinformatics (Oxford, England)*, *21*(11), 2667–2673. PubMed doi:10.1093/bioinformatics/bti384doi:10.1093/bioinformatics/bti384

Holm, L., Ouzounis, C., Sander, C., Tuparev, G., & Vriend, G. (1992). A database of protein structure families with common folding motifs. *Protein Science*, *1*(12), 1691–1698. PubMed doi:10.1002/pro.5560011217doi:10.1002/pro.5560011217

Hou, Y., Hsu, W., Lee, M. L., & Bystroff, C. (2004). Remote homolog detection using local sequence-structure correlations. *Proteins*, *57*(3), 518–530. PubMed doi:10.1002/prot.20221doi:10.1002/prot.20221

Hulo, N., Sigrist, C. J., Le Saux, V., Langendijk-Genevaux, P. S., Bordoli, L., Gattiker, A., et al. (2004). Recent improvements to the PROSITE database. *Nucleic Acids Research*, *32*(Database issue), D134–D137. PubMed doi:10.1093/nar/gkh044doi:10.1093/nar/gkh044

Karplus, K., Barrett, C., & Hughey, R. (1998). Hidden Markov models for detecting remote protein homologies. *Bioinformatics (Oxford, England)*, *14*(10), 846–856. PubMed doi:10.1093/bioinformatics/14.10.846doi:10.1093/bioinformatics/14.10.846

Kuang, R., Ie, E., Wang, K., Wang, K., Siddiqi, M., Freund, Y., & Leslie, C. (2005). Profile-based string kernels for remote homology detection and motif extraction. *Journal of Bioinformatics and Computational Biology*, *3*(3), 527–550. PubMed doi:10.1142/S021972000500120Xdoi:10.1142/S021972000500120X

Liao, L., & Noble, W. S. (2003). Combining pairwise sequence similarity and support vector machines for detecting remote protein evolutionary and structural relationships. *Journal of Computational Biology*, *10*(6), 857–868. PubMed doi:10.1089/106652703322756113doi:10.1089/106652703322756113

Needleman, S. B., & Wunsch, C. D. (1970). A general method applicable to the search for similarities in the amino acid sequence of two proteins. *Journal of Molecular Biology, 48*(3), 443–453. PubMed doi:10.1016/0022-2836(70)90057-4doi:10.1016/0022-2836(70)90057-4

Ogul, H., & Mumcuoglu, E. U. (2007). A discriminative method for remote homology detection based on n-peptide compositions with reduced amino acid alphabets. *BioSystems, 87*(1), 75–81. PubMed doi:10.1016/j.biosystems.2006.03.006doi:10.1016/j.biosystems.2006.03.006

Orengo, C. A., Michie, A. D., Jones, S., Jones, D. T., Swindells, M. B., & Thornton, J. M. (1997). CATH--a hierarchic classification of protein domain structures. *Structure (London, England), 5*(8), 1093–1108. PubMed doi:10.1016/S0969-2126(97)00260-8doi:10.1016/S0969-2126(97)00260-8

Przytycka, T., Aurora, R., & Rose, G. D. (1999). A protein taxonomy based on secondary structure. *Nature Structural Biology, 6*(7), 672–682. PubMed doi:10.1038/10728doi:10.1038/10728

Reid, A. J., Yeats, C., & Orengo, C. A. (2007). Methods of remote homology detection can be combined to increase coverage by 10% in the midnight zone. *Bioinformatics (Oxford, England), 23*(18), 2353–2360. PubMed doi:10.1093/bioinformatics/btm355doi:10.1093/bioinformatics/btm355

Shachar, O., & Linial, M. (2004). A robust method to detect structural and functional remote homologues. *Proteins, 57*(3), 531–538. PubMed doi:10.1002/prot.20235doi:10.1002/prot.20235

Shi, J., Blundell, T. L., & Mizuguchi, K. (2001). FUGUE: sequence-structure homology recognition using environment-specific substitution tables and structure-dependent gap penalties. *Journal of Molecular Biology, 310*(1), 243–257. PubMed doi:10.1006/jmbi.2001.4762doi:10.1006/jmbi.2001.4762

Tcheremenskaia, O., Giuliani, A., & Tomasi, M. (2008). PROFALIGN algorithm identifies the regions containing folding determinants by scoring pairs of hydrophobic profiles of remotely related proteins. *Journal of Computational Biology, 15*(4), 445–455. PubMed doi:10.1089/cmb.2007.0100doi:10.1089/cmb.2007.0100

Yang, Y., Tantoso, E., & Li, K. B. (2008). Remote protein homology detection using recurrence quantification analysis and amino acid physico-chemical properties. *Journal of Theoretical Biology, 252*(1), 145–154. PubMed doi:10.1016/j.jtbi.2008.01.028doi:10.1016/j.jtbi.2008.01.028

KEY TERMS AND DEFINITIONS

Consensus Sequence: Consensus sequence can be considered as a simplified profile and was used to improve sequence alignment accuracy in the early time.

Descriptor: The phase has the same meaning as feature vector in the machine learning field.

Fold Recognition: Fold recognition methods are the algorithms that attempt to detect similarities between protein 3D structures that are not accompanied by any significant sequence similarity.

Support Vector Machine: Support vector machine is a supervised learning method can be used for classification and regression analysis.

PSI-BLAST: Position specific iterative BLAST (PSI-BLAST), refers to a feature of BLAST 2.0 in which a profile (or position specific scoring matrix, PSSM) is constructed from a multiple alignment of the highest scoring hits in an initial BLAST search.

ROC Curve: In the curve, true positive instances versus false positive instances is used to examine the number of true positives out of samples identified by varying similarity scores

SCOP: SCOP is an abbreviation of "Structural Classification Of Proteins". It is a protein classification database, which divides proteins into different homologous levels.

Chapter 6
A New Approach for DNA Sequence Similarity Analysis Based on Triplets of Nucleic Acid Bases

Dan Wei
Xiamen University, China & Fujian Key Laboratory of the Brain-like Intelligent Systems (Xiamen University), China

Qingshan Jiang
Xiamen University, China

Sheng Li
Xiamen University, China

ABSTRACT

Similarity analysis of DNA sequences is a fundamental research area in Bioinformatics. The characteristic distribution of L-tuple, which is the tuple of length L, reflects the valuable information contained in a biological sequence and thus may be used in DNA sequence similarity analysis. However, similarity analysis based on characteristic distribution of L-tuple is not effective for the comparison of highly conservative sequences. In this paper, a new similarity measurement approach based on Triplets of Nucleic Acid Bases (TNAB) is introduced for DNA sequence similarity analysis. The new approach characterizes both the content feature and position feature of a DNA sequence using the frequency and position of occurrence of TNAB in the sequence. The experimental results show that the approach based on TNAB is effective for analysing DNA sequence similarity.

INTRODUCTION

DNA sequence similarity, the degree of similarity among finite sets of strings of nucleic bases, is a basic problem in Bioinformatics, and the resulting information can be used to deduce structures, functions and evolutionary relationships of genes. Therefore, research in this realm has become an important topic in the field of Bioinformatics (Jiang et al., 2002).

DOI: 10.4018/978-1-60960-064-8.ch006

There are a number of computational and statistical methods for similarity analysis developed over the past decade. The traditional methods are mainly based on alignment of the strings including insertions, deletions and gaps in sequence (Waterman, 1995), and hence their time and space complexities expand with increasing sequence length. In addition, these methods involve some subjective factors, including determining optimal criteria and assigning scores during alignment. Thus, there are some difficulties associated with these methods in comparing DNA sequences. In recent years, some alignment-free methods, such as those based on graphical representation (Liao et al., 2005), matrices (Randic, 2000), vectors (Vinga & Almeida, 2003), and so on, have been proposed to overcome critical limitations of sequence analysis by alignment. Among them, methods based on vectors have been widely studied and applied. By constructing vectors for DNA primary sequences and calculating the distance between two vectors one can obtain the similarity of two DNA sequences. The distance between two vectors can be computed in three ways: Euclidean (Blaisdell, 1986), the cosine of the correlation angle (Stuart et al., 2002), and correlation coefficient (Petrilli, 1993).

The basic rationale for using vectors is that similar sequences will share word composition to some extent, which is then quantified by the distance among such vectors. Generally, sequence comparison is only based on the statistics of word frequency. The statistical and probabilistic properties of words in sequences (Reinert et al., 2000) were studied, with emphasis on the deductions of exact distributions and the evaluation of its asymptotic approximations. The first usage of k-word counts for biological sequence comparison was implemented by Blaisdell (1986). Two vectors of relative frequencies of k-words over a sliding window from two given DNA sequences were computed to analyze the sequences (Wu et al., 2001). Later, word-based comparisons were reviewed by Vinga and Almeida (2003). Recently,

a sixteen-component vector of the relative frequencies of the dual nucleotides has been applied to characterize and compare the coding sequences (Luo et al., 2008). Based on the short word composition of biological sequences, a new distance metric was presented (Wang & Zheng, 2008). These word-based studies determined the similarity of DNA sequences by ignoring the position of each word within a sequence and noting only its frequency. However, the position of occurrence of word in the sequence has a close relation with gene transposition, translocation and converse. Considering the positions of L-tuple, which is a DNA sequence segment with the length L, the Characteristic Distribution of L-tuple (CDLt) was presented by Liu et al. (2007). In addition, CDLt was used to compare DNA sequences (Liu, 2008). Unfortunately, the methods based on CDLt failed to measure similarity among conserved sequences.

In this chapter, the frequency and position of occurrence of Triplets of Nucleic Acid Bases (TNAB) in a DNA sequence are discussed. Based on the frequency and position, this chapter presents a new approach which can extract more information from the DNA sequence. Moreover, a new algorithm SATNAB (Similarity Analysis based on TNAB) for sequence comparison is outlined. The experimental result suggests that this new approach is suitable for the analysis of DNA sequences.

This chapter is organized as follows. First, similarity analysis based on CDLt is described. The approach based on TNAB is presented next. Afterwards, we present the experiments and the performance results, followed by the conclusions.

SIMILARITY ANALYSIS

The characteristic distribution of L-tuple was studied to extract position feature from DNA sequences by Liu et al. (2007).

L-Tuple

A sequence, *S*, of length *n*, is defined as a linear succession of *n* symbols from four letter alphabet, which contains A, C, G and T. A segment of *L* symbols, with $L \leq n$, is designated an *L*-tuple or *L*-word. The set W_L consists of all possible *L*-tuples which can be extracted from sequence *S* and has *K* elements. The definitions can be given as,

$$W_L = \{w_1, w_2, ..., w_K\} \tag{1}$$

$$K = 4^L \tag{2}$$

where w_i ($i = 1, 2, ..., K$) is the ith *L*-tuple in W_L.

CDLt and Similarity Analysis

CDLt reflects the feature and information involved in sequence. The definition of CDLt is as follow:

Given a DNA sequence *S*, α_i is the location of the ith occurrence of an *L*-tuple w_j, where $\alpha_0 = 0$. And β_i can be given as,

$$\beta_i = \begin{cases} \dfrac{\alpha_i - \alpha_{i-1}}{n}, 1 \leq i < m \\ \dfrac{n - \alpha_{i-1}}{n}, i = m \end{cases} \tag{3}$$

where *n* is the length of *S*, *m* is the number of occurrences of w_j in S. The characteristic distribution function is defined as follow:

$$P\{w_j \text{ occurs at } \alpha_i\} = \beta_i, \quad i = 1, 2, ..., m \tag{4}$$

Equation (4) is the characteristic distribution of w_j. Based on the above, CDLt can be used in analyzing DNA sequence similarity (Liu, 2008). We transform the procedure into an algorithm, and name it SACDLt (Similarity Analysis based

on CDLt) for comparison. The pseudo code is summarized as follows:

Algorithm 1 (SACDLt)

```
Input: DNA sequences, S₁, S₂,…,
S_M
  Output: distance matrix
  begin
  1 Initialization
    1.1 k is any integer with 1≤
k ≤ n, n is the length of DNA
sequence;
    1.2 Use Equation (2) to count
the number, K, of k-tuples;
    2 For m=1 to M do
      2.1 For c=1 to K do
2.1.1 Search and locate each k-
tuple in S_M;
2.1.2 For each k-tuple, use
Equation (3) and Equation (4)
to calculate and construct the
characteristic distribution;
      2.2 For each S_m, calculate
the variance of the character-
istic distribution of k-tuple
and then obtain variance values
whose number is K;
      2.3 Construct K-component
vector by the K-variance value;
      2.4 Calculate cosine of
the correlation angle between
two vectors
    3 Output distance matrix
  end
```

It can be seen from the algorithm flow that CDLt is computed and constructed by Equation (3) and Equation (4) respectively. $\alpha_i - \alpha_{i-1}$ represents the density of *L*-tuple, that is the position feature, however, β_i cannot show the content feature of *L*-tuple. Therefore, the features extracted from DNA sequences may not be enough to measure the similarity between species when using CDLt.

According to the analysis above, we consider the frequency and position of TNAB as the content feature and position feature respectively while analyzing DNA sequence similarity. Therefore we extract more information from DNA sequences to measure the similarity.

A NEW APPROACH BASED ON TRIPLETS OF NUCLEIC ACIDS BASES

In this section, we introduce how to obtain the frequency and position of TNAB, and present a new measurement approach as well as the algorithm of DNA sequence similarity analysis.

Triplets of Nucleic Acids Bases

As is known, the genetic code consists of triplets of DNA (or RNA in some virus) nucleic acids and all 64 TNAB correspond to 20 amino acids as well as a stop code. According to the hypothesis that the codon usage patterns are similar in closed species, many researchers use TNAB in analysis and comparison among DNA sequences (Balaban et al., 2003; Liao & Wang, 2004; Randic et al., 2001). Moreover, TNAB can simplify the computation considerably.

TNAB in sequence S, of length n, can be obtained by taking a sliding window 3-wide which is run through the sequence, from position 1 to n-2. For example, for the sequence S=ATGACTTTGC, where n=10, the set of TNAB would be {ATG, TGA, GAC, ACT, CTT, TTT, TTG, TGC}.

Frequency and Position of Occurrence of TNAB in DNA Sequence

Due to code degeneracy, each amino acid corresponds to at most six TNAB and at least one. For instance, the codons of serine are TCT, TCC, TCA, TCG, AGT and AGC. Amino acid sequences

is more conserved than DNA sequences in the evolutionary process, and can provide more useful information for species evolution (Nei & Kumar, 2000). As a result, we divided 64 TNAB into 21 classes. In each class, the frequencies of TNAB can be defined, taking example for serine, as follows:

$$
\begin{aligned}
f_{TCT} &= \frac{C_{TCT}}{C_{TCT} + C_{TCC} + C_{TCA} + C_{TCG} + C_{AGT} + C_{AGC}} \\
f_{TCC} &= \frac{C_{TCC}}{C_{TCT} + C_{TCC} + C_{TCA} + C_{TCG} + C_{AGT} + C_{AGC}} \\
f_{TCA} &= \frac{C_{TCA}}{C_{TCT} + C_{TCC} + C_{TCA} + C_{TCG} + C_{AGT} + C_{AGC}} \\
f_{TCG} &= \frac{C_{TCG}}{C_{TCT} + C_{TCC} + C_{TCA} + C_{TCG} + C_{AGT} + C_{AGC}} \\
f_{AGT} &= \frac{C_{AGT}}{C_{TCT} + C_{TCC} + C_{TCA} + C_{TCG} + C_{AGT} + C_{AGC}} \\
f_{AGC} &= \frac{C_{AGC}}{C_{TCT} + C_{TCC} + C_{TCA} + C_{TCG} + C_{AGT} + C_{AGC}}
\end{aligned}
\tag{5}
$$

where C_{TCT}, C_{TCC}, C_{TCA}, C_{TCG}, C_{AGT}, C_{AGC} denote the number of TCT, TCC, TCA, TCG, AGT, AGC in a DNA sequence respectively. In addition, f_{TCT}, f_{TCC}, f_{TCA}, f_{TCG}, f_{AGT}, f_{AGC} represent the frequency of TCT, TCC, TCA, TCG, AGT, AGC respectively.

A triplet, t, occurs at position p_i ($i=1,2,\ldots, m$) in a DNA sequence, S. q_i ($i=1,2,\ldots, m$) is the space between two neighboring positions of t, set p_0=0. q_i can be obtained by

$$
q_i = p_i - p_{i-1} \quad (i = 1, 2, \ldots, m)
\tag{6}
$$

For example, for the sequence ATGACTTT-GCTGATGGCTGAGGATGAATGC, ATG occurs at position 1, 13, 23, 27. In that case, the space between two neighboring positions of ATG would be (1, 12, 10, 4). q_i is only dependent on the number and positions of t and independent on other triplets. So q_i would be regarded as the position feature in S to analyze DNA sequences.

Similarity Measure between Sequences

In order to easily compare different DNA sequences, we associate each sequence with the frequency and position of occurrence of TNAB respectively, and then obtain two 64-compoment vectors.

Two vectors of frequencies, $F^X = (f_1^X, f_2^X, ..., f_{64}^X)$ and $F^Y = (f_1^Y, f_2^Y, ..., f_{64}^Y)$, correspond to two DNA sequences, X and Y, where $f_i^X (i = 1, 2, ..., 64)$ and $f_i^Y (i = 1, 2, ..., 64)$ stand for the frequency of the ith triplet in X and Y respectively. The similarity of frequencies, namely $Sim_1(X,Y)$, can be computed by

$$Sim_1(X,Y) = \frac{\sum_{i=1}^{64}(f_i^X \cdot f_i^Y)}{\sqrt{\sum_{i=1}^{64}(f_i^X)^2} \cdot \sqrt{\sum_{i=1}^{64}(f_i^Y)^2}}$$

(7)

After normalizing the position feature of each triplet in a DNA sequence and calculating its mean square deviation, we associate the sequence with the mean square deviation of 64 triplets and then construct a 64-compoment vector. For two DNA sequences, X and Y, there are two corresponding vectors: $V^X = (v_1^X, v_2^X, ..., v_{64}^X)$ and $V^Y = (v_1^Y, v_2^Y, ..., v_{64}^Y)$, where $v_i^X (i = 1, 2, ..., 64)$ and $v_i^Y (i = 1, 2, ..., 64)$ denote the position feature of the ith triplet in X and Y respectively. The similarity of positions, namely $Sim_2(X,Y)$, can be computed by

$$Sim_2(X,Y) = \frac{\sum_{i=1}^{64}(v_i^X \cdot v_i^Y)}{\sqrt{\sum_{i=1}^{64}(v_i^X)^2} \cdot \sqrt{\sum_{i=1}^{64}(v_i^Y)^2}}$$

(8)

It can be seen from the above definition that $Sim_1(X,Y)$ represents the content feature and $Sim_2(X,Y)$, is the position feature. Considering both the frequencies and positions of TNAB, the similarity between X and Y, $Sim(X,Y)$, can be computed by

$$Sim(X,Y) = \lambda_1 \cdot Sim_1(X,Y) + \lambda_2 \cdot Sim_2(X,Y)$$

(9)

where λ_1 and λ_2 are weighting coefficients. In addition, $\lambda_1 + \lambda_2 = 1$.

Similarity Analysis Algorithm Based on TNAB

Using the vectors of frequencies and position of all possible triplets, we measure the similarity of DNA sequences. The algorithm SATNAB is summarized as follows:

Algorithm 2 (SATNAB)

Input: DNA sequences, S_1, S_2, ..., S_M
  Output: distance matrix, Sim
  begin
1 Initialization
    Use Equation (2) to count the number of all possible triplets;
  2 For m=1 to M do
    2.1 For c=1 to 64 do
2.1.1 Search and locate each triplet in S_m;
2.1.2 For each triplet, use equations like Equation (5) to calculate the frequency;
2.1.3 For each triplet, use Equation (6) calculate and construct the position feature;
    2.2 For each S_m, Construct 64-component vector, F^{S_m}, by the frequencies of all triplets;
    2.3 For each S_m, Construct 64-component vector, V^{S_m}, by the

mean square deviation of normalized position feature of all
triplets;
```
   3 For i=1 to M do
     3.1 For j=1 to M do
             3.1.1 Use Equation
(7) to calculate Sim (Sᵢ, Sⱼ);
             3.1.2 Use Equation
(8) to calculate Sim (Sᵢ, Sⱼ);
             3.1.3 Use Equation
(9) to calculate Sim (Sᵢ, Sⱼ);
     4 Output Sim
   end.
```

Sim is a nonnegative matrix where the diagonal elements are 1, and its elements reflect the distances among species. The larger $Sim (S_i, S_j)$ is, the more similar the DNA sequences are, and vice versa.

EXPERIMENTS AND RESULT ANALYSIS

One of the purposes of investigating similarity of sequences is to estimate sequence homology and deduce evolutionary relationships of sequences (Sun & Lu, 2005). Therefore, we choose the known evolutionary truth to verify the validity of similarity analysis. If the results accord with the existing evolutionary truth, the approach is effective.

In this section, we evaluate the validity of our algorithm, SATNAB, on the well-conserved DNA sequences. We also compare SATNAB with SACDLt and CLUSTALW (Chenna et al., 2003) which is one of the most popular and standard multiple sequence alignment programs. SATNAB and SACDLt are both alignment-free algorithms. What's more, the time complexity of SATNAB is similar to SACDLt. Here we just show the execution time of SATNAB and CLUSTALW to compare computational efficiency. All experi-

ments were conduced on a computer with 3.00 Ghz CPU and 1GMB RAM.

Experimental Data

In the experiment, the coding sequences of the first exon of the β-globin genes of eleven species which were reported by Liao (2005) are listed in Table 1. These sequences are conserved data for genes study.

Result Analysis

The experiment results of CLUSTALW, SATNAB ($\lambda_1 = 0.7$) and SACDLt ($L=3$) are shown in Table 2, Table 3 and Table 4 respectively. The comparisons are shown in Table 5, Table 6 and Figure 1.

According to Table 2, the most similar species pairs are Gorilla-Chimpanzee, Human-Chimpanzee and Human-Gorilla. The more similar species pairs are Goat-Bovine, Rabbit-Gorilla and Rabbit-Chimpanzee. The smallest entries appear in the rows belong to Opossum and Gallus. These results are rational in biological morphology.

In Table 3, we see again the dissimilarity of Gallus and Opossum compared to the other species considered here, because their corresponding rows have smaller entries. The largest entries are associated with Gorilla-Chimpanzee (0.9274), Human-Gorilla (0.9206), Goat-Bovine (0.9033). The more similar species pairs are Human-Chimpanzee (0.8498), Gorilla-Bovine (0.8484), Mouse-Rat (0.8388), while the smallest entries appear in the rows belong to Opossum and Gallus. These results accord with biological morphology.

On above analysis, it can conclude that the results in Table 2 are basically consistent with those in Table 3.

Table 4 indicates that Gallus and Opossum are highly dissimilar to others species because their corresponding rows have small entries. This is not unexpected because Gallus is the only nonmammalian species and Opossum is distantly related to the other considered ones. Some experimental

Table 1. Exon-1 of the β-Globin genes of eleven species

Species	Coding sequence
Human	ATGGTGCACCTGACTCCTGAGGAGAAGTCTGCCGTTACTGCCCTGTGGGGCAAGGTGAACGTGGATTA-AGTTGGTGGTGAGGCCCTGGGCAG
Goat	ATGCTGACTGCTGAGGAGAAGGCTGCCGTCACCGGCTTCTGGGGCAAGGTGAAAGTGGATGAAGTTG-GTGCTGAGGCCCTGGGCAG
Opossum	ATGGTGCACTTGACTTCTGAGGAGAAGAACTGCATCACTACCATCTGGTCTAAGGTGCAGGTTGAC-CAGACTGGTGGTGAGGCCCTTGGCAG
Gallus	ATGGTGCACTGGACTGCTGAGGAGAAGCAGCTCATCACCGGCCTCTGGGGCAAGGTCAATGTGGCC-GAATGTGGGGCCGAAGCCCTGGCCAG
Lemur	ATGACTTTGCTGAGTGCTGAGGAGAATGCTCATGTCACCTCTCTGTGGGGCAAGGTGGATGTAGAGA-AAGTTGGTGGCGAGGCCTTGGGCAG
Mouse	ATGGTTGCACCTGACTGATGCTGAGAAGTCTGCTGTCTCTTGCCTGTGGGGCAAAGGTGAACCCCGAT-GAAGTTGGTGGTGAGGCCCTGGGCAGG
Rabbit	ATGGTGCATCTGTCCAGTGAGGAGAAGTCTGCGGTCACTGCCCTGTGGGGCAAGGTGAATGTG-GAAGAAGTTGGTGGTGAGGCCCTGGGC
Rat	ATGGTGCACCTAACTGATGCTGAGAAGGCTACTGTTAGTGGCCTGTGGGGAAAGGTGAACCCTGATA-ATGTTGGCGCTGAGGCCCTGGGCAG
Gorilla	ATGGTGCACCTGACTCCTGAGGAGAAGTCTGCCGTTACTGCCCTGTGGGGCAAGGTGAACGTGGAT-GAAGTTGGTGGTGAGGCCCTGGGCAGG
Bovine	ATGCTGACTGCTGAGGAGAAGGCTGCCGTCACCGCCTTTTGGGGCAAGGTGAAAGTGGATGAAGTTG-GTGGTGAGGCCCTGGGCAG
Chimpanzee	ATGGTGCACCTGACTCCTGAGGAGAAGTCTGCCGTTACTGCCCTGTGGGGCAAGGTGAACGTGGAT-GAAGTTGGTGGTGAGGCCCTGGGCAGGTTGGTATCAAGG

results comforted to the evolutionary truth, such as Goat-Bovine (0.8963), Gorilla-Chimpanzee (0.8888) and Mouse-Rat (0.879) pairs. However, the largest entries are associated with the Goat-Gorilla (0.9791), Rabbit-Gorilla (0.9727) and Goat-Rabbit (0.9612) pairs, the more similar species pairs are Goat-Chimpanzee (0.8738), Human-Lemur (0.8736), and the smallest entries are associated with Human-Gorilla (0.5702),

Table 2. Aligned score matrix for the coding sequences of Table 1 by CLUSTALW

Species	Goat	Opos-sum	Gallus	Lemur	Mouse	Rabbit	Rat	Gorilla	Bovine	Chimpanzee
Human	84	73	72	70	83	88	80	98	87	98
Goat		67	74	77	76	79	74	86	96	86
Opossum			69	57	71	73	67	73	68	73
Gallus				65	69	70	64	73	70	73
Lemur					65	65	61	70	80	70
Mouse						80	85	84	76	84
Rabbit							73	90	81	90
Rat								80	72	80
Gorilla									88	100
Bovine										88

Table 3. The similarity/dissimilarity matrix for the coding sequences of Table 1 by SATNAB

Species	Human	Goat	Opos-sum	Gallus	Lemur	Mouse	Rabbit	Rat	Gorilla	Bovine	Chimpanzee
Human	1	0.7788	0.7362	0.6787	0.7419	0.8175	0.7299	0.7781	0.9206	0.7694	0.8498
Goat		1	0.6757	0.7486	0.7818	0.8349	0.8	0.7416	0.8642	0.9033	0.8255
Opossum			1	0.7053	0.6209	0.681	0.6574	0.6174	0.722	0.6118	0.7153
Gallus				1	0.7615	0.7187	0.8383	0.63	0.7264	0.7312	0.7929
Lemur					1	0.7716	0.8157	0.7246	0.7646	0.8326	0.7294
Mouse						1	0.7746	0.8388	0.8705	0.8135	0.8358
Rabbit							1	0.7097	0.8107	0.7811	0.8301
Rat								1	0.8198	0.7343	0.7446
Gorilla									1	0.8484	0.9274
Bovine										1	0.8146
Chimpanzee											1

Table 4. Similarity/dissimilarity matrix for the coding sequences of Table 1 by SACDLt

Species	Human	Goat	Opos-sum	Gallus	Lemur	Mouse	Rabbit	Rat	Gorilla	Bovine	Chimpan-zee
Human	1	0.5416	0.7238	0.5355	0.8736	0.6098	0.499	0.6185	0.5702	0.4866	0.4937
Goat		1	0.3718	0.5742	0.6691	0.6681	0.9612	0.629	0.9791	0.8963	0.8738
Opossum			1	0.6216	0.6412	0.4708	0.3274	0.4841	0.3895	0.3426	0.3395
Gallus				1	0.5082	0.6184	0.5879	0.5799	0.5852	0.5295	0.687
Lemur					1	0.6068	0.6565	0.6421	0.6952	0.5908	0.5844
Mouse						1	0.7009	0.879	0.6745	0.6089	0.6005
Rabbit							1	0.6431	0.9727	0.8778	0.8686
Rat								1	0.6544	0.5728	0.5649
Gorilla									1	0.8945	0.8888
Bovine										1	0.8038
Chimpanzee											1

Human-Chimpanzee (0.4937) pairs. These results deviate from the truth in the evolution sense.

In Table 5, we compare the results in the three important aspects: (1) For the most similar species pairs, such as the Goat-Gorilla, Rabbit-Gorilla and Goat-Rabbit pairs, the results of SACDLt are irrational, but the results of SATNAB are rational for the Gorilla-Chimpanzee, Human-Gorilla and Goat-Bovine pairs. (2) For the similar species pairs, the disappointing results which are the Goat-Chimpanzee and Human-Lemur pairs do not appear in the results of SATNAB. (3) For the most dissimilar species pairs, the results of SACDLt, including the Human-Gorilla and Human-Chimpanzee pairs, disagree with the fact. By SATNAB, the pairs of Opossum and Gallus to the other species considered here are highly dissimilar, which coincides with the known evolutionary truth.

Table 5. Comparison of the results between SACDLt and SATNAB

	results of SACDLt	results of SATNAB
the most similar species pairs	Goat-Gorilla	Gorilla-Chimpanzee
	Rabbit-Gorilla	Human-Gorilla
	Goat-Rabbit	Goat-Bovine
the similar species pairs	Goat-Bovine	Human-Chimpanzee
	Gorilla-Bovine	Goat-Gorilla
	Gorilla-Chimpanzee	Gorilla-Bovine
	Mouse-Rat	Mouse-Rat
	Goat-Chimpanzee	Rabbit-Chimpanzee
	Human-Lemur	
	Rabbit-Chimpanzee	
the most dissimilar species pairs	Human-Gorilla	belonging to the pairs of Opossum and Gallus to the other species
	Human-Chimpanzee	
	the pairs of Opossum and Gallus to the other species	

According to the results from Table 4 and Table 3, Figure 1 shows the similarity between Human and other species by SACDLt and SATNAB. In Figure 1, the similarity between Human and other species increased with the value of its corresponding column. By SACDLt, Human is most similar to Lemur and Opossum, while rather dissimilar to Chimpanzee and Gorilla. These results are evidently unconscionable. However, the experiment by SATNAB shows that Human is most similar to Gorilla and Chimpanzee, while most dissimilar to Opossum and Gallus. The results coincide with the known evolutionary truth.

On the basis of above analysis, the results in Table 3 are more rational than those in Table 4 and it is confirmed that our similarity measurement approach based on TNAB works well. However, some disappointed values, such as the Gallus-Rabbit (0.8383), Mouse-Gorilla (0.8705), are found in the large value in Table 3. This deviation lies in the possible reasons: Each species' genome is very long and contains many exons, yet only the first exon of the β-globin genes of eleven species is applied into this study and could not reveal the truth in the full range.

In order to demonstrate that the computational efficiency of SATNAB outweighs traditional sequence comparison approaches, we compare SATNAB with CLUSTALW. Table 6 lists the execution time of SATNAB and CLUSTALW respectively. It is noted that SATNAB outperforms CLUSTALW in runtime efficiency. And the number and length of sequences have little impact on the speed of SATNAB and larger impact on that of CLUSTALW. Because of its simplicity, the computation of SATNAB is valuable for analysing long sequences.

Table 6. Comparison of the execution time of SATNAB and CLUSTALW, where letter s means second

	number and length of sequences								
	5*1400	5*2800	5*5600	10*1400	10*2800	10*5600	20*1400	20*2800	20*5600
SATNAB	0.094s	0.156s	0.312s	0.141s	0.219s	0.484s	0.297s	0.578s	1.25s
CLUSTALW	1.1s	6.7s	26.7s	4.4s	23.5s	81.6s	30.6s	136.8s	590.2s

Figure 1. Comparison of the results between SACDLt and SATNAB on the human-other species similarity

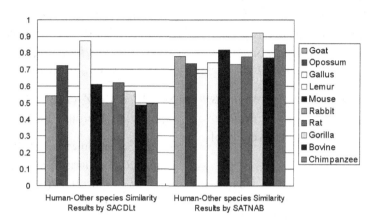

CONCLUSION AND FUTURE WORK

A new similarity measurement approach for analyzing DNA sequence has been presented in this chapter. This approach can reflect not only the content feature of DNA sequences, but also the position feature with the frequencies and positions of TNAB in DNA sequences. Based on this approach, a new algorithm aiming at analyzing DNA sequence similarity is outlined. The experimental results show that the new approach is effective for similarity analysis of DNA sequences, and more efficient than existing methods because of the simplicity of computing TNAB. Furthermore, the algorithm would not be affected by behaviors in the evolution process of genes, such as insertion, deletion, substitution and recombination. Some future work may include searching for more appropriate parameters to characterize the primary features of DNA sequence so that more useful information from DNA sequence can be obtained.

ACKNOWLEDGMENT

This work was supported by the National Natural Science Foundation of China under Grant No.10771176.

REFERENCES

Balaban, A. T., Plavsic, D., & Randic, M. (2003). DNA invariants based on nonoverlapping triplets of nucleotide bases. *Chemical Physics Letters, 379*(1-2), 147–154. doi:10.1016/j.cplett.2003.07.019

Blaisdell, B. E. (1986). A measure of the similarity of sets of sequences not requiring sequence alignment. *Proceeding of the National Academy of Sciences of the United States of America, 83*(14), 5155-5159.

Chenna, R., Sugawara, H., Koike, T., Lopez, R., Gibson, T. J., Higgins, D. G., & Thompson, J. D. (2003). Multiple sequence alignment with the Clustal series of programs. *Nucleic Acids Research, 31*(13), 3497–3500. doi:10.1093/nar/gkg500

Jiang, T., Xu, Y., & Zhang, M. (2002). *Current topics computation molecular biology*. Beijing: Tsinghua University Press.

Liao, B., Tan, M., & Ding, K. (2005). A 4D representation of DNA sequences and its application. *Chemical Physics Letters, 402*(4), 380–383. doi:10.1016/j.cplett.2004.12.062

Liao, B., & Wang, T. (2004). Analysis of similarity/dissimilarity of DNA sequences based on non-overlapping triplets of nucleotide bases. *Journal of Chemical Information and Computer Sciences, 44*(5), 1666–1670. doi:10.1021/ci034271f

Liu, Y. Z. (2008). *The Alignment-free Methods and Their Applications for Analysis of Biological Sequences*. PhD Thesis, Dalian University of Technology, China.

Liu, Y. Z., Yang, Y., & Wang, T. (2007). Characteristic Distribution of *L*-tuple for DNA Primary Sequence. *Journal of Biomolecular Structure & Dynamics, 25*(1), 85–91.

Luo, J., Li, R., & Zeng, Q. (2008). A novel method for sequence similarity analysis based on the relative frequency of dual nucleotides. *Communications in Mathematical and in Computer Chemistry / MATCH, 59*(3), 653-659.

Nei, M., & Kumar, S. (2000). *Molecular Evolution and Phylogenetics*. Oxford: Oxford University Press.

Petrilli, P. (1993). Classification of protein sequences by their dipeptide composition. *Bioinformatics (Oxford, England), 9*(2), 205–209. doi:10.1093/bioinformatics/9.2.205

Randic, M. (2000). Condensed Representation of DNA Primary Sequences. *Journal of Chemical Information and Computer Sciences, 40*(1), 50–56. doi:10.1021/ci990084z

Randic, M., Guo, X., & Basak, S. C. (2001). On the Characterization of DNA Primary Sequences by Triplet of Nucleic Acid Bases. *Journal of Chemical Information and Computer Sciences, 41*(3), 619–626. doi:10.1021/ci000120q

Reinert, G., Schbath, S., & Waterman, M. S. (2000). Probabilistic and statistical properties of words: an overview. *Journal of Computational Biology, 7*(1-2), 1–46. doi:10.1089/10665270050081360

Stuart, G. W., Moffett, K., & Baker, S. (2002). Integrated gene and species phylogenies from unaligned whole genome protein sequences. *Bioinformatics (Oxford, England), 18*(1), 100–108. doi:10.1093/bioinformatics/18.1.100

Sun, X., & Lu, Z. (2005). *The Foundation of Bioinformatics*. Beijing: Tsinghua University Press.

Vinga, S., & Almeida, J. (2003). Alignment-free sequence comparison-a review. *Bioinformatics (Oxford, England), 19*(4), 513–523. doi:10.1093/bioinformatics/btg005

Wang, J., & Zheng, X. (2008). WSE, a new sequence distance measure based on word frequencies. *Mathematical Biosciences, 215*(1), 78–83. doi:10.1016/j.mbs.2008.06.001

Waterman, M. S. (1995). *Introduction to Computational Biology: Maps, Sequences and Genomes*. Boca Raton, FL: CRC Press.

Wu, T., Hsieh, Y., & Li, L. (2001). Statistical Measure of DNA Sequence Dissimilarity under Markov Chain Models of Base Composition. *Biometrics, 57*(2), 441–448. doi:10.1111/j.0006-341X.2001.00441.x

ADDITIONAL READING

Dai, Q., Liu, X., & Wang, T. (2006). Numerical characterization of DNA sequences based on the k-step Markov chain transition probability. *Journal of Computational Chemistry, 27*(15), 1830–1842. doi:10.1002/jcc.20471

Edgar, R. C. (2004). MUSCLE: multiple sequence alignment with high accuracy and high throughput. *Nucleic Acids Research, 32*(5), 1792–1797. doi:10.1093/nar/gkh340

Feng, J., Liu, X., & Wang, T. (2008). Condensed representations of protein secondary structure sequences and their application. *Journal of Biomolecular Structure & Dynamics, 25*(6), 621–628.

Ferragina, P., Giancarlo, R., Greco, V., Manzini, G., & Valiente, G. (2007). Compression-based classification of biological sequences and structure via the Universal Similarity Metric: experimental assessment. *Bioinformatics (Oxford, England)*, *8*(1), 252–271.

Gates, M. A. (1985). Simpler DNA sequence representations. *Nature*, *316*(6025), 219. doi:10.1038/316219a0

Hamori, E. (1985). Novel DNA sequence representations. *Nature*, *314*(6012), 585–586. doi:10.1038/314585a0

He, P., & Wang, J. (2002). Characteristic sequences for DNA Primary sequence. *Journal of Chemical Information and Computer Sciences*, *42*(5), 1080–1085. doi:10.1021/ci010131z

Jeffrey, H. J. (1990). Chaos game representation of gene structure. *Nucleic Acids Research*, *18*(8), 2163–2170. doi:10.1093/nar/18.8.2163

Kantorovitz, M., Robinson, G. E., & Sinha, S. (2007). A statistical method for alignment-free comparison of regulatory sequences. *Bioinformatics (Oxford, England)*, *23*(13), 1249–1255. doi:10.1093/bioinformatics/btm211

Li, C., & Wang, J. (2005). New invariant of DNA sequences. *Journal of Chemical Information and Modeling*, *45*(1), 115–120. doi:10.1021/ci049874l

Li, M., Badger, J. H., & Chen, X. (2001). An information-based sequence distance and its application to whole mitochondrial genome phylogeny. *Bioinformatics (Oxford, England)*, *17*(2), 149–154. doi:10.1093/bioinformatics/17.2.149

Nandy, A. (1996). Two-dimensional graphical representation of DNA sequences and intron-exon discrimination in intron-rich sequence. *Bioinformatics (Oxford, England)*, *12*(1), 55–62. doi:10.1093/bioinformatics/12.1.55

Pham, T. D., & Zuegg, J. (2004). A probabilistic measure for alignment-free sequence comparison. *Bioinformatics (Oxford, England)*, *20*(18), 3455–3461. doi:10.1093/bioinformatics/bth426

Qi, J., Wang, B., & Hao, B. L. (2004). Whole proteome prokaryote phylogeny without sequence alignment: A K-String composition approach. *Journal of Molecular Evolution*, *58*(1), 1–11. doi:10.1007/s00239-003-2493-7

Randic, M., Vracko, M., & Lers, N. (2003). Analysis of similarity/dissimilarity of DNA sequences based on novel 2-D graphical representation. *Chemical Physics Letters*, *371*(1-2), 202–207. doi:10.1016/S0009-2614(03)00244-6

Randic, M., Vracko, M., & Zupan, J. (2003). Compact 2-D graphical representation of DNA. *Chemical Physics Letters*, *373*(5-6), 558–562. doi:10.1016/S0009-2614(03)00639-0

Shen, J., Zhang, S., Lee, H. C., & Hao, B. L. (2004). SeeDNA:a visualization tool for k-string content of long DNA sequences and their randomized counterparts. *Genomics, Proteomics & Bioinformatics*, *2*(3), 192–196.

Srabashi, B., Debi, P., & Probal, Ch. (2003). Words in DNA sequences: some case studies based on their frequency statistics. *Journal of Mathematical Biology*, *46*(6), 479–503. doi:10.1007/s00285-002-0185-3

Stuart, G. W., Moffett, K., & Leader, J. J. (2002). A comprehensive vertebrate phylogeny using vector representations of protein sequences from whole genomes. *Molecular Biology and Evolution*, *19*(4), 554–562.

Wu, T., Burke, J., & Davison, D. (1997). A measure of DNA sequence dissimilarity based on Mahalanobis distance between frequencies of words. *Biometrics*, *53*(4), 1431–1439. doi:10.2307/2533509

Yao, Y., Nan, X., & Wang, T. (2005). Analysis of similarity/dissimilarity of DNA sequences based on 3-D graphical representation. *Chemical Physics Letters*, *411*(1), 248–255. doi:10.1016/j.cplett.2005.06.040

Yau, S. S., Wang, J., Niknejad, A., Lu, C., Jin, N., & Ho, Y. K. (2003). DNA sequence representation without degeneracy. *Nucleic Acids Research*, *31*(12), 3078–3080. doi:10.1093/nar/gkg432

Zhang, C. T., Zhang, R., & Ou, H. (2003). The Z curve database: a graphic representation of genome sequences. *Bioinformatics (Oxford, England)*, *19*(5), 593–599. doi:10.1093/bioinformatics/btg041

KEY TERMS AND DEFINITIONS

DNA Sequence: It is a succession of nucleotide bases in the DNA molecule or strand. With regard to its biological function, which may depend on context, a sequence may be sense or anti-sense, and either coding or noncoding. DNA sequences can also contain "junk DNA".

Triplets of Nucleotide Bases: It is a segment of three nucleotide bases where the bases may be adenine, cytosine, guanine and thymine.

Similarity Analysis: It is the similarity measure between two DNA sequences. In general, it is computed by alignment and alignment-free methods.

L-Tuple: It is a segment of *L* symbols from four letter alphabet, A, C, G and T standing for nucleotide bases adenine, cytosine, guanine, and thymine, respectively.

Chapter 7
MicroRNA Precursor Prediction Using SVM with RNA Pairing Continuity Feature

Huan Yang
Jilin University, China

Yan Wang
Jilin University, China

Trupti Joshi
University of Missouri, USA

Dong Xu
University of Missouri, USA

Shoupeng Yu
Changchun Institute of Technology, China

Yanchun Liang
Jilin University, China

ABSTRACT

MicroRNAs (miRNAs) are endogenous single-stranded non-coding RNAs of ~22 nucleotides in length and they act as post-transcriptional regulators in bacteria, animals and plants. Almost all current methods for computational prediction of miRNAs use hairpin structure and minimum of free energy as characteristics to identify putative pre-miRNAs from a pool of candidates. We discovered a new effective feature named "basic-n-units" (BNU) to distinguish pre-miRNAs from pseudo ones. This feature describes pairing continuity of RNA secondary structure. Simulation results show that a classification method, called Triplet-SVM-classifier, achieved an accuracy of 97.24% when this BNU feature was used. This is a 3% increase caused solely by adding this new feature. We anticipate that this BNU feature may increase the accuracy for most classification methods.

DOI: 10.4018/978-1-60960-064-8.ch007

INTRODUCTION

A large number of m*icroRNAs* (miRNAs) have been identified through a variety of methods. But the number of miRNAs discovered is far less than that in the forecast level of theory. It is difficult to identify true pre-miRNA from their sequences. Pre-miRNA prediction methods include those that depend on sequence alignment of homologous fragments as well as those that use scoring functions based on sequences and structural characteristics. Machine learning prediction methods, which are widely applied in bioinformatics research, are becoming a common tool for pre-miRNA predictions. However, the accuracies of existing methods show that there is still room for improvement in distinguishing true pre-miRNAs from other hairpin sequences with similar stem-loops (pseudo pre-miRNAs). Because most of these algorithms rely on the characteristics of stem-loop hairpin structures, in which a large amount of pseudo pre-miRNAs can be found, it becomes increasingly important to identify more unique and essential features that define true pre-miRNAs. In our study, we discovered a new effective structural feature of pre-miRNAs whose inclusion in classification studies has improved the prediction accuracy.

BACKGROUND

MicroRNAs (miRNAs), one of the non-coding RNA families, are a class of endogenous, single-stranded, small (19-27nt) nucleic acids that have an extremely conserved structure. In the nucleus, a gene encoding miRNA is first transcribed into a pri-microRNA, which is cut into pre-miRNA with a hairpin (stem-loop) structure (Bartel, 2004) of about 70nt in length using an enzyme called "Drosha RNase" (Lee et al., 2003). The mature miRNAs are derived from cleavage of pre-miRNA by the Dicer enzyme out of the nucleus. miRNAs are essential in animal and plant development

(Bartel, 2004), stress response in plants (Bari et al., 2006), and various diseases including cancers (Blenkiron et al., 2007). They also play key roles in the regulation and control of a variety of the metabolic processes of different organisms (Hua & Xiao, 2005).

Since 2003, thousands of miRNAs have been experimentally identified. At the same time, a variety of prediction methods have been developed too. For examples, miRScan relies on the observation that the known miRNAs are derived from phylogenetically conserved stem-loop precursor RNAs (Lim et al., 2003). Xue et al. (2005) proposed an SVM-based method for classification of real and pseudo pre-miRNAs based on local contiguous structure-sequence composition feature. Nam et al. (2005; 2006) constructed hidden Markov models (HMM) to search for distant homologs of miRNA families. Yousef et al. (2006) used a Naıve Bayes classifier along with the integration of data from multiple species to predict miRNA genes. Jiang et al. (2007) tried to construct a classifier, called MiPred, between per-miRNA and pseudo miRNA using Random forest and P-value. As suggested by Helvik et al. (2007), the miRNA gene prediction methods can also be improved by reliable predictions of Drosha-processing sites. Aiming at identifying miRNAs from genomes with a few known miRNA, Xu et al. (2008) proposed and developed a novel miRNA prediction method, miRank, with a novel ranking algorithm based on random walks. RNAmicro (Hertel & Stadler, 2006) was designed to classify the surveys of large-scale comparative genomics for predicting putative RNAs. Recently, Ahmed et al. (2009) demonstrated that guide and passenger strands of miRNA precursors can be distinguished using nucleotide sequence and secondary structures.

However, new problems also occurred: the features extracted using the existing forecasting methods are limited, and the range of species that can be predicted is small. Some methods can only predict one type of pre-miRNAs from either animal, plant or bacteria; some can predict pre-miRNAs with only a single loop or with only multi-loops; some can only predict a few designated species. Therefore, to overcome these existing difficulties, this chapter presents a new feature for pre-miRNA classification. We have implemented this feature in the Triplet-SVM model with satisfactory results.

DISCOVERY OF A NOVEL FEATURE FOR MICRORNA PRECURSOR CLASSIFICATION

Basic-N-Units (Bnu) Feature

In animals, almost all pre-miRNAs of about 60~70nt in length contain a single internal loop. In contrast, the vast majority of plant pre-miRNAs with 120nt in length - much longer than animals' pre-miRNAs - contain multiple loops. As previous studies have shown, conserved sequence and stem-loop structure are the most prominent characteristics of pre-miRNA. In addition, there are also some intrinsic features of pre-miRNA with one loop: minimum of 18 base pairings on the stem of the hairpin structure (including the GU wobble pairs); maximum of -15 kcal/mol free energy of the secondary structure (Xue et al., 2005).

When observing the structures of true miRNA and pseudo miRNA data, we discovered that even if there are 18 base pairings on the stem of the hairpin structure of both real miRNA and pseudo miRNA, the continuity of matching bases in real miRNAs is better than that in pseudo miRNAs. Take Figure 1 as an example, the brackets and dots sequences are the secondary structure information where "(" or ")" and "." represent paired and unpaired nucleotides, respectively. There are longer continuous "(", especially in the mature part, in a real miRNA in contrast to pseudo miRNA, as shown in Figure 1. Therefore, the better continuity that we refer to does not have to be "perfect matching". In other words, very few non-matching sites are permitted, such as these "." in Figure 1A

in certain region. We developed a rule to capture such particular regions and express this feature as the following: count the longest continuous matching bases length with a few non-matching sites. The longest length is used as a feature and the non-matching sites separate the longest region into several blocks. We called this representation "basic-n-units" (BNU), where n-1 is the maximum number of non-matching nucleotides allowed for each gap. Take Figure 1 as an example, there are 3 gaps with 3 non-matching nucleotides in total in the block style parts, and these non-matching nucleotides divide the block style parts into 4 blocks, which is called a "basic-4-units". If there is only one gap with 2 non-matching nucleotides, it is called a "basic-3-units" (as n-1 is 2 here).

After observing abundant plants data and a number of experiments with basic-3-units, basic-4-units, basic-5-units and basic-6-units respectively, we finally chose basic-4-units, as it was demonstrated to be the best one to distinguish real from pseudo pre-miRNAs in our experiments. We named the significant basic-4-units (BFU) as basic feature units. However, it is worth noting that this case might be different in animals, as most animal pre-miRNAs are more active and the continuity of animal pre-miRNAs is not as good as that of the plants. This suggests that we may select a different "N" of basic-n-units for animal pre-miRNA prediction.

MATERIALS AND METHODS

Datasets

We used 1523 pre-miRNAs, including both single-loop and multiple-loop, which originated from 11 species of plants for training set and test set.

The real plant miRNA precursors' datasets came from the miRBase database, Release 12.0 (Griffiths-Jones et al. 2006). We chose miRNAs in 11 plant species including *Arabidopsis thaliana, Brassica napus, Chlamydomonas reinhardtii,*

Figure 1. Comparison between real pre-RNA and pseudo pre-RNA. (a) The sequence and secondary structure of ath-mir-156a. (b) The sequence and secondary structure of a tRNA from Sorghum. (c) The sequence and secondary structure in a protein-coding region randomly selected from human genome. The alphabetical sequences of "A" "C" "G" "U" are sequence information of stem-loop structures; the brackets and dots sequences are the secondary structure information where "(" or ")" and "." means paired and unpaired respectively. The block style parts on the structure and the underlined parts on the sequence are the basic-4-units.

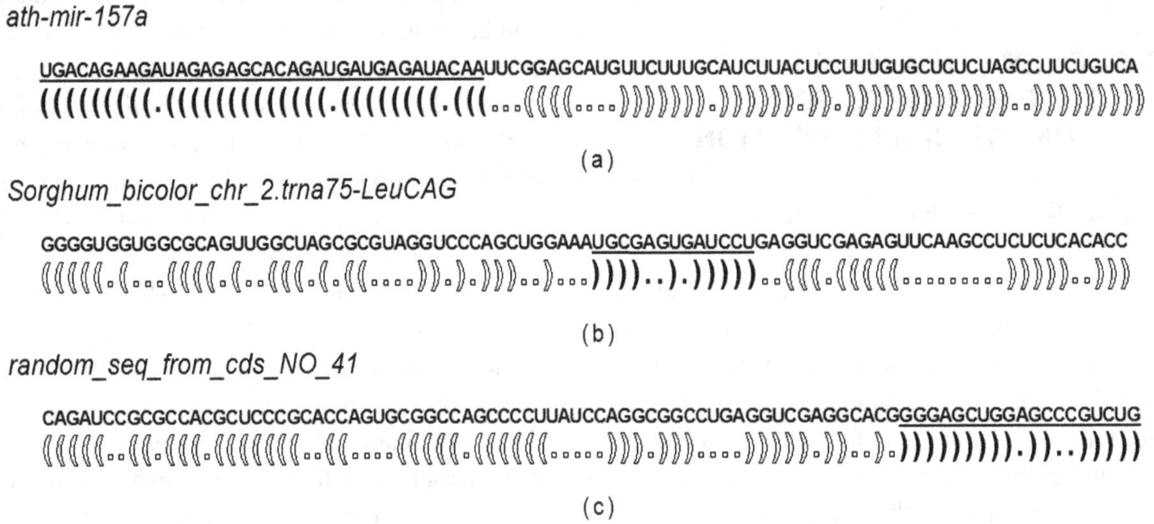

ath-mir-157a

UGACAGAAGAUAGAGAGCACAGAUGAUGAGAUACAAUUCGGAGCAUGUUCUUUGCAUCUUACUCCUUUGUGCUCUCUAGCCUUCUGUCA

((((((((((.((((((((((((.((((((((.(((...((((.....))))))))).)))))))).)).)))))))))))))))..)))))))))))

(a)

Sorghum_bicolor_chr_2.trna75-LeuCAG

GGGGUGGUGGCGCAGUUGGCUAGCGCGUAGGUCCCAGCUGGAAAUGCGAGUGAUCCUGAGGUCGAGAGUUCAAGCCUCUCUCACACC

((((((.(.(...((((.(..(.((((.(.(.((.....))).).)))).)..)...))))..).)))).))))))..(((.(.(((((.........))))))..)))

(b)

random_seq_from_cds_NO_41

CAGAUCCGCGCCACGCUCCCGCACCAGUGCGGCCAGCCCCUUAUCCAGGCGGCCUGAGGUCGAGGCACGGGGAGCUGGAGCCCGUCUG

((((((..(((.(((.(((((((((..(((.....(((((.(((((((.....))).)))).))))....)))))).))..).)))))))))).)).))))))

(c)

Glycine max, Oryza sativa, Physcomitrella patens, Populus trichocarpa, Sorghum bicolor, Selaginella moellendorffii, Vitis vinifera and *Zea mays*. It provided us 1523 pre-miRNAs entries in total.

The 1568 negative samples, as pseudo miR-NAs hairpins, were randomly selected from the genomic tRNA database (GtRNAdb) (Chan et al., 2008), which includes 78,759 tRNA genes predicted from 740 species.

In the course of the entire classification experiment, one general model was trained finally. Our training set includes 1023 pre-miRNAs entries (positive samples) and 1056 tRNA (negative samples) selected randomly from 1523 plant pre-miRNAs and 78,759 plant tRNA, respectively. The testing set comprised of the remaining 500 plant pre-miRNAs not used in training set and 516 pseudo pre-miRNAs randomly picked up from the tRNA dataset (excluding those already selected in the training sets).

Local Contiguous Triplet Structure Composition

Local features characterize various sequence properties in RNA sequences. For instance, in the predicted secondary structure there are only two conditions for each nucleotide, paired or unpaired, indicated by brackets '(' or ')' and dots '.', respectively, as shown in Figure 2. The left bracket '(' means that the paired nucleotide is located near the 5'-end and can be paired with another nucleotide at the 3'-end, which is indicated as a right bracket ')'. Here, we do not distinguish "(" and ")", and use '(' for both situations. For any three adjacent nucleotides, there are eight (2^3) possible structure compositions: '(((', '((.', '(..','...', '.((',

'..(', '.(.' and '(.('. We further differentiate each of these eight configurations by the nucleotide—A,C,G,U—in the middle position. Thus, there are 32 (4×8) possible sequence-structure configurations for each triplet in the precursors of miRNAs. Similar features have been used in some of the existing methods, such as triplet-SVM-classifier (Xue et al., 2005) and MiPred (Jiang et al. 2007). We have successfully developed this triplet-SVM method to solve precursors with both single loop and multiple loops.

The Minimum of Free Energy (MFE)

We also used the normalized minimum free energy (MFE) of folding in our method, which is a most popular global feature at the structural and topological level predicted by the RNAFold software package (Hofacker et al., 1994).

SVM Classification

Support vector machine (SVM) is used to classify real vs. pseudo pre-miRNAs with the feature vectors. The 32-dimentional features mentioned in the triplet-SVM method, MFE, BFU and the ratio of MFE/BFU have constituted 35-dimentional feature vectors as input vectors to distinguish real from pseudo. We used the LIBSVM 2.86 (http://www.csie.ntu.edu.tw/~cjlin/libsvm/) software package to train our training set with 5 fold cross-validation and then applied to the testing set.

RESULTS AND DISCUSSION

When applying SVM classifier to the testing set with 500 positive samples and 516 negative samples, 491 out of the 500 plant pre-miRNAs are correctly recognized and 512 out of the 516 pseudo-miRNAs are detected as negative, which give a sensitivity of 99.19%, specificity of 98.27%,

Figure 2. Extraction of local structure-sequence features: (a) the sequence and secondary structure of ath-mir-165a; (b) the configurations of 32 local sequence-structure features. Frequencies of the 32 features are obtained for each miRNA precursor or putative candidate, and further normalized by the length of the corresponding sequence.

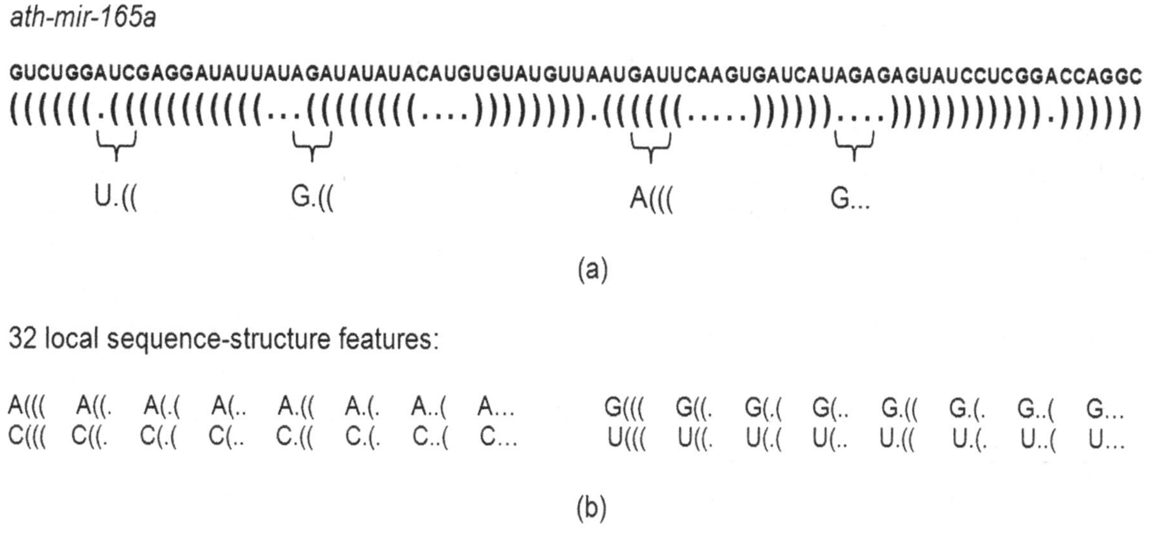

(a)

(b)

Table 1. Classification performance of the triplet-SVM classifier with BFU on test sets

Species	number of pre-miRNAs + number of tRNA	Accuracy (%)
Total	500+516	97.24
Arabidopsis thaliana	62+66	99.22
Brassica napus	14+15	100
Chlamydomonas reinhardtii	16+18	94.12
Glycine max	22+24	100
Oryza sativa	117+120	95.78
Physcomitrella patens	73+75	99.32
Populus trichocarpa	77+81	96.20
Sorghum bicolor	23+24	100
Selaginella moellendorffii	19+21	100
Vitis vinifera	46+48	97.87
Zea mays	31+33	100

and accuracy of 97.24%, respectively (shown in Table 1). The performance of Triplet-SVM-classifier with BNU feature was compared with other existing methods: Triplet-SVM-classifier (Xue et al., 2005) and MiPred (Jiang et al., 2007) which is the improvement of Triplet-SVM-classifier. These three methods used the same training set to test the same amount of human data. MiPred added random forest and p-value based on the first method. Our approach does not add any other algorithm in addition to adding a BNU feature. As shown in Table 2, the average accuracy of Triplet-SVM-classifier with BFU is better than that of other two. The detail of their algorithms can be found from these original publications. Thus, BNU feature not only can be applied in plants, but also can be extended to animals.

In order to illustrate the effectiveness of BNU feature, we also used the same training and testing datasets from (Xue et al., 2005). Their real sample datasets were downloaded from the miRNA registry database (Ambros et al. 2003; Griffiths-Jones et al., 2004), release 5.0, which contains 193 reported pre-miRNA entries from Homo sapiens whose secondary structures with one loop. Their pseudo samples dataset is called "CODING", which was made up of 8494 sequence segments that have similar stem-loop structures as genuine pre-miRNAs but have not been reported as pre-miRNAs. The testing set is a cross-species set, which was downloaded from the same database with 581 pre-miRNAs entries from 11 species besides human (see Table 3).

The classification performance of *Triplet-SVM-classifier and the improved Triplet-SVM-classifier with BFU feature are compared* (shown in Table 3). Almost all prediction accuracies for different species are improved by certain degree,

Table 2. Comparison with other methods

Methods	average sensitivity(%)	average specificity(%)	Accuracy(%)
Triplet-SVM-classifier	79.47	88.30	83.90
MiPred	89.35	93.21	91.29
Triplet-SVM-classifier with BFU	91.30	91.89	91.61

Table 3. Performance comparison between Triplet-SVM-classifier and the improved Triplet-SVM-classifier with BFU feature

Species	number of pre-miRNAs	Accuracy (%) of Triplet-SVM-classifier	Accuracy of Triplet-SVM-classifier with BFU(%)
Mus musculusi	36	94.4	97.22
Rattus norvegicus	25	80	80
Callus gallus	13	84.6	92.31
Dnio rerio	6	66.7	83.33
Caenorhabditis briggsae	73	95.9	98.63
Caenorhabditis elegans	110	86.4	88.18
Drosophila pseudoobscura	71	90.1	91.55
Drosophila melanogaster	71	91.5	92.96
Oryza sativa	96	94.8	100
Arabidopsis thaliana	75	92	97.33
Epstein Barr Virus	5	100	60
Total	581	90.9	93.63

except for Epstein-Barr virus, which has only 5 samples. Overall, the total prediction accuracy of our method was ~3% greater than the Triplet-SVM-classifier, which illustrated the effectiveness of BFU. We should note that the BFU here means basic-5-units, because almost all pre-miRNAs in animals contain single loops.

CONCLUSION

We have devised an effective feature using the triplet-SVM classifier for classification of the real pre-miRNAs and the pseudo pre-miRNAs. BNU feature can be tuned by a parameter for different species. We added this feature to an existing method, Triplet-SVM-classifier (Xue et al. 2005), and obtained an improved classification model. By adding just this new feature "BNU" to the other features already in use, the performance is improved, demonstrating the value of "BNU" as a feature. This feature may also improve the classification accuracy of other similar methods. Nevertheless, there is still room for further improvement in defining this feature. As our ongoing

study, we are developing a more sophisticated way to characterize this continuity than merely "counting" "BNU". Besides, as pre-miRNAs in plants and animals are quite different, it requires change of parameter of this feature in different biological kingdoms.

ACKNOWLEDGMENT

The authors would like to thank Chen Zhang, Zhongbo Cao, Juexin Wang, Dongyu Zhao, Ying Sun, Wei Du and Liang Chen of Jilin University for helpful discussions. The authors are grateful to the support of the NSFC (grant no.60903097, 60673023, 60703025, 60803052, 10872077); the National High-Tech R&D Program of China (863) (grant no. 2007AA04Z114, 2009AA02Z307); the Science-Technology Development Project from Jilin Province of China (grant no. 20080708, 20080172); the project of 200810026, 20091021 support by Jilin University, and "211" and "985" project of Jilin University. Trupti Joshi and Dong Xu's efforts on this project have been supported by US United Soybean Board.

REFERENCES

Ahmed, F., Ansari, H. R., & Raghava, G. P. (2009). Prediction of guide strand of microRNAs from its sequence and secondary structure. *BMC Bioinformatics, 10*, 105. doi:10.1186/1471-2105-10-105

Ambros, V., Bartel, B., Bartel, D. P., Burge, C. B., Carrington, J. C., & Chen, X. (2003). Tuschl T: A uniform system for microRNA annotation. *RNA (New York, N.Y.), 9*(3), 277–279. doi:10.1261/rna.2183803

Bari, R., Pant, B. D., Stitt, M., & Scheible, W. R. (2006). Pho2, microrna399, and phr1 define a phosphate-signaling pathway in plants. *Plant Physiology, 141*(3), 988–999. doi:10.1104/pp.106.079707

Bartel, D. (2004). MicroRNAs: genomics, biogenesis, mechanism, and function. *Cell, 116*(2), 281–297. doi:10.1016/S0092-8674(04)00045-5

Blenkiron, C., Goldstein, L. D., Thorne, N. P., Spiteri, I., Chin, S. F., & Dunning, M. J. (2007). MicroRNA expression profiling of human breast cancer identifies new markers of tumour subtype. *Genome Biology, 8*(10), R214. doi:10.1186/gb-2007-8-10-r214

Chan, P. P., & Lowe, T. M. (2008). GtRNAdb: a database of transfer RNA genes detected in genomic sequence. *Nucleic Acids Research, 37*(Database issue), D93–D97. doi:10.1093/nar/gkn787

Griffiths-Jones, S. (2004). The microRNA Registry. *Nucleic Acids Research, 32*(Database issue), D109–D111. doi:10.1093/nar/gkh023

Griffiths-Jones, S., Grocock, R. J., van Dongen, S., Bateman, A., & Enright, A. J. (2006). miRBase: microRNA sequences, targets and gene nomenclature. *Nucleic Acids Research, 34*(Database issue), D140–D144. doi:10.1093/nar/gkj112

Helvik, S. A. Jr, S. O., & Saetrom, P. (2007). Reliable prediction of Drosha processing sites improves microRNA gene prediction. *Bioinformatics (Oxford, England), 23*(2), 142–149. doi:10.1093/bioinformatics/btl570

Hertel, J., & Stadler, P. F. (2006). Hairpins in a Haystack: recognizing microRNA precursors in comparative genomics data. *Bioinformatics (Oxford, England), 22*(14), e197–e202. doi:10.1093/bioinformatics/btl257

Hofacker, I. L., Fontana, W., Stadler, P. F., Bonhoeffer, S., Tacker, M., & Schuster, P. (1994). Fast folding and comparison of RNA secondary structures. *Monatshefte fur Chemie, 125*(2), 167–188. doi:10.1007/BF00818163

Hua, Y. J., & Xiao, H. S. (2005). Progresses on the microRNA study. [in Chinese]. *Chinese Bulletin of Life Sciences, 17*(3), 5–8.

Jiang P., Wu H. N., Wang W. K., Ma W., Sun X., & Lu, Z. H. (2007). MiPred: classification of real and pseudo microRNA precursors using random forest prediction model with combined features. *Nucleic Acids Research, 35*(Web Server issue), W339-W344.

Lee, Y., Ahn, C., Han, J., Choi, H., Kim, J., & Yim, J. (2003). The nuclear RNase III Drosha initiates microRNA processing. *Nature, 425*(6956), 415–419. doi:10.1038/nature01957

Lim, L. P., Glasner, M. E., Yekta, S., Burge, C. B., & Bartel, D. P. (2003). Vertebrate microRNA genes. *Science, 299*(5612), 1540. doi:10.1126/science.1080372

Nam, J. W., Kim, J., Kim, S. K., & Zhang, B. T. (2006). ProMiR II: a web server for the probabilistic prediction of clustered, nonclustered, conserved and nonconserved microRNAs. *Nucleic Acids Research, 34*(Web Server issue), W455-W458.

Nam, J. W., Shin, K. R., Han, J., Lee, Y., Kim, V. N., & Zhang, B. T. (2005). Human microRNA prediction through a probabilistic co-learning model of sequence and structure. *Nucleic Acids Research*, *33*(11), 3570–3581. doi:10.1093/nar/gki668

Xu, Y. P., Zhou, X. F., & Zhang, W. X. (2008). MicroRNA prediction with a novel ranking algorithm based on random walks. *Bioinformatics (Oxford, England)*, *24*(13), i50–i58. doi:10.1093/bioinformatics/btn175

Xue, C. H., Li, F., He, T., Liu, G. P., Li, Y. D., & Zhang, X. G. (2005). Classification of real and pseudo microRNA precursors using local structure-sequence features and support vector machine. *BMC Bioinformatics*, *6*, 310. doi:10.1186/1471-2105-6-310

ADDITIONAL READING

Bentwich, I. (2005). Prediction and validation of microRNAs and their targets. *FEBS Letters*, *579*(26), 5904–5910. doi:10.1016/j.febslet.2005.09.040

Berezikov, E., Guryev, V., Van De Belt, J., Wienholds, E., Plasterk, R. H., & Cuppen, E. (2005). Phylogenetic shadowing and computational identification of human microRNA genes. *Cell*, *120*(1), 21–24. doi:10.1016/j.cell.2004.12.031

Bernstein, E., Caudy, A. A., Hammond, S. M., & Hannon, G. J. (2001). Role for a bidentate ribonuclease in the initiation step of RNA interference. *Nature*, *409*(6818), 363–366. doi:10.1038/35053110

Calin, G. A., Dumitru, C. D., Shimizu, M., Bichi, R., Zupo, S., & Noch, E. (2002). Frequent deletions and down-regulation of micro-RNA genes miR15 and miR16 at 13q14 in chronic lymphocytic leukemia. *Proceedings of the National Academy of Sciences of the United States of America*, *99*(24), 15524–15529. doi:10.1073/pnas.242606799

Cortes, C., & Vapink, V. (1995). Support vector networks. *Machine Learning*, *20*(3), 273–295. doi:10.1007/BF00994018

Dezulian, T., Remmert, M., Palatnik, J. F., Weigel, D., & Huson, D. H. (2005). Identification of plant microRNA homologs. *Bioinformatics (Oxford, England)*, *22*(3), 359–360. doi:10.1093/bioinformatics/bti802

Hackenberg, M., Sturm, M., Langenberger, D., Falcón-Pérez, J. M. & Aransay, A. M. (2009). miRanalyzer: a microRNA detection and analysis tool for next-generation sequencing experiments. *Nucleic Acids Research*, *37*(Web Server issue), W68-W76.

Kim, V. N., & Nam, J. W. (2006). Genomics of microRNA. *Trends in Genetics*, *22*(3), 165–173. doi:10.1016/j.tig.2006.01.003

Lau, N. C., Lim, L. P., Weinstein, E. G., & Bartel, D. P. (2001). An abundant class of tiny RNAs with probable regulatory roles in Caenorhabditis elegans. *Science*, *294*(5543), 858–862. doi:10.1126/science.1065062

Lee, R. C., Feinbaum, R. L., & Ambros, V. (1993). The C.elegans heterochronic gene lin-4 encodes small RNAs with antisense complementarity to lin-14. *Cell*, *75*(5), 843–854. doi:10.1016/0092-8674(93)90529-Y

Lund, E., Guttinger, S., Calado, A., Dahlberg, J. E., & Kutay, U. (2004). Nuclear export of microRNA precursors. *Science*, *303*(5654), 95–98. doi:10.1126/science.1090599

Pedersen, J. S., Bejerano, G., Siepel, A., Rosenbloom, K., Lindblad-Toh, K., Lander, E. S., Kent, J., Miller, W. & Haussler, D. (2006). Identification and classification of conserved RNA secondary structures in the human genome. *PLoS Comput Biology*, *2*(4), 0251-0262.

Reinhart, B. J., Slack, F. J., Basson, M., Pasquinelli, A. E., Bettinger, J. C., & Rougvie, A. E. (2000). The 21-nucleotide let-7 RNA regulates developmental timing in Caenorhabditis elegans. *Nature, 403*(6772), 901–906. doi:10.1038/35002607

Rosenblatt, F. (1958). The perceptron: a probabilistic model for information storage and organization in th brain. *Psychological Review, 65*(6), 386–408. doi:10.1037/h0042519

Rumellhart, D. E., Hinton, G. E., & Williams, R. J. (1986). Learning Internal Representations by Error Propagation. *Nature, 323*(6288), 533–536. doi:10.1038/323533a0

Ruvkun, G., Ambros, V., Coulson, A., Waterston, R., Sulston, J., & Horvitz, H. R. (1989). Molecular genetics of the Caenorbabditis elegans heterochronic gene lin-14. *Genetics, 121*(3), 501–516.

Sabah, K., Veronica, H., & Panayiotis, V. B. (2009). HHMMiR: efficient de novo prediction of microRNAs using hierarchical hidden Markov models. *BMC Bioinformatics, 10*(Suppl 1), S35–S47. doi:10.1186/1471-2105-10-S1-S35

Slack, F. J., Basson, M., Liu, Z., Ambros, V., Horvitz, H. R., & Ruvkun, G. (2000). The lin-41 RBCC gene acts in the C.elegans heterochronic pathway between the let-7 regulatory RNA and the LIN-29 transcription factor. *Molecular Cell, 5*(4), 659–669. doi:10.1016/S1097-2765(00)80245-2

Yekta, S., Shih, I. H., & Bartel, D. P. (2004). MicroRNA—directed cleavage of HOXB8 mRNA. *Science, 304*(5670), 594–596. doi:10.1126/science.1097434

Yousef, M., Nebozhy, M., Shatkay, H., Kanterakis, S., Showe, L. C., & Showe, M. K. (2006). Combining multi-species genomic data for microRNA identification using a Naive Bayes classifier. *Bioinformatics (Oxford, England), 22*(11), 1325–1334. doi:10.1093/bioinformatics/btl094

KEY TERMS AND DEFINITIONS

MicroRNA: In genetics, microRNAs (miRNA or μRNA) are single-stranded RNA molecules of 21-23 nucleotides in length, which regulate gene expression.

SVM: Short for support vector machines. A support vector machine constructs a hyperplane or set of hyperplanes in a high or infinite dimensional space, which can be used for classification, regression or other tasks. Intuitively, a good separation is achieved by the hyperplane that has the largest distance to the nearest training datapoints of any class (so-called functional margin), since in general the larger the margin the lower the generalization error of the classifier.

BNU: Short for basic-n-units. It is a new effective feature to distinguish pre-miRNAs from pseudo pre-miRNA. This feature describes pairing continuity of RNA secondary structure.

MFE: Minimum free energy.

Chapter 8
Four Long-Chain Acyl-Coenzyme:
A Synthetase Genes that Might be Involved in the Biosynthesis of Lipids *in Brassica Napus*

Fuge Zhu
Jiangsu University, China

Xiaoli Tan
Jiangsu University, China

Juan Li
Jiangsu University, China

Mingyu Wei
Jiangsu University, China

Lili Yu
Jiangsu University, China

ABSTRACT

Long chain acyl-coenzyme A synthetases (LACSs) activate free fatty acid to acyl-CoA thioesters, and play important roles in the biosynthesis and degradation of lipids. In this study, four cDNAs (Complementary DNA) encode long chain fatty acyl-CoA synthetase activity has been found in Brassica napus. Sequence analysis indicated that the four LACSs possessed typical molecular characteristics of LACS. Compared with low oil content varieties seed, the four genes are strongly expressed in high oil content varieties seeds at 35 days after pollination (DAP). The expression pattern suggested that the four LACSs might be involved in the biosynthesis of lipids and oil accumulation in rapeseed.

DOI: 10.4018/978-1-60960-064-8.ch008

INTRODUCTION

Rapeseed is a main oil crop, providing about 50% of the edible oil in China and rapeseed oil is widely applied in edible oil as well as in industry such as detergent, lubricant, paint, biodegradable plastic and bioenergy, etc. An effective way to promote the economic value of rapeseed is to increase the seed oil content.

Seed oil is a major storage compound and has significant economic value. Lipid is the main component of rapeseeds oil (Shen et al., 2006). Long-chain fatty acyl-coenzyme A (CoA) synthetases (LACSs) play a crucial role in both anabolism and catabolism of lipid. These enzymes activate free fatty acid to form acyl-CoA, a key esterification step necessary for the utilization of fatty acids in lipid metabolism (Iijima et al., 1996).

In higher plants, the LACSs play an important role in lipid catabolism. During the biosynthesis of lipid, LACSs could play a key role by providing fatty acyl-CoA, and thus link fatty acid de novo synthesis and TAG assembly (Ohlrogge & Jaworski, 1997). LACSs could provide sufficient acyl-CoA pool for TAG synthesis and are also believed to be correlated with the content and variety of TAG (Ichihara et al., 2003). The sum of CoA and acetyl-CoA levels plays an important role in plant growth, salt/osmotic stress resistance, and seed lipid storage (Rubio et al., 2008). LACS genes have been cloned from several plant species and most LACS enzymes display highest levels of activity with the fatty acids that make up the common structural and storage lipids in the plant (He, 2007). In *Arabidopsis thaliana*, AtLACS2 gene (At1g49430) is expressed in young, rapidly expanding tissues, and in leaves expression is limited to cells of the epidermal layers, suggesting that the AtLACS2 enzyme may act in the synthesis of very-long-chain fatty acids (VLCFA) (Schnurr et al., 2004). AtLACS2 has previously been shown to be involved in tolerance to biotic and abiotic stress and in the pathogenesis of *B.cinerea* (Tang et al., 2007). AtLACS1 has overlapping functions with AtLACS2 in plant's very-long-chain fatty acid (VLCFA) synthesis (Shiyou et al., 2009). AtLACS9 participates in glycerolipid synthesis in the developing seed (Shockey et al., 2002).

In *B. napus*, 4 cDNAs encoding the putative ACSs were isolated but their detail functions were still unknown (Fulda et al., 1997). In our report, we describe a bioinformatics assessment of the four *Brassica napus* LACSs(BnLACSs) genes. The investigation of potential relationship between rapeseed oil-content and *BnLACSs* was performed by RT-PCR.

MATERIALS AND METHODS

Bioinformatics Analysis

Tools and Methods

DNA and amino acid sequence manipulation were performed with DNAMAN. WU-BLAST Network Service in TAIR (http://www.arabidopsis.org) and Blast in NCBI (http://www.ncbi.nlm.nih.gov/) were used for searching genes. Phylogenetic tree was constructed using MEGA 4.0.

Accession Numbers

Brassica napus LACSs: BnLACS1: ABY77761.1 BnACS6: CAC19877.1

X94624: CAA64327.1 Z72153: CAA96523.1

Arabidopsis thaliana LACSs: AtLACS1: AF503751 AtLACS2: NP_175368.2 AtLACS3: NM_114758

AtLACS4: AAM28621.1 AtLACS5: NP_197141.1 AtLACS6: AF503765

AtLACS7: NP_188316.1 AtLACS8: AAM28625.1 AtLACS9: NP_177882.1

Plant Materials and Growth Conditions

Brassica napus cv. Ningyou16 was utilized for expression analysis of the 4 *BnLACSs* at reproductive stage. *Brassica napus* lines EM91, EM97, EM98, EM86, EM71 and EM102 with different oil contents were utilized to analyze the expression of four *Brassica napus LACSs* in pod at 35 days after pollination (DAP). All plants were grown and self-pollinated under natural conditions.

Oil Content Analysis of Whole Rapeseed Kernels

Near Infrared Reflectance Spectroscopy (NIRS) is a rapid, non-destructive and economical method of oil content analysis of seeds without the use of hazardous chemicals. In this study, NIRS was conducted to estimate the oil content of whole rapeseed kernels. The plants were chosen from different lines that showed a wide range of fatty acid composition of the seed oil. *Brassica napus* lines EM91, EM97, EM98, EM86, EM71 and EM102 with different oil contents were utilized. The analysis of rapeseed oil was performed by the method of R.Tkachuk (Tkachuk, 1981).

RNA Extractions and Reverse Transcription

The developing pods were sampled at 35 days after pollination (DAP) from EM91, EM97, EM98, EM86, EM71 and EM102. The seeds and pod coats were separated and stored at -70°C for RNA isolation. RNA was extracted by plant Trizol reagent (Tiangen Biotech Co. Ltd.). All steps were carried out following the instruction of the manufacturer. 2 µg total RNAs were used for the first strand cDNA synthesis with M-MLV Reverse Transcriptase (Takara, Japan) according to the manufacture's protocol.

Semi-Quantitative Reverse Transcription (RT)-PCR Analysis in Different *B. Napus* Lines

For RT-PCR assays, the cDNA of different *B. napus* lines were used as template. The primer sequences are shown in Table 1.

The PCR was performed using the following procedure: denaturization at 95°C for 5 min followed by 30 cycles (95°C for 30 s, 58°C for 30 s and 72°C for 30 s). The same cDNA was also used to amplify the *Actin* as an internal control. 10 µl products of each reaction were electrophoresed on 1% agarose gel stained with ethidium bromide.

Table 1. Oligonucleotide primers used in RT-PCR analysis

Genes	Primer	Nucleotide sequence	Nucleotide location
BnLACS1	F	5'-GAAGGTTGGACCGTATGTGTGG	207-228
	R	5'-ATAATCCACGGCTCCAGAACC	406-426
BnACS6	F	5'-ACGCTAAGAAAGACAAGAAACGA	72-95
	R	5'-AGCCCTGTAACGCAATAAACC	452-473
X94624	F	5'- TCATAAGCATGGAGGCATGTAA	356-378
	R	5'- ATAACTCGGTCAAAGATGTGGG	860-882
Z72153	F	5'-AGGTTTCGCTGGTATTCGTTC	506-526
	R	5'-ACCGTAGGCATTGGCACA	1380-1397
Actin	F	5'-ATGGCCGATGGTGAGGACATTC	1-22
	R	5'-GGTGCGACCACCTTGATCTTC	981-1001

Figure 1. Multiple sequence alignment of 4 BnLACSs and Arabidopsis thaliana LACSs

A	BLOCK I	BLOCK II	BLOCK III
AtLACS1	NICTIMYTSGTSGDPKGVVLTH	VVQGYGLTETLGGT	GTYRNPELTEDAHKDG.....LFHTGDIGE
BnACS6	DVAVIMYTSGTSGLPKGVHHTH	IGQGYGLTETCAGG	GTYFNEEKTKEYYKVDEKGHRLFYTGDIGQ
AtLACS2	DICTIMYTSGTTGEPKGVILNN	LSQGYGLTESCGGS	GIYHRQDLTDQVLIDG.....LFHTGDIGE
BnLACS4	DICTIMYTSGTTGDPKGVNISN	VLQGYGLTESCAGT	GTYRREDLTKEVLIDG.....ULHTGDIVG
BnLACS1	NTCTIMYTSGTSGDPKGVVLTH	VLQGYGLTETLGGT	GTYRNPKLTDEVLKDG.....LFHTGDIGE
X94624	DICTIMYTSGTTGDPKGVNISN	VLQGYGLTESCAGT	GTYRREDLSKEVLIDG.....ULHTGIVE
Z72153	DICTIMYTSGTTGEPKGVILSN	LSQGYGLTESCGGS	GIYHRQDLTNQWVING.....LFHTGDIGE

RESULT

Sequence Analysis

In order to search the homologous genes of *Arabidopsis thaliana LACSs* in oilseed rape, WU-Blast Netwok Service in TAIR was used to perform sequence alignment in *Arabidopsis thaliana* database using *BnLACS1, BnACS6, X94624* and *Z72153* as query sequences. *Arabidopsis* contains nine long chain acyl coenzyme A synthetase genes that participate in fatty acid and glycerolipid metabolism (Shockey et al., 2002). Multiple sequence alignment of *B. napus* 4 LACSs and *A. thaliana* 9 LACSs showed that some considerably conserved amino acid sequences existed in the form of blocks. Three blocks appeared among these protein, and three AMP-binding motifs – [YF] TSG [TS] [ST] GXPK, GYGXTE and GW [FL] [HK] [IVL] G–orderly located in Block I-III. The

conserved tyrosine residue which is indicated with black arrow is assumed to be involved in the adenylate formation (Figure 1).

Multiple amino acid sequence alignment of three blocks located in the 4 BnLACSs with Arabidopsis thaliana LACSs. Black shading presents strictly conserved residues, and gray presents less strictly conserved residues. The conserved tyrosine which is indicated with black arrow is assumed to be involved in the adenylate formation.

Molecular Evolution Analysis

Phylogenetic analysis was carried out based on protein sequence similarity. The phylogenetic analysis showed that the LACSs were clustered into two big groups (Figure 2).

phylogenetic tree was drawn based on the amino acid sequence from A. thaliana and B.

Figure 2. Phylogenetic analysis

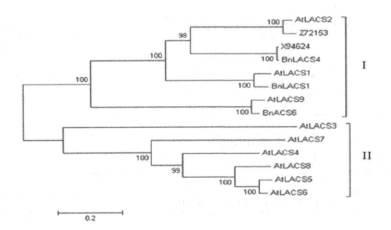

Table 2. Oil content Analysis of different Brassica napus line

B. napus lines	2006	Oil content(%) 2007	2008
EM97	29.25	35.237	36.15
EM98	28.47	33.059	33.92
EM86	50.56	44.93	44.15
EM71	48.78	45.45	44.98
EM102	50.59	47.254	46.90

napus LACS. Phylogenetic tree was constructed using MEGA4. Bar = 0.2.

The phylogenetic tree demonstrated that At-LACS1, AtLACS2 and AtLACS9 and *Brassica napus* 4 BnLACSs were in group I.

Oil Content Analysis of Different *Brassica Napus* Lines

Oil content of rapeseed of different *Brassica napus* lines grown during 2006 and 2008 was analyzed by NIRs. Table 2 shows the oil content of different *Brassica napus* lines.

Brassica napus EM97 and EM98 are low oil content lines and EM86, EM71 and EM102 are high oil content. Rapeseed oil contents are determined by many pathways include lipid biosynthesis pathway. At present, the reason that some lines are high and some lines are low in oil content is not yet clear.

Analysis of BnLACSs Expression Profile in Different *Brassica Napus* Lines

To investigate the relationship between the four BnLACSs expression levels and oil-content of rapeseeds, Low oil content *Brassica napus* lines EM97 and EM98 and high oil-content lines EM86, EM71 and EM102 were employed to analyze expression profiles in developing seeds at 35 days after pollination (DAP). As shown in Figure 3, the BnLACSs showed different level of expression in

developing seeds. The higher expression occurred in strains of high oil content.

BnLACSs expression profile in 35 DAP developing seeds of rapeseed lines EM97, EM98, EM86, EM71 and EM102. Actin gene was used as an internal control. The resulting products were separated by gel electrophoresis and stained by ethidium bromide.

CONCLUSION

In our study, we have isolated four genes from oilseed rape developing seeds, which encodes plant acyl-CoA synthetase. Sequence analysis indicated that the four BnLACSs belonged to AMP-binding super-family and contained a linker domain, which suggested the four BnLACSs presumably encoded LACS activity.

Figure 3. RT-PCR analysis of BnLACSs expression

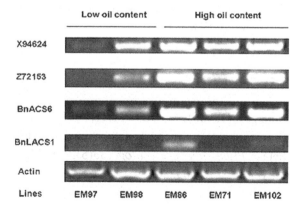

Phylogenetic analysis showed that the four BnLACSs belong to group I. In group I, AtLACS1, AtLACS2, AtLACS9, which was involved in the lipids synthesis(Shockey et al., 2002;Lü et al., 2009), BnACS6 is expressed in lipogenic tissues of *Brassica napus* and might be involved in lipid synthesis during seed development (Pongdontri and Hills, 2001). This result shows that group I LACSs might be involved in oil synthesis .

Analysis of BnLACSs expression profile showed that the higher expression occurred in developing seeds of high oil contents. In flowers and developing seeds, lipids are synthesized at high rates (Slocombe et al.,1994). The *BnLACSs* genes were expressed in lipogenic tissues and might play an important role in rapeseed oil synthesis.

Rapeseed oil contents are determined by many pathways include lipid biosynthesis pathway. Whether BnLACSs has contribution to oil contents requires further investigation, such as the over-expression of BnLACSs in transgenic plants, expression assay of BnLACSs in near isogenic lines of different oil contents. The results will provide us more information about BnLACSs and the correlation between oil contents and BnLACSs.

ACKNOWLEDGMENT

This work was supported by The National Basic Research Program (973 Program) (2006CB101600), The National High-tech Research and Development Program (863 Program) (2008AA10Z152) and The Talent Fund of Jiangsu University (05JDG003).

REFERENCE

Fulda, M., Heinz, E., & Wolter, F. P. (1997). *Brassica napus* cDNAs encoding fatty acyl-CoA synthetase. *Plant Molecular Biology*, *33*(5), 911–922. doi:10.1023/A:1005780529307

He, X. (2007). Ricinus communis contains an acyl-CoA synthetase that preferentially activates ricinoleate to its CoA thioester. *Lipids*, *42*, 931–938. doi:10.1007/s11745-007-3090-0

Ichihara, K. i., Kobayashi, N., & Saito, K. (2003). Lipid synthesis and acyl-CoA synthetase in developing rice seeds. *Lipids*, *38*(8), 881–884. doi:10.1007/s11745-003-1139-0

Iijima, H., Fujino, T., Minekura, H., Suzuki, H., & Yamamoto, T. (1996). Biochemical Studies of Two Rat Acyl-CoA Synthetases, ACS1 and ACS2. *European Journal of Biochemistry*, *242*(2), 186–190. doi:10.1111/j.1432-1033.1996.0186r.x

Ohlrogge, J. B., & Jaworski, J. G. (1997). Regulation of fatty acid synthesis. *Annual Review of Plant Physiology and Plant Molecular Biology*, *48*(1), 109. doi:10.1146/annurev.arplant.48.1.109

Pongdontri, P., & Hills, M. (2001). Characterization of a novel plant acyl-coA synthetase that is expressed in lipogenic tissues of *Brassica napus* L. *Plant Molecular Biology*, *47*(6), 717–726. doi:10.1023/A:1013652014744

Schnurr, J., Shockey, J., & Browse, J. (2004). The acyl-CoA synthetase encoded by LACS2 is essential for normal cuticle development in *Arabidopsis*. *The Plant Cell*, *16*(3), 629–642. doi:10.1105/tpc.017608

Shen, B., & Sinkevicius, K, W., Selinger, D. A., & Tarczynski, M.C. (2006). The homeobox gene GLABRA2 affects seed oil Content in *Arabidopsis*. *Plant Molecular Biology*, *60*(3), 377–387. doi:10.1007/s11103-005-4110-1

Shiyou, L., Song, T., Kosma, D. K., Parsons, E. P., Rowland, O., & Jenks, M. A. (2009). *Arabidopsis* CER8 encodes LONG-CHAIN ACYL-COA SYNTHETASE 1 (LACS1) that has overlapping functions with LACS2 in plant wax and cutin synthesis. *The Plant Journal*, *03892*, x. doi:. doi:10.1111/j.1365-313X

Shockey, J. M., Fulda, M. S., & Browse, J. A. (2002). *Arabidopsis* contains nine long-chain acyl-coenzyme A synthetase genes that participate in fatty acid and glycerolipid metabolism. *Plant Physiology, 129,* 1710–1722. doi:10.1104/pp.003269

Silvia, R., Whitehead, L., Larson, T. R., Graham, I. A., & Rodriguez, P. L. (2008). The coenzyme A biosynthetic enzyme phosphopantetheine adenylyltransferase plays a crucial role in plant growth, salt/osmotic stress resistance, and seed lipid storage. *Plant Physiology, 148,* 546–556. doi:10.1104/pp.108.124057

Slocombe, S. P., Piffanelli, P., Fairbairn, D., Bowra, S., & Murphy, D. J. (1994). Temporal and tissue-Specific regulation of a *Brassica napus* stearoyl-acyl carrier protein desaturase gene. *Plant Physiology, 104*(4), 1167–1176. doi:10.1104/pp.104.4.1167

Tang, D., Simonich, M. T., & Innes, R. W. (2007). Mutations in LACS2, a long-chain acyl-coenzyme A synthetase, enhance susceptibility to avirulent *Pseudomonas* syringae but confer resistance to *Botrytis cinerea* in *Arabidopsis. Plant Physiology, 144*(2), 1093–1103. doi:10.1104/pp.106.094318

Taylor, D. C., Barton, D. L., Giblin, E. M., Mackenzie, S. L., & Mcvetty, P. B. E. (1995). Microsomal Lyso-phosphatidic acid acyltransferase from a *Brassica oleracea* cultivar incorporates erucic acid into the sn-2 position of seed triacylglycerols. *Plant Physiology, 109*(2), 409–420.

Tkachuk, R. (1981). Oil and protein analysis of whole rapeseed kernels by near infrared reflectance spectroscopy. *Journal of the American Oil Chemists' Society, 58,* 819–822. doi:10.1007/BF02665588

ADDITIONAL READING

Bafor, M., Smith, M., Jonsson, L., Stobart, K., & Stymne, S. (1991). Ricinoleic acid biosynthesis and triacylglycerol assembly in microsomal preparations from developing castor bean endosperm. *The Biochemical Journal, 280,* 507–514.

Bafor, M., Smith, M., Jonsson, L., Stobart, K., & Stymne, S. (1993). Biosynthesis of vernoleate (*cis*-12-epoxyoctadeca-*cis*-9-enoate) in microsomal preparations from developing endosperm of *Euphorbia lagascae. Archives of Biochemistry and Biophysics, 303,* 145–151. doi:10.1006/abbi.1993.1265

Broun, P., & Somerville, C. (1997). Accumulation of ricinoleic, lesquerolic, and densipolic acids in seeds of transgenic *Arabidopsis* plants that express a fatty acyl hydroxylase cDNA from castor bean. *Plant Physiology, 113,* 933–942. doi:10.1104/pp.113.3.933

Browse, J. A., Warwick, N., Somerville, C. R., & Slack, C. R. (1986a). Fluxes through the prokaryotic and eukaryotic pathways of lipid synthesis in the 16:3 plant *Arabidopsis thaliana. The Biochemical Journal, 235,* 25–31.

Fulda, M., Heinz, E., & Wolter, F. P. (1997). *Brassica napus* cDNAs encoding fatty acyl-CoA synthetase. *Plant Molecular Biology, 33*(5), 911–922. doi:10.1023/A:1005780529307

He, X. (2007). Ricinus communis contains an acyl-CoA synthetase that preferentially activates ricinoleate to its CoA thioester. *Lipids, 42,* 931–938. doi:10.1007/s11745-007-3090-0

Ichihara, K. i., Kobayashi, N., & Saito, K. (2003). Lipid synthesis and acyl-CoA synthetase in developing rice seeds. *Lipids, 38*(8), 881–884. doi:10.1007/s11745-003-1139-0

Iijima, H., Fujino, T., Minekura, H., Suzuki, H., & Yamamoto, T. (1996). Biochemical Studies of Two Rat Acyl-CoA Synthetases, ACS1 and ACS2. *European Journal of Biochemistry, 242*(2), 186–190. doi:10.1111/j.1432-1033.1996.0186r.x

Ohlrogge, J. B., & Jaworski, J. G. (1997). Regulation of fatty acid synthesis. *Annual Review of Plant Physiology and Plant Molecular Biology, 48*(1), 109. doi:10.1146/annurev.arplant.48.1.109

Pongdontri, P., & Hills, M. (2001). Characterization of a novel plant acyl-coA synthetase that is expressed in lipogenic tissues of *Brassica napus* L. *Plant Molecular Biology, 47*(6), 717–726. doi:10.1023/A:1013652014744

Shockey, J. M., Fulda, M. S., & Browse, J. A. (2002). *Arabidopsis* contains nine long-chain acyl-coenzyme A synthetase genes that participate in fatty acid and glycerolipid metabolism. *Plant Physiology, 129*, 1710–1722. doi:10.1104/pp.003269

Shockey, J. M., Fulda, M. S., & Browse, J. A. (2003). *Arabidopsis* contains a large superfamily of acyl-activating enzymes. Phylogenetic and biochemical analysis reveals a new class of Acyl-Coenzyme A Synthetases. *Plant Physiology, 132*, 1065–1076. doi:10.1104/pp.103.020552

Sieber, P., Schorderet, M., Ryser, U., Buchala, A., Kolattukudy, P., Metraux, J. P., & Nawrath, C. (2000). Transgenic *Arabidopsis* plants expressing a fungal cutinase show alterations in the structure and properties of the cuticle and postgenital organ fusions. *The Plant Cell, 12*, 721–738.

Siloto, R. M. P., Findlay, K., Lopez-Villalobos, A., Yeung, E. C., Nykiforuk, C. L., & Moloney, M. M. (2006). The accumulation of oleosins determines the size of seed oilbodies in *Arabidopsis*. *The Plant Cell, 18*, 1961–1974. doi:10.1105/tpc.106.041269

Silvia, R., Whitehead, L., Larson, T. R., Graham, I. A., & Rodriguez, P. L. (2008). The coenzyme A biosynthetic enzyme phosphopantetheine adenylyltransferase plays a crucial role in plant growth, salt/osmotic stress resistance, and seed lipid storage. *Plant Physiology, 148*, 546–556. doi:10.1104/pp.108.124057

Slocombe, S. P., Piffanelli, P., Fairbairn, D., Bowra, S., & Murphy, D. J. (1994). Temporal and tissue-Specific regulation of a *Brassica napus* stearoyl-acyl carrier protein desaturase gene. *Plant Physiology, 104*(4), 1167–1176. doi:10.1104/pp.104.4.1167

Suh, M. C., Samuels, A. L., Jetter, R., Kunst, L., Pollard, M., Ohlrogge, J., & Beisson, F. (2005). Cuticular lipid composition, surface structure, and gene expression in *Arabidopsis* stem epidermis. *Plant Physiology, 139*, 1649–1665. doi:10.1104/pp.105.070805

Tanaka, T., Tanaka, H., Machida, C., Watanabe, M., & Machida, Y. (2004). A new method for rapid visualization of defects in leaf cuticle reveals five intrinsic patterns of surface defects in *Arabidopsis*. *The Plant Journal, 37*, 139–146. doi:10.1046/j.1365-313X.2003.01946.x

Tang, D., Simonich, M. T., & Innes, R. W. (2007). Mutations in LACS2, a long-chain acyl-coenzyme A synthetase, enhance susceptibility to avirulent *Pseudomonas* syringae but confer resistance to *Botrytis cinerea* in *Arabidopsis*. *Plant Physiology, 144*(2), 1093–1103. doi:10.1104/pp.106.094318

Thelen, J. J., Mekhedov, S., & Ohlrogge, J. B. (2001). *Brassicaceae* express multiple isoforms of biotin carboxyl carrier protein in a tissue-specific manner. *Plant Physiology, 125*, 2016–2028. doi:10.1104/pp.125.4.2016

Thelen, J. J., & Ohlrogge, J, B. (2002a). Both antisense and sense expression of biotin carboxyl carrier protein isoform 2 inactivates the plastid acetylcoenzyme A carboxylase in *Arabidopsis thaliana. The Plant Journal, 32*, 419–431. doi:10.1046/j.1365-313X.2002.01435.x

Thelen, J. J., & Ohlrogge, J. B. (2002b). Metabolic engineering of fatty acid biosynthesis in plants. *Metabolic Engineering Journal, 4*, 12–21. doi:10.1006/mben.2001.0204

Wagner, P., Furstner, R., Barthlott, W., & Neinhuis, C. (2003). Quantitative assessment to the structural basis of water repellency in natural and technical surfaces. *Journal of Experimental Botany, 54*, 1295–1303. doi:10.1093/jxb/erg127

Weber, A., Servaites, J. C., Geiger, D. R., Kofler, H., Hille, D., & Gro¨ner, F. (2000). Identification, purification, and molecular cloningof a putative plastidic glucose translocator. *The Plant Cell, 12*, 787–802.

Zou, J., Wei, Y., Jako, C., Kumar, A., Selvaraj, G., & Taylor, D. C. (1999). The *Arabidopsis thaliana* TAG1 mutant has a mutation in a diacylglycerol acyltransferase gene. *The Plant Journal, 19*, 645–653. doi:10.1046/j.1365-313x.1999.00555.x

KEY TERMS AND DEFINITIONS

Brassica Napus: Also known as oilseed rape, *Brassica napus* is one of the major sources of vegetable oil and widely grown throughout the world. *Brassica* species are now the second largest oilseed crop in the world oilseed production.

LACS: Long-chain fatty acyl-coenzyme A (CoA) synthetases. Long-chain acyl-coenzyme A synthetases (LACSs) activate free fatty acid to acyl-CoA thioesters and play an important role in lipid biosynthesis and fatty acid degradation.

RT-PCR: (Reverse transcription-polymerase chain reaction) is a sensitive method for the detection of mRNA expression levels.

NIRS: Near infrared spectroscopy is a spectroscopic method which uses the near infrared region of the electromagnetic spectrum. At present, NIRS is widely used as an efficient and non-destructive method for seed quality analysis in oilseed rape (*Brassica napus* L.).

Reverse Transcription: Is a process in which single-stranded RNA is reverse transcribed into complementary DNA (cDNA) by using total cellular RNA or poly(A) RNA, a reverse transcriptase enzyme, a primer, dNTPs and an RNase inhibitor.

DAP: Is days after pollination.

Section 2
Biological Networks and Systems Biology

Chapter 9
Topological Analysis of Axon Guidance Network for Homo Sapiens

Xuning Chen
Shanghai University, China

Weiping Zhu
Shanghai University, China

ABSTRACT

Axonal outgrowth is usually guided by a variety of guidance factors, such as netrins, ephrins, slits and semaphorins, and is one of the critical steps for the proper formation of neural networks. However, how the signal molecules function and why some of these play more important roles than others in guiding the axonal directional outgrowth has not been fully understood. In this study, we try to solve the problem by using the complex network analysis method. The signal molecules and interactions are treated as the nodes and edges to construct the axon guidance network model for Homo sapiens. The data of the model are taken from the KEGG database, and an analysis workbench named Integrative Visual Analysis Tool for Biological Networks and Pathways (VisANT) is employed to analyze the topological properties, including the degree distribution and the top co-expressed genes of the axon guidance network. This study has just opened a window into understanding the mechanism of axon guidance.

INTRODUCTION

Axon guidance is one of the critical steps for the proper formation of a neural network (Negishi et al., 2005), which relates to a variety of guidance factors, such as netrins, ephrins, slits, and semaphorins (Dickson, 2002). The growth cone at the tip of an extending axon is highly sensitive to repulsive and attractive guidance cues in its

environment. These molecules may be diffusible and work from a distance, or bound to membrane or substrate, or work at a close range. It is the complex integration of these repulsive and attractive signals that guides an axon to its target appropriately. These molecules not only play critical roles during nervous system development but may also regulate the regenerative capacity of neurons during nervous system diseases. Thus, it is necessary to fully understand how these factors

DOI: 10.4018/978-1-60960-064-8.ch009

function and which plays more important roles in the axon guidance network.

Genetics and biochemistry have identified a large set of molecules that affect axon guidance. How all of these molecules exert their effects is less understood. Growth cone signaling mechanisms are highly complex, consisting of numerous dynamic networks of biochemical reactions and signaling interactions between cellular components. This complexity makes it virtually impossible to analyze by traditional methods. Hence, network analysis method has been developed as a platform for integrating information from high-to-low throughput experiments for the analysis of biological systems (Kwoha & Ng, 2007).

A lot of research work has demonstrated that the topological property of a biosystem network implies rich biological functional information (Jeong et al., 2000; Kohn, 1999; Uetz et al., 2000). The network topology-based approach also helps to uncover potential mechanisms that contribute to their shared pathophysiology (Lee et al., 2008). In this paper, we revealed the topological property of the axon guidance network for *Homo sapiens* by using the complex network analysis method. The results show that some of the nodes are more highly connected than the others in the network. It is as expected that there are a few hubs that dominate their topology to resist random failures in a biosystem.

MODEL AND ANALYSIS TOOL

The numerous online pathway databases vary widely in coverage and representation of biological processes. An integrated network-based information system for querying, visualization and analysis promised successful integration of data on a large scale. Such integrated systems will greatly facilitate the understanding of biological interactions and experimental verification (Kwoha & Ng, 2007).

We treated the signal molecules and interactions as the nodes and edges to model the axon guidance network and used the data from the Kyoto Encyclopedia of Genes and Genomes (KEGG) Pathway (Kanehisha, 2009). In order to make these simplifications, it was necessary to neglect some of the details of the biological processes (De Silva & Stumpf, 2005). In reality, axon guidance pathway is highly interconnected and factorizing them into distinct networks will ultimately underestimate the biological complexity.

Many tools exist for visually exploring biological networks including well-known examples such as Cytoscape, VisANT, Pathway Studio and Patika (Suderman & Hallett, 2007). We employed the Integrative Visual Analysis Tool for Biological Networks and Pathways (VisANT) as the analysis workbench. VisANT not only provides network drawing capabilities, including support for very large networks, but it is also one of the first such packages to support creation, visualization and analysis of mixed networks, i.e. networks containing both directed and undirected links. The ability to use nodes to model more complex entities such as protein complexes or pathways allows for more informative visualizations (Hu et al., 2005). A model using the VisANT processing is shown in Figure 1. Signal molecules are the nodes and physical interactions among them are the edges or links in the graph. There are 69 nodes and 67 edges. A single protein/gene is represented as a filled green circle and a meta-node of the multiple proteins/genes is represented as a green box. And "-" indicates that the node is fully expanded (i.e. all connections are shown) whereas the "+" indicates that some links have not yet been displayed.

RESULTS AND DISCUSSIONS

In the following sections, we will present a basic theoretical framework oriented to describe and analyze axon guidance networks.

Figure 1. Axon guidance pathway shown in VisANT by loading KEGG Pathway (Kanehisha, 2009)

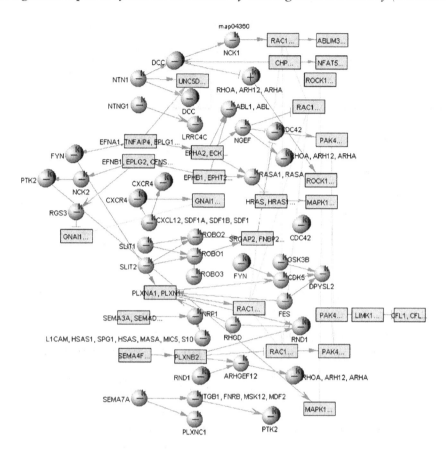

Degree and Degree Distribution

The degree of a network (node) is the number of edges adjacent to that node. The distribution of degrees among components is useful in characterizing the topology and scale of a network, and often has meaningful biological interpretations. In a directed axon guidance network, the degree is separated into 'in'-degree and 'out'-degree, depending on the directions of interaction between two given components. The degree of a hub is often the most important and essential for cell function. Degree is also a feature that distinguishes hubs (highly connected nodes) from leaves or orphans (weakly or non-connected nodes) in the network.

Using the VisANT, we can generate a scatter plot and log-linear regression fit of the degree distribution, $P(k)$, of the network (Hu *et al.*,

2005). The degree exponent, γ, of the log-linear regression, where $P(k) = A k^{\gamma}$, is a measure of the network's 'scale-free' property (Albert *et al.*, 2000; Jeong *et al.*, 2000). For $1 \le k \le k_{max}$, where k is the degree and k_{max} is the maximum degree presented in the network. Here we chose the exponent, γ, by setting the mean of the distribution to be equal to k_{mean}. The coefficient A is determined by requiring $P(k)$ to be normalized.

Furthermore, the VisANT plot allows us to quickly identify which nodes have the highest (or lowest) connectivity. As it occurs with axon guidance maps, it has been observed that very few nodes have many links, whereas most nodes have only a few. For example, plexins, a receptor of semaphorins for the repulsive axonal guidance molecules has the highest connectivity of 6 neighbors. In this model, the node shown is

Figure 2. Degree distribution of axon guidance networks by the straight line with log–log scale on both axes

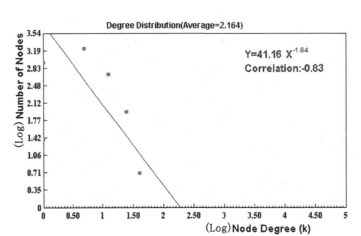

plexins, which has the highest interactions with 6 neighbors. This means that the plexin family performs important tasks on axon guidance. This result is consistent with the experimental study (reviewed by Negishi *et al.*, 2005; Tamagnone *et al.*, 1999).

Plexins are a family of transmembrane proteins that were shown to act as receptors for semaphorins either alone or in a complex together with Neuropilins. Based on structural criteria plexins were subdivided into 4 classes, A through D (Mauti *et al.*, 2006). Plexin A is a neuronal semaphorin receptor that controls axon guidance (Winberg *et al.*, 1998). Much less is known about Plexins of the other three classes. Despite the fact that Plexins are involved in the formation of neuronal circuits, the temporal changes of their expression patterns during development of the nervous system have not been analyzed in detail (Mauti *et al.*, 2006).

Finally, we have compiled a comprehensive map of known interactions in axon guidance-*Homo sapiens*. Although the network and its topology are not completely known, we can provide a useful estimate of the distribution of connectivity in axon guidance-*Homo sapiens*. Figure 2 shows the degree distribution of axon guidance-Homo sapiens using the VisANT software. The total number of nodes is 69, with a mean connectivity of 2.164.

Figure 2 also illustrates the fitted power law of the distribution. The exponent is 1.64.

Top Co-Expressed Genes of Plexins

In axon guidance networks, CDK5, RHOD, FES, FYN, and RND1 are 5 neighbors for plexins (Figure 3). Identifying various molecules involved in plexin signal transduction pathways provides a good understanding of the molecular mechanisms for plexin family-mediated axon guidance and neuronal network formation. Based on the GeneRecommender (Owen *et al.*, 2003), a package used to identify coexpressed genes in microarray data, we can pick out new genes with similar function for a given list of genes already known to have closely related function. It ranks genes according to how strongly they correlate with a set of query genes in axon guidance for which the query genes are most strongly coregulated (Figure 4).

In Comparison with other methods for studying axon guidance, the use of complex network analysis method has several advantages. A key aim of network analysis is to systematically catalogue all molecules and their interactions within a living cell. There is a clear need to understand how these molecules and the interactions between them determine the function of this

Figure 3. In axon guidance networks, CDK5, RHOD, FES, FYN, and RND1 are 5 neighbors for plexins

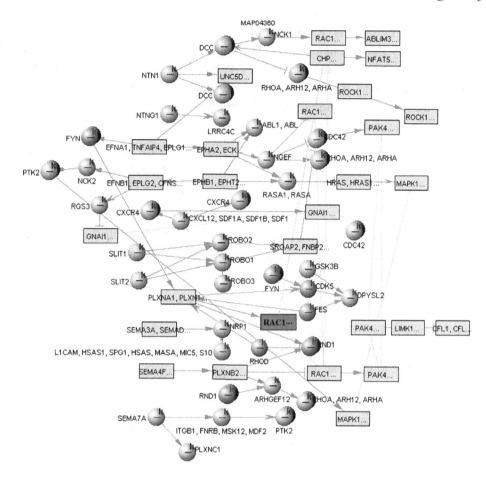

Figure 4. VisANT plugin for the GeneRecommender service searches for the top 10 co-expressed genes with a given set of query genes shown in the left panel. Scatter plot of the top 10 co-expressed genes is shown in the right panel.

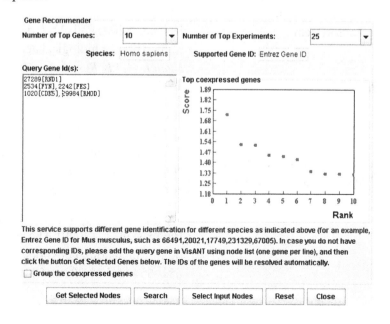

enormously complex machinery, both in isolation and when surrounded by other cells. Rapid advances in network biology indicate that cellular networks are governed by universal laws and offer a new conceptual framework that could potentially revolutionize our view of biology and disease pathologies in the twenty-first century (Barabási & Oltvai, 2004).

CONCLUSION

This study was conducted to investigate the relationship between topology and biological function in axon guidance networks. When describing axon guidance at the system level (e.g. a neuron), it is important to remember that the data are often very noisy, and the processes are highly complex: guidance cue abundances and interactions change over time and in response to external stimuli as well as to dynamical intrasystem processes. The static language of network analysis used to studying axon guidance may reach its limits when the condition and contingency of interactions need to be considered. Although network methods for the analysis of axon guidance data are still in their infancy, we believe that Topological Analysis helps researchers to gain further access to the comprehensive axon guidance pathway information, and may be a useful method for the detection and analysis of the nervous system.

ACKNOWLEDGMENT

This work was supported by the National Natural Sciences Foundation of China (Grant No. 10572085) and Shanghai Leading Academic Discipline Projects (Project Number: S30106).

REFERENCES

Albert, R., DasGupta, B., Dondi, R., & Sontag, E. D. (2008). Inferring (biological) signal transduction networks via transitive reductions of directed graphs. *Algorithmica, 51*(2), 129–159. doi:10.1007/s00453-007-9055-0

Albert, R., Jeong, H., & Barabási, A. L. (2000). Error and attack tolerance of complex networks. *Nature, 406*(6794), 378–382. doi:10.1038/35019019

Barabási, A. L., & Oltvai, Z. N. (2004). Network biology: understanding the cell's functional organization. *Nature Reviews. Genetics, 5*, 101–113. doi:10.1038/nrg1272

Christensen, C., Thakar, J., & Albert, R. (2007). Systems-level insights into cellular regulation: inferring, analysing, and modelling intracellular networks. *IET Systems Biology, 1*(2), 61–77. doi:10.1049/iet-syb:20060071

De Silva, E., & Stumpf, M. P. H. (2005). Complex networks and simple models in biology. *Journal of the Royal Society, Interface, 2*(5), 419–430. doi:10.1098/rsif.2005.0067

Dickson, B. J. (2002). Molecular mechanisms of axon guidance. *Science, 298*(5600), 1959–1964. doi:10.1126/science.1072165

Hu, Z., Mellor. J., Yamada, T., Holloway, D., & Delisi, C. (2005). VisANT: data-integrating visual framework for biological networks and modules. *Nucleic Acids Research, 33*(Web Server issue), W352–357.

Hu, Z., Mellor. J., Yamada, T., Holloway, D., & Delisi, C. (2007). VisANT 3.0: new modules for pathway visualization, editing, prediction and construction. *Nucleic Acids Research, 35*(Web Server issue), W625–632.

Jeong, H., Tombor, B., Albert, R., Oltvai, Z. N., & Barabási, A. L. (2000). The large-scale organization of metabolic networks. *Nature, 407*(6804), 651–654. doi:10.1038/35036627

Kanehisha Laboratories. (2009). Axon guidance - Homo sapiens (human), *KEGG PATHWAY*, Retrieved May 20, 2009, from http://www.genome.jp/kegg/ pathway/hsa/hsa04360.html.

Kohn, K. (1999). Molecular interaction map of the mammalian cell cycle control and DNA repair systems. *Molecular Biology of the Cell*, *10*(8), 2703–2734.

Kwoha, C. K., & Ng, P. Y. (2007). Network analysis approach for biology. *Cellular and Molecular Life Sciences*, *64*(14), 1739–1751.

Lee, D. S., Park, J., Kay, K. A., Christakis, N. A., Oltvai, Z. N., & Barabási, A. L. (2008). The implications of human metabolic network topology for disease comorbidity. *Proceedings of the National Academy of Sciences of the United States of America*, *105*(29), 9880–9885. doi:10.1073/pnas.0802208105

Mauti, O., Sadhu, R., Gemayel, J., Gesemann, M., & Stoeckli, E. T. (2006). Expression patterns of plexins and neuropilins are consistent with cooperative and separate functions during neural development. *BMC Developmental Biology*, *6*(32). doi:.doi:10.1186/1471-213X-6-32

Negishi, M., Oinuma, I., & Katoh, H. (2005). Plexins: axon guidance and signal transduction. *Cellular and Molecular Life Sciences*, *62*(12), 1363–1371. doi:10.1007/s00018-005-5018-2

Owen, A. B., Stuart, K., Mach, K., Villeneuve, A. M., & Kim, S. (2003). A gene recommender algorithm to identify coexpressed genes in C. elegans. *Genome Research*, *13*(8), 1828–1837.

Stefan, H. (2005). The Yeast Systems Biology Network: mating communities. *Biotechnology*, *16*(13), 356–360.

Suderman, M., & Hallett, M. (2007). Tools for visually exploring biological networks. *Bioinformatics (Oxford, England)*, *23*(20), 2651–2659. doi:10.1093/bioinformatics/btm401

Tamagnone, L., Artigiani, S., Chen, H., & He, Z. (1999). Plexins are a large family of receptors for transmembrane, secreted, and GPI-anchored semaphorins in vertebrates. *Cell*, *99*(1), 71–80. doi:10.1016/S0092-8674(00)80063-X

Uetz, P., Giot, L., Cagney, G., & Mansfield, T. A. (2000). A comprehensive analysis of protein-protein interactions in Saccharomyces cerevisiae. *Nature*, *403*(6770), 623–627. doi:10.1038/35001009

Winberg, M. L., Noordermeer, J. N., Tamagnone, L., Comoglio, P. M., & Spriggs, M. K. (1998). Plexin A is a neuronal semaphorin receptor that controls axon guidance. *Cell*, *95*(7), 903–916. doi:10.1016/S0092-8674(00)81715-8

ADDITIONAL READING

Albert, R., & Barabási, A. L. (2002). Statistical mechanics of complex networks. *Reviews of Modern Physics*, *74*(1), 47–97. doi:10.1103/RevModPhys.74.47

Amaral, L. A. N., & Ottino, J. M. (2004). Complex systems and networks: challenges and opportunities for chemical and biological engineers. *Chemical Engineering Science*, *59*(8–9), 1653–1666. doi:10.1016/j.ces.2004.01.043

Bhalla, U. S., & Iyengar, R. (1999). Emergent properties of networks of biological signaling pathways. *Science*, *283*(5400), 381–387. doi:10.1126/science.283.5400.381

Chou, K. C., & Cai, Y. D. (2006). Predicting protein-protein interactions from sequences in a hybridization space, *Journal of Proteome Research*, *5*(2), 316–322. doi:10.1021/pr050331g

Christopher, C. Q., & William, G. W. (2008). Axon guidance: asymmetric signaling orients polarized outgrowth. *Trends in Cell Biology*, *18*(12), 597–630. doi:10.1016/j.tcb.2008.09.005

Fenn, J. B., Mann, M., Meng, C. K., Wong, S. F., & Whitehouse, C. M. (1989). Electrospray Ionization for Mass Spectrometry of Large Biomolecules. *Science, 246*(4926), 64–71. doi:10.1126/science.2675315

Garrity, P. A. (1999). Signal transduction in axon guidance. *Cellular and Molecular Life Sciences, 55*(1420-682X), 1407–1415.

Gavin, A. C. (2002). Functional organization of the yeast proteome by systematic analysis of protein complexes. *Nature, 415*(6868), 141–147. doi:10.1038/415141a

Guelzim, N., Bottani, S., & Bourgine, P. (2002). Topological and causal structure of the yeast transcriptional regulatory network. *Nature Genetics, 31*(1), 60–63. doi:10.1038/ng873

Holme, P., Huss, M., & Jeong, H. (2003). Subnetwork hierarchies of biochemical pathways. *Bioinformatics (Oxford, England), 19*(4), 532–538. doi:10.1093/bioinformatics/btg033

Hood, L., & Perlmutter, R. M. (2004). The impact of systems approaches on biological problems in drug discovery. *Nature Biotechnology, 22*(10), 1215–1217. doi:10.1038/nbt1004-1215

Jeong, H., Mason, S., & Barabási, A. L. (2001). Lethality and centrality in protein networks. *Nature, 411*(6833), 41–42. doi:10.1038/35075138

Jeong, H., Tombor, B., & Albert, R. (2000). The large-scale organization of metabolic networks. *Nature, 407*(6804), 651–654. doi:10.1038/35036627

Kachalo, S., Zhang, R., Sontag, E., Albert, R., & DasGupta, B. (2008). NET-SYNTHESIS: A software for synthesis, inference and simplification of signal transduction networks. *Bioinformatics (Oxford, England), 24*(2), 293–295. doi:10.1093/bioinformatics/btm571

Kitano, H. (2002). Systems Biology: A brief overview. *Science, 295*(5560), 1662–1664. doi:10.1126/science.1069492

Lee, W. C. (2004). Applications of affinity chromatography in proteomics. *Analytical Biochemistry, 324*(1), 1–10. doi:10.1016/j.ab.2003.08.031

Mangan, S., & Alon, U. (2003). Structure and function of the feed-forward loop network motif. *Proceedings of the National Academy of Sciences, 100*(21), 11980–11985.

Maslov, S., & Sneppen, K. (2002). Specificity and stability in topology of proteins networks. *Science, 296*(5569), 910–913. doi:10.1126/science.1065103

Matthew, S., & Michael, H. (2007). Tools for visually exploring biological networks. *Bioinformatics (Oxford, England), 23*(20), 2651–2659. doi:10.1093/bioinformatics/btm401

Milo, R., Itzkovitz, S., & Kashtan, N. (2004). Super-families of evolved and designed networks. *Science, 303*(5663), 1538–1542.

Milo, R., Shen, O. S., & Itzkovitz, S. (2002). Network motifs: simple building blocks of complex networks. *Science, 298*(5594), 824–827. doi:10.1126/science.298.5594.824

Newman, M. E. J. (2003). The structure and function of complex networks. *SIAM Review, 45*(2), 167–256. doi:10.1137/S003614450342480

Rives, A. W., & Galitski, T. (2003). Modular organization of cellular networks. *Proceedings of the National Academy of Sciences of the United States of America, 100*(3), 1128–1133. doi:10.1073/pnas.0237338100

Shen, O. S., Milo, R., Mangan, S., & Alon, U. (2002). Network motifs in the transcriptional regulation network of Escherichia. *Nature Genetics, 31*(1), 64–68. doi:10.1038/ng881

Vidal, M., & Legrain, P. (1999). Yeast forward and reverse 'n'-hybrid systems. *Nucleic Acids Research, 27*(4919–929), 919–929.

Wuchty, S., & Stadler, P. F. (2003). Centers of complex networks. *Journal of Theoretical Biology, 223*(1), 45–53. doi:10.1016/S0022-5193(03)00071-7

KEY TERMS AND DEFINITIONS

Axon Guidance: It (also called axon pathfinding) is a subfield of neural development concerning the process by which neurons send out axons to reach the correct targets. Axons often follow very precise paths in the nervous system, and how they manage to find their way so accurately is being researched.

Complex Networks: It is a network (graph) with non-trivial topological features—features that do not occur in simple networks such as lattices or random graphs. The study of complex networks is a young and active area of scientific research inspired largely by the empirical study of real-world networks such as computer networks and social networks.

Topological Properties: A property of spaces is a topological property if whenever a space X possesses that property, every space homeomorphic to X would also possess that property. Informally, a topological property is a property of the space that can be expressed using open sets.

Degree Distribution: The degree of a node in a network is the number of connections it has to other nodes and the degree distribution is the probability distribution of these degrees over the whole network.

Neural Network: Traditionally, the term neural network had been used to refer to a network or circuit of biological neurons. The modern usage of the term often refers to artificial neural networks, which are composed of artificial neurons or nodes.

Scale-free Network: It is a network whose degree distribution follows a power law, at least asymptotically. That is, the fraction $P(k)$ of nodes in the network having k connections to other nodes goes for large values of k as $P(k) \sim k^{-\gamma}$ where γ is a constant whose value is typically in the range $2 < \gamma < 3$, although occasionally it may lie outside these bounds.

Netrins: They are a class of proteins involved in axon guidance. It is named after the Sanskrit word "netr", which means "one who guides." Netrins are genetically conserved across nematode worms, fruitflies, frogs, and mice. Structurally, netrin resembles laminin.

Ephrins: They are components of cell signaling pathways involved in animal development, and implicated in some cancers.

Slits: It is a complex extracellular protein containing at least four different motifs shared with other differentiation factors and receptors, including the vertebrate epidermal growth factor, the Drosophila receptor Toll, and the matrix protein laminin.

Semaphorins: They are a class of secreted and membrane proteins that act as axonal growth cone guidance molecules. They primarily act as short-range inhibitory signals and signal through multimeric receptor complexes. They are usually cues to deflect axons from inappropriate regions, especially important in neural system development. The major class of proteins that act as their receptors are called plexins.

Growth Cone: It is a dynamic, actin-supported extension of a developing axon seeking its synaptic target. Neuronal growth cones are situated on the very tips of nerve cells on structures called axons and dendrites. The sensory, motor, integrative, and adaptive functions of growing axons and dendrites are all contained within this specialized structure.

Neuropilin: It is a protein receptor active in neurons. There are two forms of Neuropilins, NRP-1 and NRP-2. They are transmembrane glycoproteins, and predominantly co-receptors for another class of proteins known as Semaphorins. Of the Semaphorins, NRP-1 and NRP-2 are specifically receptors for Class-3 Semaphorins, which, amongst many things, are responsible for axon guidance during the development of the nervous system in vertebrates.

Chapter 10
Evaluation of Coupled Nuclear and Cytoplasmic p53 Dynamics

Tingzhe Sun
Nanjing University, China

Meihong Cai
Nanjing University, China

Jun Cui
Nanjing University, China

Pingping Shen
Nanjing University, China

ABSTRACT

The tumor suppressor protein p53 predominantly serves as a sequence specific transcription factor that may be activated upon exposure to diverse stimuli. One potent death inducer, p53-upregulated mediator of apoptosis (PUMA), is transcriptionally induced by p53. Once released into the cytoplasm, PUMA can lead to the activation of Bcl-2 apoptotic network. The cytoplasmic proapoptotic roles of p53 have recently been discovered, and these findings have placed p53 into the chemical interaction network with Bcl-2 family members. PUMA can also relieve p53 from the sequestration of antiapoptotic members. Released p53 further enters the nucleus and induces PUMA expression. We proposed that this positive feedback loop could lead to bistability. Further sensitivity analysis suggested that the system which covers the interactions between p53 and BCL-2 family members is considerably sensitive to p53 production rate. Meanwhile, downstream network components are much more affected by certain parameters than upstream effectors. Therefore, this newly discovered positive feedback loop might play critical roles in apoptotic network.

INTRODUCTION

The p53 tumor suppressor protein is a sequence specific transcription factor and its biological roles are closely mediated by modulating the expression of numerous target genes (Whibley et al., 2009). In particular, p53 can trigger apoptosis in response to diverse stimuli, among which irradiation induced damage has caught much attention.

DOI: 10.4018/978-1-60960-064-8.ch010

Intricate regulation and manipulation of p53 and its related pathways are considerably important for consistent development and cancer evasion in harsh environment (Evan et al., 2008). Therefore, the dynamic patterns of p53 have become an active area of research. Many recent studies have established well-defined oscillation patterns in p53 dynamics and these observations motivated the constructions of many mathematical models (Lahav et al., 2004; Geva-Zatorsky et al., 2006).

Differential equation based models included either delays or combined feedback loops to reproduce p53 oscillations (damped, undamped or digital), although some of the feedback loops seem ambiguous (Bar-Or et al., 2000; Monk, 2003; Ma et al., 2005; Ciliberto et al., 2005; Chickarmane et al., 2007; Zhang et al., 2007; Batchelor et al., 2008; Proctor et al., 2008; Puszynski et al., 2008). Some other theoretical analyses focused on bistability or temporal patterns and intended to elucidate physiological roles of p53 in biological systems (Wee et al., 2006; Wee et al., 2009). Generally speaking, feedback strengths play important roles in dynamic pattern determination. The system in which positive feedback dominates confers bistability, and oscillations occur when negative feedback becomes dominant (Tyson et al., 2003). Thus, investigation of individual feedback loops could help further our understanding of network performance and provide powerful insights.

A recently discovered bcl-2 homology domain only (BH3-only) protein, p53-upregulated mediator of apoptosis (PUMA), which couples nuclear and cytoplasmic functions of p53 under stress conditions, is a potent death inducer (Chipuk et al., 2005). PUMA is a B-cell lymphoma 2 (BCL-2) family member and is able to dissociate p53 from the sequestration of anti-apoptotic members B-cell lymphoma x long (BclxL)/Bcl-2. Then, free p53 proteins enter the nucleus and induce a plethora of downstream targets including PUMA (Schuler et al., 2005). The synthesized PUMA further releases p53 from BclxL/Bcl-2 into the cytoplasm thus establishes a positive feedback

loop and bistability may occur. An eruption of p53 is devastating because p53 can directly activate Bax/Bak (proapoptotic Bcl-2 family proteins) besides its role as a transcription factor (Schuler et al., 2005). Thus, this positive feedback loop is physiologically important in apoptosis progression.

Diverse feedback loops are imbedded in p53 network and an integrated model that covers entire feedback loops is unfeasible and probably masks individual roles of feedback loops. Therefore, we took a different approach in which only one positive feedback loop is scrutinized. In this study, we investigated a positive feedback loop in p53 signaling transduction pathways and found inherent bistability which connects both nuclear (transcriptional induction) and cytoplasmic (a BH3-like function) functions of p53. Furthermore, we employed different kinds of sensitivity analyses to elucidate feedback performance as sensitivity analysis can also indicate biological effects of mutations or artificial manipulation by altering system parameters.

BACKGROUND

During early years, several p53 models have been constructed. Bar-Or et al. (2000) presented a simplified model in an attempt to explain the mechanism of damped oscillation, and similar dynamics were also presented by Monk (2003) when a time delay was introduced. In a field-breaking study of p53-MDM2 in individual cells, Lahav et al. (2004) found the expression of p53 followed a series of pulses and the mean period of the oscillations were relatively fixed and the mean number of pulses increased with irradiation dose. Ma et al. (2005) introduced a stochastic process in damage repair process and best reproduced the digital pulses. Ciliberto et al. (2005) and Chickarmane et al. (2007) moved the p53 system from steady state into a region of stable limit cycle in response to damage, which is then drawn back when damage is eliminated. Tyson's group compared these models and delineated several new scenarios although the speculated mechanisms seemed to be cell type specific (Zhang et al., 2007). All these above models concentrate on the digital pulses of p53 in single cells. Geva-Zatorsky et al. (2006) found that p53 performs sustained oscillation with γ-irradiation when observations last longer. However, some other theoretical analyses also focus on bistability or temporal patterns and intend to elucidate physiological roles of p53 in realistic biological systems (Wee et al., 2006; Wee et al., 2009). To our knowledge, PUMA is a downstream target of p53, and once produced, can dissociate p53 from the sequestration of BclxL/Bcl-2 (Figure 1). As BclxL and Bcl-2 are functionally redundant, these two species are simplified as one component (BclxL in our model) in the equations.

Meanwhile, Noxa also serves as a p53 downstream target and BH3-only proapoptotic protein although it plays less important roles. Thus, PUMA and Noxa are lumped together as one component (PUMA in our model). Overall, the minimal model is formulated as a set of differential equations and describes 5 species together with 16 independent parameters. Most parameters are adapted or directly calculated from literature (see Table 3 for details).

MAIN FOCUS OF THE CHAPTER

Inherent Positive Feedback Confirms Bistability

Positive feedback primarily contributes to the occurrence of bistability if the system contains nonlinear interactions. As nonlinear interactions are ubiquitous design patterns in biochemical reactions, we investigated whether the inherent positive feedback loops described above can confer bistability. As most parameters are adapted from literature, subsequent simulations indeed found that the steady states of p53 are bistable and sometimes irreversible (Figure 2, bifurcation parameters are shown at top right corner in corresponding panels). The system retains low steady state until k6 traverses the critical value (0.00114µM/min), at which p53 flips to high state in an all or none fashion, while p53 remains at high state until k6 falls back to 0.00071µM/min (Figure 2A). Similar dynamic patterns are also found with several other bifurcation parameters (Figure 2B, D and F). In order to determine the region where bistability merges, we then referred to the 2-parameter bifurcation diagram (Figure 2C and F). The shaded area shows bistability, while points located elsewhere are monostable (Figure

Figure 1. Schematic representation of network. The core model is illustrated in dashed box.

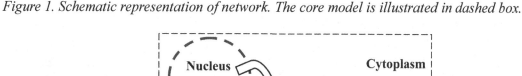
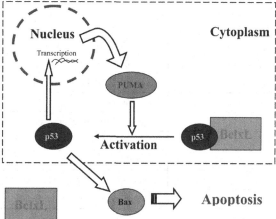

Figure 2. Bifurcation diagrams. Bifurcation diagrams of p53 with bifurcation parameters k5 (A) and k6 (B). (C) two-parameter diagram for (A) and (B). Steady state levels of BclxL with bifurcation parameters k11 (D) and k12 (E). (F) two-parameter diagram for panels (D) and (E).

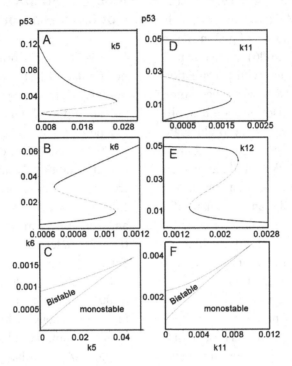

2C and F). From the bifurcation diagrams, we speculated that accelerated BclxL degradation would result in an explosion of p53 levels if the critical value is surpassed and probably trigger apoptosis as discussed above (Figure 2D). Alternatively, increased BclxL induction inhibits p53 elevation and probably contributes to cell death repression (Figure 2E). Aberrant elevation in BclxL levels are found in some tumor cell lines where apoptosis is suppressed, while increased BclxL degradation undoubtedly induces apoptosis (Certo et al., 2006; Egger et al., 2003; Egger et

Table 1. Reaction scheme and parameter for the model

No.	Reactions	Description	k_+	k_-
1	p53+Bclxl <-> p53Bclxl	Bclxl induced p53 sequestration	k1	k2
2	PUMA+Bclxl <-> PUMABclxl	Bclxl induced PUMA sequestration	k3	k4
3	null <-> P53	p53 production and degradation	k6	k5
4	PUMA -> null	PUMA degradation	k7	
5	->PUMA	p53 induced PUMA expression	k8	
6	p53Bclxl -> null	Bclxl degradation	k9	
7	PUMABclxl -> null	PUMABclxl degradation	k10	
8	null <-> Bclxl	Bclxl production and degradation	k12	k11
9	PUMA +p53Bclxl <-> p53+PUMABclxl	PUMA dissociates p53 from Bclxl	k13	k14

The parameters n and K donates Hill coefficient and EC50 for transcription term respectively.

Table 2. Ordinary differential equations and flows

Differential equations
$dp53/dt = -J_0 - J_2 + J_8$
$dBclxl/dt = -J_0 - J_1 - J_7$
$dPUMA/dt = -J_1 - J_3 + J_4 - J_8$
$dp53Bclxl/dt = J_0 - J_5 - J_8$
$dPUMABclxl/dt = J_1 - J_6 + J_8$

Flows $J_0 = k1 \cdot p53 \cdot Bclxl - k2 \cdot p53Bclxl$	$J_1 = k3 \cdot PUMA \cdot Bclxl - k4 \cdot PUMABclxl$
$J_2 = k5 \cdot p53 - k6$	$J_3 = k7 \cdot PUMA$
$J_4 = k8 \cdot p53^n/(p53^n + K^n)$ $J_6 = k10 \cdot PUMABclxl$ $J_8 = k13 \cdot PUMA \cdot p53Bclxl - k14 \cdot PUMABclxl \cdot p53$	$J_5 = k9 \cdot p53Bclxl$ $J_7 = k11 \cdot Bclxl - k12$

al., 2007; Hayward et al., 2004). Our simplified model is qualitatively consistent with these experimental results.

Stochastic Modeling Identifies Population Behavior

As deterministic approaches cannot describe individual cellular dynamics, we further employed stochastic simulations based on Chemical Langevin Equations (CLEs) to explore the stochastic nature of single cell dynamics. 1000 independent runs were performed and then averaged to take their mean values (Figure 3). Simulation results showed that the transition time at which p53 flips to the high steady state differ significantly from each other (Figure 3 *black curves*). The significant discreteness is largely attributed to the highly variable cellular environment and inherent stochasticity of biochemical reactions (e.g. collisions

Table 3. model parameters values

parameters	values	references and comments
k1	$1/(\mu M \cdot min)$	Chipuk, 2004
k2	0.06/min	Chipuk, 2004
k3	$12/(\mu M \cdot min)$	Chen, 2005
k4	0.06/min	Chen, 2005
k5	0.02/min	Ma, 2005
k6	$0.001 \mu M/min$	Estimation from Ma, 2005
k7	0.001/min	Estimation
k8	$0.003 \mu M/min$	Estimation
k9	0.015/min	Estimation
k10	0.001/min	Estimation
k11	0.0014/min	Reed, 1996, 2005;
k12	$0.0017 \mu M/min$	Estimation from Reed, 2005
k13	$10/(\mu M \cdot min)$	Estimation
k14	$0.05/(\mu M \cdot min)$	Estimation
n	3	Ciliberto, 2005
K	$0.03 \mu M$	Estimation

Figure 3. Stochastic simulation identifies population behavior. Chemical Langevin equations are imple-mented and five independent runs are shown in the figure (black curves). Population average is shown as the dark grey curve.

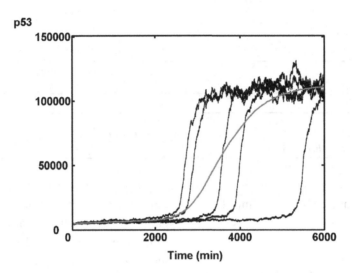

between molecules). Population average showed that p53 levels increase gradually, which is mark-edly different from the single cell dynamics. Some experiments identified a gradual increasing pattern in p53 dynamics under stress conditions, especially irradiation (Blattner et al., 1999; Okamura et al., 2001). Thus, our model was general consistent with experimental data and further clarified the stochastic nature of biological processes.

Inhibitor Effect *In Silico* Simulation

To reveal the relevance of the effect of BclxL lev-els, simulations were performed with altered pro-tein concentrations. Altered BclxL concentrations were simulated by changing the initial condition and the production rate constant to give a steady state. Under normal conditions, the upswing of p53 levels requires nearly 20000 input PUMA molecules (Figure 4, upper panel). However, when we 'knocked down' about 20% total BclxL proteins *in silico*, we found significant effects with varying input PUMA molecules (Figure 4, lower panel). However, a 20% downregulation of BclxL leads to a significantly earlier onset of high steady state

of p53 levels and lowers the PUMA threshold for high p53 levels (Figure 4, lower panel). The steady state of p53 is also increased (data not shown). In addition, 20% upregulation of BclxL, almost completely abolishes the effect of reaching a high p53 level and undoubtedly inhibits apoptosis (data not shown). The upregulation of BclxL shows that the cells can protect themselves from cell death against strong external stimuli by slight upregulation of the anti-apoptotic BclxL levels. This result is interesting because in certain tumor cells, BclxL is upregulated compared with normal cells (Hanahan et al., 2000; Konishi et al., 2006; Lebedeva et al., 2000). *In silico* simulation sug-gested that the elevation of steady state of BclxL levels profoundly represses p53 upregulation and ensuing apoptosis. It is possible that the eleva-tion of BclxL level prevents efficient removal of tumor cells and potentiates tumor progression. This result indicated that BclxL plays pivotal roles in apoptosis regulation and tumor cells may work out the strategy of upregulation of BclxL to counteract the apoptotic effects.

Local Effects of Parameter Sensitivity

To investigate the parameter effects on all the state variables in nonlinear systems, we implemented local parameter sensitivity analysis which serves as a straightforward linear approximation. We evaluated the dependence of stable steady state of state variables to 1% parameter variations. The simulation results provided a normalized output relative to the nominal steady state and parameter values. We found that for first three variables (p53, BclxL and p53BclxL), all parameters have only minor effects compared with the other two state variables (PUMA and PUMABclxL). For first three state variables, k6 (p53 production rate) is relatively positive in controlling p53 levels and has opposing effects on BclxL levels. The p53 degradation rate, k5, however, plays less important roles. The parameter k12 (BclxL production rate) negatively regulates p53 levels as BclxL neutralizes p53 (Figure 5). Interestingly, k11 which describes the process of BclxL degradation nearly duplicates the roles of k6. For last two state variables (PUMA and PUMABclxL), all parameters have much more prominent effects. PUMA and PUMABclxL levels strongly depend on k6 as PUMA is induced by p53. Three parameters, k12, n (Hill coefficient) and K (EC50 for induction term) elicit considerably negative effects on PUMA and PUMABclxL levels. The negative effect of k12 is obvious because BclxL neutralizes PUMA and sequesters its proapoptotic functions. Parameters n and K also have negative effects probably due to the fact that a decrease in these two parameters will facilitate the p53-mediated induction. All state variables are extremely insensitive to k13 and k14, indicating a dispensable role for competitive binding. These results not only consolidated critical roles

Figure 4. Initial value effects. The dynamic responses of p53 with varied input PUMA levels. Left panel: normal conditions. Right panel: 'knocked-down' cells.

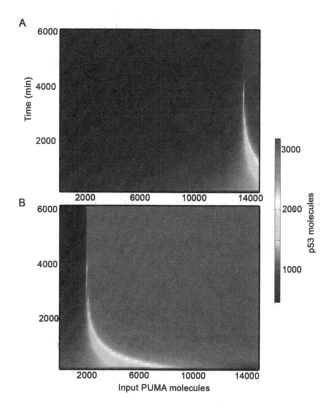

Figure 5. Local sensitivity analysis. Each parameter is perturbed 1% at both directions and the ensemble average is calculated to evaluate local sensitivities

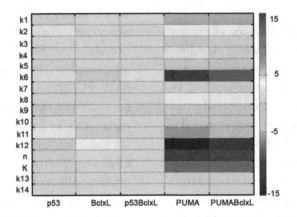

for certain parameters (e.g. p53 production rate dominates the systematic performance) but also suggested that parametric effects can be enlarged to downstream biochemical reactions (i.e. PUMA is p53 inducible and the last two state variables show much stronger overall parametric effects).

Monte Carlo Approach to Evaluate Bistability

For the minimal models, we generated stochastic parameter sets and searched for the parameters that lead to bistability. We implemented a Monte Carlo approach as its convergence rate is not affected by dimension of the systems (Eißing et al., 2005). 2000 random parameter sets were generated. All parameters are allowed to vary within predefined range (-1% to 1%) and parameter vector are randomly selected such that each parameter obeys uniform distribution. Then for each parameter vector, system is checked for the existence of bistability (e.g. p53 as our selected state variable). A detailed representation of the distribution of the parameter sets that lead to bistability is shown in Figure 6 with logarithm scale. For almost all the parameters, the effects of changing one parameter cannot be compensated by adjusting the other parameters and this illus-

Figure 6. Monte Carlo approach to evaluate bistable performance

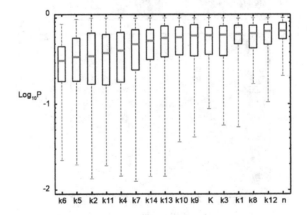

trates that each parameter plays essential roles in bistability performance. For all experiments, the bistable region appears tight as the median values are less centered within a predefined range. We sorted the parameter sets according to the median values and found that the turnover rates for p53 (k5 and k6) are allowed to vary within a relatively larger range. Although the system is sensitive to k6 (Figure 5), bistability performance shows less sensitivity to k6 (Figure 6). Association rates of p53 and PUMA (k1 and k3) largely affect bistable performance but dissociation rates (k2 and k4) seem less important. Of all the parameters, the Hill coefficient for p53 mediated induction is most significantly restricted, which probably supports a critical role for transcriptional cooperativity. The relatively narrow parameter ranges allowed for bistability are probably due to the simplified architecture of the model.

DISCUSSION

In this paper, we described a minimal model which couples the nuclear and cytoplasmic functions of p53 and illustrates the occurrence of inherent bistability. Bistability is a ubiquitous dynamic pattern involved in fate determination such as differentiation, cell cycle and apoptosis. The tumor suppressor p53 has multiple proapoptotic roles. Therefore, high levels of wild type p53 are regarded as hallmarks of apoptosis. Bistability of p53 was also discussed in previous work (Wee et al., 2006; Wee et al., 2009) and might serve as an alternative determinant for cell fate decision. Here we evaluated the interplay of p53 with Bcl-2 family members. A well-documented negative feedback loop, p53-MDM2 is not considered here as we focused on one positive feedback loop which covers p53 and Bcl-2 family. In the meantime, MDM2 induction is severely reduced in UV irradiation while p53-PUMA interplay remains intact (Chipuk et al., 2005; Kæser et al., 2002). Thus, we discuss p53 bistability in this paper.

Stochastic effects also provide more insights as stochasticity is ubiquitously distributed in biological environment. We found that ensemble average of multiple independent simulations yields a gradual increasing pattern (Figure 3) which shows considerable agreement with experimental data (Blattner et al., 1999; Okamura et al., 2001). This result suggested that asynchronous individual responses (i.e. inherent stochasticity) contribute to cell population behavior.

Further, we investigated initial value effects and found that BclxL levels play crucial roles in cell fate determination as slightly knocking down of BclxL will strongly relieve the apoptotic threshold (Figure 4). Abnormal elevation in BclxL levels is found in numerous tumor cell lines in which apoptosis is suppressed. This result further supported a notion that pharmacological intervention of BclxL might be adopted as a strategy for quelling cancer. Subsequent parameter sensitivity analysis further identified the key control elements. We found that the system is strongly sensitive to k6 (p53 production rate), but bistability shows less dependence to k6 (Figure 5 and Figure 6). On the other hand, downstream elements are more sensitive than upstream components to parameter changes (Figure 5). Mechanically speaking, signals may be amplified as information flow propagates downstream. Thus, intricate upstream control seems more important and might be subject to biotechnological manipulations.

Recently, a model was constructed to further investigate the interactions between p53 and Bcl-2 family, but this model neglected the existence of bistability (Dogu et al., 2009). Our model took a more simplified representation where p53 serves as model output variable. As p53 directly activates Bax and Bak, our model is equivalent to the Dogu et al.'s model. In the meantime, we implemented diverse approaches to evaluate the bistability performance especially parameter stochasticity. Random parameter variations allow the analysis of non-linear effects due to parameter combinations. Only few studies on the robustness of pathways have employed random parameter variations (Eißing et al., 2005). Taking different approaches allows in depth study of biological pathways.

As life death decision becomes a critical issue in scientific research, we will further explore how to elicit subtle control over the critical process in life-death decision.

CONCLUSION AND FUTURE WORK

The simulation results of our model outlined the occurrence of bistability and the importance of apoptosis regulation by manipulating BclxL levels. The analyses also indicated how tumor cells become more aggressive, speculating strategies to retard tumor progression. These theoretical studies might pave the way to the appreciable understanding of p53 pathway architecture and shed lights on future computational studies. As we explored only one positive feedback loop in the p53 system, incorporation with many other feedback loops deserves further investigation. Furthermore, some parameter values may need further refinement based on new experimental measurements.

ACKNOWLEDGMENT

This work is supported by National Basic Research Program of China (No. 2008CB418102) and National Natural Science Foundation of China (NSFC, No.30870588).

REFERENCES

Bar-Or, R. L., Maya, R., Segel, L. A., Alon, U., Levine, A. J., & Oren, M. (2000). Generation of oscillations by the p53-Mdm2 feedback loop: A theoretical and experimental study. *Proceedings of the National Academy of Sciences of the United States of America*, *97*(21), 11250–11255. doi:10.1073/pnas.210171597

Batchelor, E., Mock, C. S., Bhan, I., Loewer, A., & Lahav, G. (2008). Recurrent Initiation: A mechanism for triggering p53 pulses in response to DNA damage. *Molecular Cell*, *30*(3), 277–289. doi:10.1016/j.molcel.2008.03.016

Blattner, C., Tobiasch, E., Litfen, M., Rahmsdorf, H. J., & Herrlich, P. (1999). DNA damage induced p53 stabilization: no indication for an involvement of p53 phosphorylation. *Oncogene*, *18*(9), 1723–1732. doi:10.1038/sj.onc.1202480

Certo, M., Moore, V. D. G., Nishino, M., Wei, G., Korsmeyer, S., Armstrong, S. A., & Letai, A. (2006). Mitochondria primed by death signals determine cellular addiction to antiapoptotic BCL-2 family members. *Cancer Cell*, *9*(5), 351–365. doi:10.1016/j.ccr.2006.03.027

Chen, L., Willis, S. N., Andrew, W., Smith, B. J., Fletcher, J., & Hinds, M. G. (2005). Differential Targeting of Prosurvival Bcl-2 Proteins by Their BH3-Only Ligands Allows Complementary Apoptotic Function. *Molecular Cell*, *17*(3), 393–403. doi:10.1016/j.molcel.2004.12.030

Chickarmane, V., Ray, A., Sauro, H. M., & Nadim, A. (2007). A Model for p53 Dynamics Triggered by DNA Damage. *SIAM Journal on Applied Dynamical Systems*, *6*(1), 61–78. doi:10.1137/060653925

Chipuk, J. E., Bouchier-Hayes, L., Kuwana, T., Newmeyer, D. D., & Green, D. R. (2005). PUMA couples the nuclear and cytoplasmic proapoptotic function of p53. *Science*, *309*(5741), 1732–1935. doi:10.1126/science.1114297

Chipuk, J. E., Kuwana, T., Bouchier-Hayes, L., Droin, N. M., Newmeyer, D. D., Schuler, M., & Green, D. R. (2004). Direct Activation of Bax by p53 Mediates Mitochondrial Membrane Permeabilization and Apoptosis. *Science*, *303*(5660), 1010–1014. doi:10.1126/science.1092734

Ciliberto, A., Novak, B., & Tyson, J. J. (2005). Steady states and oscillations in the p53/Mdm2 network. *Cell Cycle (Georgetown, Tex.)*, *4*(3), 488–493.

Dogu, Y., & Díaz, J. (2009). Mathematical model of a network of interaction between p53 and Bcl-2 during genotoxic-induced apoptosis. *Biophysical Chemistry*, *143*(1-2), 44–54. doi:10.1016/j. bpc.2009.03.012

Egger, L., Madden, D. T., Rheme, C., Rao, R. V., & Bredesen, D. E. (2007). Endoplasmic reticulum stress-induced cell death mediated by the proteosome. *Cell Death and Differentiation*, *14*(6), 1172–1180. doi:10.1038/sj.cdd.4402125

Egger, L., Schneider, J., Rheme, C., Tapernoux, M., Hacki, J., & Borner, C. (2003). Serine proteases mediate apoptosis-like cell death and phagocytosis under caspase-inhibiting conditions. *Cell Death and Differentiation*, *10*(10), 1188–1203. doi:10.1038/sj.cdd.4401288

Eißing, T., Allgower, F., & Bullinger, E. (2005). Robustness properties of apoptosis models with respect to parameter variations and intrinsic noise. *IEE Proc-Systems Biology*, *152*(4), 221–228. doi:10.1049/ip-syb:20050046

Evan, G. I. (2008). The Ever-Lengthening Arm of p53. *Cancer Cell*, *14*(2), 108–110. doi:10.1016/j. ccr.2008.07.012

Geva-Zatorsky, N., Rosenfeld, N., Itzkovitz, S., Milo, R., Sigal, A., Dekel, E., Yarnitzky, T., Liron, Y., Polak, P., Lahav, G., & Alon, U. (2006). Oscillations and variability in the p53 system. *Molecular Systems Biology*, *2*, 2006.0033.

Hanahan, D., & Weinberg, R. A. (2000). The Hallmarks of Cancer. *Cell*, *100*(1), 57–70. doi:10.1016/ S0092-8674(00)81683-9

Hayward, R. L., Macpherson, J. S., Cummings, J., Monia, B. P., Smyth, J. F., & Jodrell, D. (2004). Enhanced oxaliplatin-induced apoptosis following antisense Bcl-xl down-regulation is p53 and Bax dependent: Genetic evidence for specificity of the antisense effect. *Molecular Cancer Therapeutics*, *3*(10), 169–178.

Konishi, T., Sasaki, S., Watanabe, T., Kitayama, J., & Nagawa, H. (2006). Overexpression of hRFI inhibits 5-fluorouracil-induced apoptosis in colorectal cancer cells via activation of NF-kB and upregulation of BCL-2 and BCL-XL. *Oncogene*, *25*(22), 3160–3169. doi:10.1038/sj.onc.1209342

Kæser, M. D., & Iggo, R. D. (2002). Chromatin immunoprecipitation analysis fails to support the latency model for regulation of p53 DNA binding activity in vivo. *Proceedings of National Academic Sciences of the United States of America*, *99*(1), 95–100.

Lahav, G., Rosenfeld, N., Sigal, A., Geva-Zatorsky, N., Levine, A. J., Elowitz, M. B., & Alon, U. (2004). Dynamics of the p53–Mdm2 feedback loop in individual cells. *Nature Genetics*, *36*(2), 147–150. doi:10.1038/ng1293

Lebedeva, I., Rando, R., Ojwang, J., Cossum, P., & Stein, C. A. (2000). Bcl-xL in Prostate Cancer Cells: Effects of Overexpression and Down-Regulation on Chemosensitivity. *Cancer Research*, *60*(21), 6052–6060.

Ma, L., Wagner, J., Rice, J. J., Hu, W., Levine, A. J., & Stolovitzky, G. A. (2005). A plausible model for the digital response of p53 to DNA damage. *Proceedings of the National Academy of Sciences of the United States of America*, *102*(40), 14266–14271. doi:10.1073/pnas.0501352102

Monk, N. A. M. (2003). Oscillatory Expression of Hes1, p53, and NF-κB Driven by Transcriptional Time Delays. *Current Biology*, *13*(16), 1409–1413. doi:10.1016/S0960-9822(03)00494-9

Okamura, S., Arakawa, H., Tanaka, T., Nakanishi, H., Ng, C. C., & Taya, Y. (2001). p53DINP1, a p53-Inducible Gene, Regulates p53-Dependent Apoptosis. *Molecular Cell*, *8*(1), 85–94. doi:10.1016/ S1097-2765(01)00284-2

Proctor, C. J., & Gray, D. A. (2008). Explaining oscillations and variability in the p53-Mdm2 system. *BMC Systems Biology*, *2*, 75. doi:10.1186/1752-0509-2-75

Puszynski, K., Hat, B., & Lipniacki, T. (2008). Oscillations and bistability in the stochastic model of p53 regulation. *Journal of Theoretical Biology*, *254*(2), 452–465. doi:10.1016/j.jtbi.2008.05.039

Reed, J. C. (1996). A day in the life of the Bcl2 protein: does the turnover rate of Bcl2. *Leukemia Research*, *20*(2), 109–111. doi:10.1016/0145-2126(95)00135-2

Reed, J. C., & Pellecchia, M. (2005). Apoptosis-based therapies for hematologic malignancies. *Blood*, *106*(2), 408–418. doi:10.1182/blood-2004-07-2761

Schuler, M., & Green, D. R. (2005). Transcription, apoptosis and p53:catch-22. *Trends in Genetics*, *21*(3), 182–187. doi:10.1016/j.tig.2005.01.001

Tyson, J. J., Chen, K. C., & Novak, B. (2003). Sniffers, buzzers, toggles and blinkers: dynamics of regulatory and signaling pathways in the cell. *Current Opinion in Cell Biology*, *15*(2), 221–231. doi:10.1016/S0955-0674(03)00017-6

Wee, K. B., & Aguda, B. D. (2006). Akt versus p53 in a network of oncogenes and tumor suppressor genes regulating cell survival and death. *Biophysical Journal*, *91*(3), 857–865. doi:10.1529/biophysj.105.077693

Wee, K. B., Surana, U., & Aguda, B. D. (2009). Oscillations of the p53-Akt Network: Implications on Cell Survival and Death. *PLoS ONE*, *4*(2), e4407. doi:10.1371/journal.pone.0004407

Whibley, C., Pharoah, P. D. P., & Hollstein, M. (2009). p53 polymorphisms: cancer implications. *Nature Reviews. Cancer*, *9*(2), 95–107. doi:10.1038/nrc2584

Zhang, T., Brazhnik, P., & Tyson, J. J. (2007). Exploring Mechanisms of the DNA-Damage Response. *Cell Cycle (Georgetown, Tex.)*, *6*(1), 85–94.

ADDITIONAL READING

Bakkenist, C. J., & Kastan, M. B. (2003). DNA damage activates ATM through intermolecular autophosphorylation and dimer dissociation. *Nature*, *421*(6922), 499–506. doi:10.1038/nature01368

Bose, I., & Ghosh, B. (2007). The p53-MDM2 network: from oscillations to apoptosis. *Journal of Biosciences*, *32*(5), 991–997. doi:10.1007/s12038-007-0103-3

Brandman, O., Ferrell, J. E. Jr, Li, R., & Meyer, T. (2005). Interlinked fast and slow positive feedback loops drive reliable cell decisions. *Science*, *310*(5747), 496–498. doi:10.1126/science.1113834

Chen, T., Filklov, V., & Skiena, S. S. (2001). Identifying gene regulatory networks from experimental data. *Parallel Computing*, *27*(1-2), 141–162. doi:10.1016/S0167-8191(00)00092-2

Chen, T., He, H. L., & Church, G. M. (1999). Modeling gene expression with differential equations. *Pacific Symposium on Biocomputing*, 29-40.

Deng, X., Geng, H., & Ali, H. (2005). Examine: A computational approach to reconstructing gene regulatory networks. *BioSystems*, *81*(2), 125–136. doi:10.1016/j.biosystems.2005.02.007

Eissing, T., Conzelmann, H., Gilles, E. D., Allgower, F., Bullinger, E., & Scheurich, P. (2004). Bistability analyses of a caspase activation model for receptor-induced apoptosis. *The Journal of Biological Chemistry*, *279*(35), 36892–36897. doi:10.1074/jbc.M404893200

Fuchs, S. Y., Adler, V., Buschmann, T., Wu, X., & Ronai, Z. (1998). Mdm2 association with p53 targets its ubiquintination. *Oncogene, 17*(19), 2543–2547. doi:10.1038/sj.onc.1202200

Fujiuchi, N., Aglipay, J. A., Ohtsuka, T., Maehara, N., Sahin, F., & Su, G. H. (2004). Requirement of IFI16 for the maximal activation of p53 induced by ionizing radiation. *The Journal of Biological Chemistry, 279*(19), 20339–20344. doi:10.1074/jbc.M400344200

Gonze, D., Halloy, J., & Goldbeter, A. (2002). Robustness of circadian rhythms with respect to molecular noise. *Proceedings of the National Academy of Sciences of the United States of America, 99*(2), 673–678. doi:10.1073/pnas.022628299

Goss, P. J., & Peccoud, J. (1998). Quantitative modeling of stochastic systems in molecular biology by using stochastic Petri Nets. *Proceedings of the National Academy of Sciences of the United States of America, 95*(12), 6750–6755. doi:10.1073/pnas.95.12.6750

Heinrich, R., & Schuster, S. (1996). *The regulation of cellular systems*. New York: Springer.

Pigolotti, S., Krishna, S., & Jensen, M. H. (2004). Oscillation patterns in negative feedback loop. *Proceedings of the National Academy of Sciences of the United States of America, 104*(16), 6533–6537. doi:10.1073/pnas.0610759104

Sengupta, S., & Harris, C. C. (2005). p53: Traffic Cop at the crossroads of DNA repair and recombination. *Nature Reviews. Molecular Cell Biology, 6*(1), 44–55. doi:10.1038/nrm1546

Stommel, J. M., & Wahl, G. M. (2004). Accelerated MDM2 auto-degradation induced by DNA-damage kinases is required for p53 activation. *The EMBO Journal, 23*(7), 1547–1556. doi:10.1038/sj.emboj.7600145

Sun, T., Chen, C., Wu, Y., Zhang, S., Cui, J., & Shen, P. (2009). Modeling the role of p53 pulses in DNA damage- induced cell death decision. *BMC Bioinformatics, 10*, 190. doi:10.1186/1471-2105-10-190

Swat, M., Kel, A., & Herzel, H. (2004). Bifurcation analysis of the regulatory modules of the mammalian G1/S transition. *Bioinformatics (Oxford, England), 20*(10), 1506–1511. doi:10.1093/bioinformatics/bth110

Tichý, A., Záškodová, D., Řezáčová, M., Vávrová, J., Vokurková, D., & Pejchal, J. (2007). Gamma-radiation-induced ATM-dependent signalling in human T-lymphocyte leukemic cells, MOLT-4. *Acta Biochimica Polonica, 54*(2), 281–287.

Tyson, J. J. Monitoring p53's pulse. (2004). *Nat Genet, 36*(2), 113-114. doi:10.1038/ng0204-113

Wang, S., & El-Deiry, W. S. (2006). p73 or p53 directly regulates human p53 transcription to maintain cell cycle checkpoints. *Cancer Research, 66*(14), 6982–6989. doi:10.1158/0008-5472.CAN-06-0511

Wang, T., Tamae, D., LeBon, T., Shively, J. E., Yen, Y., & Li, J. J. (2005). The role of peroxiredoxin II in radiation-resistant MCF-7 breast cancer cells. *Cancer Research, 65*(22), 10338–10346. doi:10.1158/0008-5472.CAN-04-4614

Wendt, J., Radetzki, S., Haefen, C. V., Hemmati, P. G., & Güner, D., chulze-Osthoff, K., Dörken, B., & Daniel, P. T. (2006). Induction of p21[CIP/WAF-1] and G2 arrest by ionizing irradiation impedes caspase-3-mediated apoptosis in human carcinoma cells. *Oncogene, 25*(3), 5972–5980.

Yu, J., Wang, Z., Kinzler, K. W., Vogelstein, B., & Zhang, L. (2003). PUMA mediates the apoptotic response to p53 in colorectal cancer cell. *Proceedings of the National Academy of Sciences of the United States of America, 100*(4), 1931–1936. doi:10.1073/pnas.2627984100

Zhang, T., Brazhnik, P., & Tyson, J. J. (2009). Computational Analysis of Dynamical Responses to the Intrinsic Pathway of Programmed Cell Death. *Biophysical Journal, 97*(2), 415–434. doi:10.1016/j.bpj.2009.04.053

Zhang, X., Liu, F., Cheng, Z., & Wang, W. (2009). Cell fate decision mediated by p53 pulses. *Proceedings of the National Academy of Sciences of the United States of America, 106*(30), 12245–12250. doi:10.1073/pnas.0813088106

KEY TERMS AND DEFINITONS

Bifurcation: Mathematically speaking, the observed states of a system correspond to solutions of nonlinear differential equations that model the biological system. If an observed stable state loses its stability when a parameter reaches a critical value, then the state is no longer observed and the system creates a new stable state that splits from the original state.

Bistability: A property of dynamic system which refers to the situations where two stable states co-exist.

Local Sensitivity: A sensitivity measure that characterizes the local effects of parameter variation. Technically speaking, the nominal set of parameters is slightly perturbed and the systematic behavior is then investigated.

P53: A tumor suppressor protein ubiquitously expressed in both nucleus and cytoplasm. Upon exposure to stress, p53 either induces apoptosis through direct activation of Bax/Bak or induces the expression of numerous proapoptotic proteins, such as Bax, PUMA and PIGs.

PUMA: P53 upregulated mediator of apoptosis.

Stochastic Simulation: A process implemented to analyze chemical reactions involving large numbers of species with complex reaction kinetics. It differs from deterministic approaches as chemical reactions proceed in a probabilistic rather than deterministic manner.

Monte Carlo: A class of computational algorithms that rely on repeated random sampling to compute their results. Monte Carlo methods are often used in simulating physical and mathematical systems

Chapter 11
Agonist Fluctuation Maintained Calcium Signaling in a Mesoscopic System

Lin Ji
Capital Normal University, China

Haiyan Wang
Capital Normal University, China

ABSTRACT

Signals in transduction cascades are widely exposed to stochastic influences. In this work, we investigate the effects of agonist release noises on calcium signaling. Besides the usually considered "amplitude noise", the case of "frequency noise" is also discussed. Simulation results show that the transduction cascades may amplify these noises when its intensity is bigger than certain critical value. The amplified noise show constructive effect to maintain the calcium signaling in critical signal-free cases. Moreover, the signal is more sensitive to the "frequency noise" than to the "amplitude noise". This suggests frequency fluctuations in signaling cascades may have greater influence than the amplitude ones, which is an important finding for signal transduction in complex pathways. Since biological systems are inherently stochastic, this work demonstrates how the calcium system takes advantage of the environmental fluctuations to maintain signaling, and therefore provide effective, sensitive signal communication.

INTRODUCTION

Signal transduction in living systems is inevitably disturbed by stochastic factors, such as the internal molecular noise, random openings and closings of voltage-gated membrane channels, thermal fluctuations of membrane potential etc. Many investigations have been done to explore the effects of stochastic factors on calcium signals

(Ullah & Jung, 2006; Falcke, 2004; Li et al., 2005; Dupont et al., 2008; Perc et al., 2008). Ullah & Jung (2006) found that signaling model that taking the stochastic channel behavior into consideration can accurately describe the statistically properties of the elementary calcium release events; Falcke (2004) reviewed the stochastic clustering character of ion channel and found that there is an optimal cluster size that best sustain the signaling; Li et al. (2005) investigated the role of internal molecular noise in intracellular calcium oscillations. In most

DOI: 10.4018/978-1-60960-064-8.ch011

of former investigations, the stochastic character is directly involved in the signaling process. Excellular signals influence calcium signaling in the form of agonist (hormone or neurotransmitter) stimulus. It triggers the signaling by binding to the receptor on the cell surface. Calcium agonist stimulus is actually another kind of signal, such as hormone or neurotransmitter signal. Environmental random perturbations or internal fluctuations may lead to stochastic changes in their release process. Related investigations have revealed that noise or external force can result in frequency (as well as the amplitude) fluctuations in oscillatory signals (Skupin et al., 2008; Ji et al., 2008; Li & He, 2005). It has been reported that the agonist stimulus plays a crucial role in calcium signaling process (Woods et al., 1986; Kawanishi et al., 1989). Under in vivo conditions, agonists are emitted as abrupt quantal "packets" in continuous pulsatile fashion, which varies not only in amplitude, but also in frequency and duration. In this work, we investigated the influence of random factors in the agonist release processes ("agonist release noise") on calcium signaling. Those that can pronouncedly influence the amplitude or frequency of the agonist signal are termed as "amplitude noise" and "frequency noise", respectively.

BACKGROUND

Agonist influences the Ca^{2+} signaling through many pathways such as Ca^{2+}-phosphatidylinositol (PI) pathway, NMDA receptor mediated synapses, derndritic calcium action potentials, and Ca^{2+} liberated by Ca^{2+} phenomena linked or not to the role of ryanodine receptors of the intracellular endoplasmic reticulum. Here, we employ the receptor-controlled model for intracellular Ca^{2+} signaling in hepatocytes proposed by Cuthbertson et al. (1991). In this model, the calcium signal (oscillation) is triggered by the binding of agonists (hormone or neurotransmitter) to their receptors, which is the basic signaling mechanism

for most of the calcium signaling systems. The influence of agonist is expressed by its concentration. The system dynamics can be described by the following equations:

$$\frac{d[G_\alpha - GTP]}{dt} = k_g[G_\alpha - GDP] - 4k_p[G_\alpha - GTP]^4[PLC] - h_g[G_\alpha - GTP]$$

$$\frac{d[DAG]}{dt} = k[PLC^*] - h_d[DAG] + l_d$$

$$\frac{d[Ca^{2+}]_i}{dt} = \rho\left\{k_c\frac{[IP_3]^3}{K_s^3 + [IP_3]^3} - h_c[Ca^{2+}]_i + l_c\right\}$$

$$\frac{d[PLC^*]}{dt} = k_p[G_\alpha - GTP]^4[PLC] - h_p[PLC^*]$$

(1)

For simplicity, it is assumed that $[DAG]$ and $[IP_3]$ increase with the same rate, i.e., $[DAG] = [IP_3]$. $[G_\alpha\text{-}GDP]$ and $[PLC]$ are determined by the relations:

$$[G_\alpha - GDP] = G_0 - [G_\alpha - GTP] - 4[PLC^*],$$

$[PLC] = P_0 - [PLC^*]$ in which G_0 and P_0 are the total concentration of G-proteins and PLC, respectively. Parameter k_g is proportional to the agonist concentration. l_d and l_c are "leak" terms of the signaling dynamics, which keeps the cell at its basal level of $[DAG]$ and $[Ca^{2+}]_i$, respectively, in the absence of external stimuli. k_p, h_p and k_d are supposed to take the form:

$$k_n = k_n'\frac{[DAG]^2}{K_D^2 + [DAG]^2} \text{ where } k_n = k_p, h_p, \text{or } k_d.$$

Detailed information about the model can be found in Ref (Cuthbertson et al., 1991).

In mesoscopic systems where the number of reactant molecules is small, internal molecular noise resulting from the stochastic nature of the discrete chemical reaction events becomes important (Hou & Xin, 2004). It is reported that this kind of internal noise can constructively induce oscillation in parameter space where only the steady-state can be observed in the corresponding macroscopic system (internal noise induced signal). In addition, the signal-to-noise ratio (SNR) of the noise-induced oscillation peaks as the noise intensity increases, indicating the occurrence of internal noise coherent resonance (INCR) (Shuai & June, 2002; Schmid et al., 2004; Hou et al.,

2005). Internal noise is also reported to be able to optimize the stochastic genetic oscillation performance (Wang et al., 2005), or sustain circadian rhythms (Li & Lang, 2008). It is generally accepted that the strength of the internal noise is scales as $1/\sqrt{V}$, where V represents the system size, a mesoscopic counterpart quantity for molecular number in microscopic systems (Xin & Hou, 2009). Therefore, INCR is also named as "system-size resonance" (Hou & Xin, 2004).

For macroscopic systems where V is infinite, the internal noise can be ignored. But for cellular or sub-cellular reaction systems where the number of reaction molecules is often small (Elowitz et al., 2002; Blake et al., 2003), internal noise must be taken into account. In calcium signaling system, the stochastic opening of the IP_3R channel is one of the main sources of internal noise, which has been reported to play an important role in determining the signal spatiotemporal pattern (Falcke, 2004). Intrinsic stochastic character of mesoscopic systems makes the deterministic models no longer strictly valid. Stochastic models such as chemical master equations (CME) should be used. Since CMEs can seldom be solved analytically, series of numerical simulation methods are developed including stochastic simulation algorithm (SSA), τ-leap method or chemical Langevin equation (CLE) (Gillespie, 2007). For systems that satisfy continuous assumption, CLE can be used to describe its stochastic dynamics, which takes much less computational time than SSA. Hou & Xin (2003) proved CLE provides good simulation results for mesoscopic reactions in cellular or sub-cellular systems, and it qualitatively agrees well with other simulation algorithms of CME. Calcium signaling is a typical mesoscopic system in which stochastic mechanisms plays a significant role whereas the state of main reactants is continuous. Therefore, CLE for the above mentioned receptor-controlled model is employed. It can be described as following:

$$
\begin{aligned}
\frac{d[G_\alpha - GTP]}{dt} &= \frac{1}{V}\left[(a_1 - 4a_2 - a_3) + \sqrt{a_1}\xi_1(t) - 4\sqrt{a_2}\xi_2(t) - \sqrt{a_3}\xi_3(t)\right] \\
\frac{d[DAG]}{dt} &= \frac{1}{V}\left[(a_4 + a_5 - a_6) + \sqrt{a_4}\xi_4(t) + \sqrt{a_5}\xi_5(t) - \sqrt{a_6}\xi_6(t)\right] \\
\frac{d[Ca^{2+}]_i}{dt} &= \frac{1}{V}\left[(a_7 + a_8 - a_9) + \sqrt{a_7}\xi_7(t) + \sqrt{a_8}\xi_8(t) - \sqrt{a_9}\xi_9(t)\right] \\
\frac{d[PLC^*]}{dt} &= \frac{1}{V}\left[(a_2 - a_{10}) + \sqrt{a_2}\xi_2(t) - \sqrt{a_{10}}\xi_{10}(t)\right]
\end{aligned}
$$

$$(2)$$

in which a_i ($i=1,\ldots 10$) are the transition rates per volume as listed in Table 1:

$\xi_i(t)$ ($i=1,\ldots 10$) are Gaussian white noises with $\langle \xi_i(t)\xi_i(t')\rangle = \delta_{ij}\delta(t-t')$ and $\langle \xi_i(t)\rangle = 0$ V is the system size.

In this work, the agonist is assumed to be released in square wave fashion instead of being

Table 1. Parameter description in the CLE

Parameter	Relation with the dynamic parameters
a_1	$k_g[G_\alpha - GDP]V$
a_2	$k_p[G_\alpha - GDP]^4[PLC]V$
a_3	$h_g[G_\alpha - GTP]V$
a_4	$k_d[PLC^*]V$
a_5	$h_d[DAG]V$
a_6	l_dV
a_7	$\rho k_c[IP_3]^3 V / \left\{K_S^3 + [IP_3]^3\right\}$
a_8	$\rho h_c[Ca^{2+}]_i V$
a_9	$\rho l_c V$
a_{10}	$h_p[PLC^*]V$

constant. Therefore, k_g in the Cuthbertson model can be expressed as:

$$k_g(t) = \begin{cases} amp & t \in \left[n \cdot per, n \cdot per + kep \right] \\ base & t \in \left(n \cdot per + kep, (n+1) \cdot per \right) \end{cases} (n = 0,1,2...)$$

(3)

Here, the agonist concentration can be characterized by three parameters: release amplitude *amp*; duration *kep* and period *per*. To satisfy the "continuous supply" requirement, another parameter "*base*", which is fixed as $0.005 \ s^{-1}$, is used to represent the stimulus strength when the "packages" are not released. The agonist release noise is introduced by incorporating white noise ingredient in the release parameters as: $\beta(t) = \beta_0(1+\gamma(t))$. β describes the agonist release parameter (*amp* or *per*). β_0 is a constant reference value. $\gamma(t)$ is Gaussian white noise with the intensity D. Our investigations show that *kep* plays similar role as *amp*, i.e., to control the received agonist amount. Therefore, only two kinds of noise are discussed here. One is the "amplitude noise" that *amp* fluctuates, the other is the "frequency noise" in which *per* is disturbed. The fluctuated stimulus sequences under these two kinds of noises are depicted in Figure 1.

RESULTS AND DISCUSSION

Description of Agonist Noise

We firstly investigate the signaling bifurcation character of the deterministic system under unperturbed square wave stimulus. Figure 2 shows the change of signal amplitude and frequency with *amp*. The deterministic system predicts Hopf bifurcation at *amp*=0.0123. The frequency of the stimulus induced signal gradually increases with *amp*. In this work, we choose reference *amp* values close to but before the bifurcation point for each given set of agonist release parameters (*per* and *kep*). That is, the system is signal free under the unperturbed square wave stimulus. For detailed discussion, we use the results under the release parameter setting *amp*=0.01 s^{-1}, *per*=50 s and *kep*=15 s as an example.

Simulation results have proved that calcium signal can be induced by either the "amplitude noise" or the "frequency noise". Low frequency signals can be induced at weak intensities, and stronger noise can further enhance the signal by increasing their frequency. Figure 3 illustrates the oscillation sequences induced by the "amplitude noise". It can be seen that the frequency of the

Figure 1. Disturbed agonist stimulation. a. agonist signal is perturbed by "amplitude noise" (D=10⁻⁵); b. agonist signal is perturbed by "frequency noise" (D=10⁻⁷); c. agonist signal is perturbed by "frequency noise" (D=10⁻⁵). (© [2010], [Lin Ji]. Used with permission.).

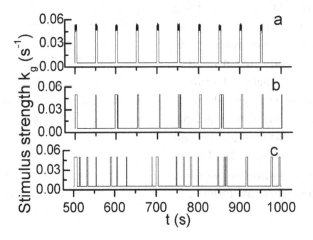

Figure 2. Calcium signaling bifurcation diagram of the deterministic system with unperturbed square wave stimulus (per=50, kep=15). The filled squares and the empty circles are the amplitude and the frequency of the signal, respectively. (© [2010], [Lin Ji]. Used with permission.).

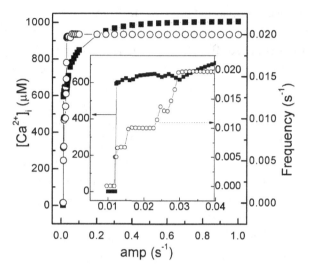

noise induced signal increases with *D*. This kind of frequency dependency can also be found in noise free system as shown in Figure 2 or in early work (Chay et al., 1995). In noise free system, it is generally believed that the increase of *amp* enhances the stimulus strength, which can

induce the signal. In certain critical range where the stimulus is not strong enough to induce the signal with intrinsic frequency, some low frequency signal appears. In our noise perturbed case, the change of *D* has similar function as *amp*, therefore, the frequency of the noise induced

Figure 3. Calcium signal induced by "amplitude noise" with different intensities as noted in each line $(V=5\times10^3)$. Dynamic parameters used in this work: $h_g = 0.0s^{-1}$, $k_d{'}=700\ s^{-1}$, $h_d=100\ s^{-1}$, $l_d=250\ nM\ s^{-1}$, $\rho k_c=9.0\times10^4\ nM\ s^{-1}$, $\rho h_c=1.0\ s^{-1}$, $\rho l_c=200\ nM\ s^{-1}$, $k_p{'}=2\times10^{-7}\ nM^4\ s^{-1}$, $h_p{'}=0.5\ s^{-1}$, $K_s=300nM$, $K_D=25\ nM$, $G_0=200\ nM$, and $P_0=10\ nM$. (© [2010], [Lin Ji]. Used with permission.).

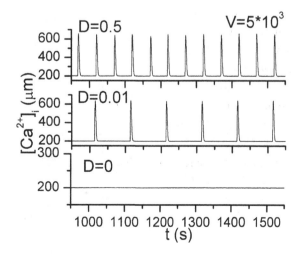

signal may also increases with D. Similar signals can also be induced by the "frequency noise", which is not shown. This indicates that the indirect perturbations in agonist release can also induce the calcium signal, and the fluctuations in both the stimulus strength and frequency are effective. However, quantitative investigations show that the "frequency noise" can induce signals with much smaller intensity.

Agonist Noise Induced Signal

It is known that the intensity of the internal noise in mesoscopic systems can be represented by the system size V, and the smaller system means the stronger internal noise (Xin & Hou, 2009). To systemically explore the agonist release noise induced calcium signal, we study the dependency of lowest noise intensity necessary to induce the signal (D_{low}) on V. Figure 4 shows the noise induced signal phase diagram for both the "amplitude noise" and "frequency noise". Note that in the agonist noise free system, calcium signals can be induced by the internal noise when V is smaller than 10^3, i.e., the internal noise intensity is big enough (internal noise induced signal). But when V is bigger, the signal may disappear. Obviously, in the "frequency noise" case, tiny fluctuations can induce the signal. The corresponding intensity is about seven orders of magnitude weaker than that of the "amplitude noise". That is to say, the "frequency noise" is more efficient in inducing the calcium signal. This may relate to the frequency-encoded character of calcium signal, and it suggests that calcium signal is also sensitive to the frequency fluctuations of its agonist signals. Since frequency fluctuations are proved to appear under the influence of noise (Skupin et al., 2008; Ji et al., 2008; Li & He, 2005) the results discovered here suggest that frequency fluctuation may be more influential for further information transduction.

"Amplitude Noise" vs. "Frequency Noise" Influence

In Figure 4 we can find that when $V<10^4$, D_{low} increases with V, but after that it is kept constant. This means when the system is large enough the internal noise becomes so weak that its influence can be ignored. Therefore, D_{low} is only determined by the signaling dynamics and the agonist release noise, and does not change with V. This indicates the internal noise only helps to induce calcium signal in small systems, but not in the big ones. Nevertheless, the D_{low} of the "frequency noise" in the phase diagram is generally six to seven orders of magnitude weaker than that of the "amplitude noise", independent of the V value. This suggests the sensitivity of the signaling to the frequency noise is an intrinsic character of the calcium system.

To quantitatively characterize the noise induced signals, their oscillation regularity Reg are calculated. The definition of Reg is:

Figure 4. Phase diagram for the appearance of calcium signal induced by agonist release noise. The filled squares stand for the "amplitude noise" situation; the empty circles represent the "frequency noise" case. (© [2010], [Lin Ji]. Used with permission.).

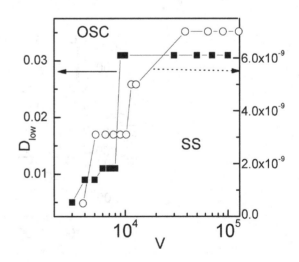

$$Reg = \sqrt{\text{var}\left(T\right)} / T \qquad (4)$$

where T denotes the time interval between two neighbored peaks in the calcium oscillation evolution sequence. Reg is also known as the coefficient of variation in other literatures (Wang et al., 2004). Obviously, smaller Reg represents more regular signal. Note that a spike is identified when the calcium concentration increases above a certain threshold value from below and it turns out that the exact value of the user-specified threshold can change in a wide range without altering the resulting oscillation dynamics. In this work, we use the threshold value 300 μM.

Figure 5 displays the influence of the two kinds of noise on the regularity of the noise induced signal. It is clear that similar tendency is obtained. With the increase of D, Reg is decreased, which means that the signal regularity is optimized. Figure 6 is the time evolution of calcium signal induced by "amplitude noise" with different intensities. It can be seen that better regularity is obtained under stronger noise. This demonstrates the well-known nontrivial "ordering" function of noise in the calcium system (Braiman et al., 1995; Ji & Li, 2004). Since the two kinds of noise influence the signal in different intensity scope, we provide the data that apparently reflect the agonist noise influence. In the "amplitude noise" case, the cooperation of agonist noise and internal noise can induce signal when both D and V are small, and the corresponding Reg are relatively big ($D<1$ cases in $V=5\times10^3$ line). When V is bigger, weak agonist noise cannot induce signal at all ($D<1$ cases in $V=10^4$ and 10^5 lines), but signals induced by stronger noise will simultaneously be regularized. With the increase of D, "amplitude noise" can help the signal reaching a "regular" state ($Reg = 0$). This situation is similar to "anticoherence resonance" in which noise can counterintuitively minimize its own destructive influence on the signal (Lacasta et al., 2002; Ji et

al., 2009). Here, the agonist release noise helps to minimize the destructive influence of internal noise. In the "frequency noise" case, all the data provided correspond to the agonist noise induced signal (these signals can be induced when log $D = -9$ according to Figure 4). Therefore, the agonist noise effect dominates, which results in much lower Reg level than the small D part in the "amplitude noise" case. When the "frequency noise" is weak, noise sustained signals have bad regularity. Similar to the "amplitude noise" case, the signal regularity can be optimized with the increase of D. But now, Reg is stabilized only at some lower value than the weak noise cases, but cannot reach 0. Generally, the value of V does not qualitatively influence these changing tendencies.

CONCLUSION

In this work, two kinds of agonist release noises are discussed with respect to their influence on calcium signaling. Simulation results prove that both of the "amplitude noise" and the "frequency noise" can induce calcium signal and optimize the signal regularity, however, the former always needs to be much stronger than the latter. This indicates that the calcium signaling is more sensitive to frequency fluctuations of the stimulation than the usually discussed amplitude noises. If we take the physical character of agonist influenced signaling, i.e. the "stimulate-respond" process as a simple "diffuse arrive and then respond process", the difference of "frequency noise" and "amplitude noise" becomes clearer. The "frequency noise" means that a second stimulus may come along before the response to the former one has fully dissipated. In this case, the pulse may add up and has a highly nonlinear effect. But in the "amplitude noise" case, the fluctuation only affects the amount of stimulus received in each pulse, which can produce only minor variations. Moreover, in the "amplitude noise" case, the agonist concentration only fluctuates when "the

Figure 5. Dependence of signal regularity with noise intensity. a. "amplitude noise" induced signal; b. "frequency noise" induced signal. (© [2010], [Lin Ji] Used with permission.).

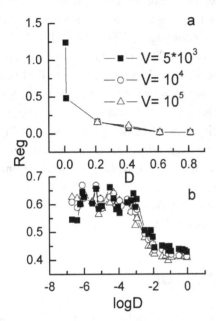

Figure 6. Time evolution of calcium signal induced by "amplitude noise" with different intensities (V=10⁴) (© [2010], [Lin Ji] Used with permission)

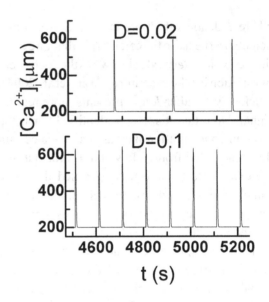

packets" are released. This means during much longer intervals (*per - kep*), there is no fluctuation. Therefore, "frequency noise" may have stronger effects than the "amplitude noise". For processes with similar "stimulate-respond" characters where the signaling is induced by excellular (or exorganelle) input, such as exocytosis or nerve firing processes, similar phenomenon may be anticipated as long as it has diffusion or first-order dissipation characters. This is of significance for living signal transduction, since stochastic fluctuations are unavoidable in transduction pathways and many signals are frequency encoded, our findings suggest the frequency fluctuations among signaling cascades may trigger more pronounced responses than the amplitude ones.

ACKNOWLEDGMENT

This work is supported by the Beijing Natural Science Foundation Program (2083027), the Beijing Young Key Talents Culture Program (PHR201008076), and Funding Project for Academic human Resources Development in Institutions of Higher Learning Under the Jurisdiction of Beijing Municipality (PHR20100718).

REFERENCES

Blake, W. J., Kærn, M., Cantor, C. R., & Collins, J. J. (2003). Noise in eukaryotic gene expression. *Nature*, *422*(6932), 633–637. doi:10.1038/nature01546

Braiman, Y., Linder, J. F., & Ditto, W. L. (1995). Taming spatiotemporal chaos with disorder. *Nature*, *378*(6556), 465–467. doi:10.1038/378465a0

Brunel, N., Chance, F. S., Fourcaud, N., & Abbott, L. F. (2001). Effects of synaptic noise and filtering on the frequency response of spiking neurons. *Physical Review Letters, 86*(10), 2186–2189. doi:10.1103/PhysRevLett.86.2186

Chay, T. R., Lee, Y. S., & Fan, Y. S. (1995). Appearance of phase-locked wenckebach-like rhythms, devil's staircase and universality in intracellular calcium spikes in non-excitable cell models. *Journal of Theoretical Biology, 174*(1), 21–44. doi:10.1006/jtbi.1995.0077

Cuthbertson, K. S. R., & Chay, T. R. C. (1991). Modelling receptor-controlled intracellular calcium oscillators. *Cell Calcium, 12*(2-3), 97–108. doi:10.1016/0143-4160(91)90012-4

Dupont, G., Abou-Lovergne, A., & Combettes, L. (2008). Stochastic aspects of oscillatory Ca^{2+} dynamics in hepatocytes. *Biophysical Journal, 95*(5), 2193–2202. doi:10.1529/biophysj.108.133777

Elowitz, M. B., Levine, A. J., Siggia, E. D., & Swain, P. S. (2002). Stochastic gene expression in a single cell. *Science, 297*(5584), 1183–1186. doi:10.1126/science.1070919

Falcke, M. (2004). Reading the patterns in living cells - the physics of Ca^{2+} signaling. *Advances in Physics, 53*(3), 255–440. doi:10.1080/00018730 410001703159

Gillespie, D. T. (2007). Stochastic Simulation of Chemical Kinetics. *Annual Review of Physical Chemistry, 58*, 35–55. doi:10.1146/annurev. physchem.58.032806.104637

Hou, Z., Rao, T., & Xin, H. (2005). Effect of internal noise for rate oscillations during CO oxidation on Platinum surfaces. *The Journal of Chemical Physics, 122*(13), 134708. doi:10.1063/1.1874933

Hou, Z., & Xin, H. (2003). Internal noise stochastic resonance in a circadian clock system. *The Journal of Chemical Physics, 119*(22), 11508–11512. doi:10.1063/1.1624053

Hou, Z., & Xin, H. (2004). Optimal system size for mesoscopic chemical oscillations. *ChemPhysChem, 5*(3), 407–412. doi:10.1002/ cphc.200300969

Ji, L., & Li, Q. (2004). Effect of spatiotemporal perturbation on Turing pattern formation. *Physics Letters. [Part A], 329*(4-5), 309–317. doi:10.1016/j.physleta.2004.07.012

Ji, L., Xu, W., & Li, Q. (2008). Noise effect on intracellular calcium oscillations in a model with delayed coupling. *Fluct. noise lett., 8*(1), L1-L9.

Ji, L., Xu, W., & Li, Q. (2009). The influence of environmental noise on circadian gene expression in Drosophila. *Applied Mathematical Modelling, 33*(4), 2109–2113. doi:10.1016/j. apm.2008.05.012

Kawanishi, T., Blank, L. M., Harootunian, A. T., Smith, M. T., & Tsien, R. Y. (1989). Ca^{2+} oscillations induced by hormonal stimulation of individual fura-2-loaded hepatocytes. *The Journal of Biological Chemistry, 264*(22), 12859–12866.

Lacasta, A. M., Sagués, F., & Sancho, J. M. (2002). Coherence and anticoherence resonance tuned by noise. *Physical Review E: Statistical, Nonlinear, and Soft Matter Physics, 66*(4), 045105. doi:10.1103/PhysRevE.66.045105

Li, H., Hou, Z., & Xin, H. (2005). Internal noise enhanced detection of hormonal signal through intracellular calcium oscillations. *Chemical Physics Letters, 402*(4-6), 444–449. doi:10.1016/j. cplett.2004.12.068

Li, Q., & He, H. (2005). Signal transduction in a coupled hormone system: Selective explicit internal signal stochastic resonance and its control. *The Journal of Chemical Physics, 123*(21), 214905. doi:10.1063/1.2135779

Li, Q., & Lang, X. (2008). Internal noise sustained circadian rhythms in a Drosophila model. *Biophysical Journal, 94*(6), 1983–1994. doi:10.1529/biophysj.107.109611

Perc, M., Green, A., Dixon, C. J., & Marhl, M. (2008). Establishing the stochastic nature of intracellular calcium oscillations from experimental data. *Biophysical Chemistry, 132*(1), 33–38. doi:10.1016/j.bpc.2007.10.002

Schmid, G., Goychuk, I., & Hänggi, P. (2004). Effect of channel block on the spiking activity of excitable membranes in a stochastic Hodgkin–Huxley model. *Physical Biology, 1*(2), 61–66. doi:10.1088/1478-3967/1/2/002

Shuai, J. W., & Jung, P. (2002). Optimal intracellular calcium signaling. *Physical Review Letters, 88*(6), 068102. doi:10.1103/PhysRevLett.88.068102

Skupin, K., Winkler, U., Wartenberg, M., Sauer, H., Tovey, S. C., Taylor, C. W., & Falcke, M. (2008). How does intracellular Ca^{2+} oscillate: by chance or by the clock? *Biophysical Journal, 94*(6), 2404–2411. doi:10.1529/biophysj.107.119495

Ullah, G., & Jung, P. (2006). Modeling the statistics of elementary calcium release events. *Biophysical Journal, 90*(10), 3485–3495. doi:10.1529/biophysj.105.073460

Wang, S., Liu, F., Wang, W., & Yu, Y. (2004). Impact of spatially correlated noise on neuronal firing. *Physical Review E: Statistical, Nonlinear, and Soft Matter Physics, 69*(1), 011909. doi:10.1103/PhysRevE.69.011909

Wang, Z., Hou, Z., & Xin, H. (2005). Internal noise stochastic resonance of synthetic gene network. *Chemical Physics Letters, 401*(1-3), 307–311. doi:10.1016/j.cplett.2004.11.064

Woods, N. M., Cuthbertson, K. S. R., & Cobbold, P. H. (1986). Repetitive transient rises in cytoplasmic free calcium in hormone-stimulated hepatocytes. *Nature, 319*(6054), 600–602. doi:10.1038/319600a0

Xin, H., & Hou, Z. (2009). *Nonlinear chemical dynamics* (2nd ed.). Hefei: China Science and Technology University Press.

ADDITIONAL READING

Berridge, M. J., Lipp, P., & Bootman, M. D. (2000). The versatility and universality of calcium signalling. *Nature Reviews. Molecular Cell Biology, 1*(1), 11–21. doi:10.1038/35036035

Carmignoto, G., & Pozzan, T. (2002). *Calcium oscillations as a signalling system that mediates the bi-directional communication between neurones and astrocytes The Tripartite Synapse: Glia in Synaptic Transmission*. Oxford: Oxford University Press.

Collins, J. J., Imhoff, T. T., & Grigg, P. (1996). Noise-enhanced information transmission in rat SA1 cutaneous mechanoreceptors via aperiodic stochastic resonance. *Journal of Neurophysiology, 76*(1), 642–645.

Falcke, M. (2003). On the role of stochastic channel behavior in intracellular Ca^{2+} dynamics. *Biophysical Journal, 84*(1), 42–56. doi:10.1016/S0006-3495(03)74831-0

Falcke, M., & Malchow, D. (2003). *Understanding calcium dynamics, experiments and theory* (Lecture Notes in Physics). Verlag Berlin Heidelberg New York: Springer.

Gammaitoni, L., Hänggi, P., Jung, P., & Marchesoni, F. (1998). Stochastic resonance. *Reviews of Modern Physics, 70*(1), 223–287. doi:10.1103/RevModPhys.70.223

Gillespie, D. T. (1977). Exact stochastic simulation of coupled chemical reactions. *Journal of Physical Chemistry, 81*(25), 2340. doi:10.1021/j100540a008

Gillespie, D. T. (2000). The chemical Langevin equation. *The Journal of Chemical Physics, 113*(1), 297–306. doi:10.1063/1.481811

Gillespie, D. T. (2001). Approximate accelerated stochastic simulation of chemically reacting systems. *The Journal of Chemical Physics, 115*(4), 1716–1733. doi:10.1063/1.1378322

Goldbeter, A. (1996). *Biochemical oscillations and cellular rhythms: the molecular bases of periodic and chaotic behavior.* Cambridge: Cambridge University Press. doi:10.1017/CBO9780511608193

Gong, Y. B., Hou, Z., & Xin, H. (2004). Optimal particle size for reaction rate oscillation in CO oxidation on nm-sized palladium particles. *The Journal of Physical Chemistry B, 108*(46), 17796–17799. doi:10.1021/jp0477250

Hänggi, P. (2002). Stochastic resonance in biology. *ChemPhysChem, 3*(3), 285–290.

Hou, Z., Qu, K., & Xin, H. (2005). Transfer of noise into signal through one-way coupled chemical oscillators. *ChemPhysChem, 6*(1), 58–61. doi:10.1002/cphc.200400222

Ji, L., & Li, Q. (2005). Turing pattern formation in coupled reaction-diffusion system with distributed delays. *The Journal of Chemical Physics, 123*(9), 094509. doi:10.1063/1.2041427

Jung, P., & Shuai, J. W. (2001). Stochastic resonance and optimal size of ion channel clusters. *Europhysics Letters, 56*(1), 29–35. doi:10.1209/epl/i2001-00483-y

Kadar, S., Wang, J., & Showalter, K. (1998). Noise-supported traveling waves in subexcitable media. *Nature, 391*(6668), 700–702. doi:10.1038/35636

Leloup, J.-C., Gonze, D., & Goldbeter, A. (2006). Computational models for circadian rhythms: Deterministic versus stochastic approaches. In Kriete, A., & Eils, R. (Eds.), *Computational Systems Biology.* Burlington, San Diego: Elsevier Academic Press. doi:10.1016/B978-012088786-6/50032-0

Lindner, B., Garcia-Ojalvo, J., Neiman, A., & Schimansky-Geier, L. (2004). Effects of noise in excitable systems. *Physics Reports, 392*(6), 321–424. doi:10.1016/j.physrep.2003.10.015

Mar, D. J., Chow, C. C., Gerstner, W., Adams, R. W., & Collins, J. J. (1999). Noise shaping in populations of coupled model neurons. *Proceedings of the National Academy of Sciences of the United States of America, 96*(18), 10450–10455. doi:10.1073/pnas.96.18.10450

Ochab-Marcinek, A., Schmid, G., Goychuk, I., & Hänggi, P. (2009). Noise-assisted spike propagation in myelinated neurons. *Physical Review E: Statistical, Nonlinear, and Soft Matter Physics, 79*(1), 011904. doi:10.1103/PhysRevE.79.011904

Perc, M., & Marhl, M. (2004). Frequency dependent stochastic resonance in a model for intracellular Ca^{2+} oscillations can be explained by local divergence. *Physica A, 332*(1), 123–140. doi:10.1016/j.physa.2003.09.046

Rudiger, S., Shuai, J. W., Huisinga, W., Nagaiah, C., Warnecke, G., Parker, I., & Falcke, M. (2007). Hybrid stochastic and deterministic simulations of calcium blips. *Biophysical Journal, 93*(6), 1847–1857. doi:10.1529/biophysj.106.099879

Schmid, G., Goychuk, I., & Hänggi, P. (2001). Stochastic resonance as a collective property of ion channel assemblies. *Europhysics Letters, 56*(1), 22–28. doi:10.1209/epl/i2001-00482-6

Schmid, G., & Hänggi, P. (2007). Intrinsic coherence resonance in excitable membrane patches. *Mathematical Biosciences, 207*(2), 235–245. doi:10.1016/j.mbs.2006.08.024

Shuai, J. W., & Jung, P. (2002). Stochastic properties of Ca^{2+} release of inositol 1,4,5-trisphosphate receptor clusters. *Biophysical Journal, 83*(1), 87–97. doi:10.1016/S0006-3495(02)75151-5

Shuai, J. W., & Jung, P. (2003). Optimal ion channel clustering for intracellular calcium signaling. *Proceedings of the National Academy of Sciences of the United States of America, 100*(2), 506–510. doi:10.1073/pnas.0236032100

Shuai, J. W., & Jung, P. (2003). Selection of intracellular calcium patterns in a model with clustered Ca^{2+} release channels. *Physical Review E: Statistical, Nonlinear, and Soft Matter Physics, 67*(3), 031905. doi:10.1103/PhysRevE.67.031905

Tang, J., Yang, X., Ma, J., & Jia, Y. (2009). Noise effect on persistence of memory in a positive-feedback gene regulatory circuit. *Physical Review E: Statistical, Nonlinear, and Soft Matter Physics, 80*(1), 011907. doi:10.1103/PhysRevE.80.011907

Tessone, C. J., Ullner, E., Zaikin, A. A., Kurths, J., & Toral, R. (2006). Noise-induced inhibitory suppression of frequency-selective stochastic resonance. *Physical Review E: Statistical, Nonlinear, and Soft Matter Physics, 74*(4), 046220. doi:10.1103/PhysRevE.74.046220

Thul, R., & Falcke, M. (2004). Release currents of ip_3 receptor channel clusters and concentration profiles. *Biophysical Journal, 86*(5), 2660–2673. doi:10.1016/S0006-3495(04)74322-2

Ullah, G., & Jung, P. (2006). Modeling the statistics of elementary calcium release events. *Biophysical Journal, 90*(10), 3485–3495. doi:10.1529/biophysj.105.073460

Zhang, J. Q., Hou, Z., & Xin, H. (2004). System size Bi-Resonance for intracellular Calcium signalling. *ChemPhysChem, 5*(7), 1041–1045. doi:10.1002/cphc.200400089

KEY TERMS AND DEFINITIONS

Signal Transduction Pathway: The substep(s) in generating or transferring signals and allow cells to respond to environmental signals. In these pathways, the signal is amplified such that each step in the pathway results in a larger number of activated components than in the previous step.

Agonist: A chemical that binds to a receptor of a cell and triggers a signaling response by the cell. An agonist often mimics the action of a naturally occurring substance.

Noise Effect: The counterintuitive influence of noise in nonlinear systems. Such as stochastic resonance, coherence resonance, noise induced signal, noise enhanced wave transmission, et al.

Mesoscopic System: Are those that are larger than atoms and yet very much smaller than the largescale everyday objects that we can see and touch. i.e., the scale between macroscopic and microscopic systems

Amplitude Noise: The stochastic character of noise lies in the variation in its amplitude, i.e., the noise amplitude is randomly distributed.

Frequency Noise: The stochastic character of noise lies in the variation in its frequency, i.e., the noise frequency is randomly distributed.

Noise Induced Signal: Near the critical bifurcation point of a nonlinear system, the presence of noise can induce nonlinear signals that may exist after the bifurcation point. This kind of signal is noise induced signal.

Section 3
Computational Predictions of Drug Properties

Chapter 12
Theoretical Study on the Antioxidant Activity of Alizarin, Purpurin, and Pseudopurpurin

Ruifa Jin
Chifeng University, China

Hongzheng Bao
Chifeng University, China

Yin Bai
Chifeng University, China

Xiuhua Li
Chifeng University, China

ABSTRACT

Hydroxyanthraquinone derivatives are a large group of natural polyphenolic compounds found widely in plants. The cytotoxic activities of hydroxyanthraquinone derivatives have been demonstrated using cancer cell lines. The pharmacological effect can be explained by their antioxidant activity and their inhibition of certain enzymes. There are two main kinds of mechanism, H-atom transfer and one-electron transfer, by which antioxidants can play their role. The structural and electronic properties of hydroxyanthraquinone derivatives, alizarin, purpurin, pseudopurpurin, and their radicals were investigated using density functional theory. It turned out that these three molecules appear to be good candidates for high antioxidant activity species, particularly for pseudopurpurin. Taking this system as an example, we present an efficient method for the investigation of antioxidant activity for such kind of hydroxyanthraquinone derivatives from theoretical point of view. With the current work, we hope to highlight the antioxidant activity of hydroxyanthraquinone derivatives and stimulate the interest for further studies and exploitation in pharmaceutical industry.

DOI: 10.4018/978-1-60960-064-8.ch012

INTRODUCTION

Hydroxyanthraquinone derivatives are a large group of natural polyphenolic compounds found widely in plants, and some of these are used as herbal medicines or food pigments. Investigations have demonstrated the preventive effect of hydroxyanthraquinone against genotoxicity or cytotoxicity (Wu & Yen, 2004; Chen et al., 2004) and the modulation of metabolic enzyme activities in response to xenobiotics (Marczylo et al., 2000; Marczylo et al., 2003; Sun et al., 2000; Wang et al., 2001). It has been demonstrated that purpurin and alizarin inhibit the activity of human recombinant cytochrome P450 (CYP), isozymes CYP 1A1, CYP 1A2, and CYP 1B1, resulting in the antimutagenic effect observed in recombinant salmonella that possess these CYPs (Takahashi et al., 2002). Some papers have been published on the cytotoxic activities of hydroxyanthraquinone derivatives using cancer cell lines such as L1210 (Koyama et al., 1989), HL-60 (Koyama et al., 1989), LNCap (Cha et al., 2005), PC3, and A431 (Zhou et al., 2006). The intake of antimutagens and anticarcinogens present in food ingredients may lead to a decreased risk of cancer onset. Modern authorised physicians are increasing their use of hydroxyanthraquinone derivatives to treat many important common diseases, due to their proven ability to inhibit specific enzymes, and to scavenge free radicals (Havsteen, 2002). In fact, the structures, the procedures of isolation, and approaches to the organic synthesis of hydroxyanthraquinone derivatives have been studied extensively in experiment. Experimental and theoretical studies of flavonols by Van Acker et al. (1996) revealed that the excellent antioxidant activity of the flavonols could be explained by the formation of an intramolecular hydrogen bond. The antioxidant activity of apigenin, luteolin, and taxifolin were studied using the B3LYP functional coupled with the 6-311++G(d,p) basis set (Leopoldini et al., 2004). The phenolic antioxidants action mechanisms were investigated using DFT/

B3LYP method (Klein & Lukes, 2006). Several interesting classes of phenolic antioxidants are studied using the density functional theory (DFT) method, including commercial antioxidants used as food additives, compounds related to Vitamin E, flavonoids in tea, aminophenols, stilbenes related to resveratrol, and sterically hindered phenols (Wright et al 2001). Quercetin is one of the most representative flavonoid compounds. The structural, electronic, and energetic characteristics of quercetin, as well as the influence of a copper ion on all of these parameters, are studied by means of quantum chemical electronic structure calculations (Fiorucci et al. 2007). However, to the best of our knowledge, no calculation about the antioxidant activity of hydroxyanthraquinone derivatives has been reported so far.

In this work, we have investigated the conformational and electronic features of three hydroxyanthraquinone derivatives: alizarin (1,2-dihydroxyanthraquinone), purpurin (1,2,4-trihydroxyanthraquinone), and pseudopurpurin (1,2,4-trihydroxy-3-carboxyanthraquinone) at the DFT level. They were chosen for their peculiar chemical structure, to evaluate the effect of the functional groups on the antioxidant ability. Bond dissociation energy (BDE) and ionization potential (IP) values computed for these systems were used as indicators of the ease by which hydroxyanthraquinone derivatives can deactivate free radicals. The spin densities were reported to give better insight into delocalization of the unpaired electron and conjugation effects. The geometrical structures studied in this work are shown in Figure 1, along with the atom numbering.

COMPUTATIONAL DETAILS

Phenols are widely used as antioxidants in living organisms. Phenoxyl radicals represent important intermediates in many biological applications (Halliwell & Gutteridge, 1989; Gugumus, 1990). The function of phenolic antioxidants (ArOH)

Figure 1. Main geometrical parameters of (A) alizarin, (B) purpurin, and (C) pseudopurpurin, along with the atom numbering

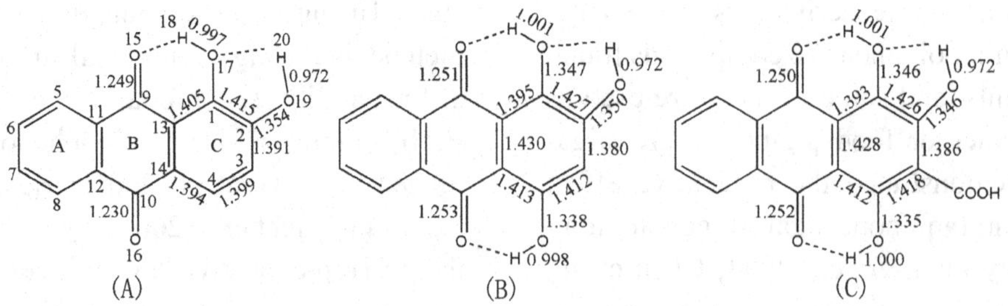

is to intercept and react with free radicals faster than the substrate (Gugumus, 1990; Wright et al., 2001). Two main kinds of mechanism are reported for the radical scavenging processes of chain-breaking antioxidants ArOH (Wright et al., 2001): H-atom transfer, Equation (1), and one-electron transfer, Eq. (2).

In the H-atom transfer, a free radical R· removes a hydrogen atom from the antioxidant (ArOH):

$$R^\bullet + ArOH \rightarrow RH + ArO^\bullet \qquad (1)$$

The efficiency of the antioxidant ArOH depends on the stability of the radical ArO·. It is usually possible to guess the most stable geometry through application of the following rules: (a) maximize hydrogen bonds in the parent and radical; (b) when no hydrogen bond is possible minimize nonbonded repulsions (Wright et al., 2001). Furthermore, the conjugation and resonance effects lead to the electron can flow easily from electron-donating moiety to the electron-withdrawing moiety. As a consequence, the stability of the radical ArO· can be increased by conjugation and resonance effects. The BDE of the O-H bonds is an important parameter to evaluate the antioxidant action, because the weaker the O-H bond the easier the reaction of free radical inactivation will be.

In the one-electron transfer mechanism, the antioxidant can give an electron to the free radical:

$$R^\bullet + ArOH \rightarrow R^- + ArOH^{+\bullet} \qquad (2)$$

Again, the radical cation arising from the electron transfer must be stable, so it does not react with substrate molecules. In this case, the IP is the most significant energetic factor for the scavenging activity evaluation.

All calculations have been performed by Gaussian 03 code (Frisch et al., 2004). B3LYP exchange correlation potential, in connection with the 6-31+G(d,p) basis set, was used for optimizing geometries without symmetry constraints. Harmonic vibrational frequencies calculations using the same methods as for the geometry optimizations were performed for both parent molecule (ArOH) and radicals (ArO· and ArOH⁺·), to characterize all their conformations as minima or saddle points and to evaluate the zero-point energy (ZPE) corrections, which we have included in all the relative energies, bond dissociation energies, and ionization potentials.

The gas-phase bond dissociation enthalpy (BDE) was calculated at 298 K as the enthalpy difference for Eq. (3):

$$ArOH \rightarrow ArO^\bullet + H^\bullet \qquad (3)$$

The adiabatic ionization potential (IP) was obtained as the energy difference between the ArOH and ArOH⁺· species.

RESULTS AND DISCUSSION

Hydrogen Atom Transfer of Hydroxyanthraquinone Derivatives

The main optimized geometric parameters of alizarin, purpurin, and pseudopurpurin are presented in the ground-state equilibrium structures of the alizarin and purpurin optimized at the B3LYP/6-31+G(d,p) level are completely planar. In the case of the pseudopurpurin, the optimized structure is almost planar except of a pyramidalization of the carboxyl group. According to the suggested cutoff definition for D–H --- A H-bond (H --- A distances < 3.0 Å and D–H---A angles > 110°) (Steiner & Desiraju, 1998; Steiner, 2002), the interaction between hydroxy-H and oxygen of keto group and in ortho-hydroxy functionality have been considered as H-bond, which has been named as incipient (frozen) proton transfer reaction from D to A (Steiner, 2002). In the conformations of minimum energy of alizarin, purpurin, and pseudopurpurin, the hydroxyl groups are oriented in such a way to maximize H-bond-like interactions. Alizarin presents two hydrogen bonds between 1-OH and the 9-keto groups and in ortho-dihydroxy functionality. Purpurin has three hydrogen bonds established between 1-OH/4-OH and 9-keto/10-keto groups, and in ortho-dihydroxy functionality, respectively. Pseudopurpurin is formed by introducing electron-withdrawing (–COOH) group on 3-position and is characterized by similar interactions as in purpurin. The optimized H-bond lengths $R_{O15---H18}$ are 1.666, 1.651, and 1.659 Å, and $R_{O17---H20}$ are 2.143, 2.128, 2.120 Å in alizarin, purpurin, and pseudopurpurin, respectively. The H-bond lengths $R_{O16---H}$ in purpurin and pseudopurpurin are 1.662 and 1.647 Å, respectively. It suggests that the introduction of the electron-donating (–OH) group on 4-position and/or the electron-withdrawing (–COOH) group on 3-position of alizarin leads to enhancement the strength of the interaction of the hydrogen bonds $O_{15}---H_{18}$ and $O_{17}---H_{20}$. The introduction of the electron-withdrawing (–COOH) group on

3-position of purpurin leads to enhancement the strength of the interaction of the hydrogen bonds $O_{17}---H_{20}$ and $O_{16}---H$ while decrease the strength of the interaction of the hydrogen bond $O_{15}---H_{18}$.

The relative energies and BDE values of alizarin, purpurin, and pseudopurpurin radical species are presented in Table 1. Starting from the absolute minima of each system, two radicals from alizarin and three from purpurin and pseudopurpurin were obtained upon H-atom abstraction from every hydroxyl phenolic group, while a single radical cation for each parent molecule was obtained by removing one electron. The most stable radical arising from alizarin is the 2-OH radical, obtained by abstraction of a hydrogen atom from the hydroxyl attached to the carbon C_2. The energy of the 1-OH radical is higher by 5.51 kcal/mol than that of 2-OH radical. The radicalization of the 1-OH group involves the breaking of the hydrogen bond established with the 9-keto group, while the radicalization of the 2-OH group involves the breaking of the hydrogen bond in ortho-dihydroxy functionality. It confirms that the hydrogen bond between 1-OH and 9-keto groups is stronger than that in ortho-dihydroxy functionality, so 1-OH radical is the less stable one. For purpurin and pseudopurpurin, their 1-OH and 2-OH radicals are found to be practically isoenergetic (0.48 and 0.39 kcal/mol, respectively) because of the introduction of the electron-donating (–OH) and/ or the electron-withdrawing (–COOH) groups. Their isomers 4-OH radicals are found at 9.28 and 8.70 kcal/mol, respectively, above the absolute minimum.

In Figure 2 are reported the spin densities for the most stable radicals. Hydroxyanthraquinone derivatives are usually considered radical scavengers thanks to their excellent delocalization possibility. For the all the most stable radicals of alizarin, purpurin, and pseudopurpurin, the unpaired electron is delocalized over the B and C rings because of the planar conformation assumed by these species. The spin distribution of 2-OH radical for alizarin indicates the oxygen O_{19} from

Table 1. Relative energies (ΔE) and bond dissociation energy (BDE) (all in kcal/mol) for alizarin, purpurin, and pseudopurpurin radical species

radical specie	ΔE	BDE	ΔBDE*
1-OH-alizarin	5.51	91.31	8.07
2-OH-alizarin	0.00	85.64	2.40
1-OH-purpurin	0.00	87.28	4.04
2-OH-purpurin	0.48	87.70	4.46
4-OH-purpurin	9.26	96.71	13.47
1-OH-pseudopurpurin	0.39	87.67	4.43
2-OH-pseudopurpurin	0.00	87.23	3.99
4-OH-pseudopurpurin	8.70	96.17	12.93

*ΔBDE are referred to phenol. Gas-phase BDE for phenol is 83.24 kcal/mol.

which the H atom is removed as the most probable radical center, followed by the atoms C_1, O_{17}, C_3, and O_{16}. The spin densities of O_{19}, C_1, O_{17}, C_3, and O_{16} are 0.031, 0.022, 0.020, 0.018, and 0.013, respectively. For the 1-OH radical of purpurin the hydrogen bonds between the 2-OH group and the oxygen O_{17} and between the 4-OH and 10-keto groups contribute to the radical stability. The unpaired electron center remains on the oxygen atom O_{17} from which the H atom is removed, followed by the atoms C_4, O_{15}, O_{16}, and O atom of 4-OH. The spin densities of O_{17}, C_4, O_{15}, O_{16}, and O atom of 4-OH are 0.040, 0.015, 0.012, 0.010, and 0.015, respectively. In the 2-OH radical of pseudopurpurin the unpaired electron center remains on the oxygen atom O_{19} from which we remove the H atom, followed by the atoms C_{14}, O_{16}, O_{17}, and C_4. The spin densities of O_{19},

C_{14}, O_{16}, O_{17}, and C_4 are 0.031, 0.024, 0.022, 0.019, and 0.014, respectively.

The BDE values that characterize the hydrogen atom donating ability of alizarin, purpurin, and pseudopurpurin in the gas phase are presented in Table 2. On the basis of gas phase BDE values, it is evident that the 2-OH radical of alizarin and both 1-OH and 2-OH radicals of purpurin and pseudopurpurin are predicted to be the most efficient radical scavengers among the radicals. Such efficiency is related to the further stabilization of the derived phenoxy radical via formation of intramolecular hydrogen bonds. The 1-OH radical of alizarin and 4-OH radicals of both purpurin and pseudopurpurin are expected to be of low activity since the corresponding BDE values were 6-10 kcal/mol higher than those obtained for 2-OH radical of alizarin and both 1-OH and/or 2-OH radicals of purpurin and pseu-

Figure 2. Spin densities for the most stable radical of (A) alizarin, (B) purpurin, and (C) pseudopurpurin

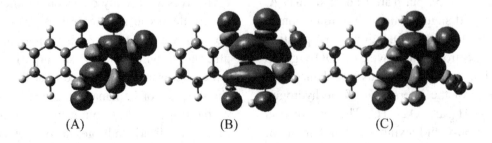

(A)   (B)   (C)

Table 2. Ionization potential (IP) (in kcal/mol) for alizarin, purpurin, and pseudopurpurin

Cationic Radical Species	IP	ΔIP*
Alizarin	184.56	-6.12
Purpurin	179.19	-11.49
Pseudopurpurin	181.94	-8.74

ΔIP are referred to phenol. Gas-phase IP for phenol is 190.68 kcal/mol.

dopurpurin, respectively. Furthermore, the ΔBDE values of the 2-OH radical of alizarin and both 1-OH and 2-OH radicals of purpurin and pseudopurpurin are increased slightly compared with that of tocopherol (Leopoldini et al., 2004), which is the biological reference compound for the antioxidant activity, with the maximum deviation being less than 9 kcal/mol. For these systems, the particular H-atom donating ability can be attributed to the catechol moiety. Tocopherol, characterized by the same functional group, is the biological reference compound for the antioxidant activity and is the major lipid-soluble chain-breaking antioxidant normally in human blood plasma. It indicates that the ortho-dihydroxy and the hydrogen bond between them influence decidedly the stability of the radical. The ortho-dihydroxy is the most important site for the H-atom transfer. The trend of BDE values for the examined compounds suggests that an essential factor for a good activity as antioxidant is the ortho-dihydroxy-type structure, and the introduction of the –OH and/or –COOH groups for the molecules does not significantly affect the activities of antioxidants.

Single Electron Transfer of Hydroxyanthraquinone Derivatives

According to the one-electron transfer, an electron is removed from the HOMO of the parent molecules, giving rise to radical cation species. All cationic radical species are planar and thus completely conjugated. Hydrogen bonds are normally retained as in the parent molecule, contributing to a further stabilization. The spin densities for the radical cation species arising from alizarin, purpurin, and pseudopurpurin are shown in Figure 3. The spin distributions or these three species show the unpaired electron delocalized over the B and C rings. For alizarin, the oxygen atoms of 1-OH and 2-OH hydroxyl groups can be considered the more accredited radical centers, even if there is a possibility of finding the spin density on the C_2 and C_4 atoms of the C ring and O_{16} atom of B ring. For purpurin and pseudopurpurin, the oxygen atoms of 1-OH and 4-OH hydroxyl groups can be considered the more accredited radical centers, even if there is a possibility of finding the spin density on the C_1, C_4, and O_{19} atoms of the C ring and O_{15} and O_{16}

Figure 3. Spin densities for the radical cation of (A) alizarin, (B) purpurin, and (C) pseudopurpurin

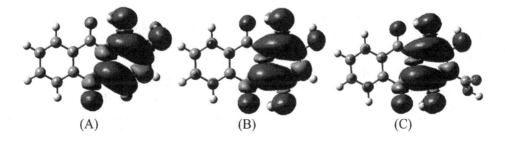

(A) (B) (C)

atom of B ring. Furthermore, the strength of the interaction of the hydrogen bonds is stronger than those in their neutral molecules. The optimized the H-bond lengths $R_{O15\text{---}H18}$ and $R_{O17\text{---}H20}$ in alizarin, purpurin, and pseudopurpurin cationic radicals are 1.467, 1.550, and 1.554, and 2.246, 2.219, and 2.210 Å, respectively. The H-bond lengths $R_{O16\text{---}H}$ of purpurin and pseudopurpurin cationic radicals are 1.633, and 1.612 Å, respectively. It indicates that the stability of the cationic radicals can be increased by hydrogen bonds. As a consequence, the one-electron transfer mechanism of molecules containing hydrogen bonds can take place more easily than those molecules without hydrogen bonds.

Table 2 lists the IP values for alizarin, purpurin, and pseudopurpurin. The trend for computed IPs is slightly different from that of BDEs. The lowest value is found for Purpurin (179.19 kcal/mol), followed by Pseudopurpurin (181.94 kcal/mol), and alizarin (184.56 kcal/mol). The electron donating ability of hydroxyanthraquinone derivatives seems to be related to an extended electronic delocalization over all the molecules. Furthermore, the introduction of the –OH and/or –COOH groups for the molecules leads to different changes of the IPs. The value of IP decreases when –OH group is introduced into alizarin, whereas the corresponding value increases when –COOH group is introduced into purpurin. Furthermore, the ΔIP values of alizarin, purpurin, and pseudopurpurin are similar to that of taxifolin (Leopoldini et al., 2004), with the maximum deviation being less than 2 kcal/mol. The IP is dependent on the HOMO energy of the parent molecule. For conjugated system, the IP is raised in energy, so the abstraction of an electron becomes very easy. The trend of IP values for the examined compounds suggests that an essential factor for a good activity as antioxidant is the ortho-dihydroxy-type structure, and it can be further improved by the introduction of the –OH and/or –COOH groups for the molecules.

CONCLUSION

The antioxidant properties of three hydroxyanthraquinone derivatives were investigated at the B3LYP/6-31+G(d,p) level of theory, to establish what and how the functional groups can affect the radical scavenging activity. Based on the obtained results, the following conclusions can be drawn. The ability of compounds to form intramolecular hydrogen bonds is important for good antioxidant activity. The hydrogen bonds between hydroxyl in C ring and keto group in B ring and in ortho-dihydroxy functionality confer high stability for the radical species. Moreover, the 2-OH radical of alizarin and both 1-OH and 2-OH radicals of purpurin and pseudopurpurin are the most active in donating an H atom, as confirmed by their low BDE values. These three molecules appear to be good candidates for the one-electron-transfer mechanism, particularly for pseudopurpurin. Their planar conformation and the extended electronic delocalization between adjacent rings determine low IP values. Although our results are obtained in gas phase, while the hydroxyanthraquinone derivatives act normally in solution, we think that gas-phase BDE and IP are, however, excellent primary indicators of free radical scavenging activity.

ACKNOWLEDGMENT

We gratefully acknowledge the Research Program of Sciences at Universities of Inner Mongolia Autonomous Region (NJzy08148) for financial support.

REFERENCES

Cha, T.-L., Qiu, L., Chen, C.-T., Wen, Y., & Hung, M.-C. (2005). Emodin down-regulates androgen receptor and inhibits prostate cancer cell growth. *Cancer Research*, 65(6), 2287–2295. doi:10.1158/0008-5472.CAN-04-3250

Chen, H. C., Hsieh, W. T., Chang, W. C., & Chung, J. G. (2004). Aloe-emodin induced in vitro G2/M arrest of cell cycle in human promyelocytic leukemia HL-60 cells. *Food and Chemical Toxicology, 42*(8), 1251–1257. doi:10.1016/j.fct.2004.03.002

Fiorucci, S. B., Golebiowski, J., Cabrol-Bass, D., & Antonczak, S. (2007). DFT study of quercetin activated forms involved in antiradical, antioxidant, and prooxidant biological processes. *Journal of Agricultural and Food Chemistry, 55*(3), 903–911. doi:10.1021/jf061864s

Frisch, M. J., et al. (2004). *Gaussian 03, revision B.03*. Wallingford, CT: Gaussian, Inc.

Gugumus, F. (1990). *Oxidation inhibition in organic mMaterials*. Boca Raton: CRC Press.

Halliwell, B., & Gutteridge, J. M. C. (1989). *Free radicals in biology and medicine*. Oxford: Oxford University.

Havsteen, H. B. (2002). The biochemistry and medical significance of the flavonoids. *Pharmacology & Therapeutics, 96*(2-3), 67–202. doi:10.1016/S0163-7258(02)00298-X

Klein, E., & Lukes, V. (2006). DFT/B3LYP study of the substituent effect on the reaction enthalpies of the individual steps of single electron transfer-proton transfer and sequential proton loss electron transfer mechanisms of phenols antioxidant action. *The Journal of Physical Chemistry A, 110*(44), 12312–12320. doi:10.1021/jp063468i

Koyama, M., Takahashi, K., Chou, T.-C., Darzynkiewicz, Z., Kapuscinski, J., Kelly, T. R., & Watanabe, K. A. (1989). Intercalating agents with covalent bond forming capability. A novel type of potential anticancer agents. 2. Derivatives of chrysophanol and emodin. *Journal of Medicinal Chemistry, 32*(7), 1594–1599. doi:10.1021/jm00127a032

Leopoldini, M., Marino, T., Russo, N., & Toscano, M. (2004). Antioxidant properties of phenolic compounds: H-atom versus electron transfer mechanism. *The Journal of Physical Chemistry A, 108*(22), 4916–4922. doi:10.1021/jp037247d

Leopoldini, M., Marino, T., Russo, N., & Toscano, M. (2004). Density functional computations of the energetic and spectroscopic parameters of quercetin and its radicals in the gas phase and in solvent. *Theo Chem Acc, 111*(2-6), 210-216.

Leopoldini, M., Pitarch, I. P., Russo, N., & Toscano, M. (2004). Structure, conformation, and electronic properties of apigenin, luteolin, and taxifolin antioxidants. A first principle theoretical study. *The Journal of Physical Chemistry A, 108*(1), 92–96. doi:10.1021/jp035901j

Marczylo, T., Arimoto-Kobayashi, S., & Hayatsu, H. (2000). Protection against Trp-P-2 mutagenicity by purpurin: mechanism of in vitro antimutagenesis. *Mutagenesis, 15*(3), 223–228. doi:10.1093/mutage/15.3.223

Marczylo, T., Sugiyama, C., & Hayatsu, H. (2003). Protection against Trp-P-2 DNA adduct formation in C57bl6 mice by purpurin is accompa nied by induction of cytochrome P450. *Journal of Agricultural and Food Chemistry, 51*(11), 3334–3337. doi:10.1021/jf026072m

Steiner, T. (2002). The hydrogen bond in the solid state. *Angewandte Chemie International Edition, 41*(1), 48–76. doi:10.1002/1521-3773(20020104)41:1<48::AID-ANIE48>3.0.CO;2-U

Steiner, T., & Desiraju, G. R. (1998). Distinction between the weak hydrogen bond and the van der waals interaction. *Chemical Communications (Cambridge), 8*, 891–892. doi:10.1039/a708099i

Sun, M., Sakakibara, H., Ashida, H., Danno, G., & Kanazawa, K. (2000). Cytochrome P4501A1-inhibitory action of antimutagenic anthraquinones in medicinal plants and the structure–activity relationship. *Bioscience, Biotechnology, and Biochemistry, 64*(7), 1373–1378. doi:10.1271/bbb.64.1373

Takahashi, E., Fujita, K., Kamataki, T., Arimoto-Kobayashi, S., Okamoto, K., & Negishi, T. (2002). Inhibition of human cytochrome P450 1B1, 1A1 and 1A2 by antigenotoxic compounds, purpurin and alizarin. *Mutation Research, 508*(1-2), 147–156. doi:10.1016/S0027-5107(02)00212-9

Van Acker, S. A. B. E., De Groot, M. J., Van den Berg, D. J., Tromp, M. N. J. L., Den Kelder, G. D. O., Van der Vijgh, W. J. F., & Bast, A. (1996). A quantum chemical explanation of the antioxidant activity of flavonoids. *Chemical Research in Toxicology, 9*(8), 1305–1312. doi:10.1021/tx9600964

Wang, H. W., Chen, T. L., Yang, P. C., & Ueng, T. H. (2001). Induction of cytochromes P450 1A1 and 1B1 by emodin in human lung adenocarcinoma cell line CL5. *Drug Metabolism and Disposition: the Biological Fate of Chemicals, 29*(9), 1229–1235.

Wright, J. S., Johnson, E. R., & Di Labio, G. A. (2001). Predicting the activity of phenolic antioxidants: Theoretical method, analysis of substituent effects, and application to major families of antioxidants. *Journal of the American Chemical Society, 123*(6), 1173–1183. doi:10.1021/ja002455u

Wu, C.-H., & Yen, G.-C. (2004). Antigenotoxic properties of Cassia Tea (*Cassia tora* L.): mechanism of action and the influence of roasting process. *Life Sciences, 76*(1), 85–101. doi:10.1016/j.lfs.2004.07.011

Zhou, X., Song, B., Jin, L., Hu, D., Diao, C., & Xu, G. (2006). Isolation and inhibitory activity against ERK phosphorylation of hydroxyanthraquinones from rhubarb. *Bioorganic & Medicinal Chemistry Letters, 16*(1), 563–568. doi:10.1016/j.bmcl.2005.10.047

Zhu, Q., Zhang, X. M., & Fry, A. J. (1997). Bond dissociation energies of antioxidants. *Polymer Degradation & Stability, 57*(1), 43–50. doi:10.1016/S0141-3910(96)00224-8

ADDITIONAL READING

Babula, P., Adam, V., Havel, L., & Kizek, R. (2007). Naphthoquinones and their pharmacological properties [Naftochinony a jejich farmakologické vlastnosti]. *Ceska a Slovenska Farmacie, 56*(3), 114–120.

Cai, Y., Sun, M., Xing, J., & Corke, H. (2004). Antioxidant phenolic constituents in roots of rheum officinale and rubia cordifolia: Structure-radical scavenginq activity relationships. *Journal of Agricultural and Food Chemistry, 52*(26), 7884–7890. doi:10.1021/jf0489116

Colaric, M., Veberic, R., Solar, A., Hudina, M., & Stampar, F. (2005). Phenolic acids, syringaldehyde, and juglone in fruits of different cultivars of Juglans regia L. *Journal of Agricultural and Food Chemistry, 53*(16), 6390–6396. doi:10.1021/jf050721n

Gunduc, N., & El, S. N. (2003). Assessing antioxidant activities of phenolic compounds of common turkish food and drinks on in vitro low-density lipoprotein oxidation. *Journal of Food Science, 68*(8), 2591–2595. doi:10.1111/j.1365-2621.2003.tb07066.x

Halvorsen, B. L., Holte, K., Myhrstad, M. C. W., Barikmo, I., Hvattum, E., & Remberg, S. F. (2002). A systematic screening of total antioxidants in dietary plants. *The Journal of Nutrition, 132*(3), 461–471.

Hazra, B., Sur, P., Roy, D. K., Sur, B., & Banerjee, A. (1984). Biological activity of diospyrin towards Ehrlich ascites carcinoma in Swiss a mice. *Planta Medica, 51*(4), 295–297. doi:10.1055/s-2007-969713

Huang, Q., Lu, G., Shen, H. M., Chung, M. C., & Ong, C. N. (2007). Anti-cancer properties of anthraquinones from rhubarb. *Medicinal Research Reviews, 27*(5), 609–630. doi:10.1002/med.20094

Inbaraj, J. J., & Chignell, C. F. (2004). Cytotoxic action of juglone and plumbagin: A mechanistic study using HaCaT Keratinocytes. *Chemical Research in Toxicology, 17*(1), 55–62. doi:10.1021/tx034132s

Jang, M., Cai, L., Udeani, G. O., Slowing, K. V., Thomas, C. F., & Beecher, C. W. (1997). Cancer chemopreventive activity of resveratrol, a natural product derived from grapes. *Science, 275*(5297), 218–220. doi:10.1126/science.275.5297.218

Leopoldini, M., Marino, T., Russo, N., & Toscano, M. (2004). Antioxidant properties of phenolic compounds: H-atom versus electron transfer mechanism. *The Journal of Physical Chemistry A, 108*(22), 4916–4922. doi:10.1021/jp037247d

Leopoldini, M., Russo, N., Chiodo, S., & Toscano, M. (2006). Iron chelation by the powerful antioxidant flavonoid quercetin. *Journal of Agricultural and Food Chemistry, 54*(17), 6343–6351. doi:10.1021/jf060986h

Li, S. C. (1982). *Ben cao gang mu.* Beijing, China: People's Health Publishing Press.

Matsuda, H., Morikawa, T., Toguchida, I., Park, J. Y., Harima, S., & Yoshikawa, M. (2001). Antioxidant constituents from rhubarb: Structural requirements of stilbenes for the activity and structures of two new anthraquinone glucosides. *Bioorganic & Medicinal Chemistry, 9*(1), 41–50. doi:10.1016/S0968-0896(00)00215-7

Nenadis, N., & Sigalas, M. P. (2008). A DFT study on the radical scavenging activity of maritimetin and related aurones. *The Journal of Physical Chemistry A, 112*(47), 12196–12202. doi:10.1021/jp8058905

Osman, S. A. A., Abdalla, A. A., & Alaib, M. O. (1983). Synthesis of sulfanilamido-naphthoquinones as potential antituberculous agents. *Journal of Pharmaceutical Sciences, 72*(1), 68–71. doi:10.1002/jps.2600720116

Parra, R. D., & Ohlssen, J. (2008). Cooperativity in intramolecular bifurcated hydrogen bonds: An ab initio study. *The Journal of Physical Chemistry A, 112*(15), 3492–3498. doi:10.1021/jp711956u

Perry, N. B., & Blunt, J. W. (1991). A cytotoxic and antifungal 1,4-naphthoquinone and related compounds from a New Zealand brown alga, Landsburgia Quercifolia. *Journal of Natural Products, 54*(4), 978–985. doi:10.1021/np50076a009

Russo, N., Toscano, M., & Uccella, N. (2000). Semiempirical molecular modeling into quercetin reactive site: Structural, conformational, and electronic features. *Journal of Agricultural and Food Chemistry, 48*(4), 3232–3237. doi:10.1021/jf990469h

Salmon-Chemin, L., Buisine, E., Yardley, V., Kohler, S., Debreu, M. A., & Landry, V. (2001). 2-and 3-substituted 1,4-naphthoquinone derivatives as subversive substrates of trypanothione reductase and lipoamide dehydrogenase from Trypanosoma cruzi: Synthesis and correlation between redox cycling activities and in vitro cytotoxicity. *Journal of Medicinal Chemistry, 44*(4), 548–565. doi:10.1021/jm0010791

Thomson, R. H. (1971). *Naturally occurring quinones.* London, UK: Academic Press.

Visioli, F., Bellomo, G., & Galli, C. (1998). Free radical-scavenging properties of olive oil polyphenols. *Biochemical and Biophysical Research Communications, 247*(1), 60–64. doi:10.1006/bbrc.1998.8735

Wright, J. S., Johnson, E. R., & DiLabio, G. A. (2001). Predicting the activity of phenolic antioxidants: Theoretical method, analysis of substituent effects, and application to major families of antioxidants. *Journal of the American Chemical Society, 123*(6), 1173–1183. doi:10.1021/ja002455u

Wu, X. Y., Wu, Q. T., & Liu, L. J. (1995). Study of pharmacology and application of rhubarb. *Acta Chin Med Pharmacol, 2*(2), 54–55.

Yardley, V., Snowdon, D., Croft, S., & Hazra, B. (1996). In vitro activity of diospyrin and derivatives against leishmania donovani, trypanosoma cruzi and trypanosoma brucei brucei. *Phytotherapy Research, 10*(7), 559–562. doi:10.1002/(SICI)1099-1573(199611)10:7<559::AID-PTR891>3.0.CO;2-V

Zhou, X., Song, B., Jin, L., Hu, D., Diao, C., & Xu, G. (2006). Isolation and inhibitory activity against ERK phosphorylation of hydroxyanthraquinones from rhubarb. *Bioorganic & Medicinal Chemistry Letters, 16*(3), 563–568. doi:10.1016/j.bmcl.2005.10.047

KEY TERMS AND DEFINITIONS

Density Functional Methods: Density functional methods include the effects of electron correlation—the fact that electrons in a molecular system react to one another's motion and attempt to keep out of one another's way in their model. Hartree-Fock calculations consider this effect only in an average—each electron sees and reacts to an averaged electron density, while methods including electron correlation account for the instantaneous interactions of pairs of electron with opposite spin.

Antioxidant Activity: Antioxidant activity of compound is the ability to inhibit the oxidation of materials of both commercial and biological importance. The function of antioxidants is to intercept and react with free radicals at a rate faster than the substrate, and since free radicals are able to attack a variety of targets including lipids, fats, and proteins, it is believed that they are implicated in a number of important degenerative diseases.

Hydrogen Bond: A typical hydrogen bond (H bond) is defined in terms of a proton donor D-H and a proton acceptor A. The H atom is bound covalently to an electronegative atom in D, and noncovalently to an electronegative atom in A. According to the suggested cutoff definition for D–H --- A H-bond definition, the distances between proton donor and hydrogen H---A is less than 3.0 Å and D–H---A angles is larger than 110°.

One-Electron Transfer Mechanism: In this mechanism, by which antioxidants can play their role, a free radical R· removes a hydrogen atom from the antioxidant (ArOH): R· + ArOH → RH + ArO·. The efficiency of the antioxidant ArOH depends on the stability of the radical ArO·, which in turn is determined by the number of hydrogen bonds, conjugation, and resonance effects. The BDE of the O-H bonds is an important parameter to evaluate the antioxidant action, because the weaker the O-H bond the easier the reaction of free radical inactivation will be.

H-atom Transfer Mechanism: In this mechanism, the antioxidant can give an electron to the free radical: R· + ArOH → R⁻ +ArOH⁺·. Again, the radical cation arising from the electron transfer must be stable, so it does not react with substrate molecules. In this case, the IP is the most significant energetic factor for the scavenging activity evaluation.

Bond Dissociation Enthalpy (BDE): BDE is the enthalpy difference for the reaction ArOH →ArO· + H·. The BDE of the O-H bonds is an important parameter to evaluate the antioxidant action, because the weaker the O-H bond the easier the reaction of free radical inactivation will be. Molecules with the low PDE values are expected to have high activity.

Ionization Potential (IP): IP is the energy difference between the ArOH and ArOH⁺· species. In the one-electron transfer mechanism, the IP is the most significant energetic factor for the scavenging activity evaluation. Molecules with the low IP values are expected to have high activity.

Chapter 13
Human Oral Bioavailability Prediction of Four Kinds of Drugs

Aixia Yan
Beijing University of Chemical Technology, China

Zhi Wang
Beijing University of Chemical Technology, China

Jiaxuan Li
Beijing University of Chemical Technology, China

Meng Meng
Beijing University of Chemical Technology, China

ABSTRACT

In the development of drugs intended for oral use, good drug absorption and appropriate drug delivery are very important. Now the predictions for drug absorption and oral bioavailability follow similar approach: calculate molecular descriptors for molecules and build the prediction models. This approach works well for the prediction of compounds which cross a cell membrane from a region of high concentration to one of low concentration, but it does not work very well for the prediction of oral bioavailability, which represents the percentage of an oral dose which is able to produce a pharmacological activity. The models for bioavailability had limited predictability because there are a variety of pharmacokinetic factors influencing human oral bioavailability. Recent study has shown that good quantitative relationship could be obtained for subsets of drugs, such as those that have similar structure or the same pharmacological activity, or those that exhibit similar absorption and metabolism mechanisms. In this work, using MLR (Multiple Linear Regression) and SVM (Support Vector Machine), quantitative bioavail-

DOI: 10.4018/978-1-60960-064-8.ch013

ability prediction models were built for four kinds of drugs, which are Angiotensin Converting Enzyme Inhibitors or Angiotensin II Receptor Antagonists, Calcium Channel Blockers, Sodium and Potassium Channels Blockers and Quinolone Antimicrobial Agents. Explorations into subsets of compounds were performed and reliable prediction models were built for these four kinds of drugs. This work represents an exploration in predicting human oral bioavailability and could be used in other dataset of compounds with the same pharmacological activity.

INTRODUCTION

In drug development, a large amount of possible drug candidate molecules, called "lead compounds", may be predicted through drug design and computational modeling. However, about 95% of lead compounds have failed in the development stages, and 50% of these failures were shown to be due to unfavorable absorption, distribution, metabolism, and excretion (ADME) properties (Beresford et al., 2002). In the development of drugs intended for oral use, good drug absorption and appropriate drug delivery are very important (Hou & Xu, 2004).

Inadequate bioavailability is one of the main reasons that cause many promising drug candidates failed in clinical trials. Bioavailability represents the percentage of an oral dose which is able to produce a pharmacological activity, in other words, the fraction of the oral dose that reaches the arterial blood in an active form. Oral bioavailability is related to several factors, such as gastrointestinal transition and absorption, intestinal membrane permeation, and intestinal/hepatic first-pass metabolism. Moreover, during absorption, many researchers have suggested that gut wall Cytochrome P_{450} 3A4 and P-glycoprotein, the multidrug transporter, act in a concerted manner to control the absorption of their substrates (Van Asperen et al., 1998; Lampen et al., 1998; Hall et al., 1999). One possible method to maximize oral absorption would be to design a molecule that acts as a substrate of P-glycoprotein and CYP3A4 (Van de Waterbeemd, 2001).

Some researchers have summarized general molecular properties of drug molecules that may lead to good drug absorbency. Veber et al. (2002) reported studies on rat bioavailability data for 1100 drug candidates. It was found that drug molecules having fewer than 10 rotatable bonds and less than 140 Å² PSA (Polar Surface Area) (or a hydrogen bond count less than 12) usually showed more than 20% rat oral bioavailability. Lu et al. (2004) investigated the relationship between number of rotatable bonds and PSA for rat oral bioavailability of 434 molecules. Compared to Veber's work (Veber et al., 2002), Lu et al. reported that the prediction results were dependent on the calculation methods.

There are also quantitative studies in order to predict bioavailability. Hirono et al. (1994) reported a quantitative structure-bioavailability model for 188 noncongeneric organic drugs; the drugs were separated into three groups: nonaromatics, aromatics, and heteroaromatics. Based on each group's chemical and physical properties, a quantitative model was developed. Andrews et al. (2000) reported a QSAR (Quantitative Structure and Activity Relationship) model based on 591 compounds and 85 descriptors. The model achieved a good correlation (r^2=0.71), but overfitting problem may exist from the cross-validation result (q^2=0.58).

Yoshida et al. (2000) published a classification model for human oral bioavailability. This model can get a correct rate of 60% for the test group. Turner et al. (2003) reported a QSAR model for a dataset of 169 compounds using stepwise regression method. The regression model were built based on a training set including 159 compounds and validated by a test set including 10 compounds. Although the correlation coefficient of 0.72 was obtained for the test set, due to the small size of the test set, the validation was not statistically reliable. Turner et al. (2004) developed another artificial neural network (ANN) model for oral bioavailability. The correlation coefficients for training set and test set of the model were 0.736 and 0.897, respectively. Wang et al. (2006) reported a correlation model for the predictions of oral bioavailability. The models were built based on the counts of molecular fragments descriptors using a genetic algorithm (GA) and consensus score was employed for a molecule which was simply defined as the average of the values predicted by the best 20 GA-QSAR models. However, the prediction capability of this model is also questionable due to the low correlation coefficient value of cross-validation.

Hou et al. (2007) conjectured that there are no simple rules based on molecular descriptors that can be used to predict human oral bioavailability accurately and reliably by analyzing a diverse dataset of 773 compounds with experimental human oral bioavailability values.

In our recent study (Wang et al., 2008), we explored the modeling of human oral bioavailability based on Hou's dataset. At first, a quantitative model of the whole dataset was built using multiple linear regression (MLR) analysis. This model had limited predictability, emphasizing that a variety of pharmacokinetic factors influence human oral bioavailability. In order to explore whether better models can be built when the compounds share the same ADME properties, four subsets were chosen from the whole dataset to build quantitative models and better models were obtained by multiple linear regression analysis. At first, 161 compounds, whose experimental human intestinal absorption (HIA) values were available, were investigated by using HIA value as a descriptor. Afterwards, 51 sulfonamide drug compounds were chosen for building quantitative models, and the correlation coefficient of the best model obtained was r=0.77; 29 β-lactam drug compounds were chosen for building quantitative models, and the

correlation coefficient of the best model obtained was r=0.78; 58 central nervous system (CNS) drug compounds were chosen for quantitative models, and the correlation coefficient of the best model obtained was r=0.80.

Our recent study has shown that good quantitative relationship could be obtained for subsets of drugs, which have similar structure or the same pharmacological activity, and which exhibit similar absorption and metabolism mechanisms (Wang et al., 2008). In this work, four subsets of drugs were collected to further investigate the applicability of this approach. Drugs in each subset were considered to have the same pharmacological activity.

MATERIALS AND METHODS

Data Set

The human oral bioavailability dataset was taken from http://modem.ucsd.edu/adme, which was collected by Hou and colleagues (Hou et al., 2007). From this dataset, four subsets of drugs were collected manually according to the pharmacological activity, which were (1) Angiotensin Converting Enzyme Inhibitors and Angiotensin II Receptor Antagonists, (2) Calcium Channel Blockers, (3) Sodium and Potassium Channels Blockers and (4) Quinolone Antimicrobial Agents.

Molecular Descriptors

Parameter Client(Tetko et al., 2005; VCCLAB, http://www.vcclab.org, 2005)was used to produce the molecular descriptors. There are more than 3000 descriptors that can be calculated for each molecule. Each descriptor belongs to one of the 24 groups as shown in Table 1.

Descriptors used in each model were selected according to the following steps:

Table 1. Calculated 24 groups of descriptors in Parameter Client

N	Group	Count
1	Constitutional descriptors	47
2	Topological descriptors	118
3	Walk and path counts	47
4	Information indices	47
5	Molecular properties	29
6	Geometrical descriptors	73
7	2D autocorrelations	96
8	3D-MoRSE descriptors	160
9	WHIM descriptors	99
10	GETAWAY descriptors	197
11	RDF descriptors	149
12	Connectivity indices	33
13	Edge adjacency indices	107
14	Topological charge indices	21
15	Eigenvalue-based indices	44
16	BCUT descriptors	64
17	Randic molecular profiles	41
18	Functional group counts	121
19	Atom-centred fragments	120
20	ET-state Indices	>300
21	ET-state Properties	3
22	GSFRAG Descriptor	307
23	GSFRAG-L Descriptor	886
24	Charge descriptors	14

1. Removing the redundant descriptors of each group. The pairwise correlation of all descriptors (and bioavailability) in each group were calculated. Then the descriptors which are not statistically significantly correlated to bioavailability were removed. Furthermore, a descriptor was eliminated if the correlation coefficient was higher than 0.85. The remainder descriptors were kept for the following analysis.

2. Selecting proper descriptors from the combination of the remainder descriptors (from step1) of each group (for building model).

The pairwise correlation of all descriptors (and bioavailability) in each combination was done. A descriptor was eliminated if the correlation coefficient was higher than 0.85. After that, from the remainder descriptors the stepwise linear regression variable selection method was used for choosing the descriptors. Stepwise variable entry and removal examines the variables in the block at each step for entry or removal (Criteria: Probability of F to enter <=0.50, Probability of F to remove >=0.100).

Support Vector Machine (SVM)

The SVM technique is widely used for its classification ability. There exist a number of excellent introductions into SVM (Vapnik & Chapelle, 2000; Cortes & Vapnik, 1995; Scholkopf et al., 1997; Burges, 1998). SVM originated as an implementation of Vapnik's Structural Risk Minimization (SRM) principle from statistical learning theory. The special property of SVMs is that they simultaneously minimize the empirical classification error and maximize the geometric margin. Thus, SVM is also known as a maximum margin classifier.

SVMs can also be applied to regression problems by the introduction of an alternative loss function. In this study, LIBSVM software developed by Chang and Lin was used for SVM analysis (Chang & Lin, 2001). There are four basic kernels in LIBSVM software. The kernel matrix using sigmoid may not be positive definite and in general its accuracy is not better than RBF. Polynomial kernels could be used but if a high degree is used, numerical difficulties tend to happen. Thus, Radial Basis Function (RBF) which is suggested as a reasonable first choice was used in this work. The RBF kernel nonlinearly maps samples into a higher dimensional space, so it can handle the case when the relation between property and attributes is nonlinear. There are four types of SVM in LIBSVM software. The type of SVM was set as nu-SVR (nu-support vector regression) for building regression models. "nu" in nu-SVR approximates the fraction of training errors and support vectors.

Prediction Models for Bioavailability

Through the descriptor selection method above, four models were built based on the selected descriptors using MLR (Multiple Linear Regression) and SVM (Support Vector Machine), respectively.

Models 1. 19 drugs of the Angiotensin Converting Enzyme Inhibitors or Angiotensin II Receptor Antagonists were chosen for building quantitative model. Four descriptors were selected according to the selection method above. The intercorrelations between the four descriptors and bioavailability are given in Table 2.

In the selected four descriptors, one can see that H8e and R7m from GETAWAY descriptors show high correlation with bioavailability, which can be deduced that bioavailability of Angiotensin Converting Enzyme Inhibitors or Angiotensin II Receptor Antagonists is related to the atomic weightings such as atomic mass and electronegativity.

With the four selected descriptors, prediction models were built by the MLR (Multiple Linear Regression) and SVM (Support Vector Machine), respectively. Leave-one-out (Loo) cross validation was performed to validate the obtained models. For the MLR model, r=0.91, MAE (Mean absolute error) =5.97, r_{Loo}=0.85; for the SVM model, r=0.91, MAE (Mean absolute error) =6.12, r_{Loo}=0.89. It can be seen from the validation results that both models obtained are reliable. The results of Models 1 were shown in Figure 1.

Models 2. 16 drugs of Calcium Channel Blockers were chosen for building quantitative model. Five descriptors were selected according to the selection method above. The intercorrelations between the five descriptors and bioavailability are given in Table 3.

In the selected five descriptors, SsssN(ar) from ET-state indices show a high correlation with bioavailability. It can be seen that the aromatic amines group plays an important role for bioavailability of Calcium Channel Blockers.

With the five selected descriptors, prediction models were built by the MLR (Multiple Linear Regression) and SVM (Support Vector Machine), respectively. Leave-one-out (Loo) cross validation was performed to validate the obtained models. For the MLR model, r=0.98, MAE (Mean absolute error)=2.93, r_{Loo}=0.96; for the SVM model, r=0.98, MAE (Mean absolute error) =3.46, r_{Loo}=0.94. It can be seen from the validation results that both models obtained are reliable. The results of Models 2 were shown in Figure 2.

Models 3. 17 drugs of Sodium and Potassium Channels Blockers were chosen for building quantitative model. Five descriptors were selected according to the selection method above.

Table 2. The intercorrelations between the four descriptors and bioavailability data for 19 Angiotensin Converting Enzyme Inhibitors or Angiotensin II Receptor Antagonists

	Bioavailability	EEig01r	H8e	R7m	FDI
Bioavailability	1				
EEig01r	0.34	1			
H8e	-0.53	0.26	1		
R7m	-0.71	-0.28	0.25	1	
FDI	0.37	0.022	0.18	-0.38	1

EEig01r (edge adjacency indices): eigenvalue 01 from edge adj. matrix weighted by resonance integrals; H8e (GETAWAY): H autocorrelation of lag 8 / weighted by atomic Sanderson electronegativities; R7m (GETAWAY): R autocorrelation of lag 7 / weighted by atomic masses; FDI (geometrical): folding degree index. (http://www.vcclab.org/lab/indexhlp/)

Figure 1. (a) Calculated vs. experimental values of bioavailability for 19 Angiotensin Converting Enzyme Inhibitors or Angiotensin II Receptor Antagonists in Models 1 by MLR analysis. For the dataset of this model, r=0.91, MAE (Mean absolute error) =5.97, r_{Loo} =0.85. (b) Calculated vs. experimental values of bioavailability for 19 Angiotensin Converting Enzyme Inhibitors or Angiotensin II Receptor Antagonists in Models 1 by SVM. For the dataset of this model, r=0.91, MAE (Mean absolute error) =6.12, r_{Loo} =0.89.

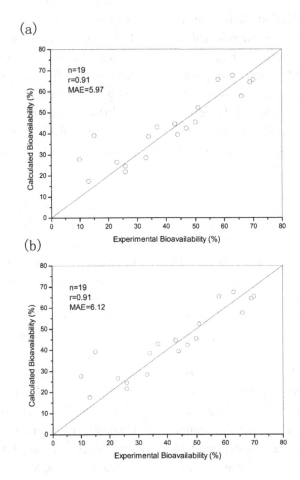

Table 3. The intercorrelations between the five descriptors and bioavailability data for 16 Calcium Channel Blockers

	Bioavailability	ZM2V	RDF035m	R6u	G2v	SsssN(ar)
Bioavailability	1					
ZM2V	-0.55	1				
RDF035m	-0.57	0.57	1			
R6u	0.29	-0.50	-0.10	1		
G2v	-0.25	0.069	-0.0038	0.21	1	
SsssN(ar)	-0.79	0.37	0.32	0.17	0.19	1

ZM2V (topological descriptor): second Zagreb index by valence vertex degrees; RDF035m (RDF descriptors): Radial Distribution Function - 3.5 / weighted by atomic masses; R6u (GETAWAY): R autocorrelation of lag 6 / unweighted; G2v (WHIM): 2nd component symmetry directional WHIM index / weighted by atomic van der Waals volumes; SsssN(ar) (ET-state indices): ET-state indices of aromatic amines group. (http://www.vcclab.org/lab/indexhlp/)

Figure 2. (a) Calculated vs. experimental values of bioavailability for 16 Calcium Channel Blockers in Models 2 by MLR analysis. For the dataset of this model, r=0.98, MAE =2.93, r_{Loo} =0.96. (b) Calculated vs. experimental values of bioavailability for 16 Calcium Channel Blockers in Models 2 by SVM. For the dataset of this model, r=0.98, MAE =3.46, r_{Loo} =0.94.

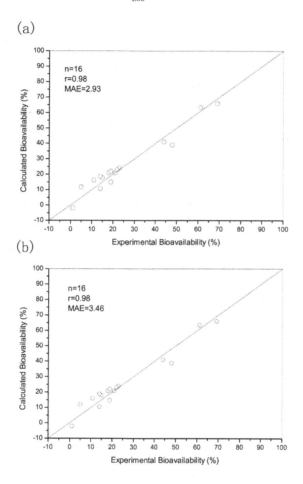

The intercorrelations between the five descriptors and bioavailability are given in Table 4.

Among the selected five descriptors, Mor21u from 3D-MoRSE descriptors and MATS7m from 2D autocorrelations descriptors have shown good correlation with bioavailability. It can be seen that bioavailability of Sodium and Potassium Channels Blockers is related to the summer of atomic mass by certain function.

With the five selected descriptors, prediction models were built by the MLR (Multiple Linear Regression) and SVM (Support Vector Machine), respectively. Leave-one-out (Loo) cross validation was performed to validate the obtained models. For the MLR model, r=0.97, MAE (Mean absolute error)=6.29, r_{Loo}=0.93; for the SVM model, r=0.98, MAE (Mean absolute error) =6.11, r_{Loo}=0.94. It can be seen from the validation results that both models obtained are reliable. The results of Models 3 were shown in Figure 3.

Model 4. 19 drugs which belong to Quinolone Antimicrobial Agents were chosen for building quantitative model. Three descriptors were selected according to the selection method above. The intercorrelations between the three descriptors and bioavailability are given in Table 5.

Table 4. The intercorrelations between the five descriptors and bioavailability data for 17 Sodium and Potassium Channels Blockers

	Bioavailability	EEig15r	nCbH	MATS7m	GATS1m	Mor21u
Bioavailability	1					
EEig15r	-0.24	1				
nCbH	-0.29	0.46	1			
MATS7m	-0.60	0.18	0.18	1		
GATS1m	0.34	-0.14	0.10	0.11	1	
Mor21u	0.66	-0.55	-0.72	-0.41	-0.20	1

EEig15r (edge adjacency indices): Eigenvalue 15 from edge adj. matrix weighted by resonance integrals; nCbH (functional group counts): number of unsubstituted benzene C(sp2); MATS7m (2D autocorrelations): Moran autocorrelation- lag 7 / weighted by atomic masses; GATS1m (2D autocorrelations): Geary autocorrelation- lag 1 / weighted by atomic masses; Mor21u (3D-MoRSE): 3D-MoRSE - signal 21 / unweighted. (http://www.vcclab.org/lab/indexhlp/)

Figure 3. (a) Calculated vs. experimental values of bioavailability for 17 Sodium and Potassium Channels Blockers in Models 3 by MLR analysis. For the dataset of this model, r=0.97, MAE =6.29, r_{Loo}=0.93. (b) Calculated vs. experimental values of bioavailability for 17 Sodium and Potassium Channels Blockers in Models 3 by SVM. For the dataset of this model, r=0.98, MAE =6.11, r_{Loo}=0.94.

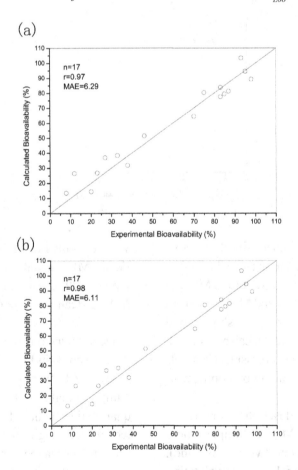

Table 5. The intercorrelations between the three descriptors and bioavailability data for 19 Quinolone Antimicrobial Agents

	Bioavailability	**Infective-50**	**R4e+**	**SdssC**
Bioavailability	1			
Infective-50	-0.24	1		
R4e+	-0.32	0.005	1	
SdssC	-0.80	-0.11	0.63	1

Infective-50 (molecular properties): Ghose-Viswanadhan-Wendoloski anti-infective-like index at 50%; R4e+ (GETAWAY): R maximal autocorrelation of lag 4 / weighted by atomic Sanderson electronegativities; SdssC (ET-state indices): ET-state indices of C atom. (http://www.vcclab.org/lab/indexhlp/)

It is not surprised that Infective-50 which represents the anti-infective-like index at 50% was selected because of the pharmacological activity of Quinolone Antimicrobial Agents. The descriptor SdssC, representing a substructure of the carbon atom with two single bonds and one double bond, has shown a high correlation with bioavailability of Quinolone Antimicrobial Agents.

With the five selected descriptors, prediction models were built by the MLR (Multiple Linear Regression) and SVM (Support Vector Machine), respectively. Leave-one-out (Loo) cross validation was performed to validate the obtained models. For the MLR model, r=0.91, MAE (Mean absolute error)=6.72, r_{Loo}=0.81; for the SVM model, r=0.90, MAE (Mean absolute error) =7.11, r_{Loo}=0.84. It can be seen from the validation results that both models obtained are reliable. The results of Models 4 were shown in Figure 4.

From these four models, one can see that models of different subsets of drugs are built based on sets of different descriptors. Obviously, it can be seen GETAWAY descriptors are frequently used in the models. GETAWAY descriptors match 3D-molecular geometry provided by the molecular influence matrix and atom relatedness by molecular topology, with chemical information by using different atomic property weightings. In this study, it can be seen that bioavailability of the subset of compounds with the same pharma-cological activity is related to the atomic weightings such as atomic mass and electronegativity.

The models of these four subsets have performed well. However, the prediction power for the external compounds still need to be validated and the number of the training data needs to be increased to obtain more powerful models.

CONCLUSION

In this study, quantitative structure activity relationship was performed on four subsets of drugs which were (1) Angiotensin Converting Enzyme Inhibitors and Angiotensin II Receptor Antagonists, (2) Calcium Channel Blockers, (3) Sodium and Potassium Channels Blockers and (4) Quinolone Antimicrobial Agents.

By now, QSAR models do not work well for the prediction of oral bioavailability because there are a variety of pharmacokinetic factors influencing human oral bioavailability, such as hepatic metabolism. Thus, it is a very promising research direction to introduce descriptors to model the first pass metabolism in the future. Another research direction can be seen from our study, which is to build models for compounds owning specific substructure or the same pharmacological activity. One can see that good quantitative relationship can be built for these four subsets of drugs which were considered having the same pharmacological activity.

Figure 4. (a) Calculated vs. experimental values of bioavailability for 19 Quinolone Antimicrobial Agents in Models 4 by MLR analysis. For the dataset of this model, r=0.91, MAE =6.72, r_{Loo}=0.81. (b) Calculated vs. experimental values of bioavailability for 19 Quinolone Antimicrobial Agents in Models 4 by SVM. For the dataset of this model, r=0.90, MAE =7.11, r_{Loo}=0.84.

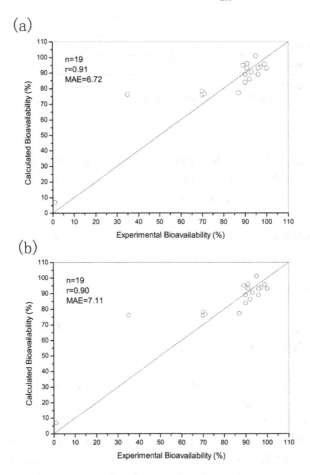

The pharmacokinetic factors influencing human oral bioavailability are just too divers. Due to these influences, no general model for the prediction of human oral bioavailability for a diverse set of compounds might be achievable. However, explorations into subsets of compounds were performed and good quantitative relationship was shown for subsets of drugs, which have similar structure or the same pharmacological activity. Further wok will prove the applicability of this approach extends to other subsets of compounds with similar structure or the same pharmacological activity.

ACKNOWLEDGMENT

This work was supported by the National Natural Science Foundation of China (20605003 and 20975011), National High Tech Project (2006AA02Z337), the Fundamental Research Funds for the Central Universities (ZZ0911) of Beijing University of Chemical Technology, and the Scientific Research Foundation of Graduate School (09Li001) of Beijing University of Chemical and Technology.

REFERENCES

Andrews, C. W., Bennett, L., & Yu, L. X. (2000). Predicting Human Oral Bioavailability of a Compound: Development of a Novel Quantitative Structure-Bioavailability Relationship. *Pharmaceutical Research*, *17*(6), 639–644. doi:10.1023/A:1007556711109

Beresford, A. P., Selick, H. E., & Tarbit, M. H. (2002). The emerging importance of predictive ADME simulation in drug discovery. *Drug Discovery Today*, *7*(2), 109–116. doi:10.1016/S1359-6446(01)02100-6

Burges, C. J. C. (1998). A tutorial on Support Vector Machines for pattern recognition. *Data Mining and Knowledge Discovery*, *2*(2), 121–167. doi:10.1023/A:1009715923555

Chang, C. C., & Lin, C. J. (2001). LIBSVM: a library for support vector machine. Software available at http://www.csie.ntu.edu.tw/~cjlin/libsvm.

Cortes, C., & Vapnik, V. (1995). Support-Vector Networks. *Machine Learning*, *20*(3), 273–297. doi:10.1007/BF00994018

Hall, S. D., Thummel, K. E., Watkins, P. B., Lown, K. S., Benet, L. Z., & Paine, M. F. (1999). Molecular and physical mechanisms of first pass extraction. *Drug Metabolism and Disposition: the Biological Fate of Chemicals*, *27*(2), 161–166.

Hirono, S., Nakagome, I., Hirano, H., Matsushita, Y., Yoshi, F., & Moriguchi, I. (1994). Noncongeneric structure-pharmacokinetic property correlation studies using fuzzy adaptive least-squares: Oral bioavailability. *Biological & Pharmaceutical Bulletin*, *17*(2), 306.

Hou, T. J., Wang, J. M., Zhang, W., & Xu, X. J. (2007). ADME Evaluation in Drug Discovery. 6. Can Oral Bioavailability in Humans Be Effectively Predicted by Simple Molecular Property-Based Rules? *Journal of Chemical Information and Modeling*, *47*(2), 460–463. doi:10.1021/ci6003515

Hou, T. J., & Xu, X. J. (2004). Recent development and application of virtual screening in drug discovery: An overview. *Current Pharmaceutical Design*, *10*(9), 1011–1033. doi:10.2174/1381612043452721

Lampen, A., Zhang, Y., Hackbarth, I., Benet, L. Z., Sewing, K. F., & Christians, U. (1998). Metabolism and transport of the acrolide immunosuppresant sirolimus in the small intestine. *The Journal of Pharmacology and Experimental Therapeutics*, *285*(3), 1104–1112.

Lu, J. J., Crimin, K., Goodwin, J. T., Crivori, P., Orrenius, C., & Xing, L. (2004). Influence of molecular flexibility and polar surface area metrics on oral bioavailability in the rat. *Journal of Medicinal Chemistry*, *47*(24), 6104–6107. doi:10.1021/jm0306529

Scholkopf, B., Sung, K. K., Burges, C. J. C., Girosi, F., Niyogi, P., Poggio, T., & Vapnik, V. (1997). Comparing support vector machines with Gaussian kernels to radial basis function classifiers. *IEEE Transactions on Signal Processing*, *45*(11), 2758–2765. doi:10.1109/78.650102

Tetko, I. V., Gasteiger, J., Todeschini, R., Mauri, A., Livingstone, D., & Ertl, P. (2005). Virtual computational chemistry laboratory - design and description. *Journal of Computer-Aided Molecular Design*, *19*(6), 453–463. doi:10.1007/s10822-005-8694-y

Turner, J. V., Glass, B. D., & Agatonovic-Kustrin, S. (2003). Prediction of drug bioavailability based on molecular structure. *Analytica Chimica Acta*, *485*(1), 89–102. doi:10.1016/S0003-2670(03)00406-9

Turner, J. V., Maddalena, D. J., & Agatonovic-Kustrin, S. (2004). Bioavailability Prediction Based on Molecular Structure for a Diverse Series of Drugs. *Pharmaceutical Research*, *21*(1), 68–82. doi:10.1023/B:PHAM.0000012154.09631.26

Van Asperen, J., Van Tellingen, O., & Beijnen, J. H. (1998). The pharmacological role of P-glycoprotein in the intestinal epithelium. *Pharmaceutical Research, 37*(6), 429–435. doi:10.1006/phrs.1998.0326

Van de Waterbeemd, H., Smith, D. A., Beaumont, K., & Walker, D. K. (2001). Property-Based Design: Optimization of Drug Absorption and Pharmacokinetics. *Journal of Medicinal Chemistry, 44*(9), 1313–1333. doi:10.1021/jm000407e

Vapnik, V., & Chapelle, O. (2000). Bounds on error expectation for support vector machines. *Neural Computation, 12*(9), 2013–2036. doi:10.1162/089976600300015042

VCCLAB. (2005). *Virtual Computational Chemistry Laboratory*. Retrieved from http://www.vcclab.org

Veber, D. F., Johnson, S. R., Cheng, H. Y., Smith, B. R., Ward, K. W., & Kopple, K. D. (2002). Molecular properties that influence the oral bioavailability of drug candidates. *Journal of Medicinal Chemistry, 45*(12), 2615–2623. doi:10.1021/jm020017n

Wang, J. M., Krudy, G., Xie, X. Q., Wu, C. D., & Holland, G. (2006). Genetic Algorithm-Optimized QSPR Models for Bioavailability, Protein Binding, and Urinary Excretion. *Journal of Chemical Information and Modeling, 46*(6), 2674–2683. doi:10.1021/ci060087t

Wang, Z., Yan, A. X., Yuan, Q. P., & Gasteiger, J. (2008). Explorations into Modeling Human Oral Bioavailability. *European Journal of Medicinal Chemistry, 43*(11), 2442–2452. doi:10.1016/j.ejmech.2008.05.017

Yoshida, F., & Topliss, J. G. (2000). QSAR model for drug human oral bioavailability. *Journal of Medicinal Chemistry, 43*(13), 2575–2585. doi:10.1021/jm0000564

ADDITIONAL READING

Andrew, R. L. (2001). *Molecular modelling: principles and applications*. Englewood Cliffs, N.J: Prentice Hall.

Bjorkroth, J. P., Pakkanen, T. A., Lindroos, J., Pohjala, E., Hanhijarvi, H., & Lauren, L. (1991). Comparative molecular field analysis of some clodronic acid eaters. *Journal of Medicinal Chemistry, 34*(8), 2338–2343. doi:10.1021/jm00112a004

Brown, F. K. (1998). Chapter 35. Chemoinformatics: What is it and How does it Impact Drug Discovery. *Annual Reports in Medicinal Chemistry, 33*, 375–384. doi:10.1016/S0065-7743(08)61100-8

Ekins, S., & Rose, J. (2002). In silico ADME/Tox: the state of the art. *Journal of Molecular Graphics & Modelling, 20*(4), 305–309. doi:10.1016/S1093-3263(01)00127-9

Gasteiger, J., & Engel, T. (2004). *Chemoinformatics: A Textbook*. New York: Wiley.

Hann, M., & Green, R. (1999). Chemoinformatics - a new name for an old problem? *Current Opinion in Chemical Biology, 3*(4), 379–383. doi:10.1016/S1367-5931(99)80057-X

Hodgson, J. (2001). ADMET-turning chemicals into drugs. *Nature Biotechnology, 19*, 722–726. doi:10.1038/90761

Leonard, J. T., & Roy, K. (2006). On selection of training and test sets for the development of predictive QSAR models. *QSAR & Combinatorial Science, 25*(3), 235–251. doi:10.1002/qsar.200510161

Livingstone, D. J. (2000). The Characterization of Chemical Structures Using Molecular Properties - A Survey. *Journal of Chemical Information and Computer Sciences, 40*(2), 195–209. doi:10.1021/ci990162i

Lombardo, F., Gifford, E., & Shalaeva, M. Y. (2003). In Silico ADME Prediction: Data, Models, Facts and Myths. *Mini Reviews in Medicinal Chemistry*, *3*(8), 861–875. doi:10.2174/1389557033487629

Martin, Y. C. (2005). A bioavailability score. *Journal of Medicinal Chemistry*, *48*(9), 3164–3170. doi:10.1021/jm0492002

Nikolova, N., & Jaworska, J. (2003). Approaches to Measure Chemical Similarity - a review. *QSAR & Combinatorial Science*, *22*(9-10), 1006–1026. doi:10.1002/qsar.200330831

Purcell, W. P., Bass, G. E., & Clayton, J. M. (1973). Experimental Determination of Partition Coefficients. In Purcell, W. P. (Ed.), *Strategy of Drug Design: A Molecular Guide to Biological Activity* (pp. 126–142). New York: Wiley.

Roy, K. (2007). On some aspects of validation of predictive quantitative structure-activity relationship models. *Expert Opin. Drug Dis.*, *2*(12), 1567–1577. doi:10.1517/17460441.2.12.1567

Selassie, C. D. (2003). History of Quantitative Structure-Activity Relationships. In Abraham, D. J. (Ed.), *Burger's medicinal Chemistry and Drug Discovery* (6th ed., pp. 1–48). New York: Wiley. doi:10.1002/0471266949.bmc001

Selick, H. E., Beresford, A. P., & Tarbit, M. H. (2002). The emerging importance of predictive ADME simulation in drug discovery. *Drug Discovery Today*, *7*(2), 109–116. doi:10.1016/S1359-6446(01)02100-6

Svetnik, V., Liaw, A., Tong, C., Culberson, J. C., Sheridan, R. P., & Bradley, P. F. (2003). A Classification and Regression Tool for Compound Classification and QSAR Modeling. *Journal of Chemical Information and Computer Sciences*, *43*(6), 1947–1958. doi:10.1021/ci034160g

Sykora, V. J., & Leahy, D. E. (2008). Chemical Descriptors Library (CDL): A Generic, Open Source Software Library for Chemical Informatics. *Journal of Chemical Information and Modeling*, *48*(10), 1931–1942. doi:10.1021/ci800135h

Tropsha, A. (2003). Recent trends in quantitative structure-activity relationships. In Abraham, D. J. (Ed.), *Burger's medicinal chemistry and drug discovery* (pp. 49–77). New York: Wiley. doi:10.1002/0471266949.bmc002

Wold, S., & Eriksson, L. (1995). Statistical validation of QSAR results. In Van de Waterbeemd, H. (Ed.), *Chemometric methods in molecular design* (pp. 309–318). Weinheim: VCH. doi:10.1002/9783527615452.ch5

Xue, Y., Li, Z. R., Yap, C. W., Sun, L. Z., Chen, X., & Chen, Y. Z. (2004). Effect of molecular descriptor feature selection in support vector machine classification of pharmacokinetic and toxicological properties of chemical agents. *Journal of Chemical Information and Computer Sciences*, *44*(5), 1630–1638. doi:10.1021/ci049869h

Yang, S. Y., & Jefferson, G. B. (1996). Quantative structure-activity relationship study with micellar electrokinetic chromatography influence of surfactant type and mixer miceller on estimation of hydrophobicity and bioavailability. *Journal of Chromatography. A*, *721*(2), 323–328. doi:10.1016/0021-9673(95)00773-3

KEY TERMS AND DEFINITIONS

Human Oral Bioavailability: Bioavailability represents the percentage of an oral dose which is able to produce a pharmacological activity, in other words, the fraction of the oral dose that reaches the arterial blood in an active form.

MLR: Multiple Linear Regression; it attempts to model the relationship between two or more explanatory variables and a response variable by fitting a linear equation to observed data.

ADME: Absorption, Distribution, Metabolism, and Excretion; it is used to describe the disposition of a pharmaceutical compound within an organism.

QSAR: Quantitative Structures-Activity Relationships; it is the process by which chemical structure is quantitatively correlated with a well defined process, such as biological activity or chemical reactivity.

SVM: Support Vector Machine, a set of related supervised learning methods used for classification and regression.

Chapter 14

In Silico Prediction of Blood Brain Barrier Permeability:
A Support Vector Machine Model

Zhi Wang
Beijing University of Chemical Technology, China

Aixia Yan
Beijing University of Chemical Technology, China

Jiaxuan Li
Beijing University of Chemical Technology, China

ABSTRACT

The ability of penetration of the blood-brain barrier is an important property for the development of Central Nervous System drugs, which is commonly expressed by logBB (logBB = log(C_{brain}/C_{blood}). In this work, a support vector machine was used to build quantitative models of blood brain barrier permeability. Molecular descriptors for 182 compounds were calculated by ADRIANA.Code and 12 descriptors were selected using the automatic variable selection function in Weka. Based on two common physicochemical descriptors (xlogP and Topological Polar Surface Area (TPSA)) and 10 2D property autocorrelation descriptors on atom pair properties, an SVM regression model was built. The built model was validated by an external test set. The reliable predictions of the test set demonstrate that this model performs well and can be used for estimation of logBB values for drug and drug-like molecules.

INTRODUCTION

In the discovery and development process of a central nervous system (CNS) targeted drug, one important property is the ability of a drug to penetrate the blood-brain barrier (BBB) (Norinder et

al., 2002). Usually, BB is defined as the brain-blood concentration ratio of a compound at steady state, which is commonly expressed by logBB (logBB = log(C_{brain}/C_{blood}), which C_{brain} and C_{blood} are the equilibrium concentrations of the drug in the brain and the blood, respectively) to present the extent of a drug passing through the blood-brain barrier.

DOI: 10.4018/978-1-60960-064-8.ch014

However, it is expensive and time-consuming to obtain the experimental data on blood-brain distribution ratio of a compound. Therefore, it is necessary to use a reliable in silico model to predict logBB for drug candidates.

Numerous models on quantitative prediction of logBB models have been published. Earlier reported models were built by Linear Regression and Multiple Linear Regression (MLR) based on some simple physicochemical descriptors. Young et al. (1988) used the important physicochemical properties (ΔlogP) for brain penetration employing the linear regression method on centrally acting histamine H_2 antagonists. Based on Young's data set, Van de Waterbeemd and Kansy (1992) investigated the importance of hydrogen bonding on logBB by the MLR method and obtained a good relationship with logBB using the Polar Surface Area (PSA) and molecular volume as descriptors. Calder and Ganellin (1994) also investigated Young's data set using experimental ΔlogP values and theoretically computed descriptors such as PSA and molecular volume by the MLR method.

In order to get more reliable models, researchers tried to (1) enlarge the data set to extend the chemical space (Abraham et al., 1994; Salminen et al,. 1997; Subramanian & Kitchen, 2003; Garg & Verma, 2006); (2) investigate more related descriptors (Lombardo, 1996; Kaliszan & Markuszewski, 1996; Clark, 1999; Ertl et al., 2000; Hutter, 2003; Hou & Xu, 2003; Abraham, 2004; Sun, 2004); and (3) build models by advanced data mining methods such as Partial Least Square (PLS) analysis, Genetic Algorithms and Artificial Neural Networks (Norinder et al., 1998; Luco, 1999; Platts et al., 2001; Iyer et al., 2002; Winkler & Burden, 2004; Yap & Chen, 2005).

In our recent research, it is found that 2D property autocorrelation descriptors have worked well in determining whether a compound may cross the blood-brain barrier or not (Wang et al., 2009). In this work, the 2D property autocorrelation descriptors and some other 2D physicochemical descriptors were used to build a quantitative model

for prediction of logBB using a Support Vector Machine (SVM).

MATERIALS AND METHODS

Data Set

182 compounds with logBB experimental values and SMILES strings were collected from published work by Garg & Verma (2006). The experimental logBB of all these compounds were provided in Appendix. CORINA (CORINA, Molecular Networks GmbH, Erlangen, Germany, http://www.molecular-networks.com) was used to add hydrogen atoms and to compute 3D structures. For each molecule, only a single 3D conformation was generated. Then the whole data set were spilt into as training set (122 compounds) and test set (60 compounds) randomly. The training set (122 compounds) was subjected to 10-fold cross validation, and the test set (60 compounds) was used as an external validation set.

Molecular Descriptors

In our study, a total of 62 descriptors were calculated using ADRIANA.Code (ADRIANA.Code, Molecular Networks GmbH, Erlangen, Germany, http://www.molecular-networks.com), including 6 global molecular descriptors and 56 2D property autocorrelation descriptors.

Global molecular descriptors, expressed by a single value, represent a chemical structure by a structural, chemical or physicochemical feature or property of the molecule. In this study, six important molecular physicochemical descriptors related to brain penetration were calculated. They are molecular weight, number of H-bond donors, number of H-bond acceptors, topological polar surface area (TPSA) (Ertl et al., 2000), octanol/water distribution coefficient (xlogP) (Wang et al., 2000) and mean molecular polarizability (Miller, 1990).

The 2D property autocorrelation uses the molecular 2D structure and atom pair properties as a basis to obtain vectorial molecular descriptors (Bauknecht et al., 1996; Moreau et al, 1980). The atom pair properties are summed up for certain topological distances which count the number of bonds on the shortest path between two atoms. The 2D molecular autocorrelation vectors (Wagener et al., 1995) are calculated by the following equation (Equation 1):

$$A\left(d\right) = \sum_{ij} p_i p_j \qquad (1)$$

$A(d)$ is the topological autocorrelation coefficient referring to atom pairs i, j which are separated by d bonds. $p_i p_j$ is an atomic property such as partial atomic charge on atom i or j, respectively. Thus, for each compound, a series of coefficients for different topological distances d, a so-called autocorrelation vector is obtained. The 2D molecular autocorrelation vectors (Wagener et al., 1995) were calculated based on the following seven atomic properties: σ charge (SigChg) (Gasteiger & Marsili, 1978; Gasteiger & Marsili, 1980), π charge (PiChg), total charges (TotChg), σ electronegativity (SigEN), π electronegativity (PiEN), lone-pair electronegativity (LpEN) and atomic polarizability (Apolariz) (Gasteiger & Hutchings, 1984). For each property, the autocorrelation values for eight distances (0 to 7 bonds) were calculated.

Taking ethanol for example (Chart 1), ethanol has three pairs of atoms that are separated by four bonds: H1-H2, H1-H3 and H1-H4. Thus, the corresponding autocorrelation for the topological distance four computes to

$$A(4) = p_1 p_2 + p_1 p_3 + p_1 p_4 \qquad (2)$$

Chart 1. An Example for Autocorrelation Coefficient Calculation

Support Vector Machine (SVM)

The SVM technique is widely used for its classification ability. There exist a number of excellent introductions for SVM (Vapnik & Chapelle, 2000; Cortes & Vapnik, 1995; Scholkopf et al., 1997; Burges, 1998). SVM originated as an implementation of Vapnik's Structural Risk Minimization (SRM) principle from statistical learning theory. The special property of SVMs is that they simultaneously minimize the empirical classification error and maximize the geometric margin. Thus, SVM is also known as a maximum margin classifier.

SVMs can also be applied to regression problems by the introduction of an alternative loss function. In this study, LIBSVM software developed by Chang and Lin was used for SVM analysis (Chang & Lin, 2001). There are four basic kernels in LIBSVM software. The kernel matrix using sigmoid may not be positive definite and in general its accuracy is not better than RBF. Polynomial kernels could be used but if a high degree is used, numerical difficulties tend to happen. Thus, Radial Basis Function (RBF) which is suggested as a reasonable first choice was used in this work. The RBF kernel nonlinearly maps samples into a higher dimensional space, so it can handle the case when the relation between property and attributes is nonlinear. There are four types of SVM in LIBSVM software. The type of SVM was set as nu-SVR (nu-support vector regression) for building regression models. "nu" in nu-SVR approximates the fraction of training errors and support vectors.

RESULTS AND DISCUSSION

Automatic Variable Selection

The program Weka (Weka, 2007; Witten & Frank, 2005) was used to automatically select subsets of variables that are highly correlated with the class while having low intercorrelation (attribute evaluator CfsSubsetEval combined with either the BestFirst or the ExhaustiveSearch search method). In this work, the selection of variables was repeated for 10-fold during cross-validation. The attribute evaluator CfsSubsetEval was used to estimate the worth of a subset of descriptors, which is accomplished by considering the individual predictive ability of each feature and the intercorrelation between these features. Automatic variable selection using the BestFirst method yielded a subset of 12 descriptors (Table 1). The occurrence of how often these descriptors were chosen in the 10-fold cross-validation run is given in the last column of this table. The details of the 12 descriptors and the experimental logBB of all these compounds were provided in Appendix.

It is not surprising that XlogP and TPSA were chosen because these two descriptors are useful to interpret the mechanism of passive transportation and are also used in other logBB models (Young et al., 1988; Van de Waterbeemd & Kansy, 1992; Calder & Ganellin, 1994; Garg & Verma, 2006).

There are 10 2D autocorrelation descriptors that were selected. These descriptors lend themselves to a very clear physicochemical interpretation. The first member of an autocorrelation vector is always the product of an atomic property with itself, thus the following descriptors were selected: The sum over all atoms of the

Table 1. Descriptors Selected by Automatic Variable Selection and Percentage of Their Occurrence in a 10-fold Cross-Validated Variable Selection

Descriptors	Description			Occurrence in 10-fold cross validation[%]
XlogP	octanol/water distribution coefficient			100
TPSA	topological polar surface area			100
2DACorr_SigChg_5	2D-autocorrelation	σ-charge	Bond distance 4	80
2DACorr_SigChg_7	2D-autocorrelation	σ-charge	Bond distance 6	40
2DACorr_SigChg_8	2D-autocorrelation	σ-charge	Bond distance 7	70
2DACorr_PiChg_1	2D-autocorrelation	π-charge	Bond distance 0	60
2DACorr_PiChg_5	2D-autocorrelation	π-charge	Bond distance 4	100
2DACorr_PiChg_7	2D-autocorrelation	π-charge	Bond distance 6	60
2DACorr_TotChg_6	2D-autocorrelation	total charges	Bond distance 5	70
2DACorr_TotChg_7	2D-autocorrelation	total charges	Bond distance 6	100
2DACorr_TotChg_8	2D-autocorrelation	total charges	Bond distance 7	100
2DACorr_SigEN_1	2D-autocorrelation	σ-electronegativity	Bond distance 0	100

Figure 1.Predicted vs. experimental values of LogBB. Using the 12 selected descriptors as inputs, SVM regression model was built based on the training set (122 compounds); test set including 60 compounds was used to validate the obtained model. For the training set of the obtained SVM model, r = 0.92, sd=0.24; for the test set, r=0.85, sd=0.29.

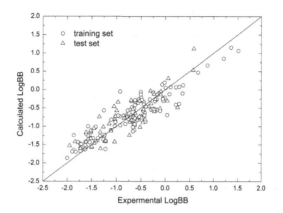

square of q_π and χ_σ ($\sum_{i=1}^{N} q_{\pi i}^2$ and $\sum_{i=1}^{N} \chi_{\sigma i}^2$) as well as the sum of all products of partial atomic charge between two atoms separated by certain number of bonds. The descriptors encoding the σ charge emphasize that the charge distribution is very important, the descriptors with q_π emphasizing the importance of the electronic distribution is the π-sphere.

Models Based on Support Vector Machine

Using the 12 selected descriptors as inputs, SVM regression model was built based on the training set (122 compounds); test set including 60 compounds was used to validate the obtained model.

When using RBF kernels, there are two parameters C and γ which are keys to achieve high training accuracy. Using gridregression.py selec-

tion tool, a grid-search is recommended on C and γ using cross-validation. Basically, pairs of (C, γ) are tried and the one with the best cross-validation accuracy is picked. Based on the 12 descriptors selected above, the best pair (C, γ) (0.5, 1) with 10-fold cross-validation rate is found through grid search. After the best pair (C, γ) was found, the whole training set is trained again to generate the final model. The result of the regression model for training set and test set were shown in Figure 1 and Table 2.

For the training set of the obtained SVM model, r = 0.92, sd=0.24, n=122; for the test set, r=0.85, sd=0.29, n=60. It can be seen the model built is reliable through the validation by test set.

Comparison with Other Models

Based on the results obtained from SVM, it was of interest to compare and validate this model with

Table 2. Regression Result of SVM Model

	N	correlation coefficient (r)	standard deviation (sd)
Training set	122	0.92	0.24
Test set	60	0.85	0.29

Table 3. Comparison with other models

parameter	Cerius2	CSBBB	PreADME	Garg's model	Our model
correlation coefficient (r)	0.66	0.76	0.76	0.90	0.90
coefficient of determination (R^2)	0.44	0.57	0.58	0.81	0.82
adjusted R square	0.43	0.57	0.58	0.81	0.81
standard error	0.52	0.43	0.54	0.30	0.29
observations	158	182	182	182	182
training set size	>120	103	88	132	122
test set size		74	42	50	60

The prediction results of other models were obtained from the work of Garg and colleagues (Garg & Verma, 2006).

Cerius2: from Accelrys Software Inc., U.S.A., based on the MLR method (Cerius2, Accelrys, Inc., 10188 Telesis Court, Suite 100, San Diego, CA 92121, U.S.A.);

CSBBB: from Chem-Silico LLC, Tewksbury, based on the ANN method (ChemSilico; http://www.chemsilico.com/CS_prBBB/BBBhome.html);

PreADME: from Research Institute of Bioinformatics and Molecular Design, Korea, based on the ANN method (PreADME, Yonsei Engineering Research Complex, Yonsei University 134 Sinchon-dong, Seodaemun-gu, Seoul 120-749, Korea.).

other models. As we used the same dataset that was employed in Garg's work, we can directly compare our model with that of Garg's work; in addition, their work included the comparisons of their models with others' (Garg & Verma, 2006), which were also listed in Table 3.

It can be seen that our SVM model shows similar prediction result with Garg's ANN model (Garg & Verma, 2006) and better than other models. The SVM model has shown very good logBB predictions ($R^2 =0.82$) followed by Garg's ANN model ($R^2 =0.81$), PreADME ($R^2 =0.58$), CSBBB ($R^2 =0.57$), and then Cerius2 ($R^2 =0.44$).

CONCLUSION

A LogBB regression model has been developed based on two common physicochemical descriptors (xlogP and TPSA) and ten 2D property autocorrelation descriptors. It is known that xlogP and TPSA are meaningful descriptors to interpret the BBB penetration mechanism. The selected 10 2D property autocorrelation descriptors also lend themselves to a very clear physicochemical interpretation.

An SVM was used to build reliable regression models. The predictions to the test set demonstrate that this model performs well and can be used for estimation of logBB values for drug and drug-like molecules.

ACKNOWLEDGMENT

This work was supported by the National Natural Science Foundation of China (20605003 and 20975011), National High Tech Project (2006AA02Z337), the Fundamental Research Funds for the Central Universities (ZZ0911) of Beijing University of Chemical Technology,and the Scientific Research Foundation of Graduate School (09Li001) of Beijing University of Chemical and Technology. We thank Molecular Networks GmbH, Erlangen, Germany for making the programs ADRIANA.Code and CORINA available for our scientific work.

REFERENCES

Abraham, M. H. (2004). The factors that influence permeation across the blood-brain barrier. *European Journal of Medicinal Chemistry, 39*(3), 235–240. doi:10.1016/j.ejmech.2003.12.004

Abraham, M. H., Chadha, H. S., & Mitchell, R. C. (1994). Hydrogen bonding. 33. Factors that influence the distribution of solutes between blood and brain. *Journal of Pharmaceutical Sciences, 83*(9), 1257–1268. doi:10.1002/jps.2600830915

ADRIANA. Code, version 1.0, Molecular Networks GmbH, Erlangen, Germany, http://www.molecular-networks.com (accessed March 2010).

Bauknecht, H., Zell, A., & Bayer, P. H., Levi, Wagener, M., Sadowski, J., & Gasteiger, J. (1996). Locating Biologically Active Compounds in Medium-Sized Heterogeneous Datasets by Topological Autocorrelation Vectors: Dopamine and Benzodiazepine Agonists. *Journal of Chemical Information and Computer Sciences, 36*(6), 1205–1213. doi:10.1021/ci960346m

Burges, C. J. C. (1998). A tutorial on Support Vector Machines for pattern recognition. *Data Mining and Knowledge Discovery, 2*(2), 121–167. doi:10.1023/A:1009715923555

Calder, J. A., & Ganellin, C. R. (1994). Predicting the brain-penetrating capability of histaminergic compounds. *Drug Design and Discovery, 11*(4), 259–268.

Cerius2, ver 4.8.1, Accelrys, Inc., 10188 Telesis Court, Suite 100, San Diego, CA 92121, U.S.A.

Chang, C. C., & Lin, C. J. (2001). LIBSVM: a library for support vector machine. Software available at http://www.csie.ntu.edu.tw/~cjlin/libsvm.

ChemSilico. CSBBB - A new Log BB Predictor; http://www.chemsilico.com/CS_ prBBB/BBBhome.html.

Clark, D. E. (1999). Rapid calculation of polar molecular surface area and its application to the prediction of transport phenomena. 2. Prediction of blood-brain barrier penetration. *Journal of Pharmaceutical Sciences, 88*(8), 815–821. doi:10.1021/js980402t

CORINA. Molecular Networks GmbH, Erlangen, Germany, http://www.molecular-networks.com (accessed March 2010).

Cortes, C., & Vapnik, V. (1995). Support-Vector Networks. *Machine Learning, 20*(3), 273–297. doi:10.1007/BF00994018

Ertl, P., Rohde, B., & Selzer, P. (2000). Fast calculation of molecular polar surface area as a sum of fragment-based contributions and its application to the prediction of drug transport properties. *Journal of Medicinal Chemistry, 43*(21), 3714–3717. doi:10.1021/jm000942e

Garg, P., & Verma, J. (2006). In Silico Prediction of Blood Brain Barrier Permeability: An Artificial Neural Network Model. *Journal of Chemical Information and Modeling, 46*(1), 289–297. doi:10.1021/ci050303i

Gasteiger, J., & Hutchings, M. G. (1984). Quantitative Models of Gas-Phase Proton Transfer Reaction Involving Alcohols, Ethers and Their Thio Analogs. Correlation Analyses Based On Residual Electronegativity and Effective Polarizability. *Journal of the American Chemical Society, 106*(22), 6489–6495. doi:10.1021/ja00334a006

Gasteiger, J., & Marsili, M. (1978). A New Method for Calculating Atomic Charges in Molecules. *Tetrahedron Letters, 19*(34), 3181–3184. doi:10.1016/S0040-4039(01)94977-9

Gasteiger, J., & Marsili, M. (1980). Iterative Partial Equalization of Orbital Electronegativity - A Rapid Access to Atomic Charges. *Tetrahedron, 36*(22), 3219–3228. doi:10.1016/0040-4020(80)80168-2

Hou, T. J., & Xu, X. J. (2003). ADME Evaluation in Drug Discovery. 3. Modeling Blood-Brain Barrier Partitioning Using Simple Molecular Descriptors. *Journal of Chemical Information and Computer Sciences, 43*(6), 766–770. doi:10.1021/ci034134i

Hutter, M. C. (2003). Prediction of blood-brain barrier permeation using quantum chemically derived information. *Journal of Computer-Aided Molecular Design, 17*(7), 415–433. doi:10.1023/A:1027359714663

Iyer, M., Mishru, R., Han, Y., & Hopfinger, A. J. (2002). Predicting blood-brain barrier partitioning of organic molecules using membrane-interaction QSAR analysis. *Pharmaceutical Research, 19*(11), 1611–1621. doi:10.1023/A:1020792909928

Kaliszan, R., & Markuszewski, M. (1996). Brain/blood distribution described by a combination of partition coefficient and molecular mass. *International Journal of Pharmaceutics, 145*(1-2), 9–16. doi:10.1016/S0378-5173(96)04712-6

Lombardo, F., Blake, J. F., & Curatolo, W. J. (1996). Computation of brain-blood partitioning of organic solutes via free energy calculations. *Journal of Medicinal Chemistry, 39*(24), 4750–4755. doi:10.1021/jm960163r

Luco, J. M. (1999). Prediction of the brain-blood distribution of a large set of drugs from structurally derived descriptors using partial least-squares (PLS) modeling. *Journal of Chemical Information and Computer Sciences, 39*(2), 396–404. doi:10.1021/ci980411n

Miller, K. J. (1990). Additivity Methods in Molecular Polarizability. *Journal of the American Chemical Society, 112*(23), 8533–8542. doi:10.1021/ja00179a044

Moreau, G., & Broto, P. (1980). The autocorrelation of a topological structure: a new molecular descriptor. *Nouveau Journal de Chimie, 4*, 359–360.

Norinder, U., & Haeberlein, M. (2002). Computational approaches to the prediction of the blood-brain distribution. *Advanced Drug Delivery Reviews, 54*(3), 291–313. doi:10.1016/S0169-409X(02)00005-4

Norinder, U., Sjoberg, P., & Osterberg, T. (1998). Theoretical calculation and prediction of brain-blood partitioning of organic solutes using MolSurf parametrization and PLS statistics. *Journal of Pharmaceutical Sciences, 87*(8), 952–959. doi:10.1021/js970439y

Platts, J. A., Abraham, M. H., Zhao, Y. H., Hersey, A., Ijaz, L., & Butina, D. (2001). Correlation and prediction of a large blood-brain distribution data sets: an LFER study. *European Journal of Medicinal Chemistry, 36*(9), 719–730. doi:10.1016/S0223-5234(01)01269-7

PreADME, ver 1.0, B138A, Yonsei Engineering Research Complex, Yonsei University 134 Sinchon-dong, Seodaemun-gu, Seoul 120-749, Korea.

Salminen, T., Pulli, A., & Taskinen, J. (1997). Relationship between immobilized artificial membrane chromatographic retention and the brain penetration of structurally diverse drugs. *J. Pharmceut. Biomed., 15*(4), 469–477. doi:10.1016/S0731-7085(96)01883-3

Scholkopf, B., Sung, K. K., Burges, C. J. C., Girosi, F., Niyogi, P., Poggio, T., & Vapnik, V. (1997). Comparing support vector machines with Gaussian kernels to radial basis function classifiers. *IEEE Transactions on Signal Processing, 45*(11), 2758–2765. doi:10.1109/78.650102

Subramanian, G., & Kitchen, D. B. (2003). Computational models to predict blood-brain barrier permeation and CNS activity. *Journal of Computer-Aided Molecular Design, 17*(10), 643–664. doi:10.1023/B:JCAM.0000017372.32162.37

Sun, H. (2004). A Universal Molecular Descriptor System for Prediction of LogP, LogS, LogBB, and Absorption. *Journal of Chemical Information and Computer Sciences, 44*(2), 748–757. doi:10.1021/ci030304f

Van de Waterbeemd, H., & Kansy, M. (1992). Hydrogen-bonding capacity and brain penetration. *Chimia, 46*(7-8), 299–303.

Vapnik, V., & Chapelle, O. (2000). Bounds on error expectation for support vector machines. *Neural Computation, 12*(9), 2013–2036. doi:10.1162/089976600300015042

Wagener, M., Sadowski, J., & Gasteiger, J. (1995). Autocorrelation of Molecular Surface Properties for Modeling Corticosteroid Binding Globulin and Cytosolic Ah Receptor Activity by Neural Networks. *Journal of the American Chemical Society, 117*(29), 7769–7775. doi:10.1021/ja00134a023

Wang, Z., Yan, A. X., & Yuan, Q. P. (2009). Classification of blood-brain barrier permeation by Kohonen's self-organizing Neural Network (KohNN) and Support Vector Machine (SVM). *QSAR & Combinatorial Science, 28*(9), 989–994. doi:10.1002/qsar.200960008

Weka: Waikato Environment for Knowledge Analysis; University of Waikato, New Zealand. http://www.cs.waikato.a c.nz/ml/weka/ (accessed March, 2010).

Winkler, D. A., & Burden, F. R. (2004). Modelling blood-brain barrier partitioning using Bayesian neural nets. *Journal of Molecular Graphics & Modelling, 22*(6), 499–505. doi:10.1016/j.jmgm.2004.03.010

Witten, I. H., & Frank, E. (2005). *Data Mining: Practical machine learning tools and techniques*. San Francisco: Morgan Kaufmann.

Yap, C. W., & Chen, Y. Z. (2005). Quantitative Structure-Pharmacokinetic Relationships for drug distribution properties by using general regression neural network. *Journal of Pharmaceutical Sciences, 94*(1), 153–168. doi:10.1002/jps.20232

Young, R. C., Mitchell, R. C., Brown, T. H., Ganellin, C. R., Griffiths, R., & Jones, M. (1988). Development of a new physicochemical model for brain penetration and its application to the design of centrally acting H2 receptor histamine antagonists. *Journal of Medicinal Chemistry, 31*(3), 656–671. doi:10.1021/jm00398a028

ADDITIONAL READING

Andrew, R. L. (2001). *Molecular modelling: principles and applications*. Englewood Cliffs, NJ: Prentice Hall.

Arbaham, M. H., Chadha, H. S., & Mitchell, R. C. (1995). Hydrogen bonding. 36. Determination of blood brain distribution using octanol-water partition coefficients. *Drug Design and Discovery, 13*(2), 123–131.

Brown, F. K. (1998). Chemoinformatics: What is it and How does it Impact Drug Discovery. *Annual Reports in Medicinal Chemistry, 33*, 375–384. doi:10.1016/S0065-7743(08)61100-8

Butina, D., Segall, M. D., & Frankcombe, K. (2002). Predicting ADME properties in silico: methods and models. *Drug Discovery Today, 7*(11), S83–S88. doi:10.1016/S1359-6446(02)02288-2

Ekins, S., & Rose, J. (2002). In silico ADME/Tox: the state of the art. *Journal of Molecular Graphics & Modelling, 20*(4), 305–309. doi:10.1016/S1093-3263(01)00127-9

Gasteiger, J., & Engel, T. (2004). *Chemoinformatics: A Textbook*. New York: Wiley.

Hann, M., & Green, R. (1999). Chemoinformatics - a new name for an old problem? *Current Opinion in Chemical Biology*, 3(4), 379–383. doi:10.1016/S1367-5931(99)80057-X

Kelder, J., Grootenhuis, P. D. J., & Bayada, D. M. (1999). Polar molecular surface as a dominating determinant for oral absorption and brain penetration of drugs. *Pharmaceutical Research*, 16(10), 1514–1519. doi:10.1023/A:1015040217741

Ooms, F., Weber, P., Carrupt, P. A., & Testa, B. (2002). A simple model to predict blood-brain barrier permeation from 3D molecular fields. *Biochimica et Biophysica Acta*, 1587(2), 118–125.

Purcell, W. P., Bass, G. E., & Clayton, J. M. (1973). Experimental Determination of Partition Coefficients. In Purcell, W. P. (Ed.), *Strategy of Drug Design: A Molecular Guide to Biological Activity* (pp. 126–142). New York: Wiley.

Roy, K. (2007). On some aspects of validation of predictive quantitative structure-activity relationship models. *Expert Opin. Drug Dis.*, 2(12), 1567–1577. doi:10.1517/17460441.2.12.1567

Selassie, C. D. (2003). History of Quantitative Structure-Activity Relationships. In Abraham, D. J. (Ed.), *Burger's medicinal Chemistry and Drug Discovery* (6th ed., pp. 1–48). New York: Wiley. doi:10.1002/0471266949.bmc001

Selick, H. E., Beresford, A. P., & Tarbit, M. H. (2002). The emerging importance of predictive ADME simulation in drug discovery. *Drug Discovery Today*, 7(2), 109–116. doi:10.1016/S1359-6446(01)02100-6

Timmerman, H., Roberto, T., Consonni, V., Mannhold, R., & Kubinyi, H. (2002). *Handbook of Molecular Descriptors*. Weinheim: Wiley-VCH.

Tropsha, A. (2003). Recent trends in quantitative structure-activity relationships. In Abraham, D. J. (Ed.), *Burger's medicinal chemistry and drug discovery* (pp. 49–77). New York: Wiley. doi:10.1002/0471266949.bmc002

Vapnik, V., & Chapelle, O. (2003). Bounds on error expectation for support vector machines. *Neural Computation*, 12(9), 2013–2036. doi:10.1162/089976600300015042

Wold, S., & Eriksson, L. (1995). Statistical validation of QSAR results. In Van de Waterbeemd, H. (Ed.), *Chemometric methods in molecular design* (pp. 309–318). Weinheim: VCH. doi:10.1002/9783527615452.ch5

Xue, Y., Li, Z. R., Yap, C. W., Sun, L. Z., Chen, X., & Chen, Y. Z. (2004). Effect of molecular descriptor feature selection in support vector machine classification of pharmacokinetic and toxicological properties of chemical agents. *Journal of Chemical Information and Computer Sciences*, 44(5), 1630–1638. doi:10.1021/ci049869h

KEY TERMS AND DEFINITIONS

BBB: Blood Brain Barrier; it is a separation of circulating blood and cerebrospinal fluid (CSF) maintained by the choroid plexus in the central nervous system.

CNS: Central Nervous System; it is the part of the nervous system that functions to coordinate the activity of all parts of the bodies of bilaterian animals—that is, all animals more advanced than sponges or jellyfish.

SVM: Support Vector Machine, a set of related supervised learning methods used for classification and regression.

Weka: Weka is data mining software in Java. It is a collection of machine learning algorithms for data mining tasks.

APPENDIX

Table 4. The experimental logBB and the 12 calculated descriptors. (X3: 2DACorr_SigChg_5, X4: 2DACorr_SigChg_7, X5: 2DACorr_SigChg_8, X6: 2DACorr_PiChg_1, X7: 2DACorr_PiChg_5, X8: 2DACorr_PiChg_7, X9: 2DACorr_TotChg_6, X10: 2DACorr_TotChg_7, X11: 2DACorr_TotChg_8, X12: 2DACorr_SigEN_1)

Name	BBB	XlogP	TPSA	X3	X4	X5	X6	X7	X8	X9	X10	X11	X12
1,1,1-Trichloroethane	0.40	2.47	0.00	0.00	0.00	0.00	0.00	0.00	0.00	0.00	0.00	0.00	705.06
1,1,1-Trifluoro-2-chloroethane	0.08	1.98	0.00	0.00	0.00	0.00	0.00	0.00	0.00	0.00	0.00	0.00	921.01
1,2,3,4-Tetrahydroquinoline	0.65	1.88	12.03	-0.04	0.02	0.01	0.01	0.00	0.00	-0.01	0.02	0.01	1308.99
1-Hydroxymidazolam	-0.07	4.15	47.86	0.06	-0.19	0.12	0.11	-0.01	0.00	-0.01	-0.17	0.08	2928.24
1-Propanol	-0.16	0.25	20.23	-0.02	0.00	0.00	0.00	0.00	0.00	0.01	0.00	0.00	725.07
2,2-Dimethylbutane	1.04	3.72	0.00	0.00	0.00	0.00	0.00	0.00	0.00	0.01	0.00	0.00	1085.24
2-Methylpentane	0.97	3.66	0.00	0.01	0.01	0.00	0.00	0.00	0.00	-0.01	0.01	0.00	1084.80
2-Methylpropanol	-0.17	0.57	20.23	-0.05	0.00	0.00	0.00	0.00	0.00	0.03	0.00	0.00	889.33
2-Propanol	-0.15	0.38	20.23	0.04	0.00	0.00	0.00	0.00	0.00	0.00	0.00	0.00	726.47
3-Methylhexane	0.90	4.21	0.00	0.00	0.00	0.00	0.00	0.00	0.00	0.00	0.00	0.00	1248.68
3-Methylpentane	1.01	3.66	0.00	-0.01	0.00	0.00	0.00	0.00	0.00	0.01	0.00	0.00	1084.83
4-Hydroxyalprazolam	-1.48	4.59	62.78	-0.21	-0.22	0.12	0.27	0.05	0.01	0.09	-0.32	0.20	2796.10
4-Hydroxymidazolam	-0.30	3.64	49.89	-0.05	-0.08	0.05	0.22	0.05	0.01	-0.08	-0.17	0.05	2885.97
9-Hydroxy risperidone	-0.67	1.65	82.17	-0.21	-0.04	-0.03	0.32	0.06	0.00	0.54	-0.21	-0.05	4252.36
Acetaminophen	-0.31	0.44	49.33	-0.05	-0.25	0.20	0.08	0.01	0.00	0.15	-0.28	0.29	1541.41
Acetylsalicylic acid	-0.50	1.44	63.60	0.31	0.21	-0.11	0.09	0.02	0.02	-0.54	0.39	-0.16	1873.21
Albuterol	-1.03	1.44	72.72	0.01	0.19	-0.06	0.00	0.00	0.00	-0.15	0.17	-0.05	2482.46
Alprazolam	0.04	4.94	42.55	-0.10	-0.10	0.06	0.27	0.05	0.01	0.01	-0.21	0.15	2649.52
Aminopyrine	0.00	1.63	26.79	0.10	0.02	-0.01	0.45	0.04	0.02	-0.23	0.02	-0.05	2396.09
Amitriptyline	0.89	4.93	3.24	0.01	0.03	0.04	0.00	0.00	0.00	-0.02	0.03	0.04	2701.38
Amobarbital	0.04	2.06	75.27	0.36	0.19	-0.21	0.26	0.08	0.00	-0.21	0.23	-0.25	2582.39
Amphetamine	0.93	1.78	26.02	0.06	-0.02	0.00	0.00	0.00	0.00	-0.02	-0.01	0.00	1396.95
Antipyrine	-0.10	1.08	23.55	0.07	-0.02	0.00	0.48	0.03	0.02	-0.13	-0.01	-0.04	1895.12
Argon	0.03	0.00	0.00	0.00	0.00	0.00	0.00	0.00	0.00	0.00	0.00	0.00	0.00
Atenolol	-0.87	0.46	84.58	-0.03	-0.21	0.26	0.07	-0.01	0.00	0.13	-0.29	0.30	2818.32

continued on following page

Table 4. Continued

Atropine	-0.06	1.80	49.77	0.47	0.02	-0.09	0.04	0.00	0.00	-0.29	0.08	-0.10	2958.92
BBcpd10	-1.17	1.55	83.72	-0.16	0.03	0.06	0.26	-0.09	-0.02	0.61	-0.17	-0.07	2074.42
BBcpd12 (cimetidine derivative)	-0.67	3.82	86.53	0.17	0.02	-0.02	0.59	-0.17	-0.01	-0.31	-0.04	-0.01	2798.99
BBcpd13 (cimetidine derivative)	-0.66	3.03	86.53	0.16	0.05	-0.08	0.59	-0.17	-0.01	-0.30	-0.02	-0.06	2719.21
BBcpd14 (cimetidine derivative)	-0.12	4.68	86.53	0.17	0.11	-0.08	0.59	-0.17	-0.01	-0.42	0.08	-0.02	3536.68
BBcpd15 (guanidinothiazole der.)	-0.18	1.40	77.29	0.36	-0.01	0.10	0.24	-0.07	0.00	-0.22	-0.07	0.06	1898.28
BBcpd16 (guanidinothiazole der.)	-1.57	0.65	106.39	0.39	-0.14	0.27	0.32	-0.08	-0.03	-0.10	-0.44	0.58	2536.83
BBcpd17 (ranitidine analog)	-1.12	2.61	90.02	0.20	0.17	-0.14	0.60	-0.17	0.01	-0.42	0.02	-0.02	3299.71
BBcpd18 (ranitidine analog)	-0.27	4.63	90.02	0.04	-0.19	0.22	0.65	-0.22	0.05	-0.35	0.05	0.02	3223.88
BBcpd19 (ranitidine analog)	-0.28	2.80	86.01	0.15	0.00	-0.02	0.44	-0.12	0.04	-0.22	0.10	-0.04	3488.26
BBcpd21 (ranitidine analog)	-0.24	4.08	41.57	0.06	0.06	-0.04	0.07	0.00	-0.01	-0.15	0.13	-0.11	3572.89
BBcpd22 (ranitidine analog)	-0.02	2.15	32.70	0.08	0.03	-0.06	0.00	0.00	0.00	-0.03	0.05	-0.07	2579.74
BBcpd23 (ranitidine analog)	0.69	3.80	37.39	0.02	0.12	-0.07	0.04	0.00	-0.01	-0.08	0.17	-0.14	3282.22
BBcpd24 (ranitidine analog)	0.44	2.88	37.39	0.01	0.14	-0.08	0.09	0.00	-0.01	-0.10	0.17	-0.12	3149.78
BBcpd26 (ranitidine analog)	0.22	4.01	50.53	0.07	0.20	-0.18	0.11	0.00	-0.01	-0.16	0.24	-0.24	3652.87
BBcpd57 (guanidinothiazole der)	-1.15	0.58	103.31	0.34	-0.12	0.22	0.25	-0.09	-0.02	0.02	-0.38	0.38	2060.60
BBcpd58 (guanidinothiazole der)	-1.54	0.74	137.50	0.51	-0.15	0.31	0.77	-0.26	-0.03	-0.34	-0.43	0.61	2964.20
BBcpd60 (ranitidine analog)	-0.73	4.26	90.02	0.21	0.23	-0.14	0.60	-0.17	0.01	-0.54	0.11	0.02	4117.18
BCNU	-0.52	1.46	61.77	-0.13	-0.01	-0.01	0.16	0.01	0.00	0.10	-0.02	-0.01	1963.75
Benzene	0.37	2.02	0.00	0.00	0.00	0.00	0.00	0.00	0.00	0.01	0.00	0.00	750.27
Bishydroxy L-663,581 metabolite	-1.82	0.87	116.99	0.77	-0.09	0.11	0.34	-0.26	0.07	-0.55	-0.12	0.43	3782.44
Bromocriptine	-1.10	3.46	118.21	-0.27	0.13	-0.31	0.26	-0.07	-0.01	0.40	0.21	-0.38	5937.43
Bromperidol	1.38	3.81	40.54	0.11	0.12	-0.27	0.02	0.00	0.00	-0.12	0.13	-0.32	3256.26
Buspirone	0.48	2.21	69.64	0.00	-0.16	0.07	0.21	0.03	0.00	0.19	-0.26	0.20	4063.44
Butanone	-0.08	0.46	17.07	-0.02	0.00	0.00	0.01	0.00	0.00	0.01	0.00	0.00	887.52
Caffeine	-0.06	-0.43	58.44	0.02	0.00	0.01	0.39	0.20	0.00	-0.09	-0.07	-0.03	2081.90
Carbamazepine	-0.14	2.32	46.33	-0.04	-0.14	-0.01	0.17	0.02	0.01	0.19	-0.15	-0.05	2215.93
Carbamazepine-10,11-epoxide	-0.35	1.54	58.86	0.08	0.04	-0.07	0.18	0.02	0.01	-0.10	0.09	-0.11	2304.35

continued on following page

Table 4. Continued

Carbon disulphide (CS2)	0.60	1.99	0.00	0.00	0.00	0.00	0.09	0.00	0.00	0.00	0.00	0.00	0.00	344.61
Cefotetan	-1.89	-2.55	219.93	0.33	0.02	0.67	0.55	-0.06	-0.02	0.00	0.00	-0.58	0.68	5114.78
CF3CH2Cl	0.08	1.98	0.00	0.00	0.00	0.00	0.00	0.00	0.00	0.00	0.00	0.00	0.00	921.01
CF3CH2OCH=CH2	0.13	2.22	9.23	0.00	-0.05	0.00	0.01	0.00	0.00	0.00	0.09	-0.05	0.00	1243.30
Chlorpromazine	1.06	4.87	6.48	0.05	-0.06	0.05	0.03	0.00	0.00	0.00	-0.03	0.01	0.05	2669.84
Cimetidine	-1.42	0.77	88.89	0.10	0.00	-0.03	0.65	-0.14	-0.05	0.00	-0.08	-0.13	-0.16	2512.12
Clobazam	0.35	2.29	40.62	0.16	0.00	-0.02	0.18	-0.03	0.03	0.00	0.01	0.03	-0.04	2692.34
Clonidine	0.11	2.59	36.42	-0.11	-0.10	-0.07	0.15	-0.01	-0.01	0.00	0.12	-0.07	-0.06	1776.80
Codeine	0.55	1.09	41.93	-0.16	0.28	-0.16	0.00	0.00	0.00	0.00	-0.17	0.27	-0.16	2864.75
Cyclohexane	0.92	3.32	0.00	0.00	0.00	0.00	0.00	0.00	0.00	0.00	0.01	0.00	0.00	983.13
Cyclopropane	0.00	1.66	0.00	0.00	0.00	0.00	0.00	0.00	0.00	0.00	0.00	0.00	0.00	485.68
Desflurane	0.11	1.95	9.23	-0.25	0.00	0.00	0.00	0.00	0.00	0.00	0.11	0.00	0.00	1554.79
Desipramine	1.20	3.70	15.27	-0.02	0.03	0.04	0.03	0.00	0.00	0.00	-0.04	0.08	0.02	2618.53
Desmethylclobazam	0.36	2.15	49.41	0.19	-0.02	0.01	0.18	-0.03	0.03	0.00	-0.06	0.03	-0.01	2524.19
Desmethyldesipramine	1.06	3.32	29.26	-0.01	0.06	0.01	0.03	0.00	0.00	0.00	-0.06	0.10	-0.03	2452.00
Desmethyldiazepam	0.50	2.78	41.46	-0.13	-0.09	0.04	0.14	0.01	0.00	0.00	0.09	-0.14	0.08	2307.66
Desmonomethylpromazine	0.59	3.99	15.27	0.02	-0.01	0.07	0.03	0.00	0.00	0.00	-0.05	0.03	0.04	2409.10
Diazepam	0.52	2.92	32.67	-0.14	-0.03	0.01	0.14	0.01	0.00	0.00	0.05	-0.10	0.06	2475.81
Dichloromethane	-0.11	1.50	0.00	0.00	0.00	0.00	0.00	0.00	0.00	0.00	0.00	0.00	0.00	437.37
Didanosine	-1.30	-0.75	88.74	0.08	0.06	0.08	0.35	0.01	0.00	0.00	-0.29	0.06	0.25	2368.00
Diethylether	0.00	0.87	9.23	0.01	0.01	0.00	0.00	0.01	0.00	0.00	0.01	0.01	0.00	896.13
Divinyl ether	0.11	1.25	9.23	0.01	0.01	0.00	0.02	0.01	0.00	0.00	-0.01	0.01	0.00	759.95
Enflurane	0.24	2.10	9.23	-0.07	0.00	0.00	0.00	0.00	0.00	0.00	0.05	0.00	0.00	1510.74
Ethanol	-0.16	-0.09	20.23	0.01	0.00	0.00	0.00	0.00	0.00	0.00	0.00	0.00	0.00	561.02
Ethylbenzene	0.20	2.93	0.00	-0.01	0.00	0.00	0.00	0.00	0.00	0.00	0.01	0.00	0.00	1079.88

continued on following page

Table 4. Continued

Etoposide	-2.00	1.10	160.83	-0.46	-0.60	0.13	0.05	-0.01	0.01	0.43	-0.69	0.16	5680.56
Flunitrazepam	0.06	2.35	78.49	-0.05	0.10	-0.06	0.58	0.14	0.11	-0.63	0.60	-0.62	3127.60
Fluphenazine	1.51	4.14	29.95	-0.12	0.09	0.03	0.03	0.00	0.00	-0.08	0.09	0.04	4002.27
Gentisic acid	0.08	1.38	77.76	0.05	-0.39	0.12	0.05	0.00	0.00	0.36	-0.41	0.12	1529.23
Haloperidol	1.34	3.98	40.54	-0.03	0.22	-0.08	0.02	0.00	0.00	-0.10	0.22	-0.07	3435.10
Halothane	0.35	2.76	0.00	0.00	0.00	0.00	0.00	0.00	0.00	0.00	0.00	0.00	1004.05
Heptane	0.81	4.24	0.00	0.00	0.00	0.00	0.00	0.00	0.00	0.00	0.00	0.00	1248.44
Hexane	0.80	3.69	0.00	0.00	0.00	0.00	0.00	0.00	0.00	0.00	0.00	0.00	1084.59
Hexobarbital	0.10	1.18	66.48	0.26	-0.04	-0.02	0.26	0.08	0.00	0.03	-0.04	-0.02	2574.49
Hydroxyzine	0.39	2.76	35.94	-0.04	0.18	0.01	0.00	0.00	0.00	-0.21	0.17	0.00	3467.14
Ibuprofen	-0.18	3.65	37.30	0.02	-0.05	0.04	0.04	0.00	0.00	0.01	-0.07	0.05	2202.01
ICI 17148	-0.04	-1.01	77.29	0.38	0.02	-0.02	0.23	-0.07	0.00	-0.28	0.00	0.00	1406.57
Icotidine	-2.00	1.80	88.50	0.06	0.15	-0.08	0.42	-0.13	0.07	-0.40	0.44	-0.42	3820.44
Imipramine	1.06	3.95	6.48	-0.01	0.00	0.06	0.03	0.00	0.00	-0.03	0.06	0.07	2785.30
Indinavir	-0.75	2.94	118.03	-0.11	0.17	-0.33	0.15	0.00	0.01	0.18	0.18	-0.37	6191.19
Indomethacin	-1.26	3.35	68.53	-0.13	-0.60	0.48	0.18	0.05	-0.03	0.17	-0.89	0.81	3273.65
Isoflurane	0.42	2.09	9.23	-0.26	0.00	0.00	0.00	0.00	0.00	0.11	0.00	0.00	1515.91
Krypton	-0.16	0.00	0.00	0.00	0.00	0.00	0.00	0.00	0.00	0.00	0.00	0.00	0.00
L-663,581	-0.30	2.92	76.53	0.28	-0.09	-0.02	0.35	-0.26	0.07	-0.23	-0.09	0.13	3350.36
Levodopa	-0.77	-1.76	103.78	-0.39	-0.12	0.16	0.04	0.00	0.01	0.16	-0.15	0.15	2007.31
Levorphanol	0.00	3.25	23.47	0.02	-0.14	0.10	0.00	0.00	0.00	0.06	-0.14	0.09	2566.86
Lin_test_35	-1.82	0.86	116.99	0.22	-0.05	0.07	0.34	-0.26	0.07	-0.34	0.04	0.16	3626.95
Lin_train_45	0.35	3.10	0.00	0.09	0.00	0.00	0.00	0.00	0.00	0.00	0.00	0.00	1157.93
Lin_train_55	0.27	2.83	0.00	0.12	0.00	0.00	0.00	0.00	0.00	0.00	0.00	0.00	1191.87
Lupitidine	-1.06	1.42	82.76	0.10	0.26	-0.30	0.43	-0.13	0.08	-0.40	0.42	-0.49	4009.11
Mepyramine	0.49	3.20	28.60	-0.12	0.18	-0.17	0.04	0.00	0.02	0.09	0.15	-0.26	2893.67
Mesoridazine	-0.36	3.83	23.55	-0.03	-0.04	0.03	2.24	0.16	-0.06	-0.06	0.02	0.08	3463.80
Methamphetamine	0.99	2.16	12.03	0.04	-0.03	-0.01	0.00	0.00	0.00	0.00	-0.03	-0.01	1563.51
Methane	0.04	0.21	0.00	0.00	0.00	0.00	0.00	0.00	0.00	0.00	0.00	0.00	265.59

continued on following page

Table 4. Continued

Methohexital	-0.06	1.81	66.48	0.36	-0.14	0.07	0.26	0.08	0.00	0.06	-0.14	0.12	2877.78
Methotrexate	-1.52	1.41	210.54	-0.16	0.54	-0.20	0.34	-0.03	-0.06	-0.44	0.42	0.09	4625.37
Methoxyflurane	0.25	1.78	9.23	-0.02	0.00	0.00	0.00	0.00	0.00	-0.03	0.00	0.00	1197.07
Methylcyclopentane	0.93	3.29	0.00	0.00	0.00	0.00	0.00	0.00	0.00	0.01	0.00	0.00	983.38
Mianserin	0.99	3.47	6.48	0.03	-0.03	-0.03	0.01	0.00	0.00	0.03	-0.03	-0.04	2519.00
Midazolam	0.36	4.00	29.66	0.01	-0.07	0.03	0.22	0.05	0.01	-0.04	-0.18	0.05	2740.85
Mirtazapine	0.53	2.93	19.37	-0.04	-0.01	-0.08	0.04	0.00	0.00	0.12	-0.01	-0.12	2538.82
Monohydroxy L-663,581 metabolite	-1.34	1.99	96.76	0.15	-0.02	0.00	0.34	-0.26	0.07	-0.28	0.09	-0.01	3491.92
Morphine	-0.16	0.78	52.93	-0.25	0.28	-0.23	0.00	0.00	0.00	-0.08	0.27	-0.23	2693.64
m-Xylene	0.30	2.89	0.00	0.00	0.02	0.00	0.00	0.00	0.00	-0.01	0.02	0.00	1081.22
N-Desmethylclobazam	0.00	2.15	49.41	0.19	-0.02	0.01	0.18	-0.03	0.03	-0.06	0.03	-0.01	2524.19
Neon	0.20	0.00	0.00	0.00	0.00	0.00	0.00	0.00	0.00	0.00	0.00	0.00	0.00
Nevirapine	0.00	2.47	58.12	0.11	-0.02	-0.09	0.16	-0.01	0.01	-0.05	0.06	-0.19	2556.71
Nitrogen	0.03	0.00	47.58	0.00	0.00	0.00	0.00	0.00	0.00	0.00	0.00	0.00	491.74
Nitrous oxide	0.03	-0.50	48.38	0.00	0.00	0.00	7.31	0.00	0.00	0.00	0.00	0.00	606.07
Nor-1-chlorpromazine	1.37	4.62	15.27	0.04	-0.03	0.05	0.03	0.00	0.00	-0.04	0.03	0.02	2503.06
Nor-2-chlorpromazine	0.97	4.24	29.26	0.05	0.00	0.04	0.03	0.00	0.00	-0.06	0.05	-0.01	2336.54
Northioridazine	0.75	5.63	15.27	0.05	-0.04	0.04	0.03	0.00	0.00	-0.03	0.04	0.02	3078.09
Norverapamil	-0.64	4.42	72.74	-0.05	0.32	0.08	0.17	0.00	0.00	-0.66	0.36	0.20	4607.27
Oxazepam	0.61	2.86	61.69	-0.31	-0.18	0.08	0.15	0.01	0.00	0.20	-0.22	0.11	2455.56
o-Xylene	0.37	2.89	0.00	-0.02	0.01	0.00	0.00	0.00	0.00	0.01	0.01	0.00	1081.24
Paraxanthine	0.06	-0.57	67.23	0.09	0.02	-0.01	0.39	0.20	0.00	-0.19	-0.01	-0.05	1913.43
Pentane	0.76	3.13	0.00	0.00	0.00	0.00	0.00	0.00	0.00	0.00	0.00	0.00	920.73
Pentobarbital	0.12	2.06	75.27	0.48	0.15	-0.11	0.26	0.08	0.00	-0.30	0.21	-0.15	2582.66
Pergolide	0.30	4.01	19.03	-0.02	-0.05	-0.04	0.07	0.00	0.00	-0.03	-0.04	0.00	2944.69
Phencyclidine	0.68	4.12	3.24	-0.02	-0.03	0.01	0.00	0.00	0.00	-0.03	-0.03	0.01	2515.10
Phenserine	1.00	3.39	44.81	-0.09	-0.06	0.06	0.14	0.00	0.01	0.08	-0.09	0.04	3355.16
Phenylbutazone	-0.52	3.68	40.62	0.01	0.07	-0.08	0.28	0.06	0.01	0.24	0.09	-0.09	3101.74
Phenytoin	-0.04	2.25	58.20	0.09	-0.02	-0.03	0.20	0.06	0.00	0.14	0.01	-0.05	2433.16

continued on following page

Table 4. Continued

	0.08	1.81	44.81	-0.19	-0.07	0.10	0.12	0.00	0.01	0.10	-0.14	0.09	2861.07
Physostigmine	0.08	1.81	44.81	-0.19	-0.07	0.10	0.12	0.00	0.01	0.10	-0.14	0.09	2861.07
Primidone	-0.07	1.53	58.20	0.40	-0.03	-0.03	0.13	0.00	0.00	-0.22	-0.03	-0.04	2253.90
Promazine	1.23	4.24	6.48	0.03	-0.05	0.07	0.03	0.00	0.00	-0.03	0.01	0.07	2575.88
Propan-1-ol	-0.16	0.25	20.23	-0.02	0.00	0.00	0.00	0.00	0.00	0.01	0.00	0.00	725.07
Propan-2-ol	-0.15	0.38	20.23	0.04	0.00	0.00	0.00	0.00	0.00	0.00	0.00	0.00	726.47
Propanone	-0.15	0.20	17.07	0.01	0.00	0.00	0.01	0.00	0.00	0.00	0.00	0.00	723.08
Propranolol	0.64	3.04	41.49	-0.07	-0.01	0.04	0.00	0.00	0.00	-0.01	-0.02	0.04	2593.85
p-Xylene	0.31	2.89	0.00	-0.01	-0.01	0.01	0.00	0.00	0.00	0.02	-0.01	0.01	1081.21
Quinidine	-0.46	2.58	45.59	-0.19	0.13	0.00	0.02	0.00	0.00	0.13	0.12	-0.01	3153.12
Ranitidine	-1.23	1.30	86.26	0.23	0.13	-0.12	0.60	-0.13	0.01	-0.21	-0.11	-0.07	3291.67
Risperidone	-0.02	2.43	61.94	0.03	0.02	0.00	0.32	0.06	0.00	0.20	-0.06	-0.02	4114.25
Salicylic acid	-1.10	2.21	57.53	0.34	0.05	0.01	0.05	0.00	0.00	-0.32	0.04	0.01	1376.38
Salicyluric acid	-0.44	0.83	86.63	-0.06	-0.19	0.40	0.11	-0.04	-0.01	0.21	-0.36	0.50	2010.18
SB-222200	0.30	6.36	41.99	-0.17	-0.01	-0.01	0.08	-0.02	0.00	0.29	-0.06	-0.01	3617.94
SK&F 93319	-1.30	3.62	69.87	0.10	0.08	-0.15	0.41	-0.16	0.01	-0.10	-0.07	-0.14	4232.43
SKF101468	-0.30	2.24	32.34	0.01	-0.03	0.02	0.08	0.00	0.00	0.07	-0.12	0.07	2763.67
SKF89124	-0.06	1.83	52.57	-0.25	-0.14	0.14	0.08	0.00	0.00	0.37	-0.28	0.18	2918.04
Sulforidazine	0.18	4.63	40.62	-0.07	-0.02	0.02	0.33	0.04	-0.05	0.00	0.04	0.06	3710.42
Sulphur hexafluoride (SF6)	0.36	2.24	0.00	0.00	0.00	0.00	0.35	0.00	0.00	0.00	0.00	0.00	1327.11
Tacrine	-0.13	2.21	38.91	0.09	0.00	0.02	0.05	-0.01	0.00	-0.17	0.01	0.02	1895.01
Teflurane	0.27	2.49	0.00	0.00	0.00	0.00	0.00	0.00	0.00	0.00	0.00	0.00	1040.91
Temelastine	-1.88	2.91	79.27	0.07	0.18	-0.19	0.42	-0.13	0.07	-0.33	0.45	-0.54	3740.02
Tertbutylchlorambucil	1.00	5.53	29.54	0.04	0.12	-0.02	0.05	0.00	-0.01	-0.10	0.09	0.08	3368.66
Theobromine	-0.28	-0.57	67.23	0.07	0.03	-0.02	0.39	0.20	0.00	-0.12	-0.03	-0.06	1913.24
Theophylline	-0.29	-0.75	69.30	-0.11	-0.04	0.01	0.39	0.20	0.00	0.06	-0.17	0.01	1913.30
Thiopental	-0.14	2.61	58.53	0.49	0.10	-0.10	0.23	0.03	0.00	-0.39	0.14	-0.13	2485.09
Thioperamide	-0.16	2.15	43.95	-0.03	0.01	0.02	0.42	-0.01	0.02	-0.02	-0.12	0.32	2828.77
Thioridazine	0.24	5.88	6.48	0.04	-0.07	0.05	0.03	0.00	0.00	-0.01	0.02	0.05	3244.93
Tibolone	0.40	2.97	37.30	-0.15	0.09	-0.01	0.01	0.00	0.00	-0.02	0.10	-0.01	3210.64

continued on following page

Table 4. Continued

Tiotidine	-0.82	-0.29	137.50	0.42	0.00	-0.07	0.75	-0.21	-0.04	-0.27	-0.14	-0.28	2891.20
Toluene	0.37	2.46	0.00	0.00	0.00	0.00	0.00	0.00	0.00	0.01	0.00	0.00	915.74
Triazolam	0.74	5.56	42.55	-0.04	-0.12	0.07	0.27	0.05	0.02	0.03	-0.30	0.14	2744.04
Trichloroethene	0.34	2.62	0.00	0.00	0.00	0.00	0.00	0.00	0.00	0.00	0.00	0.00	631.27
Trichloromethane	0.29	2.07	0.00	0.00	0.00	0.00	0.00	0.00	0.00	0.00	0.00	0.00	536.98
Trifluoperazine	1.44	4.84	9.72	-0.07	0.01	0.06	0.03	0.00	0.00	-0.03	0.01	0.06	3704.80
Valproic acid	-0.22	2.67	37.30	0.00	-0.09	0.03	0.04	0.00	0.00	0.07	-0.10	0.03	1711.58
Verapamil	-0.70	4.66	63.95	-0.04	0.29	0.18	0.17	0.00	0.00	-0.66	0.29	0.36	4774.08
Xenon	0.03	0.00	0.00	0.00	0.00	0.00	0.00	0.00	0.00	0.00	0.00	0.00	0.00
Y-G14	-0.42	0.53	24.92	0.09	-0.05	0.00	0.02	0.00	0.00	-0.04	-0.05	0.01	1414.75
Y-G15	-0.06	0.78	16.13	0.09	-0.08	-0.01	0.02	0.00	0.00	0.03	-0.11	0.01	1581.53
Y-G16	-0.42	-0.49	38.91	0.13	-0.03	0.03	0.03	0.00	0.00	-0.10	-0.03	0.03	1113.96
Y-G19	-0.43	1.77	38.91	0.13	-0.01	0.05	0.03	0.00	0.00	-0.13	-0.01	0.05	1771.85
Y-G20	0.25	-0.37	43.32	0.05	-0.01	0.00	0.24	0.01	0.00	-0.23	0.08	0.01	1594.36
Zidovudine	-0.72	-0.88	130.17	0.17	0.06	-0.03	1.67	0.05	0.28	-0.53	0.99	-0.79	2828.10
Zolantidine	0.14	4.23	37.39	0.08	0.09	-0.12	0.10	0.00	-0.01	-0.12	0.15	-0.17	3558.92
B1-Hydroxyalprazolam	-1.27	3.91	62.78	-0.20	-0.03	-0.05	0.27	0.05	0.01	-0.01	-0.13	0.04	2786.21

Section 4
Medical Signal Processing and Analysis

Chapter 15
The Study of Transesophageal Oxygen Saturation Monitoring

Zhiqiang Zhang
Sichuan University, China

Bo Gao
Sichuan University, China

Guojie Liao
Sichuan University, China

Ling Mu
West China Hospital, China

Wei Wei
West China Hospital, China

ABSTRACT

In this chapter, the transesophageal oxygen saturation (SpO_2) monitoring system was proposed based on the early experiments, to provide a new program of SpO_2 acquisition and analysis and avoid the limitation of traditional methods. The PPG (photoplethysmographic) signal of descending aorta and left ventricular was monitored in the experiment. The analysis of the peak-to-peak values, the standard deviation and the position of peaks in signal waveforms showed that in vivo signal was more stable and sensitive; and the physiological information was reflected in the left ventricular PPG waveform. Therefore, it can be concluded that the transesophageal SpO_2 monitoring technology has better guidance in clinical applications.

INTRODUCTION

Oxygen saturation (SpO_2) is the percentage of oxyhemoglobin (HbO_2) with respect to the sum of hemoglobin (Hb) and HbO_2 in blood, which

DOI: 10.4018/978-1-60960-064-8.ch015

is an important physiological parameter to assess human health condition. Therefore, oximetry has become an indispensable guardianship and diagnostic equipment and there is a wide range of applications in clinical practice, such as surgery, anaesthesia and intensive care units (ICU) (Kyriacou, 2006). There are some reports that

Oximeters are placed in fingers, foreheads (Kim et al., 2007), tongues (Jobes & Nicolson, 1988), faces (O'Leary et al., 1992) and other parts of body surface to monitor oxygen saturation. However, in some cases, such as trauma (burn), surgery, or the unstable peripheral circulation, there are some limitations in clinical applications (Kyriacou et al., 2002; Ahrens, 1999; Pal et al., 2005).

Before this study, Zhu et al. (2005) had verified the feasibility of transesophageal pulse oximetry through the animal experiments, then, the human experiments that monitoring pulmonary artery through trachea could be achieved (Wei et al., 2005). In this work, based on the anatomical relationship that the esophagus was close to the descending aorta (Kyriacou et al., 2003), a method of transesophageal SpO_2 monitoring was proposed, to provide a new method for in vivo monitoring. As the blood vessels of descending aorta and left ventricular are larger than surface vessels, which means that the light absorption of internal vessels is larger, so we expected that the signals from these parts would be more stable and sensitive, to make the SpO_2 monitoring accurate and timely. Also, more biological information was expected to be obtained from the signal waveforms.

SPO$_2$ MONITORING SYSTEM

Theoretical Principle of SpO$_2$ Monitoring

Timely monitoring of blood oxygen saturation is an important indicator to determine human respiratory system, circulatory system, or whether there are anoxic obstacles in the surrounding environment. The measurement of SpO_2 is based on the Hb and HbO_2 with different light absorption characteristics (Sola et al., 2006), as shown in Figure 1.

Studies have shown that human blood is sensitive to the light in the range of 600 nm to 1000 nm wavelength (Sola et al., 2006). In Figure 1, HbO_2 and Hb have different light absorption coefficients in different wavelength regions. In the infrared spectrum, their absorption curves changed smoothly and are close to each other, so there is little difference in absorption of Hb and HbO_2. However, in the red spectrum, HbO_2 and Hb are more sensitive to the changes in blood oxygen, because of their large difference in absorption coefficient, especially around 660 nm where the difference between HbO_2 and Hb absorption coefficient is the greatest. With these factors considered, light sources at 660 nm and

Figure 1. The light absorption coefficients of HbO_2 and Hb in the red and infrared spectrum

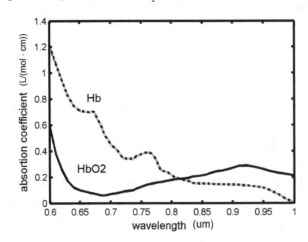

940 nm were selected for the oxygen saturation measurement.

Generally, the human's blood SpO_2 is determined by measuring photoplethysmographic (PPG) signal, which is caused by the fluctuations of vessels volume. The SpO_2 calculation is shown in empirical Equation (1).

$$SpO_2 = A_S - B_S \bullet \frac{(I_{AC}^{\lambda_1} / I_{DC}^{\lambda_1})}{(I_{AC}^{\lambda_2} / I_{DC}^{\lambda_2})} \qquad (1)$$

A_S, B_S are the coefficients of empirical equation, and λ_1, λ_2 are red and infrared light wavelengths, respectively, and I_{AC}, I_{DC} are light intensity. In the experiment, I_{AC} is calculated by the peak-to-peak values of PPG waveforms, whereas I_{DC} is a constant. Therefore, as the blood volume alters, the changes of light intensity will be shown in the PPG signal waveforms. For example, when blood backward flow caused by heart beating occurs, the changes of blood volume will be reflected in the PPG waveforms.

Methodology

In order to overcome the limitation of traditional SpO_2 measurement in some circumstances, the transesophageal SpO_2 measurement method was proposed in this work. It uses red light (660 nm) and infrared light (940 nm) as the light sources, which are controlled by FPGA, at the same time, the sensors are inspired with the trigger pulse to gather the reflected light intensity through the blood vessel. And then, current to voltage, amplification and analog to digital. At last, the signal will be put into the computer to filter, real-time display and calculate the SpO_2, pulse and other physiological information by MATLAB software. Figure 2 is the block diagram of SpO_2 measurement system.

EXPERIMENT

This study had been approved by the Hospital Ethics Committee and agreed by patients. Basic vital signs such as BP (Blood Pressure), HR (Heart Rate) and SpO_2 were monitored when patients went into the operating room. After anesthesia was induced, the self-made probe (Patent No. ZL200320115080.2) against narcotic-induced tube was inserted into the esophagus and adjusted to the proper position. Method is shown in Figure 3.

In the clinical experiment, the researchers first gathered the PPG signal from fingers using self-made equipment. Then, the measurements were place into esophagus to monitor the PPG signal of descending aorta and left ventricle. It should be emphasized that it was not in the same time when the PPG signal was collected in different parts, so the pulses calculated from the waveforms were not same with each other, whereas they were same with the hospital's patient monitor, respectively, which was place on finger.

Figure 2. The block diagram of SpO_2 measurement system

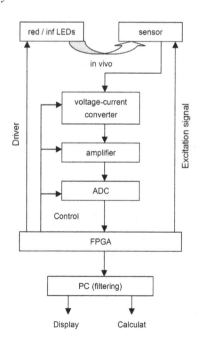

Figure 3. The diagram of transesophageal monitoring SpO₂ method

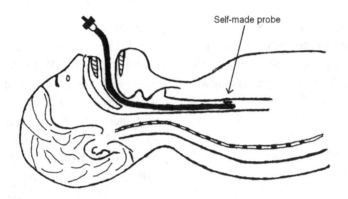

Finger PPG Signal

In the experiment 1, the researchers used the device to collect finger PPG signal, as shown in Figure 4.

In Figure 4, the finger PPG signal waveform is smooth, but has a small peak-to-peak value. There are mostly capillary vessels in fingers, which have small blood volume, so the changes of blood volume are small. As a result, it can be concluded the sensitivity of the body surface PPG is lower.

Descending Aorta PPG Signal

In the experiment 2, the SpO₂ acquisition tube was placed into the lower esophagus to collect descending aorta PPG signal. The red and infrared rays were launched by self-made probe through esophagus mucosa and directly into the descending aorta. Because the light absorptions of Hb and HbO₂ are different, so the red and infrared rays' intensity change in varying degrees, which are collected by the probe sensors. The waveform is shown in Figure 5.

In Figure 5, the PPG signal waveform is continuous, smooth and clean. The distance between peak 1 is calculated and normalized, then calculates the position of peak 2 between peak 1. After analysis, the location of peak 2 is very stable, which concentrates in 0.618-0.632, but its phys-

Figure 4. Finger PPG signal (a is red and b is infrared)

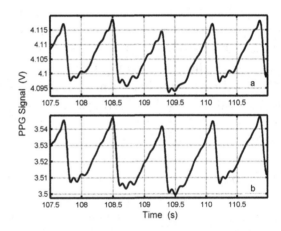

iological significance need to be studied in the subsequent experiments.

Left Ventricle PPG Signal

Figure 6 is the left ventricle PPG signal waveform. From this waveform, the "double peak" phenomenon is found, which is unique characteristic of heart. As we know, heart keeps up the circulation of the blood by alternately contracting and expanding. The waveform peak is corresponding to ejection time, which the heart's blood volume is least, and the amount of light absorbed is smallest. After ejection, the measured signal value decreases in a period of time, then the value is

Figure 5. Descending aorta PPG signal (a is red and b is infrared)

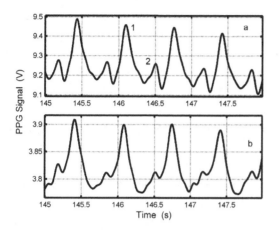

Figure 6. Left ventricle PPG signal (a is red and b is infrared)

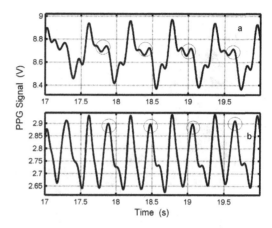

fluctuating between heart and vessel, which will make a process of repeated shocks, as shown in Figure 6 circle tag. This phenomenon can be seen intuitively, however, the relationship between this phenomenon and the cardiovascular status still need further experiments.

DISCUSSION

In order to calculate SpO_2, the peak-to-peak values are calculated, and larger value could be more sensitive to the SpO_2 in different parts. The researchers select 30 seconds PPG waveforms of the left ventricle, descending aorta and finger to calculate the average of peak-to-peak values, which are shown in Figure 7.

The peak-to-peak values of infrared and red of left ventricle are 0.269 and 0.503, and the values of descending aorta are 0.154 and 0.274, while the values of finger are 0.019 and 0.050, respectively. Consequently, the peak-to-peak values in vivo are larger than in finger, and that is more than 5 times. The reason is that heart and descending aorta are close to the esophagus, SpO_2 in aorta can be monitored directly. However, finger blood vessels are mostly terminal capillary vessels, which contain less blood than the aorta,

so the absorption of light is less than the aorta. As a result, the peak-to-peak values of PPG signal in vivo are much larger than body surface's, which means in vivo signal is more sensitive to evaluate the SpO_2 timely and accurate.

In order to measure the stability of waveforms, standard deviation was used to assess the degree of fluctuation in PPG waveforms in this work. Standard deviation is proposed to measure the difference between individuals and their average. Therefore, the greater the standard deviation is, the more different the individual would be from

Figure 7. Comparison of left ventricle, descending aorta and finger PPG peak-to-peak value

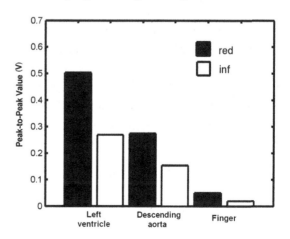

Figure 8. Comparison of left ventricle, descending aorta and finger PPG standard deviation

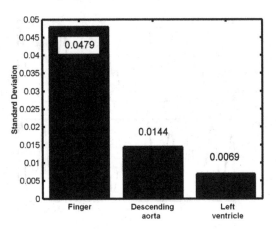

their average, which may impact the stability of the pulse calculation. The researchers choose the 30 seconds PPG waveforms in finger, descending aorta and left ventricle to calculate the standard deviation, to assess the stability of PPG waveforms. The standard deviation is shown in Figure 8.

In Figure 8, the standard deviation of left ventricular and descending aorta is much smaller than finger's. That means in vivo PPG waveform is more stable, so it is better to analyze the SpO_2 and pulse.

The descending aorta and left ventricle signal were monitored in this study, so the degree of interference was minimal. In Figure 5, 30 seconds PPG signal waveform was selected and 70% of the peak values are concentrative, whereas the peak values out of this range are significantly larger. The patient breathes through the breathing machine in the same frequency as the peak value out of range occurrence. Therefore, the peak values out of range are caused by the breathing machine. Excluding this impact of breathing machine, the signal waveforms are stable.

CONCLUSION

As the SpO_2 measurement on the body surface is difficult to achieve in some clinical applications, the in vivo PPG signal is monitored directly in this chapter, which can achieve continuous, non-invasive assessment of the oxygen saturation. The experimental analysis shows that the PPG waveforms of descending aorta and left ventricular are more stable and sensitive, so the application of this study may allow the measurement of body oxygen supply directly and accurately. Meanwhile, the echo information of heart can be seen in the left ventricular waveform. This information merits further evaluation and development. Therefore, this study is significant to clinical assessment, and may act as a better guide to surgery and the SpO_2 monitoring.

ACKNOWLEDGMENT

We would like to thank Prof. Min GONG for proofreading of this chapter and his constructive feedback and comments. This study was supported by the National Natural Science Foundation of China.

REFERENCES

Ahrens, T. (1999). Continuous mixed venous (SvO_2) monitoring: Too expensive or indispensable? *Critical Care Nursing Clinics of North America, 11*(1), 33–48.

Jobes, D. R., & Nicolson, S. C. (1988). Monitoring of arterial hemoglobin oxygen saturation using a tongue sensor. *Anesthesia and Analgesia, 67*(2), 186–188. doi:10.1213/00000539-198802000-00014

Kim, S. H., Ryoo, D. W., & Bae, C. (2007). Adaptive Noise Cancellation Using Accelerometers for the PPG Signal from Forehead. *Conference Proceedings; ... Annual International Conference of the IEEE Engineering in Medicine and Biology Society. IEEE Engineering in Medicine and Biology Society. Conference*, 2564–2567.

Kyriacou, P. A. (2006). Pulse oximetry in the oesophagus. *Physiological Measurement, 27*(1), 1–35. doi:10.1088/0967-3334/27/1/R01

Kyriacou, P. A., Powell, S. L., Jones, D. P., & Langford, R. M. (2002). Esophageal pulse oximetry utilizing reflectance photoplethysmography. *IEEE Transactions on Bio-Medical Engineering, 49*(11), 1360–1368. doi:10.1109/TBME.2002.804584

Kyriacou, P. A., Powell, S. L., Jones, D. P., & Langford, R. M. (2003). Evaluation of esophageal pulse oximetry in patients undergoing cardio-thoracic surgery. *Anaesthesia, 58*(5), 422–427. doi:10.1046/j.1365-2044.2003.03091.x

O'Leary, R. J., Landon, M., & Benumof, J. L. (1992). Buccal pulse oximeter is more accurate than finger pulse oximeter in measuring oxygen saturation. *Anesthesia and Analgesia, 75*(4), 495–498.

Pal, S., Kyriacou, P. A., Kumaran, S., Fadheel, S., Emamdee, R., Langford, R., & Jones, D. (2005). Evaluation of oesophageal reflectance pulse oximetry in major burns patients. *Burns: journal of the International Society for Burn Injuries, 31*(3), 337-341.

Sola, J., Castoldi, S., Chetelat, O., Correvon, M., Dasen, S., & Droz, S. (2006). SpO₂ Sensor Embedded in a Finger Ring: design and implementation. *Conference Proceedings; ... Annual International Conference of the IEEE Engineering in Medicine and Biology Society. IEEE Engineering in Medicine and Biology Society. Conference, 1*, 4295–4298.

Wei, W., Zhu, Z. Q., Liu, L. X., Zuo, Y. X., Gong, M., Xue, F. S., & Liu, J. (2005). A pilot Study of Continuous Transtracheal Mixed Venous Oxygen Saturation Monitoring. *Anesthesia and Analgesia, 101*(2), 440–443. doi:10.1213/01.ANE.0000156949.91614.E9

Zhu, Z. Q., Wei, W., Yang, Z. B., Liu, A. J., & Liu, J. (2005). Transesophageal Arterial Oxygen Saturation Monitoring: An Experimental Study. [Medical Science Edition]. *Journal of Sichuan University, 36*(1), 124–126.

ADDITIONAL READING

Addison, P. S., & Watson, J. N. (2005). Oxygen Saturation Determined Using a Novel Wavelet Ratio Surface. *Medical Engineering & Physics, 27*(3), 245–248. doi:10.1016/j.medengphy.2004.10.002

Alexander, C. M., Teller, L. E., & Gross, J. B. (1989). Principles of Pulse Oximetry: Theoretical and Practical Considerations. *Anesthesia and Analgesia, 68*(3), 368–376.

Asada, H., Shaltis, P., Reisner, A., Rhee, S., & Hutchinson, R. C. (2003). Wearable PPG-Biosensors. *IEEE Engineering in Medicine and Biology Magazine, 22*(3), 28–40. doi:10.1109/MEMB.2003.1213624

Barker, S. J., Tremper, K. K., & Hyatt, J. (1989). Effects of methemoglobinemia on pulse oximetry and mixed venous oximetry. *Anesthesiology, 70*(1), 112–117. doi:10.1097/00000542-198901000-00021

Birmingham, P. K., Cheney, F. W., & Ward, R. J. (1986). Esophageal Intubation: A Review of Detection Techniques. *Anesthesia and Analgesia, 65*(8), 886–891.

Brimacombe, J., Keller, C., & Margreiter, J. (2000). A Pilot Study of Left Tracheal Pulse Oximetry. *Anesthesia and Analgesia, 91*(4), 1003–1006. doi:10.1097/00000539-200010000-00043

Clayton, D. G., Webb, R. K., Ralston, A. C., Duthie, D., & Runciman, W. B. (1991). A comparison of the performance of 20 pulse oximeters under conditions of poor perfusion. *Anaesthesia, 46*(1), 3–10. doi:10.1111/j.1365-2044.1991.tb09303.x

Coetzee, F. M., & Elghazzawi, Z. (2000). Noise-Resistant Pulse Oximetry Using a Synthetic Reference Signal. *IEEE Transactions on Bio-Medical Engineering, 47*(8), 1018–1026. doi:10.1109/10.855928

Comtois, G., & Mendelson, Y. (2007). A Noise Reference Input to an Adaptive Filter Algorithm for Signal Processing in a Wearable Pulse Oximeter. *Bioengineering Conference, IEEE*, 106-107.

Comtois, G., Mendelson, Y., & Ramuka, P. (2007). A Comparative Evaluation of Adaptive Noise Cancellation Algorithms for Minimizing Motion Artifacts in a Forehead-Mounted Wearable Pulse Oximeter. *Conference Proceedings; ... Annual International Conference of the IEEE Engineering in Medicine and Biology Society. IEEE Engineering in Medicine and Biology Society. Conference*, 1528–1531.

Crerar-Gilbert, A. J., Kyriacou, P. A., Jones, D. P., & Langford, R. M. (2002). Assessment of Photoplethysmographic Signals for the Determination of Splanchnic Oxygen Saturation in Humans. *Anaesthesia, 57*(5), 442–445. doi:10.1046/j.0003-2409.2001.02453.x

Dildy, G. A. (2004). Fetal Pulse Oximetry: A Critical Appraisal. *Best Practice & Research. Clinical Obstetrics & Gynaecology, 18*(3), 477–484. doi:10.1016/j.bpobgyn.2004.02.010

Engler, E. L., & Holm, K. (1990). Perspectives on the Interpretation of Continuous Mixed Venous Oxygen Saturation. *Heart & Lung, 19*(5), 578–580.

Finlay, J. C., & Foster, T. H. (2004). Hemoglobin Oxygen Saturations in Phantoms and In Vivo from Measurements of Steady-state Diffuse Reflectance at a Single, Short Source–detector Separation. *Medical Physics, 31*(7), 1949–1959. doi:10.1118/1.1760188

Kyriacou, P. A., Moye, A. R., Gregg, A., Choi, D. M. A., Langford, R. M., & Jones, D. P. (1999). A System for Investigating Oesophageal Photoplethysmographic signals in Anaesthetized Patients. *Medical & Biological Engineering & Computing, 37*(5), 639–643. doi:10.1007/BF02513360

Kyriacou, P. A., Powell, S., Langford, R. M., & Jones, D. P. (2002). Investigation of Oesophageal Photoplethysmographic Signals and Blood Oxygen Saturation Measurements in Cardiothoracic Surgery Patients. *Physiological Measurement, 23*(3), 533–545. doi:10.1088/0967-3334/23/3/305

Margreiter, J., Keller, C., & Brimacombe, J. (2002). The Feasibility of Trans-esophageal Echocardiograph-Guided Right and Left Ventricular Oximetry in Hemodynamically Stable Patients Undergoing Coronary Artery bypass Grafting. *Anesthesia and Analgesia, 94*, 794–798. doi:10.1097/00000539-200204000-00005

Mendelson, Y., Duckworth, R. J., & Comtois, G. (2005). A Wearable Reflectance Pulse Oximeter for Remote Physiological Monitoring. *Conference Proceedings; ... Annual International Conference of the IEEE Engineering in Medicine and Biology Society. IEEE Engineering in Medicine and Biology Society. Conference, 1*, 912–915.

Palve, H., & Vuori, A. (1989). Pulse Oximetry during Low Cardiac Output and Hypothermia States Immediately after Open Heart Surgery. *Critical Care Medicine, 17*(1), 66–69. doi:10.1097/00003246-198901000-00014

Priclipp, R. C., Scuderi, P. E., Hines, M. H., Atlee, J. L., & Butterworth, J. F. (2000). Comparison of a Prototype Esophageal Oximetry Probe with Two Conventional Digital Pulse Oximetry Monitors in Aortocoronary bypass Patients. *Journal of Clinical Monitoring and Computing, 16*(3), 201–209. doi:10.1023/A:1009941610320

Relente, A. R., & Sison, L. G. (2002). Characterization and Adaptive Filtering of Motion Artifacts in Pulse Oximetry Using Accelerometers. *EMBS/BMES Conference, 2*, 1769-1770.

Ren, J. F., Marchlinski, F. E., & Callans, D. J. (2006). Real-time Intracardiac Echocardiographic Imaging of the Posterior Left Atrial Wall Contiguous to Anterior Wall of the Esophagus. *Journal of the American College of Cardiology, 48*(3), 594–595. doi:10.1016/j.jacc.2006.05.019

Reuss, J. L. (2004). Factors Influencing Fetal Pulse Oximetry Performance. *Journal of Clinical Monitoring and Computing, 18*(1), 13–24. doi:10.1023/B:JOCM.0000025278.82852.b3

Sanjit, K. M., & James, F. K. (1993). *Handbook for Digital Signal Processing*. New York.

Shafqat, K., Jones, D. P., Langford, R. M., & Kyriacou, P. A. (2006). Filtering Techniques for the Removal of Ventilator Artefact in Oesophageal Pulse Oximetry. *Medical & Biological Engineering & Computing, 44*(8), 729–737. doi:10.1007/s11517-006-0089-2

Shimada, Y., Yoshiya, I., Oka, N., & Hamaguri, K. (1984). Effects of Multiple Scattering and Peripheral Circulation on Arterial Oxygen Saturation Measured with Pulse-type Oximeter. *Medical & Biological Engineering & Computing, 22*(5), 475–478. doi:10.1007/BF02447712

Tachibana, C., Fukada, T., Hasegawa, R., Satoh, K., Furuya, Y., & Ohe, Y. (1996). Accuracy of A Pulse Oximeter during Hypoxia. *Masui, 45*(4), 479–482.

Tong, D. A., Bartels, K. A., & Honeyager, K. S. (2002). Adaptive Reduction of Motion Artifact in the Electrocardiogram. *EMBS/BMES Conference, 2*, 1403-1404.

Tremper, K. K., & Barker, S. J. (1989). Pulse Oximetry. *Anesthesiology, 70*(1), 98–108. doi:10.1097/00000542-198901000-00019

Vicenzi, M. N., Gombotz, H., Krenn, H., Dorn, C., & Rehak, P. (2000). Tran esophageal versus Surface Pulse Oximetry in Intensive Care Unit Patients. *Critical Care Medicine, 28*(7), 2268–2270. doi:10.1097/00003246-200007000-00014

Widrow, B., & Glover, J. R. (1975). Adaptive Noise Canceling: Principles and Applications. *Proceedings of the IEEE, 63*(12), 1692–1716. doi:10.1109/PROC.1975.10036

Wood, L. B., & Asada, H. H. (2006). Noise Cancellation Model Validation for Reduced Motion Artifact Wearable PPG Sensors Using MEMS Accelerometers. *Conference Proceedings; ... Annual International Conference of the IEEE Engineering in Medicine and Biology Society. IEEE Engineering in Medicine and Biology Society. Conference, 1*, 3525–3528.

Yao, J., & Warren, S. (2004). A Novel Algorithm to Separate Motion Artifacts from Photoplethysmographic Signals Obtained with a Reflectance Pulse Oximeter. *Conference Proceedings; ... Annual International Conference of the IEEE Engineering in Medicine and Biology Society. IEEE Engineering in Medicine and Biology Society. Conference, 3*, 2153–2156.

KEY TERMS AND DEFINITIONS

Esophagus: Is a channel formed by the muscles connecting the throat to the stomach.

SpO$_2$: Is the percentage of HbO$_2$ to the sum of hemoglobin Hb and HbO$_2$ in blood.

PPG: Photoplethysmographic, which is caused by the fluctuations of vessels volume.

Oximetry: By detecting the absorbance of the finger or other parts of the body, in red and infrared wavelength, calculate human SpO$_2$.

AC/ DC: The PPG waveform is composed of two parts. One is changing with the pulse change, that we call AC, the other one is not changing with the pulse change, that we call DC.

Left Ventricle: Is one of the four ventricular of human heart ventricles, which include two atrium and two ventricles. It receives oxygenated blood from the left atrium, and then pumps into the arteries to supply oxygenated blood to the body.

Descending Aorta: Is a part of the circulation of the artery.

Standard Deviation: Is proposed to measure a difference between data and its average.

Peak-to-Peak Value: The distance between maximum and minimum.

Chapter 16

Digital Auscultation System of Traditional Chinese Medicine and Its Signals Acquisition:
Analysis Methods

Fanpeng Zhou
East China University of Science and Technology, China

Jianjun Yan
East China University of Science and Technology, China

Yiqin Wang
Shanghai University of Traditional Chinese Medicine, China

Fufeng Li
Shanghai University of Traditional Chinese Medicine, China

Chunming Xia
East China University of Science and Technology, China

Rui Guo
Shanghai University of Traditional Chinese Medicine, China

Haixia Yan
Shanghai University of Traditional Chinese Medicine, China

ABSTRACT

Digital auscultation of Traditional Chinese Medicine (TCM) is a relatively new technology which has been developed for several years. This system makes diagnoses by analyzing sound signals of patients using signal processing and pattern recognition. The paper discusses TCM auscultation in both traditional and current digital auscultation methods. First, this article discusses demerits of traditional TCM auscultation methods. It is through these demerits that a conclusion is drawn that digital auscultation of TCM is indispensable. Then this article makes an introduction to voice analysis methods from lin-

DOI: 10.4018/978-1-60960-064-8.ch016

ear and nonlinear analysis aspects to pattern recognition methods in common use. Finally this article establishes a new TCM digital auscultation system based on wavelet analysis and Back-propagation neural network (BPNN).

INTRODUCTION

Traditional Chinese Medicine (TCM) is a world-renowned cultural achievement. It has been playing an important role in Chinese people's lives since ancient ages. TCM diagnosis methods can be categorized into four basic means, observation, listening, interrogation, and pulse-taking. Observation means observing facial expression, color or shape of the patient. Listening means detecting changes of patient's voice. Interrogation involves asking patients and their family about disease development, current symptoms, and circumstances related to the diseases. Pulse-taking is palpating his (her) pulse (Xu, 2006).

TCM auscultation is the diagnostic tool commonly known as listening. As is known to all of us, voice is generated by the speech organs which reflect different body status. So we can identify people's body status from their voice (Wang, 1997). Human's brain is an automatic system of information extraction, analysis and identification. Brain commands ears to capture sound signals, and these signals are sent into brain for processing. Sound signals, together with memory and experiences, are used to make judgment. Yet, this manual approach meets some problems when used in medical field in which high accuracy is needed. The most typical problems are as follows: (Mo, 1996)

1. First, different individuals may feel or react differently about the same sound or voice. Therefore, auscultation done by human lacks unified standard.
2. Second, it takes a long time to learn TCM auscultation. An inexperienced TCM doctor cannot diagnose as correctly as those with rich clinical experiences.

3. Third, people's organs will recess, so are ears, and this makes it difficult for an aged TCM doctor to auscultate correctly.
4. Finally, a noisy environment may mask sound or voice, thus cause misdiagnosis.

Considering all these problems, it has become an imperative job to make auscultation accurate and standardized. Effective approach towards this aim is to establish an objective digital auscultation system. This new approach can also serve to increase the efficiency of TCM auscultation (Liu, 2008).

Before solving this problem in traditional TCM auscultation methods, an introduction to TCM signal analysis methods and pattern recognition methods is given. This article will introduce these methods about both basic theory and application in common use.

ANALYSIS METHODS AND FEATURES

In TCM digital auscultation system, there must be features extracted from the signals (voice) for pattern recognition. Generally speaking, voice signals' features are changeable, and this is so called "an unstable process"; but in a small amount of time, the features are relatively unchangeable, so voice signals can be considered as a stable process in a small time interval.

Signal analysis method can be divided into two kinds: linear and nonlinear analysis.

Linear Analysis

In linear analysis method signals are separated into several small intervals. There are several linear analysis methods such as time domain analysis, frequency domain analysis, and time-frequency domain analysis and so on.

Time domain analysis is a method of analyzing and extracting time domain parameters. It is easy to realize time domain analysis and extract important voice parameters.

Frequency domain analysis is to analyze frequency-domain parameters and decompose complex time course waveform into a number of single harmonic components. In this method, frequency structure, amplitude of harmonic component, and phase information can be obtained. There are several frequency domain analysis methods such as Fourier-transform spectrum analysis, Linear Prediction Analysis and so on.

The principle of time-frequency domain analysis is to establish a joint function composed of time and frequency. This function can express energy density and intensity in different time and frequency. In this analysis, one dimension time domain signal $x(n)$ and frequency domain signal $X(e^{jw})$ are united to create a new two dimension signal. Wavelet analysis is a typical representative of time-frequency domain analysis.

Some feature parameters have been used to analyze the signals of TCM Auscultation. There are short-term energy, short-term zero-crossing rate, short-term autocorrelation function and short-term AMDF (Average magnitude difference function) in time-domain. And there is spectrum, power spectrum density and inverse spectrum in frequency-domain. Some of those parameters are shown as following.

$$M_n = \sum_{m=0}^{N-1} \left| x_n(m) \right| \qquad (1)$$

where length of the frame is N, $X_n(m)$ expresses the nth frame signal, and M_n expresses short-term AMDF.

$$Z_n = \frac{1}{2} \sum_{m=0}^{N-1} \left| \mathrm{sgn}\left[x_n(m) \right] - \mathrm{sgn}\left[x_n(m-1) \right] \right| \qquad (2)$$

where Z_n expresses short-term zero-crossing rate.

In practical application, there are also some other normal feature parameters. Some of these parameters are listed in Table 1.

Nonlinear Analysis

Based on chaos theory and fractal theory, nonlinear analysis revealed more information of nonlinear signal.

There are several nonlinear analysis methods, such as Delay Vector Variance (Yan et al., 2008) and so on.

In nonlinear analysis basic feature parameters also exist, for example, Fourier spectrum, attractor, fractal dimension and Lyapunov Coefficients (LC) (Yu et al., 2001).

If an aggregate A is covered by a rectangle, and the rectangle is divided into several little rectangles with area of ε. Then fractal dimension is expressed as the following.

$$d = \lim_{\varepsilon \to 0} \left[\frac{\log N(\varepsilon)}{\log(\frac{1}{\varepsilon})} \right] \qquad (3)$$

where $N(\varepsilon)$ is number of the grids that cover the entire A.

In fact, it is not sufficient for just one parameter to indicate TCM voice characteristics, but rather a group of integrated parameters. Combining linear and nonlinear analysis methods can then capture the characteristics of voice.

Table. 1 Feature parameters used to analyze sound

Parameters	Researchers
spectrogram graphics	Xu et al., 2000
glottis noise energy	Xu et al., 2000; Gong et al., 2002
frequency chattering, formant	Gong et al., 2000; Hou, 2002; Lin, 2003
average fundamental frequency, maximum fundamental frequency, minimum fundamental frequency, custom fundamental frequency, SDFo	Liu et al., 2002
standardization noise energy	Hou et al., 2002
frequency perturbation	Xu et al., 2000; Hou et al., 2002; Liao et al., 2001
HNR	Liao et al., 2001
pitch	Zheng, 2000; Hou, 2002; Liao, 2001; Lin 2003; Branco et al., 2007; Yu et al., 2001
zero-crossing rate	Chen, 2005
low frequency energy ratio, high frequency energy ratio, fractal dimension value, resonance Spectrum proportion parameter, resonance Spectrum proportion parameter, resonance Spectrum energy parameter	Lin, 2003
average zero-crossing rate, peak-or-valley transformation	Chen, 2005; Yang et al., 2000
amplitude perturbation	Xu et al., 2000; Gong et al., 2000; Liao et al., 2001; Yu et al., 2001
fundamental frequency perturbation	Gong et al., 2000; Yu et al., 2001
maximum phonatory time (MPT)	Hou et al., 2002; Yu, et al., 2001
sound intensity; oral airflow (OAF)	Yu et al., 2001

PATTERN RECOGNITION METHODS

In order to get a digital diagnosis conclusion, pattern recognition methods must be introduced. General speaking, there are several recognition methods which are used in different situations. The methods are shown as following.

Template Matching Methods

In the method representative characteristic vectors will be extracted from every speaker's training conversation. These vectors are used to form a feature vector consequence. And the consequence is optimized to calculate a feature aggregate based on some optimizing method. This aggregate is used as a reference template. When recognizing, feature vector consequence is similarly attracted from the test sound signals, then consequence is compared with reference template based on ef-

fective matching rule (Wei et al., 1996). In voice recognition system the most frequent template matching methods are Dynamic Time Warping (DTW) and Vector Quantization (VQ).

Probabilistic Model Methods

In the methods, effective feature vectors are extracted from one or more pronunciation. These vectors are used to form a mathematical model which can effectively portray the regular distribution of the feature vectors in feature space. When recognizing, feature vector consequence is matched with mathematical model, then similarity of test sound and the model is calculated. This similarity is the final recognition criterion. The most frequent model is Hidden Markov Model (HMM) which can depict placidity and variability of the sound signals (Fakotakis et al., 1996).

Artificial Neural Network

Artificial neural network (ANN) is similar to biological nervous systems in information process. It is a unique and complex system composed of parallel units. The system has an advantage of self-organization and self-study, and it also can improve their performance with accumulation of experiences. Because of such merits ANN can contain more accurate chrematistics of the voice samples, so it is obviously helpful for sound recognition (Setlur & Jacobs, 1995).

Generally speaking, template matching method, for example, DTW, is used more in embedded small words recognition system because of its simple structure (Robert, 1990). And probabilistic model method, such as HMM, is used in connective recognition system. ANN is a developing realm, and with the development of various algorithms ANN is used more and more in both small words and connective words recognition system. In this article ANN will be utilized to classify and recognize TCM symptoms.

DIGITAL AUSCULTATION SYSTEM OF TCM

This article establishes an automatic TCM auscultation system. The system construction is shown in Figure 1, from which a general system structure can be gained.

Samples are provided by Shanghai University of TCM. There are 27 healthy samples shown in

Figure 1. System construction of digital auscultation system of TCM. The system consists of several parts, which are preprocessing, feature extraction, training, and matching calculating.

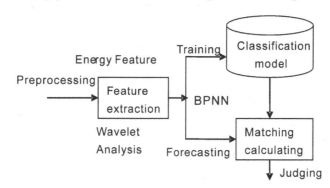

Figure 2. Vowel [a:] of a healthy person. This signal is acquired from the pronunciation of vowel [a:] of a healthy person. And this signal will be compared with those acquired from the patients.

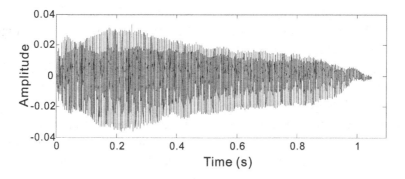

Figure 3. Vowel [a:] of a patient with deficiency syndrome. This signal is also acquired from the pronunciation while this is made by a patient who has the deficiency syndrome.

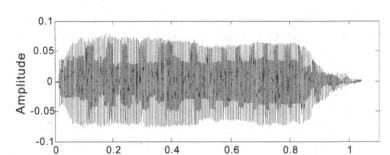

Figure 2 and 185 deficient samples shown in Figure 3, and these samples are all collected from vowel [a:] pronunciation.

Feature Extraction Based on Wavelet Analysis

Wavelet analysis is a new technology developed in the recent 20 years. The emergency of wavelet theory has provided a new analysis method for non-stationary signal, and wavelet has received a few successes in voice signal analysis and voice expression. Because of the capacity of anti-noise robust parameters extracted by wavelet, wavelet can be used more effectively in voice feature extraction. As features extracted by wavelet are not limited in short-term assumption, wavelet application is not limited by voice signal type and obviously more extensive.

In wavelet analysis a set of coefficients called wavelet coefficients are acquired after the decomposition of signals. Therefore the signal can be reconstructed as a linear combination of the wavelet functions weighted by the wavelet coefficients. In order to reconstruct the signal exactly, sufficient number of coefficients should be extracted. The basic theory of wavelet is a time-frequency localization method. And it is obvious that the energy of the wavelet is restricted to a finite time interval. In this method time window and frequency can be changed, which can be expressed as following,

there is a high frequency and low time resolution in low-frequency parts, and there is a high time and low frequency resolution in high parts (Meyer, 1993). This produces a segmentation, or tiling of the time-frequency plane that is appropriate for most physical signals, especially those of a transient nature. This technology applied to the voice signals of TCM will reveal features related to the transient nature of the signal.

Time-frequency localization is realized through decomposition of the signal. The decomposition of the signal into different frequency bands is merely obtained by consecutive of high-pass and low-pass filtering of time domain signal. Each step of the decomposition involves two digital filters and two down-samples. The first filter, a high-pass filter, is the mother wavelet, while the second filter, a low-pass filter, is the mirror version. And outputs of the two filters provide the signal details, which are called D1 in high-pass filter and A1 in low-pass filter. Then A1 is further decomposed and this decomposition process is continued. The procedure of decomposition of a vowel [a:] signal is shown in Figure 4.

It is very important to select a suitable wavelet function and the number of decomposition levels in wavelet analysis of voice signals of TCM. The number of decomposition levels is decided based on the dominant frequency components of voice signal. The levels is chosen as most as possible to retain those parts in wavelet coefficients

Figure 4. Decomposition procedure of vowel [a:]. In this decomposition procedure wavelet analysis is introduced, and there are seven layers in this procedure so that useful information in the signals can be acquired as much as possible.

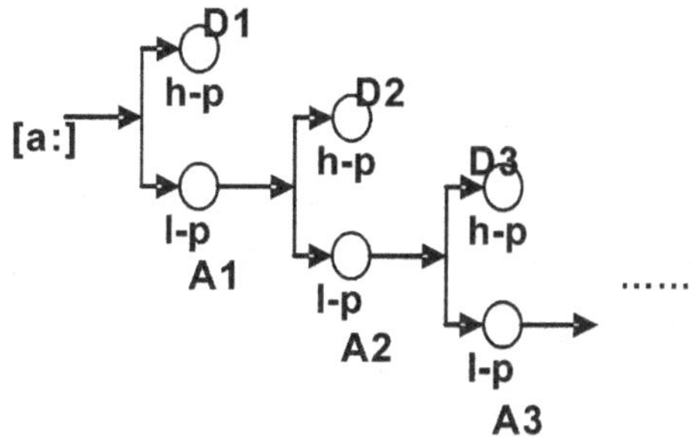

related to the necessary information for pattern recognition. In this study, since the signals don't have useful frequency components above 8000HZ, so the system chooses seven levels. And details of the signal are decomposed into D1~D7 and one approximation, A7. In voice application fields, lots of experiments have been conducted to see which functions work more effectively. Final result shows the smoothing features of the db4 made it more appropriate to analyze voice signals.

In this article wavelet analysis is used to distill and analyze seven-layer Energy features of signals, and the wavelet function is db4. Energy parameter is defined as below.

$$E_n = \sum_{m=0}^{N-1} x^2{}_n(m) \qquad (4)$$

where $x_n(m)$ is the signal processed by windowing treatment, N is the length of window function, E_n expresses amplitude variation of voice.

After feature extraction, this system acquired sixty-five features.

Pattern Recognition Based on BPNN

Features distilled by wavelet analysis are sent to NN (neural network) for pattern recognition. And this article utilizes BPNN to recognize and analyze. BPNN is a multi-layer perceptions neural network based on Error Back Propagation. There are three layers through which signals and error can be transported layer by layer in BPNN (Jacek, 1992; Miner, 2000). BPNN have an advantage of self-study, expanding, linear mapping and non-linear mapping. In this article, the parameters of BPNN are shown as following:

1. Number of input layer nodes: 65. This number is decided by feature number extracted by wavelet analysis. ($n=2^{i-1}+1$, i is wavelet decomposition level, $n=2^{7-1}+1=65$)
2. Number of output layer nodes: 2. Output of BPNN is 1 and 0 which express deficient and healthy result.
3. Number of hidden layer nodes: 10. From empirical formula ($m = \sqrt{n+l} + \alpha$, m is number of hidden layer nodes, n is number of input layer nodes, l is number of output layer nodes, and α express a number between one and ten) (Miner, 2000), we can gain number of hidden layer nodes.
4. Initial learning rate: 0.01. This parameter is acquired from empirical experiments.
5. Max training epochs: 5000.
6. Target error: 0.0001. The lower the target error, the higher accuracy the TCM auscultation system is.

RESULTS

In these samples there are 70% being used for training and 30% for forecasting. Training and forecasting process is repeated for ten times. After that, the average is calculated. Results are acquired as following.

From Table 2 we can see:

Table 2. Comparison of the results in two groups. In this table the recognition accuracy results of healthy group and patients group are compared, and finally total accuracy is concluded.

Group	Numbers		Accuracy %	
	Training	Forecasting	Average	Total
Deficient	130	55	99.38	91.63
Healthy	19	5	36.11	

1. Total recognition accuracy is up to as high as 91.63%, so there can be a conclusion that the method based on Wavelet Analysis and NN is effective and reliable.
2. Deficient samples recognition accuracy is as high as 99.38%, and healthy samples recognition accuracy is 36.11%.

CONCLUSION

As is shown above, beginning with discussion of traditional TCM Auscultation, this article summarizes the merits and demerits of traditional TCM Auscultation, and concludes the necessity of establishing a reliable digital TCM Auscultation system. The article makes an introduction to voice analysis method from aspects of linear analysis and nonlinear analysis and presents a list of stable feature parameters. Then several different pattern recognition methods are also introduced. Digital TCM auscultation system is established based on wavelet analysis and BPNN in this article. The system uses wavelet analysis to extract seven-level energy features and these features are sent to BPNN for pattern recognition. Finally, a satisfactory result shows that this method is feasible and may be applicable and extended for further research.

ACKNOWLEDGMENT

This project was supported by the National Natural Science Foundation of China (No. 30701072), National Science & Technology Pillar Program in the Eleventh Five-year Plan Period (No. 2006BAI08B01-04), Construction Fund for Key Subjects of Shanghai (No. S30302), the Fundamental Research Funds for the Central Universities and Undergraduates' Innovation Experimental Program of Shanghai (S0814). The test data were provided by TCM Syndrome Lab of Shanghai University of TCM.

REFERENCES

Branco, A., Fekete, S., & Rugolo, L. (2007). The newborn pain cry: Descriptive acoustic spectrographic analysis. *International Journal of Pediatric Otorhinolaryngology*, *1*(71), 39–46.

Chen, L. Y. (2005). *The Development of Objective Auscultation System Using Neural Networks*. Unpublished master's theses, Feng chia University, Taiwan.

Fakotakis, N., & Sirigos, J. (1996). *A high performance text independent speaker recognition system based on Vowel Sotting and Neural Nets*. Paper presented at 1996 IEEE International Conference on Acoustics, Speech, and Signal Processing, Atlanta.

Gong, Q., Shen, W., Huang, Z. M., & Chen, Y. Y. (2000). Cases of Computer Analysis on Voice Acoustic Parameters in 896 Adults. *Journal of Audiology and Speech Pathology*, *1*(8), 34–36.

Hou, L. Z., Han, D. M., Xu, W., & Zhang, L. (2002). Study on voice characteristics of people with different sexes and ages. *Journal of Clinical Otorhinolaryngology, 1*(16), 667–669.

Jacek, M. (1992). *Introduction to Artificial Neural Systems*. Chicago, US: West Publishing Company.

Liao, H. R., Chen, J., & Xu, Z. R. (2001). Detection for Objective Acoustics of Morbid Voice. *Journal of Gansu College of Traditional Chinese Medicine, 1*(18), 26–27.

Lin, G. H. (2003). A Study of Automatic Analysis for Listening Examination of Chinese Medicine - Classification and Recognition. In *Vacuity Patient's Voice. Unpublished master's theses*. Chun Yuan Christian University, Chungli.

Liu, N. W. (2008). The objective symptoms of Chinese medicine diagnosis. *Shanxi Journal of Traditional Chinese Medicine, 1*(24), 56–58.

Liu, Q. M., Zhang, J. Q., & Huang, M. Q. (2002). Quantitative analysis of pathological voice. *Journal of Preclinical Medicine College of Shandong Medical University, 1*(16), 89–95.

Meyer, Y. (1993). *Wavelets: Algorithms and Applications. Society for Industrial and Applied Mathematics*. Philadelphia: Baker & Taylor Books.

Miner, B. (2000). *Robust Voice Recognition over IP and Mobile Networks*. Paper presented at the symposium of Proceeding of the Alliance Engineering, Dallas, US.

Mo, X. M. (1996). The status quo and prospect of voice diagnosis. *Journal of tradtional chinese veterinary medicine, 1*(16), 66-67.

Robert, H. (1990). *Neurocomputing*. Massachusetts, US: Addison-Wesley Publishing Company.

Setlur, A., & Jacobs, T. (1995). *Results of a speaker verification service trial using HMM models*. Paper presented at the Proc. Eurospeech, Budapest, Hungary.

Wang, E. Y. (1997). Significance of Sound in clinical diagnosis. *Journal of tradtional chinese veterinary medicine, 1*(4), 47-54.

Wei, G., & Lu, Y. Q. (1996). Chaos and Fractal Theories for Speech Signal Processing. In S. J. Wang (Ed.), *Acta Electronica Sinica: vol. 24. Communication and signal processing* (pp. 34-39). Chinese Institute of Electronics Press.

Xu, J. J., Qiao, Z. M., Qi, Q. H., & Yin, M. (2000). Quantitative Evaluation of Voice in Laryngeal Diseases by Computer Technique. *Acta Universitatis Medicinalis Nanjing, 1*(20), 121–124.

Xu, J. T. (2006). Characteristics of four traditional diagnostic methods and their relationship. *Modern Medicine*, (16): 4–11.

Yan, J. J., Wang, Y. Q., Wang, H. J., Li, F. F., Xia, C. M., Guo, R., & Ma, T. C. (2008, May). *Nonlinear analysis in TCM acoustic diagnosis using Delay Vector Variance*. Paper presented at The 2nd International Conference on Bioinformatics and Biomedical Engineering, Shanghai, PRC.

Yang, M. T., Chiu, C. C., & Yang, Z. X. (2000). *Pilot Study on Vacuity Patient's Speech by Fractal Demension Method*. Paper presented at Engineering Technique's Application on Chinese Medicine and Western Medicine 2000 Annual Symposium, Taipei.

Yu, P., Ouaknine, M., Revis, J., & Giovanni, A. (2001). Objective Voice Analysis for Dysphonic Patients: A Multiparametric Protocol Including Acoustic and Aerodynamic Measurements. *Journal of Voice, 1*(15), 29–42.

Zheng, Y. R. (2000). *An Expert System with Inquiring Diagnosis and Auscultical Diagnosis of Chronic Renal Failure in Chinese Medicine. Unpublished master's theses*. Chun Yuan Christian University, Chungli.

ADDITIONAL READING

Bland, A. (1995). Logistic regression. In Brank, B. (Ed.), *An Introduction to Medical statistics* (pp. 317–320). London, UK: Oxford University Press.

Booth, J. R., & Childers, D. G. (1979). Automated analysis of ultra high speed larynx geal films. *IEEE Transactions on Bio-Medical Engineering*, (26): 185–192. doi:10.1109/TBME.1979.326556

Deller, J. R., Proakis, J. G., & Hansen, J. H. L. (1993). Example short-term features and applications. In A. M () Discrete-Time Processing of Speech Signals. New York, 1993, pp.236–262.

Deng, T. T. (1993). Basic theory of traditional Chinese medicine. In Deng, T. T. (Ed.), *Diagnostics of Chinese Medicine* (pp. 5–11). Taipei, Taiwan: Chih-Yin Publishing Company.

Dickinson, R. J., & Kitney, R. (2004). Miniature ultra sonic probe construction for minimal access surgery. *Physics in Medicine and Biology*, (49): 3527–3538. doi:10.1088/0031-9155/49/16/002

Fenster, A., Downey, D. B., & Cardinal, H. N. (2001). Three-dimensional ultra sound imaging. *Physics in Medicine and Biology*, *1*(46), 67–99. doi:10.1088/0031-9155/46/5/201

Giovanni, A., Ouaknine, M., Guelfucci, B., Yu, P., Zanaret, M., & Triglia, J. M. (1999). Nonlinear behavior of vocal fold vibration, the role of coupling between the vocal folds. *Voice*, *1*(13), 465–476. doi:10.1016/S0892-1997(99)80002-2

Horng, C. H. (1993). The principles and methods of diagnostics. In Wang, X. (Ed.), *The Illustrations of Chinese Medicine* (pp. 13–18). Taipei, Taiwan: Lead Press.

Kiritani, S. (2000). High-speed digital image recording for observing vocal fold vibration. In Kent, R. D., & Ball, M. (Eds.), *Voice Quality Measurement* (pp. 145–152). San Diego: Singular Publishing.

Kiritani, S. (2000). High-speed digital image recording for observing vocal fold vibration. In Kent, R. D., & Ball, M. (Eds.), *Voice Quality Measurement* (pp. 145–167). San Diego: Singular Publishing.

Lang, A. E., & Lozano, A. M. (1998). Parkinson's disease. *The New England Journal of Medicine*, *1*(339), 1044–1053. doi:10.1056/NEJM199810083391506

Lieberman, P. (1963). Some acoustic measures of the fundamental periodicity of normal and pathologic larynges. *Acoust Soc Am*, *1*(35), 344–353. doi:10.1121/1.1918465

Marek, K., & Seibyl, J. (2000). A molecular map for neurode generation. *Science*, *1*(289), 409–411. doi:10.1126/science.289.5478.409

Markel, J. D. (1972). Digital in verse filtering: a new tool for formant trajectory estimation. *IEEE Trans. Audio Elec*, *1*(20), 129–137. doi:10.1109/TAU.1972.1162367

Metter, J., & Hanson, W. (1986). Clinical and acoustical variability in hypo kinetic dysarthria. *Journal of Communication Disorders*, *1*(19), 347–366. doi:10.1016/0021-9924(86)90026-2

Michalis, D., Gramss, T., & Strube, H. W. (1995). Lottal-to-noise excitation ratio a new measure for describing pathological voices. *Acustica*, *1*(81), 700–706.

Parkinson's disease. *Advances in Neurology*, *1*(37), 1–7.

Richards, M., Marder, K., Cote, L., & Mayeux, R. (1994). Interrater reliability of the unified Parkinson's disease rating scale motor examination. *Movement Disorders*, *1*(9), 89–91. doi:10.1002/mds.870090114

Schulz, G. M., & Grant, M. K. (2000). Effects of speech therapy and pharmacologic and surgical treatments on voice and speech in Parkinson's disease: are view of the literature. *Journal of Communication Disorders*, *1*(33), 59–88. doi:10.1016/S0021-9924(99)00025-8

Shaughnessy, D. O. (1987). *Speech production and acoustic-phonetics, Speech Communication, Human and Machine*. Reading, MA: Addison-Wesley.

Shipley, K., & McAfee, J. (1992). *Assessment in speech language pathology: are source manual*. San Diego: Singular Publishing Group.

The Dysarthrias: physiology, acoustics, perception, management (pp.101–130). San Diego, US: College-Hill Press.

Timke, R., Leden, H., & Moore, P. (1959). Laryngeal vibrations: measurements of the glottis wave. *Arch Otolaryngol, 1*, (69): 438–444.

Titze, I. R., Baken, R., & Herzel, H. (1993). Evidence of chaos in vocal fold vibration. In I. R. Titze (Ed.), *Vocal Fold Physiology New Frontier in Basic Science* (pp. 143-188) *y*. San Diego: Singular Pbulishing.

Titze, I. R., Horii, Y., & Scherer, R. C. (1987). Some technical considerations in voice perturbation measurements. *Speech. Hearing Research*, (30): 252–260.

Ward, C. D., Sanes, J. N., Dambrosia, J. M., & Calne, D. B. (1983). *Methods for evaluating treatment in Weismer, G. (1984). Articulatory characteristics of Park insomnia dysarthria: segmental and phrase-level timing, spirantization, and glottal-supra glottal coordination* (Mc, M., Rosenbeck, J., & Aronson, A., Eds.).

Whittingham, T. A. (2003). Transducers and beamforming. In Hoskins, P. R., Thrush, A., Martin, K., & Whittingham, T. A. (Eds.), *Diagnostic Ultra sound: Physics and Equipment* (pp. 23–48). London, UK: Greenwich Medical Media.

Yan, Y., Ahmad, K., Kunduk, M., & Bless, D. (2005). Analysis of vocal fold vibrations from high speed laryngeal images using a Hilberttrans form based methodology. *Voice, 1*(19), 161–175. doi:10.1016/j.jvoice.2004.04.006

Yan, Y., Chen, X., & Bless, D. (2006). Automatic tracing of the vocal fold motion from high speed digital images. *IEEE Transactions on Bio-Medical Engineering*, (53): 1394–1400. doi:10.1109/TBME.2006.873751

Zwirner, P., & Barnes, G. (1992). Vocal tract steadiness: ameasure of phonatory stability and upper airway motor control during phonation in dysarthria. *Journal of Speech and Hearing Research*, *1*(35), 761–768.

KEY TERMS AND DEFINITIONS

Digital Auscultation: This refers to a new auscultation system based on digital technology. And in this system advanced digital process methods will be introduced in order to realize the objective of auscultation system.

TCM: This word is short of traditional Chinese medicine. And in this medicine methods observation, listening, interrogation, and pulse-taking will be introduced to cure the patients.

Voice Analysis: Voice analysis is just the method of auscultation, in which patients' voice will be used to diagnose .And in this article patients' voice is acquired by digital methods for further research.

Pattern Recognition: This refers to recognition of different diseases. In this article new recognition method based on BPNN is introduced.

Wavelet Analysis: This refers to a new digital process technology which is generally used for feature extraction in this digital auscultation system.

BPNN: BPNN is a multi-layer perceptions neural network based on Error Back Propagation.

Energy Feature: This refers to one of the most important features extracted by wavelet analysis.

Chapter 17

Pulse Wave Analysis of Traditional Chinese Medicine Based on Hemodynamics Principles

Rui Guo
Shanghai University of Traditional Chinese Medicine, China

Yiqin Wang
Shanghai University of Traditional Chinese Medicine, China

Haixia Yan
Shanghai University of Traditional Chinese Medicine, China

Fufeng Li
Shanghai University of Traditional Chinese Medicine, China

Jianjun Yan
East China University of Science and Technology, China

Zhaoxia Xu
Shanghai University of Traditional Chinese Medicine, China

ABSTRACT

From the perspective of hemodynamics principles, the pressure pulse wave marked in the radial artery is the comprehensive result of pulse wave propagation and reflection in the arterial conduit. The most common pulse charts (also called pulse wave) obtained by Traditional Chinese Medicine (TCM) pulse-taking technique, if quantified and standardized, may become a universal and valuable diagnostic tool. The methods of feature extraction of TCM pulse charts currently involve time-domain analysis, frequency-domain analysis and time-frequency joint analysis. The feature parameters extracted by these methods have no definite clinical significance. Therefore, these feature parameters cannot essentially

DOI: 10.4018/978-1-60960-064-8.ch017

differentiate different types of TCM pulse. In this chapter, the harmonic analysis method was applied to analyze the common TCM pulse charts (plain pulse, wiry pulse, slippery pulse). Velocity and reflectivity coefficients of pulse were calculated. We found that wave velocities and reflection coefficients of different TCM pulse have different distributions. Furthermore, we studied the clinical significance of velocities and reflection coefficients. The result suggests that wave velocity and reflection coefficient are the feature parameters of TCM pulse with physiological and pathological significance, which can be used to interpret formation of Chinese medicine pulse. Our study reveals the mechanism of TCM pulse formation and promotes non-invasive TCM pulse diagnostic method.

INTRODUCTION

Pulse diagnosis of Traditional Chinese Medicine (TCM), as a non-invasive detection method, has won the praises and attention in both China and around the globe. Nevertheless, the traditional pulse diagnosis lacks objective evaluation standards, which has severely restricted the research and clinical application of pulse diagnosis, as 〖Sphygmology Classic〗 states that "the theory of pulse is abstruse and the conditions of pulse are difficult to differentiate". Therefore, objective and digital pulse diagnosis becomes important for the modernization of this ancient and valuable traditional Chinese medicine technique.

For many years, the objective and quantification problem of TCM pulse has been a hotly-pursued area of multi-disciplinary research. Currently, a lot of researchers in China and abroad have put forward different methods concerning pulse wave signal analysis, involving time-domain analysis, frequency-domain analysis and time-frequency joint analysis, etc. The extracted parameters include waveform amplitude and area, power spectrum, cepstral (logarithm of power spectrum Inverse Fourier Transform called cepstral), wavelet energy at different scales, etc. However, there are still some limitations that remain to be overcome: ① the research on TCM pulse is limited to the application of signal processing methods for analyzing the waveform of pulse, without much consideration regarding the formation principle of pulse wave. ② the extracted feature and parameter

are insufficient for interpreting clinical pathology, i.e., diagnostic purposes.

A classical treatise of pulse has pointed out that: "the heart is the basis of life and the origin of blood vessel" (〖Suwen · Thesis on Zangxiang〗). The contraction and relaxation of the aortic pulse result from the periodic contraction and relaxation of the heart that propagate from the bottom of aortic pulse and along the arterial duct in waveform. This waveform is called the pulse wave. The information acquired from radial artery is actually the comprehensive reflection of wave form (shape), velocity (fast or slow), period (rhythm) and swing (intensity) of the pulse wave presented in radial artery (Liu & Li, 1982). This result informs us that the scientific nature of pulse may be revealed via studying the propagation law of pulse wave in arterial conduit. In recent years, we have studied the variation range of the pulse wave velocity and reflection coefficient of slippery pulse, wiry pulse and plain pulse gathered from hundreds of healthy people based on theory of pulse wave propagation and reflection of hemodynamic principles, and we have obtained some meaningful results that are presented in this chapter.

HEMODYNAMIC PRINCIPLE BASIS OF TCM PULSE WAVE

In TCM, pulse refers to what the doctor senses by palpating the examinee's radial artery with fingers. Diagnosis information is then extracted based on the association of the pulse with pathology and physiology. The sensed pulse pulsation originates from radial direction pulsation of radial artery (change of the semidiameter of blood vessel); whereas the blood pressure of arterial conduit represents the change of semidiameter of blood vessel as a function of time. Therefore, the detected changeable waveform of arterial conduit semidiameter could nearly match the waveform of blood pressure.

From hemodynamic standpoint, the pressure pulse wave generates when blood pass through the heart after heart contracts, then it transmits into the brachial artery and reach to radial artery. The reflected wave generates in brachial artery and radial artery. The pressure wave in radial artery is actually the integrative result of the pressure wave and reflected wave (Liu, 1982). In other words, the pressure pulse wave marked in the radial artery is a superposition of pressure pulse and reflected wave in the radial artery.

Propagation Characteristics of Pulse Wave

The fastness or slowness of the pulse wave propagation shall depend on the propagation velocity of pulse wave; whereas the propagation velocity of the pulse wave shall directly relate to the elastic feature of arterial wall. As for certain confirmed arterial conduit section, whenever the blood pressure in the conduit changes dp, the relative variation of the sectional area of blood vessels would be dA / A. Generally the expanding degree of the blood vessels is denoted as (Liu, 1982):

$$D = \frac{1}{A} \frac{dA}{dp} \tag{1}$$

Obviously, the blood vessel becomes stiffener, the expanding degree D becomes smaller; on the contrary, the blood vessel has better elasticity, the expanding degree D becomes larger. Under certain circumstances, the propagation velocity of

pulse wave c could be expressed by the expanding degree D (Liu, 1982):

$$c = \sqrt{\frac{1}{\rho D}} \tag{2}$$

ρ in Formula (2) is the blood density. Thus, it can be seen that the blood vessel becomes stiffener, the pulse wave spreads faster; whereas the blood vessel has better elasticity, the propagation velocity of pulse wave becomes smaller. Therefore, we could judge the elasticity of blood vessel via testing the velocity of pulse wave.

Reflection Properties of Pulse Wave

The pulse wave caused due to heart ventricle intermittent ejection shall propagandize along with the arterial conduit and the pulse wave shall eject whenever the geometric property (cross section area of blood vessel) and physical property (elasticity of blood vessel wall) change. The ejected amount of characterized pulse wave is the ratio of reflected pressure pulse wave to incident pressure pulse wave (Liu & Li, 1997), namely

$$R = \frac{P_{refletion}}{P_{travel}} \tag{3}$$

R is the reflection coefficient of pressure pulse wave. Liu (1997) states that the reflection of pulse wave shall bring the property of aorta far end and peripheral blood vessel resistance. The larger peripheral blood vessel resistance, the greater reflection coefficient. Therefore, the reflection coefficient could be used for diagnosing the features of microcirculation of organs and tissues. From Hemodynamics Principles and Methods (Liu & Li, 1997) and Blood Flow in Artery (McDonald, 1982), we could learn that the influence of reflection wave, despite of being reflected from the farthest artery terminal, shall surely appear in the pulse wave of the same heart period. In other words, the reflection wave shall overlap in the incident wave of the same period so as to make the wave form change. Nevertheless, the delayed time of the reflection wave each time shall depend on the propaganda velocity of the pulse wave. Therefore, the velocity of pulse wave and end reflection coefficient of the arterial conduit shall exert the direct influence to the pulse waveform.

To sum up, the pressure pulse wave marked in the radial artery is the comprehensive result of the propaganda and reflection of artery conduit in the radial artery. However, some cardiovascular diseases or organ tissue diseases would cause the change of reflection regularity of pulse wave and then affect the form features of pulse wave, such as the blood vessel of the aged has generally become stiffened, the pulse wave velocity becomes larger, the reflection wave could faster reach to the diastolic period, or even to contraction period and overlap with the traveling wave so as to form into the characteristics of wiry pulse (Figure 1). Therefore, the pulse wave velocity and the end reflection coefficient of the artery conduit shall exert the direct influence to the pulse wave form. The reason is that the pulse wave velocity and reflection coefficient have the direct relation-ship with the physical parameters such as blood vessel elasticity, blood viscosity and peripheral resistance. Supposing that we could analyze the pulse wave in terms of the propaganda property and reflection property of the pulse wave, it is expected to find out the index of the physical meanings.

WAVE HARMONIC WAVE ANALYSIS OF PULSE WAVE

In our laboratory, we use ZM_III type pulse wave sensor to collect 38 examples of wiry pulse, 31 examples of plain pulse and 40 examples of slip-pery pulse. We carry out Fourier decomposition of typical periodical pulse wave and analyze the harmonic wave amplitude of the *1st* to *8th* harmonic wave. According to the principle of Fourier series, periodic functions can be expanded into a constant and a group common cycle of sine and cosine functions. In expanded form, the part that minimum period equal to the original function cycle is called the primary harmonic or first-harmonic wave. The wave of 8 times the

Figure 1. The feature of pulse wave formed after combining the reflecting wave with traveling wave, which looks like the pulse chart of wiry pulse in TCM, prg denotes traveling wave, ref denotes reflection wave, pulse denotes the superposition of traveling wave and reflection wave

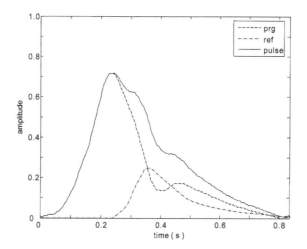

Figure 2.This figure contains a typical pulse chart of slippery pulse in TCM and its analysis of harmonic wave. Panel A contains a typical pulse chart of slippery pulse in TCM. Panel B contains amplitude-frequency characteristic of slippery pulse. The abscissa shows different harmonic number n of Fourier analysis of slippery pulse, and the vertical ordinate shows corresponding amplitude of Fourier analysis. Arrow points to the position n_{min} where the first local minimum harmonic amplitude P_{min} appears.

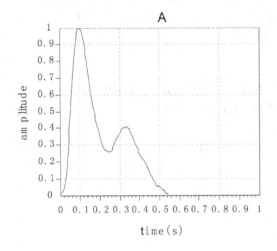
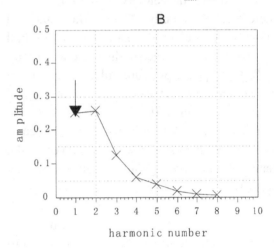

fundamental frequency is called the 8th harmonic wave. The result is as follows:

(1) The harmonic wave analysis of slippery pulse (see Figure2)

By statistics of pulse amplitude-frequency characteristic of 40 slippery pulses, we find that whenever the first minimum harmonic amplitude of slippery pulse appears, 70% of the corresponding minimum harmonic number n_{min} shall rest upon 1 or 2, more in 2.

Figure 3.This figure contains a typical pulse chart of plain pulse in TCM and its analysis of harmonic wave. Panel A contain a typical pulse chart of plain pulse in TCM. Panel B contains amplitude-frequency characteristic of plain pulse. The abscissa shows different harmonic number n of Fourier analysis of plain pulse, and the vertical ordinate shows corresponding amplitude of Fourier analysis. Arrow points to the position n_{min} where the first local minimum harmonic amplitude P_{min} appears.

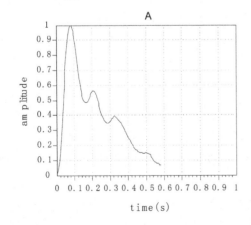
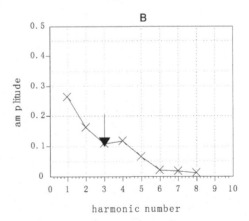

(2) The harmonic wave analysis of plain wave (see Figure3)

By statistics of pulse amplitude-frequency characteristic of 31 plain pulses, we find that whenever the first minimum harmonic amplitude of plain pulse appears, 73% of the corresponding minimum harmonic number n_{min} shall rest upon 3 or 4.

(3) The harmonic wave analysis of wiry wave (see Figure 4)

By statistics of pulse amplitude-frequency characteristic of 38 wiry pulses, we find that whenever the first minimum harmonic amplitude of wiry pulses appears, 74% of the corresponding minimum harmonic number n_{min} shall rest upon 4 or 5.

From the statistics result above, we find that n_{min} of different Chinese medicine pulse have taken on certain rules. Harmonic frequency corresponding to n_{min} is denoted by f_{min}. In accordance with hemodynamics principle, n_{min}, P_{min} and f_{min} are related to the propagation and reflection of pulse wave. Then we shall seek for rules of velocity

and reflection coefficient based on the harmonic analysis of pulse wave.

ANALYSIS OF PULSE WAVE PROPAGATION AND REFLCTION PROPERTY

Calculating Method of Wave Velocity and Reflection Coefficient

Liu & Liu (2007) introduced the calculating method of wave velocity and coefficient on the basis of amplitude-frequency characteristic of pressure wave; we have found out the minimum harmonic wave n_{min} corresponding to the first minimum harmonic amplitude and then get the corresponding minimum frequency. According to the principle of Fourier transform, f_{min} is n_{min} times heart frequency. That is:

$$f_{min} = n_{min} * (heart\ rate\ /\ 60) \qquad (4)$$

According to the definition of wavelength, we know wavelength λ corresponding to f_{min}:

Figure 4. This figure contains a typical pulse chart of wiry pulse in TCM and its analysis of harmonic wave. Panel A contain a typical pulse chart of wiry pulse in TCM. Panel B contains amplitude-frequency characteristic of wiry pulse. The abscissa shows different harmonic number n of Fourier analysis of wiry pulse, and the vertical ordinate shows corresponding amplitude of Fourier analysis. Arrow points to the position n_{min} where the first local minimum harmonic amplitude P_{min} appears.

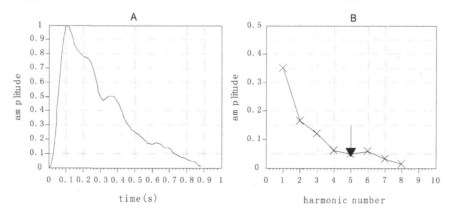

$$\lambda = \frac{c}{f_{min}} \qquad (5)$$

Where a c refers to pulse velocity. According to $\frac{1}{4}$ Wavelength Law of propagation and reflection of pressure pulse wave, the position is $\frac{1}{4}$ from terminal where the first minimum harmonic amplitude of pulse appears. Pressure wave is collected at the radial artery in this research; therefore, the distance of the reflection wave transmitting from terminal to radial artery is $\frac{1}{4}$ the wavelength corresponding to f_{min}:

$$L = \frac{1}{4} \times \lambda \qquad (6)$$

Calculate the pulse velocity c based on the minimum frequency:

$$c = L*(4* f_{min}) \qquad (7)$$

Where L is generally valued 0.8.

Calculate the first minimum amplitude P_{min} and corresponding amplitude P_1 of harmonic number $n=1$ based on amplitude-frequency characteristic of pressure wave and then calculates the reflection coefficient of pressure wave R:

$$R = (P_1 - P_{min}) / P_1 \qquad (8)$$

Wave Velocity Distribution of Wiry Pulse, Slippery Pulse and Plain Pulse

Wave velocity is an index of propagation property of pulse wave. By the analysis of wiry pulse, slippery pulse and plain pulse above, we know that we could get f_{min} of each type of pulse respectively based on Formula (4). Then we could estimate

wave velocity c based on Formula (7). We can get the following distribution of 38 wiry pulses, 40 slippery pulses and 31 plain pulses: the scope of wave velocity of wiry pulse is within $c \geq 12.6 m/s$, the wave velocity of plain pulse within $9.0 \leq c \leq 16.4 m/s$; whereas the scope of wave velocity of slippery pulse is within $3.6 \leq c \leq 10.8 m/s$.

Reflection Coefficient Distribution of Wiry Pulse, Slippery Pulse and Plain Pulse

Reflection coefficient is an index of reflection characteristic of pulse wave. We could get the following distribution law of pulse reflection coefficient of 38 wiry pulses, 40 slippery pulses and 31 plain pulses: the scope reflection coefficient R of wiry pulse is within $R \geq 0.7$, the reflection coefficient of plain pulse within $0.5 \leq R \leq 0.7$; whereas the scope of the reflection coefficient of slippery pulse is within $0.2 \leq R \leq 0.5$ (see Figure 5).

To sum up, we could draw the distribution Figure 5 of wiry pulse, slippery pulse and plain pulse based on the wave velocity and reflection coefficient of pulse wave. From Figure 5, we could know some distribution laws of wiry pulse, slippery pulse and plain pulse: the wiry pulse usually appears in the area with faster wave velocity and greater reflection coefficient; the slippery pulse usually appears in the area with slower wave velocity and smaller reflection coefficient whereas the plain pulse shall take on in the area between the two kinds of pulses.

CONCLUSION

The feature extraction methods of pulse taken in TCM often include time-domain analysis, frequency-domain analysis and time-frequency joint analysis. The clinical significance of feature parameters of time-domain pulse chart has been mostly studied nowadays. However, the results often show discrepancies with respect to clinical

Figure 5. The distribution of reflection coefficients and wave velocities of wiry pulse, slippery pulse and plain pulse

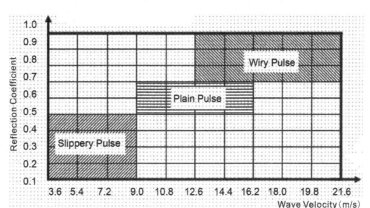

studies. Feature parameters of other types of pulse charts have not shown definite clinical significance. Therefore, these feature parameters cannot differentiate the different types of pulse obtained from TCM practice.

Based on hemodynamics principles, we know that the propagation and reflection of pulse wave is the source of difference in pulse charts. Each pulse chart appears to be specific to one TCM pulse type. Presumably, differences in TCM pulse charts are related to superposition between propagation and reflection of pulse wave. This chapter has studied the propagation property and refection property of pressure pulse wave of wiry pulse, plain pulse and slippery pulse in TCM. It was found that wave velocity characterizing propagation property and reflection coefficient characterizing reflection property of different TCM pulse (wiry pulse, plain pulse and slippery pulse) appear regularly-distributed. The understanding of these parameters as the characteristics for the classification of TCM pulse may help improve the recognition accuracy of existing classification method of TCM pulse. Different TCM pulse often corresponds to different clinical significance, reflecting pathological change of the Zang-Fu organs, Qi and blood. Therefore, wave velocity and reflection coefficients are feature parameters of pulse charts with physiological and pathological significance. With the study on formation mechanism of TCM pulse, combined with wave velocity and reflection coefficient of pulse, there may be new breakthroughs in the understanding and quantification of pulse.

ACKNOLWLEDGMENT

This project was supported National 11th Five Supportive Project (N0. 2006BAI08B01-04), Shanghai 3th Leading Academic Discipline Project (No. S30302), Shanghai Science Foundation for The Excellent Youth Scholar)

REFERENCES

Liu, Z., & Liu, Z. R. (2007) Pulse Processing. Patent No.: 200710045229.7

Liu, Z. R. (1982). Pulse and Hemodynamics in Traditional Chinese Medicine. *Chinese Journal of Science*, 5(6), 411–413.

Liu, Z. R. (1982). Blood Flow in Artery. *Science Press*. Beijing. (In Chinese). Translation from D.A.McDonald (1974). Blood Flow in Arteries, EdwardArnold, London.

Liu, Z. R. & Li, X. X. (1982). Change of Pressure Wave of Radial Artery with Physical Parameter. *Chinese Journal of Theoretical and Applied Mechanics* (3), 244

Liu, Z. R., & Li, X. X. (1997). *Hemodynamics Principles and Methods* (1st ed.). Fudan University Press.

'Sphygmology Classic' was written in the 3d century AD by Wang shu he in Western Jin Dynasty, and 'Sphygmology Classic' is the earliest extant Sphygmology monograph.

'Suwen' is a part of 'The Huang Di's Canon of Internal Medicine', and is a seminal text of ancient Chinese medicine, covering the areas such as the Theory of Traditional Chinese Medicine. The book is writted by more than one person and there is not a final conclusion yet about writing time of the book.

ADDITIONAL READING

Hanon, O., Haulon, S., Lenoir, H., Seux, M. L., Rigaud, A. S., & Safar, M. (2005). Relationship between arterial stiffness and cognitive function in elderly subjects with complaints of memory loss. *Stroke, 36*(10).

Hashimoto, J., Nichols, W. W., O'Rourke, M. F., & Imai, Y. (2008). Association Between Wasted Pressure Effort and Left Ventricular Hypertrophy in Hypertension:Influence of Arterial Wave Reflection. *American Journal of Hypertension, 21*(3).

Lukman, S., He, Y. L., & Hui, S. C. (2007). *Computational methods for Traditional Chinese Medicine: A survey*. Computer Methods and Programs in Biomedicine.

Saijo, Y., Utsugi, M., Yoshioka, E., Fukui, E., & Sata, T., F., Nakagawa, N., Hasebe, N., Yoshida, T., & Kishi, R. (2009). Inflammation as a cardiovascular risk factor and pulse wave velocity as a marker of early-stage atherosclerosis in the Japanese population. *Environmental Health and Preventive Medicine*, 14.

Sugawara, J., Komine, H., Hayashi, K., Maeda, S., & Matsuda, M. (2007). Relationship between augmentation index obtained from carotid and radial artery pressure waveforms. *Journal of Hypertension, 25*(2).

Toprak, A., Reddy, J., Chen, W., Srinivasan, S., & Berenson, G. (2009). Relation of Pulse Pressure and Arterial Stiffness to Concentric Left Ventricular Hypertrophy in Young Men (from the Bogalusa Heart Study). *The American Journal of Cardiology, 103*(7).

Utsugi, M., Saijo, Y., & Kishi, R. (2005). A review of epidemiological studies about pulse wave velocity for prevention of cardiovascular disease. *Japanese Journal of Public Health*, 52.

Wang, Y. Q. (1994). *Diagnostics of Traditional Chinese Medicine*. Beijing: Higher Education Press.

Yan, J. J., Wang, Y. Q., & Li, F. F. Y, H.X., Xia, C.M., G, R. (2008). Analysis and Classification of Wrist Pulse using Sample Entropy. *2008 IEEE International Symposium on IT in Medicine & Education*. 12-14, Dec, Xiamen, China.

Yan, J. J., Wang, Y. Q., Xia, C. M., & Li, F. F. Y, H.X., G, R. (2007). Detecting Nonlinearity in Wrist Pulse Using Delay Vector Variance Method, *International Conference on Cognitive Neurodynamics in Shanghai*.

KEY TERMS AND DEFINITIONS

Pulse Chart: A chart that consist of the recorded pulse wave.

Pulse Diagnosis in TCM: The pulse diagnosis, i.e., the pulse-taking, is an approach to understand the disease condition and differentiate syndrome patterns by feeling the patients' pulsation with the physician's fingers.

Reflection Coefficient of Pulse Wave: The ejected amount of characterized pulse wave is the ratio of reflected pressure pulse wave to incident pressure pulse wave.

The Plain Pulse: There are pulsations in three regions, around 4 beats in a cycle of respiration, neither superficial nor deep, neither big nor small, moderate, gentle, forceful and regular rhythm with certain force in chi region by pressing, which may correspondingly change along with the changes of physiological activities and weather changes.

The Slippery Pulse: The pulse comes and goes smoothly and feels like beads rolling on a plate.

The Wiry Pulse: The pulse is long and straight, feeling like palpating the string of musical instrument.

Wave Velocity of Pulse Wave: The velocity or speed of the pulse wave propagation.

Hemodynamics: The branch of physiology that studies the circulation of the blood and the forces involved.

Section 5
Computational Biology

Chapter 18
A New Mechanical Algorithm for Calculating the Amplitude Equation of the Reaction–Diffusion Systems

Houye Liu
Wenzhou University, China

Weiming Wang
Wenzhou University, China

ABSTRACT

Amplitude equation may be used to study pattern formatio. In this chapter, we establish a new mechanical algorithm AE_Hopf for calculating the amplitude equation near Hopf bifurcation based on the method of normal form approach in Maple. The normal form approach needs a large number of variables and intricate calculations. As a result, deriving the amplitude equation from diffusion-reaction is a difficult task. Making use of our mechanical algorithm, we derived the amplitude equations from several biology and physics models. The results indicate that the algorithm is easy to apply and effective. This algorithm may be useful for learning the dynamics of pattern formation of reaction-diffusion systems in future studies.

INTRODUCTION

Turing (1952) showed that under certain conditions, reaction and diffusion processes alone could lead to the symmetry-breaking instability (i.e., Turing instability) of a system (i.e., Turing system) from a homogeneous state to a stationary patterned state (Setayeshgar & Cross, 1999). Turing system can generate stationary patterns such as stripes and/or spots. Turing instability

mechanism has particular relevance to pattern formation in nonlinear complex systems. Nowadays, pattern formation is one of the central problems of the natural, social, and technological science (Medvinsky et al., 2002). Especially in population dynamics, pattern can clarify the distribution and development of different species. There are a number of theoretical and numerical studies of pattern formation by using weakly nonlinear analysis (Chen & Vinals, 1999; Dufiet & Boissonade, 1996; Ipsen et al., 1998; Ipsen et al., 2000; Malomed,

DOI: 10.4018/978-1-60960-064-8.ch018

1993; Pena & Perez-Garca, 2000). Among these studies, the authors have focused on pattern formation from a spatially uniform state that is near the transition from linear stability to linear instability by using the standard bifurcation-theoretic tools such as amplitude equations (Pearson, 1993). The amplitude equation formalism is a natural scheme to extract universal properties of pattern formation (Gunaratne et al., 1994). Briefly, the idea of an amplitude equation for an oscillatory reaction-diffusion system is to represent the state of the system through a complex amplitude (real amplitude and phase) which varies much more slowly in space and time than the original dynamical variables (Ipsen et al., 1998).

Near supercritical Hopf bifurcation, the amplitude equation of reaction-diffusion system can be reduced to the complex Ginzburg-Landau equation (CGLE). CGLE describes the time evolution of the amplitude of the oscillatory system, shows rich behavior and has been applied in a variety of contexts (Leppanen, 2004). The CGLE, i.e., amplitude equation, takes the form:

$$\frac{dA}{dt} = (1 - i\varpi)A - (1 + i\alpha)|A|^2 A + (1 + i\beta)\nabla^2 A,$$

(1)

Where a is the complex amplitude of the oscillation. I is the imaginary unit, and ϖ, α, β are adjustable parameters.

Some valid methods for obtaining the coefficients of the amplitude equation have been developed in recent years, such as multi-scale expansion (Newell, et al., 1993), center manifold reduction (Callahan & Knobloch, 1999), etc. Besides, there is another method called normal form approach presented by Ispen et al. (1998). This method can derive normal forms and related amplitude equations for flows and discrete dynamics on the center manifold of a dynamical system at local bifurcations.

However, the normal form approach method requires a huge number of calculations. The ob-

jective of this chapter is to establish a promising mechanical algorithm in **Maple** for calculating the amplitude equation near Hopf bifurcation.

BASIC METHODS

Let us first recall the basic principles of the method of normal form approach for calculating the coefficients of amplitude equation. For more details, we refer to (Ipsen et al., 1998; Ipsen et al., 2000). Here we pay attention to the following reaction-diffusion system:

$$\begin{cases} \dfrac{\partial u}{\partial t} = f(u, v, \mu) + d_1 \nabla^2 u, \\ \dfrac{\partial v}{\partial t} = g(u, v, \mu) + d_2 \nabla^2 v, \end{cases}$$

(2)

where u and v stand for the density of two species, μ the bifurcation parameter, f and g nonlinear function, and d_1, d_2 the diffusion coefficients. $\nabla^2 = \dfrac{\partial}{\partial u^2} + \dfrac{\partial}{\partial v^2}$ is the usual Laplacian operator in two-dimensional space. To simplify, system (2) can be rewritten as

$$\dot{V} = F(V, \mu) + D\nabla^2 V,$$

(3)

where V is a vector ($V \in R^2$), and μ is a set of parameters ($\mu \in R^5$). The stationary point of system (2) is $V_s(\mu)$. $D = diag(d_1, d_2)$ is the diffusive matrix. And J, the so-called Jacobian matrix at the stationary point $V_s(\mu)$, yields

$$J = \begin{bmatrix} f_u(u, v) & f_v(u, v) \\ g_u(u, v) & g_v(u, v) \end{bmatrix}_{V_s(\mu)}.$$

The process of getting the amplitude equation of system (2) is given as follows:

We first consider the stationary point $V_s(\mu)$ of system (3) at which the Jacobian matrix J has two pure imaginary eigenvalues $\lambda_1 = \bar{\lambda}_2 = i\varpi$ near Hopf bifurcation threshold, and all other eigenvalues have nonzero real parts. Denote the right and left eigenvectors of J corresponding to λ_1 by u_1 and u_1^*, and those of λ_2 by u_2 and u_2^*. To simplify, we denote $u = u_1$ and $u^* = u_1^*$. By this choice, the two dimensional center subspace E_c is spanned by any linear combinations of $\mathrm{Re}u$ and $\mathrm{Im}u$, and the center manifold W_c can be locally parameterized by point $A \in E_c$ through a smooth transformation $V = A + h(A,\mu)$. However the motion in the two dimensional center manifold is determined by an amplitude equation which is formulated in term of the two complex eigenvalues and complex conjugate amplitudes $a, \bar{a}$ with $A = au + \bar{a}\bar{u} \in E_c$, Then we can get following parameters using center manifold and normal form theory (Ipsen et al., 1998).

$$\dot{A} = i\varpi_0 A + g_{101}\mu A + g_{210}|A|^2 A + g_{320}|A|^4 A + ...$$

To derive expressions for the coefficients of (6),we first determine the constant vectors f_{pq} by substitution of

$$V = ua + \bar{u}\bar{a} + h_{200}a_2 + h_{110}|a|^2 + h_{020}\bar{a}^2 + h_{001}\mu + h_{101}\mu a + h_{011}\mu\bar{a}.$$

Collecting separate order in $a, \bar{a},$ and μ, we find the following parameters

$$f_{210} = F_{VV}(u,h_{110}) + F_{VV}(\bar{u},h_{200}) + \frac{1}{2}F(u,u,\bar{u}),$$
$$f_{101} = F_{V\mu}(V,\mu)u + F_{VV}(u,h_{001}),$$
$$\tag{4}$$

Where

$$F_{VV}(\varsigma,\eta) = \sum_{i,j=1}^{2}\frac{\partial^2 F}{\partial V_i \partial V_j}\varsigma_i\eta_j, F_{VVV}(\varsigma,\eta,\theta) = \sum_{i,j,k=1}^{2}\frac{\partial^3 F}{\partial V_i \partial V_j \partial V_k}\varsigma_i\eta_j\theta_k, F_{V\mu}(\varsigma,\mu) = \sum_{i=1}^{2}\sum_{j=1}^{2}\frac{\partial^2 F}{\partial V_i \partial \mu_j}\varsigma_i\mu_j.$$
$$\tag{5}$$

Then we can get the coefficients h_{200} and h_{110} of the transformation at second order from the following equations

$$(J - 2\lambda_1 I)h_{200} = -\frac{1}{2}F_{VV}(u,u),$$
$$Jh_{110} = -F_{VV}(u,\bar{u}),$$
$$\tag{6}$$

where $\lambda_1 = i\varpi$, $F_{VV}(u,u)$ and $F_{VV}(u,\bar{u})$ can be solved according to Equation (5). Because the second order coefficients h_{200} and h_{110} have been solved, the third order nonlinear coefficient g_{210} of amplitude equation then becomes

$$g_{210} = u^* f_{210} = u^* F_{VV}(u,h_{110}) + u^* F_{VV}(\bar{u},h_{200}) + u^*\frac{1}{2}F_{VVV}(u,u,\bar{u}).$$
$$\tag{7}$$

For unfolding terms, the coefficient vector h_{001} can be found by solving the following equation

$$Jh_{001} = -F_\mu$$
$$\tag{8}$$

After obtaining h_{001}, the first nontrivial coefficient of the unfold amplitude equation becomes

$$g_{101} = u^* f_{101} = u^* F_{V\mu}u + u^* F_{VV}(u,h_{001}).$$
$$\tag{9}$$

For the diffusion term we have $d = u^* Du$, $D = diag(d_1, d_2)$ is the diffusive matrix.

After setting $\alpha = g_{101}$ and $\beta = g_{210}$ and truncating the higher order, we can obtain the following amplitude equation

$$\frac{\partial A}{\partial t} = (i\varpi + \alpha\mu)A + \beta A|A|^2 + d\nabla^2 A,$$
$$\tag{10}$$

where

$$\alpha = u^* f_{101} = u^* F_{V\mu} \mu + u^* F_{VV}(u, h_{001}),$$

$$\beta = u^* f_{210} = u^* F_{VV}(u, h_{110}) + u^* F_{VV}(\bar{u}, h_{200}) + u^* \frac{1}{2} F_{VVV}(u, u, \bar{u}),$$

$$d = u^* D u.$$

$$(11)$$

It is easy to see that the complexity of the above calculating process can be very hard in practice. In the following section, we will give a mechanical algorithm for calculation Equation (11).

NEW MECHANICAL ALGORITHM

It is a new development orientation in the field of mathematics and computer to conduct science calculation by computer. For a long time, the mathematicians and computer scientists have dreamed of replacing human brain with computer to conduct symbolic operation and any kind of mathematical processes, leading the mathematics to a mechanizing way and making the computer itself become more intelligent.

Maple, an international mathematical software, is an exchanged computer algebra system with great ability of symbolic operation, numerical calculation, coping with graphics, etc. Its powerful functions library and unique interior programming language provide scientific calculation and programming with friendly platform (Wang, 2006).

Formulae (4-11) can be well adapted to calculate the coefficients of amplitude equation by applying **Maple**. The whole process of the normal form approach could be programmed in **Maple**. Now if we want to obtain the coefficients (11) of the amplitude equation based on the normal form approach method, everything we have to do is just to input the information about the system, then the program will give out the exact expression of the amplitude Equation (10) and (11). The main algorithm of **AE_Hopf** is as follows:

INPUT the system, the variables and the Hopf bifurcation condition.

Step 1. Calculate the stationary point $V_s(\mu)$ of the system and sign as sol = u^*, v^*).

Step 2. Calculate the eigenvalues eig = eigenvalues(J) of matrix J.

If type(eig,`sqrt') then
vec=eigenvectors(J);
vec:=op(map(algsubs,op(1,eig[1]) = -1,[vec]));
goto step3;
elif has(eig[i],I) or type(eig[i],`+') then
vec=[eigenvectors(J)]
goto step3
else
error "There is not two pure imaginary eigenvalues of the system";
  end if
  Step 3.
  for i from 1 to nops(vec) do
if type(op(1,vec[i]),`*') then
temp:=op(1,vec[i]);
temp:=op(1,temp);
elif nops(op(1,vec[i])) = 1 then
temp:=op(1,vec[i]);
end if;
if op(1,temp) = 1 and op(2,vec[i]) = 1 then
u*:=op(op(3,vec[i]));
elif op(1,temp) = -1 and op(2,vec[i]) = 1 then
u:=op(op(3,vec[i]));
else
error "The error occurs when the eigenvectors is selected";
end if;
  end do:
  Step 4.
  Obtaining parameters F_{VV}, F_{VVV}, $F_{V\mu}$, h_{110} and h_{200} from (5) and (11);
  Defining parameters α, β, d as (11).
  OUTPUT The amplitude equation.

EXAMPLES

The mechanical algorithm **AE_Hopf** of this study is useful in calculating the amplitude equation of the reaction-diffusion system (2). Here are some examples to illustrate the mechanized process.

A. The Brusselator System

We consider the following Brusselator system (Nicolis & Prigogine, 1977):

$$\begin{cases} \dfrac{\partial x}{\partial t} = a - (b+1)x + x^2 y + d_x \nabla^2 x, \\ \dfrac{\partial y}{\partial t} = bx - x^2 y + d_y \nabla^2 y. \end{cases} \quad (12)$$

Let b be the bifurcation parameter, then we can get the Hopf bifurcation condition at the stationary point, $b = a^2 + 1$. For obtaining the amplitude equation of the system near Hopf bifurcation, one just need to input the following commands in **Maple**.

sys:=[a-(b+1)*x+(x^2)*y,b*x-(x^2)*y];

var:=[x,y];

AE_Hopf(sys,var,b=a^2+1);

Then we can get the following results about system (12) with the mechanical algorithm **AE_Hopf**:

"The amplitude equation takes the form:"

$$\frac{\partial A}{\partial t} = (i\varpi + \alpha b)A + \beta A |A|^2 + d\nabla^2 A,$$

where

$$\alpha = \frac{i}{a}, \quad \beta = \frac{6ai + 3a^3 i - 4 - 4a^4 + 7a^2}{-3a^4},$$

$$d = \frac{id_x + ad_x + id_y - ad_y}{a}.$$

B. Holling-II Predator-Prey System

Next, we consider the predator-prey system with Holling-II functional response:

$$\begin{cases} \dfrac{\partial x}{\partial t} = x(r_1 - ax) - \dfrac{\alpha xy}{1 + \varpi x} + d_x \nabla^2 x, \\ \dfrac{\partial y}{\partial t} = -r_2 y + k \dfrac{\alpha xy}{1 + \varpi x} + d_y \nabla^2 y. \end{cases} \quad (13)$$

where $\dfrac{\alpha xy}{1 + \varpi x}$ is Holling-II functional response.

After some substitution, the system can be written as

$$\begin{cases} \dfrac{\partial x}{\partial t} = x(a_1 + a_2 x + a_3 x^2 - y) + d_x \nabla^2 x, \\ \dfrac{\partial y}{\partial t} = y(x - 1) + d_y \nabla^2 y. \end{cases}$$

$$(14)$$

From an ecological viewpoint, we only consider the positive stationary point $s(1, a_1 + a_2 + a_3)$. We select a_2 as the bifurcation parameter, and Hopf bifurcation occurs if $a_2 = -2a_3$. Then with the commands

sys:=[x*(a_1+a_2*x+a_3*x^2-y),y*(x-1)];

var:=[x,y];

AE_Hopf(sys,var,a[2]=-2*a[3],3);

We can get the following results immediately:
"The amplitude equation takes the form:"

$$\frac{\partial A}{\partial t} = (i\varpi + \alpha a_2)A + \beta A |A|^2 - d\nabla^2 A, \quad (15)$$

where

$$\alpha = -\sqrt{a_3 - a_1} + 1$$

$$\beta = \frac{-1}{3}a_1 - \frac{4}{3}a_3^2 - 2a_3\sqrt{a_3 - a_1} - \frac{1}{3} + 2a_3$$

$$d = \sqrt{a_3 - a_1}\, d_x + \sqrt{a_3 - a_1}\, d_y$$

CONCLUSION

The mechanical algorithm **AE_Hopf** of normal form approach for deriving coefficients of amplitude equation from reaction-diffusion system was proposed in this study. The mechanical algorithm **AE_Hopf** of normal form approach method has several advantages over existing approaches, including its simple concept, ease in operation, and powerful performance. The results of the examples indicated that the algorithm **AE_Hopf** is effective for these reaction-diffusion systems. This algorithm may be useful for establishing the amplitude equation near Hopf bifurcation. Furthermore, it may be helpful for learning the dynamics of pattern formation of the reaction-diffusion systems.

ACKNOWLEDGMENT

This research was supported by the Science Foundation of Zhejiang Province (Y7080041).

REFERENCES

Callahan, T. K., & Knobloch, E. (1999). Pattern formation in three-dimensional reaction-diffusion systems. *Physica D. Nonlinear Phenomena, 132*(3), 339–362. doi:10.1016/S0167-2789(99)00041-X

Chen, P., & Vinals, J. (1999). Amplitude equation and pattern selection in Faraday waves. *Physical Review E: Statistical Physics, Plasmas, Fluids, and Related Interdisciplinary Topics, 60*(1), 559–570. doi:10.1103/PhysRevE.60.559

Dufiet, V., & Boissonade, J. (1996). Dynamics of Turing pattern monolayers close to onset. *Physical Review E: Statistical Physics, Plasmas, Fluids, and Related Interdisciplinary Topics, 53*(5), 4883–4892. doi:10.1103/PhysRevE.53.4883

Gunaratne, G. H., Ouyang, Q., & Swinney, H. L. (1994). Pattern formation in the presence of symmetries. *Physical Review E: Statistical Physics, Plasmas, Fluids, and Related Interdisciplinary Topics, 50*(4), 2802–2820. doi:10.1103/PhysRevE.50.2802

Ipsen, M., Hynne, F., & Sørensen, P. G. (1998). Systematic derivation of amplitude equations and normal forms for dynamical systems. *Chaos (Woodbury, N.Y.), 8*(4), 834–852. doi:10.1063/1.166370

Ipsen, M., Hynne, F., & Sørensen, P. G. (2000). Amplitude equations for reaction--diffusion systems with a Hopf bifurcation and slow real modes. *Physica D. Nonlinear Phenomena, 136*(1-2), 66–92. doi:10.1016/S0167-2789(99)00149-9

Leppanen, T. (2004). *Computational studies of pattern formation in Turing systems*. Finland: Helsinki University of Technology.

Malomed, B. A. (1993). Ramp-induced wavenumber selection for traveling waves. *Physical Review E: Statistical Physics, Plasmas, Fluids, and Related Interdisciplinary Topics, 47*(4), 2257–2260. doi:10.1103/PhysRevE.47.R2257

Medvinsky, A. B., Petrovskii, S. V., Tikhonova, I. A., Malchow, H., & Li, B. L. (2002). Spatiotemporal Complexity of Plankton and Fish Dynamics. *SIAM Review, 44*(3), 311–370. doi:10.1137/S0036144502404442

Newell, A. C., Passot, T., & Lega, J. (1993). Order parameter equations for patterns. *Annual Review of Fluid Mechanics, 25*(1), 399–453. doi:10.1146/annurev.fl.25.010193.002151

Nicolis, G., & Prigogine, I. (1977). *Self-organization in nonequilibrium systems: From dissipative structures to order through fluctuations*. New York: Wiley.

Pearson, J. E. (1993). Complex patterns in a simple system. *Science, 261*(5118), 189–192. doi:10.1126/science.261.5118.189

Pena, B., & Perez-Garca, C. (2000). Selection and competition of Turing patterns. *Europhysics Letters, 51*(3), 300–306. doi:10.1209/epl/i2000-00352-3

Setayeshgar, S., & Cross, M. C. (1999). Numerical bifurcation diagram for the two-dimensional boundary-fed chlorine-dioxide-iodine-malonic-acid system. *Physical Review E: Statistical Physics, Plasmas, Fluids, and Related Interdisciplinary Topics, 59*(4), 4258–4264. doi:10.1103/PhysRevE.59.4258

Turing, A. M. (1952). The Chemical Basis of Morphogenesis. *Philosophical Transactions of the Royal Society of London, 237*(641), 37–72. doi:10.1098/rstb.1952.0012

Wang, W. (2006). A new mechanical algorithm for solving the second kind of Fredholm integral equation. *Applied Mathematics and Computation, 172*(2), 946–962. doi:10.1016/j.amc.2005.02.026

ADDITIONAL READING

Aranson, I. S., & Kramer, L. (2002). The world of the complex Ginzburg-Landau equation. *Reviews of Modern Physics, 74*(1), 99–143. doi:10.1103/RevModPhys.74.99

Barrio, R. A., Varea, C., Aragon, J. L., & Maini, P. K. (1999). A two-dimensional numerical study of spatial pattern formation in interacting Turing systems. *Bulletin of Mathematical Biology, 61*(3), 483–505. doi:10.1006/bulm.1998.0093

Chen, C., Jin, L., & Zhu, X. (1983). *Mathematical Analysis*. Beijing: Higher Education Press.

Ciliberto, S., Coullet, P., Lega, J., Pampaloni, E., & Perez-Garcia, C. (1990). Defects in roll-hexagon competition. *Physical Review Letters, 65*(19), 2370–2373. doi:10.1103/PhysRevLett.65.2370

Conway, J. M., & Riecke, H. (2007). Pattern Selection in the Complex Ginzburg-Landau Equation with Multi-Resonant Forcing. *Physical Review E: Statistical, Nonlinear, and Soft Matter Physics, 76*, 1–5. doi:10.1103/PhysRevE.76.057202

Cross, M. C., & Hohenberg, P. C. (1993). Pattern formation outside of equilibrium. *Reviews of Modern Physics, 65*(3), 851–1112. doi:10.1103/RevModPhys.65.851

Dewel, G., Borckmans, P., De Wit, A., Rudovics, B., Perraud, J. J., & Dulos, E. (1995). Pattern selection and localized structures in reaction-diffusion systems. *Physica A, 213*(181), 4.

Dubey, B., Das, B., & Hussain, J. (2001). A predator--prey interaction model with self and cross-diffusion. *Ecological Modelling, 141*(1-3), 67–76. doi:10.1016/S0304-3800(01)00255-1

Harris, J. W., & Stocker, H. (1998). *Handbook of mathematics and computational science*. Berlin: Springer.

Ipsen, M., Kramer, L., & Sørensen, P. G. (2000). Amplitude equations for description of chemical reaction-diffusion systems. *Physics Reports, 337*, 193–235. doi:10.1016/S0370-1573(00)00062-4

Kamerich, E. (2000). *Maple Enchiridion*. Berlin, Heidelberg: Springer.

Lengyel, I., & Epstein, I. R. (1992). A chemical approach to designing Turing patterns in reaction-diffusion systems. *Proceedings of the National Academy of Sciences of the United States of America, 89*(9), 3977–3979. doi:10.1073/pnas.89.9.3977

Levin, S. A. (1992). The problem of pattern and scale in ecology: the Robert H. MacArthur award lecture. *Ecology, 73*(6), 1943–1967. doi:10.2307/1941447

Longhi, S., & Geraci, A. (1996). Swift-Hohenberg equation for optical parametric oscillators. *Physical Review A., 54*(5), 4581–4584. doi:10.1103/PhysRevA.54.4581

Ma, T., Park, J., & Wang, S. (2004). Dynamic Bifurcation of the Ginzburg–Landau Equation. *SIAM Journal on Applied Dynamical Systems, 5*(4), 620–635. doi:10.1137/040603747

Mayol, C., Toral, R., & Mirasso, C. R. (2004). Derivation of amplitude equations for nonlinear oscillators subject to arbitrary forcing. *Physical Review E: Statistical, Nonlinear, and Soft Matter Physics, 69*(6), 66141. doi:10.1103/PhysRevE.69.066141

Niu, B., & Wei, J. (2008). Stability and bifurcation analysis in an amplitude equation with delayed feedback. *Chaos, Solitons, and Fractals, 37*(5), 1362–1371. doi:10.1016/j.chaos.2006.10.034

Okubo, A., & Levin, S. A. (2001). *Diffusion and Ecological Problems: Modern Perspectives.* New York: Springer.

Ouyang, Q., & Swinney, H. L. (1991). Transition from a uniform state to hexagonal and striped Turing patterns. *Nature, 352*(6336), 619–612. doi:10.1038/352610a0

Petrov, V., Ouyang, Q., & Swinney, H. L. (1997). Resonant pattern formation in achemical system. *Nature, 388*(6643), 655–657. doi:10.1038/41732

Renardy, M., & Renardy, Y. (1993). Derivation of amplitude equations and analysis of sideband instabilities in two-layer flows. *Physics of Fluids. A, Fluid Dynamics, 5*(11), 2738–2762. doi:10.1063/1.858737

Saez, E., & Gonzalez-Olivares, E. (1999). Dynamics of a predator-prey model. *SIAM Journal on Applied Mathematics, 59*, 1867–1878. doi:10.1137/S0036139997318457

Schopf, W., & Kramer, L. (1991). Small-amplitude periodic and chaotic solutions of the complex Ginzburg-Landau equation for a subcritical bifurcation. *Physical Review Letters, 66*(18), 2316–2319. doi:10.1103/PhysRevLett.66.2316

Varea, C., Aragon, J. L., & Barrio, R. A. (1997). Confined Turing patterns in growing systems. *Physical Review E: Statistical Physics, Plasmas, Fluids, and Related Interdisciplinary Topics, 56*(1), 1250–1253. doi:10.1103/PhysRevE.56.1250

Walgraef, D. (1997). *Spatio-temporal pattern formation.* New York: Springer.

Wu, W. (2000). *Mathematics Mechanization.* Beijing: Science press and Kluwer academic publishers.

Yang, L., & Epstein, I. R. (2003). Oscillatory turing patterns in reaction-diffusion systems with two coupled layers. *Physical Review Letters, 90*(17), 178303. doi:10.1103/PhysRevLett.90.178303

KEY TERMS AND DEFINITIONS

Amplitude Equation: It is an equation for describing the amplitude, which is the magnitude of change in the oscillating variable, with each oscillation, within an oscillating system.

Mechanical Algorithm: It tries to deal with mathematics in a constructive and algorithmic manner so that the reasoning become mechanical, automatically, and as much as possible to be intelligence-lacking. The basis of it is algorithm establishing and programming techniques.

Reaction-Diffusion Systems: Reaction-diffusion systems are systems involving constituents locally transformed into each other by chemical reactions and transported in space by diffusion. They arise, quite naturally, in chemistry and chemical engineering but also serve as a reference for the study of a wide range of phenomena encountered beyond the strict realm of chemical science such as environmental and life sciences.

Pattern: A pattern is a type of theme of recurring events of or objects, sometimes referred to as elements of a set. These elements repeat in a predictable manner. It can be a template or model which can be used to generate things or parts of a thing, especially if the things that are created have enough in common for the underlying pattern to be inferred, in which case the things are said to exhibit the unique pattern. The question of how a pattern emerges is accomplished through the work of the scientific field of pattern formation.

Hopf Bifurcation: Hopf bifurcation is the birth of a limit cycle from an equilibrium in dynamical systems generated by ODEs, when the equilibrium changes stability via a pair of purely imaginary eigenvalues. The bifurcation can be supercritical or subcritical, resulting in stable or unstable (within an invariant two-dimensional manifold) limit cycle, respectively.

Normal Form: A normal form of a mathematical object, broadly speaking, is a simplified form of the object obtained by applying a transformation (often a change of coordinates) that is considered to preserve the essential features of the object.

Stationary Point: An input to a function where the derivative is zero (equivalently, the gradient is zero): where the function "stops" increasing or decreasing (hence the name).

Chapter 19

Pattern Formation Controlled by External Forcing in a Spatial Harvesting Predator–Prey Model

Feng Rao
East China Normal University, P.R. China

ABSTRACT

Predator–prey models in ecology serve a variety of purposes, which range from illustrating a scientific concept to representing a complex natural phenomenon. Due to the complexity and variability of the environment, the dynamic behavior obtained from existing predator–prey models often deviates from reality. Many factors remain to be considered, such as external forcing, harvesting and so on. In this chapter, we study a spatial version of the Ivlev-type predator-prey model that includes reaction-diffusion, external periodic forcing, and constant harvesting rate on prey. Using this model, we study how external periodic forcing affects the stability of predator-prey coexistence equilibrium. The results of spatial pattern analysis of the Ivlev-type predator-prey model with zero-flux boundary conditions, based on the Euler method and via numerical simulations in MATLAB, show that the model generates rich dynamics. Our results reveal that modeling by reaction-diffusion equations with external periodic forcing and nonzero constant prey harvesting could be used to make general predictions regarding predator-prey equilibrium, which may be used to guide management practice, and to provide a basis for the development of statistical tools and testable hypotheses.

INTRODUCTION

Ecology has grown to be an enormous field of science in recent years (Murray, 2003; Wang et al., 2007). The topics of research include the study of the interrelationship between species and their

environment, predator-prey and competition interactions, renewable resource management, evolution of pesticide resistant strains, ecological and genetic engineering in pest control, multi-species societies, plant-herbivore systems, and so on.

Predation, a complex natural phenomenon, exists widely in the world, e.g., in the sea, on the plain, in the forest, in the desert, and so on

DOI: 10.4018/978-1-60960-064-8.ch019

(Cantrell & Cosner, 2003). Since the pioneering work of Lotka and Volterra (reviewed in Kendall, 2001), the predator-prey model has been widely studied. The predator-prey model is a type of "pursuit and evasion" system in which the prey tries to evade the predator and the predator tries to catch the prey when they interact (Murray, 2003). Pursuit means that the predator tries to shorten the spatial distance between the predator and the prey, whereas evasion means that the prey tries to widen this spatial distance. The predator-prey model is a mathematical model approximating such real-world phenomenon. Predator-prey model will likely continue to be widely researched due to its universality and importance (Berryman, 1992; Kuang & Beretta, 1998).

A typical spatial extended model, reaction-diffusion model, involves not only time but also space and consists of several species which react with each other and diffuse within the spatial domain. It normally uses a pair of partial differential equations to represent the time course of reacting and diffusing processes. In the spatial extended predator-prey model, the reaction represents the event when the predator catches and consumes the prey, and the diffusion is a spatial process and describes the predator's "pursuit" and the prey's "evasion". The reaction-diffusion model describes the evolution of the predator and the prey as a function of time (Zhang, 2008).

Harvest is the process of gathering mature crops from the fields. The harvest marks the end of the growing season, or the growing cycle for a particular crop. Harvesting, in general usage, includes an immediate post-harvest handling, such as all of the actions taken immediately after removing the crop—cooling, sorting, cleaning, packing—up to the point of further on-farm processing, or shipping to the wholesale or consumer market. The exploitation of biological resources and the harvesting are commonly practiced in fishery, forestry, and wildlife management. Concerning the conservation, for the long-term benefits of humanity, there is a wide-range of interest in the use of bioeconomic modeling of proper harvesting to gain insight on the scientific management of renewable resources such as fisheries and forestries (Xiao et al., 2006). Harvesting is also an important factor affecting the predator-prey system.

For a spatial extended predator-prey model, it is well known that the internal source is the dynamics of the individuals of the model and the external source is the variability of the environment. These two sources act together in deciding the evolution of the model (Zhou & Kurths, 2005). Some of the variability is periodic, such as temperature, water, food supply of the prey, and mating habits. It is necessary and important to consider models with periodic ecological parameters or perturbations. These periodic factors are regarded as the external periodic forcing in the predator-prey model. The external forcing can affect the populations of the predator and the prey, which would go extinct in a deterministic environment (Huang & Jing, 2009; Liu et al., 2008).

In this chapter, we consider the Ivlev-type predation-diffusion model with constant harvest, which has not been widely studied. Ivlev (1961) studied the spatiotemporal complexity of a predator-prey model with Ivlev-type functional response (Ivlev, 1961). Functional response, that is, the prey consumption rate by an average single predator, increases with the prey consumption rate. Functional response can be influenced by the predator density. Functional response of the predator to the prey density refers to the change in the density of prey attached per unit time per predator as the prey density changes. Wang et al, (2010) focused on the following diffusive model:

$$
\frac{\partial N}{\partial t} = N(1-N) - P(1-e^{-\gamma N}) + d_1 \nabla^2 N,
$$
$$
\frac{\partial P}{\partial t} = \varepsilon P(1-e^{-\gamma N}) - \beta P + d_2 \nabla^2 P.
$$

$$(1)$$

where N and P represent population density of prey and predator at time t, respectively, ε, β, γ are positive constants whose biological meanings are obvious. ε stands for the conversion rate of prey captured by predator, β is the death rate of predator, and γ the efficiency of predator capture of prey. From the second equation of (1), we know $\varepsilon > \beta$. And d_1, d_2 are the diffusion coefficients of prey and predator, respectively. For diffusive instability of the model, the mobility of predator should be much higher than that of the prey (i.e. $d_1 < d_2$). $\nabla^2 = \dfrac{\partial}{\partial x^2} + \dfrac{\partial}{\partial y^2}$ is the usual Laplacian operator in two-dimensional space.

Based on the results of previous work (Wang et al, 2008), we mainly focus on the effect of external forcing on pattern formation in the Ivlev-type predator-prey diffusion model with constant harvest in this chapter.

THE MODEL

The diffusive Ivlev-type predator-prey model with external periodic forcing and constant harvest we employ is:

$$\frac{\partial N}{\partial t} = N(1-N) - P(1-e^{-\gamma N}) - h + A\sin(\omega t) + d_1 \nabla^2 N,$$

$$\frac{\partial P}{\partial t} = \alpha\beta P(1-e^{-\gamma N}) - \beta P + d_2 \nabla^2 P.$$

$$(2)$$

where $\alpha = \dfrac{\varepsilon}{\beta} > 1$, $h>0$ represents the rate of harvesting or removal. And $A\sin(\omega t)$ denotes the periodic forcing with amplitude A and angular frequency ω.

Model (2) is to be analyzed under the following non-zero initial condition and zero flux boundary conditions with a system size of $\Omega = 200 \times 200$:

$N(x, y, 0) > 0, P(x, y, 0) > 0 (x, y) \in \Omega = [0, R] \times [0, R]$,

$N(x, y, 0) > 0, P(x, y, 0) > 0, (x, y) \in \Omega = [0, R] \times [0, R]$, (3)

$$\frac{\partial N}{\partial n} = \frac{\partial P}{\partial n} = 0, (x, y) \in \partial\Omega. \ (4)$$

the zero flux boundary conditions imply that no external input is imposed from outside.

In the above, n is the outward unit normal vector of the boundary $\partial\Omega$ which we will assume is smooth. The main reason for choosing such boundary conditions is that we are interested in the self-organization of pattern(Chattopadhyay & Tapaswi, 1997; Murray, 1990).

By calculating we can get that the non-spatial model (2) has three stationary states in the positive quadrant:

(i) trivial stationary state (N_i, P_i) $(i = 1,2)$, i.e., extinct of the predator only:

$$N_i = \frac{1 + (-1)^i \sqrt{1 - 4h}}{2}, P_i = 0. \ (5)$$

(ii) a nontrivial stationary state (N^*, P^*) (coexistence of prey and predator), where

$$N^* = -\frac{\ln(\frac{\alpha-1}{\alpha})}{\gamma}, P^* = -\frac{\alpha(\ln(\frac{\alpha-1}{\alpha})\gamma + \ln(\frac{\alpha-1}{\alpha})^2 + h\gamma^2)}{\gamma^2}.$$

$$(6)$$

In this chapter, we mainly focus on the dynamics of nontrivial stationary state (N^*, P^*). For cyclical populations, this coexistence state may be unstable and lie inside a stable limit cycle in the kinetic phase plane. Then we may start our numerical simulations to analyze the dynamic behavior of model (2) and choose parameters value $\alpha = 2.5, \beta = 1.5, \gamma = 1.5, d_1 = 0.01, d_2 = 0.1$ in two-dimensional space using a finite difference approximation for the spatial derivatives and an explicit Euler method for the time integration (Garive, 2007) with a time step $\Delta t = 1/24$ and space stepsize $\Delta x = \Delta y = 1/3$. Initially, model (2) is integrated from the homogeneous steady state $(N^*, P^*) = (0.3405504159, 0.0614395750)$ with small random perturbation superimposed. The initial conditions are always a small amplitude random perturbation $\pm 5 \times 10^{-4}$ around the steady state and patterns develop spontaneously.

NUMERICAL RESULTS

In this section, we present some numerical simulation results of model (2) with external periodic forcing and harvest. In the following, we can show that the dynamic behavior of model (2) gradu-

ally changes with different values of the harvest parameter h and magnitude of external forcing.

When we adopt $h = 0.12$ and fix the amplitude $A = 0.0001$, Figure 1 shows the dynamical behavior of model (2) with different angular frequency ω. The first row of Figure 1, i.e., (A) $\omega = \pi/40$; the second row, (B) $\omega = \pi/50$; and the last row of Figure 1, (C)$\omega = \pi/80$. And the first column of Figure 1, marked as (i), shows the snapshots of spatiotemporal pattern of model (2) at $t = 1000$ with different angular frequency, respectively, we can see that some changes gradually occur in these patterns with different angular frequency. The second column of Figure 1, marked as (ii), displays the phase portraits of model (2) with different angular frequency, respectively. In this case, we can also see that a limit cycle emerges,

Figure 1. Dynamical behavior of model (2) with h=0.12, α = 2.5, β = 1.5, γ = 1.5, d_1=0.01, d_2=0.1, The amplitude A=0.0001, and angular frequency are respectively: (A)$\omega = \pi/40$; (B)$\omega = \pi/50$; (C)$\omega = \pi/80$. And (i) Grey-scaled snapshots of spatiotemporal pattern of model (2) at t = 1000; (ii)Phase portrait.

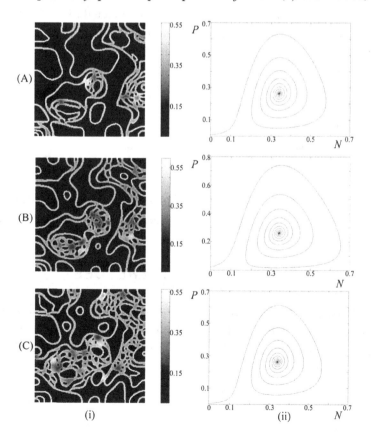

Figure 2. Time-series plots of predator P with h = 0.14, α = 2.5, β = 1.5, γ = 1.5, d₁ = 0.01, d₂ = 0.1. The amplitude and angular frequency are respectively: (a) A = 0.00005, ω = π / 10; (b) A = 0.00005, ω = π / 8; (c) A = 0.00025, ω = π / 10

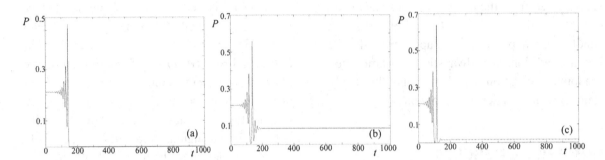

and with different angular frequency the limit cycle takes place some change.

For the sake of learning the dynamics of model (2) with the parameter $h = 0.14$, further, we illustrate time-series plots of predator P in Figure 2, where (a) the amplitude $A = 0.00005$ and angular frequency $\omega = \pi / 10$; (b) $A = 0.00005$, $\omega = \pi / 8$; (c) $A = 0.00025$, $\omega = \pi / 10$.

Comparing with every one of Figure 2, we can note that time-series plots have drastically changed. It is comprehensible that the external periodic forcing can enhance the oscillations of the species' density with different values of the amplitude and the effect of external forcing on predator-prey model (2) is drastic. From the obove discussion, we may draw a conclusion that the external periodic forcing plays a constructive role on the model in the space.

CONCLUSION

In this chapter, we present a spatial predator-prey model that contains several important factors, such as the external periodic forcing, harvest and diffusion processes. In our analytic model, the external forcing term is assumed as $A\sin(\omega t)$. The use of the external forcing term presents continuous external fluctuations connected to the random variation of environmental parameters such as temperature and natural resources and so on.

We demonstrate that the external periodic forcing plays a key role in the predation-diffusion model with constant harvest. Our model for spatially extended systems composed by two species could be useful to explain spatiotemporal behaviors of populations whose dynamics are strongly affected by the environmental physical variables, and the results of this chapter are an important step toward providing the theoretical biology community with simple practical numerical methods for investigating the key dynamics of realistic predator-prey models.

ACKNOWLEDGMENT

This research was supported by the Natural Science Foundation of Zhejiang Province (Y7080041).

REFERENCES

Berryman, A. A. (1992). The origins and evolution of predator-prey theory. *Ecology*, *75*(3), 1530–1535. doi:10.2307/1940005

Cantrell, R. S., & Cosner, C. (2003). *Spatial ecology via reaction-diffusion equations*. England: John Wiley & Sons Ltd.

Chattopadhyay, J., & Tapaswi, P. K. (1997). Effect of cross-diffusion on pattern formation a nonlinear analysis. *Acta Applicandae Mathematicae, 48*(1), 1–12. doi:10.1023/A:1005764514684

Garvie, M. R. (2007). Finite-difference schemes for reaction-diffusion equations modelling predator-prey interactions in matlab. *Bulletin of Mathematical Biology, 69*(3), 931–956. doi:10.1007/s11538-006-9062-3

Huang, J., & Jing, Z. (2009). Bifurcations and chaos in three-well duffing system with one external forcing. *Chaos, Solitons, and Fractals, 40*(3), 1449–1466. doi:10.1016/j.chaos.2007.09.045

Ivlev, V. (1961). *Experimental ecology of the feeding fishes*. New Haven: Yale University Press.

Kendall, B. E. (2001). Cycles, chaos, and noise in predator-prey dynamics. *Chaos, Solitons, and Fractals, 12*(2), 321–332. doi:10.1016/S0960-0779(00)00180-6

Kuang, Y., & Beretta, E. (1998). Global qualitative analysis of a ratio-dependent predator-prey system. *Journal of Mathematical Biology, 36*(4), 389–406. doi:10.1007/s002850050105

Liu, Q. X., Jin, Z., & Li, B. L. (2008). Resonance and frequency-locking phenomena in spatially extended phytoplankton-zooplankton system with additive noise and periodic forces. *Journal of Statistical Mechanics*, P05011. doi:10.1088/1742-5468/2008/05/P05011

Murray, J. D. (1990). Discussion: Turing's theory of morphogenesis-its influence on modelling biological pattern and form. *Bulletin of Mathematical Biology, 52*(1), 117–152. doi:10.1007/BF02459571

Murray, J. D. (2003). *Mathematical biology. I. An introduction*, 3rd edn., Interdisciplinary Applied Mathematics 18, Springer, New York.

Murray, J. D. (2003). *Mathematical biology. II. Spatial models and biomedical applications*, 3rd edn., Interdisciplinary Applied Mathematics 18, Springer, New York.

Wang, W. M., Liu, Q. X., & Jin, Z. (2007). Spatiotemporal complexity of a ratio-dependent predator-prey system. *Physical Review E: Statistical, Nonlinear, and Soft Matter Physics, 75*(5), 51913. doi:10.1103/PhysRevE.75.051913

Wang, W. M., Zhang, L., Wang, H. L., & Li, Z. (2010). Pattern formation of a predator-prey system with Ivlev-type functional response. *Ecological Modelling, 221*(2), 131–140. doi:10.1016/j.ecolmodel.2009.09.011

Xiao, D. M., Li, W. X., & Han, M. A. (2006). Dynamics in a ratio-dependent predator-prey model with predator harvesting. *Journal of Mathematical Analysis and Applications, 324*(1), 14–29. doi:10.1016/j.jmaa.2005.11.048

Zhang, L., Wang, W. M., Xue, Y. K., & Jin, Z. (2008). Complex dynamics of a Holling-type IV predator-prey model. *arXiv:0801.4365v1*.

Zhou, C., & Kurths, J. (2005). Noise-sustained and controlled synchronization of stirred excitable media by external forcing. *New Journal of Physics, 7*, 18. doi:10.1088/1367-2630/7/1/018

ADDITIONAL READING

Ahamadi, M., & Gervais, J. J. (2003). Symbolic-numerical methods for the computation of normal forms of PDEs. *Journal of Computational and Applied Mathematics, 158*(2), 443–472. doi:10.1016/S0377-0427(03)00482-5

Basson, M., & Fogarty, M. J. (1997). Harvesting in discrete-time predator-prey systems. *Mathematical Biosciences, 141*(1), 41–74. doi:10.1016/S0025-5564(96)00173-3

Biktashev, V. N., Brindley, J., Holden, A. V., & Tsyganov, M. A. (2004). Pursuit-evasion predator-prey waves in two spatial dimensions. *Chaos: An Interdisciplinary Journal of Nonlinear Science, 14*, 988. doi:10.1063/1.1793751

Dawes, J. H. P., & Tsai, T. L. (2006). Frequency locking and complex dynamics near a periodically forced robust heteroclinic cycle. *Physical Review E: Statistical, Nonlinear, and Soft Matter Physics, 74*(5), 55201. doi:10.1103/PhysRevE.74.055201

Gakkhar, S., & Singh, B. (2007). The dynamics of a food web consisting of two preys and a harvesting predator. *Chaos, Solitons, and Fractals, 34*(4), 1346–1356. doi:10.1016/j.chaos.2006.04.067

Gierer, A., & Meinhardt, H. (1972). A theory of biological pattern formation. *Biological Cybernetics, 12*(1), 30–39. doi:10.1007/BF00289234

Guan, S. G., Wang, X. G., & Lai, C. H. (2006). Frequency locking by external force from a dynamical system with strange nonchaotic attractor. *PHYSICS LETTERS A, 354*(4), 298–304. doi:10.1016/j.physleta.2006.01.067

Guo, H. J., & Chen, L. S. (2009). Time-limited pest control of a Lotka-Volterra model with impulsive harvest. *Nonlinear Analysis Real World Applications, 10*(2), 840–848. doi:10.1016/j.nonrwa.2007.11.007

harvested one-predator-two-prey model. *Applied Mathematics and Computation, 129*(1), 107–118.

Hoekstra, J., & Van den Bergh, J. C. J. M. (2005). Harvesting and conservation in a predator-prey system. *Journal of Economic Dynamics & Control, 29*(6), 1097–1120. doi:10.1016/j.jedc.2004.03.006

Koch, A. H., & Meinhardt, H. (1994). Biological pattern formation: from basic mechanisms to complex structres. *Reviews of Modern Physics, 66*(4), 1481–1507. doi:10.1103/RevModPhys.66.1481

Kooij, R. E., & Zegeling, A. (1996). A predator-prey model with Ivlev's functional response. *Journal of Mathematical Analysis and Applications, 198*(2), 473–489. doi:10.1006/jmaa.1996.0093

Kuang, Y., Huisman, J., & Elser, J. J. (2004). Stoichiometric plant-herbivore models and their interpretation. *Mathematical Biosciences and Engineering, 1*, 215–222.

Kumar, S., Srivastava, S. K., & Chingakham, P. (2002). Hopf bifurcation and stability analysis in a

Ou, Y. Q. (2000). *Pattern formation in reaction-diffusion systems*. Shanghai: Shanghai Scientific and Technological Education Pubishing House.

Pearce, I. G., Chaplain, M. A. J., Schofield, P. G., Anderson, A. R. A., & Hubbard, S. F. (2006). Modelling the spatio-temporal dynamics of multi-species host-parasitoid interactions: heterogeneous patterns and ecological implications. *Journal of Theoretical Biology, 241*(4), 876–886.

Pearson, J. E. (1993). Complex patterns in a simple system. *Science, 261*(5118), 189. doi:10.1126/science.261.5118.189

Sandstede, B., & Scheel, A. (2007). Period-doubling of spiral waves and defects. *SIAM Journal on Applied Dynamical Systems, 6*, 494–547. doi:10.1137/060668158

Stegemann, G., & Scholl, E. (2007). Two-dimensional spatiotemporal pattern formation in the double barrier resonant tunnelling diode. *New Journal of Physics, 9*, 55. doi:10.1088/1367-2630/9/3/055

Sugie, J. (1998). Two-parameter bifurcation in a predator-prey system of Ivlev type. *Journal of Mathematical Analysis and Applications, 217*(2), 349–371. doi:10.1006/jmaa.1997.5700

Uriu, K., & Iwasa, Y. (2007). Turing pattern formation with two kinds of cells and a diffusive chemical. *Bulletin of Mathematical Biology, 69*(8), 2515–2536. doi:10.1007/s11538-007-9230-0

Walgraef, D. (1997). *Spatiotemporal pattern formation*. New York: Springer.

Wang, H. L., & Wang, W. M. (2008). The dynamical complexity of a Ivlev-type prey-predator system with impulsive effect. *Chaos, Solitons, and Fractals, 38*(4), 1168–1176. doi:10.1016/j.chaos.2007.02.008

Wang, H. L., Zhang, K., & Ou, Y. Q. (2006). Resonant-pattern formation induced by additive noise in periodically forced reaction-diffusion systems. *Physical Review E: Statistical, Nonlinear, and Soft Matter Physics, 74*(3), 036210. doi:10.1103/PhysRevE.74.036210

Xiang, Z. Y., & Song, X. Y. (2009). The dynamical behaviors of a food chain model with impulsive effect and Ivlev functional response. *Chaos, Solitons, and Fractals, 39*(5), 2282–2293. doi:10.1016/j.chaos.2007.06.124

Yang, L. F., Dolnik, M., Zhabotinsky, A. M., & Epstein, I. R. (2002). Pattern formation arising from interactions between Turing and wave instabilities. *The Journal of Chemical Physics, 117*(15), 7259. doi:10.1063/1.1507110

KEY TERMS AND DEFINITIONS

Predator-Prey System: A system takes the form of a pair of ordinary differential equations, one representing a prey species, the other its predator. The predator-prey system illustrates some of the salient features of ecological models: modeled biological populations experience growth, interact with other populations (as either predators, prey or competitors) and suffer mortality.

Ivlev Model: Ivlev's equation describes the effect of consumer satiation on the rate of re-

source consumption in a similar way to Holling's disk equation; i.e., it describes a cyrtoid or Type II functional response. However, although the model has an identical form, it is derived from different assumptions and has a different explicit mathematical structure. Notice also that Ivlev's model is derived from a differential equation that has not been integrated over time and, as such, must be considered an instantaneous consumption equation.

External Forcing: A force outside the system under consideration. The classification of forces as external or internal is largely a matter of convenience and depends on how the system is defined. In biomechanics, the human body is generally regarded as the system and any force acting on it from the outside environment, such as air resistance or the impact force of an external object, is regarded as an external force.

Harvest: In agriculture, the harvest is the processes of gathering mature crops from the fields. The harvest marks the end of the growing season, or the growing cycle for a particular crop, and this is the focus of seasonal celebrations of many religions. Harvesting in general usage includes an immediate post-harvest handling, all of the actions taken immediately after removing the crop—cooling, sorting, cleaning, packing—up to the point of further on-farm processing, or shipping to the wholesale or consumer market.

Pattern Formation: A pattern is a type of theme of recurring events of or objects: sometimes referred to as elements of a set. These elements repeat in a predictable manner. It can be a template or model which can be used to generate things or parts of a thing, especially if the things that are created have enough in common for the underlying pattern to be inferred, in which case the things are said to exhibit the unique pattern. The question of how a pattern emerges is accomplished through the work of the scientific field of pattern formation.

Chapter 20

Repetitive Firing and Bursting due to Different Bifurcation Mechanism in Unmyelinated Fibre

Junran Zhang
Southwest Science and Technology University and The Forth Military Medical University, China

Yongguo Han
Southwest Science and Technology University, China

Guangcan Xiao
Southwest Science and Technology University, China

Sanjue Hu
The Forth Military Medical University, China

ABSTRACT

In neural science, different action potential (AP) firing patterns are typically considered to be dominated by different dynamical mechanisms. Different AP firing patterns in unmyelinated fibres can contribute to pain and sensory information transmission. Experiments in rabbit unmyelinated nerve (axon) show some interesting phenomena, mainly concerned with the AP firing patterns that changed regularly. Investigating the dynamical mechanism of unmyelinated fibre during various kinds of AP firing patterns is useful to understand the neural information processing in axon and pain information transmission. Here, we reproduced these phenomena by constructing a mathematical model, where the discharge of the Hodgkin-Huxley (H-H) neuron under square wave stimulation was studied by simulation. It is shown that square wave can induce bursting firing, especially with long time-course duration. This is different from the popular theory that explained repetitive and bursting firing due to stimulus intensity and instantaneous fluctuation. Through dynamical analysis, we found that the mechanism of the action potential pattern changed according to Hopf bifurcation, a dynamical behavior that emergence and stability of limit cycles of bifurcating from a stable equilibrium. The finding may support the neural information coding hypothesis in unmyelinated axon.

DOI: 10.4018/978-1-60960-064-8.ch020

INTRODUCTION

It is commonly agreed that different regions of the neuron perform specific signaling tasks. The pattern of firing is determined in a number of special regions responsible for signal integration, such as receptors, axon hillock and synapse. In contrast, the axon is usually believed to be specialized for carrying signals faithfully over long distances and to work as a relatively simple relay line (Mackenzie, et al., 1996). Recently, some experimental and theoretical data suggest that the functional capabilities of axons are much more diverse than traditionally thought. In other words, the function of the axon is no longer limited to the conduction of the action potential, but is also involved in the regulation of patterns of firing (Debanne et al., 2004; Philip et al., 2006).

Our previous experiment (Zhu et al., 2009) investigating the changes in action potential (AP) firing patterns in C-fibres of rabbit suggested that information processing may occurr in the axonal region. The C-fibers are unmyelinated fibers, and have a slower conduction velocity (compared with myelinated fiber). The fibers are associated with sensations of warmth and chronic or dull pain. These fibers are archaic in evolution and maintain some basic characteristics related to AP propagation. Therefore, investigating the mechanism of

AP pattern changes in C-fiber axon is important to understand elementary neural information processing principles, pain information transmission rules, etc.

In our experiment, we observed some interesting phenomena in AP firing pattern changes in C-fiber by electrophysiological method (we exposed about 10 cm of rabbit's unmyelinated nerve, stimulated the nerve bundle at one terminal, and recorded single nerve firing at the other terminal). Its results can be concluded from three aspects:

The first firing pattern is irregular when stationary stimulation is imposed on the nerve bundle. We called this pattern irregular firing pattern, which was shown in Figure 1.

The second firing pattern is regular when stationary stimulation is imposed on the nerve bundle. In this case, the action potential is maintained in stable status even in a high stimulus frequency (50 Hz). Normally, the range of normal biological condition in the unmyelinated nerve fiber is from 4 to 32 Hz (Derjean et al., 2003). We called this pattern the repetitive firing pattern, which was shown in Figure 2.

The third firing pattern has repetitive firing and silence occurring in turns when stationary stimulation is imposed on the nerve bundle. We called this pattern the bursting firing pattern, which was shown in Figure 3.

Figure 1. Irregular firing pattern of C-fiber

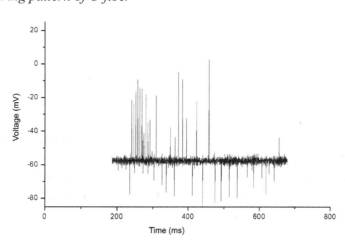

Figure 2. Repetitive firing pattern of C-fiber

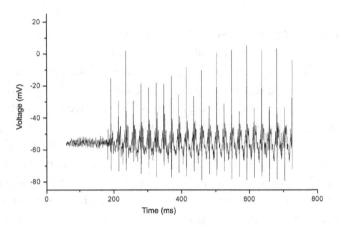

Figure 3. Bursting firing pattern of C-fiber

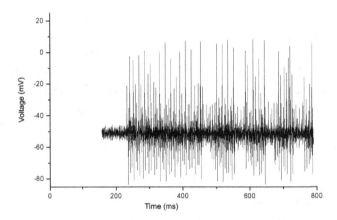

Computational models are useful in the analysis of neural dynamical system. For example, experimental data and dynamic equations (Scriven, 1981) were adopted to build such models. Bifurcations (means the splitting of a main body into two parts) play an important role in dynamical systems, especially when there are qualitative changes in systematic behavior. A typical example of bifurcation in neuron dynamics is the transition that changes from rest to periodic spiking activity in one neuron. *Hopf* bifurcation is an important type of bifurcation that has been observed in neural dynamics. It describes the onset (or disappearance) of periodic activity, which is a ubiquitous phenomenon in the brain. Many studies have shown the bifurcation patterns in the H-H neuron. For example, Fukai et al.,

(2003) examined a global bifurcation structure of the H-H neuron in the multiple-parameter space. In this chapter, our studies focus on the discharge of neurons under stimulation of different intensities by model simulation and dynamics analysis.

COMPUTATIONAL MODELS AND METHODS

The C-Fiber Firing Model

Based on Scriven's work (Scriven, 1981), we built the model into three separate systems: sodium-potassium (*Na-K*), Chloride-(*Cl*) and (*Ca*). We mainly consider the *Na-K* pump's contribution in reproducing various firing pattern. The *Na-K* pump are strongly dependent on the external potassium concentration and weakly dependent on internal sodium concentration (Baker et al., 1969). To simplify the simulation, we assumed that the *Na-K* pump's action dependent on the external potassium concentration only.

The membrane potential equation was presented like this:

$$C\frac{dV}{dt} = I_{total} = I_{Na} + I_{Nap} + I_K + I_{Kp} + I_{Ca} + I_{Cap+}I_{CL} + I_{inj}$$

$$(1)$$

where

$$I_{Na} = -g_{Na} *h*m*m*m*(v-E_{Na})$$ $$(2)$$

$$I_K = -(g_K *n*n*n*n + G_{kca}/(1+0.01/Ca_{in}))*(v-E_K)$$

$$I_{Kp} = a/((1+b1/K_{sp})*(1+b1/K_{sp})*(1+b2/Na_{in}))$$

$$(4)$$

$$I_{Nap} = -r*I_{kp}$$ $$(5)$$

$$r = 1.5$$ $$(6)$$

$$I_{Ca} = -g_{Ca}*mc*h*(v-E_{ca})$$ $$(7)$$

$$I_{Cap} = I_{cap}*0.001*Ca_{in}/Ca_{in} = 0.5)$$ $$(8)$$

$$I_{Cl} = -g_{Cl}*(v-E_{cl})$$ $$(9)$$

The membrane capacitance C is constant; thus, the transmembrane voltage V changes with the total transmembrane current I_{total} according to the equation. I_{Na}, I_K, I_{Ca} and I_{Cl} are currents conveyed through the local sodium channels, potassium channels, calcium channels, and chlorine channels, respectively. Here g_{Na} and g_K denote the maximum conductance of fast sodium current and fast potassium current, respectively. G_{Ca} is the maximum value of the calcium conductance. G_{Cl} is

the maximum value of the chlorinum conductance. V is the membrane potential in millivolts, and I_{inj} is the injected current. *ENa*, E_K, E_{Ca} and E_{Cl} are corresponding reversal potentials of the sodium, potassium, calcium, and chlorine currents. The I_{Kp} and I_{Nap} are the currents caused by the *Na-K* pump system. The *Na-K* pump are strongly dependent on the external potassium concentration and weakly dependent on internal sodium concentration (Baker et al., 1969). I_{Ca} is the calcium current described by Brown et al. (1978). g_{Ca} is the maximum value of calcium conductance. I_{cap} is the calcium pump current and was referenced from Sacchi et al (Athanasiades et al., 2000). m and h are gating variables for activation and inactivation, respectively, representing the fraction of the maximum conductance available at any given time and voltage. The gating variables n are same as m for activation in potassium channels. mc similar to m but changed the V variable to V-20 (Scriven, 1981). The parameters were summarized in Table 1 (Basic parameters).

Hopf Bifurcation Theorem and Numerical Detection

Consider an autonomous system of nonlinear ordinary differential equation

$$\frac{dy}{dt} = f(y,\lambda) \quad f: \quad R^n \times R \to R^n \quad y \in R^n \quad \lambda \in R$$

$$(10)$$

where λ is the parameter. The steady-state solution of (1) satisfies $f(y,\lambda) = 0$ (11)

At the critical value λ_0 of the parameter λ, from the *Hopf* bifurcation theory, a *Hopf* bifurcation could be characterized by the following conditions.

$$f(y_0, \lambda_0) = 0$$ $$(12)$$

$$f_y(y_0, \lambda_0) = 0$$ $$(13)$$

The equations has a simple pair of purely imaginary eigenvalues

$$\mu(\lambda_0) = \pm\, i\beta \qquad (14)$$

and no other eigenvalue with zero real part.

$$d(\operatorname{Re}\mu\,(\lambda_0))\,/\,d\lambda \neq 0 \qquad (15)$$

The orbit structure near $(y, \lambda) = y_0, \lambda_0)$ can be determined by center manifold theorem. But that's very difficult to solve for practical nonlinear problems, and sometimes it is almost impossible for large systems. Thus, the application of the above method is limited. A combined analytical/numerical computational approach can be used to simplify the problem. Wen (2005) presented a criterion for simple *Hopf* bifurcation in terms of the coefficients of the characteristic equations. And numerical computation has been widely used as a main tool to detect *Hopf* bifurcation points of nonlinear systems (Lin et al., 1997). We used the numerical computation to detect the bifurcation points in our neural model.

DIFFERENT FIRING PATTERN AND THEIR DYNAMICS

Repetitive firing can be induced with an injected current of *10nA* .With the appropriate choice in pump parameters, two mainly phenomena, repetitive firing and bursting firing, can be simulated .In the model, the two phenomena were simulated by adjusting the *Na-K* pump parameters according to experimental result which we recorded from rabbit's unmyelinated nerve. The second firing pattern and the third firing pattern also based on the experiment. To investigate the mechanisms under these different firing patterns, we used the nonlinear analysis tool- *XPPAUTO* to probe the factors which decided difference firing pattern (Izhikevich,2000).

Repetitive Firing Pattern and Dynamic Analysis

The model reproduced repetitive firing pattern based on Scriven's work (Scriven, 1981). Here the parameters were presented in Table 1 (Variables changed in repetitive).

After a length of subthreshold oscillation, the model emerge repetitive firing which can last for a long time, this can be seen in Figure 4. The repetitive firing due to *Na-K* pump activity, which

Figure 4. Simulation of repetitive firing pattern

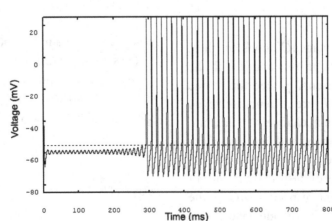

Figure 5. Bifurcation diagrams of an H-H neuron as a function of I

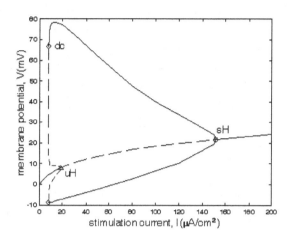

balance the ion losing. If the balance was kept well, the repetitive firing will lasting constantly.

The action potential trains often show various kinds of temporal patterns. How are these rich and colorful rhythms given rise to? Is the inherent contact existed between the different patterns? What are the functional meanings of these temporal patterns in action potential trains? These problems have caused the concern of more and more neurophysiologists. What is worth attention is that rhythms of spontaneous discharge of nerve is very various, the period rhythm can transformed to each other via period-adding bifurcation. The experimental neural activity in C-fibres become a good biological model for exploring the dynamical mechanism of firing pattern because of its merits: easy to functioning the electric field stimulus, easy to long time recording with electrical physiology characters. Combining with the nonlinear dynamics theory, deeper mechanism underlying different firing patterns as well as the inherent contact between the various patterns can be elucidated.

Here, one-parameter bifurcation diagrams (*1BDs*) was used, which plot the equilibrium potentials and the maximal/minimal values of the membrane potentials for periodic solutions as a function of *I*.

When $T=18.5°C$, the *1BDs* is shown in Figure 5.Nomenclature: *uH*-subcritical Hopf, *sH*-super-critical Hopf, *dc*-double cycle. $I_{uH} = 18.5673\mu A/cm^2$, $I_{sH}=151.5824\mu A/cm^2$, $I_{dc}=8.035\mu A/cm^2$.

$T=18.5°C$. Here *I* is the bifurcation parameter and *V* is the membrane potential of the limit states. Nomenclature: *uH*-subcritical Hopf, *sH*-super-critical Hopf, *dc*-double cycle. Solid lines represent stable periodic solutions and equilibrium points. Dashed lines represent unstable periodic solutions and equilibrium points

From Figure 5, it can be seen clearly that the onset (or disappearance) of periodic activity depends on the intensity of the stimulation current *I*.

Bursting Firing Pattern and Dynamic Analysis

The model reproduced bursting firing pattern by adjusted the *Na-K* pump parameter. Here the parameters were presented in Table 1 (Variables changed in bursting).

Bursting(periods of firing separated by periods of silence) is, in this model, a natural extension of adaptation. If *Na-K* pump is sufficiently strong to stop the fiber firing, diffusion from the periaxonal space and activity of the pump restores the ionic concentrations to equilibrium. This, in turn,

Table 1. Parameters of the model

Variable	Value	Source
Basic parameters		
C	*1μF*	squid: Hodgkin and Huxley (1952)
gNa	*120mS*	present work
gK	*36mS*	present work
gCa	*0.03mS*	Brown et al., 1978
gCl	*0.07mS*	present work
gkca	*0.2mS*	Scriven, 1981
E_{Na}	*50mV*	present work
E_K	*-77mV*	present work
E_{Ca}	*126.3mV*	Brown et al., 1978
E_{CL}	*-65mV*	present work
a	*1*	present work
b1	*1*	Scriven, 1981
b2	*0*	present work
Dk	*100nm/s*	Scriven, 1981
Dca	*0.001um/s*	Scriven, 1981
Icap	*0. 12nA*	Athanasiades et al., 2000
Variables changed in repetitive		
gkca	*0.25mS*	
J	*10 nA*	
Variables changed in Bursting		
gkca	*0.3mS*	
J	*12.1nA*	
b1	*4*	

reduces the activity of the pump and allows the never fiber to recommence firing (Scriven, 1981). The simulative result of bursting firing pattern was shown in Figure 6.

CONCLUSION

Traditionally, it was well known that stimulation must be of not only enough intensity but also enough steepness to activate an action potential. This phenomena was known as accommodation. Our results show that square wave stimulation can make a neuron bursting, especially the long time-course bursting. The onset (or disappearance) of bursting under square wave stimulation is related to *Hopf* bifurcation. This finding is complementary to the traditional theory in the accommodation of neurons.

Besides, a long time-course bursting, which represents supernormal excitability of neurons and is characteristic of some special event, can make a synapse serve as an integron of information of events. Moreover, the slow passage effect (characterized by a slow transition of the system through a Hopf bifurcation) can be shortened significantly by noise or weak input from other bursters (AP firing with bursting pattern), which provides a

Figure 6. Simulation of Bursting firing pattern

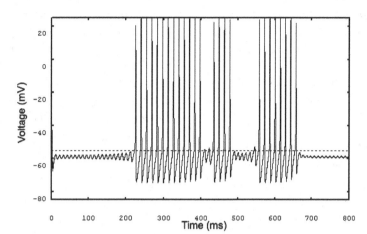

powerful trend for instantaneous synchronization of bursters. These results imply that some excitatory synaptic reactions with large enough intensity may be the cause for pain perception.

The irregular firing pattern was not studied here. Nonetheless, we can offer possible reasons of this pattern which may have contributed to adaptation, i.e., irregular firing may be the transition phase for adaptation between the AP repetitive firing and the burster. The key to adaptation is the *Na-K* pump activity. By adjusting the *Na-K* pump parameters, we can obtain the irregular firing pattern from repetitive firing and the bursting firing, respectively. Moreover, the contribution of temperature to bifurcation is not investigated in this model. In the normal physiological condition, there is no *Hopf* bifurcation, the bursting also can not be induced by slow wave stimulation (Zhu et al., 2001). Therefore, the model does not yet fit the real central neuron perfectly. To further understand the reason of firing pattern changes, more work must be done, including incorporating other currents, parameter adjustment for other experimental conditions, and including temperature effect.

Because the different AP firing patterns were simulated in the model as well as being produced and recorded in the axon of C-fiber, the complex AP firing patterns and corresponding dynamical analysis suggest that there may be information processing and coding potentiality in the C-fiber axon.

ACKNOWLEDGMENT

I would like to thank Limin Angela Liu and Huimin Lei for their help in the proofreading of this chapter and the anonymous reviewers for constructive feedback and comments. The present study was supported by National Natural Science Foundation of China (Grant No. 81000605) and the Key project of SWUST (09zx7102).

REFERENCES

Athanasiades, A., Clark, J. W., Ghorbel, F., & Bidani, A. (2000). An ionic current model for medullary respiratory neurons. *Journal of Computational Neuroscience*, *9*(3), 237–257. doi:10.1023/A:1026583620467

Baker, P. F., Blaustei.Mp, Keynes, R. D., Manil, J., Shaw, T. I., & Steinhar.Ra. (1969). Ouabain-sensitive fluxes of sodium and potassium in squid giant axons. *Journal of Physiology-London*, *200*(2), 459.

Brown, A. M., Akaike, N., & Lee, K. S. (1978). The calcium conductance of neurons. *Annals of the New York Academy of Sciences, 307*, 330–344. doi:10.1111/j.1749-6632.1978.tb41960.x

Debanne, D. (2004). Information processing in the axon. *Nature Reviews. Neuroscience, 5*, 303–316. doi:10.1038/nrn1397

Derjean, D., Bertrand, S., Le Masson, G., Landry, M., Morisset, V., & Nagy, F. (2003). Dynamic balance of metabotropic inputs causes dorsal horn neurons to switch functional states. *Nature Neuroscience, 6*(3), 274–281. doi:10.1038/nn1016

Fukai, H., Doi, S., Nomura, T., & Sato, S. (2000). Hopf bifurcations in multiple-parameter space of the Hodgkin-Huxley equations I. Global organization of bistable periodic solutions. *Biological Cybernetics, 82*(3), 215–222. doi:10.1007/s004220050021

Izhikevich, E. M. (2000). Neural excitability, spiking and bursting. *International Journal of Bifurcation and Chaos in Applied Sciences and Engineering, 10*(6), 1171–1266. doi:10.1142/S0218127400000840

Lin, R., Leng, G., & Lee, H. P. (1997). A method for the numerical computation of Hopf bifurcation. *Applied Mathematics and Computation, 86*(2-3), 137–156. doi:10.1016/S0096-3003(96)00178-6

Mackenzie, P. J., Umemiya, M., & Murphy, T. H. (1996). Ca 2+ imaging of CNS axons in culture indicates reliable coupling between single action potentials and distal functional release sites. *Neuron, 16*, 783–795. doi:10.1016/S0896-6273(00)80098-7

Philip, M. L., Gila, M. T., David, J. T., Hugh, B., & Peter, G. (2006). Activity-dependent modulation of axonal excitability in unmyelinated peripheral rat nerve fibers by the 5-HT 3. *Journal of Neurophysiology, 96*, 2963–2971. doi:10.1152/jn.00716.2006

Scriven, D. R. L. (1981). Modeling repetitive firing and bursting in a small unmyelinated nerve-fiber. *Biophysical Journal, 35*(3), 715–730. doi:10.1016/S0006-3495(81)84823-0

Wen, G. (2005). Criterion to identify Hopf bifurcations in maps of arbitrary dimension. *Physical Review E: Statistical, Nonlinear, and Soft Matter Physics, 72*(2 Pt 2), 026201. doi:10.1103/PhysRevE.72.026201

Zhu, J. L., Shen, Q., & Jiang, D. Z. (2001). Bursting of nenrons under slow wave stimulation. *In: Building new bridges at the frontiers of engineering and medicine-23rd annual international conference of the IEEE engineering in medicineand biology society.*Istanbul Turkey.

Zhu, Z. R., Tang, X. W., & Wang, W, T., Ren, W., Xing, J. L., Zhang, J. R., Duan J. H., Wang, Y. Y., Jiao, X, Y., Hu, S. J. (2009). Conduction Failures in Rabbit Saphenous Nerve Unmyelinated Fibers. *Neuro-Signals, 17*, 181–195. doi:10.1159/000209279

ADDITIONAL READING

Chen, X., & Levine, D. (2001). Hyper-responsivity in a subset of C-fiber nocicepters in a model of painful diabetic neuropathy in the rat. *Neuroscience, 102*, 185–192. doi:10.1016/S0306-4522(00)00454-1

Destexhe, A., Mainen, Z. F., & Sejnowski, T. J. (1994). Synthesis of models for excitable membranes, synaptic transmission and neuromodulation using a common kinetic formalism. *Journal of Computational Neuroscience, 1*(3), 195–230. doi:10.1007/BF00961734

Gee, M. D., Lynn, B., & Cotsell, B. (1996). Activity-dependent slowing of conduction velocity provides a method for identifying different functional classes of C-fiber in the rat saphenous nerve. *Neuroscience, 73,* 667–675. doi:10.1016/0306-4522(96)00070-X

Hu, S. J., Yang, H. J., Jian, Z., Long, K. P., Duan, Y. B., & Wan, Y. H. (2000). Adrenergic sensitivity of neurons with non-periodic firing activity in rat injured dorsal root ganglion. *Neuroscience, 101*(3), 689–698. doi:10.1016/S0306-4522(00)00414-0

Izhikevich, E. M. (1998). Multiple cusp bifurcations. *Neural Networks, 11*(3), 495–508. doi:10.1016/S0893-6080(97)00117-2

Izhikevich, E. M. (2000). Phase equations for relaxation oscillators. *SIAM Journal on Applied Mathematics, 60*(5), 1789–1804. doi:10.1137/S0036139999351001

Izhikevich, E. M. (2001). Resonate-and-fire neurons. *Neural Networks, 14*(6-7), 883–894. doi:10.1016/S0893-6080(01)00078-8

Izhikevich, E. M. (2003). Simple model of spiking neurons. *IEEE Transactions on Neural Networks, 14*(6), 1569–1572. doi:10.1109/TNN.2003.820440

Izhikevich, E. M. (2004). Which model to use for cortical spiking neurons? *IEEE Transactions on Neural Networks, 15*(5), 1063–1070. doi:10.1109/TNN.2004.832719

Izhikevich, E. M., Desai, N. S., Walcott, E. C., & Hoppensteadt, F. C. (2003). Bursts as a unit of neural information: selective communication via resonance. *Trends in Neurosciences, 26*(3), 161–167. doi:10.1016/S0166-2236(03)00034-1

Izhikevich, E. M., Gally, J. A., & Edelman, G. M. (2004). Spike-timing dynamics of neuronal groups. *Cerebral Cortex, 14*(8), 933–944. doi:10.1093/cercor/bhh053

Izhikevich, E. M., & Hoppensteadt, F. (2004). Classification of bursting mappings. *International Journal of Bifurcation and Chaos in Applied Sciences and Engineering, 14*(11), 3847–3854. doi:10.1142/S0218127404011739

Jian, Z., Xing, J. L., Yang, G. S., & Hu, S. J. (2004). A novel bursting mechanism of type A neurons in injured dorsal root ganglia. *Neuro-Signals, 13*(3), 150–156. doi:10.1159/000076569

Kubota, Y., & Bower, J. M. (1999). Decoding time-varying calcium signals by the postsynaptic biochemical network: Computer simulations of molecular kinetics. *Neurocomputing, 26-7,* 29–38. doi:10.1016/S0925-2312(99)00085-5

Lisman, J. E. (1997). Bursts as a unit of neural information:making unreliable synapses reliable. *Trends in Neurosciences, 20*(1), 38–43. doi:10.1016/S0166-2236(96)10070-9

Liu, Y. H., Yang, J., & Hu, S. J. (2008). Transition between two excitabilities in mesencephalic V neurons. *Journal of Computational Neuroscience, 24*(1), 95–104. doi:10.1007/s10827-007-0048-4

Orstavik, K., Weidner, C., Schmidt, R., Schmelz, M., Hilliges, M., & Jorum, E. (2003). Pathological C-fibers in patients with a chronic painful condition. *Brain, 126,* 567–578. doi:10.1093/brain/awg060

Segev, I., & Schneidman, E. (1999). Axons as computing devices: basic insights gained from models. *Journal of Physiology, Paris, 93,* 263–270. doi:10.1016/S0928-4257(00)80055-8

Seth, A. K., Izhikevich, E., Reeke, G. N., & Edelman, G. M. (2006). Theories and measures of consciousness: An extended framework. *Proceedings of the National Academy of Sciences of the United States of America, 103*(28), 10799–10804. doi:10.1073/pnas.0604347103

Soleng, A. F., Chiu, D., & Raastad, M. (2003). Unmyelinated axons in the rat hippocampus hyperpolarize and activate an H current when spike frequency exceeds 1HZ. *The Journal of Physiology, 552*, 459–470. doi:10.1113/jphysiol.2003.048058

Wan, Y. H., & Hu, S. J. (2003). Short-term depression at primary afferent synapses in rat substantia gelatinosa region. *Neuroreport, 14*(2), 197–200. doi:10.1097/00001756-200302100-00007

Wan, Y. H., Jian, Z., Hu, S. J., Xu, H., Yang, H. J., & Duan, Y. B. (2000). Detection of determinism within time series of irregular burst firing from the injured sensory neuron. *Neuroreport, 11*(14), 3295–3298. doi:10.1097/00001756-200009280-00049

Wan, Y. H., Jian, Z., Wen, Z. H., Wang, Y. Y., Han, S., & Duan, Y. B. (2004). Synaptic transmission of chaotic spike trains between primary afferent fiber and spinal dorsal horn neuron in the rat. *Neuroscience, 125*(4), 1051–1060. doi:10.1016/j.neuroscience.2004.02.035

Xing, J. L., Hu, S. J., Jian, Z., & Duan, J. H. (2003). Subthreshold membrane potential oscillation mediates the excitatory effect of norepinephrine in chronically compressed dorsal root ganglion neurons in the rat. *Pain, 105*(1-2), 177–183. doi:10.1016/S0304-3959(03)00200-8

Yang, H.-J., Hu, S.-J., Jian, Z., Wan, Y.-H., & Long, K.-P. (2000). Relationship between the sensitivity to tetraethylammonium and firing patterns of injured dorsal root ganglion neurons. *Sheng Li Xue Bao, 52*(5), 395–401.

Zhang, J. R., Wang, J. N., Liu, Y. H., & Hu, S. J. (2008). Simulation of primary afferent synapses in unmyelinated nerve fiber. *Bmei 2008. Proceedings of the International Conference on Biomedical Engineering and Informatics, 1*, 723–727.

KEY TERMS AND DEFINITIONS

H-H Equations: The Hodgkin: Huxley model is a scientific model that describes how action potentials in neurons are initiated and propagated. It is a set of nonlinear ordinary differential equations that approximate the electrical characteristics of excitable cells such as neurons and cardiac myocytes.

Membrane Potential: The membrane potential is the voltage difference (or electrical potential difference) between the interior and exterior of a cell. Because the fluid inside and outside a cell is highly conductive, whereas a cell's plasma membrane is highly resistive, the voltage change in moving from a point outside to a point inside occurs largely within the narrow width of the membrane itself. Therefore, it is common to speak of the membrane potential as the voltage across the membrane.

Action Potential: An action potential (or nerve impulse) is a transient alteration of the transmembrane voltage (or membrane potential) across an excitable membrane in an excitable cell (such as a neuron or myocyte) generated by the activity of voltage-gated ion channels embedded in the membrane. The best known action potentials are pulse-like waves of voltage that travel along the axons of neurons.

Firing Pattern: The cells show different modes of firing with different amounts of current injection.

Bifurcation: It means the splitting of a main body into two parts.

Hopf Bifurcation: In bifurcation theory, a Hopf or Andronov–Hopf bifurcation, named after Eberhard Hopf and Aleksandr Andronov, is a local bifurcation in which a fixed point of a dynamical system loses stability as a pair of complex conjugate eigenvalues of the linearization around the fixed point cross the imaginary axis of the complex plane. Under reasonably generic assumptions about the dynamical system, we can expect to see a small amplitude limit cycle branching from the fixed point.

Unmyelinated Fibre: A fibre having no myelin covering (CNS); a naked axon; in the Peripheral nervous system represented by all axons lying in troughs in a single Schwann cell (Schwann cell unit); a slow conducting fibre.

Supercritical / Subcritical Hopf Bifurcations: The limit cycle is orbitally stable if a certain quantity called the first Lyapunov coefficient is negative, and the bifurcation is supercritical. Otherwise it is unstable and the bifurcation is subcritical.

Chapter 21
The Mathematical Modeling and Computational Simulation for Error–Prone PCR

Lixin Luo
South China University of Technology, China

Fang Zhu
South China Universityof Technology, China

Si Deng
South China University of Technology, China

ABSTRACT

Many enzymes have been widely used in industrial production, for they have higher catalytic efficiency and catalytic specificity than the traditional catalysts. Therefore, the performance of enzymes has attracted wide attention. However, due to various factors, enzymes often cannot show their greatest catalytic efficiency and the strongest catalytic ability in industrial production. In order to improve the enzyme activity and specificity, people become increasingly interested in the transformation and modification of existing enzymes. For the structure modification of proteinase, this chapter introduces a computational method for modelling error-prone PCR. Error-prone PCR is a DNA replication process that intentionally introduces copying errors by imposing mutagenic reaction condition. We then conclude about the mathematical principle of error-prone PCR which may be applied to the quantitative analysis of directed evolution in future studies.

INTRODUCTION

The successful application of enzymes as industrial biocatalysts requires the availability of suitable enzymes with high activity, specificity and stability in process conditions. However, naturally procreant enzymes are often not optimized to meet these requirements(Zhao et al., 2002). Using the method of directed evolution, we can not only produce useful biocatalyst for the organic chemistry domain, but also improve the properties of the biocatalyst and even create biocatalysts that possess novel catalytic activities and properties (Raillard et al., 2001). Directed evolution has

DOI: 10.4018/978-1-60960-064-8.ch021

been used increasingly in academic and industrial laboratories to modify and improve important biocatalysts (Arnold & Volkov, 1999). It is a fast way that simulates Darwinian evolution in the test tube to improve protein with a certain purpose (Zhao et al., 2002). Relative to the traditional "rational design", this method is called "irrational design". Error-prone PCR protocols, which use a low fidelity replication step to introduce random point mutations into DNA sequences at each round of amplification, were used in early directed evolution experiments (Moore & Arnold, 1996; Zaccolo & Gherardi, 1999).

Error-prone PCR is a DNA replication process that introduces copying errors in PCR process by changing reaction conditions. The key to the error-prone PCR is to control the DNA mutation frequency (Leung et al., 1989). If the DNA mutation frequency is too high, the vast majority of the procreant enzymes will lose their activity; if the mutation frequency is too low, the amount of wild-type enzymes will be too high and the diversity of the sample will be too low. The observed mutational frequency resulted in 0.25-20 mutations per 1000 base pairs in the error-prone PCR. The ideal rate of basic group displacement and the optimal error-prone PCR condition depend on the length of the target DNA fragment, the running time of PCR and the mutational frequency ω (Moore & Arnold, 1996).

MODELING FOR ERROR-PRONE PCR

The top priority of mutagenic PCR is to introduce various types of mutations in an unbiased form rather than to achieve a high overall level of amplification (Cadwell & Joyce, 1994). As in the regular PCR, the first step is the denaturing which the double-stranded DNA is separated into two single strands by heating; the second step is the annealing which is the primer binds to the complementary single-strand DNA; the third step is extension which the template sequence is extended by DNA polymerase. As non-complementary nucleotides can bind to the extended-chain, mutation occurs in the third step (Gregory & Costas, 2000). The error rate of *Taq* polymerase is the highest of the known thermostable DNA polymerases, in the range of 0.1×10^{-4} to 2×10^{-4} per nucleotide per pass of the polymerase, and depending on reaction conditions (Leung et al., 1989). It is important to control these highly variable copying errors for obtaining "useful" mutations and excluding "useless" mutations (Gregory & Costas, 2000). Simulation technique has become extremely important in almost every aspect of scientific and engineering endeavor(Neim, 1995). Simulation is experimentation with models(Korn & Wait, 1978).Therefore, we introduce computational method model into error-prone PCR and make a conclusion about mathematic law of error-prone PCR, then it can play a guiding role in the analysis.

In the proposed model, mutations will occur during the extending process and every mutation can be considered as a contrary event to the others. Let ω represent different mutation rates and a single mutation rate M_{ij} stands for the mutative probability from nucleotide i to nucleotide j.

$$\omega = \begin{bmatrix} M_{AA} & M_{AT} & M_{AC} & M_{AG} \\ M_{TA} & M_{TT} & M_{TC} & M_{TG} \\ M_{CA} & M_{CT} & M_{CC} & M_{CG} \\ M_{GA} & M_{GT} & M_{GC} & M_{GG} \end{bmatrix} \qquad (1)$$

These values depend on the experimental conditions. ω can be used to describe mutation rate ω^n after n extension steps. When $n=0$, $M_{ij}^n=0$ (but if $i=j$, $M_{ij}^n=1$); when $n=1$, $M_{ij}^n = M_{ij}$; when $n \geq 1$, $M_{ij}^n = \sum_{k=A,T,C,G} M_{kj} M_{ik}^{n-1}$ (Gregory & Costas, 2000).

The Computational Method:
Algorithm M_{ij}^n

```
Input i j n;
If n=0
```

```
If i=j return 1;
else return 0;
else if n=1 return M_ij;
else return  ∑       M_kj M_ik^{n-1}
           k=A,T,C,G
```

Not all the sequences go through N extended steps of N PCR cycles.

Let $Z_{N,n}$ represent the number of sequences after N PCR cycles and n extended steps. For example, after three PCR cycles, 16 single strands of DNA are produced. Before the first PCR cycle, the extended step is 0, there are two original single-strands; after the first PCR cycle, the extended step is 1, another two single-strands are produced from original sequences; after the second PCR cycle, the extended step is 2, two new double-strands are produced; the rest may be deduced by analogy. So, $Z_{3,0}=2$, $Z_{3,1}=6$, $Z_{3,2}=6$, $Z_{3,3}=2$. After N PCR cycles, the reaction mixture contains a number of strands that have been through n extension steps. These strands ($Z_{N,n}$) originate from: either old templates that have been through n extension step prior to the Nth PCR cycle ($Z_{N-1,n}$); or new strands extended from templates that had already been through n-1 extension steps ($Z_{N-1,n-1}$)(Gregory & Costas, 2000).

$$Z_{N,n} = Z_{N-1,n} + Z_{N-1,n-1} \tag{2}$$

According to the above formula, we can obtain the result that $Z_{N,n} = 2\binom{N}{n}$, and the total number of the sequences is 2^{N+1}.

$\binom{N}{n}$ Computational Method:

Algorithm $\binom{N}{n}$

```
Input N, n;
Define Accumulation _
N=1,Accumulation_n=1,i;
For i=N-n+1 to N step 1
Accumulation _N = Accumulation
_N×i;
```

```
Go back to For
For i=1 to n step 1
Accumulation _n = Accumulation
_n×i;
Go back to For
```
$$\text{return } \frac{Accumulation\_N}{Accumulation\_n};$$

The sequences produced through n extended steps in the ratio of the total sequences is $\frac{1}{2^N}\binom{N}{n}$ and the mutation rate of nucleotide i mutates to nucleotide j after N PCR cycles is

$$p_{ij}^N = \frac{1}{2^N} \sum_{n=0}^{N} \binom{N}{n} M_{ij}^n \tag{3}$$

The Computational Method:
Algorithm p_{ij}^N

```
Define t,
Accumulation=1,counter=0;
For t=0 to N step 1
counter=counter+  (N)  × M_ij^n;
                  (n)
Accumulation=2×Accumulation;
Go back to For
```
$$\text{return } \frac{2 \times counter}{Accumulation};$$

This is just a research concerned about the mutation rate at a single-point, then we will discuss the mutation rate $\sum_{s^0,s}^{N}$ of the entire sequences.

$$\sum_{s^0,s}^{N} = \frac{1}{2^N} \sum_{n=0}^{N} \left(\binom{N}{n} \frac{\sum_{j=1}^{B} [P^n]_{s_j^0, s_j}}{B} \right) \tag{4}$$

$$\left[P^n\right]_{S^0_j,S_j} = \left[1 - P^n_{jj}\right]_{S^0_j,S_j} = \left[\sum_{k=A,T,C,G;\exp ect=j} P^n_{jk}\right]_{S^0_j,S_j}$$

(5)

Let S^0, S represent the original sequence and the sequence after N PCR cycles, respectively; let B represents S^0 and S sequence length.

Let $\left[P^n\right]_{S^0_j,S_j}$ stand for the mutation rate after n extended steps while the sequence position is j. The computational Method:

Algorithm $\sum_{S^0,S}^{N}$

```
Obtain all sequence S⁰
Define n, j,
Sum=0,Counter,Accumulation=1;
For n=0 to N step 1
For j=1 to B step
Counter=Counter+[Pⁿ]_{S⁰_j,S_j};

Go back to For
```

$$\text{Sum=Sum+} \frac{\binom{N}{n} \times counter}{B};$$

```
Accumulation=Accumulation×2;
Go back to For
```

$$\text{Return } \frac{2 \times sum}{Accumulation};$$

Data Analysis

In the mathematical methods above, we can see that mutation rate p^N_{ij} increases with the number of PCR cycles (range from 0 to 17 PCR cycles). The relationship between mutation rate and the number of PCR cycles is linear. It is consistent with the simple formulae that is proposed by Eckert & Lunkel:

$$f = \frac{Np}{2}$$

(6)

N and P stand for cycle numbers and mutation rate respectively.

We also use this method to analyze the mutation rate $\sum_{S^0,S}^{N}$ of *Bacillus subtilis* Lipase complete gene at the same time: Changes in mutation rate and PCR cycles remain the linear relationship.

In our experiment, ω is the mutation rate that was measured in the condition that the concentration of Mn²⁺ is 0 (Shafkhani et al., 1997). All of the above discussions are based on their reaction conditions.

The analysis of the case is based on the following data (the concentration of Mn²⁺ is 0):

$$\omega = \begin{bmatrix} 99.926\% & 0.035\% & 0.007\% & 0.032\% \\ 0.035\% & 99.926\% & 0.032\% & 0.007\% \\ 0.007\% & 0.021\% & 99.972\% & 0.000\% \\ 0.021\% & 0.007\% & 0.000\% & 99.972\% \end{bmatrix} \begin{matrix} (A) \\ (T) \\ (C) \\ (G) \end{matrix}$$

(7)

The data figured out in our experiment is line with Shafkhani's data

$$p^{13}_{ij} = \begin{bmatrix} 99.522\% & 0.227\% & 0.046\% & 0.205\% \\ 0.227\% & 99.522\% & 0.205\% & 0.046\% \\ 0.046\% & 0.137\% & 99.817\% & 0.000\% \\ 0.137\% & 0.046\% & 0.000\% & 99.817\% \end{bmatrix} \begin{matrix} (A) \\ (T) \\ (C) \\ (G) \end{matrix}$$

(8)

The fact is based on the discussion between *Bacillus Subtilis* Lipase complete gene (the average mutation rate of every PCR cycle $\sum_{S^0,S}^{1}$ =0.0135%) and the mutation rate of different GC contents (12 PCR cycles in our experiment):

Changes in GC contents directly affect mutation rate, but the result from traditional $f = \frac{Np}{2}$ have no relation with it, this is inconsistent with the actual situation. This method shows better pertinence of the different ratio of GC contents and different mutation rates of different chain.

DISCUSSION AND CONCLUSION

We established a mathematical frame for describing error-prone PCRs. And then we discussed the changes in the mutation rate of different PCR cycles and GC contents.

Using *Bacillus subtilis* Lipase as an example, we tested how well our method works. The target gene fragment of the lipase enzyme can be amplified by PCR. In the process, we can introduce a certain frequency of random mutation to the target gene by adjusting reaction conditions such as increasing Mg^{2+} concentration or changing the concentration of the four dNTP in the system to improve the error rate of the amplified reaction. Then we can construct the corresponding mutant library and obtain the required mutant through corresponding screening methods (Tang et al., 2003). Based on this, we obtained the mutation rate of the Lipase complete gene in *Bacillus subtilis* under one condition. The mathematical model established in the paper may be widely applicable for predicting and calculating various DNA sequences in the error-prone environment.

The model above is based on perfect reaction condition and introduces a series of parameters for different conditions. For instance, (1) it is possible that only a part of the single strand is extended in every PCR cycle, so the total number of strands should be equal to $(1+\gamma)^N$ instead of 2^N, $0<\gamma<1$; (2) mutation rate ω may be different under various conditions.

This chapter intends to give a corresponding mathematic description of the primary quality of error-prone PCR. There are many details remain to be investigated in our future work.

REFERENCES

Arnold, F. H., & Volkov, A. A. (1999). Directed evolution of biocatalysts. *Current Opinion in Chemical Biology*, *3*(1), 54–59. doi:10.1016/S1367-5931(99)80010-6

Cadwell, R. C., & Joyce, G. F. (1994). Mutagenic PCR. *PCR Methods and Applications*, *3*(6), S136–S140.

Gregory, L., & Costas, D. (2000). Modeling DNA Mutation and Recombination for Directed Evolution Experiment. *Journal of Theoretical Biology*, *205*(3), 483–503. doi:10.1006/jtbi.2000.2082

Korn, G. A., & Wait, J. V. (1978). *Didital Continuous System Simulation*. Englewood Cliffs, NJ: Prentice Hall.

Leung, D., Chen, E., & Goeddel, D. (1989). A method for random mutagenesis of a defined DNA segment using modified polymerase chain reaction. *Technique*, *1*, 11–15.

Moore, J., & Arnold, F. (1996). Directed evolution of a para-nitrobenzyl esterase for aqueous-organic solvents. *Nature Biotechnology*, *14*(4), 458–467. doi:10.1038/nbt0496-458

Neim, A. K. (1996). *Systems modeling and computer simulation*. New York: Marcel Dekker, Inc.

Raillard, S., Krebber, A., & Chen, Y. (2001). Novel enzyme activities and functional plasticity revealed by recombining highly homologous enzymes. *Chemistry & Biology*, *8*(9), 891–898. doi:10.1016/S1074-5521(01)00061-8

Shafkhani, S., Siesel, R., Ferrari, E., & Schellenberger, V. (1997). Generation of large libraries of random mutants in bacillus subtilis by PCR-base plasmid multimerization. *BioTechniques*, *23*(2), 304–310.

Tang, L. H., Xia, L. M., & Su, M. (2003). The research of microbial lipase molecular transformation. *Biotechnology*, *13*(3), 42–44.

Zaccolo, M., & Gherardi, E. (1999). The effect of high-frequency random mutagenesis on in vitro protein evolution: a study on TEM-1 beta-lactamase. *Molecular Biology*, *285*(2), 775–783. doi:10.1006/jmbi.1998.2262

Zhao, H. M., & Chockal, I. N., GAM, K., & Chen, Z. L. (2002). Directed Evolution of Enzymes and Pathways for Industrial Biocatalysis. *Current Opinion in Biotechnology, 13*(2), 104–110. doi:10.1016/S0958-1669(02)00291-4

ADDITIONAL READING

Arnold, F. (1996). Directed evolution: Creating biocatalysts for the future. *Chemical Engineering Science, 51*(23), 5091–5102. doi:10.1016/S0009-2509(96)00288-6

Arnold, F. H. (1998). Design by directed evolution. *Accounts of Chemical Research, 31*(3), 125–131. doi:10.1021/ar960017f

Arnold, F. H., & Volkov, A. A. (1999). Directed evolution of biocatalysts. *Current Opinion in Chemical Biology, 3*(1), 54–59. doi:10.1016/S1367-5931(99)80010-6

Bailey, J. E. (1998). Mathematical modeling and analysis in biochemical engineering, past accomplishments and future opportunities. *Biotechnology Progress, 14*(1), 8–20. doi:10.1021/bp9701269

Biles, B. D., & Connolly, B. A. (2004). Low-fidelity Pyrococcus furiosus DNA polymerase mutants useful in error-prone PCR. *Nucleic Acids Research, 32*(22), 176–182. doi:10.1093/nar/gnh174

Crameri, A., Dawes, G., Rodriguez, E. Jr, Silver, S., & Stemmer, W. (1997). Molecular evolution of an arsenate detoxification pathway by DNA shuffling. *Nature Biotechnology, 15*(5), 436–438. doi:10.1038/nbt0597-436

Curis, E., Nicolis, I., Bensaci, J., Deschamps, P., & Bénazeth, S. (2009). Mathematical modeling in metal metabolism: overview and perspectives. *Biochimie, 91*(10), 1238–1254. doi:10.1016/j.biochi.2009.06.019

Henke, E., & Bornscheuer, U. T. (1999). Directed evolution of an esterase from Psueudomonas fluorescens. Random mutagenesis by error-prone PCR or a mutator strain and identification of mutants showing enhanced enantioselectivity by a resorufin-based fluorescence assay. *Biological Chemistry, 380*(7-8), 1029–1033. doi:10.1515/BC.1999.128

Ho, S. N., Hunt, H. D., Horton, R. M., Pullen, J. K., & Pease, L. R. (1989). Site-directed mutagenesis by overlap extension using the polymerase chain reaction. *Gene, 77*(1), 51–59. doi:10.1016/0378-1119(89)90358-2

Hsu, J., Das, S., & Mohapatra, S. (1997). Polymerase chain reaction engineering. *Biotechnology and Bioengineering, 55*(2), 359–366. doi:10.1002/(SICI)1097-0290(19970720)55:2<359::AID-BIT13>3.0.CO;2-C

Lio, Z. Q., Sun, Z. H., Zheng, P., Leng, Y., & Qian, J. R. (2005). Directed evolution of D-lactonohydrolase by error-prone PCR and DNA shuffling. *Sheng Wu Gong Cheng Xue Bao, 21*(5), 773–781.

Moore, G. L., & Maranas, C. D. (2000). Modeling DNA mutation and recombination for directed evolution experiments. *Journal of Theoretical Biology, 205*(3), 483–503. doi:10.1006/jtbi.2000.2082

Moore, J., & Arnold, F. (1996). Directed evolution of a para-nitrobenzyl esterase for aqueous-organic solvents. *Nat. Biotect., 14*(4), 458–467. doi:10.1038/nbt0496-458

Nixon, A. E., & Firestine, S. M. (2000). Rational and "irrational" design of proteins and their use in biotechnology. *IUBMB Life, 49*(3), 181–187.

Orita, M., Suzuki, Y., Sekiya, T., & Hayashi, K. (1989). Rapid and sensitive detection of point mutation and DNA polymorphisms using the polymerase chain reaction. *Genomics, 5*(4), 874–879. doi:10.1016/0888-7543(89)90129-8

Pritchard, L., Corne, D., Kell, D. B., Rowland, J., & Winson, M. (2005). A general model of error-prone PCR. *Journal of Theoretical Biology, 234*(4), 497–509. doi:10.1016/j.jtbi.2004.12.005

Schaefer, B. C. (1995). Revolutions in rapid amplification of cDNA ends:new strategies for polymerase chain reaction cloning of full3length cDNA ends. *Analytical Biochemistry, 227*(2), 255–273. doi:10.1006/abio.1995.1279

Schmidt, M., Bottcher, D., & Bornscheuer, U. T. (2009). Protein engineering of carboxyl esterases by rational design and directed evolution. *Protein and Peptide Letters, 16*(10), 1162–1171. doi:10.2174/092986609789071216

Smolen, P., Baxter, D. A., & Byrne, J. H. (2000). Mathematical modeling of gene networks. *Neuron, 26*(3), 567–580. doi:10.1016/S0896-6273(00)81194-0

Stemmer, W. (1994). Rapid evolution of a protein in vitro by DNA shuffling. *Nature, 370*(6488), 389–391. doi:10.1038/370389a0

Sun, F. (1995). The polymerase chain reaction and branching processes. *Journal of Computational Biology, 2*(1), 63–86. doi:10.1089/cmb.1995.2.63

Sun, F. (1999). Modeling DNA shuffling. *Journal of Computational Biology, 6*(1), 77–90. doi:10.1089/cmb.1999.6.77

Tobin, M. B., Gustafsson, C., & Huisman, G. W. (2000). Directed evolution: the 'rational' bas is for 'irrational' design. *Current Opinion in Structural Biology, 10*(4), 421–427. doi:10.1016/S0959-440X(00)00109-3

Van, L. B., Spelberg, J. H., Kingma, J., Wubbolts, M. G., & Janssen, D. B. (2004). Directed evolution of epoxide hydrolase from A. radiobacter toward higher enantioselectivity by error-prone PCR and DNA shufffing. *Chemistry & Biology, 11*(7), 981–990. doi:10.1016/j.chembiol.2004.04.019

Wang, D., Zhao, C., Cheng, R., & Sun, F. Z. (2000). Estimation of the mutation rate during error-prone polymerase chain reaction. *Journal of Computational Biology, 7*(1-2), 143–158. doi:10.1089/10665270050081423

KEY TERMS AND DEFINITIONS

Directed Revolution: It is a method used in protein engineering to use the power of natural selection to evolve proteins with desirable properties not found in nature. And a typical directed evolution experiment involves three steps: diversification, selection, amplification.

Enzyme: Enzymes are biocatalysts that can speed up the rate of reactions by lowering the activation energy. As with all catalysts, enzymes are not consumed by the reactions they catalyze, nor do they alter the equilibrium of these reactions.

Error -Prone PCR: Error-prone PCR is a modification of standard PCR methods, designed to alter and enhance the natural error rate of the polymerase. This technique is based on the principle that Taq polymerase is capable of annealing incompatible base-pairs to each other during amplification under imperfect PCR conditions.

PCR: Polymerase chain reaction (PCR) is a technique to amplify a single or few copies of a piece of DNA across several orders of magnitude, generating thousands to millions of copies of a particular DNA sequence.

Rational Design: Rational design is a method used in protein engineering. It attempts to obtain new protein with desired properties by making some changes of the protein. And this is based on the knowledge of structure and function of protein.

Section 6
Structure and Modeling

Chapter 22
Molecular Dynamics Simulation of Interlayer Structure and Hydration Properties of Glycine Intercalated Layered Double Hydroxides

Guo-Xiang Pan
Huzhou Teachers College, China

Zhe-Ming Ni
Zhejiang University of Technology, China

Feng Cao
Huzhou Teachers College, China

Jin-Tian Yang
Huzhou Teachers College, China

Pei-Song Tang
Huzhou Teachers College, China

Li-Geng Wang
Zhejiang University of Technology, China

Hai-Feng Chen
Huzhou Teachers College, China

Min-Hong Xu
Huzhou Teachers College, China

ABSTRACT

Interlayer structure, hydrogen-bond, hydration and swelling properties of glycine intercalated layered double hydroxides (LDHs-Gly) were investigated with molecular dynamics (MD) methods. The results show that the interlayer spacing d_c increases as hydration level increases. The computed hydration energies reach the most negative values at low water contents and change rapidly over the range $1 \leq N_W \leq 6$, and slowly and gradually approach the potential energy for bulk SPC water at $N_W > 6$. But there are no local minima in the energy over the entire hydration range. This result suggests that LDHs-Gly tend to absorb water continuously in water-rich environments and enhance swelling to delaminate the hydroxide layers. The interlayers of LDHs-Gly exhibit complex hydrogen-bond network. With water content increasing, the glycine molecules progressively change their orientation from parallel to the

DOI: 10.4018/978-1-60960-064-8.ch022

layers to nearly perpendicular. Water molecules firstly form hydrogen-bond with M-OH layers at low water contents. While the hydroxide layers gradually get to saturation state at $N_w > 3$. And then water molecules continuously fill the interlayer to expand interlayer spacing.

INTRODUCTION

Layered double hydroxides, also known as anionic clays or hydrotalcite-like compounds (HTlcs), may be considered as analogous to the magnesium hydroxide mineral brucite. In the largest group of anionic clays some of the Mg^{2+} is substituted by a M^{3+} species, for example Al^{3+}, Fe^{3+} or Ga^{3+}. Other varieties of anionic clays exist where the M^{2+} species is for example Zn^{2+} or Ni^{2+}, giving rise to the family of compounds of general formula $M^{2+}_{1-x}M^{3+}_x(OH)_2A^{x-}\cdot nH_2O$. In each case the resulting structure consists of layers bearing a net positive charge, which is compensated by the introduction of anions in the interlayer region, as well as at the edges and surfaces of layered double hydroxides (Cavani et al., 1991).

Incorporation of bio- and organic species into LDHs interlayers using ion-exchange method has gained significant attention in recent years. Amino acids, as important components of proteins, enzymes and biomolecules, can serve as pillars in cationic and anionic clays. Intercalation compounds of amino acids offer the perspective applications in separation science as chiral catalyst, as well as in drug delivery systems.

In recent times there has been a growing interest in anionic clays although, historically, attention has been focused almost exclusively on the cationic clay materials. Experimental techniques have been used to determine or at least to infer the local structure of the clay sheet or intercalated material. However, clays are polycrystalline materials and precise experimental location of interlayer species is extremely difficult. Because of these limitations, interest in and the use of computational methods for studying these layered solids has increased in order that observed physical and chemical properties may be rationalised and even predicted.

By applying initial velocities to a configuration of atoms and solving Newton's equations of motion the potential energy surface may be traversed in a deterministic fashion and the temporal evolution of a system followed. This is known as molecular dynamics (MD). In this technique thermal energy is included using a thermostat, which allows potential energy barriers to be overcome in a realistic manner. The main advantage of the method is that the dynamical evolution of a system, with time, may be followed, which allows comparison with additional experimental techniques such as NMR and quasi-elastic neutron scattering. It still remains a challenge, however, to follow the evolution of a system beyond the timescale of 1–10 ns, even when using classical mechanics simulations.

Force-fields are often parameterised to fit a set of experimental data, or based upon detailed electronic structure calculations. However, there are relatively few force-fields able to reliably model well both the interlayer (often organic) species and the octahedral metal ion environments peculiar to the clay structure, particularly in the case of anionic clays. Force-fields that are specifically parameterised to model clay–organic interactions (Teppen et al., 1997; Cygan et al., 2004). The more generic Dreiding force-field has also been utilised, in a modified form, for modelling clay systems, especially LDHs (Newman, et al., 2001). Force-field based molecular dynamics simulations have been used to determine the elastic properties of clay sheets, an important property for the prediction of bulk materials properties.

Recent experimental studies have shown that glycine intercalated layered double hydroxides (LDHs-Gly) can be obtained via hydrothermal synthesis, and enhanced swelling leading to delamination of the LDHs layers can be achieved in a solution environment (Li et al., 2006; Aisawa et al.,

2006; Hibino, 2004). For amino acids intercalated LDHs systems, its interlayer information is not generally obtainable from experimental measurements due to the inherent structural disorder and generally low crystallinity of anionic clays. In the present work, however, molecular dynamics (MD) computer simulations are used to probe the interlayer structure and provide fresh insight into the microscopic origin of the swelling behavior upon hydration of LDHs-Gly.

COMPUTATIONAL MODELS AND METHODS

The simulation supercells consist of 4*4*1 hexagonal (2H) unit cells of glycine intercalated LDHs ($Mg_{24}Al_8(OH)_{64}(8Gly) \cdot 8N_wH_2O$), containing two metal-hydroxide layers, eight glycine ions (four per each interlayer), and a variable number of water molecules. The carboxylic groups of the glycines are considered to be deprotonated in the interlayer of LDHs-Gly, since their pKa_1 values are 9.60.

The interatomic potentials employed here are based on the universal force field (Pan et al., 2009; Rappe et al.,1992). Starting from energy and stress minimized structures, NPT- ensemble MD simulations of 50 ps duration were carried out at 298 K and 1 bar pressure for different hydration states, N_w, of the system. After an initial 30 ps period of equilibration, the average unit cell parameters and hydration energy were calculated over the remaining 20 ps (Kumar et al., 2006; Kumar et al., 2007). For selected hydration values of N_w = 0~8, the longer NVE-MD simulations of 200 ps duration, including an initial 50 ps for equilibration, which starting from the final atomic configurations and average interlayer spacings obtained from the NPT-MD simulations. All MD simulations were performed with a time step of 0.5 fs. And periodic boundary conditions and Ewald summation techniques were employed.

Result and Discussion

The cell parameter of LDHs-Gly, *a* value, computed from NPT-ensemble MD simulations are all about 0.27 nm, which are lower than the literature values of *a* =0.31 nm, whereas the *c*-axis (d_c value) increases with water content increasing as shown in Figure 1, the variation is linear in N_w, and the linear equation can be expressed as d_c=0.1162N_W+1.007 (R^2=0.999).

The hydration energy, is a simple and effective measure of the affinity of water for the interlayer. Which is defined as following: $\Delta U_H = (U(8N_W) - U(0))/8N_W$ (1)

Where $U(0)$ is the energy of hydrotalcite without containing H_2O molecules. $8N_W$ is the total number of water molecules and $U(8N_W)$ is the total potential energy of the system.

The computed hydration energies show the most negative values at low water contents, the rapid changes over the range $1 \leq N_W \leq 6$, and a slower, gradual approach to the potential energy for bulk SPC water from $N_W > 6$ (Figure 1). Remarkably, these hydration energies remain lower than that of the bulk water (-10 kcal/mol for the SPC water model) to very high water contents, and there are no local minima in the energy over the entire hydration process. This behavior is the

Figure 1. Variation of interlayer spacing (d_c) and hydration energy as a function of the number of water molecules per formula unit, N_w, from NPT-MD simulation at 298 K and 1 atm pressure

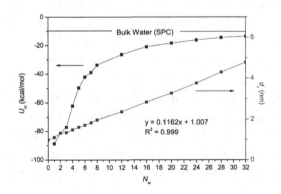

similar to the computed swelling energetics of citrate as well as monocarboxylic acids formate, acetate, and propanoate intercalated LDHs found in previous MD studies (Kumar et al., 2006; Kumar et al., 2007). The present MD results thus suggest the absence of specifically preferred hydration states and a tendency for the system to adsorb water continuously in water-rich environments such as high relative humidity (RH) conditions or in aqueous solution. The practical outcome of this enhanced swelling is delamination of the layers, similar to that observed in the recent experimental observations of LDHs-Gly in solution environments (Li et al., 2006; Aisawa et al., 2006; Hibino, 2004).

Understanding of the orientation of the intercalated glycine molecules in LDHs interlayers is important to many practical applications of amino acids intercalated material, but there are few detailed theoretical and experimental studies. The results show significant changes in glycine orientation with the hydration state, as shown by the representative snapshots in Figure 2. In the dry system, $N_w = 0$, the glycine molecules are aligned parallel to the metal hydroxide layers so as to maximize the number of H-bonds they accept from the M-OH groups.

With increasing water content, the glycine anions progressively change their orientation from parallel to the layers to nearly perpendicular. In all hydration state, the carboxyls tend to bind with metal hydroxides layers. Whereas, water molecules firstly bind with the hydroxides layer to satisfy the hydroxyls, and then fill the interspace between the glycines. At moderate hydration levels (Figure 2B, $N_w = 6$), the glycine molecules tend to orient perpendicular to the layers, and water molecules near the metal-hydroxide layers exhibit strong preference for surface sites directly above M-OH. Furthermore, interlayer swelling spacing is obtained by water molecules filling the central of layer-layer, and the hydroxide layers separate to each other up to delamination at higher water contents.

To understand the microscopic origin of the enhanced swelling behavior of LDHs-Gly, detailed analysis of the hydrogen bond (H-bond) statistics between the different donor-acceptor pairs are carried out. We use here a common H-bond definition in which an H-bond is considered to exist if the acceptor-hydrogen of donor distance is less than 0.25 nm and simultaneously the donor- hydrogen-acceptor angle is larger than 90° (Yin et al., 2006). We define three types H-bonds

Figure 2. Snapshots of interlayer glycine orientation with different hydration levels. (A) parallel to the layer in the dry system ($N_W = 0$) and (B) perpendicular to the layer at intermediate hydration values ($N_W = 6$).

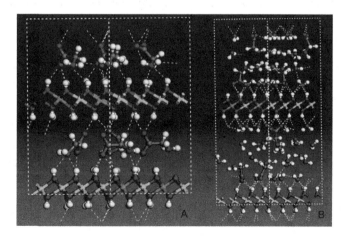

exist in the interlayer of LDHs-Gly: L-A denotes Layer-glycine type H-bond, A-W denotes glycine-water type H-bond, and L-W denotes layer-water type H-bond.

The glycine anion functions not only as H-bond acceptor through the carboxyl group and amido group, but also as H-bond donor because of the hydrogen of its amido group. The statistics of H-bonds between the relevant donor/acceptor pairs in LDHs-Gly are listed in Figure 3. As the water contents increasing, L-A Type and A-W type H-bonds contain invariable, and reach their respective characteristic saturation values are about 3 and 1. The H-bonds analysis result consists with interlayer glycine orientation at various hydration states.

The M-OH groups of metal hydroxide layers act as pure H-bond donors, consistent with previous MD studies. The total number of H-bonds donated by the M-OH groups (Figure 3B) is 0.5 per hydroxyl at $N_w = 0$. As the hydration level increasing, the number of L-W type H-bonds rapidly increase at $N_w \leq 3$. But L-W type and L-A type H-bonds contain invariable at higher water contents. So the total number of H-bond donated by M-OH reaches a saturation value of 1.0 ~1.2 per hydroxyl, a bit higher than the ideal value of

1.0 due to the different H-bonds statistic standard reported (Kumar et al., 2006).

CONCLUSION

Similar to LDHs intercalated with citrate, LDHs-Gly show no minima in the hydration energy at any investigated water content, suggesting high water affinity of the system and a tendency for enhanced swelling in the hydration process. The simulation results are consistent with the experimental observation of the delamination of LDHs-Gly in solution environments. Simulation results also show that the swelling behavior is due to the development of an integrated interlayer H-bond network. With increasing water content, the glycine molecules progressively change their orientation from parallel to the layers to nearly perpendicular. The water molecules near the metal-hydroxide layers exhibit strong preference for surface sites directly above M-OH at low water contents. When $N_w >$ 3, the total number of H-bond donated by M-OH reaches a saturation value of 1.0~1.2 per hydroxyl group. Furthermore, the swelling interlayer spacing resulted from water molecules continuously filling the interlayer region of LDHs-Gly.

Figure 3. Hydrogen bond statistics for the different species as a function of N_w: (A) the average number of H-bonds accepted by glycine anions from hydroxide layers and water molecules; (B) the average number of H-bonds donated by the hydroxide layers to glycine and water molecules

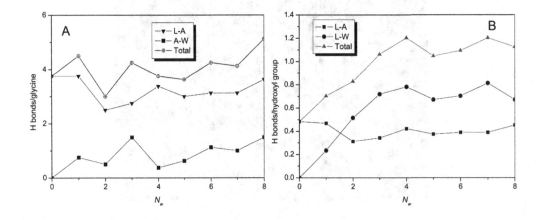

ACKNOWLEDGMENT

We gratefully acknowledge the financial support for this work by science & research program of Zhejiang province (Grant 2009R10050) and analysis measurement of science and technology planning project of zhejiang province(2008F70042).

REFERENCES

Aisawa, S., Sasaki, S., Takahashi, S., Hirahara, H., Nakayama, H., & Narita, E. (2006). Intercalation of amino acids and oligopeptides into Zn-Al layered double hydroxide by coprecipitation reaction. *Journal of Physics and Chemistry of Solids, 67*(5-6), 920–925. doi:10.1016/j.jpcs.2006.01.004

Cavani, F., Trifiro, F., & Vaccari, A. (1991). Hydrotalcite-type anionic clays: preparation, properties and applications. *Catalysis Today, 11*(2), 173–301. doi:10.1016/0920-5861(91)80068-K

Cygan, R. T., Liang, J. J., & Kalinichev, A. G. (2004). Molecular models of hydroxide, oxyhydroxide, and clay phases and the development of a general force field. *The Journal of Physical Chemistry B, 108*(4), 1255–1266. doi:10.1021/jp0363287

Hibino, T. (2004). Delamination of layered double hydroxides containing amino acids. *Chemistry of Materials, 16*(25), 5482–5488. doi:10.1021/cm048842a

Kumar, P. P., Kalinichev, A. G., & Kirkpatrick, R. J. (2007). Molecular dynamics simulation of the energetics and structure of layered double hydroxides intercalated with carboxylic acids. *The Journal of Physical Chemistry C, 111*(36), 13517–13523. doi:10.1021/jp0732054

Kumar, P. P., Kalinichev, A. G., Kirkpatrick, R. J., & James, R. (2006). Hydration, swelling, interlayer structure, and hydrogen bonding in organolayered double hydroxides: insights from molecular dynamics simulation of citrate-intercalated hydrotalcite. *The Journal of Physical Chemistry B, 110*(9), 3841–3844. doi:10.1021/jp057069j

Li, B. G., Hu, Y., & Chen, Z. Y. (2006). Hydrothermal synthesis of exfoliative LDH in the presence of glycine. *Chinese Journal of Chemical Physicals, 19*(3), 253–258.

Newman, S. P., Greenwell, H. C., Coveney, P. V., & Jones, W. (2001). Computer modelling of layered double hydroxides. In Rives, V. (Ed.), *Layered Double Hydroxides: Present and Future.* Nova Science, New York.

Pan, G. X., Ni, Z. M., Wang, F., Wang, J. G., & Li, X. N. (2009). Molecular dynamics simulation on structure, hydrogen-Bond and hydration properties of diflunisal intercalated layered double hydroxides. [in Chinese]. *Acta Physico-Chimica Sinica, 25*(2), 223–228.

Rappe, A. K., Casewit, C. J., Colwell, K. S., Goddard, W. A., & Skiff, W. M. (1992). UFF, a Full Periodic Table Force Field for Molecular Mechanics and Molecular Dynamics Simulations. *Journal of the American Chemical Society, 114*(25), 10024–10039. doi:10.1021/ja00051a040

Teppen, B. J., Rasmussen, K., Bertsch, P. M., Miller, D. M., & Schafer, L. (1997). Molecular Dynamics Modeling of Clay Minerals. 1. Gibbsite, Kaolinite, Pyrophyllite, and Beidellite. *The Journal of Physical Chemistry B, 101*(9), 1579–1587. doi:10.1021/jp961577z

Yin, K. L., Zou, D. H., Yang, B., Zhang, X. H., Xia, Q., & Xu, D. J. (2006). Investigation of H-bonding for the related force fields in materials studio software. [in Chinese]. *Computers and Applied Chemistry, 23*(12), 1335–1340.

ADDITIONAL READING

Allada, R. K., Navrotsky, A., & Berbeco, H. T. (2002). Thermochemistry and aqueous solubilities of hydrotalcite-like solids. *Science*, *296*(5568), 721–723. doi:10.1126/science.1069797

Boulet, P., Greenwell, H. C., Stackhouse, S., & Coveney, P. V. (2006). Recent advances in understanding the structure and reactivity of clays using electronic structure calculations. *Journal of Molecular Structure THEOCHEM*, *762*(1-3), 33–48. doi:10.1016/j.theochem.2005.10.028

Cavani, F., Trifiro, F., & Vaccari, A. (1991). Hydrotalcite-type anionic clays: preparation, properties, and applications. *Catalysis Today*, *11*(2), 173–301. doi:10.1016/0920-5861(91)80068-K

Cygan, R. T., Liang, J. J., & Kalinichev, A. G. (2004). Molecular models of hydroxide, oxyhydroxide, and clay phases and the development of a general force field. *The Journal of Physical Chemistry B*, *108*(4), 1255–1266. doi:10.1021/jp0363287

Evans, D. G., & Duan, X. (2006). Preparation of layered double hydroxides and their applications as additives in polymers, as precursors to mag-netic materials and in biology and medicine. *Chemical Communications (Cambridge)*, *6*(5), 485–496. doi:10.1039/b510313b

Greenwell, H. C., Jones, W., Coveney, P. V., & Stackhouse, S. (2006). On the application of computer simulation techniques to anionic and cationic clays: A materials chemistry perspective. *Journal of Materials Chemistry*, *16*(8), 708–723. doi:10.1039/b506932g

Greenwell, H. C., Jones, W., Newman, S. P., & Coveney, P. V. (2003). Computer simulation of interlayer arrangement in cinnamate intercalated layered double hydroxides. *Journal of Molecular Structure*, *647*(1-3), 75–83. doi:10.1016/S0022-2860(02)00514-8

Hou, X. Q., Bish, D. L., Wang, S. L., Johnston, C. T., & Kirkpatrick, R. J. (2003). Hydration, expansion, structure, and dynamics of layered double hydroxides. *The American Mineralogist*, *88*(1), 167–179.

Kirkpatrick, R. J., Kalinichev, A. G., Hou, X., & Struble, L. (2005). Experimental and molecular dynamics modeling studies of interlayer swelling: water incorporation in kanemite and ASR gel. *Materials and Structures*, *38*(278), 449–458. doi:10.1617/14344

Kirkpatrick, R. J., Kalinichev, A. G., & Wang, J. (2005). Molecular dynamics modelling of hydrated mineral interlayers and surfaces: structure and dynamics. *Mineralogical Magazine*, *69*(3), 289–308. doi:10.1180/0026461056930251

Kumar, P. P., Kalinichev, A. G., & Kirkpatrick, R. J. (2006). Hydration, swelling, interlayer structure, and hydrogen bonding in organolayered double hydroxides: Insights from molecular dynamics simulation of citrate-intercalated hydrotalcite. *The Journal of Physical Chemistry B*, *110*(9), 3841–3844. doi:10.1021/jp057069j

Li, H., Ma, J., Evans, D. G., Zhou, T., Li, F., & Duan, X. (2006). Molecular dynamics modeling of the structures and binding energies of alpha-nickel hydroxides and nickel-aluminum layered double hydroxides containing various interlayer guest anions. *Chemistry of Materials*, *18*(18), 4405–4414. doi:10.1021/cm060867h

Li, Q., Kumar, P. P., Babu, P. K., Kalinichev, A. G., & Kirkpatrick, R. J. (2005). Structure and dynamics of citrate ions in Mg/Al layered double hydroxide: C-13 NMR and molecular dynamics simulation studies. *Geochimica et Cosmochimica Acta*, *69*(10), A816–A816.

Lombardo, G. M., Pappalardo, G. C., Punzo, F., Costantino, F., Costantino, U., & Sisani, M. (2005). A novel integrated X-ray powder diffraction (XRPD) and molecular dynamics (MD) approach for modelling mixed-metal (Zn, Al) layered double hydroxides (LDHs). *European Journal of Inorganic Chemistry*, (24): 5026–5034. doi:10.1002/ejic.200500666

Mohanambe, L., & Vasudevan, S. (2005). Structure of a cyclodextr in functionalized anionic clay: XRD analysis, spectroscopy, and computer simulations. *Langmuir*, *21*(23), 10735–10742. doi:10.1021/la050628t

Mohanambe, L., & Vasudevan, S. (2005). Anionic clays containing anti-inflammatory drug molecules: Comparison of molecular dynamics simulation and measurements. *The Journal of Physical Chemistry B*, *109*(32), 15651–15658. doi:10.1021/jp050480m

Ni, Z. M., Pan, G. X., Wang, L. G., & Chen, L. T. (2006). Theoretical studies on supra-molecular interaction between host layer and halide anion of layered double hydroxides. *Acta Physico-Chimica Sinica*, *22*(11), 1321–1324.

Roeffaers, M. B. J., Sels, B. F., & Uji-I, H. (2006). Spatially resolved observation of crystal-face-dependent catalysis by single turnover counting. *Nature*, *439*(7076), 572–575. doi:10.1038/nature04502

Toth, R., Ferrone, M., Miertus, S., Chiellini, E., Fermeglia, M., & Pricl, S. (2006). Structure and energetics of biocompatible polymer nanocomposite systems: A molecular dynamics study. *Biomacromolecules*, *7*(6), 1714–1719. doi:10.1021/bm050937y

Trave, A., Selloni, A., Goursot, A., Tichit, D., & Weber, J. (2002). First principles study of the structure and chemistry of Mg-based hydrotalcite-like anionic clays. *The Journal of Physical Chemistry B*, *106*(47), 12291–12296. doi:10.1021/jp026339k

Wang, J. W., Kalinichev, A. G., Amonette, J. E., & Kirkpatrick, R. J. (2003). Interlayer structure and dynamics of Cl-bearing hydrotalcite: far infrared spectroscopy and molecular dynamics modeling. *The American Mineralogist*, *88*(2-3), 398–409.

Wang, J. W., Kalinichev, A. G., & Kirkpatrick, R. J. (2004). Molecular modeling of the 10-angstrom phase at subduction zone conditions. *Earth and Planetary Science Letters*, *222*(2), 517–527. doi:10.1016/j.epsl.2004.03.013

Wang, J. W., Kalinichev, A. G., & Kirkpatrick, R. J. (2006). Effects of substrate structure and composition on the structure, dynamics, and energetics of water at mineral surfaces: A molecular dynamics modeling study. *Geochimica et Cosmochimica Acta*, *70*(3), 562–582. doi:10.1016/j.gca.2005.10.006

KEY TERMS AND DEFINITIONS

Glycine: It is an organic compound with the formula NH_2CH_2COOH. With only a hydrogen atom as its side chain, glycine is the smallest of the 20 amino acids commonly found in proteins.

Layered Double Hydroxides: They comprise an unusual class of layered materials with positively charged layers and charge balancing anions located in the interlayer region. This is unusual in solid state chemistry: many families of materials have negatively charged layers and cations in the interlayer spaces.

Interlayer: A layer placed between other layers.

Hydration: The process of combining with water, usually reversible.

Delamination: In laminated materials repeated cyclic stresses, impact, and so on can cause layers to separate, forming a mica-like structure of separate layers, with significant loss of mechanical toughness.

Hydrogen Bond: A chemical bond consisting of a hydrogen atom between two electronegative atoms (e.g., oxygen or nitrogen) with one side being a covalent bond and the other being an ionic bond.

Molecular Dynamics (MD): It is a form of computer simulation in which atoms and molecules are allowed to interact for a period of time by approximations of known physics, giving a view of the motion of the particles. It is an atomistic simulation method where each atom is treated as a point mass, simple force rules describe the interactions between atoms. Newton's equations are integrated to advance the atomic positions and velocities, and thermodynamic statistics are extracted from the motion of the atoms.

Chapter 23
Structure of Hydrogenase in Biohydrogen Production Anaerobic Bacteria

Ming Du
Harbin Institute of Technology, China

Lu Zhang
Harbin Institute of Technology, China

ABSTRACT

Hydrogenase plays an important role in the process of biohydrogen production. Hydrogenases have very unique active sites and are classified into three groups according to the metal composition of the active sites: the [Ni-Fe] hydrogenase, [Fe-Fe] hydrogenase, and [Fe-only] hydrogenase. In this paper, the crystal structures and active sites of three kinds of hydrogenases are examined and compared. These enzymes have an unusual structural feature in common. Their similar active site indicates that the catalytic mechanism of hydrogen activation is probably similar. The understanding of the catalytic mechanisms for the three kinds of hydrogenases may help achieve the industrialization process of hydrogen energy production. Moreover, the future research direction about the hydrogenases from auto-aggregative bacteria and the chemical mimic of hydrogenases structure is discussed.

INTRODUCTION

The aim of this chapter is to review the research development of hydrogenase (Hase) in anaerobic bacteria and to provide reliable information regarding the structure of Hase in anaerobic bacteria. Toward this goal, the advancement in molecular structure discovery and active site studies of Hase in anaerobic bacteria is presented. Future research directions of Hase are then presented.

DOI: 10.4018/978-1-60960-064-8.ch023

BACKGROUND

With the increasing demand for energy around the globe, the fossil fuel reserves are being depleted. In addition, the excessive use of fossil fuels is one of the primary causes for global climate change and air pollution. It is urgent to find alternative sources of energy to solve this issue (Zhu et al., 1999; Ren et al., 1997; Lay, 2000; Kataoka, 1997). Microorganisms have effective systems for hydrogen production by utilizing carbohydrate in pyruvate route of metabolic pathway. Due to the pathway of carbohydrate metabolism and the bacterial hydrogen production, the specific rate of hydrogen conversion can reach to $10mo1H^2/$ mol-glucose theoretically (Tanisho, 2000), which is a high level in the industrialization of hydrogen production. Hydrogen, as a clean energy source, is expected to be a substitute for fossil fuel in the 21st century, since it only generates water when combusted. With the sharp increase in energy requirements, hydrogen, as a clean fuel produced from bacteria, has been a much-pursued topic for researchers.

In some anaerobic microorganism, some proteins were identified in 1891 that decomposed formic acid to hydrogen and carbon dioxide, and were named as hydrogenases by Stephenson and Strickland (1931). Hydrogenase was first isolated and purified from *Clostridium pasteurianum* by Chen and Mortenson (1974). However, at that time, the discovery of hydrogenases didn't attract too much research interest. Because of the abundance of oil and the lack of concern for climate change in those days, the benefits of low environmental pollution and potentials for sustainable development from hydrogen were not pursued.

Hydrogenases (Hase) are enzymes that catalyze the reversible oxidation process or production of molecular hydrogen. They can be found in a wide variety of organisms. Hydrogenase is the key terminal enzyme in electron delivery within biological hydrogen metabolism. There are three possible pathways of bacterial hydrogen production: pyruvate dehydrogenase pathway, pyruvate-formylrendase pathway, and $NADH + H^+ \rightarrow H_2$ pathway (He et al., 2004; Tanisho, 2000; Gray & Gest, 1965). Hydrogenase catalyses the formation and decomposition of the simplest molecule, i.e., hydrogen. It plays a very important role in hydrogen metabolism and the energy production in bacteria (Nicolet, 2000; Tamagnini et al., 2002).

Over the past a few decades, researchers have paid much attention on the biochemical and biophysical properties of hydrogenases. Most of the studies focused on the structure and expression of

gene, the stereo structure and the active center of hydrogenases, and the electron delivery mechanism and so on. Now, the structures and catalytic mechanisms of different hydrogenases from a myriad of microorganisms have been illustrated in varying degrees of detail. The study on the structures, functions and catalytic mechanisms of hydrogenases would provide an important theoretical basis for the research and application of biological hydrogen production. In recent years, more and more attention has been paid to identifying and developing new bacterial strains and modifying bacteria or hydrogenases through genetic engineering. Many promising results have shown the importance of studies on hydrogenases.

STRUCTURE AND ACTIVE SITE OF HYDROGENASES

In recent years, with the rapid development of biotechnology and protein identification technology, the studies of structures and functions of Hase have made great strides. One type of Hase, [Ni-Fe] Hase, which is comprised of a large subunit and a small subunit, was found in rod and vibrio shaped bacteria. The active center of [Ni-Fe] Hase is comprised of nonprotein diatomic ligands of the Fe atom, and there are two cyanide ligands (CN) and one carbon monoxide bridge (CO) bound to the Fe atom. The active site is located in the large subunit, and there are [Fe-S] clusters in the small subunit (Volbeda et al., 2005). Another type of Hase, [Fe-Fe] Hase, was found in bacteria and eukaryotes. The X-ray crystallographic structures and the spectroscopic data have been reported by Peters et al. (1998). The [H] cluster, the active site at which protons are reduced to dihydrogen (or dihydrogen oxidised to protons) can be viewed as a conventional [4Fe-4S]-cluster which is linked to a [2Fe-3S]-subsite by a protein backbone bridging cysteinyl sulfur ligand. At the subsite, a terminal carbon monoxide, a bridging carbon monoxide and a cyanide ligand are bound at each iron atom that also share two bridging sulfur ligands of a 1, 3-propanedithiolate or possibly related di(thiomethyl) oxo or di(thiomethyl)amine units (Peters et al., 1998; Nicolet et al., 1999). In 2006, the crystal structure of [Fe-only] Hase ([Fe-S cluster-free] Hase) was reported (Oliver et al., 2006).

[Ni-Fe] Hydrogenase

The structures of many [Ni-Fe] Hases from bacteria were illustrated, such as *Desulfovibrio vulgaris* (Higuchi et al., 1987) and *Desulfovibrio desulfuricans* (Matias et al., 2001) and so on. The clarified overall folds of the enzymes structures were quite similar. However, the structures of non-protein ligands bound at the [Ni-Fe] active sites were different (Volbeda et al., 2002). Stereo structures of *Desulfovibrio gigas* [Ni-Fe] Hase (pdb code 2FRV) and *Moorella thermoacetica* carbon monoxide dehydrogenase/acetyl coenzyme A synthase (CODH/ACS, pdb code 1OAO) have been described in previous study (Volbeda & Fontecilla-Camps, 2005). The large and the small subunit of the Hase, the two CODH subunits and the three domains of the two ACS subunits, gas accessible tunnels, Ni, Fe, Mg and S atoms are shown as different colors or shapes. For details, please refer to the review article by Volbeda & Fontecilla-Camps (2005).

[Fe-Fe] Hydrogenase

Peters et al. (1998) reported the crystal structure of Hase from *Clostridium pasteurianum*. The active site is comprised of five [Fe-S] clusters, one of which was a special [H] cluster. The [H] cluster contains two iron atoms in organic form distinctly. The combination of metal and carbon atom is established by CO and CN ligands. Nicolet et al. (1999) reported the crystal structure of [Fe-Fe] Hase from *Desulfovibrio desulfuricans* at 1.6 angstrom resolution. The structural properties of CpI [Fe-Fe]-Hase from *Clostridium pasteurianum* were reported (Cohen et al., 2005), when they focused on the gas diffusion process of the Hase. CpI Hase demonstrating embedded [H] cluster and iron-sulfur clusters. The residues linking the two principal gas pathways connect the external solution to the buried [H] cluster. In general, the hydrogen producing activity of [Fe-Fe] Hase is the highest among the three Hase groups (Cohen et al., 2005).

[Fe-only] Hydrogenase

[Fe-only] Hase (Hmd) is a homodimer with dimensions of about $90 \text{Å} \times 50 \text{ Å} \times 40 \text{ Å}$ that can be subdivided into a central globular unit attached to two peripheral units in a linear manner. Each of the peripheral units corresponds to the N-terminal domain (residues 1~250) of one subunit and is composed of an alpha or beta structure that belongs to the Rossmann fold protein family. The crystal structure of [Fe-only] Hase from *Methanocaldococcus jannaschii* was illustrated by Oliver et al. (2006). Hmd is composed of three globular units: two identical peripheral units consisting of a Rossmann fold like N-terminal segment of two subunits and one central unit composed of the intertwined C-terminal segment of both subunits. The ribbon diagram and fold topology diagram of the dimer are shown in a previous study (Oliver et al., 2006).

Differences of Hydrogenase Structures

For the three kinds of Hases, their active site iron has cyanide and CO or only CO as natural ligands, which are not found in any other metalloenzymes. This common feature is a sign of convergent evolution, indicating that the catalytic mechanism of hydrogen activation in different Hase is probably similar, and therefore information can be extrapolated from one enzyme to another. The differences of them are summarized in Table 1.

Table 1. Physical and chemical properties of Hase

Item	[Ni-Fe]		[Fe-Fe] (D. desulfuricans)	[Fe-only] (M. jannaschii or M. kandleri)
	[Ni-Fe] (D. gigas)	[Ni-Fe-Se] (Dm. baculatum)		
Position in cell	Cytoplasm	Cytoplasm	Cytoplasm	Cytoplasm
Molecular weight	89.5 KD	85 KD	53 KD	76 KD
Subunit number	2	2	2	3
Fe atom number	12	14	14	4 (an iron-containing cofactor)
Ni atom number	1	1	0	0
Other atom	1 Mg	1 Se	0	0
Non-protein ligands	2 CN, 1 CO	2 CN, 1 CO	2 CN, 3 CO, 1 azadithiolate	1CN, 2 CO, one sulphur and a pyridone derivative
$[4Fe-4S]^{2+/1+}$	2	3	3	0
$[3Fe-4S]^{2+/1+}$	1	0	0	0

FUTURE RESEARCH DIRECTIONS

An enhancement of the hydrogen production rate and a stable operation of the system are essential to realize the industrialization of fermentative biohydrogen production. The key problem is that how to improve the transforming rate of sugar, how to decrease the cost of substitute, and how to produce hydrogen effectively by bioreactor (Adams et al., 1981). At present, most of the fermentative biohydrogen production bacteria are *Clostridium and Enterobacter*, whose activities are relatively high (20-30 mmol H_2/g-drycell·h). YUAN-3, a strain of *Ethanoligenens* was separated from the hydrogen-production bioreactor by our previous study. It is an auto-aggregative (self-flocculating) bacteria strain with the hydrogen producing activity of 27.6 mmol H_2/g-drycell·h (Xing et al., 2006). The presence of non-flocculating bacteria is often considered as a nuisance, responsible for an increase in cells escaping from the reactor. All reported hydrogen-producing bacteria are non-aggregating bacteria. Efficient aggregation and settling of flocs are important for holding biomass in bioreactor. YUAN-3 can keep the amount of bacteria cells due to its high auto-aggregative

specialty. Thus, the hydrogen evolution rate can be increased by non-immobilized bacteria (purified YUAN-3 stains). Sequentially, the cost of biohydrogen producing decreases significantly. To our best knowledge, there were few reports on hydrogen production bacteria with auto-aggregative performance. Hase from effective hydrogen evolution bacteria is deemed to exhibit high catalytic activity, and the Hase in super efficient bacteria with novel specialty may has superior performance on hydrogen production. Considering the advantages of hydrogen yield and cell characteristics of bacteria, further research on the structure and function of Hase from the auto-aggregative bacteria, YUAN-3, has great scientific and industrial significance.

CONCLUSION

There are three classes of hydrogenases and they are [Ni-Fe] hydrogenase, [Fe-Fe] hydrogenase and [Fe-only] hydrogenase. These enzymes are necessary in the process of hydrogen production of bacteria and are not related phylogenetically but have an unusual structural feature in common. To promote the progress of biohydrogen production industrialization, we need to understand and make good use of these similarities and differences. The studies on the Hases in hydrogen producing bacteria with auto-aggregative property will help to promote the industrialization of hydrogen energy production.

ACKNOWLEDGMENT

The subject was financially supported by "China Postdoctoral Science Foundation (20070420861)" and "Heilongjiang Postdoctoral Fund (LBH-Z07115)".

REFERENCES

Adams, M. W., Mortenson, L. E., & Chen, J. S. (1981). Hydrogenase. *Biochimica et Biophysica Acta, 594*(2-3), 105–176.

Chen, J. S., & Mortenson, L. E. (1974). Purification and properties of hydrogenase from *Clostridium pasteurianum* W5. *Biochimica et Biophysica Acta, 371*(2), 283–298.

Cohen, J., Kim, K., & King, P. (2005). Finding gas diffusion pathways in proteins: application to O_2 and H_2 transport in CpI [Fe-Fe]-hydrogenase and the role of packing defects. *Structure (London, England), 13*(9), 1321–1329. doi:10.1016/j.str.2005.05.013

Gray, C. T., & Gest, H. (1965). Biological formation of molecular hydrogen production. *Science, 148*(3667), 186–192. doi:10.1126/science.148.3667.186

He, C., Wang, M., Li, M., & Sun, L. (2004). Advance in chemical mimic of Fe-only hydrogenase. *Progress in Chemistry, 16*(2), 250–255.

Higuchi, Y., Yasuoka, N., & Kakudo, M. (1987). Single crystals of hydrogenase from *Desulfovibrio vulgaris. Journal of Biochemistry, 262*(6), 2823–2825.

Kataoka, N., Miya, A., & Kiriyama, K. (1997). Studies on hydrogen production by continuous culture system of hydrogen-producing anaerobic bacteria. *Water Science and Technology, 36*(6-7), 41–47. doi:10.1016/S0273-1223(97)00505-2

Lay, J. J. (2000). Modeling and optimization of anaerobic digested sludge converting starch to hydrogen. *Biotechnology and Bioengineering, 68*(3), 269–278. doi:10.1002/(SICI)1097-0290(20000505)68:3<269::AID-BIT5>3.0.CO;2-T

Matias, P. M., Soares, C. M., & Saraiva, L. M. (2001). [Ni-Fe] hydrogenase from *D. desulfuricans* ATCC 27774: gene sequencing, three dimensional structure determination and refinement at 1·8 and modelling studies of its interaction with the tetrahaem cytochrome C3. *Journal of Biological Inorganic Chemistry, 6*(1), 63–68. doi:10.1007/s007750000167

Nicolet, Y., Lemon, B. J., Fontecilla-Camps, J. C., & Peters, J. W. (2000). A novel FeS cluster in [Fe-only] hydrogenases. *Trends in Biochemical Sciences, 25*(3), 138–143. doi:10.1016/S0968-0004(99)01536-4

Nicolet, Y., Piras, C., & Legrand, P. (1999). *Desulfovibrio desulfuricans* iron hydrogenase: the structure shows unusual coordination to an active site Fe binuclear center. *Structure (London, England), 7*(1), 13–23. doi:10.1016/S0969-2126(99)80005-7

Oliver, P., Björn, M., & Sonja, V. (2006). The crystal structure of the apoenzyme of the iron-sulphur cluster-free hydrogenase. *Journal of Molecular Biology, 358*(3), 798–809. doi:10.1016/j.jmb.2006.02.035

Peters, J. W., Lanailotta, W. N., & Lemon, B. J. (1998). X-Ray Crystal structure of the Fe-only hydrogenase (CpI) from *Clostridium pasteurianum* to 1.8 Angstrom Resolution. *Science, 282*(5395), 1853–1858. doi:10.1126/science.282.5395.1853

Ren, N., Wang, B., & Huang, J. C. (1997). Ethanol-type fermentation from carbohydrate in high rate acidogenic reactor. *Biotechnology and Bioengineering, 54*(5), 428–433. doi:10.1002/(SICI)1097-0290(19970605)54:5<428::AID-BIT3>3.0.CO;2-G

Stephenson, M., & Stickland, L. H. (1931). Hydrogenase: a bacterial enzyme activating molecular hydrogen. I. The properties of the enzyme. *The Biochemical Journal, 25*(1), 205–214.

Tamagnini, P., Axelsson, R., & Lindberg, P. (2002). Hydrogenases and hydrogen metabolism of cyanobacteria. *Microbiology and Molecular Biology Reviews, 66*(1), 1–20. doi:10.1128/MMBR.66.1.1-20.2002

Tanisho, S. (2000). *A strategy for improving the yield of molecular hydrogen by fermentation.* Paper presented at Proceedings of 13th World Hydrogen Energy Conference, Beijing, China.

Volbeda, A., & Fontecilla-Camps, J. C. (2005). Structure–function relationships of nickel–iron sites in hydrogenase and a comparison with the active sites of other nickel–iron enzymes. *Coordination Chemistry Reviews, 249*(15-16), 1609–1619. doi:10.1016/j.ccr.2004.12.009

Volbeda, A., Martin, L., & Cavazza, C. (2005). Structural differences between the ready and unready oxidized states of [Ni-Fe] hydrogenases. *Journal of Biological Inorganic Chemistry, 10*(3), 239–249. doi:10.1007/s00775-005-0632-x

Volbeda, A., Montet, Y., & Vernède, X. (2002). High-resolution crystallographic analysis of *Desulfovibrio fructosovorans* [Ni-Fe] hydrogenase. *International Journal of Hydrogen Energy, 27*(11-12), 1449–1461. doi:10.1016/S0360-3199(02)00072-1

Xing, D., Ren, N., & Li, Q. (2006). *Ethanoligenens harbinense* gen. nov., sp. nov., isolated from molasses wastewater. *International Journal of Systematic and Evolutionary Microbiology, 56*(4), 755–760. doi:10.1099/ijs.0.63926-0

Zhu, H., Suzuki, T., Tsygankov, A. T., Asada, Y., & Miyake, J. (1999). Hydrogen production from tofu wastewater by *Rhodobacter sphaeroides* immobilized in agar gels. *International Journal of Hydrogen Energy, 24*(4), 305–310. doi:10.1016/S0360-3199(98)00081-0

ADDITIONAL READING

Adams, M. W. W., & Hall, D. O. (1979). Properties of the solubilized membrane-bound hydrogenase from the photosysthetic bacteriam *Rhodospirillum rubrum. Archives of Biochemistry and Biophysics, 195*(2), 288–299. doi:10.1016/0003-9861(79)90355-2

Arp, D. J., & Burris, R. H. (1979). Purification and properties of the particulate hydrogenase from the bacteroids of soybean root nodules. *Biochimica et Biophysica Acta, 570*(2), 221–230.

Casalot, L., Hatchikian, C. E., Forget, N., de Philip, P., Dermoun, Z., Belaich, J. P., & Rousset, M. (1998). Molecular study and partial characterization of iron-only hydrogenase in *Desulfovibrio fructosovorans. Anaerobe, 4*(1), 45–55. doi:10.1006/anae.1997.0137

Darensbourg, M. Y., Lyon, E. J., & Smee, J. J. (2000). The bio-organometallic chemistry of active site iron in hydrogenase. *Coordination Chemistry Reviews, 206-207,* 533–561. doi:10.1016/S0010-8545(00)00268-X

Davidson, E. A., van der Giezen, M., Horner, D. S., Embley, T. M., & Howe, C. J. (2002). An [Fe] hydrogenase from the anaerobic hydrogenosome-containing fungus *Neocallimastix frontalis* L2. *Gene, 296*(1-2), 45–52. doi:10.1016/S0378-1119(02)00873-9

Feio, M. J., Beech, I. B., Carepo, M., Lopes, J. M., Cheung, C. W., & Franco, R. (1998). Isolation and characterisation of a novel sulphate-reducing bacterium of the *Desulfovibrio Genus. Anaerobe, 4*(2), 117–130. doi:10.1006/anae.1997.0142

Garcin, E., Vernede, X., Hatchikian, E. C., Volbeda, A., Frey, M., & Fontecilla-Camps, J. C. (1999). The crystal structure of a reduced [NiFeSe] hydrogenase provides an image of the activated catalytic center. *Structure (London, England), 7*(5), 557–566. doi:10.1016/S0969-2126(99)80072-0

Gitlitz, P. H., & Krasna, A. I. (1975). Structural and catalytic properties of hydrogenase from *Chromatium. Biochemistry, 14*(12), 2561–2568. doi:10.1021/bi00683a001

Hallenbeck, P. C., & Benemann, J. R. (1978). Characterization and partial purification of the reversible hydrogenase of *Anabaena cylindrica. FEBS Letters, 94*(2), 261-264.

Hatchikian, E. C., Bruschi, M., & LeGall, J. (1978). Characterization of the periplasmic hydrogenase from *Desulfovibrio gigas. Biochemical and Biophysical Research Communications, 82*(2), 451–461. doi:10.1016/0006-291X(78)90896-3

Kim, M. S., Choi, E. H., & Oh, Y. K. (2008). Characterization of hydrogenase from purple sulfur bacterium *Thiocapsa roseopersicina* and its prolonged *in vitro* hydrogen evolution. *International Journal of Hydrogen Energy, 33*(5), 1496–1502. doi:10.1016/j.ijhydene.2007.09.043

Laska, S., & Kletzinm, A. (2000). Improved purification of the membrane-bound hydrogenase-sulfurreductase complex from thermophilic archaea using e-aminocaproic acid-containing chromatography buffers. *Journal of Chromatography. B, Analytical Technologies in the Biomedical and Life Sciences, 737*(1-2), 151–160. doi:10.1016/S0378-4347(99)00362-X

Lojou, E., & Bianco, P. (2004). Electrocatalytic Reactions at hydrogenase-modified electrodes and their applications to biosensors: from the isolated enzymes to the whole cells. *Electroanalysis, 16*(13-14), 1093–1100. doi:10.1002/elan.200403002

Marr, A. C., Spencer, D. J. E., & Schuroder, M. (2001). Structural mimics for the active site of [Ni-Fe] hydrogenase. *Coordination Chemistry Reviews, 219-221,* 1055–1074. doi:10.1016/S0010-8545(01)00396-4

Ogata, H., Hirota, S., Nakahara, A., Komori, H., Shibata, N., & Kato, T. (2005). Activation process of [NiFe] hydrogenase elucidated by high-resolution X-Ray analyses: Conversion of the ready to the unready state. *Structure (London, England), 13*(11), 1635–1642. doi:10.1016/j.str.2005.07.018

Orengo, C. A., & Thornton, J. M. (2005). Protein families and their evolution-A structural perspective. *Annual Review of Biochemistry, 74,* 867–900. doi:10.1146/annurev.biochem.74.082803.133029

Ren, N., Wang, X., Xiang, W., Lin, M., Li, J., & Guo, W. (2002). Hydrogen production with high evolution rate and high yield by immobilized cells of hydrogen producing bacteria strain B49 in a column reactor. *High Technology Letters, 8*(4), 21–25.

Schnackenberg, J., Schulz, R., & Senger, H. (1993). Characterization and purification of a hydrogenase from the eukaryotic green alga *Scenedesmus obliquus. FEBS Letters, 327*(1), 21–24. doi:10.1016/0014-5793(93)81030-4

Shima, S., & Thauer, R. K. (2007). A third type of hydrogenase catalyzing H_2 activation. *Chemical Record (New York, N.Y.), 7*(1), 37–46. doi:10.1002/tcr.20111

Ueno, Y., Kurano, N., & Miyachi, S. (1999). Purification and characterization of hydrogenase from the marine green alga, *Chlorococcum littorale. FEBS Letters, 443*(2), 144–148. doi:10.1016/S0014-5793(98)01699-8

Vignais, P. M., & Billoud, B. (2007). Occurrence, classification, and biological function of hydrogenases: An overview. *Chemical Reviews, 107*(10), 4206–4272. doi:10.1021/cr050196r

Volbeda, A., Charon, M. H., Piras, C., Hatchikian, E. C., Frey, M., & Fontecilla-Camps, J. C. (1995). Crystal structure of the nickel-iron hydrogenase from *Desulfovibrio gigas. Nature, 373*(6515), 580–587. doi:10.1038/373580a0

Winter, G., Buhrke, T., Lenz, O., Jones, A. K., Forgber, M., & Friedricha, B. (2005). A model system for [Ni-Fe] hydrogenase maturation studies, Purification of an active site-containing hydrogenase large subunit without small subunit. *FEBS Letters, 579*(20), 4292–4296. doi:10.1016/j.febslet.2005.06.064

Xing, D., Ren, N., & Wang, A. (2008). Continuous hydrogen production of auto-aggregative *Ethanoligenens harbinense* YUAN-3 under non-sterile condition. *International Journal of Hydrogen Energy, 33*(5), 1489–1495. doi:10.1016/j.ijhydene.2007.09.038

Yanke, L. J., Bryant, R. D., & Laishley, E. J. (1995). Hydrogenase I of *Clostridium pasteurianum* functions as a novel selenite reductase. *Anaerobe, 1*(1), 61–67. doi:10.1016/S1075-9964(95)80457-9

Zirngibl, C., Hedderich, R., & Thauer, R. K. (1990). N^5, N^{10}-Methylenete trahydromethanopterin dehydrogenase from *Methanobacterium thermoautotrophicum* has hydrogenase activity. *FEBS Letters, 261*(1), 112–116. doi:10.1016/0014-5793(90)80649-4

KEY TERMS AND DEFINITIONS

Hydrogen Energy: The physical and chemical properties of hydrogen are what make hydrogen an ideal candidate for a clean energy source because it contains a large amount of energy in its chemical bond and its burning reaction forms water only.

Hydrogenase: It is the enzyme that catalyzes the reversible oxidation or production of molecular hydrogen and is the key terminal enzyme in electron delivery within biological hydrogen metabolism.

Biohydrogen Production Anaerobic Bacteria: A group of bacteria which can only grow and produce hydrogen under the conditions without oxygen.

Hydrogenase Classification: Hydrogenases are classified into three groups according to the metal composition of the active sites.

Section 7
Problems and Solutions in Environmental Sciences

Chapter 24

Seasonal Trade–Off between Water– and Nitrogen–Use Efficiency of Constructive Plants in Desert Riparian Forest in Hyperarid Region of China

Shengkui Cao
Qinghai Normal University, China & Chinese Academy of Sciences, China

Qi Feng
Chinese Academy of Sciences, China

Jianhua Si
Chinese Academy of Sciences, China

Yonghong Su
Chinese Academy of Sciences, China

Zongqiang Chang
Chinese Academy of Sciences, China

Haiyang Xi
Chinese Academy of Sciences, China

ABSTRACT

Foliar $\delta^{13}C$ values are often used to denote the long-term water use efficiency (WUE) of plants whereas long-term nitrogen use efficiency (NUE) are usually estimated by the ratio of C to N in the leaves. Seasonal variations of $\delta^{13}C$ values, foliar nitrogen concentration and C/N ratios of Populus euphratica and Tamarix ramosissima grown under five different microhabitats of Ejina desert riparian oasis of northwestern arid regions in China were studied. The results indicated that T. ramosissima had higher $\delta^{13}C$ value compared with that of P. euphratica. The N concentration and C/N ratios of two species were not significantly different. The seasonal pattern of three indexes in two species was different. The $\delta^{13}C$ values and N concentration decreased during the plant's growth period. However, the change of C/N ratios was increased. Among microhabitats, there were higher $\delta^{13}C$ values and N concentration as well as lower C/N ratios in the Dune and Gobi habitats. Foliar $\delta^{13}C$ values significantly and positively correlated with N concentration in P. euphratica and T. ramosissima, whereas a significantly negative correlation between $\delta^{13}C$ values and C/N ratios was found for P. euphratica. This relation in T. ramosissima was weak, but there was a significant quadratic curve relationship between $\delta^{13}C$ values and C/N ratios, which

DOI: 10.4018/978-1-60960-064-8.ch024

revealed that there was a trade-off between WUE and NUE for P. euphratica and in natural condition, P. euphratica could not improve WUE and NUE simultaneously. T. ramosissima could simultaneously enhance WUE and NUE. The above characters of WUE and NUE in two plants reflected the different adaptations of desert species to environmental condition.

INTRODUCTION

The adaptive use of limited resources by plants is a central topic of plant ecology, as the amount of resources required to support plant growth is one of the key factors that determines species persistence in a community (Aerts & Chapin, 2000). Plant adaptation to resource availability is often reflected as resource-use efficiency (Binkley et al., 2004). Water and nitrogen (N) are two key resources for plant life and associated physiological processes. The supplies of water and N in most natural arid and semi-arid ecosystems cannot meet the demand of plants. Therefore, water and N limitations may serve as evolutionary pressures on plants to utilize water and N more efficiently (Yasumura et al., 2002).

Water-use efficiency (WUE) is one important trait that can contribute to growth, survival, and distribution of plant species in water-limited habitats. WUE is traditionally defined either as the ratio of dry matter accumulation to water consumption over a season (WUET, T means longer period of time, for example, a growing season) or as the ratio of net photosynthesis (A) to transpiration (E) over a period of seconds or minutes (WUEi, where i means a short period of time) (Sinclair et al., 1984). During the past several decades, carbon isotope composition ($\delta^{13}C$) of plant tissues has been substantially studied (Farquhar & Richards, 1984; Martin & Thorstenson, 1988; Leroux et al., 1996; Amdt et al., 2001). Because a strong positive correlation was found between $\delta^{13}C$ and WUE (Farquhar et al., 1989), the $\delta^{13}C$ has been developed as an indirect indicator of WUE of C3 plants. C3 refers to the firstly formed compounds consisting of three carbon atoms after CO_2 is fixed.

Nitrogen use efficiency (NUE) has also been widely studied (Vitousek, 1982; Bridgham et al.,

1995; Aerts & Chapin, 2000; Binkley et al., 2004). Nitrogen is an essential component of photosynthetic proteins. Because of its limited availability, nitrogen is one of the primary factors that limit plant growth in many ecosystems (Kachi & Hirose, 1983). Berendse and Aerts (1987) defined nitrogen-use efficiency (NUE) as the amount of dry matter produced per g or kg of nitrogen. Hiremath (2000) developed a concept to study the different components that determine leaf life time NUE in a detailed and integrated manner. She defined cumulative NUE as the ratio of total carbon assimilation by a leaf to total nitrogen investment in that leaf over its lifetime. Recently, long-term NUE has been estimated by plant C/N ratios in several studies (Patterson et al., 1997; Livingston et al., 1999; Chen et al., 2005). So far, almost all the studies on NUE have exclusively addressed the species in subarctic tundra or tropical rain forests, while few such studies have ever been conducted of the plants in the arid regions of the world (Yuan et al., 2006).

Water shortage is becoming a serious problem for the desert riparian forest in the extreme arid region. The Ejina oasis is a typical hyperarid desert oasis at the downstream end of the Heihe River basin in northwestern China; it is also a natural ecological screen to protect the Hexi Corridor region, or even to northwest China and north China. During the past several decades, because of the combined effects of natural and man-made factors, the eco-environment of the oasis has deteriorated markedly, with the area of the oasis decreasing and its ecological function declining. Riparian plant communities in the lower reaches of the Heihe River showed patterns of patchiness (He and Zhao, 2006). *P. euphratica* (arbor species) and *T. ramosissima* (bush species), as the main constructive species in desert riparian ecosystem in the regions, have largely decreased in number. The former mainly consists of over-matured forest, and the latter has become sparsely distributed and forms dwarf communities (Si et al., 2005). Their degradation has seriously threatened desert oases' ecological safety of the lower reach in Heihe River in China. Many other inland basins in the arid areas of Northwest China face the same problems. To protect the desert riparian community, many studies have been done, such as on water use (Si et al., 2005, 2007), on the eco-physiological and biochemical response to water (Chen et al., 2003a; Wang et al., 2007) and to salt stress (Ma et al., 2002, Chen et al., 2004), etc. However, there is lack of research on water- and nitrogen-use efficiency of main plants of the desert riparian forest in the Heihe River basin.

Plant water-use efficiency (WUE) and nitrogen use efficiency (NUE) were specifically used as surrogates of potential resource use efficiency to facilitate comparisons among leaves under similar environmental conditions. In natural conditions, plant will enhance rate of photosynthesis at given nutrient status to meet plant growth and development. However, at the same time, the water loss from stoma (small holes are formed between guard cells in the Leaf epidermis) increases correspondingly. The variations of NUE and WUE can influence plant growth and reproduction, and can be the key to understanding the interaction of individuals with their environment. The present study aims to characterize seasonal trade-off between water- and nitrogen-use efficiency of *P. euphratica* and *T. ramosissima* growing in locations naturally subjected to different water conditions throughout the growing season of 2008. We studied nitrogen, C/N ratios and carbon isotope compositions ($\delta^{13}C$), thereby addressing the question whether two different constructive species from desert riparian forest in extreme arid regions of Northwestern China have the capacity to cope with the equilibrium between water and nitrogen. They were analyzed as follows: (1) seasonal changes in N concentration,

C/N ratios and $\delta^{13}C$ in leaves of *P. euphratica* and *T. ramosissima* under different microhabitats, and (2) the correlations between $\delta^{13}C$ values and N, C/N ratios in both *P. euphratica* and *T. ramosissima* to determine the trade-off between water and nitrogen use efficiency.

MATERIAL AND METHOD

The Experimental Site

The experiment was conducted at the *P. euphratica* Reserve (101°10' E, 41°59' N, elevation 920.46 m) during the growing season of May–September, 2008, in the Ejina oasis in the lower reaches of the Heihe River, Northwestern China (Figure 1). The study region is one of the extreme arid regions in China. According to local meteorological data from 1961 to 2005, the monthly average precipitation at the study site was less than 10 mm. Potential evaporation ranged from 36.01 to 555.75 mm. Annual average temperature ranged from -11.3 to 26.8 °C, with the minimum and maximum values of -7.0 and 29.8 °C, respectively, and relative humidity from 22.36 to 49.38% (Table 1). The dominant woody species in this area are *P. euphratica* and *T. ramosissima*, the former is the dominant native woody species, capable of forming an imposing canopy (>20 m tall) in some areas; the latter is a weedy, invasive xerophytic shrub species, which can form monospecific stands at a maximum height varying between 2 and 3 m.

Sampling Process

Sampled leaves of *P. euphratica* and *T. ramosissima* were collected on 18 May, 21 June, 23 July, 20 August, and 20 September 2008 in the *P. euphratica* Reserve. To objectively assess the water use efficiency and nutrient status of *P. euphratica* and *T. ramosissima*, in April, there were selected five typical sampling plots with the area of 50 m×50 m, which represented widespread habitats grow-

Figure 1. The sketch of Heihe River and the site of the study

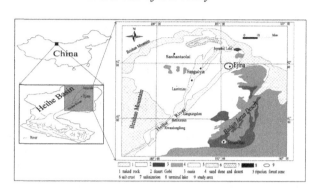

ing them at present, such as Dune, Gobi, Riparian sandpile, Riparian lowland, Typical *P. euphratica* Flatland (Table.2). Five individuals each species in every plot were selected and tagged as sample trees, which they had similar DBH (diameter at breast height) and coverage. At each sampling time, there were collected the mature leaves and the assimilating new twigs for *P. euphratica* and *T. ramosissima* from sample trees, respectively. The mature leaves/twigs from the light-facing side and the same heights were taken between 8 and 10 a.m., and about 20 leaves/twigs from each

tree were pooled as a sample from each species. Plant samples were first ultrasonically washed with distilled water and air-dried, then oven-dried at 70°C for at least 48 h to a constant mass and ground with a plant-sample mill (*1093* Sample Mill, Sweden) into uniformly fine powder. It was finally sieved with a 0.25-mm-mesh screen.

Meanwhile, imbedding a groundwater well in every plot, the depth was measured two weekly by electronic conductance method. Soil moisture content was measured from the surface to a depth of 2.0 m using a time domain reflectory (TDR;

Table 1. Monthly average of main climate variables at Ejina country (1961-2005)

Month	Air temperature (°C)[a]	Maximum air temperature (°C)	Precipitation (mm)	Relative humanity (%)	Evaporation (mm)[b]	Wind speed (m/s)
Jan.	-11.3	-7.0	0.2	48.22	36.01	2.58
Feb.	-6.3	-1.4	0.2	36.38	69.17	2.83
Mar.	2.1	6	1.1	28.33	180.34	3.38
Apr.	11.3	15.7	1.2	23.33	342.22	4.14
May	19.2	21.4	3.1	22.36	495.03	4.13
Jun.	24.8	26.7	5.2	26.22	553.08	3.92
Jul.	26.8	29.8	9.4	32.69	555.75	3.64
Aug.	24.6	27.3	8.4	34.91	482.82	3.36
Sept.	17.7	20.3	3.6	33.11	339.14	2.98
Oct.	8.2	10.5	2.3	35.09	200.53	2.87
Nov.	-1.8	2.8	0.5	40.67	92.58	3.12
Dec.	-9.9	-4.6	0.2	49.38	39.99	2.74

a Measured at 1 m above the surface

b Water evaporation measured at the station.

Table 2. The condition of five typical plots

Plots	Latitude and longitude	Altitude (m)	Soil type	Org. matter (g/kg)		Org. carbon (g/kg)	Total N (g/kg)	C/N	Available K (mg/kg)	Groundwater depth (m) (May-Sept.)	Mean depth (m)
Gobi(G)	41°57'35.3"N, 101°01'36.5"E	970	Coarse sand		0.63	0.37	0.07	5.29	87.61	-3.67~-4.05	-3.86
Riparian sandpile(S)	41°59'00.0"N, 101°07'30.7"E	975	Fine sand	1.09		0.63	0.11	5.73	99.94	-2.60~-3.78	-3.00
Riparian lowland(O)	41°58'11.8"N, 101°05'00.9"E	986	Fine sand	1.18		0.68	0.13	5.23	153.26	-1.85~-2.43	-2.15
Typical *P.euphratica* Flatland(N)	41°57'20.5"N, 101°04'44.6"E	995	clay loam	4.99		2.89	0.41	7.05	170.61	-2.02~-2.61	-2.33
Dune(D)	42° 1'40.86"N, 101° 3'45.12"E	990	Fine sand	0.89		0.52	0.08	6.5	80.16	-4.89~-5.59	-5.32

IMKO, Germany). In the present study, the whole unit of the soil water content expressed as volumetric water content.

Determination of Foliar δ¹³C and Total C and N Content

For carbon and nitrogen analysis, samples of 0.5–1.0 mg were transferred into tin capsules (SA76980502, IVA Analysentechnik, Meerbusch, Germany). The samples for carbon and nitrogen analyses were injected into an elemental analyser (NC 2500; CE Instruments, Milan, Italy) coupled to an isotope ratio mass spectrometer (Delta Plus; Finnigan MAT, Bremen, Germany) by a Conflo II interface (Finnigan MAT, Bremen, Germany) for $\delta^{13}C$ and total C and N determination. The $\delta^{13}C$ values are expressed relative to the PDB (Pee Dee Belemnite) standard. The δ values were defined as: $\delta^{13}C$ (‰) = $[(R_{sample}/R_{ST}) - 1] \times 1000$, where R_{sample} and R_{ST} are the $^{13}C/^{12}C$ ratios of the sample and standard (PDB for $\delta^{13}C$), respectively.

Statistic Analysis

All statistical analyses were performed using SPSS 13.0. The effect of plots or species was analyzed using a one-way variance (ANOVA) ($p<0.05$). Differences between treatment means were compared by Duncan's multiple range tests at 0.05 probability level. Linear regression was also used to evaluate the relationship between leaf nitrogen concentration (leaf N), the C/N ratios and carbon isotope composition ($\delta^{13}C$).

M O, N, S, G, D represented irrigated riparian flatland, riparian lowland, typical *P.euphratica* flatland, riparian sandpile, Gobi and Dune, respectively. Data represented mean±SE from 3 replicates. Different small letters indicated significant differences between months in the same plot ($p<0.05$); Different capital letters in a row showed significant differences between plots in the same month ($p<0.05$).

RESULTS

Variation of δ¹³C Values

Table 3, 4 showed seasonal changes in foliar $\delta^{13}C$ values of *P. euphratica* and *T. ramosissima* in different plots, which indicated that, the foliar $\delta^{13}C$ values in *P. euphratica* were significantly lower than those in *T.ramosissima*, ranged from

-29.14±0.07‰, -28.13±0.03‰ to -25.85±0.06‰, -24.58±0.06‰, the mean was -27.70±0.15‰, -26.66±0.12‰, respectively. Among habitats, there were significant differences in $\delta^{13}C$ values of two species under different plots. The levels of $\delta^{13}C$ values from the Dune and Gobi plots were higher than from the riparian lowland, typical *P. euphratica* stand and riparian sandpile during the same periods and showed a decreasing trend from May to September under every plot. However, the seasonal pattern of $\delta^{13}C$ values in the leaves of *P. euphratica* and *T. ramosissima* were slightly different. For *P. euphratica,* its values were becoming richer from June to September. They were the highest in May in five plots during the growing season, but the lowest in different months among different plots. For example, in the typical P.euphratica Flatland and Dune plots, it appeared in July; in the riparian sandpile site, the lowest $\delta^{13}C$ value appeared in August; and in the Riparian lowland and Gobi plots, it appeared in September. For *T.ramosissima,* the $\delta^{13}C$ signature was depleted by the end of the growing season; its lowest values appeared in August or September under different plots.

Seasonal Variations in Foliar Nitrogen Concentration

Foliar N concentration in *P. euphratica* differed between each plot. The highest N concentration in leaves of *P. euphratica* appeared in the Dune during the whole growth period, the N concentration became near between the riparian lowland with typical *P. euphratica* stand, between the riparian sandpile and Gobi plots (Figure 2A). The sequence mean N concentration among five plots in turn was the Dune, riparian lowland, typical *P. euphratica* stands, Gobi and riparian sandpile. However, the N concentration in *T. ramosissima* was similar or a little different among plots except in the Dune, where there had the highest N content in growth season, with the mean of 1.56±0.06% (Figure 2B). There was not a significantly difference in N concentration between *P. euphratica* and *T. ramosissima*. The N concentration of *P. euphratica* and

Table 3. Seasonal variations of foliar $\delta^{13}C$ of P. euphratica under different plots

Plot	May	June	July	Aug.	Sept.	Mean
O	-26.95±0.05[aA]	-27.30±0.08[bA]	-28.43±0.05[cA]	-28.34±0.05[cA]	-28.54±0.10[cA]	-27.91±0.18[A]
N	-27.49±0.01[aB]	-28.96±0.04[bB]	-29.14±0.07[cB]	-28.36±0.05[dA]	-28.37±0.08[dA]	-28.47±0.16[B]
S	-27.37±0.11[aB]	-28.23±0.07[bC]	-28.41±0.04[bdC]	-28.66±0.05[cA]	-28.53±0.09[cdA]	-28.24±0.13[B]
G	-26.38±0.05[aC]	-27.55±0.09[bD]	-27.55±0.05[bD]	-27.38±0.03[cB]	-27.82±0.02[dB]	-27.34±0.14[C]
D	-25.85±0.06[aD]	-26.64±0.05[bE]	-27.36±0.06[cD]	-26.38±0.08[dC]	-26.40±0.03[dC]	-26.53±0.13[D]

Table 4. Seasonal variations of foliar $\delta^{13}C$ of T. ramosissima under different plots

Plots	May	June	July	Aug.	Sept.	Mean
O	-26.12±0.07[aA]	-26.85±0.04[bA]	-27.35±0.07[cA]	-27.44±0.03[cA]	-27.68±0.08[dA]	-27.09±0.15[A]
N	-27.37±0.06[aB]	-27.04±0.04[bB]	-27.36±0.04[aA]	-27.77±0.03[cA]	-27.17±0.05[bB]	-27.34±0.07[AB]
S	-27.76±0.02[aC]	-27.35±0.05[bB]	-27.86±0.03[cB]	-27.72±0.08[cA]	-28.13±0.03[dC]	-27.56±0.13[B]
G	-24.97±0.04[aD]	-26.26±0.05[bC]	-25.99±0.07[cC]	-26.59±0.08[dB]	-25.68±0.04[eD]	-25.90±0.15[C]
D	-24.58±0.06[aD]	-25.35±0.11[bD]	-25.45±0.03[bD]	-25.90±0.02[cC]	-25.72±0.02[cD]	-25.40±0.12[D]

T. ramosissima in growing season in 2008 ranged from 0.98±0.05%, 0.96±0.06% to 2.95±0.11%, 2.96±0.06%, the mean 1.68±0.06%, 1.56±0.06%, respectively. And the seasonal pattern of two species was similar, which the N concentration was decreased from May to September. The highest N concentration appeared in May, the lowest was in September (Figure 2A, B).

Seasonal Variations in Foliar C/N Ratios

There was an increasing pattern of C/N in both *P. euphratica* and *T. ramosissima* from May to September under different plots (Figure 3A, B). In addition, the values were close, with the mean of 27.65±0.77, 27.41±0.91, respectively. Among plots, the lowest C/N of *P. euphratica* and *T. ramosissima* was in the Dune, with the mean of 18.63±0.56, 19.13±0.94, respectively. The C/N value of *P. euphratica* was the highest in the ripar-

ian sandpile, with the mean of 33.99±1.36, next was the Gobi and the value was not significantly different between the riparian lowland and the typical *P. euphratica* stand, between the riparian sandpile and the Gobi. For *T. ramosissima*, the highest C/N value was in the Gobi, with the mean of 34.52 ± 2.16. There was not significant difference in C/N among other three plots.

Correlations between Foliar δ¹³C with N Concentration and C/N Ratios

As Figure 4A, B showed, with data pooled across five plots during the whole growth season, foliar $\delta^{13}C$ values were significantly and positively correlated with foliar N concentration ($p<0.0001$) in both *P. euphratica* and *T. ramosissima*. The difference only was intercept, with the value of -29.88 and -28.68, respectively. The slope was close, with the value o f 1.30. Furthermore, when data in all plots in growing season were pooled

Figure 2. Seasonal variations of nitrogen content of P. euphratica (A) and T. ramosissima (B) in 2008. M O, N, S, G, D represented irrigated riparian flatland, riparian lowland, typical P.euphratica flatland, riparian sandpile, Gobi and Dune, respectively. Data represented mean±SE from 3 replicates. Different small letters indicated significant differences (p<0.05).

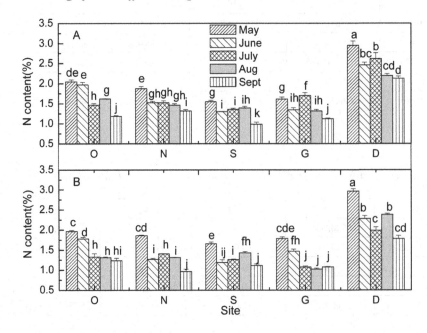

Figure 3. Seasonal variations of C/N in P. euphratica (A) and T. ramosissima (B) in 2008. Symbols and abbreviations as in Figure 2. Vertical bars represented SE of the mean (n=3)

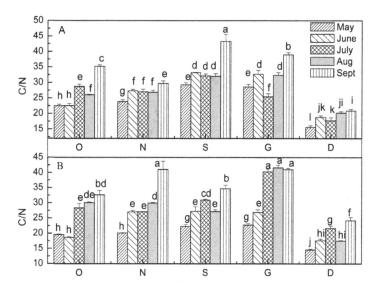

(Figure 5A, B), the relationship between foliar $\delta^{13}C$ values and C/N was significantly negative in *P. euphratica* (*p*<0.0001), but for the *T. ramosissima*, this correlation was quadratic curve.

Changes in carbon isotopic composition ($\delta^{13}C$) values are more susceptible to plant water status change and it can assess the drought tolerance of different species (Ehleringer et al., 1992). The

DISCUSSION

Because foliar $\delta^{13}C$ is related to the ratio of photosynthesis and stomatal conductance (A/g_s, g_s represents the stomatal conductance) or transpiration (A/E), it can be used as an integrated indicator of long-term WUE in natural ecosystems and a strong positive correlation existed between the foliar $\delta^{13}C$ and WUE (Farquhar et al., 1984, 1989; Ehleringer et al., 1992). In the present, the average $\delta^{13}C$ values in *P. euphratica* and *T. ramosissima* were -27.70±0.15‰, -26.66±0.12‰ respectively, which is generally much higher than the lowland average (−28.74‰) of the global survey (Körner et al., 1988). This pattern of $\delta^{13}C$ values indicated that *T. ramosissima* has higher WUE than that of *P. euphratica*. Moreover, they reinforced the significance of higher WUE in the adaptive strategies of desert plants to arid environments.

Figure 4. Relationships between $\delta^{13}C$ values and N concentration in P. euphratica (A) and T. ramosissima (B). Symbols and abbreviations as in Figure 2.

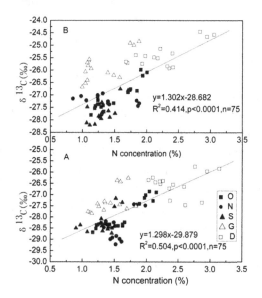

Figure 5. Relations between $\delta^{13}C$ and C/N in P. euphratica (A) and T. ramosissima (B). Symbols and abbreviations as in Figure 2

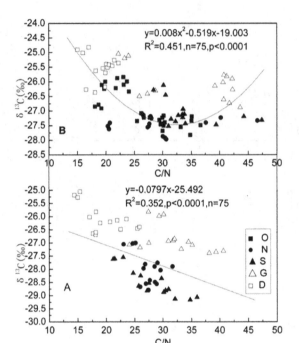

higher $\delta^{13}C$ signatures under all plots indicated that *T. ramosissima* has stronger drought tolerance than *P. euphratica*. Their drought tolerance also agreed with their field distribution, which the riparian community dominated by *P. euphratica* generally distributes within 500 m of the river, but *T. ramosissima* dominated communities are the most prevalent riparian communities located between 500 and 1500 m from the river (He et al., 2006).

However, markedly higher foliar $\delta^{13}C$ values of *P. euphratica* and *T. ramosissima* were found in Dune and Gobi than other three plots (Table 3, 4). These results showed soil water, especially groundwater, was a key factor limiting two species growth. The significantly negative relationship between foliar monthly mean $\delta^{13}C$ values and groundwater depth (data not showed) also documented that soil water availability was one key factor controlling variation of foliar $\delta^{13}C$ values in both species. Previous studies have found

negative correlations between $\delta^{13}C$ and indices of water availability (Miller et al., 2001; Wang et al., 2003). The carbon isotope discrimination model suggested that increased $\delta^{13}C$ by drought was due to decreased WUE through increased stomatal and/ or mesophyll conductance. Those results also suggested that the two species growing in droughty habitats tend to improve their WUE and employ more conservative water-use patterns to survive in unfavorable environments, and there must maintain within a range of groundwater depth, because groundwater is the main water source of two desert riparian constructive species according to reports by Zhao et al. (2008). Foliar $\delta^{13}C$ values of the five habitats in both *P.euphratica* and *T.ramosissima* followed a declining seasonal trend with the highest values in May (Table 3, 4) probably due to the diverse signatures of storage-derived C as compared to autotrophic organic matter, which is increasingly dominating the foliar signature with advancing growth (Damesin & Lelarge, 2003; Helle & Schleser, 2004).

A strong positive correlation has been observed between the light saturated rate of photosynthesis of a leaf and its nitrogen content (Reich et al., 1994). That is, generally, higher nitrogen content is associated with higher rates of maximum photosynthesis. The reason for this strong relationship is the large amount of leaf organic nitrogen (up to 75%) present in the chloroplasts, most of it in the photosynthetic machinery (Shangguan et al., 2000). In this study, the similar mean content of foliar N in *P. euphratica* and *T. ramosissima* showed that they co-exited similar conditions and had similar photosynthetic capacity. Meanwhile, the N content in the leaves of *P. euphratica* and *T. ramosissima* was the highest in May at all study sites and declined with the growth season (Figure 2A, B). Seasonal maximum of foliar N concentration at the beginning of the growing season was also detected at European beech forest stands growing on different soil types under different climatic conditions (Geßler, 1999; Nahm et al., 2005a, 2006) and is attributed to N remobilization from storage tissues to promote protein and chlorophyll synthesis in the growing leaves. It indicated that their photosynthetic capacity decreased with increasing transpiration in growing period advancing. Among the habitats, difference was observed in early, middle and later stage of the growing season and the foliar nitrogen concentration in Dune site was the highest. Those indicated that they had enhanced their photosynthetic capacity when they encountered water stress. There were robust positive correlations between foliar $\delta^{13}C$ and nitrogen content (Figure 4A, B), which demonstrated that high leaf nitrogen content corresponded to increased photosynthetic capacities and decreased internal leaf CO_2 concentration. Many studies have also shown increased N supply could increase $\delta^{13}C$ values and water-use efficiency of plants (Gordon et al., 1999; Shangguan et al., 2000).

Plant C/N ratio was used to estimate the long-term NUE (Livingston et al., 1999; Chen et al., 2005). Water stress may limit nitrogen uptake and availability, leading to a decrease in leaf nitrogen content, exacerbating senescence (Guenni et al., 2004). However, moderate drought is considered to increase NUE (Yuan et al., 2006). In this study, declining total foliar nitrogen content resulted in increasing foliar C/N ratios throughout the growing season at all sites (Figure 3A, B). Variations of N and C/N ratios in both species demonstrated that the highest foliar photosynthetic nitrogen content of both species in the Dune led to the lowest C/N ratios, suggesting that plants need to expend more nitrogen to maintain carbon assimilation and growth under dry conditions. Additional nitrogen supply might also limit the severity of water stress (Bennett et al., 1986).

Water and nitrogen are two of the most important resources for plant. Drought severely restricts the mobility of nitrogen through dehydrated soil and thus a co-occurrence of water deficits and nitrogen limitations is common in the extreme arid desert riparian forest ecosystem. Thus, efficient use of resources is great important for growth and survival of desert plants. However, an increase in the efficiency in the use of one resource sometimes led to a reduction in the efficiency with which another is utilized (Hirose & Bazzaz, 1998). Any increase in stomata conductance tended to increase leaf intercellular CO_2 concentration leading to increase of NUE while increasing water loss through stomata and then decreasing WUE of plants. Traits of plants that improve nutrient use might be conflicting with traits leading to an efficient use of water. Previous studies have verified that plants would show different life strategies with different water and nitrogen conditions in controlled environment (Field et al., 1983; Chen et al., 2005), which showed a trade-off between tolerance of adverse environment and growth potential. However, investigations in natural conditions are apparently limited. In this study, plant C/N ratio was used to estimate the long-term NUE. This ratio indicates the amount of carbon fixed per unit nitrogen, and is an index of the efficiency by which N is distributed and utilized for carbon acquisition (Patterson et al., 1997). This study found a significant and negative correlation between $\delta^{13}C$ values and C/N ratios in *P. euphratica* ($r^2 = 0.35$, $p<0.0001$) (Figure 5A). For *T. ramosissima*, this relationship was weak ($r^2 = 0.14$, $p = 0.0009$, figure not showed) but significantly quadratic curve relation ($r^2 = 0.51$, $p<0.0001$) (Figure 5B) was found. The negative correlation between WUE and NUE of *P. euphratica* was a similar result to those reported for California evergreen and American elm (Field et al., 1983 and Reich et al., 1989, respectively). Those results showed that *P. euphratica* achieved higher WUE at the expense of decreasing NUE. In such a case, NUE will be lower but WUE higher. Thus the cost of a high WUE is low NUE and vice versa. *P. euphratica* in water-well habitats (for example, higher soil water content or shallower groundwater depth) might fully use nitrogen resources to maximize their assimilation gain per unit of leaf nitrogen, despite decreasing their WUE. Conversely, *P. euphratica* growing in dry conditions (deeper groundwater level) might well under-utilize its nitrogen source in order to maximize their WUE. However, *T. ramosissima* could simultaneously maintain relative higher WUE and NUE. The quadratic curve indicated that there was a range of soil water content (including groundwater depth). The significantly quadratic curve relationship between foliar $\delta^{13}C$ and C/N in the *T. ramosissima* suggested that simultaneously maintaining relative higher WUE and NUE need to keep a certain water condition of below -3.5 m. That indicated *T. ramosissima* had the characteristics of raising the NUE and WUE at the same time to the benefit of maintenance of its growth, when it suffered from water stress. In all, this inter-specific difference in the trade-off of plasticity between NUE and WUE may partially explain the regional distribution of these two species.

CONCLUSION

The NUE and WUE of desert riparian constructive plant species in natural conditions at the Ejina desert oasis in northwestern of China were investigated. The results indicated that *T. ramosissima* had higher WUE and stronger drought tolerance than *P. euphratica*. Variation of WUE and NUE among different microhabitats and growth season showed the cost of higher WUE in *P. euphratica* was decreased NUE, less carbon accumulation, and reduced growth rate. On the contrary, *T. ramosissima* could simultaneously enhance WUE and NUE, but that may need to be within a range of water conditions to be further determined in a future study.

ACKNOWLEDGMENT

This work was supported by the National Natural Science Foundation of China (40901048, 40725001, 40671010, 40701054).

REFERENCES

Aerts, R., & Chapin, F. S. III. (2000). The mineral nutrition of wild plants revisited: a re-evaluation of processes and patterns. *Advances in Ecological Research*, 30(1), 1–67.

Arndt, S. K., Clifford, S. C., Wanek, W., Jones, H. G., & Popp, M. (2001). Physiological and morphological adaptations of the fruit tree *Ziziphus rotundifolia* in response to progressive drought stress. *Tree Physiology*, 21(11), 705–715.

Bennett, J. M., Jones, J. W., Zur, B., & Hammond, L. C. (1986). Interactive effects of nitrogen and water stresses on the water relations of field-grown corn leaves. *Agronomy Journal*, 78(2), 273–280. doi:10.2134/agronj1986.0002196200 7800020012x

Berendse, F., & Aerts, R. (1987). Nitrogen-use-efficiency: a biologically meaningful definition? *Functional Ecology, 1*(3), 293–296.

Binkley, D., Stape, J. L., & Ryan, M. G. (2004). Thinking about efficiency of resource use in forests. *Forest Ecology and Management, 193*(1), 5–16. doi:10.1016/j.foreco.2004.01.019

Bridgham, S. D., Pastor, J., McClaugherty, C. A., & Richardson, C. J. (1995). Nutrient-use efficiency: a litterfall index, a model, and a test along a nutrient-availability gradient in North Carolina peatlands. *American Naturalist, 145*(1), 1–21. doi:10.1086/285725

Chen, S. P., Bai, Y. F., Zhang, L. X., & Han, X. G. (2005). Comparing physiological responses of two dominant grass species to nitrogen addition in Xilin River Basin of China. *Environmental and Experimental Botany, 53*(1), 65–75. doi:10.1016/j.envexpbot.2004.03.002

Chen, Y. N., Chen, Y. P., Li, W. H., & Zhang, H. F. (2003a). Response of the accumulation of proline in the bodies of *Populus euphratica* to the change of ground water level at the lower reaches of Tarim River. *Chinese Science Bulletin, 48*(18), 1995–1999.

Chen, Y. N., Wang, Q., Ruan, X., Li, W. H., & Chen, Y. P. (2004). Physiological response of *Populus euphratica* to artificial water recharge of the lower reaches of Tarim River. *Acta Botanica Sinica, 46*(12), 1393–1401.

Damesin, C., & Lelarge, C. (2003). Carbon isotope composition of current year shoots from *Fagus sylvatica* in relation to growth, respiration and use of reserves. *Plant, Cell & Environment, 26*(2), 207–219. doi:10.1046/j.1365-3040.2003.00951.x

Ehleringer, J. R., Phillips, S. L., & Comstock, J. P. (1992). Seasonal variation in the carbon isotope composition of desert plants. *Functional Ecology, 6*(3), 396–404. doi:10.2307/2389277

Farquhar, G. D., Ehleringer, J. R., & Hubick, K. T. (1989). Carbon isotope discrimination and photosynthesis. *Annual Review of Plant Physiology and Plant Molecular Biology, 40*(6), 503–537. doi:10.1146/annurev.pp.40.060189.002443

Farquhar, G. D., & Richards, R. A. (1984). Isotope composition of plant carbon correlations with water-use efficiency of wheat cultivars. *Australian Journal of Plant Physiology, 11*(6), 539–552. doi:10.1071/PP9840539

Field, C., Merino, J., & Mooney, H. A. (1983). Compromises between water-use efficiency and nitrogen-use efficiency in five species of California evergreens. *Oecologia, 60*(3), 384–389. doi:10.1007/BF00376856

Geßler, A. (1999). *Untersuchungen zum Stickstoffhaushalt von Buchen (Fagus sylvatica) in einem stickstoff übersättigten Waldökosystem.* PhD thesis, University of Freiburg, Germany.

Gordon, C., Woodin, D. J., Mullins, C. E., & Alexander, I. J. (1999). Effects of environmental change, including drought, on water use by competing *Calluna vulgaris* (Heather) and *Pteridium aquilinum* (bracken). *Functional Ecology, 13*(Suppl.1), 96–106. doi:10.1046/j.1365-2435.1999.00012.x

Guenni, O., Baruch, Z., & Marín, D. (2004). Responses to drought of five Brachiaria species. II. Water relations and leaf gas exchange. *Plant and Soil, 258*(1), 249–260. doi:10.1023/B:PLSO.0000016555.53797.58

He, Z. B., & Zhao, W. Z. (2006). Characterizing the spatial structures of riparian plant communities in the lower reaches of the Heihe River in China using geostatistical techniques. *Ecological Research, 21*(5), 551–559. doi:10.1007/s11284-006-0160-3

Helle, G., & Schleser, G. H. (2004). Beyond CO_2-fixation by Rubisco—an interpretation of C-13/C-12 variations in tree rings from novel intraseasonal studies on broad-leaf trees. *Plant, Cell & Environment, 27*(3), 367–380. doi:10.1111/j.0016-8025.2003.01159.x

Hiremath, A. J. (2000). Photosynthetic nutrient-use efficiency in three fast-growing tropical trees with differing leaf longevities. *Tree Physiology, 20*(14), 937–944.

Hirose, T., & Bazzaz, F. A. (1998). Trade-off between light- and nitrogen-use efficiency in canopy photosynthesis. *Annals of Botany, 82*(2), 195–202. doi:10.1006/anbo.1998.0668

Kachi, N., & Hirose, T. (1983). Limiting nutrients for plant growth in coastal sand dune soils. *Journal of Ecology, 71*(6), 937–944. doi:10.2307/2259603

Körner, C., Farquhar, G. D., & Roksandic, Z. (1988). A global survey of carbon isotope discrimination in plants from high altitude. *Oecologia, 74*(4), 623–632. doi:10.1007/BF00380063

Leroux, D., Stock, W. D., Bond, W. J., & Maphanga, D. (1996). Dry mass allocation, water use efficiency and $\delta^{13}C$ in clones of *Eucalyptus grandis, E. grandis×camaldulensis* and *E. grandis×nitens* grown under two irrigation regimes. *Tree Physiology, 16*(5), 497–502.

Livingston, N. J., Guy, R. D., & Ethier, G. J. (1999). The effects of nitrogen stress on the stable carbon isotope composition, productivity and water use efficiency of white spruce (*Picea glauca* (Moench) Voss) seedlings. *Plant, Cell & Environment, 22*(3), 281–289. doi:10.1046/j.1365-3040.1999.00400.x

Ma, T. J., Liu, Q. L., Li, Z., & Zhang, X. J. (2002). Tonoplast H^+-ATPase in response to salt stress in *Populus euphratica* cell suspensions. *Plant Science, 163*(3), 499–505. doi:10.1016/S0168-9452(02)00154-1

Martin, B., & Thorstenson, Y. R. (1988). Stable carbon isotope composition ($\delta^{13}C$), water use efficiency and biomass productivity of *Lycopersicon esculentum, Lycopersicon pennellii*, and the F1 hybrid. *Plant Physiology, 88*(2), 213–217. doi:10.1104/pp.88.1.213

Miller, J. M., Williams, R. J., & Farquhar, G. D. (2001). Carbon isotope discrimination by a sequence of Eucalyptus species along a subcontinental rainfall gradient in Australia. *Functional Ecology, 15*(3), 222–232. doi:10.1046/j.1365-2435.2001.00508.x

Nahm, M., Holst, T., Matzarakis, A., Mayer, H., Rennenberg, H., & Geßler, A. (2005a). Soluble N compound profiles and concentration in European beech (*Fagus sylvatica* L.) are influenced by local climate and thinning. *European Journal of Forest Research, 125*(1), 1–14. doi:10.1007/s10342-005-0103-5

Nahm, M., Radoglou, K., Halyvopoulos, G., Geßler, A., Rennenberg, H., & Fotelli, M. N. (2006). Seasonal changes in nitrogen, carbon and water balance of adult *Fagus sylvatica* L. grown at its south-eastern distribution limit in Europe. *Plant Biology, 8*(1), 52–63. doi:10.1055/s-2005-872988

Patterson, T. B., Guy, R. D., & Dang, Q. L. (1997). Whole-plant nitrogen- and water-relations traits, and their associated trade-offs, in adjacent muskeg and upland boreal spruce species. *Oecologia, 110*(2), 160–168. doi:10.1007/s004420050145

Reich, P. B., Walters, M. B., Ellsworth, D. S., & Uhl, C. (1994). Photosynthesis-nitrogen relations in Amazonian tree species. I. Patterns among species and communities. *Oecologia, 97*(1), 62–72. doi:10.1007/BF00317909

Reich, P. B., Waters, M. B., & Tabone, T. J. (1989). Response of *Ulmus americana* seedlings to varying nitrogen and water status- Water and nitrogen use efficiency in photosynthesis. *Tree Physiology, 5*(2), 173–184.

Shangguan, Z. P., Shao, M. A., & Dyckmans, J. (2000). Nitrogen nutrition and water stress effects on leaf photosynthetic gas exchange and water use efficiency in winter wheat. *Environmental and Experimental Botany, 44*(1), 141–149. doi:10.1016/S0098-8472(00)00064-2

Si, J. H., Feng, Q., Zhang, X. Y., & Chang, Z. Q. (2007). Sap Flow of *Populus euphratica* in a Desert Riparian Forest in an Extreme Arid Region during the Growing Season. *Journal of Integrative Plant Biology, 49*(4), 425–436. doi:10.1111/j.1744-7909.2007.00388.x

Si, J. H., Feng, Q., Zhang, X. Y., Liu, W., Su, Y. H., & Zhang, Y. W. (2005). Growing season Evapotranspiration from Tamarix ramosissima stands under extreme arid conditions in northwest China. *Environ. Geol., 48*(7), 861–870. doi:10.1007/s00254-005-0025-z

Si, J. H., Feng, Q., Zhang, X. Y., Su, Y. H., & Zhang, Y. W. (2005). Vegetation changes in the lower reaches of the Heihe River after its water import. *Acta Bot. Boreal.* [in Chinese]. *Occident Sin., 25*(4), 631–640.

Sinclair, T. R., Tanner, C. B., & Bennett, J. M. (1984). Water-use efficiency in crop production. *Bioscience, 34*(1), 36–40. doi:10.2307/1309424

Vitousek, P. M. (1982). Nutrient cycling and nitrogen use efficiency. *American Naturalist, 119*(4), 553–572. doi:10.1086/283931

Wang, G. H. (2003). Differences in leaf $\delta^{13}C$ among four dominant species in a secondary succession sere on the Loess Plateau of China. *Photosynthetica, 41*(4), 525–531. doi:10.1023/B:PHOT.0000027516.43278.c4

Wang, Q., Ruan, X., Chen, Y. N., & Li, W. H. (2007). Eco-physiological response of *Populus euphratica Oliv* to water release of the lower reaches of the Tarim River, China. *Environ. Geol., 53*(2), 349–357. doi:10.1007/s00254-007-0650-9

Yasumura, Y., Hikosaka, K., Matsui, K., & Hirose, T. (2002). Leaf-level nitrogen-use efficiency of canopy and understorey species in a beech forest. *Functional Ecology, 16*(6), 826–834. doi:10.1046/j.1365-2435.2002.00691.x

Yuan, Z. Y., Li, L. H., Han, X. G., Chen, S. P., Wang, Z. W., Chen, Q. S., & Bai, Y. F. (2006). Nitrogen response efficiency increased monotonically with decreasing soil resource availability: a case study from a semiarid grassland in northern China. *Oecologia, 148*(4), 564–572. doi:10.1007/s00442-006-0409-0

Zhao, L. J., Xiao, H. L., Cheng, G. D., & Song, Y. X. (2008). A preliminary study of water sources of riparian plants in the lower reaches of the Heihe Basin. [in Chinese]. *Acta Geoscientica Sinica, 29*(6), 709–718.

ADDITIONAL READING

Aerts, R., & de Caluwe, H. (1994). Nitrogen use efficiency of Carex species in relation to nitrogen supply. *Ecology, 75*(8), 2362–2372. doi:10.2307/1940890

Ahmad, A., Khan, I., & Abrol, Y. P. (2008). Muhammad Iqbal. Genotypic variation of nitrogen use efficiency in Indian mustard. *Environmental Pollution, 154*(3), 462–466. doi:10.1016/j.envpol.2007.10.007

Alongi, D. M., Clough, B. F., & Robertson, A. I. (2005). Nutrient-use efficiency in arid-zone forests of the mangroves Rhizophora stylosa and Avicennia marina. *Aquatic Botany, 82*(2), 121–131. doi:10.1016/j.aquabot.2005.04.005

Baligar, V. C., Fageria, N. K., & He, Z. L. (2001). Nutrient use efficiency in plants. *Communications in Soil Science and Plant Analysis, 32*(7), 921–950. doi:10.1081/CSS-100104098

Charles, R. W., McGrath, J. F., & Adams, M. A. (2001). Water availability and carbon isotope discrimination in conifers. *Oecologia, 127*(4), 476–486. doi:10.1007/s004420000609

Dawson, J. C., Huggins, D. R., & Jones, S. S. (2008). Characterizing nitrogen use efficiency in natural and agricultural ecosystems to improve the performance of cereal crops in low-input and organic agricultural systems. *Field Crops Research, 107*(2), 89–101. doi:10.1016/j.fcr.2008.01.001

Hamerlynck, E. P., Huxman, T. E., McAuliffe, J. R., & Smith, S. D. (2004). Carbon isotope discrimination and foliar nutrient status of *Larrea tridentate* (creosote bush) in contrasting Mojave Desert soils. *Oecologia, 138*(2), 210–215. doi:10.1007/s00442-003-1437-7

Han, X., Li, L., & Yuan, Z. (2004). Nitrogen use efficiency of competing individuals in a dense stand of an annual herb, *Chenopodium album.* [in Chinese]. *Acta Phytoecologica Sinica, 28*(3), 294–299.

Hendrik, P., & Evans, J. R. (1998). Photosynthetic nitrogen-use efficiency of species that differ inherently in specific leaf area. *Oecologia, 116*(1), 26–37. doi:10.1007/s004420050560

Huggins, D. R., & Pan, W. L. (2003). Key indicators for assessing nitrogen use efficiency in cereal-based agroecosystems. *Journal of Crop Production, 8*(4), 157–185. doi:10.1300/J144v08n01_07

Marshall, J. D., & Zhang, J. (1994). Carbon isotope discrimination and water use efficiency of native plants of the north-central Rockies. *Ecology, 75*(7), 1887–1895. doi:10.2307/1941593

Paponov, I. A., & Sambo, P., aufm Erley, G. S., Presterl, T., Geiger, H. H., & Engels, C. (2005). Kernel set in maize genotypes differing in nitrogen use efficiency in response to resource availability around flowering. *Plant and Soil, 272*(2), 101–110. doi:10.1007/s11104-004-4210-8

Pastor, J., & Bridgham, S. D. (1999). Nutrient efficiency along nutrient availability gradients. *Oecologia, 118*(1), 50–58. doi:10.1007/s004420050702

Poorter, H., & Evans, J. R. (1998). Photosynthetic nitrogen-use efficiency of species that differ inherently in specific leaf area. *Oecologia, 116*(1), 26–37. doi:10.1007/s004420050560

Reich, P. B., Ellsworth, D. S., & Uhl, C. (1995b). Leaf carbon and nutrient assimilation and conservation in species of different successional status in an oligotrophic Amazonian forest. *Functional Ecology, 9*(1), 65–76. doi:10.2307/2390092

Samborski, S., Kozak, M., & Azevedo, R. A. (2008). Does nitrogen uptake affect nitrogen uptake efficiency, or vice versa? *Acta Physiologiae Plantarum, 30*(4), 419–420. doi:10.1007/s11738-008-0164-4

Saurer, M., Siegwolf, R. T. W., & Schweingruber, F. H. (2004). Carbon isotope discrimination indicates improving water-use efficiency of trees in northern Eurasia over the last 100 years. *Global Change Biology, 10*(12), 2109–2120. doi:10.1111/j.1365-2486.2004.00869.x

Silla, F., & Escudero, A. (2004). Nitrogen-use efficiency: trade-offs between N productivity and mean residence time at organ, plant and population levels. *Functional Ecology, 18*(4), 511–521. doi:10.1111/j.0269-8463.2004.00872.x

Smedley, M. P., Dawson, T. E., & Comstock, J. P. (1991). Seasonal carbon isotope discrimination in a grassland community. *Oecologia, 85*(3), 314–320. doi:10.1007/BF00320605

Sparks, J. P., & Ehleringer, J. R. (1997). Leaf carbon isotope discrimination and nitrogen content for riparian trees along elevation transects. *Oecologia, 109*(3), 362–367. doi:10.1007/s004420050094

Tsialtas, J. T., Handley, L. L., Kassioumi, M. T., Veresoglou, D. S., & Gagianas, A. A. (2001). Interspecific variation in potential water-use efficiency and its relation to plant species abundance in a water-limited grassland. *Functional Ecology*, *15*(5), 605–614. doi:10.1046/j.0269-8463.2001.00555.x

KEY TERMS AND DEFINITIONS

Plant Water Use Efficiency: Traditionally defined either as the ratio of dry accumulation to water consumption over a season (WUET) or as the ratio of net photosynthesis (A) to transpiration (E) over a period of seconds or minutes (WUEi).

Plant Nitrogen Use Efficiency: Is defined as the ratio of total carbon assimilation by a leaf to total nitrogen investment in that leaf over its lifetime.

Stable Carbon Isotope Composition ($\delta^{13}C$): Expressed relative to the PDB (Pee Dee Belemnite) standard.

Ejina Oasis: A typical hyperarid desert oasis at the downstream end of the Heihe River basin in northwestern China.

Populus Euphratica: The dominant native woody species in the desert riparian ecosystem, capable of forming an imposing canopy (>20 m tall) in some areas

Tamarix Ramosissima: A weedy, invasive xerophytic shrub species in the desert riparian ecosystem, which can form monospecific stands at a maximum height varying between 2 and 3 m.

Chapter 25
Root Water Uptake Model of *Populus Euphratica* in Desert Riparian Forest in Extreme Arid Region

Yongzheng Tian
Chinese Academy of Sciences, China & Alxa League of Inner Mongolia Autonomous Region, China

Jianhua Si
Chinese Academy of Sciences, China

Qi Feng
Chinese Academy of Sciences, China

Shengkui Cao
Qinghai Normal University, China & Chinese Academy of Sciences, China

ABSTRACT

Plant root water uptake is a key way to transfer soil water to the atmosphere. It is an important part of the research on water transforming patterns in the SPAC (Soil-Plant-Air Continuum). So understanding the water absorption patterns of plant root system is a base to recognize the SPAC. Recently there are many studies on the water absorption patterns of plant root system. However, the researched plants are mostly crops and the main researched areas are regions with adequate precipitation. There are only a few studies on the water absorption of natural plants in extreme arid desert regions. This paper studied the root water absorption patterns of Populus euphratica and established the corresponding mathematical model based on the data of root density and soil water dynamics in root zone in desert riparian forest in extreme arid region. The finite difference method was used to discretize the soil water movement equation with evaporation boundary conditions. Numerical simulation analysis of soil water movement in root zone of Populus euphratica showed that the simulated values were consistent with the measurement values with 92-98% precision. This work provides a theoretical basis for the study of water movement in the SPAC.

DOI: 10.4018/978-1-60960-064-8.ch025

INTRODUCTION

Root water uptake is an important process of water cycle and an important part of the research on water transforming patterns in the SPAC (Soil-Plant-Air Continuum). A quantitative means of describing root water uptake may help guide efficient water use (Gong et al., 2006). The research on the water uptake model of plant roots was started in the 1940's. Van den Honert (1948) put forward the theoretical pattern of water flow, which established the model of root water-uptake mechanism. Gardner (1960) developed the first single-root water uptake model. Afterwards, many different models were developed, among which the water-uptake models proposed by Molz & Remson (1970), Nimah & Hanks(1973), Feddes et al. (1976, 1978), Hillel et al.(1976), Raats(1975), Herlelrath et al.(1977) and Molz (1976, 1981), had broadened and improved the model. Since the beginning of the 1960's, a number of scholars have improved the acquisition of parameters involved in root water-uptake models and the measurement methods. They also established the two and three-dimensional models. Green (1997; 1999) established the root water uptake model of apple trees. Vrugt et al. (2001) developed the two and three-dimensional models of almond trees, and compared them in detail. Pagesl (1989) and Diggle (1998) constructed the three-dimensional models. These models mostly consist of three quantitative descriptors, namely, the atmospheric condition, effective root distribution, and root water uptake efficiency dependent on soil water potential that is controlled by soil water availability. These studies further improved and optimized the water uptake model of plant roots.

Scholars have extensively researched the distribution of root system and water uptake and established the water uptake models, of oaks (Katul et al.,1997), apple trees (Green & Clothier 1997,1999)and almond trees (Vrugt et al., 2001) and so on. In China, the study of water uptake model of root system was mainly concentrated on the establishment of root water uptake model of crops, except the root system distribution and root water uptake model of the apple trees (He et al., 2000; Yao et al., 2004; Gong et al., 2006), other trees have not been researched.

As the most important forest resources in desert regions of Northwest China, *Populus euphratica* forests are an important ecological screen in northern area of China. They play an irreplaceable role in the maintenance of ecological security. Therefore, to clearly understand the consumption of ground water by *Populus euphratica* forests, the study of water uptake of the root system in *Populus euphratica* trees in the desert riparian forest has an important and practical significance. The aims of this study are as follows: 1)To establish the fine root distribution pattern of *Populus euphratica* in desert riparian forest in the extreme arid region; 2) to ascertain the main parameters affecting the water uptake of root system, the function of water potential influence, the distribution function of root-length density and the amount of transpiration; 3) to set up the root water uptake model of *Populus euphratica* in desert riparian forest in the extreme arid region; 4) to validate the water-uptake model.

MATERIALS AND METHODS

Experimental Site and Plant Material

The experiment was conducted in the *Populus euphratica* Forest Reserve (101°10′E 41°59′N, 920.46 m elev.) in the Ejina oasis in the lower Heihe basin in northwest China. The site is one of the extreme arid regions in China. Annual rainfall in the region is less than 50 mm, of which 84% falls during the rainy season (May-September) and evaporation is larger than 3700 mm. The average yearly air temperature is about 8.2 °C. Prevailing wind directions are northwest in winter and spring, and southwest to south in summer and autumn. The yearly average wind speed is about 3.4 to

Table 1. The physical characters of soil profile at the experimental district

Depth (cm)	Texture	Bulk density (g cm⁻³)	Saturation moisture content (g·cm⁻³)	Field capacity (g cm⁻³)	Wilting moisture (g cm⁻³)
0-80	sand	1.402	21.70	3.55	2.28
80-100	clay	1.644	22.32	3.67	2.34
>100	sand	1.548	21.93	3.62	2.30

4.0 m/s. Soil in the *Populus euphratica* Forest Reserve is a sandy loam of about 2 m depth, and has a saturated volumetric water content of 0.35 m³m⁻³, and the water content of 1.2 m³m⁻³ is equal to a soil matrix potential of -1.7 Mpa. The physical characteristics of the site are presented in Table 1.

The organic content at the depth of 0–30 cm is 0.73% and 0.13% at 30–200 cm. The groundwater level ranges from 1.5 to 3.5 m. Dominant tree species is *Populus euphratica*, and it is also the dominant native tree species in Ejina oasis, and it forms an imposing canopy >20 m tall in some locations.

Firstly we investigated the distribution rule of the DBH (diameter at breast) of the standing forest, and chose a 20 m×50 m area as a sample standard land. After that, we conducted investigation on breast diameter, height, density and shade density of the sample trees, and the result are: average

age, 25; shade density, 0.8; tree density, 800/hm²; average tree height, 10 m; average breast diameter, 19 cm. We set the diameter class by 2cm, and it shows the diameter of the biggest trunk as 18-20 cm, and the result is as Figure 1.

On the ground of the standing forest investigation and internalization results, we chose the standard trees on the principle of trunk not overshadowed. We selected 2 well-developed straight and healthy ones as experimental standard trees (breast diameter, 18cm, 20 cm respectively).

Root Length Density Determination

The experiment was conducted during May to October, 2006, when the weather was clear almost every day. Since the roots of *Populus euphratica* trees were distributed unevenly both in vertical and horizontal directions and the root system was

Figure 1. The diameter at breast height (DBH) and frequency

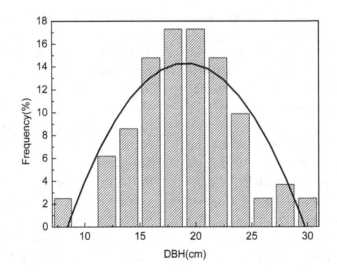

large, normally samples were collected from the soil-root zone. The roots of *Populus euphratica* are oriented towards water sources and circle the trunk symmetrically. We conducted 3-dimensional stratified sampling. At first, we excavated a profile in a prearranged direction around the trunk. In horizontal direction we collected soil samples every 20 cm continuously along a length from 0–400 cm of the profile, with a sample volume 20 cm long, 10 cm wide and 20 cm high. Vertically, we collected soil samples with the same dimensions every 20 cm continuously from 0–120 cm depth (Figure 2). In the laboratory, we separated the roots from the soil with a 2 mm sieve. The roots were separated from soil, packed in packages. They were then cleaned with water and the roots less than 2 mm in diameter were selected as the absorbing roots. They were cleaned and dried in the sun for a day. Then we obtained the length of all samples by using Equation (1) and the root length density of each soil cores from Equation (2) (Zhang et al., 2002; 2004).

$$L = \frac{11}{14} \times N \times \gamma \qquad (1)$$

$$RD = \frac{L}{V} \qquad (2)$$

Where L is length of root (cm), N is the number of roots that cross a point of intersection, γ is

a constant related to the form of the grid, RD is density of root length (cm/cm^3) and V is the volume of soil core (cm^3).

Soil Moisture Determination

Soil moisture were measured weekly from the surface to 160cm depth using the TDR (Time Domain Reflectory) (IMKO Company, Germany). The depth ranges of soil moisture measurement are 0~20 cm, 20~40 cm, 40~60 cm, 60~80 cm, 80~100 cm, 100~120 cm, 120~140 cm and 140~160 cm.

Transpiration Intensity Determination

There was used heat pulse meter (SF-300, Greenspan technology Pty Ltd., Australian), with 4 probes, to measure the stem sap flow of *Populus euphratica* trees.

Signals from the heat-pulse equipment were analyzed using the standard compensation technique, so only the salient details are repeated here. The temperature rise following the release of a pulse of heat was measured at distances X_d (15 mm) downstream and X_u (-5 mm) upstream from the heater needle. The heat-pulse velocity, V (cm h^{-1}), was then calculated:

$$V = (X_d + X_u) / 2t_z \qquad (3)$$

Figure 2. Schematic diagram of the root length density determination experiment

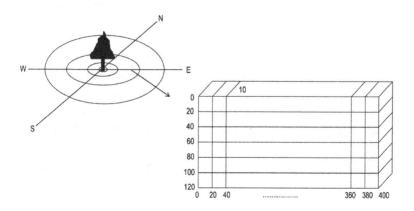

Where t_z (s) is the time delay for the temperatures to become equal at the points X_d and X_u. The heat-pulse velocity V must be corrected to account for the probe-induced effects of wounding and the thermal heterogeneity caused by finite probes of different thermal properties. According to Swanson and Whitfield (1981), the corrected heat-pulse velocity HPV (cm h^{-1}) was derived from the measured heat-pulse velocity V using

$$HPV = a + bV + cV^2 + dV^3 \qquad (4)$$

Where a, b, c, and d are the correction factors that depend on the probe size, spacing and material composition. Given that our intent is to use heat-pulse more extensively in *Populus euphratica* trees, we deemed it prudent to check that the standard coefficients are indeed appropriate. From the corrected heat pulse velocity, HPV, it is possible to infer the sap flux. Sap flow velocity (V_s, cm h^{-1}) was calculated from Edwards and Warwick formula (1984):

$$V_s = HPV(0.505F_m + F_1) \qquad (5)$$

Where F_m is the volume fraction of the wood and F_1 is the volume fraction of water. The calculation of the F_m and F_1 for each tree requires the input of the fresh weight, oven-dried weight and the immersed weight. F_m is:

$$F_m = \frac{W_d}{1.53W_i} \qquad (6)$$

And F_1 is:

$$F_1 = \frac{W_f - W_d}{W_i} \qquad (7)$$

Where W_f is the fresh weight, W_d is the oven-dried weight and Wi is the immersed weight or the sapwood sample. Sap flux in liters per unit time

(Q) is a function of the velocity of sap flow and the area, over which the flow occurs,

$$Q = V_s A \qquad (8)$$

Where A is conducting wood area.

Measurement of Soil Water Potential

Soil water potential was measured by WP4 Dewpoint Potentiameter. It has a measurement range from 0 to -40 Mpa (saturation to air-dried) with an accuracy of 0.1MPa or better. Daily courses of soil water potential, from dawn to sunset (8:00-20:00), were recorded three times per month from May to October.

Model Selection

The root water uptake model of *Populus euphratica* used the improved Feddes model, it was constructed by increasing root density term based on the Feddes model, at the same time, the model considered both soil water potential and root distribution in soil profile, which could simulate the soil water change more correctly under different soil water conditions and root length dense distributions, it has the advantage of simple form and is easy to obtain the parameter solution, and is convenient for application. Its objective functions are:

$$S_r(z,t) = \frac{\alpha(h)L(z)}{\int_0^{z_r} \alpha(h)L(z)dz} T_r(t) \qquad (9)$$

where z is the soil depth (cm), z_r is the root length(cm), $T_r(t)$ is the transpiration rate of *Populus euphratica* trees (cm/h), $S_r(z,t)$ is the root water uptake intensity(L/h), $L(z)$ is the root length density(L/cm^3);$\alpha(h)$ is the Feddes reduction function.

RESULTS AND DISCUSSION

Feddes Reduction Function $\alpha(h)$

The calculation method of Feddes reduction function $\alpha(h)$ is as follow:

$$\alpha(h) = \begin{cases} \dfrac{h}{h_1} & h_1 \leq h \leq 0 \\ 1 & h_2 \leq h \leq h_1 \\ \dfrac{h - h_3}{h_2 - h_3} & h_3 \leq h \leq h_2 \\ 0 & h \leq h_3 \end{cases} \quad (10)$$

where, h is soil water potential(cm); $\alpha(h)$ is Feddes reduction function; h_1, h_2, h_3 are soil water potential thresholds which affect root water uptake.

h_1 is soil water potential of 80% of field capacity, h_2 is soil water potential of 60% of field capacity, h_3 is soil water potential of 80% of wilting moisture. The field capacity, saturated water content and wilting moisture is 3.55%, 31.7% and 0.73% respectively. Based on these data, h_1, h_2, h_3 can be determined (Table 2).

The parameters in Table 1 are introduced in the formula (2) to obtain the values of Feddes reduction function $\alpha(h)$ (Table 3).

The Distribution Function of Root Length Density

First, there was drew a scatter point graph. The graph shows that negative e-exponent function was suitable, so we simulated one-dimension RLD function in vertical direction (Figure 3), and it was

$$L(z) = 1.7153 L_{\max} e^{-6.048z/Z} \,, \quad R^2 = 0.8884 \quad (11)$$

Where z is soil depth (cm); Z is the depth of the longest root in vertical direction (cm); $RLD(z)$ is root length density in vertical direction (cm/cm^{-3}); $RLD(z)$ is maximum root length density of each soil core (cm/cm^{-3}); in this experiment Z=120 cm and RLD_{max}= 0.517cm/cm^3.

The results showed that root length density lowers with increasing soil depth in vertical direction. The majority of the fine roots occur in 0~80 cm soil layer, accounting for 97.60% of its total, there are few fine roots in 100~120 cm soil layer, accounting for only 0.19% of its total. Most fine roots occur in 0~20 cm soil layer, accounting for 58.25% of its total.

The results of calculations show that the average density of fine root length of *Populus euphratica* in the horizontal direction is a negative e-exponent as a function of the horizontal distance from the trunk. We carried out a regression analysis on the density of the root lengths and

Table 2. Soil water potential thresholds of Feddes reduction function

	Field capacity	80% of field capacity	60% of field capacity	Wilting moisture
Moisture content (cm³/cm³)	0.0355	0.0284	0.0213	0.0073
Soil water potential (cm)	-381.261	-516.705	-764.622	-3288.47

Table 3. Feddes reduction function $\alpha(h)$ of root system of Populus euphratica

Depth(cm)	0-20	20-40	40-60	60-80	80-100	100-120
$\alpha(h)$	0.8219	0.6244	0.2258	0.1447	0.0869	0.0783

Figure 3. One-dimension root length densities in vertical direction of Populus Euphratica

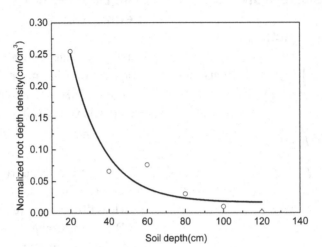

the horizontal distance to the trunk at a range of 0–400 cm (Figure 4). The equation is:

$$L(r) = \begin{cases} 0.0468 L_{max} e^{1.914r/R_1} & 0 \le r < 220 \quad R^2 = 0.68 \\ 0.3275 L_{max} e^{-1.28r/R_2} & 220 \le r < 400 \quad R^2 = 0.73 \end{cases}$$

(12)

Where r is root length in horizontal radial direction (cm); $L(r)$ is root length density in horizontal radial direction (cm.cm⁻³); R is maximum length in horizontal radial direction (cm); R= 400 cm in this experiment.

It shows that $L(r)$ of fine roots increases from 0-220 cm of horizontal radial distance to the stem, but it decreases from 220 to 400cm. Few fine roots are from 0-20cm to the stem, making up only 0.47%; more fine roots are from 160 to 220cm in horizontal radial direction, occupying 18.57%.

Transpiration Intensity of *Populus euphratica $T_r(t)$*

Based on the measured data of stem sap flow *Populus euphratica*, the piecewise fitting method was adopted to set up a mathematic model of diurnal

Figure 4. One-dimension root length density of P.euphratica in horizontal direction

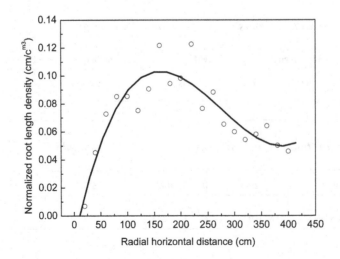

variation of transpiration rate, thus obtained the curve equation of diurnal variation of transpiration rate as follows:

$$T_r(t) = \begin{cases} -2E-08t^5+7E-07t^4+8E-05t^3-0.004t^2+0.0663t+0.0346 & 1 \leq t \leq 45 \\ -5E-09t^6+2E-06t^5-0.0003t^4+0.0296t^3-1.4411t^2+36.913t-387.37 & 46 \leq t \leq 99 \\ -3E-07t^4+0.0001t^3-0.222t^2+1.7624t-51.51 & 100 \leq t \leq 149 \end{cases}$$

(13)

where the t is Julian day.

Root Water Uptake Model of *Populus euphratica*

The parameters including $\alpha_{(h)}, L(z), L(r), T_r(t)$ were introduced into the formula (9), and obtained the root water uptake model of *Populus euphratica*.

One-dimension model in vertical direction is:

$$S(z,t) = \begin{cases} 0.0675L(z)T_r(t) & 0 < z \leq 20 \\ 0.0513L(z)T_r(t) & 20 < z \leq 40 \\ 0.0186L(z)T_r(t) & 40 < z \leq 60 \\ 0.0119L(z)T_r(t) & 60 < z \leq 80 \\ 0.0071L(z)T_r(t) & 80 < z \leq 100 \\ 0.0064L(z)T_r(t) & 100 < z \leq 120 \end{cases}$$

(14)

One-dimension model in horizontal radial direction is:

$$S(r,t) = \begin{cases} 0.6665e^{1.914r/220}T_r(t) & 0 < r \leq 220 \\ 4.664e^{-1.28r/400}T_r(t) & 220 < r \leq 400 \end{cases}$$

(15)

Model Validation

The macroscopic model of soil water movement in root zone is as follows:

$$\partial\theta / \partial t = \Delta[K(\theta)\Delta\phi] - S$$

(15)

Where φ is total soil water potential, t is time, S is root water uptake term, $K(\theta)$ is soil water conductivity, θ is the soil volume water content.

In the calculation of interval K and D, we selected geometric mean of upper and lower node sin space and used arithmetic mean of pre-and post nodes in temporal scale. Then we made grid enmeshment of the area $(0 \leq z \leq 120, 0 \leq t \leq 7, \Delta z = 20cm, \Delta t = 1day)$ according to rectangular pattern, for any inner points, wrote out the corresponding difference equation according to implicit difference scheme.

$$\frac{\theta_i^{j+1} - \theta_i^j}{\Delta t} = \frac{D_{i+1/2}^{j+1}(\theta_{i+1}^{j+1} - \theta_i^{j+1}) - D_{i-1/2}^{j+1}(\theta_i^{j+1} - \theta_{i-1}^{j+1})}{(\Delta z)^2}$$

$$- \frac{(K_{i+1}^{j+1} + K_i^{j+1}) - (K_i^{j+1} + K_{i-1}^{j+1})}{2(\Delta z)} - S_i^{j+1/2}$$

(16)

A difference equation is supplemented when z=0 in the case of the known soil evaporation rate at surface boundary conditions, a difference equation is listed out at the boundary node interface (i=0), $\partial\theta / \partial z$ using the forward difference method,

$$-D_0^{j+1} \frac{\theta_1^{j+1} - \theta_0^{j+1}}{\Delta z} + K_0^{j+1} = -E_s^{j+1/2}$$

Where D_0^{j+1}, K_0^{j+1} are $D(\theta_0^{j+1})$ and $K(\theta_0^{j+1})$, $E_s^{j+1/2}$ is average soil evaporation rate from j to $j+1$ time interval.

Solving the end soil moisture content of each node according to the initial known soil moisture content, and using the matrix chase-after method to solve the algebraic equations, θ_{n-2}, θ_2, θ_1, to obtain θ_0, and then compare the measured values for validating the model.

A model of root water uptake of *Populus euphratica* was set up based on root length den-

Table 4. Simulated and measured soil water contents in Populus euphratica forest soil (M represents measured value; S represents simulated value)

Soil depth (cm)	15,Jun.	30,Jun.		15,Jul.		31,Jul.		15,Aug.		30,Aug.		15,Sep.	
	M	M	S	M	S	M	S	M	S	M	S	M	S
0	25.0	24.9	24.9	24.5	24.5	23.9	23.9	23.1	23.1	22.1	22.1	21.0	21.0
10	25.3	25.2	25.1	24.9	24.7	24.2	24.0	23.1	23.1	22.1	22.1	21.0	21.0
20	25.9	25.7	25.7	25.1	25.1	23.9	24.2	23.3	23.3	22.6	22.2	21.1	21.1
30	27.9	26.9	26.8	26.9	25.7	25.1	24.6	24.6	23.5	23.9	22.3	21.1	21.1
40	30.0	28.1	27.6	27.4	26.1	25.2	24.7	23.9	23.5	22.2	22.2	20.9	20.9
50	29.2	27.9	27.5	26.8	25.8	24.6	24.4	23.4	23.0	21.7	21.7	20.4	20.4
60	27.2	26.1	25.8	24.8	24.5	23.9	23.3	22.2	22.1	21.8	20.8	19.1	19.6
70	23.5	23.1	23.0	22.6	22.4	21.5	21.6	20.4	20.7	19.6	19.7	18.7	18.6
80	21.0	20.3	20.6	19.8	20.5	19.5	20.1	19.1	19.5	18.5	18.8	17.6	17.8
90	21.4	20.8	20.9	20.7	20.6	20.1	20.3	19.4	19.7	18.9	19.0	18.1	18.2
100	24.7	24.0	24.1	23.2	23.4	22.5	22.7	21.9	22.0	20.8	21.1	20.0	20.1
110	30.2	29.1	29.1	28.2	28.4	26.6	26.8	25.3	25.6	24.1	24.3	23.0	23.1
120	34.9	33.6	33.0	31.9	31.3	30.1	29.7	28.6	28.2	26.8	26.6	25.3	25.1
130	31.7	30.9	30.5	29.4	29.1	27.6	27.5	25.9	25.9	24.5	24.4	22.9	22.8
140	20.3	17.9	17.2	17.0	16.7	16.6	16.3	16.3	16.1	15.9	15.8	15.8	15.5

sity, soil water potential and transpiration. The results obtained from the numerical simulation computation of soil water movement in root zone of *Populus euphratica* showed that the simulated values had a relative error of 7.0%, this may be related to the root system distribution in 30-70cm (Table 4; Figure 5). On the whole, the simulation values are consistent well with the measurement values with a precision ranging between 92% and 98%, therefore, this simulation model is highly accurate and practical, it can be used to research and predict soil water dynamic changes in the *Populus euphratica* forest in Ejina oasis.

CONCLUSION

At present, the study of root water uptake model of plant is mainly concentrated on crops, the water uptake of root system of desert riparian tree species have not been researched. A one-dimensional root water uptake model of *Populus euphratica* trees was verified with sap flow and soil water content in Ejina oasis. The model has proved to be practical and requires a simple computer program, and it can reach a high simulation precision as long as the effective root length density is determined.

Figure 5. The mean relative errors between the simulation and measurement values

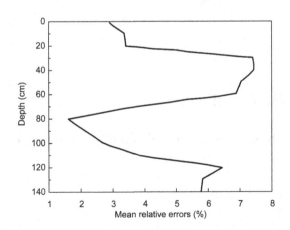

The model and the solution can basically reflect the real situation of soil water movement.

However, for the arbor species- *Populus euphratica*, the above mentioned method involves a large amount of work, such as root system sampling, root length measurement, which can severely damage the *Populus euphratica* trees. In addition, the model also has several limitations since it is set up based on a certain time interval and a certain environment. The model still requires further testing and optimization using more data in practice. In the future, we need to strengthen the research on the basic parameters of soil water movement and the distribution patterns of root system of plants so as to provide a theoretical basis for the study of soil water movement in the SPAC system.

ACKNOWLEDGMENT

This work was supported by the National Natural Science Foundation of China (40901048, 40501012;40725001;40671010) and the Knowledge Innovation Program from Chinese Academy of Sciences (KZCX2-XB2-04). The authors wish to thank the anonymous reviewers for their reading of the manuscript, and for their suggestions and critical comments.

REFERENCES

Diggle, A. J. (1988). Rootmap: a model in three-dimensional coordinates of the growth and structure of fibrous root systems. *Plant and Soil, 105*(2), 169–178. doi:10.1007/BF02376780

Dirksen, C., & Augustijn, D. C. (1988). Root water uptake function for nonuniform pressure and osmotic potentials. *Agric.*, (abstract), (pp. 188).

Dirksen, C., Kool, J. B., & Koorevaar, P. (1993). *Simulation model of hysteretic water and solute transport in the root zone* (pp. 99–122). Berlin: Springer-Verlag.

Feddes, R. A., Kowalik, P., Kolinska-Malinka, K., & Zaradny, H. (1976). Simulation of field water uptake by plants using a soil water dependent root extraction function. *Hydrol., 31*(1), 13–26. doi:10.1016/0022-1694(76)90017-2

Feddes, R. A., Kowalik, P., & Zaradny, H. (1978). *Simulation of field water use and crop yield simulation monograph series*. PUDPC, Wageningen, Simulation Monographs, (pp, 189).

Gardner, W. R. (1960). Dynamic aspects of water availability to plants. *Soil Science, 89*(1), 63–73. doi:10.1097/00010694-196002000-00001

Gong, Z. D., & Kang, S. Z. (2006). A 2-d model of root water uptake for single apple trees and its verification with sap flow and water content measurements. *Agricultural Water Management, 83*(2), 119–129. doi:10.1016/j.agwat.2005.10.005

Green, S. R., & Clothier, B. E. (1999). The root zone dynamics of water uptake by a mature apple tree. *Plant and Soil, 206*(1), 61–77. doi:10.1023/A:1004368906698

Green, S. R., Clothier, B. E., & Mcleod, D. J. (1997). The response of sap flow in apple roots to localized irrigation. *Agricultural Water Management, 33*(1), 63–78. doi:10.1016/S0378-3774(96)01277-2

Hao, Z. Y., Yang, P. L., Liu, H. L., & Yao, C. M. (1998). Experimental investigation on root system distribution of apple tree. [in Chinese]. *Journal of China Agricultural University, 3*(1), 63–66.

Herlelrath, W. N., Miller, E. E., & Gardner, W. R. (1977). Water uptake by plant: I. Divided root experiment. *Soil Science Society of America Journal, 41*(6), 1033–1038. doi:10.2136/sssaj1977.03615995004100060003x

Hillel. (1976). A macroscopic scale model of water uptake by a non-uniform root system and salt movement in the soil profile. *Soil Sci., 121*(4), 242-255.

Homaee, M., Dirksen, C., & Feddes, R. A. (2002). Simulation of root water uptake I. Non-uniform transient salinity using different macroscopic reduction functions. *Agricultural Water Management, 57*(2), 89–109. doi:10.1016/S0378-3774(02)00072-0

Homaee, M., Dirksen, C., & Feddes, R. A. (2002). Simulation of root water uptake II. Non-uniform transient salinity using different macroscopic reduction functions. *Agricultural Water Management, 57*(2), 111–126. doi:10.1016/S0378-3774(02)00071-9

Homaee, M., Feddes, R. A., & Dirksen, C. (2002). Simulation of root water uptake III. Non-uniform transient combined salinity and water stress. *Agricultural Water Management, 577*(2), 127–144. doi:10.1016/S0378-3774(02)00073-2

Homaee, M., Feddes, R. A., & Dirksen, C. (2002). A macroscopic water extraction model for nouniform transient salinity and water stress. *Soil Science Society of America Journal, 66*(6), 1764–1772. doi:10.2136/sssaj2002.1764

Kang, S. Z., Liu, X. M., & Xiong, Y. Z. (1992). Research on the model of water uptake by winter wheat root system. [in Chinese]. *Acta University Agricultural Boreali-occidentalis, 20*(1), 5–12.

Katul, G., Todd, P., & Pataki, D. (1997). Soil water depletion by oak trees and the influence of root water uptake on the moisture content spatial statistics. *Water Resources Research, 33*(4), 611–623. doi:10.1029/96WR03978

Luo, Y., Yu, Q., Ou, Y. Z., Tang, D. Y., & Xie, X. Q. (2000). The evaluation of water uptake models by using precise field observation data. [in Chinese]. *Journal of Hydraulic Engineering, 125*(4), 73–80.

Molz, F. J. (1976). Water transport in the soil-root system: Transient analysis. *Water Resources Research, 12*(4), 805–807. doi:10.1029/WR012i004p00805

Molz, F. J. (1981). Models of water transport in the soil- plant system: A review. *Water Resources Research, 17*(5), 1254–1260. doi:10.1029/WR017i005p01245

Molz, F. J., & Remson, I. (1970). Extracting term models of soil moisture use of transpiring plant. *Water Resources Research, 6*(5), 1346–1356. doi:10.1029/WR006i005p01346

Nimah, M. N., & Hanks, R. J. (1973). Model for estimating soil water, plant and atmosphere interrelations:Field test of model. *Soil Sci Soc. Am. Proc., 37*(4), 522–527. doi:10.2136/sssaj1973.03615995003700040018x

Pagesl. (1989). A simulation model of the three-dimensional architecture of the maize root system. *Plant Soil, 119*(1), 147-154.

Raats, P. A. C. (1975). Distributions of salts in the root zone. *Journal of Hydrology (Amsterdam), 27*(1-2), 237–248. doi:10.1016/0022-1694(75)90057-8

Shao, M. A., Yang, W. Z., & Li, Y. S. (1987). Numerical model of root water uptake by plant. [in Chinese]. *Acta Pedologica Sinica, 24*(4), 295–304.

Van den Honert, T. H. (1948). Water transport in plants as a catenary process. *Discussions of the Faraday Society, 3*(2), 146–153. doi:10.1039/df9480300146

Vrugt, J. A., Hopmans, J. W., & Simunek, J. (2001). Calibration of a 2-d root water uptake model. *Soil Science Society of America Journal, 65*(4), 1027–1037. doi:10.2136/sssaj2001.6541027x

Yao, J. W. (1989). An numerical model of predicting soil moisture content under the condition of crop growing. [in Chinese]. *Journal of Hydraulic Engineering, 9*(1), 32–38.

Yao, L. M., Kang, S. Z., Gong, D. Z., Jia, H. Z., & Pang, X. M. (2004). The apple tree root water uptake models established through two kinds of methods and the comparison of these models. [in Chinese]. *Journal of Irrigation and Drainage*, *23*(1), 67–70.

Zhang, J. S., & Meng, P. (2004). Spatial distribution characteristics of fine roots of pomegranate tree. [in Chinese]. *Journal of Nanjing Forestry University*, *28*(4), 89–91.

Zhang, J. S., Meng, P., & Yin, C. J. (2002). Spatial distribution characteristics of apple tree roots in the apple-wheat intercropping. [in Chinese]. *Scientia Silvae Sinicae*, *38*(4), 30–33.

Zuo, Q., Sun, Y. X., & Yang, P. L. (1988). Study on water uptake by the winter wheat's roots with the application of microlysimeter. [in Chinese]. *Journal of Hydraulic Engineering*, *6*(1), 69–76.

ADDITIONAL READING

Adiku, S. G. K., Rose, C. W., & Braddock, R. D. (2000). On the simulation of root water extraction: examination of a minimum energy hypothesis. *Soil Science*, *165*(3), 226–236. doi:10.1097/00010694-200003000-00005

Arora, V. K., & Boer, G. J. (2003). A representation of variable root distribution in dynamic vegetation models. *Earth Interactions*, *7*(6), 1–19. doi:10.1175/1087-3562(2003)007<0001:AROVRD>2.0.CO;2

Aura, E. (1996). Modelling non-uniform soil water uptake by a single plant root. *Plant and Soil*, *186*(2), 237–243. doi:10.1007/BF02415519

Bai, W. M., & Zuo, Q. (2001). Effect of water supply on root growth and water uptake of alfalfa in wulanbuhe sandy region. *Acta Phytoecologica Sinica*, *25*(1), 35–41.

Belcher, J. W., Keddy, P. A., & Twolan-Strutt, L. (1995). Root and shoot competition intensity along a soil depth gradient. *Journal of Ecology*, *83*(4), 673–682. doi:10.2307/2261635

Buysee, J., Smolders, E., & Merchx, R. (1996). Modelling the uptake of nitrate by a growing plant with an adjustable root nitrate capacity. *Plant and Soil*, *181*(1), 19–23. doi:10.1007/BF00011287

Choudhury, B. (1983). Modeling the effect of weather condition and soil water potential on canopy temperature for corn. *Agricultural Meteorology*, *29*(2), 169–182. doi:10.1016/0002-1571(83)90064-X

Clothier, B. E., & Green, S. R. (1997). Roots: the big movers of water and chemical in soil. *Soil Science*, *162*(8), 534–543. doi:10.1097/00010694-199708000-00002

Flerching, G. W. (1996). Modelling evapotranspiration and surface budgets across a watershed. *Water Resources Research*, *32*(8), 2539–2548. doi:10.1029/96WR01240

Jackson, R. B., & Caldwell, M. M. (1996). Integrating resource heterogeneity and plant plasticity: modelling nitrate and phosphate uptake in a patchy soil environment. *Journal of Ecology*, *84*(5), 891–903. doi:10.2307/2960560

Jackson, R. B., Manwaring, J. H., & Caldwell, M. M. (1990). Rapid physiological adjustment of roots to localized soil enrichment. *Nature*, *344*(1), 58–60. doi:10.1038/344058a0

Jackson, R. B., Sperry, J. S., & Dawson, T. E. (2000). Root water uptake and transport: using physiological processes in global predictions. *Trends in Plant Science*, *5*(11), 482–488. doi:10.1016/S1360-1385(00)01766-0

Kang, S. Z., Zhang, F. C., & Zhang, J. H. (2001). A simulation model of water dynamics in winter wheat field and its application in a semiarid region. *Agricultural Water Management, 49*(2), 115–129. doi:10.1016/S0378-3774(00)00137-2

Lynch, J. P., Nielsen, K. L., Davis, R. D., & Jablokow, A. G. (1997). SimRoot: modelling and visualization of root systems. *Plant and Soil, 188*(1), 139–151. doi:10.1023/A:1004276724310

Ma, H. Y., & Gong, J. D. (2005). Study on the characteristics of space-time change on soil moisture in arid region. [in Chinese]. *Research of Soil and Water Conservation, 12*(6), 231–234.

Rengel, Z. (1993). Mechanistic simulation models of nutrient uptake: a review. *Plant and Soil, 152*(1), 1–173.

Sa, R. L., Hao, S. Q., & Zhang, Q. L. (2006). A study on soil moisture variation of natural populus euphratica forest stand in Ejina. [in Chinese]. *Forest Resources Management, 1*(1), 59–62.

Scott, R. (1997). Timescales of land surface evapotranspiration response. *Journal of Climate, 10*(4), 559–566. doi:10.1175/1520-0442(1997)010<0559:TOLSER>2.0.CO;2

Smith, D. M., & Roberts, J. M. (2003). Hydraulic conductivities of competing root systems of Grevillea robusta and maize in agroforestry. *Plant and Soil, 251*(2), 343–349. doi:10.1023/A:1023085002828

Vercambre, G., & Pages, L. (2003). Architectural analysis and synthesis of the plum tree root system in an orchard using a quantitative modeling approach. *Plant and Soil, 251*(1), 1–11. doi:10.1023/A:1022961513239

Yang, L., Zhang, Q. L., & Chang, J. B. (2006). Spatial distribution ccharacteristics of roots of *populus euphratica*. [in Chinese]. *Journal of Inner Mongolia Agricultural University, 27*(1), 15–17.

KEY TERMS AND DEFINITIONS

Desert Riparian Forest: Defined that the forest system distributes at both sides of river in desert zone of arid area, depending on the river and groundwater. It is composed of the drought-tolerance tree, shrub and glass.

Populus Euphratica: The dominant native woody species in the desert riparian ecosystem, capable of forming an imposing canopy (>20 m tall) in some areas

Root Water Uptake Model: A mathematic tool quantifying root absorption in plant.

Root Density: An important parameter in studying root water uptake model in plant.

Soil Moisture: Is indicated that there contains water in soil. It is expressed by soil relative water content.

Extreme Arid Region: The area where its aridity is less than 0.03.

Chapter 26
The Fuzzy Integrated Energy Prior-Warning Model Based on Entropy Weight

Yaqun He
China University of Mining and Technology, China

Hua Wei
China University of Mining and Technology, China

Weiran Zuo
China University of Mining and Technology, China

Xiaobing Wu
China University of Mining and Technology, China

Xin Ge
China University of Mining and Technology, China

Shan Wu
China University of Mining and Technology, China

Baofeng Wen
China University of Mining and Technology, China

ABSTRACT

Based on the analysis of five factors affecting energy risks, including supply and demand, economy, environment, transport, and disaster, this chapter establishes the prior-warning index system of the energy risk by covering 3 sub-systems and 37 indexes. The three sub-systems are the coal sub-system, the petroleum and natural gas sub-system, and the integrated factors sub-system. Fuzzy synthesis evaluation was applied to confirm the internal estimated index weight of the sub-systems. Moreover, the risk prior-warning model of the energy sub-systems was established by the method. The weights of the three

DOI: 10.4018/978-1-60960-064-8.ch026

sub-systems were determined through the concept of entropy weight, and the prior-warning indexes of energy risk were applied to evaluate the total energy security of the three sub-systems. Finally, the prior-warning model of energy risk in China was established. The entire situation of energy safety of China was summarized via empirical analysis.

INTRODUCTION

Energy is one of the material basis for human society evolution, as well as an important resource for the economic development and social improvement. The energy economic issue has been studied by a number of specialists from different point of views. These studies are mostly involved in the relationship of the energy consumption and affecting factors, the forecast of energy supply and demand, the energy security strategy and so on. A series of achievements have been made.

Goto (1995) and Richels & Sturm (1996) had studied the influence of greenhouse gas emission and control as well as its impact to economy, energy, and environment. Huntington & Brown (2002) established the relational models of energy and climate to study how to increase energy security by adjusting the energy consumption structure. Wang & Chen (1996) proposed the design principles and the basic framework of establishing the coal prior-warning systems and early warning index system. Wu (2002) put forward the security evaluation index system of petroleum resources, which included eight indexes. Wang (2002) established a resource security assessment system, which contained 14 indexes, based on the analysis of five key factors affecting resource security and conducted a preliminary assessment on China's petroleum and food security situation.

The above-mentioned studies have built a foundation to the energy prior-warning system. But the existing evaluation systems are still mainly qualitative. Even when they adopt empirical analysis, the research in general lacks comprehensiveness and systemization. In this chapter, 37 prior-warning indexes which covered coal, petroleum and natural gas, and integrated energy economy sub-systems were selected to establish the prior-warning model of China's energy risk by applying fuzzy synthesis evaluation based on entropy weight. The empirical analysis of the results was made.

THE SELECTION OF PRIOR-WARNING INDEXES

Energy security is influenced by many interrelated factors and their combined effects. In general, there are mainly five influencing factors. In view of the important role of coal, petroleum and natural gas in our domestic primary energy structure, the prior-warning research of the entire energy system, which is composed of coal sub-system, petroleum and natural gas sub-system, integrated sub-system, was researched extensively.

The integrated sub-system is not just a simple addition of each sub-system. The system mainly focuses on the analysis of comprehensive indexes, including primary energy supply and demand, energy consumption elasticity, unit Gross Domestic Product (GDP) energy consumption and so on. Considering that the new energy takes up a smaller proportion of the energy consumption, it is not considered as a sub-system, but only reflected in the integrated sub-system. The selection principles of energy prior-warning indexes are based on science, comprehensiveness, comparability, dynamic, sensitivity and availability. The prior-warning indexes' Matrix of the energy risk is shown in Table 1.

Table 1. Prior-warning indexes' matrix of the energy risk

Energy systems	Coal sub-system	Petroleum and gas sub-system	Integrated sub-system
Supply and demand factors	Reserve-production ratio of Coal Supply and demand ratio of Coal Coal reserve rate Supply and demand balance of Coal Region Coal quality grades	Petroleum reserve-production ratio Natural Gas reserve-production ratio Petroleum supply and demand ratio Natural Gas supply and demand ratio Supply and demand balance of Petroleum and Natural Gas Region Petroleum reserve days Dependence degree on foreign petroleum Concentration degree of petroleum and natural gas import Quality level of petroleum and natural gas	Energy self-sufficiency rate Energy consumption growth rate Growth of renewable energy
Economic factors	Profit percentage of Coal industry cost	Risk indicator of International crude petroleum price	Elasticity index of energy consumption
Environmental factors	Input-output ratio of the Coal industry	Profit percentage of Petroleum and Natural gas mining industry cost Input-output ratio of Petroleum and Natural gas industry	Unit GDP energy consumption growth rate Technology saving rate
	Impact factor of Coal environment	Impact factors of Petroleum and Natural gas environment	Emission reduction rate of SO_2 Emission growth rate of CO_2 Emission growth rate of Soot
Transport factors	Carrier rate of Coal railway transportation	The concentration of Petroleum import transportation corridors Imported petroleum carrier ratio of the domestic fleet	Security degree of major Energy transportation project
Disaster factors	Mortality per millions tons coal production	Geopolitics influence factor	Impact factor of Energy catastrophic

THE PRIOR-WARNING MODEL OF ENERGY SYSTEM BASED ON FUZZY SYNTHESIS EVALUATION

It is difficult to decide precise extent, which has significant impact on various indexes, from the view of numerical value. This fact means that the energy prior-warning index system has certain degrees of ambiguity. This phenomenon requires selecting a suitable evaluation model according to the characteristic of prior-warning problems in the energy risk prior-warning process. Methods used in energy risk evaluation mainly include fuzzy synthesis evaluation method, AHP, gray gathering classification method, GIS method, and so on. Fuzzy synthesis evaluation method is a unitive analysis and evaluation method with the qualitative and quantitative combination, and accuracy and non-accuracy unify. It can integrate

the actual situation and the views of experts to calculate the levels of energy risk and solve the issues of energy risk prior-warning.

It is only selected the coal sub-system to give an explanation and other sub-systems are similar.

The basic steps of fuzzy synthesis evaluation contain six elements.

(1) U is a discourse domain of evaluating factors, and it is on behalf of a collection of indexes of the coal prior-warning sub-system. Such as $U=\{$ Reserve-production ratio of coal, The ratio of supply and demand of coal,…,Mortality per million tons of coal $\}$

(2) V presents a discourse domain of comment grade, and it is on behalf of a collection of reviews of the coal prior-warning system, which is essentially a division of change

for each interval of every prior-warning index. Evaluation is divided into five grades; they are a high degree of safety, security, a cause for concern, danger and high danger. The results of evaluation are judged by the triangular membership function:

(3) Fuzzy relationship matrix R is the result of the single factor evaluation, which is a fuzzy vector set of the coal sub-system. The integrated subject of fuzzy synthesis evaluation is to R. Then the fuzzy evaluation matrix of the coal sub-system is obtained.

(4) Evaluation index weight vector W is on behalf of the relative importance of the prior-warning indexes of coal sub-system, which is used to make a weight of R in the comprehensive evaluation. Weight vector uses a hyper standard weighting method, according to the situation that the indexes are weighted over, the more the index over-weight, the greater the weight will be. Weight value formula is as below,

$$W_i = C_i / S_i, \quad V_i = W_i / \sum_{i=1}^{m} W_i \qquad (1)$$

Where: W_i——overweight index of No. i index based on an average standard, which is the weight value; C_i——the actual value of No. I index; S_i——Standards of No. i index at all levels of the arithmetic mean value; V_i—— Normalized weight of No. i index.

(5) Composite operator refers to the calculation method in synthesis of W and R.

(6) Evaluation results vector B is the description of grading extent of the situation in the coal sub-system. Calculation result of fuzzy synthesis evaluation can be achieved by the use of MATLAB. B is the result of fuzzy synthesis evaluation of the coal sub-system.

Finally, a score vector $C = [1\ 3\ 5\ 7\ 9]$ is given, and the result of the risk prior-warning evaluation of the coal sub-system is $b = B \cdot C^T$, in which, 1 is the high degree of safety, 3 is the security, 5 is a cause for concern, 7 is the danger, and 9 is the high-danger.

THE PRIOR-WARNING MODEL BASED ON THE MULTI-OBJECTIVE OF ENTROPY WEIGHT

Because each sub-system of prior-warning indexes system reflects only one particular aspect of energy system, if we want the prior-warning indexes system to reflect and monitor the safety state of energy system, it is necessary to synthesize tolerance of all sub-systems. As a result, this paper established the prior-warning indexes of China's energy risk system to calculate the synthesis safety of the three sub-systems, coal system, petroleum and natural gas system and integrated sub-system. The calculating formula is as below,

$$V = w_1 b_1 + w_2 b_2 + w_3 b_3 \qquad (2)$$

Where, w_i stands for the weight of the coal sub-system, petroleum and natural gas system and integrated system.

$b_n (n = 1, 2, 3)$ Stands the prior-warning index of the coal sub-system, petroleum and natural gas system and integrated system.

The three sub-systems' weights in the whole energy risk-warning system were given via asking energy specialists, and then, the method of entropy weight theory was used to correct these weights. Finally, the entropy weight vector was available.

Definition 1. The Entropy Weight: The entropy weight calculation is that among the evaluating problems (m,n) (m stands for the number of evaluation systems and n stands for the number of evaluation specialists), if $e_i = -k \sum_{j=1}^{n} f_{ij} \ln f_{ij}$

Table 2. The Weight of Sub-system (coal sub-system's weight is 1)

factor	Special-ist 1	Special-ist 2	Special-ist 3	Special-ist 4	Special-ist 5	Special-ist 6	Special-ist 7	Special-ist 8	Special-ist 9	Specialist 10
R2	1.5	1	0.6	1	1	0.5	1	1	3	1.67
R3	0.75	1	1	1	1.5	1.5	1	1	1	1

is the entropy value of the evaluation system i and $k = 1 / \ln n, f_{ij} = R_{ij} / \sum_{j=1}^{n} R_{ij}$, R is the evaluation matrix of the weight of the evaluation system by specialists.

Definition 2. Among the problem of evaluation (m,n), the entropy weight of the evaluation system i is defined as below,

$$w_i = \frac{1 - e_i}{m - \sum_{1}^{m} e_i}, (i = 1, 2, ..., m), \ 0 \le w_i \le 1, \sum_{i=1}^{m} w_i = 1 \tag{3}$$

The weights hereby are decided by the inherent information of the given system, and the values of weight are different for different systems with the same standard.

By using the entropy equation to normalize and correct the weights above given by ten spe-cialists, then the entropy weights of the evaluation system-the comparatively weights of information were got. Finally the weights of the three systems were 0.1828, 0.3833 and 0.4339; hence, the energy risk prior-warning index calculation formula is as below,

$$V = 0.1828b_1 + 0.3833b_2 + 0.4339b_3 \tag{4}$$

DISCUSSION AND CONCLUSION

The energy risk prior-warning indexes of 1995-2008 were calculated by the prior-warning model of the energy security. The results are shown in Figure 1.

We can draw the following conclusions from Figure 1 by analyzing the prior-warning indexes of China's energy risk system.

Figure 1. China's energy risk prior-warning indexes of 1995-2008 and the trends of each sub-system

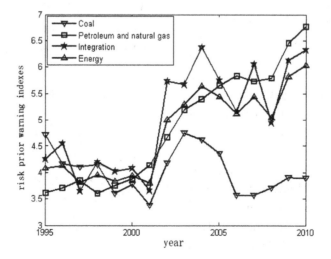

1) The calculated values of prior-warning indexes of energy risk indicate that China's energy security was well as a whole before 2008. The index of 2008 was 5.05 that is a cause for concern. The prior-warning indexes of the three sub-systems increased rapidly at 2001, and as a result, the China's energy security decreased. China's prior-warning indexes fluctuated around 4.0 during 1995-2001, and in 2001 increased rapidly to 5.0, and then fluctuated between 5.00 and 5.63 since then.

2) Since the year of 2000, the indexes of energy risk prior-warning of the coal sub-system has been significantly lower among the three sub-systems, and in 2008 it even decreased to 3.7, approaching the security state. After the substantial increasing in indexes from the year of 2001 to 2003 in the coal sub-system, they decreased steadily during 2003-2006. During 2006-2008, it fluctuated around 3.6, close to the values in 1999 and 2000.

3) As petroleum importation dependence increased since 2002, petroleum and natural gas risk prior-warning indexes were also substantially increasing. These indexes reached a peak value of 5.83 and then plateaued. Although the petroleum and natural gas security risk has not reached the danger state, it is higher than the state of a cause for concern.

4) Although the prior-warning risk indexes of the integrated sub-system were fluctuating significantly, the value of 2001 was higher than previous years. The affecting mechanism among the indexes of the sub-systems is complex and the effect still needs to be verified.

In summary, the prior-warning model of China's energy risk was established and the prior-warning indexes of the coal sub-system, petroleum and natural gas sub-system, and the integrated factors sub-system were evaluated. It was found that although the energy risk related to coal is under control, the risks associated with other types of energy sources are not yet satisfactorily managed. The results are important to consider for policy makers to achieve sustainable growth of China's economy and related issues. Proper evaluation model of the energy risk for entire China will be established in future research.

ACKNOWLEDGMENT

The financial support from China Lixin Risk Management Research Institute 2008 Open Project(NO. TSFZLXKF2007-2).

REFERENCES

Goto, M. (1995). Macroeconomic and sectoral impacts of carbon taxation. *Energy Economics, 17*(4), 277–292. doi:10.1016/0140-9883(95)00021-L

Huntington, H. G., & Brown, S. P. A. (2002). Energy security and global climate change mitigation. *Energy Policy, 32*, 715–718. doi:10.1016/S0301-4215(03)00105-8

Richels, R., & Sturm, P. (1996). The costs of CO_2 emission reductions. *Energy Policy, 24*(10), 875–887. doi:10.1016/S0301-4215(96)00083-3

Wang, H. M., & Chen, B. S. (1996). The basic framework of prior index system of coal industry. [In Chinese]. *Journal of China Coal Economic College, 4*, 10–13.

Wang, L. M. (2002). The effect factors and evaluation indexes of resource safety. [In Chinese]. *Journal of Natural Resources, 4*, 401–408.

Wu, W. S. (2002). The research of safety evaluation and prior-warning to China's petroleum resource. *Geological Techno economic Management, 5*, 13-18. (In Chinese)

ADDITIONAL READING

Chang, H. J. (2003). New horizons for Korean energy industry-shifting paradigms and challenges ahead. *Energy Policy, 31*, 1073–1084. doi:10.1016/S0301-4215(02)00213-6

Chi, C. J. (2006). Prior-warning research on energy security. *Statistics and decision, 11*, 9-31.

Edward, S., & John, F. (2001). Holistic Environmental Assessment and Offshore Oil Field Exploration and Production. *Marine Pollution Bulletin, 42*(1), 45–58. doi:10.1016/S0025-326X(00)00115-6

Franco, R. (2004). The risks of the nuclear policies. *Energy Policy, 26*(3), 239–246.

Guo, X. Z., & Duan, Z. F. (2005). China energy security multi-objective and multi-factor inspecting prior-warning system. *Natural Resource Economics of China, 2*, 13–15.

He, Y. Q., Lao, G. H., & Osuch, C. E. (2008). Co-integration based analysis of energy assurance of steady economic growth in China. *Journal of China Univ. of Mining and Tech., 18*(2), 250–254. doi:10.1016/S1006-1266(08)60053-X

He, Y. Q., Wei, H., Wang, S. Z., et al. (2008). Assessment and prediction model of china's energy assurance sustainability. *The 2nd international conference on bioinformatics and biomedical engineering.*

Li, J. Z. (2007). The establishment of China's energy prior-warning model and indexes. [Edition of Natural Science]. *Journal of China University of Petroleum, 6*, 161–166.

Wang, L. M. (2002). The effect factors and evaluation indexes of resource safety. [In Chinese]. *Journal of Natural Resources, 4*, 401–408.

Wu, W. S. (2002). The research of safety evaluation and warning to China's petroleum resource. [In Chinese]. *Geological Technoeconomic Management, 5*, 13–18.

KEY TERMS AND DEFINITIONS

Index System: This refers to the organization that is consisted of several interrelated statistical indicators.

Energy Risk: The challenges associated with different kinds of energies, such as coal, petroleum, natural gas and so on.

Fuzzy Synthesis Evaluation: It means to carry out an overall and comprehensive non-deterministic evaluation of objects according to multiple indicators.

Entropy Weight: Entropy mainly refers to a precise measure of the amount of disorder. Weight mainly refers to the relative important degree of one indicator in the overall evaluation. Entropy Weight is an objective weighting method. It has been widely used in the field of physics and economics.

Matrix: A rectangular array of elements (or entries) set out by rows and columns.

Energy Economic Issue: It means the issue that is closed related to the economic of energy.

New Energy: It is also known as non-conventional energy. It refers to all types of energy forms that are not the traditional energy. Some types of new energy include solar enegy, geothermal energy, wind energy, ocean energy, biomass and fusion energy, etc.

Empirical Analysis: It means that the conclusions will be obtained according to the previous typical examples. Then the issues will be analyzed further based on the examples.

GDP: Gross Domestic Product.

Chapter 27
A Novel Flowsheet for the Recycling of Valuable Constituents from Waste Printed Circuit Boards

Jingfeng He
China University of Mining and Technology, China

Yaqun He
China University of Mining and Technology, China

Nianxin Zhou
China University of Mining and Technology, China

Chenlong Duan
China University of Mining and Technology, China

Shuai Wang
China University of Mining and Technology, China

Hongjian Zhang
China University of Mining and Technology, China

ABSTRACT

Waste printed circuit boards (PCBs) contain a number of valuable constituents. It is of great significance to separate precious metals and non-metallic constituents from waste PCBs with appropriate methods for resource recycling and environment protection. A novel flowsheet for the recycling of waste PCBs using physical beneficiation methods was constructed. Waste PCBs were disassembled into substrates and slots firstly. The substrates were crushed to the size below 1mm through wet impact crushing and separated with a tapered column separation bed. The results indicated that products with integrated separation efficiency of 93.9% and metal recovery ratio of 93.7% were obtained by the primary separation with the water discharge of 5.5 m³/h, feed-rate of 250g/min and inclination angle of 35°. Waste PCBs slots components were crushed to the size of 0.5-5mm through impact crushing and separated

DOI: 10.4018/978-1-60960-064-8.ch027

with an active pulsing air classifier. The separation results showed that products with integration separation efficiency of 92.4% and metal recovery ratio of 96.2% were obtained with the airflow velocity of 2.90m/s and pulsing frequency of 2.33Hz. Precious metals could be obtained by further separation and purification of the metal components and the non-metal components could be used as refuse derived fuel. The flowsheet has great potential to be applied in the field of waste PCBs treatment and recycling.

INTRODUCTION

As more and more electronic waste is generated around the world with the continuous development of electronics industry, recycling and reuse of electronic waste has been recognized as a great challenge. Obsolete electronic equipments contain a large amount of metal, glass, plastics and other materials. Waste printed circuit boards (PCB) are common e-waste. How to achieve the reuse of waste PCBs is an important topic in the field of environment protection and resource recycling.

Waste PCBs contain metallic elements such as Cu, Pb, Sn, Ni, Fe, Al, Cd, Be, Pd, etc., including the precious metals Ag, Au, etc. On the one hand, a number of toxic and hazardous metal components, such as Pb, Cd, Pd, etc., exist in the waste PCBs in multiple existing states. These heavy metals may cause serious environment pollution. On the other hand, wastes PCBs are rich in numerous valuable constituents and have high value for recycling. Therefore, separating the hazardous components from e-waste and recycling valuable constituents would be of significant importance.

Substantial studies have been done and reported in literature. A number of processing methods were applied to recycle waste PCBs. Zhang et al. (1998) recovered aluminum from waste PCBs with an eddy current high-pressure separator and also recycled metal-rich components of PCBs by electric separation. Araujo & Chaves (2008) recovered valuable materials from discarded cables with a dense medium separator and electric separators. Au, Ag and other kinds of precious metals were extracted from waste PCBs by chemical methods (Young & Derek, 2009). William & Paul (2007) recovered valuable constituents from the PCBs of discarded computers, televisions, mobile phones,

etc., by high temperature pyrolytic cracking. Cui & Eric (2007) invented a dry separation method for recovering valuable metals from PCBs. It was based on new equipment named pneumatic table.

In conclusion, the common recycling technologies of waste PCBs are hydrometallurgy, pyrometallurgy, mechanical recycling process or in conjunction with above methods (He et al., 2006). For the recycling of PCBs, hydrometallurgy processes are used for recycling precious metals with higher grade and recovery, such as gold, silver and non-ferrous metals such as copper and zinc, but the residual leaching in waste water may cause more serious secondary pollution. Pyrometallurgy is another feasible method for e-waste recycling. However, this method suffers from the loss of valuable resources and the emission of fugitive odor and dust as it generates volatile metallic components. (He et al., 2006). Mechanical recycling processes include dismantling, shredding, classification and separation (Zhao et al., 2006). Compared with hydrometallurgy and pyrometallurgy, mechanical processes are geared towards better environmental protection, lower cost, higher material recovery and easier industrialization. In addition, the metals after separation could be concentrated again by purification. The mechanical recycling processes of PCBs can achieve full constituent recovery including ferrous metals, non-ferrous metals, precious metals, and organic substances in PCBs (Duan, 2007). Therefore, the mechanical recycling processes gradually dominate the reutilization of waste PCBs (Vetri et al., 2007; Eswaraiah et al., 2008).

As mentioned above, several latest research achievements have been listed and summarized. Despite these achievements, however, the existing methods have several disadvantages, such as their complicated processing method, difficulty in operation, high cost, serious pollution, etc. Therefore, it is necessary and important to establish improved flowsheet to overcome these problems.

In this work, a fundamental study has been carried out on the mechanical recycling processes. A novel beneficiation flowsheet was developed to recover valuable metal constituents and non-metallic constituents from waste PCBs. The size-classification method of wet impact crushing has been applied to control the pollution caused by fugitive dust and odor. The tapered column separation bed and the active pulsing air classifier have been used to achieve the effective classification of materials with different particle size distribution. The experiment indicated that both metal and non-metal constituents could be recovered and recycled efficiently with this novel flowsheet.

EXPERIMENT RESEARCH OF WASTE PCBS SUBSTRATES

Experiment Material

For the primary shredding, a self-designed double toothed roll crusher was used to crush down PCBs into 20×20mm by both compression and shearing action. For the second stage crushing, a special impact crusher was employed to achieve liberation of metals from other components contained in PCBs. The metals degree of dissociation of PCB substrates could be above 90% with particle size decreasing to the size range of below 1mm While using slippery hammerhead, the rotate speed 882r/min, flux of water 5m³/h and aperture of the sieve plate 2.2mm.

The test result of crushing productions of waste PCBs substrates is shown in Table 1. It can be seen that 96.8% of the crushed productions were distributed below 2mm, and 97.2% of the metal grade was achieved.

The productions with size below 1mm were taken as experimental raw material. With the synthesized consideration of degree of dissociation, distribution ratio of metal and technical simplification, a tapered column separation bed was used to recover metal concentration and non-metal concentration from waste PCBs.

Experiment System

The structure diagram and the actual separation system of tapered column separation bed are shown in Figure 1 and Figure 2.

Table 1. Test result of waste PCBs substrates by wet impact crushed productions

Size (mm)	Production rate		Degree of liberation (%)	Metal grade (%)	Distribution ratio (%)
	Weight ratio (%)	Positive Cumulation (%)			
-2.2+2	3.2	3.2	66.0	22.8	2.8
-2+1	11.3	14.5	70.0	44.8	19.5
-1+0.5	19.0	33.5	95.0	54.0	39.6
-0.5+0.25	13.9	47.4	100.0	38.2	20.5
-0.25+0.125	10.9	58.3	100.0	21.0	8.8
-0.125+0.074	5.5	63.8	100.0		
-0.074	36.2	3.2	100.0	6.3	8.8
Total	100.0	——	——	26.5	100.0

Figure 1. The structure diagram of tapered column separation bed

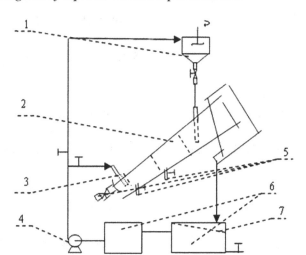

1 Beater 2 Separation bed 3 Distributor 4 Water pump

5 Discharge outlet 6 Circulation water tank 7 Filter cloth

Experiment Results

The evaluating indicators of separation include recovery rate, grade, productive rate, rich ore ratio, concentration ratio and so on. The main factors which may affect separation results include water discharge, feeding capacity and inclination angle.

The separation results of PCBs substrates below 1mm are listed in Table 2. Experimental results showed that about 93.9% integrated efficiency and 93.7% recovery rate could be achieved for PCBs of below 1mm substrates when the water discharge was 5.5m³/h, feeding capacity was 250g/min and inclination angle was 35°. Compared with other mechanical methods, the distribution of particle size was broaden using tapered column separation bed with water medium to recovery metals from PCBs, and lower limit size of separation almost approached to zero.

Figure 2. The actual separation system of tapered column separation bed

EXPERIMENT RESEARCH OF WASTE PCBS SLOTS

Experiment Material

The monomer dissociation of waste PCBs slots can be achieved in a larger size distribution, and the density differences of materials after impact crushing are comparatively large. So the crushing products can satisfy the experimental requirements of the raw materials size, density differences and liberation degree. To this end, the separation experiment for 0.5-5mm crushing products of waste PCBs slots was conducted with the active pulsing air classifier.

Table 3 Shows test result of crushing productions of waste PCBs slots. The leading particle size of slots crushing products is 0.5-5mm and takes up 92.8% of the total productions. In the crushing productions, almost all the metals distribute into the particle size of 0.5-5mm and account for 99.4%.

Experiment System

Figure 3 shows the laboratory scale system of active pulsing air separation and its main constituent elements.

①Air blast ②Flow valve ③Rotor flow meter ④Pulsing valve ⑤Separation column ⑥Screw feeder ⑦Cyclone dust collector ⑧Pipe line ⑨Electromotor ⑩Transducer

Experiment Results

According to the separation mechanism of the active pulsing air classification and the results of basic experiments, airflow velocity, pulsing frequency, feeding capacity, etc. were selected as

Table 2. Separation experimental results of PCBs substrates below 1mm

NO	Water discharge (m³/h)	Feeding Capacity (g/min)	Inclination angle (°)	Product	Grade (%)	Recovery (%)	Integration Efficiency (%)
1	3.5	200	35	Concentrate	79.0	96.3	87.2
				Tailing	1.4		
2	3.5	300	40	Concentrate	83.5	96.1	89.6
				Tailing	1.3		
3	3.5	250	30	Concentrate	74.1	97.4	84.9
				Tailing	0.9		
4	4.5	200	40	Concentrate	82.5	93.7	87.9
				Tailing	2.1		
5	4.5	300	30	Concentrate	87.9	95.8	91.8
				Tailing	1.4		
6	4.5	250	35	Concentrate	86.5	96.1	91.2
				Tailing	1.3		
7	5.5	200	30	Concentrate	90.7	94.1	92.4
				Tailing	1.9		
8	5.5	250	35	Concentrate	94.1	93.7	93.9
				Tailing	2.0		
9	5.5	300	40	Concentrate	90.1	94.1	92.1
				Tailing	1.9		

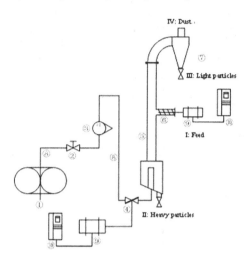

Figure 3. The laboratory scale system of active pulsing air separation

the main factors influencing separation efficiency. The relational experiments indicated the influence caused by feeding capacity was relatively smaller than the other two factors. So the airflow velocity and pulsing frequency were chosen as the leading factors of this experiment. An orthogonal test with two factors and three levels was designed and conducted in order to study the influence caused by the main factors.

Experimental results of the orthogonal test are shown in Table 4(Among which, β refers to the Concentrate Grade and θ refers to the Tailing Grade).It can be seen from the Table 4 that the highest separation efficiency of 92.4% and metal recovery ratio of 96.2% could be obtained with the airflow velocity of 2.90m/s and pulsing frequency of 2.33Hz.

A NOVEL BENEFICIATION FLOWSHEET

Based on above two basic processes to deal with waste PCBs, a novel and effective beneficiation flowsheet to recover metal concentration and non-metal concentration from PCBs was proposed. The experimental results indicated that high integration separation efficiency and metal recovery ratio could be achieved with this flowsheet. Precious metals could be obtained by further separation and purification of the metal concentration, and the non-metal concentration could be used as refuse derived fuel.

Figure 4 shows the details of this technology. Waste PCBs were disassembled into waste printed circuit boards substrates and slots firstly. Waste

Table 3. Test result of waste PCBs slots by impact crushed productions

Size (mm)	Production rate		Degree of liberation (%)	Metal grade (%)	Distribution ratio (%)
	Weight ratio	Positive Cumulation			
	(%)	(%)			
-5+2	37.5	37.5	72.0	22.8	32.9
-2+1	34.7	72.2	85.0	44.9	49.8
-1+0.5	20.6	92.8	100.0	54.0	16.7
-0.5	7.2	100.0	100.0	38.2	0.6
Total	100.0	——	——	26.5	100.0

Table 4. Experimental results of 0.5-5mm PCBs slots separation

NO	Airflow Velocity m/s	Pulsing Frequency Hz	Product Grade,%		Recovery, γ, %	Integration Efficiency, η, %
1	2.76	1.96	β 76.3	θ 2.1	96.2	89.7
2	2.76	2.14	β 79.4	θ 2.5	95.5	90.3
3	2.76	2.33	β 80.9	θ 2.3	96.0	91.3
4	2.90	1.96	β 82.4	θ 3.0	95.3	90.6
5	2.90	2.14	β 83.4	θ 3.0	95.2	91.1
6	2.90	2.33	β 84.6	θ 2.9	96.2	92.4
7	3.04	1.96	β 82.4	θ 3.4	94.2	90.2
8	3.04	2.14	β 82.8	θ 3.3	94.4	91.7
9	3.04	2.33	β 83.9	θ 2.7	95.4	92.2

Figure 4. The novel flowsheet for recycling waste PCBs

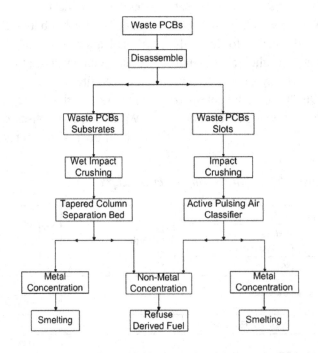

PCBs substrates were crushed to the size below 1mm through wet impact crushing and separated with a tapered column separation bed. Waste PCBs slots components were crushed to the size of 0.5-5mm through impact crushing and separated with an active pulsing air classifier.

CONCLUSION

In order to realize high-efficiency crushing and separation of waste PCBs components, and solve the problem of secondary pollution of fugitive odor and dust generated during the crushing and separation process, a wet crusher and tapered column separation bed were adopted to achieve the liberation and to obtain a complete size separation of waste PCBs constituents. The experimental results indicated that products with integrated separation efficiency of 93.9% and metal recovery ratio of 93.7% were obtained by the primary separation with the water discharge of 5.5m³/h, material feed-rate of 250g/min and inclination angle of 35°.

The effective classification of the crushing products of waste PCBs slots were realized with the active pulsing air classifier. The separation results showed that products with integrated separation efficiency of 92.4% and metal recovery ratio of 96.2% were obtained with the airflow velocity of 2.90m/s and pulsing frequency of 2.33Hz.

A novel flowsheet to recover and recycle the valuable constituents from waste PCBs was developed to realize the effective beneficiation of materials with a wide particle size distribution. The serious pollution generated by chemical treatment methods could be avoided using this physical beneficiation flowsheet. The experimental results indicate that the separation and enrichment effects were satisfactory. Therefore, the flowsheet has great potential to be applied in the field of waste PCBs treatment and recycling.

ACKNOWLEDGMENT

The financial support from Development Program of China (863 program 2007AA05Z318), China Education Ministry Key Lab Open Project (CPEUKF06-11, 08-08), Graduate Student Scientific and Technological Innovation Projects of Jiangsu Province (CX09S_006Z) and Youth Science Foundation of CUMT (2007A021).

REFERENCES

Araujo, M. C.P.Bd., & Chaves, A. P. (2008). Electronic scraps- Recovering of valuable materials from parallel wire cables. *Waste Management (New York, N.Y.)*, *28*(11), 2177–2182. doi:10.1016/j.wasman.2007.09.019

Cui, J. R., & Eric, F. (2007). Characterization of shredded television scrap and implications for materials recovery of metals from shredded television scrap. *Waste Management (New York, N.Y.)*, *27*(3), 415–424. doi:10.1016/j.wasman.2006.02.003

Duan, C. L. D. (2007). Research on comminution mechanism of discarded printed circuit boards. *China University of Mining and Technology, Xuzhou. (PhD thesis, In Chinese)*

Eswaraiah, C., Kavitha, T., & Vidyasagar, S. (2008). Classification of metals and plastics from printed circuit boards (PCB) using air classifier. *Chemical Engineering and Processing*, *47*(4), 565–576. doi:10.1016/j.cep.2006.11.010

He, W. Z., Li, G. M., & Ma, X. F. (2006). WEEE recovery strategies and the WEEE treatment status in China. *Journal of Hazardous Materials*, *136*(3), 502–512. doi:10.1016/j.jhazmat.2006.04.060

He, Y. Q., Duan, C. L., Wang, H. F., et al. (2006). Reutilization disposal of electronic scrap. *Beijing: Chemical industry press. (In Chinese)*

Vetri, M. R., Bharat, A. S., & Deshpande, P. (2008). Milling and separation of the multi-component printed circuit board materials and analysis of elutriation based on a single particle model. *Powder Technology*, *183*(2), 169–176. doi:10.1016/j.powtec.2007.07.020

William, J. H., & Paul, T. W. (2007). Separation and recovery of materials from scrap printed circuit boards. *Resources, Conservation and Recycling*, *51*(3), 691–709. doi:10.1016/j.resconrec.2006.11.010

Young, J. P., & Derek, J. F. (2009). Recovery of high purity precious metals form printed circuit boards. *Journal of Hazardous Materials*, *164*(2-3), 1152–1158. doi:10.1016/j.jhazmat.2008.09.043

Zhang, S. L., & Eric, F. (1998). Optimization of electrodynamic separation for metals recovery from electronic scraps. *Resources, Conservation and Recycling*, *22*(3-4), 143–162. doi:10.1016/S0921-3449(98)00004-4

Zhang, S. L., Eric, F., Arvidson, B., & Moss, W. (1998). Aluminum recovery from electronic scrap by High-Force eddy-current separators. *Resources, Conservation and Recycling*, *23*(4), 225–241. doi:10.1016/S0921-3449(98)00022-6

Zhao, Y. M., Wen, X. F., & Li, B. B. (2004). Recovery of copper from waste printed circuit board. *Journal of Minerals & Metallurgical Processing*, *21*(2), 99–102.

ADDITIONAL READING

Brandl, H., Bosshard, R., & Wegmann, M. (2001). Computer-munching microbes: metal leaching from electronic scrap by bacteria and fungi. *Journal of Hydrometallurgy*, *59*(2-3), 319–326. doi:10.1016/S0304-386X(00)00188-2

Cui, J. R., & Eric, F. (2003). Mechanical recycling of waste electric and electronic equipment: a review. *Journal of Hazardous Materials*, *99*(3), 243–263. doi:10.1016/S0304-3894(03)00061-X

Duan, C. L., Zhao, Y. M., & Wen, X. F. (2005). Research on the gas from pyrolysis during crushing of discarded printed circuit boards. *Journal of China University of Mining & Technology*, *34*(6), 730–734.

He, Y. Q., Duan, C. L., Wang, H. F., et al. (2006). Reutilization disposal of electronic scrap. *Beijing: Chemical industry press. (In Chinese)*

Iji, M., & Ikuta, Y. J. (1998). Pyrolysis-based Material Recovery from Molding Resin for Electronic Parts. *Journal of Environmental Engineering*, *124*, 821–828. doi:10.1061/(ASCE)0733-9372(1998)124:9(821)

Koyanaka, S., Endoh, S., & Ohya, H. (1997). Particle shape of copper milled by swing-hammer-type impact mill. *Powder Technology*, *90*(2), 135–140. doi:10.1016/S0032-5910(96)03213-5

Rubenstein & Julius. Method of processing and recovery of electronic and electric scrap. *US Patent#:5547134, 1996-08-20.*

Wen, X. F. D. (2004). Study on metals recovery from discarded printed circuit boards by physical methods. *China University of Mining and Technology, Xuzhou. (PhD thesis, In Chinese)*

Zhao, Y. M., Duan, C. L., Zhang, H. J., et al. (2008) Research on metals recycling from waste printed circuit board by mechanical processing of wet crushing and wet separation. *Proceedings of XXIV International Mineral Processing Congress, Science Press, Beijing, China, September*, 3765-3773.

Zhao, Y. M., Wang, Q. Q., & Jiao, H. G. (2005). Selectivity crushing of discarded printed circuit boards. *Journal of China University of Mining & Technology*, *34*(6), 683–687.

Zhao, Y. M., Wen, X. F., Li, B. B., et al. (2004). Recovery of copper from waste printed circuit board. *Journal of minerals & metallurgical processing, 21*(2), 99-102.

Zhao, Y. M., Wen, X. F., Li, B. B., et al. (2004). Recovery of copper from waste printed circuit board. *Journal of minerals & metallurgical processing, 21*(2), 99-102.

Zhou, L., Bai, Q. Z., & Li, J. H. (2006). Research on cryogenic comminution of discarded printed wiring boards. *Journal of China University of Mining & Technology, 35*(2), 220–224.

KEY TERMS AND DEFINITIONS

Waste Printed Circuit Boards: Typical and fundamental component for almost all electric and electronic equipment. It contains a number of metallic elements such as Cu, Pb, Sn, Ni, Fe, Al, Cd, Be, Pd, etc. including the precious metals such as Ag, Au, etc.

Wet Impact Crushing: The waste printed circuit boards are secondary crushed using the wet impacting crusher. Compared with the ways of dry crushing process for discarded PCB, wet impact crushing has the advantages of higher crushing efficiency, lower excessive crushing rate and less secondary pollution.

Tapered Column Separation Bed (TCSB): Tapered column separation bed in water medium was designed to recycle metals from WPCBs. In order to monitor the process of separation, the organic glass is used as the manufacture materials for TCSB. According to density, size of WPCBs materials, hydraulic conditions, secondary concentrate of metals from waste WPCBs, the laboratory scale TDSB with top diameter 200mm, bottom diameter 120mm, 800mm high was designed.

Active Pulsing Air Classifier: It is a type of dry classification equipment which can achieve the high-efficient separation of specific materials by density.

Metal Component: It mainly contains a number of metallic elements such as Cu, Pb, Sn, Ni, Fe, Al, Cd, Be, Pd, etc. including the precious metals such as Ag, Au, etc.

Non-Metal Concentration: Non-metal Concentration products have better combustion and mechanical characteristics than traditional fuels, materials and fillers.

Beneficiation: A separation process of particle size according to the difference in settling velocities of solid particles in the fluid medium.

Distribution Ratio: A probability distribution constructed as the ratio of two random variables having two other known distributions.

Hydrometallurgy: Extraction of metal from ore by dissolving the metal (as one of its salts) and then recovering it from the solution.

Pyrometallurgy: A branch of extractive metallurgy. It consists of the thermal treatment of minerals and metallurgical ores and concentrates to bring about physical and chemical transformations in the materials to enable recovery of valuable metals.

Eddy Current High-Pressure Separator: A kind of separation technology based on the conductivity difference of materials. The separation mechanism originates from two basic physical phenomena, which include the Faraday law of electromagnetic induction and Biot-Savart law.

Dense Medium Separator: It is a kind of separator which is mainly used in the field of mineral processing. It mainly achieves the effective separation of materials with different densities. Solid medium is used to realize the proper distribution in the suspension.

Electric Separator: The equipment which is applied in mineral processing. It is mainly based on the differences in electrifications of different materials to achieve the effective separation.

High Temperature Pyrolytic Cracking: A kind of processing which is used for the recycling of valuable constituents. According to the differences in melting points and volatility, different kinds of materials may be separated using this method.

Pneumatic Table: A type of equipment which takes the air as the medium to achieve gravity separation based on difference in densities. It has the advantages of simple structure and easy operation. It is widely used in the field of minerals separation.

Compilation of References

Abraham, M. H. (2004). The factors that influence permeation across the blood-brain barrier. *European Journal of Medicinal Chemistry*, *39*(3), 235–240. doi:10.1016/j.ejmech.2003.12.004

Abraham, M. H., Chadha, H. S., & Mitchell, R. C. (1994). Hydrogen bonding. 33. Factors that influence the distribution of solutes between blood and brain. *Journal of Pharmaceutical Sciences*, *83*(9), 1257–1268. doi:10.1002/jps.2600830915

Adams, M. W., Mortenson, L. E., & Chen, J. S. (1981). Hydrogenase. *Biochimica et Biophysica Acta*, *594*(2-3), 105–176.

ADRIANA. Code, version 1.0, Molecular Networks GmbH, Erlangen, Germany, http://www.molecular-networks.com (accessed March 2010).

Aerts, R., & Chapin, F. S. III. (2000). The mineral nutrition of wild plants revisited: a re-evaluation of processes and patterns. *Advances in Ecological Research*, *30*(1), 1–67.

Ahmed, F., Ansari, H. R., & Raghava, G. P. (2009). Prediction of guide strand of microRNAs from its sequence and secondary structure. *BMC Bioinformatics*, *10*, 105. doi:10.1186/1471-2105-10-105

Ahrens, T. (1999). Continuous mixed venous (SvO$_2$) monitoring: Too expensive or indispensable? *Critical Care Nursing Clinics of North America*, *11*(1), 33–48.

Aisawa, S., Sasaki, S., Takahashi, S., Hirahara, H., Nakayama, H., & Narita, E. (2006). Intercalation of amino acids and oligopeptides into Zn-Al layered double hydroxide by coprecipitation reaction. *Journal of Physics and Chemistry of Solids*, *67*(5-6), 920–925. doi:10.1016/j.jpcs.2006.01.004

Albert, R., DasGupta, B., Dondi, R., & Sontag, E. D. (2008). Inferring (biological) signal transduction networks via transitive reductions of directed graphs. *Algorithmica*, *51*(2), 129–159. doi:10.1007/s00453-007-9055-0

Albert, R., Jeong, H., & Barabási, A. L. (2000). Error and attack tolerance of complex networks. *Nature*, *406*(6794), 378–382. doi:10.1038/35019019

Almeida, J. S., Carrico, J. A., & Maretzek, A., Nobl,e P. A., & Fletcher, M. (2001). Analysis of genomic sequences by Chaos Game Representation. *Bioinformatics (Oxford, England)*, *17*(5), 429–437. doi:10.1093/bioinformatics/17.5.429

Altschul, S. F., Gish, W., Miller, W., Myers, E. W., & Lipman, D. J. (1990). Basic local alignment search tool. *Journal of Molecular Biology*, *215*(3), 403–410.

Altschul, S. F., Madden, T. L., Schaffer, A. A., Zhang, J., Zhang, Z., Miller, W., & Lipman, D. J. (1997). Gapped BLAST and PSI-BLAST: a new generation of protein database search programs. *Nucleic Acids Research*, *25*(17), 3389–3402. doi:10.1093/nar/25.17.3389

Ambros, V., Bartel, B., Bartel, D. P., Burge, C. B., Carrington, J. C., & Chen, X. (2003). Tuschl T: A uniform system for microRNA annotation. *RNA (New York, N.Y.)*, *9*(3), 277–279. doi:10.1261/rna.2183803

Anand, B., Gowri, V. S., & Srinivasan, N. (2005). Use of multiple profiles corresponding to a sequence alignment enables effective detection of remote homologues. *Bioinformatics (Oxford, England)*, *21*(12), 2821–2826. doi:10.1093/bioinformatics/bti432

Andreeva, A., Howorth, D., Brenner, S. E., Hubbard, T. J., Chothia, C., & Murzin, A. G. (2004). SCOP database in 2004: refinements integrate structure and sequence family data. *Nucleic Acids Research, 32*(Database issue), D226–D229. doi:10.1093/nar/gkh039

Andrews, C. W., Bennett, L., & Yu, L. X. (2000). Predicting Human Oral Bioavailability of a Compound: Development of a Novel Quantitative Structure-Bioavailability Relationship. *Pharmaceutical Research, 17*(6), 639–644. doi:10.1023/A:1007556711109

Araujo, M. C.P.Bd., & Chaves, A. P. (2008). Electronic scraps- Recovering of valuable materials from parallel wire cables. *Waste Management (New York, N.Y.), 28*(11), 2177–2182. doi:10.1016/j.wasman.2007.09.019

Arndt, S. K., Clifford, S. C., Wanek, W., Jones, H. G., & Popp, M. (2001). Physiological and morphological adaptations of the fruit tree *Ziziphus rotundifolia* in response to progressive drought stress. *Tree Physiology, 21*(11), 705–715.

Arnold, F. H., & Volkov, A. A. (1999). Directed evolution of biocatalysts. *Current Opinion in Chemical Biology, 3*(1), 54–59. doi:10.1016/S1367-5931(99)80010-6

Athanasiades, A., Clark, J. W., Ghorbel, F., & Bidani, A. (2000). An ionic current model for medullary respiratory neurons. *Journal of Computational Neuroscience, 9*(3), 237–257. doi:10.1023/A:1026583620467

Baker, P. F., Blaustei.Mp, Keynes, R. D., Manil, J., Shaw, T. I., & Steinhar.Ra. (1969). Ouabain-sensitive fluxes of sodium and potassium in squid giant axons. *Journal of Physiology-London, 200*(2), 459.

Balaban, A. T., Plavsic, D., & Randic, M. (2003). DNA invariants based on nonoverlapping triplets of nucleotide bases. *Chemical Physics Letters, 379*(1-2), 147–154. doi:10.1016/j.cplett.2003.07.019

Baldi, P., Brunak, S., Chauvin, Y., Andersen, C. A., & Nielsen, H. (2000). Assessing the accuracy of prediction algorithms for classification: an overview. *Bioinformatics (Oxford, England), 16*(5), 412–424. doi:10.1093/bioinformatics/16.5.412

Barabási, A. L., & Oltvai, Z. N. (2004). Network biology: understanding the cell's functional organization. *Nature Reviews. Genetics, 5*, 101–113. doi:10.1038/nrg1272

Bari, R., Pant, B. D., Stitt, M., & Scheible, W. R. (2006). Pho2, microrna399, and phr1 define a phosphate-signaling pathway in plants. *Plant Physiology, 141*(3), 988–999. doi:10.1104/pp.106.079707

Bar-Or, R. L., Maya, R., Segel, L. A., Alon, U., Levine, A. J., & Oren, M. (2000). Generation of oscillations by the p53-Mdm2 feedback loop: A theoretical and experimental study. *Proceedings of the National Academy of Sciences of the United States of America, 97*(21), 11250–11255. doi:10.1073/pnas.210171597

Bartel, D. (2004). MicroRNAs: genomics, biogenesis, mechanism, and function. *Cell, 116*(2), 281–297. doi:10.1016/S0092-8674(04)00045-5

Basu, S., Pan, A., Dutta, C., & Das, J. (1998). Chaos game representation of proteins. *Journal of Molecular Graphics & Modelling, 15*(5), 279–289. doi:10.1016/S1093-3263(97)00106-X

Batchelor, E., Mock, C. S., Bhan, I., Loewer, A., & Lahav, G. (2008). Recurrent Initiation: A mechanism for triggering p53 pulses in response to DNA damage. *Molecular Cell, 30*(3), 277–289. doi:10.1016/j.molcel.2008.03.016

Bauknecht, H., Zell, A., & Bayer, P. H., Levi, Wagener, M., Sadowski, J., & Gasteiger, J. (1996). Locating Biologically Active Compounds in Medium-Sized Heterogeneous Datasets by Topological Autocorrelation Vectors: Dopamine and Benzodiazepine Agonists. *Journal of Chemical Information and Computer Sciences, 36*(6), 1205–1213. doi:10.1021/ci960346m

Ben-Hur, A., & Noble, W. S. (2005). Kernel methods for predicting protein-protein interactions. *Bioinformatics (Oxford, England), 21*(Suppl 1), i38–i46. doi:10.1093/bioinformatics/bti1016

Bennett, J. M., Jones, J. W., Zur, B., & Hammond, L. C. (1986). Interactive effects of nitrogen and water stresses on the water relations of field-grown corn leaves. *Agronomy Journal, 78*(2), 273–280. doi:10.2134/agronj1986.00021962007800020012x

Berendse, F., & Aerts, R. (1987). Nitrogen-use-efficiency: a biologically meaningful definition? *Functional Ecology*, *1*(3), 293–296.

Beresford, A. P., Selick, H. E., & Tarbit, M. H. (2002). The emerging importance of predictive ADME simulation in drug discovery. *Drug Discovery Today*, *7*(2), 109–116. doi:10.1016/S1359-6446(01)02100-6

Berry, D. A., & Stangl, D. K. (2000). *Meta-Analysis in Medicine and Health Policy*. Boca Raton, FL: CRC Press.

Berryman, A. A. (1992). The origins and evolution of predator-prey theory. *Ecology*, *75*(3), 1530–1535. doi:10.2307/1940005

Binkley, D., Stape, J. L., & Ryan, M. G. (2004). Thinking about efficiency of resource use in forests. *Forest Ecology and Management*, *193*(1), 5–16. doi:10.1016/j.foreco.2004.01.019

Blaisdell, B. E. (1986). A measure of the similarity of sets of sequences not requiring sequence alignment. *Proceeding of the National Academy of Sciences of the United States of America*, *83*(14), 5155-5159.

Blake, W. J., Kæ rn, M., Cantor, C. R., & Collins, J. J. (2003). Noise in eukaryotic gene expression. *Nature*, *422*(6932), 633–637. doi:10.1038/nature01546

Blattner, C., Tobiasch, E., Litfen, M., Rahmsdorf, H. J., & Herrlich, P. (1999). DNA damage induced p53 stabilization: no indication for an involvement of p53 phosphorylation. *Oncogene*, *18*(9), 1723–1732. doi:10.1038/sj.onc.1202480

Blenkiron, C., Goldstein, L. D., Thorne, N. P., Spiteri, I., Chin, S. F., & Dunning, M. J. (2007). MicroRNA expression profiling of human breast cancer identifies new markers of tumour subtype. *Genome Biology*, *8*(10), R214. doi:10.1186/gb-2007-8-10-r214

Bock, J. R., & Gough, D. A. (2001). Predicting protein-protein interactions from primary structure. *Bioinformatics (Oxford, England)*, *17*(5), 455–460. doi:10.1093/bioinformatics/17.5.455

Bosotti, R., Locatelli, G., Healy, S., Scacheri, E., Sartori, L., & Mercurio, C. (2007). Cross platform microarray analysis for robust identification of differentially expressed genes. *BMC Bioinformatics*, *8*(Suppl 1), S5. doi:10.1186/1471-2105-8-S1-S5

Braiman, Y., Linder, J. F., & Ditto, W. L. (1995). Taming spatiotemporal chaos with disorder. *Nature*, *378*(6556), 465–467. doi:10.1038/378465a0

Branco, A., Fekete, S., & Rugolo, L. (2007). The newborn pain cry: Descriptive acoustic spectrographic analysis. *International Journal of Pediatric Otorhinolaryngology*, *1*(71), 39–46.

Bridgham, S. D., Pastor, J., McClaugherty, C. A., & Richardson, C. J. (1995). Nutrient-use efficiency: a litterfall index, a model, and a test along a nutrient-availability gradient in North Carolina peatlands. *American Naturalist*, *145*(1), 1–21. doi:10.1086/285725

Brown, A. M., Akaike, N., & Lee, K. S. (1978). The calcium conductance of neurons. *Annals of the New York Academy of Sciences*, *307*, 330–344. doi:10.1111/j.1749-6632.1978.tb41960.x

Brunel, N., Chance, F. S., Fourcaud, N., & Abbott, L. F. (2001). Effects of synaptic noise and filtering on the frequency response of spiking neurons. *Physical Review Letters*, *86*(10), 2186–2189. doi:10.1103/PhysRevLett.86.2186

Burges, C. J. C. (1998). A tutorial on Support Vector Machines for pattern recognition. *Data Mining and Knowledge Discovery*, *2*(2), 121–167. doi:10.1023/A:1009715923555

Cadwell, R. C., & Joyce, G. F. (1994). Mutagenic PCR. *PCR Methods and Applications*, *3*(6), S136–S140.

Cai, C. Z., Han, L. Y., Ji, Z. L., Chen, X., & Chen, Y. Z. (2003). SVM-Prot: Web-based support vector machine software for functional classification of a protein from its primary sequence. *Nucleic Acids Research*, *31*(13), 3692–3697. doi:10.1093/nar/gkg600

Calder, J. A., & Ganellin, C. R. (1994). Predicting the brain-penetrating capability of histaminergic compounds. *Drug Design and Discovery*, *11*(4), 259–268.

Callahan, T. K., & Knobloch, E. (1999). Pattern formation in three-dimensional reaction-diffusion systems. *Physica D. Nonlinear Phenomena, 132*(3), 339–362. doi:10.1016/S0167-2789(99)00041-X

Cantrell, R. S., & Cosner, C. (2003). *Spatial ecology via reaction-diffusion equations*. England: John Wiley & Sons Ltd.

Causton, H. C., Quackenbush, J., & Brazma, A. (2003). *Microarray gene expression data analysis: A beginner's guide*. Blackwell Science Ltd.

Cavani, F., Trifiro, F., & Vaccari, A. (1991). Hydrotalcite-type anionic clays: preparation, properties and applications. *Catalysis Today, 11*(2), 173–301. doi:10.1016/0920-5861(91)80068-K

Cerius2, ver 4.8.1, Accelrys, Inc., 10188 Telesis Court, Suite 100, San Diego, CA 92121, U.S.A.

Certo, M., Moore, V. D. G., Nishino, M., Wei, G., Korsmeyer, S., Armstrong, S. A., & Letai, A. (2006). Mitochondria primed by death signals determine cellular addiction to antiapoptotic BCL-2 family members. *Cancer Cell, 9*(5), 351–365. doi:10.1016/j.ccr.2006.03.027

Cha, T.-L., Qiu, L., Chen, C.-T., Wen, Y., & Hung, M.-C. (2005). Emodin down-regulates androgen receptor and inhibits prostate cancer cell growth. *Cancer Research, 65*(6), 2287–2295. doi:10.1158/0008-5472.CAN-04-3250

Chan, P. P., & Lowe, T. M. (2008). GtRNAdb: a database of transfer RNA genes detected in genomic sequence. *Nucleic Acids Research, 37*(Database issue), D93–D97. doi:10.1093/nar/gkn787

Chang, C. C., & Lin, C. J. (2001). *LIBSVM: a library for support vector machines*. Computer Program.

Chang, C. C., & Lin, C. J. (2001). LIBSVM: a library for support vector machine. Software available at http://www.csie.ntu.edu.tw/ ~cjlin/libsvm.

Chattopadhyay, J., & Tapaswi, P. K. (1997). Effect of cross-diffusion on pattern formation a nonlinear analysis. *Acta Applicandae Mathematicae, 48*(1), 1–12. doi:10.1023/A:1005764514684

Chay, T. R., Lee, Y. S., & Fan, Y. S. (1995). Appearance of phase-locked wenckebach-like rhythms, devil's staircase and universality in intracellular calcium spikes in non-excitable cell models. *Journal of Theoretical Biology, 174*(1), 21–44. doi:10.1006/jtbi.1995.0077

Cheadle, C., Becker, K. G., Cho-Chung, Y. S., Nesterova, M., Watkins, T., & Wood, W. III (2007). A rapid method for microarray cross platform comparisons using gene expression signatures. *Molecular and Cellular Probes, 21*(1), 35–46. doi:10.1016/j.mcp.2006.07.004

ChemSilico. CSBBB - A new Log BB Predictor; http://www.chemsilico.com/CS_ prBBB/BBBhome.html.

Chen, L., Willis, S. N., Andrew, W., Smith, B. J., Fletcher, J., & Hinds, M. G. (2005). Differential Targeting of Prosurvival Bcl-2 Proteins by Their BH3-Only Ligands Allows Complementary Apoptotic Function. *Molecular Cell, 17*(3), 393–403. doi:10.1016/j.molcel.2004.12.030

Chen, H. C., Hsieh, W. T., Chang, W. C., & Chung, J. G. (2004). Aloe-emodin induced in vitro G2/M arrest of cell cycle in human promyelocytic leukemia HL-60 cells. *Food and Chemical Toxicology, 42*(8), 1251–1257. doi:10.1016/j.fct.2004.03.002

Chen, P., & Vinals, J. (1999). Amplitude equation and pattern selection in Faraday waves. *Physical Review E: Statistical Physics, Plasmas, Fluids, and Related Interdisciplinary Topics, 60*(1), 559–570. doi:10.1103/PhysRevE.60.559

Chen, J. S., & Mortenson, L. E. (1974). Purification and properties of hydrogenase from *Clostridium pasteurianum* W5. *Biochimica et Biophysica Acta, 371*(2), 283–298.

Chen, S. P., Bai, Y. F., Zhang, L. X., & Han, X. G. (2005). Comparing physiological responses of two dominant grass species to nitrogen addition in Xilin River Basin of China. *Environmental and Experimental Botany, 53*(1), 65–75. doi:10.1016/j.envexpbot.2004.03.002

Chen, Y. N., Chen, Y. P., Li, W. H., & Zhang, H. F. (2003a). Response of the accumulation of proline in the bodies of *Populus euphratica* to the change of ground water level at the lower reaches of Tarim River. *Chinese Science Bulletin, 48*(18), 1995–1999.

Chen, Y. N., Wang, Q., Ruan, X., Li, W. H., & Chen, Y. P. (2004). Physiological response of *Populus euphratica* to artificial water recharge of the lower reaches of Tarim River. *Acta Botanica Sinica, 46*(12), 1393–1401.

Chen, L. Y. (2005). *The Development of Objective Auscultation System Using Neural Networks.* Unpublished master's theses, Feng chia University, Taiwan.

Cheng, J., & Baldi, P. (2006). A machine learning information retrieval approach to protein fold recognition. *Bioinformatics (Oxford, England), 22*(12), 1456–1463. doi:10.1093/bioinformatics/btl102

Chenna, R., Sugawara, H., Koike, T., Lopez, R., Gibson, T. J., Higgins, D. G., & Thompson, J. D. (2003). Multiple sequence alignment with the Clustal series of programs. *Nucleic Acids Research, 31*(13), 3497–3500. doi:10.1093/nar/gkg500

Chickarmane, V., Ray, A., Sauro, H. M., & Nadim, A. (2007). A Model for p53 Dynamics Triggered by DNA Damage. *SIAM Journal on Applied Dynamical Systems, 6*(1), 61–78. doi:10.1137/060653925

Chipuk, J. E., Bouchier-Hayes, L., Kuwana, T., Newmeyer, D. D., & Green, D. R. (2005). PUMA couples the nuclear and cytoplasmic proapoptotic function of p53. *Science, 309*(5741), 1732–1935. doi:10.1126/science.1114297

Chipuk, J. E., Kuwana, T., Bouchier-Hayes, L., Droin, N. M., Newmeyer, D. D., Schuler, M., & Green, D. R. (2004). Direct Activation of Bax by p53 Mediates Mitochondrial Membrane Permeabilization and Apoptosis. *Science, 303*(5660), 1010–1014. doi:10.1126/science.1092734

Choi, J. K., Choi, J. Y., Kim, D. G., Choi, D. W., Lee, K. H., & Yeom, Y. (2004). Integrative analysis of multiple gene expression profiles applied to liver cancer study. *FEBS Letters, 565*(1-3), 93–100. doi:10.1016/j.febslet.2004.03.081

Choi, J. K., Yu, U., & Kim, S. (2003). Combining multiple microarray studies and modeling interstudy variation. *Bioinformatics (Oxford, England), 19*(Suppl 1), i84–i90. doi:10.1093/bioinformatics/btg1010

Christensen, C., Thakar, J., & Albert, R. (2007). Systems-level insights into cellular regulation: inferring, analysing, and modelling intracellular networks. *IET Systems Biology, 1*(2), 61–77. doi:10.1049/iet-syb:20060071

Ciliberto, A., Novak, B., & Tyson, J. J. (2005). Steady states and oscillations in the p53/Mdm2 network. *Cell Cycle (Georgetown, Tex.), 4*(3), 488–493.

Clark, D. E. (1999). Rapid calculation of polar molecular surface area and its application to the prediction of transport phenomena. 2. Prediction of blood-brain barrier penetration. *Journal of Pharmaceutical Sciences, 88*(8), 815–821. doi:10.1021/js980402t

Cohen, J., Kim, K., & King, P. (2005). Finding gas diffusion pathways in proteins: application to O_2 and H_2 transport in CpI [Fe-Fe]-hydrogenase and the role of packing defects. *Structure (London, England), 13*(9), 1321–1329. doi:10.1016/j.str.2005.05.013

Conlon, E., Song, J., & Liu, A. (2007). Bayesian meta-analysis models for microarray data: a comparative study. *BMC Bioinformatics, 8*(80).

CORINA. Molecular Networks GmbH, Erlangen, Germany, http://www.molecular-networks.com (accessed March 2010).

Cortes, C., & Vapnik, V. (1995). Support-Vector Networks. *Machine Learning, 20*(3), 273–297. doi:10.1007/BF00994018

Cortés, S. M., Rodríguez, F. V., Sánchez, P. I., & Perona, R. (2008). The role of the NFkappaB signalling pathway in cancers. *Clinical & Translational Oncology, 10*(3), 143–147. doi:10.1007/s12094-008-0171-3

Cui, J., Han, L. Y., Li, H., Ung, C. Y., Tang, Z. Q., & Zheng, C. J. (2007). Computer prediction of allergen proteins from sequence-derived protein structural and physicochemical properties. *Molecular Immunology, 44*(4), 514–520. doi:10.1016/j.molimm.2006.02.010

Cui, J. R., & Eric, F. (2007). Characterization of shredded television scrap and implications for materials recovery of metals from shredded television scrap. *Waste Management (New York, N.Y.)*, *27*(3), 415–424. doi:10.1016/j.wasman.2006.02.003

Cuthbertson, K. S. R., & Chay, T. R. C. (1991). Modelling receptor-controlled intracellular calcium oscillators. *Cell Calcium*, *12*(2-3), 97–108. doi:10.1016/0143-4160(91)90012-4

Cygan, R. T., Liang, J. J., & Kalinichev, A. G. (2004). Molecular models of hydroxide, oxyhydroxide, and clay phases and the development of a general force field. *The Journal of Physical Chemistry B*, *108*(4), 1255–1266. doi:10.1021/jp0363287

Damesin, C., & Lelarge, C. (2003). Carbon isotope composition of current year shoots from *Fagus sylvatica* in relation to growth, respiration and use of reserves. *Plant, Cell & Environment*, *26*(2), 207–219. doi:10.1046/j.1365-3040.2003.00951.x

De Silva, E., & Stumpf, M. P. H. (2005). Complex networks and simple models in biology. *Journal of the Royal Society, Interface*, *2*(5), 419–430. doi:10.1098/rsif.2005.0067

Debanne, D. (2004). Information processing in the axon. *Nature Reviews. Neuroscience*, *5*, 303–316. doi:10.1038/nrn1397

Dennis, G., Sherman, B. T., Hosack, D. A., Yang, J., Gao, W., Lane, H. C., & Lempicki, R. A. (2003). DAVID: Database for Annotation, Visualization, and Integrated Discovery. *Genome Biology*, *4*(5), 3. doi:10.1186/gb-2003-4-5-p3

Denoeux, T. (1995). A k-nearest neighbor classification rule based on Dempster-Shafer theory. *IEEE Transactions on Systems, Man, and Cybernetics*, *25*(5), 804–813. doi:10.1109/21.376493

Derjean, D., Bertrand, S., Le Masson, G., Landry, M., Morisset, V., & Nagy, F. (2003). Dynamic balance of metabotropic inputs causes dorsal horn neurons to switch functional states. *Nature Neuroscience*, *6*(3), 274–281. doi:10.1038/nn1016

Deschavanne, P. J., Giron, A., Vilain, J., Fagot, G., & Fertil, B. (1999). Genomic Signature: Characterization and Classification of Species Assessed by Chaos Game Representation of Sequences. *Molecular Biology and Evolution*, *16*(10), 1391–1399.

Dickson, B. J. (2002). Molecular mechanisms of axon guidance. *Science*, *298*(5600), 1959–1964. doi:10.1126/science.1072165

Diggle, A. J. (1988). Rootmap: a model in three-dimensional coordinates of the growth and structure of fibrous root systems. *Plant and Soil*, *105*(2), 169–178. doi:10.1007/BF02376780

Ding, C. H., & Dubchak, I. (2001). Multi-class protein fold recognition using support vector machines and neural networks. *Bioinformatics (Oxford, England)*, *17*(4), 349–358. doi:10.1093/bioinformatics/17.4.349

Dirksen, C., Kool, J. B., & Koorevaar, P. (1993). *Simulation model of hysteretic water and solute transport in the root zone* (pp. 99–122). Berlin: Springer-Verlag.

Dirksen, C., & Augustijn, D. C. (1988). Root water uptake function for nonuniform pressure and osmotic potentials. *Agric.*, (abstract), (pp. 188).

Dogu, Y., & Díaz, J. (2009). Mathematical model of a network of interaction between p53 and Bcl-2 during genotoxic-induced apoptosis. *Biophysical Chemistry*, *143*(1-2), 44–54. doi:10.1016/j.bpc.2009.03.012

Dowling, T. E., Moritz, C., Palmer, J. D., & Rieseber, L. H. (1996). *Nucleic acids III: analysis of fragments and restriction sites*. Sunderland, Mass.: Sinauer.

Duan, C. L. D. (2007). Research on comminution mechanism of discarded printed circuit boards. *China University of Mining and Technology, Xuzhou*. (PhD thesis, In Chinese)

Dubchak, I., Muchnik, I., Holbrook, S. R., & Kim, S. H. (1995). Prediction of protein folding class using global description of amino acid sequence. *Proceedings of the National Academy of Sciences of the United States of America*, *92*(19), 8700–8704. doi:10.1073/pnas.92.19.8700

Dubchak, I., Muchnik, I., Mayor, C., Dralyuk, I., & Kim, S. H. (1999). Recognition of a protein fold in the context of the Structural Classification of Proteins (SCOP) classification. *Proteins*, *35*(4), 401–407. doi:10.1002/(SICI)1097-0134(19990601)35:4<401::AID-PROT3>3.0.CO;2-K

Dufiet, V., & Boissonade, J. (1996). Dynamics of Turing pattern monolayers close to onset. *Physical Review E: Statistical Physics, Plasmas, Fluids, and Related Interdisciplinary Topics*, *53*(5), 4883–4892. doi:10.1103/PhysRevE.53.4883

Dupont, G., Abou-Lovergne, A., & Combettes, L. (2008). Stochastic aspects of oscillatory Ca^{2+} dynamics in hepatocytes. *Biophysical Journal*, *95*(5), 2193–2202. doi:10.1529/biophysj.108.133777

Edelman, E., Porrello, A., Guinney, J., Balakumaran, B., Bild, A., Febbo, P. G., & Mukherjee, S. (2006). Analysis of sample set enrichment scores: assaying the enrichment of sets of genes for individual samples in genome-wide expression profiles. *Bioinformatics (Oxford, England)*, *22*(14), 108–116. doi:10.1093/bioinformatics/btl231

Edelman, E. J., Guinney, J., Chi, J. T., Febbo, P. G., & Mukherjee, S. (2008). Modeling cancer progression via pathway dependencies. *PLoS Computational Biology.*. doi:10.1371/journal.pcbi.0040028

Egger, L., Madden, D. T., Rheme, C., Rao, R. V., & Bredesen, D. E. (2007). Endoplasmic reticulum stress-induced cell death mediated by the proteosome. *Cell Death and Differentiation*, *14*(6), 1172–1180. doi:10.1038/sj.cdd.4402125

Egger, L., Schneider, J., Rheme, C., Tapernoux, M., Hacki, J., & Borner, C. (2003). Serine proteases mediate apoptosis-like cell death and phagocytosis under caspase-inhibiting conditions. *Cell Death and Differentiation*, *10*(10), 1188–1203. doi:10.1038/sj.cdd.4401288

Ehleringer, J. R., Phillips, S. L., & Comstock, J. P. (1992). Seasonal variation in the carbon isotope composition of desert plants. *Functional Ecology*, *6*(3), 396–404. doi:10.2307/2389277

Eißing, T., Allgower, F., & Bullinger, E. (2005). Robustness properties of apoptosis models with respect to parameter variations and intrinsic noise. *IEE Proc-Systems Biology*, *152*(4), 221–228. doi:10.1049/ip-syb:20050046

Elowitz, M. B., Levine, A. J., Siggia, E. D., & Swain, P. S. (2002). Stochastic gene expression in a single cell. *Science*, *297*(5584), 1183–1186. doi:10.1126/science.1070919

Ertl, P., Rohde, B., & Selzer, P. (2000). Fast calculation of molecular polar surface area as a sum of fragment-based contributions and its application to the prediction of drug transport properties. *Journal of Medicinal Chemistry*, *43*(21), 3714–3717. doi:10.1021/jm000942e

Eswaraiah, C., Kavitha, T., & Vidyasagar, S. (2008). Classification of metals and plastics from printed circuit boards (PCB) using air classifier. *Chemical Engineering and Processing*, *47*(4), 565–576. doi:10.1016/j.cep.2006.11.010

Evan, G. I. (2008). The Ever-Lengthening Arm of p53. *Cancer Cell*, *14*(2), 108–110. doi:10.1016/j.ccr.2008.07.012

Factor, V., Oliver, A. L., Panta, G. R., Thorgeirsson, S. S., Sonenshein, G. E., & Arsura, M. (2001). Roles of Akt/PKB and IKK complex in constitutive induction of NF-kappaB in hepatocellular carcinomas of transforming growth factor alpha/c-myc transgenic mice. *Hepatology (Baltimore, Md.)*, *34*(1), 32–41. doi:10.1053/jhep.2001.25270

Fakotakis, N., & Sirigos, J. (1996). *A high performance text independent speaker recognition system based on Vowel Sotting and Neural Nets.* Paper presented at 1996 IEEE International Conference on Acoustics, Speech, and Signal Processing, Atlanta.

Falcke, M. (2004). Reading the patterns in living cells - the physics of Ca^{2+} signaling. *Advances in Physics*, *53*(3), 255–440. doi:10.1080/00018730410001703159

Farquhar, G. D., Ehleringer, J. R., & Hubick, K. T. (1989). Carbon isotope discrimination and photosynthesis. *Annual Review of Plant Physiology and Plant Molecular Biology*, *40*(6), 503–537. doi:10.1146/annurev.pp.40.060189.002443

Farquhar, G. D., & Richards, R. A. (1984). Isotope composition of plant carbon correlations with water-use efficiency of wheat cultivars. *Australian Journal of Plant Physiology, 11*(6), 539–552. doi:10.1071/PP9840539

Feddes, R. A., Kowalik, P., Kolinska-Malinka, K., & Zaradny, H. (1976). Simulation of field water uptake by plants using a soil water dependent root extraction function. *Hydrol., 31*(1), 13–26. doi:10.1016/0022-1694(76)90017-2

Feddes, R. A., Kowalik, P., & Zaradny, H. (1978). *Simulation of field water use and crop yield simulation monograph series*. PUDPC, Wageningen, Simulation Monographs, (pp. 189).

Field, C., Merino, J., & Mooney, H. A. (1983). Compromises between water-use efficiency and nitrogen-use efficiency in five species of California evergreens. *Oecologia, 60*(3), 384–389. doi:10.1007/BF00376856

Fiorucci, S. B., Golebiowski, J., Cabrol-Bass, D., & Antonczak, S. (2007). DFT study of quercetin activated forms involved in antiradical, antioxidant, and prooxidant biological processes. *Journal of Agricultural and Food Chemistry, 55*(3), 903–911. doi:10.1021/jf061864s

Fiser, A., Tusnady, G. E., & Simon, I. (1994). Chaos game representation of protein structures. *Journal of Molecular Graphics, 12*(4), 302–304. doi:10.1016/0263-7855(94)80109-6

Frisch, M. J., et al. (2004). *Gaussian 03, revision B.03*. Wallingford, CT: Gaussian, Inc.

Fukai, H., Doi, S., Nomura, T., & Sato, S. (2000). Hopf bifurcations in multiple-parameter space of the Hodgkin-Huxley equations I. Global organization of bistable periodic solutions. *Biological Cybernetics, 82*(3), 215–222. doi:10.1007/s004220050021

Garcia-Echeverria, C., Sellers, & W. R. (2009). Drug discovery approaches targeting the PI3K/Akt pathway in cancer. *Oncogene, 27*(41), 5511–5526. doi:10.1038/onc.2008.246

Gardner, W. R. (1960). Dynamic aspects of water availability to plants. *Soil Science, 89*(1), 63–73. doi:10.1097/00010694-196002000-00001

Garg, P., & Verma, J. (2006). In Silico Prediction of Blood Brain Barrier Permeability: An Artificial Neural Network Model. *Journal of Chemical Information and Modeling, 46*(1), 289–297. doi:10.1021/ci050303i

Garvie, M. R. (2007). Finite-difference schemes for reaction-diffusion equations modelling predator-prey interactions in matlab. *Bulletin of Mathematical Biology, 69*(3), 931–956. doi:10.1007/s11538-006-9062-3

Gasteiger, J., & Hutchings, M. G. (1984). Quantitative Models of Gas-Phase Proton Transfer Reaction Involving Alcohols, Ethers and Their Thio Analogs. Correlation Analyses Based On Residual Electronegativity and Effective Polarizability. *Journal of the American Chemical Society, 106*(22), 6489–6495. doi:10.1021/ja00334a006

Gasteiger, J., & Marsili, M. (1978). A New Method for Calculating Atomic Charges in Molecules. *Tetrahedron Letters, 19*(34), 3181–3184. doi:10.1016/S0040-4039(01)94977-9

Gasteiger, J., & Marsili, M. (1980). Iterative Partial Equalization of Orbital Electronegativity - A Rapid Access to Atomic Charges. *Tetrahedron, 36*(22), 3219–3228. doi:10.1016/0040-4020(80)80168-2

Geßler, A. (1999). *Untersuchungen zum Stickstoffhaushalt von Buchen (Fagus sylvatica) in einem stickstoff übersättigten Waldökosystem*. PhD thesis, University of Freiburg, Germany.

Geva-Zatorsky, N., Rosenfeld, N., Itzkovitz, S., Milo, R., Sigal, A., Dekel, E., Yarnitzky, T., Liron, Y., Polak, P., Lahav, G., & Alon, U. (2006). Oscillations and variability in the p53 system. *Molecular Systems Biology, 2*, 2006.0033.

Gewehr, J. E., Szugat, M., & Zimmer, R. (2007). Bio-Weka-extending the Weka framework for bioinformatics. *Bioinformatics (Oxford, England), 23*(5), 651–653. doi:10.1093/bioinformatics/btl671

Gillespie, D. T. (2007). Stochastic Simulation of Chemical Kinetics. *Annual Review of Physical Chemistry, 58*, 35–55. doi:10.1146/annurev.physchem.58.032806.104637

Ginalski, K., Pas, J., Wyrwicz, L. S., von Grotthuss, M., Bujnicki, J. M., & Rychlewski, L. (2003). ORFeus: Detection of distant homology using sequence profiles and predicted secondary structure. *Nucleic Acids Research, 31*(13), 3804–3807. doi:10.1093/nar/gkg504

Goldman, N. (1993). Nucleotide, dinucleotide and trinucleotide frequencies explain patterns observed in chaos game representations of DNA sequences. *Nucleic Acids Research, 21*(10), 2487–2491. doi:10.1093/nar/21.10.2487

Gomez, S. M., Noble, W. S., & Rzhetsky, A. (2003). Learning to predict protein-protein interactions from protein sequences. *Bioinformatics (Oxford, England), 19*(15), 1875–1881. doi:10.1093/bioinformatics/btg352

Gong, Q., Shen, W., Huang, Z. M., & Chen, Y. Y. (2000). Cases of Computer Analysis on Voice Acoustic Parameters in 896 Adults. *Journal of Audiology and Speech Pathology, 1*(8), 34–36.

Gong, Z. D., & Kang, S. Z. (2006). A 2-d model of root water uptake for single apple trees and its verification with sap flow and water content measurements. *Agricultural Water Management, 83*(2), 119–129. doi:10.1016/j.agwat.2005.10.005

Gordon, C., Woodin, D. J., Mullins, C. E., & Alexander, I. J. (1999). Effects of environmental change, including drought, on water use by competing *Calluna vulgaris* (Heather) and *Pteridium aquilinum* (bracken). *Functional Ecology, 13*(Suppl.1), 96–106. doi:10.1046/j.1365-2435.1999.00012.x

Goto, M. (1995). Macroeconomic and sectoral impacts of carbon taxation. *Energy Economics, 17*(4), 277–292. doi:10.1016/0140-9883(95)00021-L

Gray, C. T., & Gest, H. (1965). Biological formation of molecular hydrogen production. *Science, 148*(3667), 186–192. doi:10.1126/science.148.3667.186

Green, S. R., & Clothier, B. E. (1999). The root zone dynamics of water uptake by a mature apple tree. *Plant and Soil, 206*(1), 61–77. doi:10.1023/A:1004368906698

Green, S. R., Clothier, B. E., & Mcleod, D. J. (1997). The response of sap flow in apple roots to localized irrigation. *Agricultural Water Management, 33*(1), 63–78. doi:10.1016/S0378-3774(96)01277-2

Gregory, L., & Costas, D. (2000). Modeling DNA Mutation and Recombination for Directed Evolution Experiment. *Journal of Theoretical Biology, 205*(3), 483–503. doi:10.1006/jtbi.2000.2082

Gribskov, M. a. R., N. L. (1996). Use of receiver operating characteristic (ROC) analysis to evaluate sequence matching. *Computers & Chemistry, 20*(1), 25–33. doi:10.1016/S0097-8485(96)80004-0

Griffiths-Jones, S. (2004). The microRNA Registry. *Nucleic Acids Research, 32*(Database issue), D109–D111. doi:10.1093/nar/gkh023

Griffiths-Jones, S., Grocock, R. J., van Dongen, S., Bateman, A., & Enright, A. J. (2006). miRBase: microRNA sequences, targets and gene nomenclature. *Nucleic Acids Research, 34*(Database issue), D140–D144. doi:10.1093/nar/gkj112

Guenni, O., Baruch, Z., & Marín, D. (2004). Responses to drought of five Brachiaria species. II. Water relations and leaf gas exchange. *Plant and Soil, 258*(1), 249–260. doi:10.1023/B:PLSO.0000016555.53797.58

Gugumus, F. (1990). *Oxidation inhibition in organic mMaterials*. Boca Raton: CRC Press.

Gunaratne, G. H., Ouyang, Q., & Swinney, H. L. (1994). Pattern formation in the presence of symmetries. *Physical Review E: Statistical Physics, Plasmas, Fluids, and Related Interdisciplinary Topics, 50*(4), 2802–2820. doi:10.1103/PhysRevE.50.2802

Guo, X., & Gao, X. P. (2008). A novel hierarchical ensemble classifier for protein fold recognition. *Protein Engineering, Design & Selection, 21*(11), 659–664. doi:10.1093/protein/gzn045

Hall, S. D., Thummel, K. E., Watkins, P. B., Lown, K. S., Benet, L. Z., & Paine, M. F. (1999). Molecular and physical mechanisms of first pass extraction. *Drug Metabolism and Disposition: the Biological Fate of Chemicals, 27*(2), 161–166.

Halliwell, B., & Gutteridge, J. M. C. (1989). *Free radicals in biology and medicine*. Oxford: Oxford University.

Han, S., Lee, B. C., Yu, S. T., Jeong, C. S., Lee, S., & Kim, D. (2005). Fold recognition by combining profile-profile alignment and support vector machine. *Bioinformatics (Oxford, England), 21*(11), 2667–2673. doi:10.1093/bioinformatics/bti384

Hanahan, D., & Weinberg, R. A. (2000). The Hallmarks of Cancer. *Cell, 100*(1), 57–70. doi:10.1016/S0092-8674(00)81683-9

Hao, Z. Y., Yang, P. L., Liu, H. L., & Yao, C. M. (1998). Experimental investigation on root system distribution of apple tree. [in Chinese]. *Journal of China Agricultural University, 3*(1), 63–66.

Havsteen, H. B. (2002). The biochemistry and medical significance of the flavonoids. *Pharmacology & Therapeutics, 96*(2-3), 67–202. doi:10.1016/S0163-7258(02)00298-X

Hayward, R. L., Macpherson, J. S., Cummings, J., Monia, B. P., Smyth, J. F., & Jodrell, D. (2004). Enhanced oxaliplatin-induced apoptosis following antisense Bcl-xl down-regulation is p53 and Bax dependent: Genetic evidence for specificity of the antisense effect. *Molecular Cancer Therapeutics, 3*(10), 169–178.

He, C., Wang, M., Li, M., & Sun, L. (2004). Advance in chemical mimic of Fe-only hydrogenase. *Progress in Chemistry, 16*(2), 250–255.

He, Z. B., & Zhao, W. Z. (2006). Characterizing the spatial structures of riparian plant communities in the lower reaches of the Heihe River in China using geostatistical techniques. *Ecological Research, 21*(5), 551–559. doi:10.1007/s11284-006-0160-3

He, W. Z., Li, G. M., & Ma, X. F. (2006). WEEE recovery strategies and the WEEE treatment status in China. *Journal of Hazardous Materials, 136*(3), 502–512. doi:10.1016/j.jhazmat.2006.04.060

He, Y. Q., Duan, C. L., Wang, H. F., et al. (2006). Reutilization disposal of electronic scrap. *Beijing: Chemical industry press. (In Chinese)*

Helle, G., & Schleser, G. H. (2004). Beyond CO_2-fixation by Rubisco—an interpretation of C-13/C-12 variations in tree rings from novel intraseasonal studies on broadleaf trees. *Plant, Cell & Environment, 27*(3), 367–380. doi:10.1111/j.0016-8025.2003.01159.x

Helvik, S. A. Jr, S. O., & Saetrom, P. (2007). Reliable prediction of Drosha processing sites improves microRNA gene prediction. *Bioinformatics (Oxford, England), 23*(2), 142–149. doi:10.1093/bioinformatics/btl570

Herlelrath, W. N., Miller, E. E., & Gardner, W. R. (1977). Water uptake by plant: I. Divided root experiment. *Soil Science Society of America Journal, 41*(6), 1033–1038. doi:10.2136/sssaj1977.03615995004100060003x

Hertel, J., & Stadler, P. F. (2006). Hairpins in a Haystack: recognizing microRNA precursors in comparative genomics data. *Bioinformatics (Oxford, England), 22*(14), e197–e202. doi:10.1093/bioinformatics/btl257

Hibino, T. (2004). Delamination of layered double hydroxides containing amino acids. *Chemistry of Materials, 16*(25), 5482–5488. doi:10.1021/cm048842a

Higuchi, Y., Yasuoka, N., & Kakudo, M. (1987). Single crystals of hydrogenase from *Desulfovibrio vulgaris*. *Journal of Biochemistry, 262*(6), 2823–2825.

Hillel. (1976). A macroscopic scale model of water uptake by a non-uniform root system and salt movement in the soil profile. *Soil Sci., 121*(4), 242-255.

Hiremath, A. J. (2000). Photosynthetic nutrient-use efficiency in three fast-growing tropical trees with differing leaf longevities. *Tree Physiology, 20*(14), 937–944.

Hirono, S., Nakagome, I., Hirano, H., Matsushita, Y., Yoshi, F., & Moriguchi, I. (1994). Noncongeneric structure-pharmacokinetic property correlation studies using fuzzy adaptive least-squares: Oral bioavailability. *Biological & Pharmaceutical Bulletin, 17*(2), 306.

Hirose, T., & Bazzaz, F. A. (1998). Trade-off between light- and nitrogen-use efficiency in canopy photosynthesis. *Annals of Botany, 82*(2), 195–202. doi:10.1006/anbo.1998.0668

Hofacker, I. L., Fontana, W., Stadler, P. F., Bonhoeffer, S., Tacker, M., & Schuster, P. (1994). Fast folding and comparison of RNA secondary structures. *Monatshefte fur Chemie, 125*(2), 167–188. doi:10.1007/BF00818163

Homaee, M., Dirksen, C., & Feddes, R. A. (2002). Simulation of root water uptake I. Non-uniform transient salinity using different macroscopic reduction functions. *Agricultural Water Management, 57*(2), 89–109. doi:10.1016/S0378-3774(02)00072-0

Homaee, M., Feddes, R. A., & Dirksen, C. (2002). A macroscopic water extraction model for nouniform transient salinity and water stress. *Soil Science Society of America Journal, 66*(6), 1764–1772. doi:10.2136/sssaj2002.1764

Hong, F., Breitling, R., McEntee, C. W., Wittner, B. S., Nemhauser, J. L., & Chory, J. (2006). RankProd: a bioconductor package for detecting differentially expressed genes in meta-analysis. *Bioinformatics (Oxford, England), 22*(22), 2825–2827. doi:10.1093/bioinformatics/btl476

Hou, Z., Rao, T., & Xin, H. (2005). Effect of internal noise for rate oscillations during CO oxidation on Platinum surfaces. *The Journal of Chemical Physics, 122*(13), 134708. doi:10.1063/1.1874933

Hou, Z., & Xin, H. (2003). Internal noise stochastic resonance in a circadian clock system. *The Journal of Chemical Physics, 119*(22), 11508–11512. doi:10.1063/1.1624053

Hou, Z., & Xin, H. (2004). Optimal system size for mesoscopic chemical oscillations. *ChemPhysChem, 5*(3), 407–412. doi:10.1002/cphc.200300969

Hou, T. J., Wang, J. M., Zhang, W., & Xu, X. J. (2007). ADME Evaluation in Drug Discovery. 6. Can Oral Bioavailability in Humans Be Effectively Predicted by Simple Molecular Property-Based Rules? *Journal of Chemical Information and Modeling, 47*(2), 460–463. doi:10.1021/ci6003515

Hou, T. J., & Xu, X. J. (2004). Recent development and application of virtual screening in drug discovery: An overview. *Current Pharmaceutical Design, 10*(9), 1011–1033. doi:10.2174/1381612043452721

Hou, T. J., & Xu, X. J. (2003). ADME Evaluation in Drug Discovery. 3. Modeling Blood-Brain Barrier Partitioning Using Simple Molecular Descriptors. *Journal of Chemical Information and Computer Sciences, 43*(6), 766–770. doi:10.1021/ci034134i

Hou, L. Z., Han, D. M., Xu, W., & Zhang, L. (2002). Study on voice characteristics of people with different sexes and ages. *Journal of Clinical Otorhinolaryngology, 1*(16), 667–669.

Hu, Z., Mellor. J., Yamada, T., Holloway, D., & Delisi, C. (2005). VisANT: data-integrating visual framework for biological networks and modules. *Nucleic Acids Research, 33*(Web Server issue), W352–357.

Hu, Z., Mellor. J., Yamada, T., Holloway, D., & Delisi, C. (2007). VisANT 3.0: new modules for pathway visualization, editing, prediction and construction. *Nucleic Acids Research, 35*(Web Server issue), W625–632.

Hua, Y. J., & Xiao, H. S. (2005). Progresses on the microRNA study. [in Chinese]. *Chinese Bulletin of Life Sciences, 17*(3), 5–8.

Huang, C. D., Lin, C. T., & Pal, N. R. (2003). Hierarchical learning architecture with automatic feature selection for multiclass protein fold classification. *IEEE Transactions on Nanobioscience, 2*(4), 221–232. doi:10.1109/TNB.2003.820284

Huang, J., & Jing, Z. (2009). Bifurcations and chaos in three-well duffing system with one external forcing. *Chaos, Solitons, and Fractals, 40*(3), 1449–1466. doi:10.1016/j.chaos.2007.09.045

Huntington, H. G., & Brown, S. P. A. (2002). Energy security and global climate change mitigation. *Energy Policy*, *32*, 715–718. doi:10.1016/S0301-4215(03)00105-8

Huson, D. H., & Bryant, D. (2006). Application of Phylogenetic Networks in Evolutionary Studies, *Mol. Biol. Evo.*, *23*(2), 254-267. *Software*: http://www.splitstree.org.

Hutter, M. C. (2003). Prediction of blood-brain barrier permeation using quantum chemically derived information. *Journal of Computer-Aided Molecular Design*, *17*(7), 415–433. doi:10.1023/A:1027359714663

Ipsen, M., Hynne, F., & Sørensen, P. G. (1998). Systematic derivation of amplitude equations and normal forms for dynamical systems. *Chaos (Woodbury, N.Y.)*, *8*(4), 834–852. doi:10.1063/1.166370

Ipsen, M., Hynne, F., & Sørensen, P. G. (2000). Amplitude equations for reaction--diffusion systems with a Hopf bifurcation and slow real modes. *Physica D. Nonlinear Phenomena*, *136*(1-2), 66–92. doi:10.1016/S0167-2789(99)00149-9

Ivlev, V. (1961). *Experimental ecology of the feeding fishes*. New Haven: Yale University Press.

Iyer, M., Mishru, R., Han, Y., & Hopfinger, A. J. (2002). Predicting blood-brain barrier partitioning of organic molecules using membrane-interaction QSAR analysis. *Pharmaceutical Research*, *19*(11), 1611–1621. doi:10.1023/A:1020792909928

Izhikevich, E. M. (2000). Neural excitability, spiking and bursting. *International Journal of Bifurcation and Chaos in Applied Sciences and Engineering*, *10*(6), 1171–1266. doi:10.1142/S0218127400000840

Jacek, M. (1992). *Introduction to Artificial Neural Systems*. Chicago, US: West Publishing Company.

Jaroszewski, L., Rychlewski, L., Li, Z., Li, W., & Godzik, A. (2005). FFAS03: a server for profile--profile sequence alignments. Nucleic Acids Res, 33(Web Server issue), W284-288.

Jeffrey, H. J. (1990). Chaos game representation of gene structure. *Nucleic Acids Research*, *18*(18), 2163–2170. doi:10.1093/nar/18.8.2163

Jeong, H., Tombor, B., Albert, R., Oltvai, Z. N., & Barabási, A. L. (2000). The large-scale organization of metabolic networks. *Nature*, *407*(6804), 651–654. doi:10.1038/35036627

Ji, L., & Li, Q. (2004). Effect of spatiotemporal perturbation on Turing pattern formation. *Physics Letters. [Part A]*, *329*(4-5), 309–317. doi:10.1016/j.physleta.2004.07.012

Ji, L., Xu, W., & Li, Q. (2009). The influence of environmental noise on circadian gene expression in Drosophila. *Applied Mathematical Modelling*, *33*(4), 2109–2113. doi:10.1016/j.apm.2008.05.012

Ji, L., Xu, W., & Li, Q. (2008). Noise effect on intracellular calcium oscillations in a model with delayed coupling. *Fluct. noise lett.*, *8*(1), L1-L9.

Jiang, T., Xu, Y., & Zhang, M. (2002). *Current topics computation molecular biology*. Beijing: Tsinghua University Press.

Jiang P., Wu H. N., Wang W. K., Ma W., Sun X., & Lu, Z. H. (2007). MiPred: classification of real and pseudo microRNA precursors using random forest prediction model with combined features. *Nucleic Acids Research*, *35*(Web Server issue), W339-W344.

Jobes, D. R., & Nicolson, S. C. (1988). Monitoring of arterial hemoglobin oxygen saturation using a tongue sensor. *Anesthesia and Analgesia*, *67*(2), 186–188. doi:10.1213/00000539-198802000-00014

Jones, D. T. (1999). Protein secondary structure prediction based on position-specific scoring matrices. *Journal of Molecular Biology*, *292*(2), 195–202. doi:10.1006/jmbi.1999.3091

Jones, D. T., Taylor, W. R., & Thornton, J. M. (1992). A new approach to protein fold recognition. *Nature*, *358*(6381), 86–89. doi:10.1038/358086a0

Joseph, J., & Sasikumar, R. (2006). Chaos game representation for comparision of whole genomes. *BMC Bioinformatics, 7*(243), 1–10.

Kachi, N., & Hirose, T. (1983). Limiting nutrients for plant growth in coastal sand dune soils. *Journal of Ecology, 71*(6), 937–944. doi:10.2307/2259603

Kæser, M. D., & Iggo, R. D. (2002). Chromatin immunoprecipitation analysis fails to support the latency model for regulation of p53 DNA binding activity in vivo. *Proceedings of National Academic Sciences of the United States of America, 99*(1), 95–100.

Kaliszan, R., & Markuszewski, M. (1996). Brain/blood distribution described by a combination of partition coefficient and molecular mass. *International Journal of Pharmaceutics, 145*(1-2), 9–16. doi:10.1016/S0378-5173(96)04712-6

Kanehisha Laboratories. (2009). Axon guidance - Homo sapiens (human), *KEGG PATHWAY*, Retrieved May 20, 2009, from http://www.genome.jp/kegg/ pathway/hsa/ hsa04360.html.

Kang, S. Z., Liu, X. M., & Xiong, Y. Z. (1992). Research on the model of water uptake by winter wheat root system. [in Chinese]. *Acta University Agricultural Boreali-occidentalis, 20*(1), 5–12.

Karchin, R., Karplus, K., & Haussler, D. (2002). Classifying G-protein coupled receptors with support vector machines. *Bioinformatics (Oxford, England), 18*(1), 147–159. doi:10.1093/bioinformatics/18.1.147

Karlin, S., Mrazek, J., & Campbell, A. M. (1997). Compositional biases of bacterial genomes and evolutionary implications. *Journal of Bacteriology, 179*(12), 3899–3913.

Kataoka, N., Miya, A., & Kiriyama, K. (1997). Studies on hydrogen production by continuous culture systerm of hydrogen-producing anaerobic bacteria. *Water Science and Technology, 36*(6-7), 41–47. doi:10.1016/S0273-1223(97)00505-2

Katul, G., Todd, P., & Pataki, D. (1997). Soil water depletion by oak trees and the influence of root water uptake on the moisture content spatial statistics. *Water Resources Research, 33*(4), 611–623. doi:10.1029/96WR03978

Kawanishi, T., Blank, L. M., Harootunian, A. T., Smith, M. T., & Tsien, R. Y. (1989). Ca^{2+} oscillations induced by hormonal stimulation of individual fura-2-loaded hepatocytes. *The Journal of Biological Chemistry, 264*(22), 12859–12866.

Kawashima, S., & Kanehisa, M. (2000). AAindex: amino acid index database. *Nucleic Acids Research, 28*(1), 374. doi:10.1093/nar/28.1.374

Kelley, L. A., MacCallum, R. M., & Sternberg, M. J. (2000). Enhanced genome annotation using structural profiles in the program 3D-PSSM. *Journal of Molecular Biology, 299*(2), 499–520. doi:10.1006/jmbi.2000.3741

Kelley, L. A., MacCallum, R. M., & Sternberg, M. J. (2000). Enhanced genome annotation using structural profiles in the program 3D-PSSM. *Journal of Molecular Biology, 299*(2), 499–520. doi:10.1006/jmbi.2000.3741

Kendall, B. E. (2001). Cycles, chaos, and noise in predator-prey dynamics. *Chaos, Solitons, and Fractals, 12*(2), 321–332. doi:10.1016/S0960-0779(00)00180-6

Kim, J., Chu, J., Shen, X., Wang, J., & Orkin, S. H. (2008). An extended transcriptional network for pluripotency of embryonic stem cells. *Cell, 132*(6), 1049–1061. doi:10.1016/j.cell.2008.02.039

Kim, S. H., Ryoo, D. W., & Bae, C. (2007). Adaptive Noise Cancellation Using Accelerometers for the PPG Signal from Forehead. *Conference Proceedings;... Annual International Conference of the IEEE Engineering in Medicine and Biology Society. IEEE Engineering in Medicine and Biology Society. Conference*, 2564–2567.

Klein, E., & Lukes, V. (2006). DFT/B3LYP study of the substituent effect on the reaction enthalpies of the individual steps of single electron transfer-proton transfer and sequential proton loss electron transfer mechanisms of phenols antioxidant action. *The Journal of Physical Chemistry A, 110*(44), 12312–12320. doi:10.1021/jp063468i

Kohn, K. (1999). Molecular interaction map of the mammalian cell cycle control and DNA repair systems. *Molecular Biology of the Cell, 10*(8), 2703–2734.

Konishi, T., Sasaki, S., Watanabe, T., Kitayama, J., & Nagawa, H. (2006). Overexpression of hRFI inhibits 5-fluorouracil-induced apoptosis in colorectal cancer cells via activation of NF-kB and upregulation of BCL-2 and BCL-XL. *Oncogene, 25*(22), 3160–3169. doi:10.1038/sj.onc.1209342

Korn, G. A., & Wait, J. V. (1978). *Didital Continuous System Simulation*. Englewood Cliffs, NJ: Prentice Hall.

Körner, C., Farquhar, G. D., & Roksandic, Z. (1988). A global survey of carbon isotope discrimination in plants from high altitude. *Oecologia, 74*(4), 623–632. doi:10.1007/BF00380063

Koyama, M., Takahashi, K., Chou, T.-C., Darzynkiewicz, Z., Kapuscinski, J., Kelly, T. R., & Watanabe, K. A. (1989). Intercalating agents with covalent bond forming capability. A novel type of potential anticancer agents. 2. Derivatives of chrysophanol and emodin. *Journal of Medicinal Chemistry, 32*(7), 1594–1599. doi:10.1021/jm00127a032

Kuang, Y., & Beretta, E. (1998). Global qualitative analysis of a ratio-dependent predator-prey system. *Journal of Mathematical Biology, 36*(4), 389–406. doi:10.1007/s002850050105

Kumar, P. P., Kalinichev, A. G., & Kirkpatrick, R. J. (2007). Molecular dynamics simulation of the energetics and structure of layered double hydroxides intercalated with carboxylic acids. *The Journal of Physical Chemistry C, 111*(36), 13517–13523. doi:10.1021/jp0732054

Kumar, P. P., Kalinichev, A. G., Kirkpatrick, R. J., & James, R. (2006). Hydration, swelling, interlayer structure, and hydrogen bonding in organolayered double hydroxides: insights from molecular dynamics simulation of citrate-intercalated hydrotalcite. *The Journal of Physical Chemistry B, 110*(9), 3841–3844. doi:10.1021/jp057069j

Kwoha, C. K., & Ng, P. Y. (2007). Network analysis approach for biology. *Cellular and Molecular Life Sciences, 64*(14), 1739–1751.

Kyriacou, P. A. (2006). Pulse oximetry in the oesophagus. *Physiological Measurement, 27*(1), 1–35. doi:10.1088/0967-3334/27/1/R01

Kyriacou, P. A., Powell, S. L., Jones, D. P., & Langford, R. M. (2002). Esophageal pulse oximetry utilizing reflectance photoplethysmography. *IEEE Transactions on Biomedical Engineering, 49*(11), 1360–1368. doi:10.1109/TBME.2002.804584

Kyriacou, P. A., Powell, S. L., Jones, D. P., & Langford, R. M. (2003). Evaluation of esophageal pulse oximetry in patients undergoing cardiothoracic surgery. *Anaesthesia, 58*(5), 422–427. doi:10.1046/j.1365-2044.2003.03091.x

Lacasta, A. M., Sagués, F., & Sancho, J. M. (2002). Coherence and anticoherence resonance tuned by noise. *Physical Review E: Statistical, Nonlinear, and Soft Matter Physics, 66*(4), 045105. doi:10.1103/PhysRevE.66.045105

Lahav, G., Rosenfeld, N., Sigal, A., Geva-Zatorsky, N., Levine, A. J., Elowitz, M. B., & Alon, U. (2004). Dynamics of the p53–Mdm2 feedback loop in individual cells. *Nature Genetics, 36*(2), 147–150. doi:10.1038/ng1293

Lampen, A., Zhang, Y., Hackbarth, I., Benet, L. Z., Sewing, K. F., & Christians, U. (1998). Metabolism and transport of the acrolide immunosuppresant sirolimus in the small intestine. *The Journal of Pharmacology and Experimental Therapeutics, 285*(3), 1104–1112.

Lay, J. J. (2000). Modeling and optimization of anaerobic digested sludge converting starch to hydrogen. *Biotechnology and Bioengineering, 68*(3), 269–278. doi:10.1002/(SICI)1097-0290(20000505)68:3<269::AID-BIT5>3.0.CO;2-T

Lebedeva, I., Rando, R., Ojwang, J., Cossum, P., & Stein, C. A. (2000). Bcl-xL in Prostate Cancer Cells: Effects of Overexpression and Down-Regulation on Chemosensitivity. *Cancer Research, 60*(21), 6052–6060.

Lee, Y., Ahn, C., Han, J., Choi, H., Kim, J., & Yim, J. (2003). The nuclear RNase III Drosha initiates microRNA processing. *Nature*, *425*(6956), 415–419. doi:10.1038/nature01957

Lee, D. S., Park, J., Kay, K. A., Christakis, N. A., Oltvai, Z. N., & Barabási, A. L. (2008). The implications of human metabolic network topology for disease comorbidity. *Proceedings of the National Academy of Sciences of the United States of America*, *105*(29), 9880–9885. doi:10.1073/pnas.0802208105

Leopoldini, M., Marino, T., Russo, N., & Toscano, M. (2004). Antioxidant properties of phenolic compounds: H-atom versus electron transfer mechanism. *The Journal of Physical Chemistry A*, *108*(22), 4916–4922. doi:10.1021/jp037247d

Leopoldini, M., Pitarch, I. P., Russo, N., & Toscano, M. (2004). Structure, conformation, and electronic properties of apigenin, luteolin, and taxifolin antioxidants. A first principle theoretical study. *The Journal of Physical Chemistry A*, *108*(1), 92–96. doi:10.1021/jp035901j

Leopoldini, M., Marino, T., Russo, N., & Toscano, M. (2004). Density functional computations of the energetic and spectroscopic parameters of quercetin and its radicals in the gas phase and in solvent. *Theo Chem Acc*, *111*(2-6), 210-216.

Leppanen, T. (2004). *Computational studies of pattern formation in Turing systems*. Finland: Helsinki University of Technology.

Leroux, D., Stock, W. D., Bond, W. J., & Maphanga, D. (1996). Dry mass allocation, water use efficiency and δ^{13}C in clones of *Eucalyptus grandis, E. grandis×camaldulensis* and *E. grandis×nitens* grown under two irrigation regimes. *Tree Physiology*, *16*(5), 497–502.

Leung, D., Chen, E., & Goeddel, D. (1989). A method for random mutagenesis of a defined DNA segment using modified polymerase chain reaction. *Technique*, *1*, 11–15.

Li, S., Li, Y. H., Wei, T., Su, E. W., Duffin, K., & Liao, B. (2006). Too much data, but little inter-changeability: a lesson learned from mining public data on tissue specificity of gene expression. *Biology Direct*, *1*, 33. doi:10.1186/1745-6150-1-33

Li, M., Badger, J. H., Chen, X., Kwong, S., Kearney, P., & Zhang, H. (2001). An information-based sequence distance and its application to whole mitochondrial genome phylogeny. *Bioinformatics (Oxford, England)*, *17*(2), 149–154. doi:10.1093/bioinformatics/17.2.149

Li, W., & Godzik, A. (2006). Cd-hit: a fast program for clustering and comparing large sets of protein or nucleotide sequences. *Bioinformatics (Oxford, England)*, *22*(13), 1658–1659. doi:10.1093/bioinformatics/btl158

Li, H., Hou, Z., & Xin, H. (2005). Internal noise enhanced detection of hormonal signal through intracellular calcium oscillations. *Chemical Physics Letters*, *402*(4-6), 444–449. doi:10.1016/j.cplett.2004.12.068

Li, Q., & He, H. (2005). Signal transduction in a coupled hormone system: Selective explicit internal signal stochastic resonance and its control. *The Journal of Chemical Physics*, *123*(21), 214905. doi:10.1063/1.2135779

Li, Q., & Lang, X. (2008). Internal noise sustained circadian rhythms in a Drosophila model. *Biophysical Journal*, *94*(6), 1983–1994. doi:10.1529/biophysj.107.109611

Li, B. G., Hu, Y., & Chen, Z. Y. (2006). Hydrothermal synthesis of exfoliative LDH in the presence of glycine. *Chinese Journal of Chemical Physicals*, *19*(3), 253–258.

Liao, B., Tan, M., & Ding, K. (2005). A 4D representation of DNA sequences and its application. *Chemical Physics Letters*, *402*(4), 380–383. doi:10.1016/j.cplett.2004.12.062

Liao, B., & Wang, T. (2004). Analysis of similarity/dissimilarity of DNA sequences based on nonoverlapping triplets of nucleotide bases. *Journal of Chemical Information and Computer Sciences*, *44*(5), 1666–1670. doi:10.1021/ci034271f

Liao, H. R., Chen, J., & Xu, Z. R. (2001). Detection for Objective Acoustics of Morbid Voice. *Journal of Gansu College of Traditional Chinese Medicine, 1*(18), 26–27.

Lim, L. P., Glasner, M. E., Yekta, S., Burge, C. B., & Bartel, D. P. (2003). Vertebrate microRNA genes. *Science, 299*(5612), 1540. doi:10.1126/science.1080372

Lin, H. H., Han, L. Y., Zhang, H. L., Zheng, C. J., Xie, B., & Chen, Y. Z. (2006). Prediction of the functional class of lipid binding proteins from sequence-derived properties irrespective of sequence similarity. *Journal of Lipid Research, 47*(4), 824–831. doi:10.1194/jlr.M500530-JLR200

Lin, G. H. (2003). A Study of Automatic Analysis for Listening Examination of Chinese Medicine - Classification and Recognition. In *Vacuity Patient's Voice. Unpublished master's theses.* Chun Yuan Christian University, Chungli.

Lin, R., Leng, G., & Lee, H. P. (1997). A method for the numerical computation of Hopf bifurcation. *Applied Mathematics and Computation, 86*(2-3), 137–156. doi:10.1016/S0096-3003(96)00178-6

Liu, Y. Z., Yang, Y., & Wang, T. (2007). Characteristic Distribution of *L*-tuple for DNA Primary Sequence. *Journal of Biomolecular Structure & Dynamics, 25*(1), 85–91.

Liu, N. W. (2008). The objective symptoms of Chinese medicine diagnosis. *Shanxi Journal of Traditional Chinese Medicine, 1*(24), 56–58.

Liu, Q. M., Zhang, J. Q., & Huang, M. Q. (2002). Quantitative analysis of pathological voice. *Journal of Preclinical Medicine College of Shandong Medical University, 1*(16), 89–95.

Liu, Z. R. (1982). Pulse and Hemodynamics in Traditional Chinese Medicine. *Chinese Journal of Science, 5*(6), 411–413.

Liu, Z. R., & Li, X. X. (1997). *Hemodynamics Principles and Methods* (1st ed.). Fudan University Press.

Liu, Q. X., Jin, Z., & Li, B. L. (2008). Resonance and frequency-locking phenomena in spatially extended phytoplankton-zooplankton system with additive noise and periodic forces. *Journal of Statistical Mechanics*, P05011. doi:10.1088/1742-5468/2008/05/P05011

Liu, Y. Z. (2008). *The Alignment-free Methods and Their Applications for Analysis of Biological Sequences.* PhD Thesis, Dalian University of Technology, China.

Liu, Z. R. & Li, X. X. (1982). Change of Pressure Wave of Radial Artery with Physical Parameter. *Chinese Journal of Theoretical and Applied Mechanics* (3), 244

Liu, Z. R. (1982). Blood Flow in Artery. *Science Press.* Beijing. (In Chinese). Translation from D.A.McDonald (1974). Blood Flow in Arteries, Edward Arnold, London.

Liu, Z., & Liu, Z. R. (2007) Pulse Processing. Patent No.: 200710045229.7

Livingston, N. J., Guy, R. D., & Ethier, G. J. (1999). The effects of nitrogen stress on the stable carbon isotope composition, productivity and water use efficiency of white spruce (*Picea glauca* (Moench) Voss) seedlings. *Plant, Cell & Environment, 22*(3), 281–289. doi:10.1046/j.1365-3040.1999.00400.x

Lombardo, F., Blake, J. F., & Curatolo, W. J. (1996). Computation of brain-blood partitioning of organic solutes via free energy calculations. *Journal of Medicinal Chemistry, 39*(24), 4750–4755. doi:10.1021/jm960163r

Lu, J. J., Crimin, K., Goodwin, J. T., Crivori, P., Orrenius, C., & Xing, L. (2004). Influence of molecular flexibility and polar surface area metrics on oral bioavailability in the rat. *Journal of Medicinal Chemistry, 47*(24), 6104–6107. doi:10.1021/jm0306529

Luco, J. M. (1999). Prediction of the brain-blood distribution of a large set of drugs from structurally derived descriptors using partial least-squares (PLS) modeling. *Journal of Chemical Information and Computer Sciences, 39*(2), 396–404. doi:10.1021/ci980411n

Luo, Y., Yu, Q., Ou, Y. Z., Tang, D. Y., & Xie, X. Q. (2000). The evaluation of water uptake models by using precise field observation data. [in Chinese]. *Journal of Hydraulic Engineering, 125*(4), 73–80.

Luo, J., Li, R., & Zeng, Q. (2008). A novel method for sequence similarity analysis based on the relative frequency of dual nucleotides. *Communications in Mathematical and in Computer Chemistry / MATCH, 59*(3), 653-659.

Ma, L., Wagner, J., Rice, J. J., Hu, W., Levine, A. J., & Stolovitzky, G. A. (2005). A plausible model for the digital response of p53 to DNA damage. *Proceedings of the National Academy of Sciences of the United States of America*, *102*(40), 14266–14271. doi:10.1073/pnas.0501352102

Ma, T. J., Liu, Q. L., Li, Z., & Zhang, X. J. (2002). Tonoplast H^+-ATPase in response to salt stress in *Populus euphratica* cell suspensions. *Plant Science*, *163*(3), 499–505. doi:10.1016/S0168-9452(02)00154-1

Mackenzie, P. J., Umemiya, M., & Murphy, T. H. (1996). Ca 2+ imaging of CNS axons in culture indicates reliable coupling between single action potentials and distal functional release sites. *Neuron*, *16*, 783–795. doi:10.1016/S0896-6273(00)80098-7

Malomed, B. A. (1993). Ramp-induced wave-number selection for traveling waves. *Physical Review E: Statistical Physics, Plasmas, Fluids, and Related Interdisciplinary Topics*, *47*(4), 2257–2260. doi:10.1103/PhysRevE.47.R2257

Marczylo, T., Arimoto-Kobayashi, S., & Hayatsu, H. (2000). Protection against Trp-P-2 mutagenicity by purpurin: mechanism of in vitro antimutagenesis. *Mutagenesis*, *15*(3), 223–228. doi:10.1093/mutage/15.3.223

Marczylo, T., Sugiyama, C., & Hayatsu, H. (2003). Protection against Trp-P-2 DNA adduct formation in C57bl6 mice by purpurin is accompa nied by induction of cytochrome P450. *Journal of Agricultural and Food Chemistry*, *51*(11), 3334–3337. doi:10.1021/jf026072m

Marot, G., Foulley, J., Mayer, C., & Jaffrézic, F. (2009). Moderated effect size and P-value combinations for microarray meta-analyses. *Bioinformatics (Oxford, England)*, *25*(20), 2692–2699. doi:10.1093/bioinformatics/btp444

Martin, B., & Thorstenson, Y. R. (1988). Stable carbon isotope composition ($\delta^{13}C$), water use efficiency and biomass productivity of *Lycopersicon esculentum, Lycopersicon pennellii*, and the F1 hybrid. *Plant Physiology*, *88*(2), 213–217. doi:10.1104/pp.88.1.213

Matias, P. M., Soares, C. M., & Saraiva, L. M. (2001). [Ni-Fe] hydrogenase from *D. desulfuricans* ATCC 27774: gene sequencing, three dimensional structure determination and refinement at 1·8 and modelling studies of its interaction with the tetrahaem cytochrome C3. *Journal of Biological Inorganic Chemistry*, *6*(1), 63–68. doi:10.1007/s007750000167

Mauti, O., Sadhu, R., Gemayel, J., Gesemann, M., & Stoeckli, E. T. (2006). Expression patterns of plexins and neuropilins are consistent with cooperative and separate functions during neural development. *BMC Developmental Biology*, *6*(32). doi:.doi:10.1186/1471-213X-6-32

Medvinsky, A. B., Petrovskii, S. V., Tikhonova, I. A., Malchow, H., & Li, B. L. (2002). Spatiotemporal Complexity of Plankton and Fish Dynamics. *SIAM Review*, *44*(3), 311–370. doi:10.1137/S0036144502404442

Meyer, Y. (1993). *Wavelets: Algorithms and Applications. Society for Industrial and Applied Mathematics.* Philadelphia: Baker & Taylor Books.

Miller, K. J. (1990). Additivity Methods in Molecular Polarizability. *Journal of the American Chemical Society*, *112*(23), 8533–8542. doi:10.1021/ja00179a044

Miller, J. M., Williams, R. J., & Farquhar, G. D. (2001). Carbon isotope discrimination by a sequence of Eucalyptus species along a subcontinental rainfall gradient in Australia. *Functional Ecology*, *15*(3), 222–232. doi:10.1046/j.1365-2435.2001.00508.x

Miner, B. (2000). *Robust Voice Recognition over IP and Mobile Networks*. Paper presented at the symposium of Proceeding of the Alliance Engineering, Dallas, US.

Mo, X. M. (1996). The status quo and prospect of voice diagnosis. *Journal of tradtional chinese veterinary medicine*, *1*(16), 66-67.

Molz, F. J. (1976). Water transport in the soil-root system: Transient analysis. *Water Resources Research*, *12*(4), 805–807. doi:10.1029/WR012i004p00805

Molz, F. J. (1981). Models of water transport in the soil-plant system: A review. *Water Resources Research*, *17*(5), 1254–1260. doi:10.1029/WR017i005p01245

Molz, F. J., & Remson, I. (1970). Extracting term models of soil moisture use of transpiring plant. *Water Resources Research*, 6(5), 1346–1356. doi:10.1029/WR006i005p01346

Monk, N. A. M. (2003). Oscillatory Expression of Hes1, p53, and NF-κB Driven by Transcriptional Time Delays. *Current Biology*, 13(16), 1409–1413. doi:10.1016/S0960-9822(03)00494-9

Moore, J., & Arnold, F. (1996). Directed evolution of a para-nitrobenzyl esterase for aqueous-organic solvents. *Nature Biotechnology*, 14(4), 458–467. doi:10.1038/nbt0496-458

Moreau, G., & Broto, P. (1980). The autocorrelation of a topological structure: a new molecular descriptor. *Nouveau Journal de Chimie*, 4, 359–360.

Mouchaty, S. K., Gullberg, A., Janke, A., & Arnason, U. (2000). The phylogenetic position of the Talpidae within eutheria based on analysis of complete mitochondrial sequences. *Molecular Biology and Evolution*, 17(1), 60–67.

Murray, J. D. (1990). Discussion: Turing's theory of morphogenesis-its influence on modelling biological pattern and form. *Bulletin of Mathematical Biology*, 52(1), 117–152. doi:10.1007/BF02459571

Murray, J. D. (2003). *Mathematical biology. I. An introduction*, 3rd edn., Interdisciplinary Applied Mathematics 18, Springer, New York.

Murray, J. D. (2003). *Mathematical biology. II. Spatial models and biomedical applications*, 3rd edn., Interdisciplinary Applied Mathematics 18, Springer, New York.

Nahm, M., Holst, T., Matzarakis, A., Mayer, H., Rennenberg, H., & Geßler, A. (2005a). Soluble N compound profiles and concentration in European beech (*Fagus sylvatica* L.) are influenced by local climate and thinning. *European Journal of Forest Research*, 125(1), 1–14. doi:10.1007/s10342-005-0103-5

Nahm, M., Radoglou, K., Halyvopoulos, G., Geßler, A., Rennenberg, H., & Fotelli, M. N. (2006). Seasonal changes in nitrogen, carbon and water balance of adult *Fagus sylvatica* L. grown at its south-eastern distribution limit in Europe. *Plant Biology*, 8(1), 52–63. doi:10.1055/s-2005-872988

Nam, J. W., Shin, K. R., Han, J., Lee, Y., Kim, V. N., & Zhang, B. T. (2005). Human microRNA prediction through a probabilistic co-learning model of sequence and structure. *Nucleic Acids Research*, 33(11), 3570–3581. doi:10.1093/nar/gki668

Nam, J. W., Kim, J., Kim, S. K., & Zhang, B. T. (2006). ProMiR II: a web server for the probabilistic prediction of clustered, nonclustered, conserved and nonconserved microRNAs. *Nucleic Acids Research*, 34(Web Server issue), W455-W458.

Nanni, L. (2006). A novel ensemble of classifiers for protein fold recognition. *Neurocomputing*, 69(16-18), 2434–2437. doi:10.1016/j.neucom.2006.01.026

Needleman, S. B., & Wunsch, C. D. (1970). A general method applicable to the search for similarities in the amino acid sequence of two proteins. *Journal of Molecular Biology*, 48(3), 443–453. doi:10.1016/0022-2836(70)90057-4

Negishi, M., Oinuma, I., & Katoh, H. (2005). Plexins: axon guidance and signal transduction. *Cellular and Molecular Life Sciences*, 62(12), 1363–1371. doi:10.1007/s00018-005-5018-2

Nei, M., & Kumar, S. (2000). *Molecular Evolution and Phylogenetics*. Oxford: Oxford University Press.

Neim, A. K. (1996). *Systems modeling and computer simulation*. New York: Marcel Dekker, Inc.

Newell, A. C., Passot, T., & Lega, J. (1993). Order parameter equations for patterns. *Annual Review of Fluid Mechanics*, 25(1), 399–453. doi:10.1146/annurev.fl.25.010193.002151

Newman, S. P., Greenwell, H. C., Coveney, P. V., & Jones, W. (2001). Computer modelling of layered double hydroxides. In Rives, V. (Ed.), *Layered Double Hydroxides: Present and Future*. Nova Science, New York.

Nicolet, Y., Lemon, B. J., Fontecilla-Camps, J. C., & Peters, J. W. (2000). A novel FeS cluster in [Fe-only] hydrogenases. *Trends in Biochemical Sciences*, 25(3), 138–143. doi:10.1016/S0968-0004(99)01536-4

Nicolet, Y., Piras, C., & Legrand, P. (1999). *Desulfovibrio desulfuricans* iron hydrogenase: the structure shows unusual coordination to an active site Fe binuclear center. *Structure (London, England), 7*(1), 13–23. doi:10.1016/S0969-2126(99)80005-7

Nicolis, G., & Prigogine, I. (1977). *Self-organization in nonequilibrium systems: From dissipative structures to order through fluctuations.* New York: Wiley.

Nikaido, M., Harad, M. M., Cao, Y., Hasegawa, M., & Okada, N. (2000). Monophyletic origin of the order chiroptera and its phylogenetic position among mammalia, as inferred from the complete sequence of the mitochondrial DNA of a japanese megabat, the ryukyu flying fox *Pteropus dasymallus. Journal of Molecular Evolution, 51*(4), 318–328.

Nimah, M. N., & Hanks, R. J. (1973). Model for estimating soil water, plant and atmosphere interrelations:Field test of model. *Soil Sci Soc. Am. Proc., 37*(4), 522–527. doi:10.2136/sssaj1973.03615995003700040018x

Norinder, U., & Haeberlein, M. (2002). Computational approaches to the prediction of the blood-brain distribution. *Advanced Drug Delivery Reviews, 54*(3), 291–313. doi:10.1016/S0169-409X(02)00005-4

Norinder, U., Sjoberg, P., & Osterberg, T. (1998). Theoretical calculation and prediction of brain-blood partitioning of organic solutes using MolSurf parametrization and PLS statistics. *Journal of Pharmaceutical Sciences, 87*(8), 952–959. doi:10.1021/js970439y

Okamura, S., Arakawa, H., Tanaka, T., Nakanishi, H., Ng, C. C., & Taya, Y. (2001). p53DINP1, a p53-Inducible Gene, Regulates p53-Dependent Apoptosis. *Molecular Cell, 8*(1), 85–94. doi:10.1016/S1097-2765(01)00284-2

O'Leary, R. J., Landon, M., & Benumof, J. L. (1992). Buccal pulse oximeter is more accurate than finger pulse oximeter in measuring oxygen saturation. *Anesthesia and Analgesia, 75*(4), 495–498.

Oliver, P., Björn, M., & Sonja, V. (2006). The crystal structure of the apoenzyme of the iron-sulphur cluster-free hydrogenase. *Journal of Molecular Biology, 358*(3), 798–809. doi:10.1016/j.jmb.2006.02.035

O'Malley, S., Su, H., Zhang, T., Ng, C., Ge, H., & Tang, C. K. (2009). TOB suppresses breast cancer tumorigenesis. *International Journal of Cancer, 125*(8), 1805–1813. doi:10.1002/ijc.24490

Owen, A. B., Stuart, K., Mach, K., Villeneuve, A. M., & Kim, S. (2003). A gene recommender algorithm to identify coexpressed genes in C. elegans. *Genome Research, 13*(8), 1828–1837.

Pagesl. (1989). A simulation model of the three-dimensional architecture of the maize root system. *Plant Soil, 119*(1), 147-154.

Pal, S., Kyriacou, P. A., Kumaran, S., Fadheel, S., Emamdee, R., Langford, R., & Jones, D. (2005). Evaluation of oesophageal reflectance pulse oximetry in major burns patients. *Burns: journal of the International Society for Burn Injuries, 31*(3), 337-341.

Pan, G. X., Ni, Z. M., Wang, F., Wang, J. G., & Li, X. N. (2009). Molecular dynamics simulation on structure, hydrogen-Bond and hydration properties of diflunisal intercalated layered double hydroxides. [in Chinese]. *Acta Physico-Chimica Sinica, 25*(2), 223–228.

Patterson, T. B., Guy, R. D., & Dang, Q. L. (1997). Whole-plant nitrogen- and water-relations traits, and their associated trade-offs, in adjacent muskeg and upland boreal spruce species. *Oecologia, 110*(2), 160–168. doi:10.1007/s004420050145

Pearson, J. E. (1993). Complex patterns in a simple system. *Science, 261*(5118), 189–192. doi:10.1126/science.261.5118.189

Pena, B., & Perez-Garca, C. (2000). Selection and competition of Turing patterns. *Europhysics Letters, 51*(3), 300–306. doi:10.1209/epl/i2000-00352-3

Perc, M., Green, A., Dixon, C. J., & Marhl, M. (2008). Establishing the stochastic nature of intracellular calcium oscillations from experimental data. *Biophysical Chemistry, 132*(1), 33–38. doi:10.1016/j.bpc.2007.10.002

Peters, J. W., Lanailotta, W. N., & Lemon, B. J. (1998). X-Ray Crystal structure of the Fe-only hydrogenase (CpI) from *Clostridium pasteurianum* to 1.8 Angstrom Resolution. *Science, 282*(5395), 1853–1858. doi:10.1126/science.282.5395.1853

Petrilli, P. (1993). Classification of protein sequences by their dipeptide composition. *Bioinformatics (Oxford, England)*, *9*(2), 205–209. doi:10.1093/bioinformatics/9.2.205

Philip, M. L., Gila, M. T., David, J. T., Hugh, B., & Peter, G. (2006). Activity-dependent modulation of axonal excitability in unmyelinated peripheral rat nerve fibers by the 5-HT 3. *Journal of Neurophysiology*, *96*, 2963–2971. doi:10.1152/jn.00716.2006

Pihur, V., Datta, S., & Datta, S. (2009). RankAggreg, an R package for weighted rank aggregation. *BMC Bioinformatics*, *10*(62).

Platts, J. A., Abraham, M. H., Zhao, Y. H., Hersey, A., Ijaz, L., & Butina, D. (2001). Correlation and prediction of a large blood-brain distribution data sets: an LFER study. *European Journal of Medicinal Chemistry*, *36*(9), 719–730. doi:10.1016/S0223-5234(01)01269-7

Pollack, D. D., Eisen, J. A., Doggett, N. A., & Cummings, M. P. (2000). A case for evolutionary genomics and the comprehensive examination of sequence biodiversity. *Molecular Biology and Evolution*, *17*(12), 1776–1788.

PreADME, ver 1.0, B138A, Yonsei Engineering Research Complex, Yonsei University 134 Sinchon-dong, Seodaemun-gu, Seoul 120-749, Korea.

Proctor, C. J., & Gray, D. A. (2008). Explaining oscillations and variability in the p53-Mdm2 system. *BMC Systems Biology*, *2*, 75. doi:10.1186/1752-0509-2-75

Przybylski, D., & Rost, B. (2008). Powerful fusion: PSI-BLAST and consensus sequences. *Bioinformatics (Oxford, England)*, *24*(18), 1987–1993. doi:10.1093/bioinformatics/btn384

Puszynski, K., Hat, B., & Lipniacki, T. (2008). Oscillations and bistability in the stochastic model of p53 regulation. *Journal of Theoretical Biology*, *254*(2), 452–465. doi:10.1016/j.jtbi.2008.05.039

Qi, J., Wang, B., & Hao, B. (2004). Whole proteome prokaryote phylogeny without sequence alignment: a K-string composition approach. *Journal of Molecular Evolution*, *58*(1), 1–11. doi:10.1007/s00239-003-2493-7

Raats, P. A. C. (1975). Distributions of salts in the root zone. *Journal of Hydrology (Amsterdam)*, *27*(1-2), 237–248. doi:10.1016/0022-1694(75)90057-8

Raillard, S., Krebber, A., & Chen, Y. (2001). Novel enzyme activities and functional plasticity revealed by recombining highly homologous enzymes. *Chemistry & Biology*, *8*(9), 891–898. doi:10.1016/S1074-5521(01)00061-8

Randic, M. (2000). Condensed Representation of DNA Primary Sequences. *Journal of Chemical Information and Computer Sciences*, *40*(1), 50–56. doi:10.1021/ci990084z

Randic, M., Guo, X., & Basak, S. C. (2001). On the Characterization of DNA Primary Sequences by Triplet of Nucleic Acid Bases. *Journal of Chemical Information and Computer Sciences*, *41*(3), 619–626. doi:10.1021/ci000120q

Rappe, A. K., Casewit, C. J., Colwell, K. S., Goddard, W. A., & Skiff, W. M. (1992). UFF, a Full Periodic Table Force Field for Molecular Mechanics and Molecular Dynamics Simulations. *Journal of the American Chemical Society*, *114*(25), 10024–10039. doi:10.1021/ja00051a040

Reed, J. C. (1996). A day in the life of the Bcl2 protein: does the turnover rate of Bcl2. *Leukemia Research*, *20*(2), 109–111. doi:10.1016/0145-2126(95)00135-2

Reed, J. C., & Pellecchia, M. (2005). Apoptosis-based therapies for hematologic malignancies. *Blood*, *106*(2), 408–418. doi:10.1182/blood-2004-07-2761

Reich, P. B., Walters, M. B., Ellsworth, D. S., & Uhl, C. (1994). Photosynthesis-nitrogen relations in Amazonian tree species. I. Patterns among species and communities. *Oecologia*, *97*(1), 62–72. doi:10.1007/BF00317909

Reich, P. B., Waters, M. B., & Tabone, T. J. (1989). Response of *Ulmus americana* seedlings to varying nitrogen and water status- Water and nitrogen use efficiency in photosynthesis. *Tree Physiology*, *5*(2), 173–184.

Reinert, G., Schbath, S., & Waterman, M. S. (2000). Probabilistic and statistical properties of words: an overview. *Journal of Computational Biology*, *7*(1-2), 1–46. doi:10.1089/10665270050081360

Ren, N., Wang, B., & Huang, J. C. (1997). Ethanol-type fermentation from carbohydrate in high rate acidogenic reactor. *Biotechnology and Bioengineering*, *54*(5), 428–433. doi:10.1002/(SICI)1097-0290(19970605)54:5<428::AID-BIT3>3.0.CO;2-G

Reyes, A., Pesole, G., & Saccone, C. (1998). Complete mitochondrial DNA sequence of the fat dormouse, *Glis glis*: further evidence of rodent parahyly. *Molecular Biology and Evolution*, *15*(5), 499–505.

Reyes, A. C., Gissi, C., Pesole, G., Catzeflis, F. M., & Saccone, C. (2000). Where do rodents fit? Evidence from the complete mitochondrial genome of *Sciurus vulgaris*. *Molecular Biology and Evolution*, *17*(6), 979–983.

Rhodes, D. R., Barrette, T. R., Rubin, M. A., Ghosh, D., & Chinnaiyan, A., M. (2002). Meta-Analysis of Microarrays: Interstudy Validation of Gene Expression Profiles Reveals Pathway Dysregulation in Prostate Cancer. *Cancer Research*, *62*(15), 4427–4433.

Richels, R., & Sturm, P. (1996). The costs of CO_2 emission reductions. *Energy Policy*, *24*(10), 875–887. doi:10.1016/S0301-4215(96)00083-3

Robert, H. (1990). *Neurocomputing*. Massachusetts, US: Addison-Wesley Publishing Company.

Rohlf, F. J., & Fisher, D. L. (1968). Test for hierarchical structure in random data sets. *Systematic Zoology*, *17*, 407–412. doi:10.2307/2412038

Sadreyev, R., & Grishin, N. (2003). COMPASS: a tool for comparison of multiple protein alignments with assessment of statistical significance. *Journal of Molecular Biology*, *326*(1), 317–336. doi:10.1016/S0022-2836(02)01371-2

Sadreyev, R. I., Tang, M., Kim, B. H., & Grishin, N. V. (2007). COMPASS server for remote homology inference. Nucleic Acids Res, 35(Web Server issue), W653-658.

Saitou, N., & Nei, M. (1987). The neighbor-joining method: a new method for reconstructing phylogenetic trees. *Molecular Biology and Evolution*, *4*(4), 406–425.

Salminen, T., Pulli, A., & Taskinen, J. (1997). Relationship between immobilized artificial membrane chromatographic retention and the brain penetration of structurally diverse drugs. *J. Pharmceut. Biomed.*, *15*(4), 469–477. doi:10.1016/S0731-7085(96)01883-3

Sankoff, D., Bryantd, D., Deneault, M., Lang, B. F., & Burger, G. (2000). Early Eukaryote Evolution Based on Mitochondrial Gene Order Breakpoints. *Journal of Computational Biology*, *7*(3-4), 521–535. doi:10.1089/106652700750050925

Schaffer, A. A., Wolf, Y. I., Ponting, C. P., Koonin, E. V., Aravind, L., & Altschul, S. F. (1999). IMPALA: matching a protein sequence against a collection of PSI-BLAST-constructed position-specific score matrices. *Bioinformatics (Oxford, England)*, *15*(12), 1000–1011. doi:10.1093/bioinformatics/15.12.1000

Schmid, G., Goychuk, I., & Hänggi, P. (2004). Effect of channel block on the spiking activity of excitable membranes in a stochastic Hodgkin–Huxley model. *Physical Biology*, *1*(2), 61–66. doi:10.1088/1478-3967/1/2/002

Scholkopf, B., Sung, K. K., Burges, C. J. C., Girosi, F., Niyogi, P., Poggio, T., & Vapnik, V. (1997). Comparing support vector machines with Gaussian kernels to radial basis function classifiers. *IEEE Transactions on Signal Processing*, *45*(11), 2758–2765. doi:10.1109/78.650102

Schuler, M., & Green, D. R. (2005). Transcription, apoptosis and p53:catch-22. *Trends in Genetics*, *21*(3), 182–187. doi:10.1016/j.tig.2005.01.001

Scriven, D. R. L. (1981). Modeling repetitive firing and bursting in a small unmyelinated nerve-fiber. *Biophysical Journal*, *35*(3), 715–730. doi:10.1016/S0006-3495(81)84823-0

Setayeshgar, S., & Cross, M. C. (1999). Numerical bifurcation diagram for the two-dimensional boundary-fed chlorine-dioxide-iodine-malonic-acid system. *Physical Review E: Statistical Physics, Plasmas, Fluids, and Related Interdisciplinary Topics*, *59*(4), 4258–4264. doi:10.1103/PhysRevE.59.4258

Setlur, A., & Jacobs, T. (1995). *Results of a speaker verification service trial using HMM models*. Paper presented at the Proc. Eurospeech, Budapest, Hungary.

Shafkhani, S., Siesel, R., Ferrari, E., & Schellenberger, V. (1997). Generation of large libraries of random mutants in bacillus subtilis by PCR-base plasmid multimerization. *BioTechniques*, *23*(2), 304–310.

Shangguan, Z. P., Shao, M. A., & Dyckmans, J. (2000). Nitrogen nutrition and water stress effects on leaf photosynthetic gas exchange and water use efficiency in winter wheat. *Environmental and Experimental Botany*, *44*(1), 141–149. doi:10.1016/S0098-8472(00)00064-2

Shao, M. A., Yang, W. Z., & Li, Y. S. (1987). Numerical model of root water uptake by plant. [in Chinese]. *Acta Pedologica Sinica*, *24*(4), 295–304.

Shen, H. B., & Chou, K. C. (2006). Ensemble classifier for protein fold pattern recognition. *Bioinformatics (Oxford, England)*, *22*(14), 1717–1722. doi:10.1093/bioinformatics/btl170

Shi, J., Blundell, T. L., & Mizuguchi, K. (2001). FUGUE: sequence-structure homology recognition using environment-specific substitution tables and structure-dependent gap penalties. *Journal of Molecular Biology*, *310*(1), 243–257. doi:10.1006/jmbi.2001.4762

Shuai, J. W., & Jung, P. (2002). Optimal intracellular calcium signaling. *Physical Review Letters*, *88*(6), 068102. doi:10.1103/PhysRevLett.88.068102

Si, J. H., Feng, Q., Zhang, X. Y., & Chang, Z. Q. (2007). Sap Flow of *Populus euphratica* in a Desert Riparian Forest in an Extreme Arid Region during the Growing Season. *Journal of Integrative Plant Biology*, *49*(4), 425–436. doi:10.1111/j.1744-7909.2007.00388.x

Si, J. H., Feng, Q., Zhang, X. Y., Liu, W., Su, Y. H., & Zhang, Y. W. (2005). Growing season Evapotranspiration from Tamarix ramosissima stands under extreme arid conditions in northwest China. *Environ. Geol.*, *48*(7), 861–870. doi:10.1007/s00254-005-0025-z

Si, J. H., Feng, Q., Zhang, X. Y., Su, Y. H., & Zhang, Y. W. (2005). Vegetation changes in the lower reaches of the Heihe River after its water import. *Acta Bot. Boreal.* [in Chinese]. *Occident Sin.*, *25*(4), 631–640.

Sinclair, T. R., Tanner, C. B., & Bennett, J. M. (1984). Water-use efficiency in crop production. *Bioscience*, *34*(1), 36–40. doi:10.2307/1309424

Skupin, K., Winkler, U., Wartenberg, M., Sauer, H., Tovey, S. C., Taylor, C. W., & Falcke, M. (2008). How does intracellular Ca^{2+} oscillate: by chance or by the clock? *Biophysical Journal*, *94*(6), 2404–2411. doi:10.1529/biophysj.107.119495

Smith, T. F., & Waterman, M. S. (1981). Identification of common molecular subsequences. *Journal of Molecular Biology*, *147*(1), 195–197. doi:10.1016/0022-2836(81)90087-5

Soding, J., Biegert, A., & Lupas, A. N. (2005). The HHpred interactive server for protein homology detection and structure prediction. Nucleic Acids Res, 33(Web Server issue), W244-248.

Sokal, R. R., & Rohlf, F. J. (1962). The comparison of dendrograms by objective methods. *Taxon*, *11*, 33–40. doi:10.2307/1217208

Sola, J., Castoldi, S., Chetelat, O., Correvon, M., Dasen, S., & Droz, S. (2006). SpO_2 Sensor Embedded in a Finger Ring: design and implementation. *Conference Proceedings;... Annual International Conference of the IEEE Engineering in Medicine and Biology Society. IEEE Engineering in Medicine and Biology Society. Conference*, *1*, 4295–4298.

Stefan, H. (2005). The Yeast Systems Biology Network: mating communities. *Biotechnology*, *16*(13), 356–360.

Steiner, T. (2002). The hydrogen bond in the solid state. *Angewandte Chemie International Edition*, *41*(1), 48–76. doi:10.1002/1521-3773(20020104)41:1<48::AID-ANIE48>3.0.CO;2-U

Steiner, T., & Desiraju, G. R. (1998). Distinction between the weak hydrogen bond and the van der waals interaction. *Chemical Communications (Cambridge)*, *8*, 891–892. doi:10.1039/a708099i

Stephenson, M., & Stickland, L. H. (1931). Hydrogenase: a bacterial enzyme activating molecular hydrogen. I. The properties of the enzyme. *The Biochemical Journal*, *25*(1), 205–214.

Stuart, G. W., Moffet, K., & Leader, J. J. (2002). A comprehensive vertebrate phylogeny using vector representations of protein sequences from whole genomes. *Molecular Biology and Evolution*, *19*(4), 554–562.

Stuart, G. W., Moffett, K., & Baker, S. (2002). Integrated gene and species phylogenies from unaligned whole genome protein sequences. *Bioinformatics (Oxford, England)*, *18*(1), 100–108. doi:10.1093/bioinformatics/18.1.100

Subramanian, A., Tamayo, P., Mootha, V. K., Mukherjee, S., Ebert, B. L., & Gillette, M. A. (2005). Gene set enrichment analysis: a knowledge-based approach for interpreting genome-wide expression profiles. *Proceedings of the National Academy of Sciences of the United States of America*, *102*(43), 15545–15550. doi:10.1073/pnas.0506580102

Subramanian, G., & Kitchen, D. B. (2003). Computational models to predict blood-brain barrier permeation and CNS activity. *Journal of Computer-Aided Molecular Design*, *17*(10), 643–664. doi:10.1023/B:JCAM.0000017372.32162.37

Suderman, M., & Hallett, M. (2007). Tools for visually exploring biological networks. *Bioinformatics (Oxford, England)*, *23*(20), 2651–2659. doi:10.1093/bioinformatics/btm401

Sun, X., & Lu, Z. (2005). *The Foundation of Bioinformatics*. Beijing: Tsinghua University Press.

Sun, M., Sakakibara, H., Ashida, H., Danno, G., & Kanazawa, K. (2000). Cytochrome P4501A1-inhibitory action of antimutagenic anthraquinones in medicinal plants and the structure–activity relationship. *Bioscience, Biotechnology, and Biochemistry*, *64*(7), 1373–1378. doi:10.1271/bbb.64.1373

Sun, H. (2004). A Universal Molecular Descriptor System for Prediction of LogP, LogS, LogBB, and Absorption. *Journal of Chemical Information and Computer Sciences*, *44*(2), 748–757. doi:10.1021/ci030304f

Takahashi, E., Fujita, K., Kamataki, T., Arimoto-Kobayashi, S., Okamoto, K., & Negishi, T. (2002). Inhibition of human cytochrome P450 1B1, 1A1 and 1A2 by antigenotoxic compounds, purpurin and alizarin. *Mutation Research*, *508*(1-2), 147–156. doi:10.1016/S0027-5107(02)00212-9

Takezaki, N., & Nei, M. (1996). Genetic distances and reconstruction of phylogenetic trees from microsatellite DNA. *Genetics*, *144*(1), 389–399.

Tamagnini, P., Axelsson, R., & Lindberg, P. (2002). Hydrogenases and hydrogen metabolism of cyanobacteria. *Microbiology and Molecular Biology Reviews*, *66*(1), 1–20. doi:10.1128/MMBR.66.1.1-20.2002

Tamagnone, L., Artigiani, S., Chen, H., & He, Z. (1999). Plexins are a large family of receptors for transmembrane, secreted, and GPI-anchored semaphorins in vertebrates. *Cell*, *99*(1), 71–80. doi:10.1016/S0092-8674(00)80063-X

Tang, L. H., Xia, L. M., & Su, M. (2003). The research of microbial lipase molecular transformation. *Biotechnology*, *13*(3), 42–44.

Tanisho, S. (2000). *A strategy for improving the yield of molecular hydrogen by fermentation*. Paper presented at Proceedings of 13th World Hydrogen Energy Conference, Beijing, China.

Teppen, B. J., Rasmussen, K., Bertsch, P. M., Miller, D. M., & Schafer, L. (1997). Molecular Dynamics Modeling of Clay Minerals. 1. Gibbsite, Kaolinite, Pyrophyllite, and Beidellite. *The Journal of Physical Chemistry B*, *101*(9), 1579–1587. doi:10.1021/jp961577z

Tetko, I. V., Gasteiger, J., Todeschini, R., Mauri, A., Livingstone, D., & Ertl, P. (2005). Virtual computational chemistry laboratory - design and description. *Journal of Computer-Aided Molecular Design*, *19*(6), 453–463. doi:10.1007/s10822-005-8694-y

Turing, A. M. (1952). The Chemical Basis of Morphogenesis. *Philosophical Transactions of the Royal Society of London*, *237*(641), 37–72. doi:10.1098/rstb.1952.0012

Turner, J. V., Glass, B. D., & Agatonovic-Kustrin, S. (2003). Prediction of drug bioavailability based on molecular structure. *Analytica Chimica Acta, 485*(1), 89–102. doi:10.1016/S0003-2670(03)00406-9

Turner, J. V., Maddalena, D. J., & Agatonovic-Kustrin, S. (2004). Bioavailability Prediction Based on Molecular Structure for a Diverse Series of Drugs. *Pharmaceutical Research, 21*(1), 68–82. doi:10.1023/B:PHAM.0000012154.09631.26

Tusher, V. G., Tibshirani, R., & Chu, G. (2001). Significance analysis of microarrays applied to the ionizing radiation response. *Proceedings of the National Academy of Sciences of the United States of America, 98*(9), 5116–5121. doi:10.1073/pnas.091062498

Tyson, J. J., Chen, K. C., & Novak, B. (2003). Sniffers, buzzers, toggles and blinkers: dynamics of regulatory and signaling pathways in the cell. *Current Opinion in Cell Biology, 15*(2), 221–231. doi:10.1016/S0955-0674(03)00017-6

Uetz, P., Giot, L., Cagney, G., & Mansfield, T. A. (2000). A comprehensive analysis of protein-protein interactions in Saccharomyces cerevisiae. *Nature, 403*(6770), 623–627. doi:10.1038/35001009

Ullah, G., & Jung, P. (2006). Modeling the statistics of elementary calcium release events. *Biophysical Journal, 90*(10), 3485–3495. doi:10.1529/biophysj.105.073460

Van Acker, S. A. B. E., De Groot, M. J., Van den Berg, D. J., Tromp, M. N. J. L., Den Kelder, G. D. O., Van der Vijgh, W. J. F., & Bast, A. (1996). A quantum chemical explanation of the antioxidant activity of flavonoids. *Chemical Research in Toxicology, 9*(8), 1305–1312. doi:10.1021/tx9600964

Van Asperen, J., Van Tellingen, O., & Beijnen, J. H. (1998). The pharmacological role of P-glycoprotein in the intestinal epithelium. *Pharmaceutical Research, 37*(6), 429–435. doi:10.1006/phrs.1998.0326

Van de Waterbeemd, H., Smith, D. A., Beaumont, K., & Walker, D. K. (2001). Property-Based Design: Optimization of Drug Absorption and Pharmacokinetics. *Journal of Medicinal Chemistry, 44*(9), 1313–1333. doi:10.1021/jm000407e

Van de Waterbeemd, H., & Kansy, M. (1992). Hydrogen-bonding capacity and brain penetration. *Chimia, 46*(7-8), 299–303.

Van den Honert, T. H. (1948). Water transport in plants as a catenary process. *Discussions of the Faraday Society, 3*(2), 146–153. doi:10.1039/df9480300146

Vapnik, V. (1998). *Statistical Learning Theory*. New York: Wiley.

Vapnik, V., & Chapelle, O. (2000). Bounds on error expectation for support vector machines. *Neural Computation, 12*(9), 2013–2036. doi:10.1162/089976600300015042

Vapnik, V., & Chapelle, O. (2000). Bounds on error expectation for support vector machines. *Neural Computation, 12*(9), 2013–2036. doi:10.1162/089976600300015042

VCCLAB. (2005). *Virtual Computational Chemistry Laboratory*. Retrieved from http://www.vcclab.org

Veber, D. F., Johnson, S. R., Cheng, H. Y., Smith, B. R., Ward, K. W., & Kopple, K. D. (2002). Molecular properties that influence the oral bioavailability of drug candidates. *Journal of Medicinal Chemistry, 45*(12), 2615–2623. doi:10.1021/jm020017n

Vetri, M. R., Bharat, A. S., & Deshpande, P. (2008). Milling and separation of the multi-component printed circuit board materials and analysis of elutriation based on a single particle model. *Powder Technology, 183*(2), 169–176. doi:10.1016/j.powtec.2007.07.020

Vinga, S., & Almeida, J. (2003). Alignment-free sequence comparison-a review. *Bioinformatics (Oxford, England), 19*(4), 513–523. doi:10.1093/bioinformatics/btg005

Vitousek, P. M. (1982). Nutrient cycling and nitrogen use efficiency. *American Naturalist, 119*(4), 553–572. doi:10.1086/283931

Volbeda, A., & Fontecilla-Camps, J. C. (2005). Structure–function relationships of nickel–iron sites in hydrogenase and a comparison with the active sites of other nickel–iron enzymes. *Coordination Chemistry Reviews, 249*(15-16), 1609–1619. doi:10.1016/j.ccr.2004.12.009

Volbeda, A., Martin, L., & Cavazza, C. (2005). Structural differences between the ready and unready oxidized states of [Ni-Fe] hydrogenases. *Journal of Biological Inorganic Chemistry*, *10*(3), 239–249. doi:10.1007/s00775-005-0632-x

Volbeda, A., Montet, Y., & Vernède, X. (2002). High-resolution crystallographic analysis of *Desulfovibrio fructosovorans* [Ni-Fe] hydrogenase. *International Journal of Hydrogen Energy*, *27*(11-12), 1449–1461. doi:10.1016/S0360-3199(02)00072-1

Vrugt, J. A., Hopmans, J. W., & Simunek, J. (2001). Calibration of a 2-d root water uptake model. *Soil Science Society of America Journal*, *65*(4), 1027–1037. doi:10.2136/sssaj2001.6541027x

Wagener, M., Sadowski, J., & Gasteiger, J. (1995). Autocorrelation of Molecular Surface Properties for Modeling Corticosteroid Binding Globulin and Cytosolic Ah Receptor Activity by Neural Networks. *Journal of the American Chemical Society*, *117*(29), 7769–7775. doi:10.1021/ja00134a023

Wang, J., & Zheng, X. (2008). WSE, a new sequence distance measure based on word frequencies. *Mathematical Biosciences*, *215*(1), 78–83. doi:10.1016/j.mbs.2008.06.001

Wang, S., Liu, F., Wang, W., & Yu, Y. (2004). Impact of spatially correlated noise on neuronal firing. *Physical Review E: Statistical, Nonlinear, and Soft Matter Physics*, *69*(1), 011909. doi:10.1103/PhysRevE.69.011909

Wang, Z., Hou, Z., & Xin, H. (2005). Internal noise stochastic resonance of synthetic gene network. *Chemical Physics Letters*, *401*(1-3), 307–311. doi:10.1016/j.cplett.2004.11.064

Wang, H. W., Chen, T. L., Yang, P. C., & Ueng, T. H. (2001). Induction of cytochromes P450 1A1 and 1B1 by emodin in human lung adenocarcinoma cell line CL5. *Drug Metabolism and Disposition: the Biological Fate of Chemicals*, *29*(9), 1229–1235.

Wang, J. M., Krudy, G., Xie, X. Q., Wu, C. D., & Holland, G. (2006). Genetic Algorithm-Optimized QSPR Models for Bioavailability, Protein Binding, and Urinary Excretion. *Journal of Chemical Information and Modeling*, *46*(6), 2674–2683. doi:10.1021/ci060087t

Wang, Z., Yan, A. X., Yuan, Q. P., & Gasteiger, J. (2008). Explorations into Modeling Human Oral Bioavailability. *European Journal of Medicinal Chemistry*, *43*(11), 2442–2452. doi:10.1016/j.ejmech.2008.05.017

Wang, Z., Yan, A. X., & Yuan, Q. P. (2009). Classification of blood-brain barrier permeation by Kohonen's self-organizing Neural Network (KohNN) and Support Vector Machine (SVM). *QSAR & Combinatorial Science*, *28*(9), 989–994. doi:10.1002/qsar.200960008

Wang, W. (2006). A new mechanical algorithm for solving the second kind of Fredholm integral equation. *Applied Mathematics and Computation*, *172*(2), 946–962. doi:10.1016/j.amc.2005.02.026

Wang, W. M., Liu, Q. X., & Jin, Z. (2007). Spatiotemporal complexity of a ratio-dependent predator-prey system. *Physical Review E: Statistical, Nonlinear, and Soft Matter Physics*, *75*(5), 51913. doi:10.1103/PhysRevE.75.051913

Wang, W. M., Zhang, L., Wang, H. L., & Li, Z. (2010). Pattern formation of a predator-prey system with Ivlev-type functional response. *Ecological Modelling*, *221*(2), 131–140. doi:10.1016/j.ecolmodel.2009.09.011

Wang, G. H. (2003). Differences in leaf $\delta^{13}C$ among four dominant species in a secondary succession sere on the Loess Plateau of China. *Photosynthetica*, *41*(4), 525–531. doi:10.1023/B:PHOT.0000027516.43278.c4

Wang, Q., Ruan, X., Chen, Y. N., & Li, W. H. (2007). Eco-physiological response of *Populus euphratica Oliv* to water release of the lower reaches of the Tarim River, China. *Environ. Geol.*, *53*(2), 349–357. doi:10.1007/s00254-007-0650-9

Wang, H. M., & Chen, B. S. (1996). The basic framework of prior index system of coal industry. [In Chinese]. *Journal of China Coal Economic College*, *4*, 10–13.

Wang, L. M. (2002). The effect factors and evaluation indexes of resource safety. [In Chinese]. *Journal of Natural Resources, 4,* 401–408.

Wang, E. Y. (1997). Significance of Sound in clinical diagnosis. *Journal of tradtional chinese veterinary medicine, 1*(4), 47-54.

Warnat, P., Eils, R., & Brors, B. (2005). Cross-platform analysis of cancer microarray data improves gene expression based classification of phenotypes. *BMC Bioinformatics, 6,* 265. doi:10.1186/1471-2105-6-265

Waterman, M. S. (1995). *Introduction to Computational Biology: Maps, Sequences and Genomes.* Boca Raton, FL: CRC Press.

Wee, K. B., & Aguda, B. D. (2006). Akt versus p53 in a network of oncogenes and tumor suppressor genes regulating cell survival and death. *Biophysical Journal, 91*(3), 857–865. doi:10.1529/biophysj.105.077693

Wee, K. B., Surana, U., & Aguda, B. D. (2009). Oscillations of the p53-Akt Network: Implications on Cell Survival and Death. *PLoS ONE, 4*(2), e4407. doi:10.1371/journal.pone.0004407

Wei, W., Zhu, Z. Q., Liu, L. X., Zuo, Y. X., Gong, M., Xue, F. S., & Liu, J. (2005). A pilot Study of Continuous Transtracheal Mixed Venous Oxygen Saturation Monitoring. *Anesthesia and Analgesia, 101*(2), 440–443. doi:10.1213/01.ANE.0000156949.91614.E9

Wei, G., & Lu, Y. Q. (1996). Chaos and Fractal Theories for Speech Signal Processing. In S. J. Wang (Ed.), *Acta Electronica Sinica: vol. 24. Communication and signal processing* (pp. 34-39). Chinese Institute of Electronics Press.

Weigelt, B., Glas, A. M., Wessels, L. F., Witteveen, A. T., Peterse, J. L., & van't Veer, L. J. (2003). Gene expression profiles of primary breast tumors maintained in distant metastases. *Proceedings of the National Academy of Sciences of the United States of America, 100*(26), 15901–15905. doi:10.1073/pnas.2634067100

Weka: Waikato Environment for Knowledge Analysis; University of Waikato, New Zealand. http://www.cs.waikato.a c.nz/ml/weka/ (accessed March, 2010).

Wen, G. (2005). Criterion to identify Hopf bifurcations in maps of arbitrary dimension. *Physical Review E: Statistical, Nonlinear, and Soft Matter Physics, 72*(2 Pt 2), 026201. doi:10.1103/PhysRevE.72.026201

Wheeler, D. L., Barrett, T., Benson, D. A., Bryant, S. H., Canese, K., & Chetvernin, V. (2008). Database resources of the National Center for Biotechnology Information. *Nucleic Acids Research, 36*(Database issue), D13–D21. doi:10.1093/nar/gkm1000

Whibley, C., Pharoah, P. D. P., & Hollstein, M. (2009). p53 polymorphisms: cancer implications. *Nature Reviews. Cancer, 9*(2), 95–107. doi:10.1038/nrc2584

William, J. H., & Paul, T. W. (2007). Separation and recovery of materials from scrap printed circuit boards. *Resources, Conservation and Recycling, 51*(3), 691–709. doi:10.1016/j.resconrec.2006.11.010

Winberg, M. L., Noordermeer, J. N., Tamagnone, L., Comoglio, P. M., & Spriggs, M. K. (1998). Plexin A is a neuronal semaphorin receptor that controls axon guidance. *Cell, 95*(7), 903–916. doi:10.1016/S0092-8674(00)81715-8

Winkler, D. A., & Burden, F. R. (2004). Modelling blood-brain barrier partitioning using Bayesian neural nets. *Journal of Molecular Graphics & Modelling, 22*(6), 499–505. doi:10.1016/j.jmgm.2004.03.010

Wishart, D. S., Knox, C., Guo, A. C., Shrivastava, S., Hassanali, M., & Stothard, P. (2006). DrugBank: a comprehensive resource for in silico drug discovery and exploration. *Nucleic Acids Research, 34*(1), D668–D672. doi:10.1093/nar/gkj067

Witten, I. H., & Frank, E. (2005). *Data Mining: Practical machine learning tools and techniques.* San Francisco: Morgan Kaufmann.

Wong, K. M., Suchard, M. A., & Huelsenbeck, J. P. (2008). Alignment uncertainty and genomic analysis. *Science, 319*(5862), 473–476. doi:10.1126/science.1151532

Woods, N. M., Cuthbertson, K. S. R., & Cobbold, P. H. (1986). Repetitive transient rises in cytoplasmic free calcium in hormone-stimulated hepatocytes. *Nature*, *319*(6054), 600–602. doi:10.1038/319600a0

Wright, J. S., Johnson, E. R., & Di Labio, G. A. (2001). Predicting the activity of phenolic antioxidants: Theoretical method, analysis of substituent effects, and application to major families of antioxidants. *Journal of the American Chemical Society*, *123*(6), 1173–1183. doi:10.1021/ja002455u

Wu, G. A., Jun, S. R., Sims, G. E., & Kim, S. H. (2009). Whole-proteome phylogeny of large dsDNA virus families by an alignment-free method. *Proceedings of the National Academy of Sciences of the United States of America*, *106*(31), 12826–12831. doi:10.1073/pnas.0905115106

Wu, T., Hsieh, Y., & Li, L. (2001). Statistical Measure of DNA Sequence Dissimilarity under Markov Chain Models of Base Composition. *Biometrics*, *57*(2), 441–448. doi:10.1111/j.0006-341X.2001.00441.x

Wu, C.-H., & Yen, G.-C. (2004). Antigenotoxic properties of Cassia Tea (*Cassia tora* L.): mechanism of action and the influence of roasting process. *Life Sciences*, *76*(1), 85–101. doi:10.1016/j.lfs.2004.07.011

Wu, W. S. (2002). The research of safety evaluation and prior-warning to China's petroleum resource. *Geological Techno economic Management, 5*, 13-18. (In Chinese)

Xiao, D. M., Li, W. X., & Han, M. A. (2006). Dynamics in a ratio-dependent predator-prey model with predator harvesting. *Journal of Mathematical Analysis and Applications*, *324*(1), 14–29. doi:10.1016/j.jmaa.2005.11.048

Xin, H., & Hou, Z. (2009). *Nonlinear chemical dynamics* (2nd ed.). Hefei: China Science and Technology University Press.

Xing, D., Ren, N., & Li, Q. (2006). *Ethanoligenens harbinense* gen. nov., sp. nov., isolated from molasses wastewater. *International Journal of Systematic and Evolutionary Microbiology*, *56*(4), 755–760. doi:10.1099/ijs.0.63926-0

Xu, H., Lin, M., Wang, W., Li, Z., Huang, J., Chen, Y., & Chen, X. (2007). Learning the drug target-likeness of a protein. *Proteomics*, *7*(23), 4255–4263. doi:10.1002/pmic.200700062

Xu, Y. P., Zhou, X. F., & Zhang, W. X. (2008). MicroRNA prediction with a novel ranking algorithm based on random walks. *Bioinformatics (Oxford, England)*, *24*(13), i50–i58. doi:10.1093/bioinformatics/btn175

Xu, J. J., Qiao, Z. M., Qi, Q. H., & Yin, M. (2000). Quantitative Evaluation of Voice in Laryngeal Diseases by Computer Technique. *Acta Universitatis Medicinalis Nanjing*, *1*(20), 121–124.

Xu, J. T. (2006). Characteristics of four traditional diagnostic methods and their relationship. *Modern Medicine*, (16): 4–11.

Xue, Y., Yap, C. W., Sun, L. Z., Cao, Z. W., Wang, J. F., & Chen, Y. Z. (2004). Prediction of P-glycoprotein substrates by a support vector machine approach. *Journal of Chemical Information and Computer Sciences*, *44*(4), 1497–1505. doi:10.1021/ci049971e

Xue, C. H., Li, F., He, T., Liu, G. P., Li, Y. D., & Zhang, X. G. (2005). Classification of real and pseudo microRNA precursors using local structure-sequence features and support vector machine. *BMC Bioinformatics*, *6*, 310. doi:10.1186/1471-2105-6-310

Yan, J. J., Wang, Y. Q., Wang, H. J., Li, F. F., Xia, C. M., Guo, R., & Ma, T. C. (2008, May). *Nonlinear analysis in TCM acoustic diagnosis using Delay Vector Variance*. Paper presented at The 2nd International Conference on Bioinformatics and Biomedical Engineering, Shanghai, PRC.

Yang, J. Y., Peng, Z. L., Yu, Z. G., Zhang, R. J., Anh, V., & Wang, D. S. (2009). Prediction of protein structural classes by recurrence quantification analysis based on chaos game representation. *Journal of Theoretical Biology*, *257*(4), 618–626. doi:10.1016/j.jtbi.2008.12.027

Yang, M. T., Chiu, C. C., & Yang, Z. X. (2000). *Pilot Study on Vacuity Patient's Speech by Fractal Demension Method*. Paper presented at Engineering Technique's Application on Chinese Medicine and Western Medicine 2000 Annual Symposium, Taipei.

Yao, J. W. (1989). An numerical model of predicting soil moisture content under the condition of crop growing. [in Chinese]. *Journal of Hydraulic Engineering, 9*(1), 32–38.

Yao, L. M., Kang, S. Z., Gong, D. Z., Jia, H. Z., & Pang, X. M. (2004). The apple tree root water uptake models established through two kinds of methods and the comparison of these models. [in Chinese]. *Journal of Irrigation and Drainage, 23*(1), 67–70.

Yap, C. W., & Chen, Y. Z. (2005). Quantitative Structure-Pharmacokinetic Relationships for drug distribution properties by using general regression neural network. *Journal of Pharmaceutical Sciences, 94*(1), 153–168. doi:10.1002/jps.20232

Yasumura, Y., Hikosaka, K., Matsui, K., & Hirose, T. (2002). Leaf-level nitrogen-use efficiency of canopy and understorey species in a beech forest. *Functional Ecology, 16*(6), 826–834. doi:10.1046/j.1365-2435.2002.00691.x

Yin, K. L., Zou, D. H., Yang, B., Zhang, X. H., Xia, Q., & Xu, D. J. (2006). Investigation of H-bonding for the related force fields in materials studio software. [in Chinese]. *Computers and Applied Chemistry, 23*(12), 1335–1340.

Yona, G., & Levitt, M. (2002). Within the twilight zone: a sensitive profile-profile comparison tool based on information theory. *Journal of Molecular Biology, 315*(5), 1257–1275. doi:10.1006/jmbi.2001.5293

Yoshida, Y., Nakamura, T., Komoda, M., Satoh, H., Suzuki, T., & Tsuzuku, J. K. (2003). Mice lacking a transcriptional corepressor Tob are predisposed to cancer. *Genes & Development, 17*(10), 1201–1206. doi:10.1101/gad.1088003

Yoshida, F., & Topliss, J. G. (2000). QSAR model for drug human oral bioavailability. *Journal of Medicinal Chemistry, 43*(13), 2575–2585. doi:10.1021/jm0000564

Young, R. C., Mitchell, R. C., Brown, T. H., Ganellin, C. R., Griffiths, R., & Jones, M. (1988). Development of a new physicochemical model for brain penetration and its application to the design of centrally acting H2 receptor histamine antagonists. *Journal of Medicinal Chemistry, 31*(3), 656–671. doi:10.1021/jm00398a028

Young, J. P., & Derek, J. F. (2009). Recovery of high purity precious metals form printed circuit boards. *Journal of Hazardous Materials, 164*(2-3), 1152–1158. doi:10.1016/j.jhazmat.2008.09.043

Yu, Z. G., Anh, V. V., & Lau, K. S. (2004). Chaos game representation, and multifractal and correlation analysis of protein sequences from complete genome based on detailed HP model. *Journal of Theoretical Biology, 226*(3), 341–348. doi:10.1016/j.jtbi.2003.09.009

Yu, Z. G., Shi, L., Xiao, Q. J., & Anh, V. (2008). Simulation for chaos game representation of genomes by recurrent iterated function systems. *J. Biomedical Sci. and Eng., 1*(1), 44–51. doi:10.4236/jbise.2008.11007

Yu, Z. G., Zhan, X. W., Han, G. S., Wang, R. W., Anh, V., & Chu, K. H. (2010). Proper Distance Metrics for Phylogenetic Analysis Using Complete Genomes without Sequence Alignment. *International Journal of Molecular Sciences, 11*(3), 1141–1154. doi:10.3390/ijms11031141

Yu, Z. G., Zhou, L. Q., Anh, V., Chu, K. H., Long, S. C., & Deng, J. Q. (2005). Phylogeny of prokaryotes and chloroplasts revealed by a simple composition approach on all protein sequences from whole genome without sequence alignment. *Journal of Molecular Evolution, 60*(4), 538–545. doi:10.1007/s00239-004-0255-9

Yu, Y. K., Gertz, E. M., Agarwala, R., Schaffer, A. A., & Altschul, S. F. (2006). Retrieval accuracy, statistical significance and compositional similarity in protein sequence database searches. *Nucleic Acids Research, 34*(20), 5966–5973. doi:10.1093/nar/gkl731

Yu, P., Ouaknine, M., Revis, J., & Giovanni, A. (2001). Objective Voice Analysis for Dysphonic Patients: A Multiparametric Protocol Including Acoustic and Aerodynamic Measurements. *Journal of Voice, 1*(15), 29–42.

Yuan, Z. Y., Li, L. H., Han, X. G., Chen, S. P., Wang, Z. W., Chen, Q. S., & Bai, Y. F. (2006). Nitrogen response efficiency increased monotonically with decreasing soil resource availability: a case study from a semiarid grassland in northern China. *Oecologia*, *148*(4), 564–572. doi:10.1007/s00442-006-0409-0

Zaccolo, M., & Gherardi, E. (1999). The effect of high-frequency random mutagenesis on in vitro protein evolution: a study on TEM-1 beta-lactamase. *Molecular Biology*, *285*(2), 775–783. doi:10.1006/jmbi.1998.2262

Zender, L., & Kubicka, S. (2008). Molecular pathogenesis and targeted therapy of hepatocellular carcinoma. *Onkologie*, *31*(10), 550–555. doi:10.1159/000151586

Zhang, L. V., Wong, S. L., King, O. D., & Roth, F. P. (2004). Predicting co-complexed protein pairs using genomic and proteomic data integration. *BMC Bioinformatics*, *5*, 38. doi:10.1186/1471-2105-5-38

Zhang, T. L., & Choua, K. C. (2006). Prediction of protein subcellular location using hydrophobic patterns of amino acid sequence. *Computational Biology and Chemistry*, *30*(5), 367–371. doi:10.1016/j.compbiolchem.2006.08.003

Zhang, Z., Kochhar, S., & Grigorov, M. G. (2005). Descriptor-based protein remote homology identification. *Protein Science*, *14*(2), 431–444. doi:10.1110/ps.041035505

Zhang, T., Brazhnik, P., & Tyson, J. J. (2007). Exploring Mechanisms of the DNA-Damage Response. *Cell Cycle (Georgetown, Tex.)*, *6*(1), 85–94.

Zhang, J. S., & Meng, P. (2004). Spatial distribution characteristics of fine roots of pomegranate tree. [in Chinese]. *Journal of Nanjing Forestry University*, *28*(4), 89–91.

Zhang, J. S., Meng, P., & Yin, C. J. (2002). Spatial distribution characteristics of apple tree roots in the apple-wheat intercropping. [in Chinese]. *Scientia Silvae Sinicae*, *38*(4), 30–33.

Zhang, S. L., & Eric, F. (1998). Optimization of electrodynamic separation for metals recovery from electronic scraps. *Resources, Conservation and Recycling*, *22*(3-4), 143–162. doi:10.1016/S0921-3449(98)00004-4

Zhang, S. L., Eric, F., Arvidson, B., & Moss, W. (1998). Aluminum recovery from electronic scrap by High-Force eddy-current separators. *Resources, Conservation and Recycling*, *23*(4), 225–241. doi:10.1016/S0921-3449(98)00022-6

Zhang, L., Wang, W. M., Xue, Y. K., & Jin, Z. (2008). Complex dynamics of a Holling-type IV predator-prey model. *arXiv:0801.4365v1*.

Zhao, H. M., & Chockal, I. N., GAM, K., & Chen, Z. L. (2002). Directed Evolution of Enzymes and Pathways for Industrial Biocatalysis. *Current Opinion in Biotechnology*, *13*(2), 104–110. doi:10.1016/S0958-1669(02)00291-4

Zhao, L. J., Xiao, H. L., Cheng, G. D., & Song, Y. X. (2008). A preliminary study of water sources of riparian plants in the lower reaches of the Heihe Basin. [in Chinese]. *Acta Geoscientica Sinica*, *29*(6), 709–718.

Zhao, Y. M., Wen, X. F., & Li, B. B. (2004). Recovery of copper from waste printed circuit board. *Journal of Minerals & Metallurgical Processing*, *21*(2), 99–102.

Zheng, Y. R. (2000). *An Expert System with Inquiring Diagnosis and Auscultical Diagnosis of Chronic Renal Failure in Chinese Medicine. Unpublished master's theses.* Chun Yuan Christian University, Chungli.

Zheng, Q., & Wang, X. J. (2008) GOEAST: a web-based software toolkit for Gene Ontology enrichment analysis. *Nucleic Acids Res*, *36*(Web Server issue):W358-63. Retrieved from http://omicslab.genetics.ac.cn/ GOEAST/index.php

Zhou, H., & Zhou, Y. (2004). Single-body residue-level knowledge-based energy score combined with sequence-profile and secondary structure information for fold recognition. *Proteins*, *55*(4), 1005–1013. doi:10.1002/prot.20007

Zhou, X., Song, B., Jin, L., Hu, D., Diao, C., & Xu, G. (2006). Isolation and inhibitory activity against ERK phosphorylation of hydroxyanthraquinones from rhubarb. *Bioorganic & Medicinal Chemistry Letters, 16*(1), 563–568. doi:10.1016/j.bmcl.2005.10.047

Zhou, C., & Kurths, J. (2005). Noise-sustained and controlled synchronization of stirred excitable media by external forcing. *New Journal of Physics, 7*, 18. doi:10.1088/1367-2630/7/1/018

Zhu, Q., Zhang, X. M., & Fry, A. J. (1997). Bond dissociation energies of antioxidants. *Polymer Degradation & Stability, 57*(1), 43–50. doi:10.1016/S0141-3910(96)00224-8

Zhu, Z. Q., Wei, W., Yang, Z. B., Liu, A. J., & Liu, J. (2005). Transesophageal Arterial Oxygen Saturation Monitoring: An Experimental Study. [Medical Science Edition]. *Journal of Sichuan University, 36*(1), 124–126.

Zhu, Z. R., Tang, X. W., & Wang, W, T., Ren, W., Xing, J. L., Zhang, J. R., Duan J. H., Wang, Y. Y., Jiao, X, Y., Hu, S. J. (2009). Conduction Failures in Rabbit Saphenous Nerve Unmyelinated Fibers. *Neuro-Signals, 17*, 181–195. doi:10.1159/000209279

Zhu, H., Suzuki, T., Tsygankov, A. T., Asada, Y., & Miyake, J. (1999). Hydrogen production from tofu wastewater by *Rhodobacter sphaeroides* immobilized in agar gels. *International Journal of Hydrogen Energy, 24*(4), 305–310. doi:10.1016/S0360-3199(98)00081-0

Zhu, J. L., Shen, Q., & Jiang, D. Z. (2001). Bursting of nenrons under slow wave stimulation. *In: Building new bridges at the frontiers of engineering and medicine-23rd annual international conference of the IEEE engineering in medicine and biology society.* Istanbul Turkey.

Zouhal, L., & Denoeus, T. (1998). An evidence-theoretic k-NN rule with parameter optimization. *IEEE Transactions on Systems, Man, and Cybernetics, 28*(2), 263–273. doi:10.1109/5326.669565

Zuo, Q., Sun, Y. X., & Yang, P. L. (1988). Study on water uptake by the winter wheat's roots with the application of microlysimeter. [in Chinese]. *Journal of Hydraulic Engineering, 6*(1), 69–76.

About the Contributors

Limin Angela Liu, PhD, obtained her BSc degree from Tsinghua University, Beijing and her PhD degree from Carnegie Mellon University, USA. After postdoctoral research at Johns Hopkins University, USA, she became Associate Professor at Shanghai Jiao Tong University. Her recent work includes the establishment of an ab initio method for the prediction of transcription factor binding sites and a novel "tethered-hopping model" for describing the effects of protein-protein interactions on the formation and stability of ternary protein-DNA complexes.

Dongqing Wei, PhD, is the acting head of the Department of Bioinformatics and Biostatistics, College of Life Science and Biotechnology, Shanghai Jiao Tong University, Shanghai, China, the editor-in-Chief of the journal "Interdisciplinary Sciences - Computational Life Sciences", and the chairman of the International Association of Scientists in the Interdisciplinary Areas (IASIA). Prof. Wei's research is in the general area of structural bioinformatics. He is best known for his ground-breaking work on theory of complicated liquids. He, along with Prof. Gren Patey, has found that strongly interacting dipolar spheres can form a ferroelectric nematic phase. This was the first demonstration that dipolar forces alone can create an orientationally ordered liquid state. It is also the first time that the existence of a ferroelectric nematic phase has been established for a model liquid. This discovery solved a long standing problem in theoretical physics, and created a new direction in search for new liquid crystal materials (Phys. Rev. Lett. 68, 2043, 1992, cited about 180 times). In recent years, Prof. Wei has developed tools of molecular simulation and applied them to study biological systems with relevance to computer-aided drug design and structural biology. With more than 150 journal papers and greater than 2000 citations (Science Citation Index), he is becoming a leading figure in the area of structural bioinformatics.

Yixue Li, PhD, was born in Xinjiang, China. Currently, he is the director in Shanghai Center for Bioinformation Technology, vice director and a full research professor of Key Laboratory of Systems Biology at Shanghai Institutes for Biological Sciences, Chinese Academy of Sciences. Dr. Li received his BSc. and Msc. degrees in theoretical physics from Xinjiang University, China, in 1982 and 1987, respectively, and his Ph.D. degree in theoretical physics from the University of Heidelberg, Germany, in 1996. After Dr. Li got his Ph.D. degree he worked as a bioinformatics research staff in European Molecular Biology Laboratory (EMBL) from 1997-2000, and came back to Shanghai, China in the middle of 2000. Dr.Li's research interests include bioinformatics, systems biology and computational biology. Dr. Li has published more than 100 journal papers in various international scientific journals, such as Science, Nature Genetics, Nature Biotechnology, PNAS, Bioinformatics, NAR, Plos Computational Biology, Plos One, Molecular Systems Biology, Molecular Cellular Proteomics, Oncogene,

BMC Bioinformatics, Genome Biology, etc., and his research results have been cited by more than 1500 researchers worldwide in books, theses, journal and conference papers. Dr. Li has served as an editorial board member for 5 scientific journals.

* * *

Vo Anh, PhD, received his BSc (Hons) and PhD degrees in mathematics from University of Tasmania in 1975 and 1978, respectively, and MEc in econometrics from University of New England in 1984. Then he worked in Queensland University of Technology (QUT) since 1988 (promoted to professor in 2004). Now he is the Director of Mathematical Sciences Cluster in QUT; an associate Editor of Journal of Probability and Statistics, Applied Mathematics and Stochastic Analysis, and Stochastic Analysis and Applications; and regional editor of Information Technology for Economics & Management.

Yin Bai was bone in 1963 in Chifeng, Inner Mongolia province, China. He graduated in Pharmacology from the Inner Mongolia Medical College, where he received his diploma in 1985. After graduation, he has worked as a Pharmacology teacher for the Medical College of Chifeng University. He became Associate Professor and Professor in 2002 and 2008, respectively. His research interest includes the study on the structures, the procedures of isolation, and the antioxidant activity of antimutagens and anticarcinogens from herbal medicines.

Hongzheng Bao was bone in 1956 in Chifeng, Inner Mongolia province, China. He started studying chemistry at the Department of Chemistry of the Bohai University of Liaoning province, where he received his diploma in 1982. After graduating, he has worked as a chemist teacher for the Chemistry Department of Chifeng University. He became Associate Professor in 1995. His recent research interests include the study of the structures, the procedures of isolation, and approaches to the organic synthesis of natural product derivatives.

Meihong Cai received her master's degree in Veterinary Medicine at the University of Nanjing Agriculture, China in 2004. She majored in animal molecular immunity and virus heredity under the mentorship of Professor Puyan Chen from 2001 to 2004. After graduation, she joined the Department of Biology Technology at the University of Jiangsu as a lecturer. In 2008, she was admitted to study in the College of Life Science at Nanjing University to pursue her doctoral degree and majored in molecular immunity under the mentorship of Professor Pingping Shen. Ms. Cai's main research is in the field of vaccine.

Feng Cao, PhD, born in July 1971, in Zhejiang Province, People's Republic of China. He graduated from Northeast University in 1993 and obtained Ph.D. degree in 2000 from University of Science and Technology, Beijing. During 2002-2005, he worked at Mineral Materials Institute of Aachen University of Technology as a postdoctoral fellow. He has published more than 80 research papers and 2 books. His main research interests are on special refractories and nano-materials. Now he is working at Huzhou University as the Vice Dean.

Shengkui Cao, PhD, Lecturer in Biological and Geographical Sciences Institute, Qinghai Normal University, P. R. China, obtained Doctor's Degree of Sciences on arid water resources and hydrology in Cold and Arid Regions Environmental and Engineering Research Institute, Chinese Academy of Sciences (CAS), P. R. China in 2010. Dr. Cao conducts research in eco-hydrology of arid region and the stable isotope. Dr. Cao has participated in 5 projects and published more than 10 papers.

Zongqiang Chang, Assistant Researcher in water and soil department of Cold and Arid Regions Environmental and Engineering Research Institute, Chinese Academy of Sciences (CAS), P. R. China, mainly studies the eco-hydrology of arid region and water resources. Chang was awarded the First Prize of Gansu Province Scientific and Technological Progress in 2010, and has published 9 SCI and EI papers.

Haifeng Chen, graduated from Zhejiang University, Hangzhou, P.R. China and obtained M.S. in Materials Science and Engineering in 2006. His main research interests are in surface science, self-assembly, micro-and nanotechnology. He joined the Department of Chemistry of Huzhou Teachers College in 2006. His paper "Preparation and Aging Behavior of Nano SiO2 Modified PEA Coating by In-Situ Polymerization" has been cited by 78 times.

Xin Chen, PhD, is an Associate professor of bioinformatics, College of Life Sciences, Zhejiang University, China. He obtained two B.Sc. degrees in Biotechnology and in Computer Sciences from Shanghai Jiao Tong University in the year 2000. Then he continued to pursue his Ph.D. degree in the Department of Computational Sciences, National University of Singapore. After working as the Manager, High-throughput biology in the private institute Blueprint Initiative Asia (the team behind the famous interaction database BIND) for a year, he joined Zhejiang University. He has published more than 30 research papers in the area of bioinformatics and drug discovery. His interests lie in the theoretical modeling of coordinated therapeutic mechanisms of all forms of combined chemotherapy.

Xuning Chen is a PhD student in Biomechanics at Shanghai Institute of Applied Mathematics and Mechanics, Shanghai University, China. She received her Bachelor's degree in Applied Mathematics from Northwest Normal University, Lanzhou, China in 2004 and her Master's degree in Biomechanics, under the supervision of Dr. Weiping Zhu, from Shanghai University in 2009. She has worked for Longdong University as a Teaching Assistant for 3 years. Since March 2009, she has been a PhD Student at the Biomechanics group at Shanghai University. Xuning's main research interests include: modeling and simulation, Complex Networks, Bioinformatics, and Systems Biology, with a special focus on signal transduction pathways involved in axon guidance and growth.

Jun Cui received his Ph.D. degree in biochemistry and molecular biology from Nanjing University in 2009. He is currently an instructor at Nanjing University. He also works as a Research Scientist at Baylor College of Medicine for the joint program between Pingping Shen's lab and Rong-Fu Wang's lab since 2007. His main research interests include the molecular mechanisms of innate immunity, the dynamic modeling of the signaling network and the development of new therapies for cancer and viral associated diseases. He tries to combine the methods of molecular immunology, systems biology and biophysics to investigate the detailed mechanisms on how signaling networks respond to diverse stimuli and exert their roles in innate immune responses and other cellular processes.

Si Deng, born in January, 1987 in Yuxi, China. She is a first year graduate student in the College of Bioscience and Bioengineering of South China University of Technology. She majors in microbiology.

She is doing research on the enzyme sortase, which can anchor surface protein to cell wall of Gram-positive bacteria. She obtained her bachelor's degree in bioengineering from Nanchang University in 2009 where she won several scholarships.

Ming Du, Ph. D., is Associate Professor at the College of Food Science & Engineering, Harbin Institute of Technology. He received his Bachelor's and Master's degrees from Dalian Polytechnic University in Food Science and Engineering and his Ph.D. from China Agriculture University in Storage and Processing of Agricultural Products in 2006. His research centers on purification and characterization of functional proteins and enzymes. He severs in the Committee of Food Science and Technology in China, the Committee of Food Science and Technology in Heilongjiang Province, and the Youth Committee of Science and Technology in Harbin Institute of Technology.

Chen-long Duan, doctor of engineering, is an Associate Professor in the School of Chemical Engineering and Technology, China University of Mining and Technology. Dr. Duan received his Bachelor's degree and Master's degree from China University of Mining and Technology in Chemical Engineering and Technology and Mineral Processing Engineering respectively. He received his PhD's degree from China University of Mining and Technology in Environmental Engineering. He has been conducting simulation research of fluidized bed as a postdoctoral fellow at China University of Mining and Technology. His main research field is Mineral Processing Engineering and the crushing mechanism of waste printed circuit boards. He has undertaken several national research projects funded by the Chinese Government and taken part in several international and national key projects since 2004. Dr. Duan has published more than 30 papers in several important Journals and International conferences.

Qi Feng, Professor and Leader in water and soil department of Cold and Arid Regions Environmental and Engineering Research Institute, Chinese Academy of Sciences (CAS), P. R. China, was awarded by the Excellent Youth Foundation of China in 2007, and was selected by the One Hundred Person Project of the Chinese Academy of Sciences in 2002. Prof. Feng mainly studies hydrology of arid region, water resources and environment. Prof. Feng was awarded the Research Fellow (NRC Fellow) from National Research Council of USA in 2000, the Research Fellow (MASHAV Fellow) from Agricultural Research Organization in Israel in 2005, the Researcher Fellow (STA Fellow) from the Science and Technology Agency in Japan in 1997, the Research Fellow (JSPS) from Japan Society for the Promotion of Science in 2000 and the First Prize of Gansu Province Scientific and Technological Progress in 2010. Prof. Feng has published more than 100 scientific papers and 1 monograph.

Bo Gao received his master's degree in Microelectronics from Sichuan University, China, 2006. He is working towards his Ph. D. degree at Sichuan University. In 2006, he joined the Provincial Key Laboratory of Micro-electronics. Now he is a teacher in Physical Science and Technology College, Sichuan University. His research interests include Microelectronic, and FPGA and Bio-electronics.

Xieping Gao was born in 1965. He received his B.S. and M.S. degrees from Xiangtan University of China in 1985 and 1988, respectively. He received his Ph.D. degree from Hunan University, China, in 2003. He is a Professor in the College of Information Engineering at Xiangtan University, China. He was a visiting scholar at the National Key Laboratory of Intelligent Technology and Systems, Tsinghua University, China, from 1995 to 1996; and at the School of Electrical & Electronic Engineering, Nanyang

Technological University, Singapore, from 2002 to 2003. He is a regular reviewer for several journals and he has been a member of the technical committees of several scientific conferences. He has authored and co-authored over 80 journal papers, conference papers and book chapters. His current research interests are in the areas of wavelets analysis, image processing, neural networks, and bioinformatics.

Xin Ge is a senior undergraduate student, majoring in Applied Chemistry, at the School of Chemical Engineering and Technology, China University of Mining and Technology. His main research field is Applied Chemistry and energy economics. During the past three years, he has participated in several research projects on energy economics. He has been awarded numerous honors and awards such as the "Excellent Achievements Award". He has also published several papers in Chinese Journals.

Rui Guo is a research associate at the Center of Traditional Chinese Medicine Information Science and Technology, Shanghai University of Traditional Chinese Medicine (TCM). She received her Bachelor's degree from Huazhong University of Science and Technology in Computer Science and Technology and her Master's degree from Tongji University in Photogrammetry and Romote Sensing under the supervision of Dr. Yinying Chen. Her research focuses on pattern recognition, image processing and signal processing. She works in the Laboratory of Diagnostic Integrated Information of Traditional Chinese Medicine. Her research mainly involves pulse diagnosis of Traditional Chinese Medicine. Her relevant scientific papers have been published in Chinese Journal of Integrated Traditional and Western Medicine, Journal of Chinese Integrative Medicine, etc.

Guo-Shen Han is a PhD student in the School of Mathematics and Computational Science, Xiangtan University, China.

Yongguo Han, PhD, Dean of Computer Science School, Southwest University of Science & Technology, senior member of the China Computer Society, Computer Society of Sichuan Executive Director of the fifth council, President of YOCSEF Chengdu (2010). He obtained MA degree in Electric Power from Chongqing University and Ph.D. degree in Computer at the University of Electronic Science and Technology, respectively. The main research directions of Prof. Han are computer control technology, knowledge management and its application in education. Han and his group developed the distribution system fault locator for electric power business in Sichuan and Yunnan provinces, promoting the effective using of power. Han published hundreds of paper in fault location algorithm of electric power, real-time data recording method and parallel computing, etc. He teaches windows programming, network computing, etc. Prof. Han was awarded "Outstanding Teacher" in Mianyang City, Sichuan Province.

Jing-feng. He is a PhD Candidate in the School of Chemical Engineering and Technology, China University of Mining and Technology. He received his Bachelor's and Master's degrees from China University of Mining and Technology in Mineral Processing Engineering. His main research field is Mineral Processing Engineering and the disposal and recycling of electronic waste. He has taken part in several international and national projects supported by the Chinese Government. He has published a number of influential papers in important Journals and International conferences. He is conducting research on the two-phase liquid simulation and experiments with the advanced software of CFD.

Ya-qun. He is Professor and PhD advisor in the School of Chemical Engineering and Technology, China University of Mining and Technology. Dr. He received a Bachelor's degree from Xuzhou Normal University in mathematics. He received his Master's and PhD's degrees from China University of Mining and Technology in Mineral Processing Technology. He is the head-director of the Centre of Modern Analysis and Calculation in China University of Mining and Technology. He visited the University of Birmingham in England as short term exchange visiting scholar during the period of 2004.06 to 2004.09. He visited the University of Kentucky as senior visiting scholar during the period of 2009.09 to 2010.02. He has undertaken several international and national projects funded by the Australian Government and the Chinese Government, including E-Waste recycling, milling grinding, economic energy and so on. Manning is off the table, all other trades considered.

San-Jue Hu graduated from the Fourth Military Medical University of China. He is a full Professor in the Institute of Neurosciences of the People Liberation Army in Xi'an, China. He conducts research work in the mechanisms of pain and nonlinear dynamics of neural activity. He has published more than 200 papers and has participated in compiling 9 monographs. He has supervised about sixty graduate students. In 2009, he was awarded the First Prize of National Science and Technology Progress by the State Department of the People's Republic of China. His major achievement includes founding the model for neuropathic pain and studying analgesic mechanisms and clinical treatment.

Lin Ji, Ph. D., is an Associate Professor at the Department of Chemistry, Capital Normal University. Ji received her Ph. D. degree from Beijing Institute of Technology under the supervision of Dr. Qianshu Li. Her research focuses on nonlinear dynamics in complex biochemical systems. She was honored as a "Beijing Novel star", "Beijing Excellent Talent", "Beijing Young Key Talents", etc. She has published many influential papers in leading journals such as J. Chem. Phys., Phys .Chem. Chem. Phys., Biophys. Chem., Chem. Phys. Lett., Phys. Rev. E, Phys. Lett. A, etc.

Qingshan Jiang received his first Ph.D. in Mathematics from Chiba Institute of Technology, Japan in 1996, and a second Ph.D. in Computer Science from University of Sherbrooke, Canada, in 2002. He is now a professor at Xiamen University, China. His research interests include Pattern Recognition, Data Mining, Artificial Intelligence Information Retrieval, Neural Networks, Image Processing, statistical analysis and fuzzy modeling. His current projects include the Fuzzy Clustering and Variable Selection for Data Mining, and Mathematical Models for High-Dimensional Data Clustering and Applications to Anti-spam, supported by the National Natural Science Foundation of China. During his more than 30 years of study and research, he has published over 120 scientific papers in international journals and conference proceedings.

Ruifa Jin was bone in 1964 in Chifeng, Inner Mongolia province, China. He studied chemistry and graduated from the Inner Mongolia University in 1986. He became Associate Professor in 2001. For 20 years, he worked as a chemist teacher for Chifeng University before relocating to Department of Chemistry at the Northeast Normal University, to pursue graduate study in functional materials. He completed his Master's degree work in functional materials from Department of Chemistry at the Northeast Normal University in 2007. Shortly before the completion of his Ph.D. in 2010 with Professor J. Zhang on quantum chemical design of multifunctional luminecent materials and chemosensors for fluoride anion, he became full Professor in 2009. His research interests include theoretical investigation of antioxidant activity of natural products, new multifunctional luminecent materials, and chemosensors for the sensing of anions.

Trupti Joshi is a Research Associate and Lab Manager in the Digital Biology Laboratory, Computer Science Department at the University of Missouri-Columbia. She earned an MS degree majoring in computational biology and bioinformatics from the University of Tennessee–Oak Ridge National Laboratory, Graduate School of Genome Science and Technology. She has extensive experience in the field of bioinformatics and its application to biology and medical fields. Her research interests are in the areas of Chip-SEQ and new generation sequencing technologies including 454 and Illumina data analysis for methylation, translocation studies and SNP discovery, mirna and target gene identification, data mining, analysis of high-throughput biological data for function and biological pathway prediction, and regulatory networks identification.

Bo Li was a MSc. student in the School of Mathematics and Computational Science, Xiangtan University, China from 2006-2009.

Fufeng Li, Ph.D., is an Associate Professor at the Teaching Experimental Center in Shanghai University of Traditional Chinese Medicine (TCM). She received her Bachelor's and Master's Degree from Shanghai University of Traditional Chinese Medicine, and her Ph.D. degree from Shanghai University of Traditional Chinese Medicine in Specialty of Traditional Chinese Medicine Diagnosis under the supervision of Dr. Yiqin Wang. Her research uses modern technology (computer science and informatics) for the standardization and modernization of TCM. She works in the Laboratory of Diagnostic Integrated Information of Traditional Chinese Medicine and Teaching Experimental Center.

Jiaxuan Li received his bachelor's degree in bioengineering from Tianjin University of Science & Technology in Jun. 2004. He then joined the research group of Prof. Aixia Yan in Beijing University of Chemical Technology. He received his master's degree in biochemical engineering from Beijing University of Chemical Technology in Jun. 2007. His research focused on the prediction of physicochemical properties such as boiling point and acid-base dissociation constant (pKa) of organic compounds.

Juan Li is a graduate student of Jiangsu University located in Zhenjiang, Jiangsu province. She worked on projects in plant molecular biology at the Institute of Life Sciences and was responsible for identifying the function of Cyanobacterium Hemoglobin gene (CHB) in bacterium, yeast and plants. Hemoglobin in animal cell can bind and transport oxygen in order to improve provision of oxygen, which in turn increases the amount of electrons in the respiratory chain. Hemoglobin in microbacteria can promote growth of microbacteria, as well as the synthesis of proteins and production of metabolites. She was the first-author of "A Rapid and Simple Method for Brassica Napus Floral-Dip Transformation and Selection of Transgenic Plantlets", International Journal of Biology (2010). She was co-author of "A New Time-saving Transformation System for Brassica napus", African Journal of Biotechnology (2009).

Miaoxin Li, Ph.D., is now a postdoctoral fellow in the Department of Biochemisty, University of Hong Kong. He graduated from Hunan University of Commerce and received his Ph.D. recently at the same department of the University of Hong Kong. His work aims to understand the molecular basis of human complex diseases. These complex diseases are caused by the interaction between genes and environmental factors. He tries to map the disease gene's location in the genome and identify novel genes through genomic screening and next-generation sequencing technologies. In order to improve the study of human complex diseases, he also developed some bioinformatics tools such as IGG (tools for the interrogation of genome-wide association data) and KGG (tools that incorporate biological function with statistical analysis).

Sheng Li, born in China in 1984, received his bachelor's degree from Software School of Xiamen University in 2007. Mr. Li is now a M.S. degree candidate majoring in Computer Software and Theory at Xiamen University. His research is focused on mining sequential patterns from DNA sequences. He has published two papers during his study: one is "An Optimized Method for Protein Motif Mining published in Journal of Computer Research and Development" (in Chinese); the other is "An Optimized Algorithm for Finding Approximate Tandem Repeats in DNA Sequences" accepted by "2010 the 2nd International Workshop on Education Technology and Computer Science" (ETCS2010).

Xiuhua Li was bone in 1967 in Chifeng, Inner Mongolia province, China. She graduated in Chemical Engineering from the Chemical Engineering College of the Inner Mongolia University of Technology in 1992. After graduation, she has worked as a chemist teacher for the Chemistry Department of Chifeng University. She became Associate Professor in 2006. She received her master's degree in functional materials from the Department of Chemistry of Nankai University in 2009. Her research interests include synthesis of new functional materials and investigation of antioxidant activity of natural products.

Yi-Quan Li, PhD, is currently an Associate Professor in the School of Mathematics and Computational Science, Xiangtan University, China. He is an expert in statistics.

Yanchun Liang is the Vice Dean of College of Computer Science and Technology, Jilin University. He was a visiting scholar in Manchester University of U.K. from 1990 to 1991, a visiting professor in National University of Singapore from 2000 to 2001, a guest professor in Institute of High Performance Computing of Singapore from 2002 to 2004, and a guest professor in Trento University, Italy from 2006 to 2008. His research interests focus on bioinformatics and computational intelligence, including computational biology, artificial neural networks, evolutionary computation, and applications of intelligent computational and machine learning methods to combinational optimization, data mining, control of ultrasonic motors, and MEMS modeling. He published two books and more than 300 papers.

Guojie Liao received his bachelor's degree in Microelectronics from Sichuan University, China, 2008. He is working towards his master's degree in Physical Science and Technology College at Sichuan University. His research interests include Microelectronic, and FPGA and DSP.

Houye Liu (1983-) is a Master degree student at the College of Mathematics and Information Science, Wenzhou University, Wenzhou, P. R. China. He is interested in using mechanical algorithm and numerical simulation to model and analyze complex biomathematics systems.

Jing Liu is a graduate student in China Agricultural University at the Department of State Key Laboratories for Agrobiotechnology. She is doing research on intrinsically unstructured protein (IUP) under the supervision of Prof. Ziding Zhang. IUP is a new field concerning proteins that do not have stable 3D structures under native condition but still play important biological roles, such as in signal transduction, cell-cycle regulation, gene expression and chaperone action.

Lixin Luo, PhD, born in August, 1966 in Xingning, Guangdong, China. He is a Member of the Biochemical Engineering Committee of Chinese Chemical Society; vice-chairman of Guangdong Society for Microbiology; and Director of Industrial Microbiology Committee of Guangdong Society for Microbiology. Dr. Luo obtained his Ph.D. degree in fermentation engineering from South China University of Technology (SCUT) in 1996 and was promoted to Professor in 2008. Since 1996, he has worked at the School of Bioscience and Bioengineering, SCUT. During 2003 to 2004, he conducted research in microbial genetics at the Institute of Food Research, UK as a visiting scholar. In recent years, Dr. Luo focuses on areas of biochemical engineering and industrial microbiology. He participates and undertakes over 20 scientific research projects at national, provincial and municipal level. He has published more than 60 papers in Chinese and international journals, and obtained 2 invention patents. He has edited 8 academic books and textbooks.

Meng Meng was an undergraduate student in the research group of Prof. Aixia Yan in the Computer-Aided Drug Design (CADD) team, where she finished her undergraduate thesis. She obtained her bachelor's degree in pharmaceutical engineering from Beijing University of Chemical Technology in Jun. 2009. Her research focused on the prediction of oral bioavailability of drugs.

Ling Mu received her bachelor's degree in Anesthesiology from the Department of Anesthesiology, Luzhou Medical College, China, 2007. She is working towards her master's degree at West China Hospital, Sichuan University. In 2007, she joined the Anesthesiology Department in West China Hospital, China. Her research interests include the monitoring of basic life function and the monitoring of transesophageal pulse oxygen saturation.

Zheming Ni, Ph.D., works in the College of Chemical Engineering and Materials Science, Zhejiang University of Technology. She is a leader of the Department of Chemistry, and a member of Zhejiang branch of the Chinese Chemical Society. She obtained her B.S. degree from the Department of Chemistry in Zhejiang University in 1982. She received a Master's degree from the Institute of Catalysis in Zhejiang University in 1994. She obtained her Ph.D. degree from Zhejiang University in industrial catalysis in 2005. Her research interests are synthesis, performance and computer simulation of layered anionic clay materials. Dr. Ni has published more than 60 research papers and presided more than 15 research projects.

Guoxiang Pan, PhD, lecturer, born in 1981 in Zhejiang Province, People's Republic of China. He graduated from Zhejiang University of Technology, and obtained his Ph.D. degree in 2009. His early work, with Prof. Xiaonian Li and Prof. Zheming Ni, aimed at the aqueous reforming of glycose to produce hydrogen gas over Ni supported catalyst, and combined hydrogenation of organic compounds using methanol as the hydrogen source. Now, he is a member of the Department of Chemistry in Huzhou Teachers College. He has published more than 40 research papers. His current interests include the preparation of inorganic layered materials and drug intercalation for release, and the use of molecular simulation technology, such as density functional theory (DFT) or molecular dynamics (MD), in modeling the structure and the properties of novel materials.

Feng Rao (born 1982) is a doctoral student at the Computer Science and Technology Department of the East China Normal University. Feng Rao received Bachelor's and Master's degrees from Fuyang Normal College in Applied Mathematics and Wenzhou University in Mathematics and Information Science, respectively. She is now studying at the East China Normal University in Computer Science and Technology Department under the supervision of Dr. Zhi-bin Li. She is interested in using mathematic methods to model and analyze complex ecological systems, such as predator-prey systems. She has worked extensively on the complex spatiotemporal dynamics of these systems. Based on the bifurcation analysis and via numerical simulation, she has studied the spatial pattern formation, the evolution process of the system near the coexistence equilibrium point. Her work has showed that modeling by reaction-diffusion equations is an appropriate tool for investigating fundamental mechanisms of complex spatiotemporal dynamics and it will be useful for studying the dynamic complexity of ecosystems.

Pingping Shen received her Ph.D. in biochemistry and molecular biology from Nanjing University in Nanjing, China. She is currently a Professor of Biochemical Science and a senior member of the Chinese Society of Immunology. Her research interests include cell signal transduction and its implication in immuno-modulation, proteomics, the relationship between macrophage and liver cancer development and the dynamic modeling of cellular signaling network. Currently the main work of her lab is focused on investigation of the role and regulation mechanisms of members of Bcl-2 protein family in signaling transduction pathways and the modulation of macrophage functions. Her group also study the signaling transduction pathways involved in the occurrence of liver diseases induced by Microcystins (MCs) and estrogen.

Yu Shyr, Ph.D., is Director and Professor of Cancer Biostatistics Center in Vanderbilt University School of Medicine, and has nearly 20 years of experience as a statistical consultant, providing experimental design and statistical analysis support for basic scientific research, clinical trials, and high-dimensional data studies. He has published more than 230 peer-reviewed papers, including many statistical methodology papers, for example, describing techniques for multivariate data analysis and a wavelet-based approach to proteomic data preprocessing, as well as collaborative research papers in the fields of cancer biology, epidemiology, and clinical trials; diabetes and nephrology; orthopedics; immunology; etc. In addition, he has taught numerous seminars and courses on statistical topics such as power and sample size calculation, clinical trial design and analysis, and statistical approaches to high-dimensional data analysis.

Jianhua Si, Assistant Professor in water and soil department of Cold and Arid Regions Environmental and Engineering Research Institute, Chinese Academy of Sciences (CAS), P. R. China, mainly studies eco-hydrology of arid region and water resources. Prof. Si was awarded the Second Prize of Inner Mongolia Scientific and Technological Progress in 2007, the Ecological Excellent Prize of SEE TNC in 2007, the First Prize of Gansu Provincial Bureau of Water Resources in 2006 and the First Prize of Gansu Province Scientific and Technological Progress in 2010. Prof. Si has published more than 30 SCI and EI papers.

Yonghong Su, Assistant Researcher in water and soil department of Cold and Arid Regions Environmental and Engineering Research Institute, Chinese Academy of Sciences (CAS), P. R. China, mainly studies water resources in arid regions. Su was awarded the First Prize of Gansu Province Scientific and Technological Progress in 2010 and has published more than 10 SCI and EI papers.

Tingzhe Sun received his bachelor's degree in biology at Nanjing University in 2008. He is working towards his master's degree under the mentorship of Professor Pingping Shen at the Department of Life Sciences, Nanjing University, China. His main research activities are in the field of mathematical biology on dynamic modeling of signaling network, especially with a focus on apoptotic network, such as BCL-2, p53 pathways. He published several papers on several critical problems related to Bax activation switch in BCL-2 family and counting mechanisms in p53 signaling transduction network.

Xiaoli Tan, PhD, Associate professor in the Institute of Life Sciences, Jiangsu University, obtained bachelor's degree in North-western Agricultural University; and has since worked in Hybrid Rapeseed Research Center of Shanxi Province for rapeseed quality breeding in Northwest A&F University for his Master's degree and the Institute of Genetics and Developmental Biology, Chinese Academy of Sciences. He received his PhD degree in the field of plant lipid metabolism in 2004. Dr. Tan's main research interest focuses on the metabolic regulation of gene expression in plant lipid synthesis and degradation. Dr. Tan worked as a visiting scholar at Ian Graham's lab in CNAP (Centre for Novel Agricultural Products), Department of Biology at the University of York, UK, to functionally identify the Long Chain Acyl CoA Synthetase (LACS) Brassica napus. The main discovery was that BnLACS is involved in the lipid synthesis, and exogenous expression of the LACS in yeast results in the significant increase of lipid content.

Peisong Tang, PhD, born in November 1975, in Sichuan Province, People's Republic of China. He graduated from Kunming University of Science and Technology in 2001 and obtained his Ph.D. degree in 2006 from Zhejiang University. He has published more than 10 research papers and 1 book. His main research interests are on nanotechnology and surface science. He joined the Department of Chemistry in Huzhou Teachers College in 2006.

Yi-Min Tao obtained his Bachelor's degree from the experimental class of China Agricultural University in three years. His research focused on biological experiments and is now shifting towards bioinformatics research. He is interested in computer programming and has mastered several programming languages, such as C++, JAVA, Perl and R. Currently, his main research interests include experimental and computational studies of RNA aiming to unravel new functions of these molecules.

Yongzheng Tian, Professor and Director in the Research Institute of Forestry, Alxa League of Inner Mongolia Autonomous Region, obtained Doctor's Degree of Sciences in arid water resources and hydrology from the Cold and Arid Regions Environmental and Engineering Research Institute, Chinese Academy of Sciences (CAS), P. R. China in 2010. Dr. Tian mainly studies ecology and environment in arid regions. Dr. Tian was awarded the First Prize of Inner Mongolia Scientific and Technological Progress in 2005. Dr. Tian has completed 4 national research projects and published more than 10 papers and 1 monograph.

Haiyan Wang, graduate student, is studying at the Department of Chemistry in Capital Normal University. Her major is nonlinear biochemical dynamics.

Ligeng Wang works in Zhejiang University of Technology as the Associate Director of the Department of Chemistry. He graduated from the Department of Chemistry, Northeast Normal University and obtained a M.S. degree in 1993. His research interests include functional materials, inorganic synthesis, and medicinal chemistry.

Ruofei Wang was born in Hunan province, China. He received his B.S. degree in Computer Science and Technology from Xiangtan University in 2007. He is a graduate student who majors in signal and information processing in Xiangtan University. His current research interests include machine learning, medical image processing, and protein structure prediction in bioinformatics.

Shuai Wang is a Master degree candidate in the School of Chemical Engineering and Technology, China University of Mining and Technology. Wang received his Bachelor's degree from China University of Mining and Technology in Mineral Processing Engineering. His main research field is air separation. He has taken part in several experimental projects at several power plants. In addition, he has published several papers in Chinese Journals.

Weiming Wang (1969-), Ph. D., is an Associate Professor at the College of Mathematics and Information Science, Wenzhou University, Wenzhou, P. R. China. He is the author of over 20 refereed papers in a variety of topics, including mechanical algorithm, population dynamics, and epidemic system. His research spans computational biology and nonlinear analysis.

Yan Wang, Ph.D., graduated from the College of Computer Science and Technology of Jilin University in 2007. He conducted research on a collaborative project as a visiting scholar at University of Georgia in USA from 2007 to 2009. His research interests focus on Computational Intelligence and Bioinformatics, such as gene expression analysis, miRNA prediction, operon prediction and some other bioinformatics fields. He has published over 30 research papers.

Yiqin Wang, Ph.D., is a full Professor at Basic Medical College, Shanghai University of Traditional Chinese Medicine (TCM). Prof. Wang received her Bachelor's degree from TCM Department of Zhejiang College of Traditional Chinese Medicine in Specialty of Traditional Chinese Medicine, her Master's degree from Shanghai University of Traditional Chinese Medicine in Pediatrics of TCM, and her Ph.D. from the Shanghai University of Traditional Chinese Medicine in Basic Study of TCM Clinical Medicine. Her research focuses on the standardization of TCM symptoms and the quantification and modernization of TCM diagnosis. She serves as a lab chief at the Laboratory of Diagnostic Integrated Information of Traditional Chinese Medicine, and is also a leader of the Chinese Medicine Diagnosis Project of Shanghai 3rd Leading Academic Discipline Project.

Zhi Wang is a PhD candidate in Prof. Aixia Yan's group in the Computer-Aided Drug Design (CADD) team at the College of Life Science and Technology, Beijing University of Chemical Technology. He received his bachelor's degree in pharmaceutical engineering from Beijing University of Chemical Technology in Jun. 2007. His research is supported by the Scientific Research Foundation of Graduate School of Beijing University of Chemical and Technology. His research interests include structure-based drug design, virtual screening and the prediction of physicochemical properties such as acid-base dissociation constant (pKa), solubility and ADME/Tox prediction.

Dan Wei received her Bachelor's and Master's degrees in China from College of Mathematics and Computer Science, Hubei University. She is currently a Ph.D. candidate in Artificial Intelligence at Xiamen University and a member of Laboratory of Data Mining Technology and Applications at the same university. Her current research interests include Data Mining, Genomics, Phylogenetic, and Sequence Analysis. She has published four papers on artificial intelligence and knowledge engineering during her Master's training and two papers related to the areas of Bioinformatics and Computational Biology during her Ph.D. She worked extensively to tackle different challenges and solved several problems associated with mining the information of biological sequences.

Hua Wei is a Master degree candidate in the School of Chemical Engineering and Technology, China University of Mining and Technology. Wei received his Bachelor's degree from China University of Mining and Technology in Applied Chemistry. His main research field is energy economics and milling grinding. He has taken part in several research projects of energy economics and energy risk. In addition, he has published several papers in Chinese Journals and international conferences.

Mingyu Wei is a Master degree student in the field of plant lipid metabolism at Jiangsu University located in Zhenjiang, Jiangsu province. Ms. Wei received her bachelor's degree from Changzhi Universty in 2008. She worked on projects in plant molecular biology at the Institute of Life Sciences and conducted algae transformation research. Methods for transformation of eukaryotic algae are very important for Genetic Engineering. At present, she focuses on method optimization of eukaryotic algae transformation.

Wei Wei received her master's degree in Anesthesiology from Sichuan University, China, 2006. She was promoted to anesthesia physician in 1997, Associate Professor in 2004 and Professor in 2010. Now she is Master Instructor in Anesthesiology at West China Hospital. In the 2004 ASA (American Society of Anesthesiology) annual meeting, she was awarded one of the two annual research award by STA (Society for Technology in Anesthesiology). She has conducted research in clinical Anesthesiology for 16 years. Now she is the leader of Anesthesiology in Thoracic and Cardiovascular Surgery who is mainly responsible for clinical anesthesiology and management.

Bao-feng Wen is a Master degree candidate in the School of Chemical Engineering and Technology, China University of Mining and Technology. Mr. Wen received his Bachelor's degree from China University of Mining and Technology in Mineral Processing Technology. His main research field is air separation technology and energy economics. He has taken part in several national research projects of Mineral Processing Engineering. He has participated in several research projects on energy economics. In addition, he has published several papers in Chinese Journals and international conferences.

Jun Wu was a research assistant in Shanghai Center for Bioinformation Technology during 2006-2009 and now is a Research Assistant in Beijing Institute of Genomics, Chinese Academy of Sciences. Her primary interest is to transform original raw genomics data to basic research insights related to leukemia. Current areas of research include: (1) Transcriptional regulation of myeloid development; (2) Genetic and epigenetic regulation of gene expression as a mechanism of leukemogenesis; (3) Genetic alterations (specifically those involving regulatory DNA sequences) in human leukemia. By employing a combination of genomic and molecular characterization strategies, she aims to dissect the transcriptional network that dictates normal blood development and the initiation/progression of acute leukemia.

Shan Wu is a sophomore undergraduate student, majoring in Mineral Processing Engineering, at the School of Chemical Engineering and Technology, China University of Mining and Technology. Her main research field is Mineral Processing Engineering and energy economics. During the past two years, she has participated in several research projects on energy economics. In addition, she has also taken part in several undergraduate innovation projects as a main participant. She has been awarded numerous honors and awards such as the "Excellent Achievements Award".

Xiao-bing Wu is a senior undergraduate student, majoring in Mineral Processing Engineering, at the School of Chemical Engineering and Technology, China University of Mining and Technology. His main research field is Mineral Processing Engineering and energy economics. During the past three years, he has undertaken a National Innovative Experimental Projects of Undergraduate Students on air separation technology. In addition, he also participated in several research projects of energy economics.

Haiyang Xi, Assistant Researcher in water and soil department of Cold and Arid Regions Environmental and Engineering Research Institute, Chinese Academy of Sciences (CAS), P. R. China, obtained Doctor's Degree of Sciences on arid water resources and hydrology in Cold and Arid Regions Environmental and Engineering Research Institute, Chinese Academy of Sciences (CAS), P. R. China in 2009. Dr. Xi mainly studies hydrology and water resources in arid regions. Dr. Xi was awarded the First Prize of Gansu Province Scientific and Technological Progress in 2010, and has published more than 10 papers.

Chunming Xia, Ph. D., is an Associate Professor in the Center for Mechatronics Engineering at the East China University of Science and Technology (ECUST). He received his Bachelor's and Master's degrees from ECUST in the automatic control and the Department of Electronic Engineering and his Ph.D. from the University of Glasgow in Mechanical Engineering. His research focuses on equipment condition monitoring and diagnostic technology management, Modern Signal Processing and systems modeling and simulation performance analysis. He has published a number of papers as well as served as reviewers for many journals and conferences.

Guangcan Xiao graduated from the Department of Mathematics, Sichuan Normal University, in 1982. He had worked as a mathematics teacher in the School of Mathematics, Mianyang Economic Specialist College for ten years. Currently, he is an Associate Professor in the School of Science, Southwest University of Science & Technology. He teaches calculus, probability theory and mathematical statistics courses for undergraduate students, and fuzzy mathematics theory for graduate students. He has published many papers in fuzzy theory and nonlinear dynamics.

Lu Xie, Ph.D., is a principal investigator of the translational medicine group in Shanghai Center for Bioinformation Technology. She received her PhD degree in Xiang Ya Medical School of Central South University and worked as a research fellow in Vanderbilt University, USA for five years. She has published more than 50 research articles. Her research direction is translational medicine related bioinformatics, including integrative analysis of mRNA and miRNA expression profiling and tumor biomarker network, decoding of high-throughput mass spectrometry data and the application in human genome annotation and phosphorylation mediated cellular signaling transduction network.

Dong Xu is a James C. Dowell Associate Professor, Chair of the Department of Computer Science and Director of the Digital Biology Laboratory in the Computer Science Department, University of Missouri, Columbia. He obtained his PhD from the University of Illinois, Urbana-Champaign in 1995. He worked as a Researcher at the National Cancer Institute and Oak Ridge National Laboratory. He has conducted research in many areas of computational biology and bioinformatics, including protein structure prediction and analysis, high-throughput biological data analyses, computational proteomics, and in silico studies of plant and microbes. He has conducted many projects in these fields and published a large number of influential papers.

Hangyang Xu is a student majoring in bioinformatics at the Department of Bioinformatics, Zhejiang university, P.R.China. He has won a series of awards, including the outstanding student at the provincial level, and a number of college scholarships. His interests in bioinformatics mainly lie in the area of data mining and data warehousing. He has taken part in several undergraduate research programs, such as building a drug target database, analyzing the shared characteristics of known drug targets, and writing a Java package to facilitate biological data mining based on protein sequences.

Minhong Xu was born in November 1982, in Zhejiang Province, People's Republic of China. She graduated from Zhejiang Sci-Tech University in 2008 and obtained a B.S. degree in Materials Science and Engineering. Now she is working at Huzhou Teachers College. Her main research is on functional polymer materials and effluent treatment.

Zhaoxia Xu, Ph. D., is a research associate at the Basic Medical College of Shanghai University of Traditional Chinese Medicine. She received her Bachelor's and Master's degrees from Hubei University of Traditional Chinese Medicine in Specialty of Traditional Chinese Medicine (TCM) Diagnosis, and also her Ph.D. degree from Hubei University of Traditional Chinese Medicine in Specialty of Traditional Chinese Medicine Diagnosis. She works in the Laboratory of Diagnostic Integrated Information of Traditional Chinese Medicine at Shanghai University of Traditional Chinese Medicine. Her research focuses on the standardization for symptom diagnosis in TCM and prevention and treatment using Chinese Medicine for respiratory diseases. She conducts six scientific research projects and has published thirty journal papers.

Aixia Yan obtained her PhD in Lanzhou University in China in 2000. From Jan. 2001 to Jan. 2003, supported by Alexander von Humboldt Foundation, she worked in the group of Prof. Johann Gasteiger, University of Erlangen in Germany. From Feb. 2003 to Jan. 2005, she worked in the group of Prof. W. Graham Richards in Oxford University. Since Feb. 2005, she worked in Beijing University of Chemical Technology in China. Her current main research field is computer-aided drug design. Her current research projects include: (1) prediction of ADME/Tox properties; (2) Application of self-organizing maps in compounds pattern recognition, virtual screening and combinatorial library design; and (3) Prediction of drugs toxicity and side effects based on biochemical pathway.

Haixia Yan, Ph.D., is a Lecturer at Basic Medical College, Shanghai University of Traditional Chinese Medicine (TCM). She received her Bachelor's and Master's Degrees from Shanghai University of Traditional Chinese Medicine, and her Ph.D. degree from Shanghai University of Traditional Chinese Medicine in Specialty of Traditional Chinese Medicine Diagnosis under the supervision of Dr. Yiqin

Wang. Her research focuses on feature extraction and classification for wrist-pulse diagnosis in TCM, and standardization for symptom diagnosis in TCM. She works in the Laboratory of Diagnostic Integrated Information of Traditional Chinese Medicine and Basic Medical College. Her relevant scientific papers have been published in Chinese Journal of Integrated Traditional and Western Medicine, Shanghai Journal of Traditional Chinese Medicine, etc.

Jianjun Yan, Ph. D., is an Associate Professor at the Center for Mechatronics Engineering of East China University of Science and Technology. He received his Bachelor's, Master's and Doctor's degrees from Huazhong University of Science and Technology. His main research areas include image processing, biomedical signal processing, artificial intelligence and the modernization of auscultation of Traditional Chinese Medicine (TCM). He focuses on the nonlinear dynamics of wrist pulse and auscultation signal in Traditional Chinese Medicine, and computational methods of Traditional Chinese Medicine symptoms differentiation. He is a senior member of Chinese Mechanical Engineering Society, and is a Committee member of Professional Committee of Diagnosis in Shanghai Association of Integrative Medicine.

Ren-Xiang Yan is a PhD candidate in Bioinformatics Center of China Agricultural University. Mr. Yan received his Bachelor's degree from Fujian Agricultural and Forestry University. He is interested in structural bioinformatics, especially in protein threading algorithms and membrane protein prediction methods. Currently, he is carrying out his research under the supervision of Dr. Ziding Zhang in China Agricultural University. Some of Yan's research work has been published in BMC Bioinformatics and BMC Structural Biology journals. Now, he is focusing on outer membrane protein (OMP) discrimination study and tries to develop new methods that can identify OMP reliably.

Huan Yang received her bachelor's degree from the College of Computer Science and Technology, Jilin University in 2007. She now studies as a graduate student in the College of Computer Science and Technology, Jilin University, majoring in Bioinformatics. She has studied Computational Biology and bioinformatics in Computation Intelligence Library for three years, while working closely with University of Missouri, USA and Norman Bethune College of Medical Science, Jilin University. She has participated in two projects and published two articles in "Research and Development of Computer" and "Journal of Jilin University".

Jintian Yang was born in January 1955 in Zhejiang, China. He graduated from the Department of Chemistry in Hangzhou University (now Zhejiang University) in 1979. He has completed 13 research projects and has published more than 30 research papers and 3 books.

Yajun Yi, Ph.D., is a Research Assistant Professor in the Department of Medicine, Vanderbilt University where he received his Ph.D. His on-going research is on cancer biology that applies gene microarray technology and bioinformatics tools to study the molecular basis of metastasis in prostate cancer. His group are now using a comprehensive survey of global gene expression to enable an efficient search for metastasis-related genes in metastatic cancer. The goal is to identify candidate genes and their genomic defects. The metastatic activity of candidate genes will be assessed by in vitro and in vivo assays. Through cooperation with other investigators at Vanderbilt University, his laboratory has established a bench research project and developed two new computational methods, EXLAT and DIGMAP for the data analysis of microarray studies.

Jian Yu is a second-year graduate student under the supervision of Professor Yixue Li at the College of Life Science, Tongji University. He also works in the Translational Group of Shanghai Center for Bioinformation Technology (SCBIT), directed by Dr. Lu Xie. His research focuses on integrative analysis of genomic data to identify novel biomarkers of cancer, especially Hepato-Celluar Carcinoma (HCC). He is trying to develop mathematical models based on clinical characteristics to predict outcome of Chinese HCC patients before surgery, by collaborating with clinicians in hospitals.

Lili Yu is a graduate student of Jiangsu University located in Zhenjiang, Jiangsu province. Ms. Yu received her bachelor's degree from Jiangsu Universty in 2008. She worked on plant molecular biology at the Institute of Life Sciences and identified the function of LACS genes cloned from Glycine max. She is studying in the Chinese Academy of Agricultural Sciences Crop Science Society of China. She was first-author of "In silicon Cloning and analysis of a LACS gene from Glycine Max(L.)", International Journal of Biology (2010).

Shoupeng Yu studied economics and management at the Changchun Institute of Technology in 1992, and received his BS Degree in 1996. He is working as an engineer now. He has published several scientific articles in the areas of network safety analysis and is interested in bioinformatics research, such as miRNA prediction and gene network reconstruction.

Zu-Guo Yu, PhD, received his Bsc. and Msc degrees in mathematics from Xiangtan University in 1991 and 1994 respectively, and PhD degree in mathematics from Fudan University in 1997. Then he worked as a postdoctoral research fellow in Institute of Theoretical Physics of Chinese Academy of Science (1997-1999) and Queensland University of Technology (2000-2003). Currently he is working as a full professor in Xiangtan University (distinguished professor from 2010) and research fellow in Queensland University of Technology. He started his research in fractals since 1994 and bioinformatics since 1997.

Hong-jian Zhang, doctor of engineering, is a Lecturer in Key Laboratory of Coal Processing and Efficient Utilization, Ministry of Education. Dr. Zhang received his Bachelor's and Master's degrees from Yangzhou University (China) in Food Science and Engineering. He received his PhD degree from China University of Mining and Technology in Environmental Engineering. His main research field is environmental engineering and the wet separation of waste printed circuit boards. He has participated in several national key research projects since 2004, and has made significant contributions in these projects. Dr. Zhang has obtained two patents regarding to the electronic waste disposal in recent years. He has also published a number of ground-breaking papers in several high-profile Journals and conferences.

Jun-Ran Zhang graduated from the Fourth Military Medical University of China, and obtained his Ph.D. in Neurobiology in 2008. He is a member of the China Computer Society, the Institute of Electrical & Electronics Engineers biological computing Branch, organization of human brain mapping. Currently he is a postdoctoral fellow at the Huaxi Magnetic Resonance Research Center (HMRRC) in the West China Hospital of Sichuan University. Dr. Zhang also supervises several graduate students in Computer Science at Southwest University of Science & Technology. Dr. Zhang's main research areas are computational neuroscience, neuroimaging, etc. He has published over 10 papers and holds a patent. He teaches Computational Neuroscience, Medical Image Analysis, etc.

Lu Zhang is a Ph.D. candidate in School of Municipal and Environmental Engineering in Harbin Institute of Technology. Lu received her Bachelor's and Master's degrees from Harbin Institute of Technology in Environmental Science and Engineering. Her Ph.D. major is Environmental Science. Her research centers on purification and characterization of hydrogenases from hydrogen production bacteria. The dissertation for her MSc degree was entitled "The relationship between hydrogenases activity of YUAN-3 and the character of hydrogen production metabolism." In her thesis, optimization of the detection method of hydrogenase activity in high efficient H2-producing bacterium E. Harbinenase YUAN-3 is discussed. The relationship between the activity and the hydrogen-producing properties and the highest activity of the hydride portfolio have been determined. These results play an important role in the studies of hydrogenases from YUAN-3, an auto-aggregative strain.

Zhiqiang Zhang received his bachelor's degree in Microelectronics from Physical Science and Technology College, Sichuan University, China, 2008. He is working toward his master's degree at Sichuan University, China. His current research focus is on Digital Circuit Design, FPGA and Bio-electronics.

Fanpeng Zhou is a graduate student at the East China University of Science and Technology of Mechanical Engineering. Zhou received his Bachelor's degree from Tianjin University in Mechanical Engineering and his Master's degree from the East China University of Science and Technology in Mechanical Engineering. His research focuses on Digital Auscultation System of Traditional Chinese Medicine (TCM). As a key researcher, he has made further development in the signals acquisition system and analysis methods in TCM. In East China University of Science and Technology, he was awarded several prizes for his ground-breaking work, such as the prize of Research and Practice, the prize of Excellent Graduate Student, etc.

Nian-xin Zhou is a Master degree candidate in the School of Chemical Engineering and Technology, China University of Mining and Technology. Zhou received his Bachelor's degree from China University of Mining and Technology in Mineral Processing Engineering. His main research field is milling grinding. He has taken part in several experimental projects at several power plants. He has published several papers in Chinese Journals.

Fang Zhu, born in August, 1986 in Tongchuan, Shanxi, China. During 2004 to 2008, she was a student at the College of Bioscience and Bioengineering of South China University of Technology (SCUT). Her major was biotechnology and she received her bachelor's degree in 2008. Now she is a graduate student of industrial microbiology of College of Bioscience and Bioengineering of South China University of Technology (SCUT). Her research interest is purification of sortase and searching for its inhibitors. She expects to obtain her Master's degree in July, 2011.

Fuge Zhu, is a graduate student of Jiangsu University located in Zhenjiang, Jiangsu province. He works on plant molecular biology at the Institute of Life Sciences and was responsible for identifying the function of LACS genes cloned from Brassica napus. Long chain acyl-coenzyme A synthetases (LACSs) activate the conversion of free fatty acid to acyl-CoA thioesters, and play important roles in the biosynthesis and degradation of lipids. In Zhu's study, four cDNAs encode long chain fatty acyl-CoA synthetase activity have been found in Brassica napus. He was first-author of "Charaterization and Functional Analysis of A LACS Gene pXT166 in Brassica napus", Chinese Journal of Oil Crops

(2009). He was co-author of "A rapid and simple method for Brasscia napus floral-dip transformation and selection of transgenic plantlets", International Journal of Biology.

Weiping Zhu, Ph.D., is a full Professor at Shanghai Institute of Applied Mathematics and Mechanics, Shanghai University, China. Dr. Zhu received his Ph.D. from the Shanghai University in Solid Mechanics. His research interests include: Biomechanics in Cell Chemotaxis, Drill String Vibration, Plate, Shell and Bellows Mechanics. He is currently a full professor and a supervisor of PhD students at Shanghai University. Dr. Zhu has published about forty articles in the fields of Mechanics and biology with topics mainly covering Mathematical Modeling and Numerical Simulation. Dr. Zhu's research includes the study on the dynamics of axon guidance in the development of nervous system; easy deviation problem of a vertical well drilled with air, etc.

Wei-ran Zuo is a PhD Candidate in the School of Chemical Engineering and Technology, China University of Mining and Technology. Zuo received his Bachelor's and Master's degrees from China University of Mining and Technology in Mineral Processing Engineering. His main research field is Mineral Processing Engineering and milling grinding. He has visited the JK centre in Australia during the period of 2006.04 to 2007.02. He has taken part in several international and national projects from Chinese Government. He has published a number of influential papers in important Journals and International conferences. He is conducting research on the establishment of a grinding model.

Index